The International Bill of Rights
The Covenant on Civil and Political Rights

THE
INTERNATIONAL
BILL OF RIGHTS

The Covenant on Civil and Political Rights

Louis Henkin
Editor

New York
Columbia University Press

Library of Congress Cataloging in Publication Data
Main entry under title:

The International Bill of Rights.

   Includes index.
   Contents: The development of the Covenant on Civil
and Political Rights / Vratislav Pechota—To respect
and to ensure, state obligations and permissible
derogations / Thomas Buergenthal—The self determination of peoples / Antonio Cassese—[etc.]
   1. Civil rights (International law)—Addresses,
essays, lectures.   I. Henkin, Louis.   II. Title:
Covenant on Civil and Political Rights.
K3240.6.I53   341.4′81   81-6112
ISBN 0-231-05180-8   AACR2

COLUMBIA UNIVERSITY PRESS
NEW YORK/GUILDFORD, SURREY

*Clothbound editions of Columbia University Press
books are Smyth-sewn and printed on permanent
and durable acid-free paper.*

Contents

Contributors

THOMAS BUERGENTHAL: Dean and Professor of Law, Washington College of Law, American University; Judge, Inter-American Court of Human Rights.

ANTONIO CASSESE: Professor of International Organization, University of Florence.

YORAM DINSTEIN: Rector, and Professor of International Law, Tel Aviv University.

LOUIS HENKIN: University Professor, Columbia University.

STIG JAGERSKIOLD: Professor of Law, Emeritus, Uppsala University.

ALEXANDRE CHARLES KISS: Director of Research, National Center for Scientific Research (Strasbourg, France); Secretary General, International Institute of Human Rights (Strasbourg).

HAJI N. A. NOOR MUHAMMAD: Member, Union Public Service Commission, New Delhi; Senior Advocate of the Supreme Court of India.

KARL JOSEF PARTSCH: Professor of Public Law, Emeritus, University of Bonn; Member of the Committee for Elimination of Racial Discrimination, 1970–.

VRATISLAV PECHOTA: Principal Legal Adviser, Ministry of Foreign Affairs, Czechoslovakia, 1965–68; Visiting Scholar, Columbia University, 1979–80.

B. G. RAMCHARAN: Special Assistant to the Director, UN Division of Human Rights (Geneva).

A. H. ROBERTSON: Professeur Associé, Emeritus, University of Paris I; Secretary General (a.i.), International Institute of Human Rights (Strasbourg), 1979–80.

OSCAR SCHACHTER: Hamilton Fish Professor of International Law and Diplomacy, Columbia University.

LOUIS B. SOHN: Bemis Professor of International Law, Harvard Law School.

FERNANDO VOLIO: Professor of Law, University of Costa Rica.

Preface

THE IDEA, and perhaps too the term "an international bill of rights," were born during the Second World War and projected to be part of the new postwar world order. Later, the term was applied to the ensemble of comprehensive instruments developed under the aegis of the United Nations pursuant to the human rights provisions of the UN Charter, namely, the Universal Declaration of Human Rights, the International Covenant on Civil and Political Rights and its protocol, and the International Covenant on Economic, Social, and Cultural Rights.

The Universal Declaration was adopted in 1948 as a "common standard of achievement" for all societies to aspire to. It has acquired some legal character, and General Assembly resolutions have unanimously proclaimed the "duty" of states to "fully and faithfully observe" its provisions.* But doubts about the legal character of the Declaration have persisted, and few would insist that every act inconsistent with any provision of the Declaration is a violation of international law in its strict sense. In any event, the members of the United Nations saw fit to move from the Universal Declaration to the two covenants—formal international agreements which restate the provisions of the Declaration as binding legal obligations, define and refine those rights as well as permissible limitations on them, and provide for their implementation. With more than a third of the states of the world already party to the covenants and more states adhering to them every year, the covenants have assumed prime place in the International Bill of Rights as the instruments that influence the behavior of states and by which the condition of individual rights in particular countries is to be judged.

No legal instrument, however well drafted, is beyond the need for interpretation. International instruments, produced by a complicated process involving many and diverse participants over many years, are subject to ambiguities and uncertainties, some unwitting, many knowing and even intentional. Authentic interpretation requires careful study of the text of each provision in the context of the whole, the preparatory work (travaux préparatoires), the practice of states and international bodies, authoritative interpretation of similar provisions in other international instruments, the views of judges and scholars, and much else that may be relevant to the quest for meaning and understanding.

* See, e.g., GA Res. 1904, 18 GAOR Supp. 15, UN Doc. A/5515 at 35 (1963).

International human rights instruments, dealing with relations between a state and its own inhabitants, are particularly vulnerable to self-serving interpretation by governments. Parties to these agreements have the right to challenge misinterpretations by other parties but they are often reluctant to do so. The institutions and special "machinery" established by the Covenants for scrutinizing compliance are too "diplomatic," and insufficiently focused and taut, to provide a comprehensive guide to interpretation. It has appeared important, therefore, that there be a scholarly, objective, impartial exposition of the provisions of the Covenants to help guide governments, international bodies, and nongovernmental organizations and concerned citizens, to help maintain the international human rights standards, and to help improve the condition of human rights everywhere.

It was decided to begin with the Covenant on Civil and Political Rights, which creates obligations that can be stated with substantial clarity and precision, and which have direct, immediate, and daily impact on the lives of millions of human beings. To make the volume more readable and even more useful, it has been projected not as a table of article-by-article annotations but as a series of interlocking essays on particular rights or groups of rights. To assure a wide perspective, it is the combined effort of many scholars, representing a variety of cultures and legal systems, but sharing ideological commitment to human rights and to scholarly integrity.

The Jacob Blaustein Institute for the Advancement of Human Rights conceived this undertaking, perceived its importance to the cause of human rights, and helped make it possible. This volume, one may hope, is a fitting sequel to an undertaking a quarter-century ago when the Institute sponsored Sir Hersch Lauterpacht's seminal study and highly influential projection, also entitled "The International Bill of Rights."

Thanks are due also to the American Society of International Law which, with assistance from the Ford Foundation, convened the authors for a valuable substantive discussion while the work was in progress.*

L.H.

---

*I am grateful to Christine Hoth and Monica Bachner, Columbia Law School, 1981, and to Darryl Rains and Karen Leaf, Columbia Law School, 1982, for research and other assistance in preparing this volume for publication. I also wish to thank Ann Wagner of the New York Bar for translating Fernando Volio's contribution (essay 7) from the Spanish.

The International Bill of Rights
The Covenant on Civil and Political Rights

1

Introduction

LOUIS HENKIN

HUMAN RIGHTS is the idea of our time. It asserts that every human being, in every society, is entitled to have basic autonomy and freedoms respected and basic needs satisfied. These claims by every individual against his society are designated "rights," presumably in some moral order, perhaps under "natural law." The society has corresponding duties to give effect to these rights through domestic laws and institutions.

Today, the human rights idea is universal, accepted by virtually all states and societies regardless of historical, cultural, ideological, economic, or other differences. It is international, the subject of international diplomacy, law, and institutions. It is philosophically respectable, even to opposed philosophical persuasions.

The universalization of human rights is a political fact. The Universal Declaration of Human Rights adopted by the General Assembly in 1948 has been accepted by virtually all of today's 150 states; even those, notably the European Communist states, which had abstained when the Declaration was approved, have now accepted it formally in the Final Act of the Conference on Security and Cooperation (Helsinki, 1975).[1] Every state has adhered to at least one human rights agreement; and more than a third of the world's states have accepted the comprehensive agreements, the International Covenant on Civil and Political Rights, and the International Covenant on Economic, Social, and Cultural Rights, with more states joining every year. The universal acceptance of the idea of human rights and its general content may be only formal and superficial, in some cases even hypocritical, but no government dissents from the ideology of human rights today or offers an alternative to it.

The steady internationalization of human rights is equally impressive.

Before the Second World War, how a state treated its own inhabitants was its own business, a matter of "domestic jurisdiction," not of "international concern." Today it is the stuff of daily diplomacy among states. Numerous international organizations deal with it regularly, and it is never absent from the agenda of every organ and agency of the United Nations and of major regional organizations. There are dozens of international human rights agreements, and some of them have been adhered to by more than one hundred states. New international bodies—commissions, committees, and courts—occupy themselves with human rights daily.

The contemporary philosophical respectability of human rights is itself remarkable. The idea of limitations on government, on majorities—even on the "public good"—in favor of individual autonomy, dignity, and need, has taken root and no present political system, no contemporary political theory, rejects it. Earlier philosophical objections have subsided or have become irrelevant. Eighteenth century notions of natural rights suffered the onslaughts of legal positivism in the nineteenth and early twentieth centuries, but human rights now are attended by resurgent "neo-natural-rights" theories, and are finding a prominent place in contemporary political, ethical, and moral philosophy, now again preoccupied with "justice," "liberty," "equality," and "rights." Today, it is human rights that claims the mantle of natural law, not—as in the past—slavery or the divine right of kings, not the inferiority of women, of particular races or of the poor. The establishment of human rights in national law and in international law has disarmed legal positivists as well. It is human rights that are positive national and international law, not the antihuman laws of Hitler or some other jurisprudence of terror. And it is individual civil-political rights as well as economic-social and cultural rights that are the law, not unmitigated collectivism or laissez-faire.

The idea of human rights is not an abstraction; it has specific content. What the world has accepted are the civil, political, economic, social, and cultural rights set forth in the Universal Declaration and the international covenants. They include rights of freedom from mistreatment and undue governmental intrusion, as well as rights to governmental support for the economic and social welfare of every human being. Although specific, the rights are flexible enough to rise above differences among political systems; they are consistent with different degrees and forms of free enterprise as well as with socialism. Debates about conflicts or priorities between rights only confirm rather than depreciate any of the rights declared in the Declaration or protected by the covenants.*

Human Rights in International Relations

Concern by some governments with the condition of individuals in other countries is not new. Centuries ago, princes and popes interceded for coreligionists and others in various countries. The nineteenth century saw a number of "humanitarian interventions" by big powers, through diplomacy and sometimes through force, to protest, end, or prevent massacres, pogroms, and other atrocities. These, however, were personal expressions of "noblesse oblige," or extraordinary reactions to egregious events; they were sharp deviations from the international political system's assumption that, in principle, how a state treated its own citizens was its own business. Surely there was no serious disposition to render the treatment of the individual human being in his own country a subject of international diplomacy and law.

Human rights did not become the concern of international politics or law until after the Second World War, but individual welfare was not wholly beyond the ken of the international system even before then. International law and human rights were linked in the history of ideas, both having antecedents in natural law and in Roman law, and com-

---

*Since the international covenants have been concluded there have been arguments for new kinds of human rights, including a right to "development" and a right to peace. These, of course, are highly important. Individual rights, whether political-civil or economic-social, cannot be maintained in vacuo; they are individual rights in society and depend on the society. Individual rights cannot be enjoyed fully if the society is at war; the International Covenant on Civil and Political Rights expressly permits derogation from many rights during public emergencies that "threaten the life of the nation." Economic-social rights in particular cannot be enjoyed as fully in a country which is underdeveloped.

Whether it is meaningful or helpful to denominate an individual (or collective) right to have one's country developed, or at peace, has been debated. But any implication that such "collective rights" generally are superior to individual rights and must be given priority is profoundly mistaken. It is the essence of the idea of human rights that a hard core of autonomy, integrity, and dignity of the individual is not to be sacrificed even to the national interest and the welfare of the group, including aspects of that welfare which might be denominated "collective" or "people's" rights. In fact, however, there is no reason or evidence to support the underlying assumption that individual repression is commonly necessary to support national development or even national security. Rather, there is both reason and evidence to show that national security as well as healthy development require programs respecting individual dignity. Surely, torture does not feed the hungry or build a factory. And the quest for a higher GNP, however important for the future, is no justification for tolerating either tyranny or starvation today.

mon progenitors in Grotius, Vattel, and Locke.[2] In fact, international law early included some of what we would today identify as human rights obligations; for example, treaty provisions in which parties undertook to tolerate heterodox religious worship and not to impose civil disabilities on religious dissenters. Customary international law, too, has long imposed on states a responsibility not to deny justice to aliens. In the last century, nations sought to mitigate the horrors of war by developing law to forbid particularly cruel weapons, and to protect prisoners of war and civilian populations during war. Following the First World War, the dominant powers required several states to adhere to "minority treaties," in which they assumed obligations to respect the rights of ethnic, national, linguistic, religious, or other minorities among their inhabitants.[3] The League of Nations Covenant provided that the mandate system established for dependent areas should be governed by the principle that "the well being and development of such peoples form a sacred trust of civilization," and imposed "conditions which will guarantee freedom of conscience and religion" and other rights. Members of the League undertook "to secure just treatment of the native inhabitants of territories under their control"; mandatory powers were required to promote the welfare and rights of the inhabitants of mandated territories. The years following the First World War also saw a major development in the law of human rights, a development that is often overlooked and commonly underestimated: the International Labour Office, now the International Labour Organisation (ILO), launched a series of conventions setting minimum standards for labor and other social conditions.[4]

This early international law of human rights, however, was limited in scope and focus, and while it had humanitarian consequences, its motivation was largely political rather than idealistic. Christian princes had gone to war on behalf of coreligionists in other countries, and religious tolerance was a condition of peace in religiously divided, war-weary Europe; agreements for mutual tolerance made possible the establishment of the secular state and the rise of modern international law. Powerful states exporting people, goods, and capital to other countries in the age of mercantilism insisted on law that would protect the interests which these represented. Denial of justice to an alien was an offense to the state whose nationality he bore and jeopardized its economic and political interests. (Aliens who were "stateless," who had no nationality, had no remedy for denial of justice, since no state was offended by such denials.) States insisted on an international standard of justice (rooted in natural law) for their nationals abroad even when these states did not recognize that standard for their citizens at home. Humanitarian laws regulating the conduct of war were reciprocal undertakings defending a state's soldiery and population against the enemy. Minority treaties were required of some states, not universal norms applicable to the big and the powerful as well. The mandate provisions were seen by many as essentially hortatory, a small rhetorical price for continuing "imperialism" instead of granting the territories self-determination and self-government. The ILO conventions were capitalism's defense against the specter of spreading socialism, and states, moreover, had direct interests in the conditions of labor in countries with which they competed in a common market.

Broader law came in the wake of Hitler. The international human rights movement was born in, and out of the Second World War. The proclaimed aims of that war included the establishment of individual rights and the "Four Freedoms" for everyone in every country, and that aim also inspired the planning for the postwar world.[5] To begin, the victors imposed human rights obligations on the vanquished in peace treaties, and included human rights violations in the Nuremberg Charter and prosecutions. Occupying powers presided at the incorporation of human rights safeguards into new constitutions and laws for West Germany, Japan, and Austria. The UN Charter ushered in a new international concern for human rights everywhere.

The Charter replaced the League of Nations' concentration on the rights of minorities in selected countries with heed to the rights of all individuals everywhere. The new commitment to "self-determination," together with universal human rights, it was apparently thought, would eliminate the minorities problem: some minorities would become independent by self-determination; the rest would find their rights protected equally with majorities by universal commitment to human rights for all.

The Preamble of the UN Charter reaffirms "faith in fundamental human rights, in the dignity and worth of the human person, in the equal rights of men and women," and declares the determination of peoples "to promote social progress and better standards of life in larger freedom." The purposes of the UN include international cooperation "in promoting and encouraging respect for human rights and for fundamental freedoms for all without distinction as to race, sex, language, or religion" (Articles 1, 55(c)). Human rights are among the responsibilities for study and recommendation of the General Assembly (Article 13) and the Economic and Social Council (Article 62(2)), and a commission on human rights is expressly required (Article 68). Human rights provisions are prominent in Chapters XI and XII dealing with non-self-governing territories and international trusteeship. Members pledged themselves to cooperate with the UN organization for the achievement of its human rights purposes (Article 56).

The various UN bodies have devoted years of arduous effort to promoting human rights. Human rights have been on every agenda of every body and have become a staple of UN activity. A universal declaration of human rights was prepared and adopted. Even particular human rights violations have received attention, early as in the case of Russian wives of non-Russians and the treatment of Indians in South Africa, more recently in Chile and elsewhere.[6] Some violations—e.g., apartheid in South Africa—are perennially on the UN agenda. Other violations in other places—the treatment of Soviet Jews, allegations of torture in Chile—were the subject of extended international debate over many years. Despite resistance, it was established that within the meaning of Article 2(7) of the Charter, UN preoccupation with human rights was not forbidden intervention. The prevailing view was that UN consideration was not intervention, and, more importantly, that human rights are an international, not a domestic concern.

The New Law of Human Rights

The UN Charter ushered in a new international law of human rights. The new law buried the old dogma that the individual is not a "subject" of international politics and law and that a government's behavior toward its own nationals is a matter of domestic, not international, concern. It penetrated national frontiers and the veil of sovereignty. It removed the exclusive identification of an individual with his government. It gave the individual a part in international politics and rights in international law, independently of his government. It also gave the individual protectors other than his government, indeed protectors and remedies against his government.

The international law of human rights differs from other international law in its motivations and impulses as well. Generally, international law is made, international obligations are undertaken, to serve common or reciprocal national interests; early human rights laws, too, we have seen, largely served states' political or economic purposes. The move to a comprehensive human rights law also sought to appeal to national and transnational interests, perhaps in an effort to de-emphasize its radical nature. Human rights, it was urged, are related to international peace, for states that violate human rights at home are not trustworthy in international relations, and violations of those rights afford occasions, temptations, and pretexts for interventions or war. (The latter argument has since found instances to support it, e.g., as regards racism in southern Africa.[7]) The international human rights law also had a different kind of political motivation: states that had had minority treaties or human rights provisions in peace treaties imposed on them resented being singled out and sought to universalize their undertakings. But whatever reasons (or rationalizations) were provided to mask it, the fact is that the new comprehensive international human rights law generally serves no patent, particular national interest. It is essentially ideological, idealistic, humanitarian; its true and deep purpose is to improve the lot of individual men and women everywhere, particularly where national institutions and nonlegal international forces are not adequate—a unique and revolutionary purpose for international law.

The international law of human rights parallels and supplements national law, superseding and supplying the deficiencies of national constitutions and laws; but it does not replace, and indeed depends on, national institutions. The constituency in every society that supports human rights law is different from the constituency that supports, say, international trade agreements, or military alliances, or peaceful settlements, or even international organization and cooperation. The pressures on a government to adhere to international human rights law are also different from those to adhere to other law, and indeed, a state's adherence to human rights conventions is far less important if in fact it behaves at home, toward its own, consistently with their terms.

In other respects, too, international law and politics see human rights in the context of the international political system. Although human rights are universal, they are the claims of an individual upon his society, not on other societies. Although the society in which one lives may be crucial to life and dignity, although a right to change one's society might well be deemed fundamental, the individual does not have an absolute right to join another society and seek his rights there. Even those who are oppressed at home do not yet have an international human right to asylum elsewhere; those who are starving at home do not have an internationally recognized human right to be taken in by the more affluent societies or to be fed by them.*

---

* To date, at least, the only trace of transnational right or obligation may be that which some see as implied in Article 2 of the Covenant on Economic, Social, and Cultural Rights, that a state must take steps to achieve those rights "individually and through international assistance and cooperation" (Article 2(1)). Parties to that covenant also commit themselves to take appropriate steps to ensure the realization of every individual's right to an adequate standard of living, "recognizing to this effect the essential importance of international cooperation based on free consent" (Article 11(1)).

Like other international law, human rights law is made by treaty or convention; there is also customary human rights law made by national practice with a developing sense of legal obligation. The declarations and resolutions of UN organs and other international bodies on human rights may have greater weight in achieving international law here than on other matters, since they purport to express the conscience of mankind on a matter of conscience. And though all law-making is a political process, humanitarian law has its own politics in both making and enforcing law.

From the UN Charter to the International Covenants

The history of the development of the covenants is described fully by Vratislav Pechota (essay 2). It is relevant here to address the antecedents of that development.

In themselves, the normative human rights provisions of the UN Charter are general and preliminary: essentially, by Articles 55 and 56, member states pledge themselves to take joint and separate action in cooperation with the United Nations to achieve respect for human rights. Human rights are not defined or specified in the Charter, and there is no clear undertaking by every state not to commit one or another violation. The institutions, procedures, and programs for inducing national respect for rights, for monitoring the condition of human rights in different countries, and for preventing, deterring, or ending violation, are not provided. But the words of the Charter are words of legal obligation and surely the pledge of Article 56 is violated if a member state itself persists in committing gross violations of rights universally recognized as fundamental.

No doubt, however, the members of the UN themselves recognized that the Charter law was insufficient. Immediately they proceeded to prepare and promulgate the Universal Declaration of Human Rights, making specific the general Charter references to human rights and freedoms for all. The Declaration is a remarkable juncture of political-civil and economic-social rights, with equality and freedom from discrimination a principal and recurrent theme. It declares the rights to life, liberty, and security of person, to fair criminal process, to freedom of conscience, thought, expression, association, and privacy; the right to seek and enjoy asylum, to leave one's country and return to it; rights to marriage and family, and rights of property. It declares the will of the people to be the basis of the authority of government, and provides for universal suffrage and bona fide elections. It speaks of the right to work and leisure, health care, and education. (Because the Declaration was designed to be universal, it includes provisions that some national constitutions assumed and took for granted or did not consider necessary or "constitution-worthy," for example, the fundamentality of the family [Article 16(3)] or the right of political asylum.)

The Universal Declaration was not generally conceived as law but as "a common standard of achievement" for all to aspire to; hence its approval without dissent.* Some thought that the United Nations should rest on the Declaration and concentrate on encouraging states to raise their national norms and conform their national behavior to its standards. Instead, governments moved to convert the Declaration into binding legal norms.

The process was very, very long. In some part this was due to the ever-increasing number of states, all of which joined in the process and slowed the negotiations. In part, delay was due to the differences between a declaration and a binding covenant. Some states that had been prepared to declare a general principle wished it carefully defined and circumscribed if it were to be clearly a legal obligation with legal consequences, for though no state was compelled to adhere to any draft covenant that might emerge, most states wanted something they might be able to adopt if it became desirable; they were reluctant, moreover, to have a covenant adopted as the international norm in whose light their behavior would appear to be wanting. The process was also extended because there were strong pressures on the other hand to develop and elaborate the generalities of the Declaration and give them more specific content so that they would afford greater protection. The Declaration, moreover, had not provided for its implementation, while many sessions were spent debating and elaborating means to enforce the new emerging legal undertakings.

In substantial part, it took eighteen years to convert the Declaration into convention because it was necessary to accommodate, bridge, sub-

*Even at the time, however, a few saw the Declaration as interpreting and particularizing the general provisions of the Charter and therefore partaking of its binding legal character. Later, General Assembly resolutions unanimously proclaimed the duty of states to "fully and faithfully observe" the provisions of the Declaration; unofficial international assemblies and conferences at Montreal and Teheran in 1968 resolved to similar effect. At the Conference on Security and Cooperation in Europe (Helsinki 1975), respect for the Declaration was included among the principles guiding relations between participating states. In time, indeed, many began to speak of the Declaration as though it had the effect of law. Others have argued that the Charter, the Declaration, repeated resolutions of international organizations and the practice of states have together created a customary international law of human rights outlawing at least persistent and gross violations of fundamental, universally recognized human rights.

merge, and conceal deep divisions and differences, especially between democratic–libertarian and socialist–revolutionary states—differences in fundamental conceptions about the relation of society to the individual, about his rights and duties, about priorities and preferences among them.

Western states fought for, and obtained, a division into two covenants, the Covenant on Civil and Political Rights and the Covenant on Economic, Social, and Cultural Rights. The two covenants recognize the difference in the character of rights in various subtle ways. For example, the Covenant on Civil and Political Rights is drafted in terms of the individual's rights: e.g., "Every human being has the inherent right to life"; "No one shall be held in slavery"; "All persons shall be equal before the courts and tribunals." The Covenant on Economic, Social, and Cultural Rights, on the other hand, speaks only to the states, not the individual: "The States Parties to the present Covenant recognize the right to work"; "The States Parties . . . undertake to ensure . . . the right of everyone to form trade unions"; "The States Parties . . . recognize the right of everyone to education." There was wide agreement and clear recognition that the means required to induce compliance with social-economic undertakings were different from those required for civil-political rights. But the Covenant on Economic, Social, and Cultural Rights is law, not merely exhortation and aspiration. The rights it recognizes are as "human," universal, and fundamental as are those of the Civil and Political Rights Covenant. The obligation for a state party is "to take steps . . . to the maximum of its available resources, with a view to achieving progressively the full realization" of these rights, and fulfillment may require national planning and major programs, and international assistance. But these limitations do not derogate from the legal character of the obligations.

Other delays resulted from sharp differences over the inclusion or scope of particular rights. Most of the states were concerned, or were more concerned, with values reflecting their struggle against colonialism but not included in the Universal Declaration and not previously part of the accepted human rights ideology. They insisted that both Covenants include the right of all peoples to self-determination as well as to "economic self-determination," to "sovereignty" over their resources. Western states resisted, arguing that both are at best rights of a "people," not of any individual, and surely not—like human rights generally—rights of individuals against their own society. They argued, too, that the content of these norms was highly uncertain and controversial. The argument did not prevail, and identical provisions on self-determination now head both covenants. Also included in the Covenant on Civil and Political Rights were other, less controversial, rights not mentioned in the Declaration—freedom from imprisonment for debt, rights of children, and rights of minorities (Articles 11, 24, 27). That Covenant also prohibits propaganda for war and incitement to national, racial, or religious hatred (Article 20). Some rights included in the Declaration were substantially elaborated. On the other hand, the right to enjoy private property, included in the Declaration, was finally omitted from the covenants. Much time was also spent in the attempt to bridge the demand of some states for effective means to enforce the covenants and the insistence of others on the "sovereignty" of states and resistance to international scrutiny and "intrusion."

In sum, the international law of human rights developed by the two covenants parallels the Universal Declaration. It provides protections like those in the constitutions and laws of enlightened democratic-liberal countries as well as the promises of socialist and "welfare" constitutions. Before, during, and since the negotiation of these two major covenants, the UN system also promoted specialized declarations and conventions—on genocide, on the status of refugees and stateless persons, on the rights of women, and on the elimination of all forms of racial discrimination.[8] These emphasize, extend, and supplement the protections afforded by the principal covenants. They have also made it possible to "extract" legal obligations on these particular subjects from governments not prepared to adhere to all the obligations of the general covenants.

How much law various covenants and conventions have made depends, of course, on the number of adherences to them. As of January 1, 1981, the Genocide Convention had 85 parties, the Convention on the Elimination of All Forms of Racial Discrimination 108, the Convention on Political Rights of Women 86, and the Convention on the Status of Refugees 81.[9] Late in 1975, the Covenant on Civil and Political Rights and the Covenant on Economic, Social, and Cultural Rights obtained the adherences necessary to bring them into effect, and adherences have continued to trickle in. (As of January 1, 1981, the former had 65, the latter 66 adherences.)[10] As to each of these conventions, some adherences are subject to reservations of greater or lesser significance. It matters, of course, whether covenants are accepted by populous nations or by those with small populations; whether the states that adhere are more or less disposed to comply with their undertakings; and whether some who have not adhered might nonetheless practice what the conventions require.

Philosophical Underpinnings of International Human Rights

International human rights instruments do not legislate human rights; they "recognize" them and build upon that recognition.[11] Human rights was an eighteenth century idea, rooted in notions of natural law and natural rights, and woven of several strands: original autonomy of the individual, converted in society to popular sovereignty; government by social compact of the people and subject to the continued consent of the governed; government for limited purposes only; the rights reserved for the individual even against the people's representatives in government. The international human rights movement took these eighteenth-century ideas of individual autonomy and freedom and combined them with nineteenth- and twentieth-century ideas of socialism and the welfare state. International human rights, however, reflect no single, comprehensive theory of the relation of the individual to society (other than what is implied in the very concept of rights). That there are "fundamental human rights" was a declared article of faith, "reaffirmed" by "the peoples of the United Nations" in the UN Charter. The Universal Declaration of Human Rights, striving for a pronouncement that would appeal to diverse political systems governing diverse peoples, built on that faith and shunned philosophical exploration. Because of that faith—and of political and ideological forces—governments accepted the concept of human rights, agreed that they were appropriate for international concern, cooperated to define them, assumed international obligations to respect them, and submitted to some international scrutiny as to their compliance with these obligations.

Those who built international human rights perhaps also saw these rights as "natural," but in a contemporary sense: human rights correspond to the nature of man and of human society, to his psychology and its sociology:[12]

> —rights "derive from the inherent dignity of the human person";[13]
> —"recognition . . . of the equal and inalienable rights of all members of the human family, is the foundation of freedom, justice and peace in the world";[14]
> —respect for, and observance of, human rights will help create "conditions of stability and well-being which are necessary for peaceful and friendly relations among nations."[15]

We are not told what theory justifies "human dignity" as the source of rights, or how the needs of human dignity are determined. We are not told what conception of justice is reflected in human rights, or how preserving human rights will promote peace in the world.

International human rights are recognized as inherent, but it is not necessarily assumed that man is in principle autonomous, or that rights antecede government. The international instruments nod to popular sovereignty, but there is no other hint of social compact or of continuing consent of the governed.★ Respect for retained rights is not a condition of government, or a basis of its legitimacy; violation of rights does not warrant undoing government by revolution.

International human rights imply rights for the individual against society, but they are not seen as against the interests of society. Rather, it is believed, a good society is one in which individual rights flourish, and the promotion and protection of individual rights is a public good. Any apparent conflict between the individual and society, between individual rights and a more general public good, is only temporary and superficial; in the longer, deeper view the society is better if the individual's rights are respected.

Like the eighteenth century idea of rights, international human rights also, inevitably, implicate the purposes for which governments are created. Rights against government imply limitations on government, but there is no a priori assumption that in general government is for limited purposes only. To the contrary, born after various socialisms were established and spreading, and after commitment to welfare economics and the welfare state was nearly universal, international human rights imply a conception of government as designed for many purposes and seasons. The rights deemed to be fundamental include not only civil and political rights which government must not invade, but also rights to economic and social well-being which government must actively provide or promote. The rights declared and enumerated imply a government that is activist, intervening, that is committed to economic-social planning for the society which would redound as economic-social rights to the individual.

Human Rights as International Law

Human rights are rights which the individual has, or should have, in his society. If societies respected these rights adequately, there would be no need for international law and institutions to help protect them.

★ The Covenant does recognize the right to vote and to participate in government (Article 25). See essay 9.

International human rights law and institutions are designed to induce states to remedy the inadequacies of their national laws and institutions so that human rights will be respected and vindicated. The individual must pursue his rights through his own laws and institutions. Even when these fail him, international law and institutions cannot provide those rights; they can only press the state to provide them. International human rights obligations are met when, and only when, national laws and institutions meet the minimum international standards and give effect to the minimum of human rights.

International human rights agreements are international agreements like all others. They create rights and duties between states parties to the agreement; they may create also rights in third parties, whether states or individuals. Failure to honor these undertakings brings the same consequences as for other international agreements: other parties can demand compliance and seek reparations, and may resort to any tribunal which has jurisdiction over such claims between these parties.[16] Some agreements also provide for special remedies before particular bodies.

International Human Rights and Domestic Jurisdiction

The United Nations Charter made human rights a legitimate subject for discussion and recommendation by the Assembly and its sub-organs. Human rights may also properly come into the ken of the Security Council when it implicates peace and security, e.g., in South Africa.[17] By discussing human rights the General Assembly does not intervene in matters "which are essentially within the domestic jurisdiction of any state" (Article 2(a)). Intervention, strictly, means dictatorial interference by force, and there have been no UN military interventions in support of human rights; discussion and recommendation are not intervention. Human rights, moreover, are a matter of international concern, not essentially within any state's domestic jurisdiction. Enforcement measures by the Security Council are in any event exempted from Article 2(7).

Article 2(7) speaks only to intervention by the UN, not by member states, but most challenges to activities by states on behalf of human rights as "intervention" are equally unfounded. Peaceful objections by states to human rights violations by other states are not interventions. Generally, human rights are no longer within a state's domestic jurisdiction. That which is governed by international law or agreement is ipso facto and by definition a matter of international concern, not a

matter of any state's domestic jurisdiction. Certainly, any state that adheres to an international human rights agreement has made the subject
of that agreement a matter of international concern. It has submitted its
performance to scrutiny and to appropriate, peaceful reaction by other
parties, and to any special procedures or machinery provided by the
agreement for its implementation.

Human Rights and International Legal Rights

The international instruments speak of human rights, but they do not
purport to create them; they recognize[18] their preexistence in some
other moral or legal order. They confirm the concept of human rights
and give it status and value in the international system. Like other international agreements, the international human rights agreements create rights and obligations among the states parties to the agreement:
every party is obligated to every other state to carry out its undertakings; every other state has the right to have the obligation carried out.
But these are the legal rights of states, not the human rights of the
individual.

If states are the promisors and promisees, however, the authentic
beneficiaries are the individual inhabitants whose "human rights" the
state promises to respect. Whether the international agreements also
create international legal rights for the individual is debated. Some have
strongly denied it. Others argue that as third-party beneficiaries, and
the true beneficiaries, individuals have rights under international law,
even when they have no direct remedy but must rely on states and
international bodies to vindicate their rights. And some instruments—
for example the Optional Protocol to the International Covenant on
Civil and Political Rights, the Convention on the Elimination of All
Forms of Racial Discrimination, and the European and the American
Conventions on Human Rights—also provide some remedy for the individual to pursue his international legal rights by international legal
remedies.

National and International Enforcement

Human rights are rights to be enjoyed by individuals in their own
societies and implemented and enforced under their laws and institutions. International undertakings are designed to help assure that national societies in fact respect the human rights of their inhabitants. International instruments require states to enact legislation and otherwise

ensure that the rights are respected. In some legal systems international human rights obligations may be "self-executing" and will be given effect by officials and courts without domestic legislation.

The international system also provides "enforcement machinery." Such international instrumentalities, however, do not operate directly to grant the individual his rights; they work on the state and are designed to induce the state to carry out its obligations. Even when the individual is given some kind of an international remedy, for example, the right to "communicate" to the Human Rights Committee pursuant to the Optional Protocol to the Covenant, the communication does not produce an international mandate conferring the right; it serves only to trigger an international process to induce the state to desist from violation or to provide a remedy for past violations.

The Covenant on Civil and Political Rights

The principal international human rights agreements are the two covenants deriving from the Universal Declaration. Both covenants have been in force since 1976. The Covenant on Economic, Social, and Cultural Rights, which requires a state to take steps "to the maximum of its available resources" with a view to achieving "progressively" rights that may depend on the society's economic-social development, has, understandably, not been a subject of international controversy or of individual complaints of violations. Compliance with that Covenant is not the charge of a special monitoring body but of political bodies, the Economic and Social Council and the General Assembly, that have not built up any substantial jurisprudence of interpretation of that Covenant.

The Covenant on Civil and Political Rights, on the other hand, is acquiring an ever-growing jurisprudence. Reports by states on their compliance have been scrutinized and discussed by the Human Rights Committee created pursuant to the Covenant.[19] Governments and especially nongovernmental organizations have invoked the Covenant. Disputes about compliance by particular parties are daily fare, reflecting differences of interpretation that cry to be discussed.

The Covenant as Law

The Covenant is binding international law, like any other international agreement. That the agreement is for the benefit of individuals, and that the beneficiaries are each state party's own citizens and inhabitants, in no way detracts from its binding legal quality. Like any international agreement it creates rights and obligations among the states parties to it and affords each party the usual remedies for inducing compliance or obtaining reparation if a violation occurs. Again, that the true beneficiaries are the state's own inhabitants does not detract from the rights, obligations, or remedies available to the parties. Neither does the fact that special machinery is provided to scrutinize and induce compliance vitiate the usual remedies between states parties to the agreement.[20]

Thomas Buergenthal (essay 3) deals with the character and implications of a state's undertakings under the Covenant, as well as with those highly exceptional circumstances in which the state is free to "derogate from" or suspend some of its obligations. Like the Declaration, like even the most enlightened and libertarian national constitutions and declarations of rights, the Covenant recognizes that some rights may have to be derogated from in "time of public emergency which threatens the life of the nation." The Covenant attempts to define the circumstances in which derogation is permitted, and the extent to which it is permitted, as strictly as possible.

The Content of the Covenant

The Covenant tracks closely the provisions of the Declaration. At the beginning of this Covenant (as well as the Covenant on Economic, Social, and Cultural Rights), however, are provisions dealing with the right of peoples to self-determination and to sovereignty over their resources, which have no counterpart in the Declaration.

Self-determination has been a major slogan and a political principle in international life in the twentieth century; that it is also a norm of international law was long disputed. Whether as political principle or legal norm, important controversies revolved about its meaning and scope. What (or who) is a people entitled to self-determination? How shall a people make and indicate its determination? Are all options available to a people, or are some precluded as inconsistent with the principle of self-determination? Does self-determination mean only freedom from classical forms of colonialism, or also from various forms of "neo-colonialism?" Does it imply the right of any part of a state to secede? Is self-determination "external" only, or does it imply also the right of people freely to determine the form and substance of their government?

Article 1 of the Covenant provides: "All peoples have the right of self-determination. By virtue of that right they freely determine their political status and freely pursue their economic, social and cultural development."

That provision does not readily resolve any of the disputes about the jurisprudential character of the principle of self-determination. Clearly, the Covenant does not create the right; it recognizes it. (It does not indicate whether it is a moral or a legal right, or in which moral or legal order.) Parties to the Covenant assume the legal obligations implied in recognizing that right. Such legal obligations presumably run towards other states parties, although any "people" entitled to such self-determination may be a third-party beneficiary of such obligations. The meaning of that article is the subject of Antonio Cassese's essay (essay 4).

There were political-ideological differences as to the appropriateness of including provisions on self-determination since they asserted rights of "peoples," not of individuals. Most governments, however, supported inclusion, arguing that these rights inured to individuals and were the foundation of all other rights. Since all now accept both political and economic self-determination in principle (although with important differences as to what they imply), it may not matter much whether these "rights of peoples" are included in the lexicon of individual human rights or in other instruments. Including them in the Covenant, however, links self-determination to the rights of individuals, as Cassese demonstrates.

The other, individual rights follow the general order of the Declaration. In the Covenant, the substantive rights appear in Part III and are not formally grouped, but in fact reflect a grouping which we have sharpened in the scheme of this volume. The order of rights suggests no hierarchy of importance but follows some rationale of organization. The right to life, physical liberty, and integrity of the person form a "natural" package and a natural place to begin. Understandably, indeed inevitably, these rights come first in the elaboration of individual rights in the Covenant. They are the matrix, the indispensable condition of all human rights, giving meaning to all others. Other rights, while they also have important, intrinsic, independent validity, can be seen as developments and elaborations of these rights. Every society, every ideology proclaims the sanctity and primacy of these rights and none would admit to violating them. But there are important issues as to the scope of these rights and of the limitations upon them. These rights include the right to life itself, to physical integrity, to treatment with dignity; freedom from coercion, slavery, and forced labor; and freedom from arbitrary detention and arrest (see essay 5 by Yoram Dinstein).

The rights to life, liberty, and physical integrity are particularly implicated in a society's criminal law. The law, the procedures, the institutions, and the sanctions of the criminal law weigh heavily on the individual and sometimes take his life; international human rights seek to assure that their reach is carefully circumscribed so that individual rights are invaded only to the extent essential to.achieve the law's legitimate purposes. The substantive provisions of the Covenant forbid making criminal what should not be. Other provisions are designed to prevent abuse of criminal law and process, as by unlawful or arbitrary arrest and detention. In a civilized system—and under international human rights—the legitimate purposes of the criminal law are not served by the conviction and punishment of the innocent. Moreover, as the most threatening form of action by the state against an individual, the criminal process in particular requires fairness, decency, and respect for individual integrity and dignity. The rights of even the guilty ought not be invaded more than need be; hence, limitations on being convicted twice for the same offense, on cruel and excessive punishment, and a general requirement that "all persons deprived of their liberty"—including those convicted of crime—"shall be treated with humanity and with respect for the inherent dignity of the human person" (Article 10(1)). The many human rights issues in the criminal process are discussed by Haji N. A. Noor Muhammad in essay 6.

Stig Jagerskiold (essay 7) deals with the freedom of movement and residence. Subject to minor limitations, this freedom includes the right to move about one's country and to select or change one's place of residence. It includes too the right to continue to reside in one's country, or to leave and return to it; even the expulsion of aliens is discouraged and circumscribed. The Covenant deals as well with the right to leave one's country permanently. International human rights live in a system of sovereign states, and governments have not been willing to recognize a human right of persons in other countries to come to their country; there is not even, as yet, a recognized right of asylum for those who are oppressed and become refugees. But the right to choose the society in which one lives is an important right on which life and other rights may depend; and when other states are prepared to receive him, the individual has a human right to seize the opportunity and to cast his lot there.

Fernando Volio (essay 8) deals with personal status, privacy, and the rights to family. Western societies tend to take these for granted but, like the Universal Declaration, the Covenant articulates those rights in ways which assume and confirm the traditional family and husband-wife, parent-child relationships. New winds in some countries, including rights for children against parents in some contexts, are not reflected, but neither are they precluded. A state must respect the liberty of parents to ensure the religious and moral education of their children in conformity with their own convictions (Article 18).

The traditional political rights and freedoms of thought, conscience, expression, assembly, and association are the subject of Karl Partsch (essay 9). Political rights, reflecting the right of self-government and popular sovereignty, are not only the foundation of all other rights in the prevailing political theory; they are in political fact the only way of assuring that individuals will enjoy the other civil-political as well as economic-social rights. Political rights include the right to take part in the conduct of public affairs, to vote and be elected in general periodic elections by universal and equal suffrage, with secret ballot to guarantee the free expression of the will of the electors. The Covenant is an authentic democratic document but, perhaps inevitably, general enough to be satisfied by different political systems. One may doubt that it is satisfied merely by infrequent "plebiscitarianism" when there is no real choice.

A dominant theme of the Covenant, as of the international human rights movement generally, is equality and nondiscrimination. The Covenant strikes that theme over and over, in different forms and contexts. If its motivation was to outlaw racial discrimination in particular, it applies as well to other invidious discriminations. But the equality enjoined is equal treatment, the equal protection of the law, equality of opportunity. There is no direct injunction towards equality in fact, an equality of enjoyment. (The Covenant on Economic, Social, and Cultural Rights, however, in effect recognizes a right to an equal minimum of adequate food, housing and clothing as well as a right to the "continuous improvement of living conditions" (Article 11).) The ramifications of equality and nondiscrimination are the subject of the essay by B. G. Ramcharan (essay 10).

Article 27 of the Covenant includes minority rights not mentioned in the Universal Declaration. That article provides: "In those States in which ethnic, religious or linguistic minorities exist, persons belonging to such minorities shall not be denied the right, in community with the other members of their group, to enjoy their own culture, to profess and practice their own religion, or to use their own language." That is not to be confused with the provisions of the older minority treaties, designed to protect basic human rights of members of minority groups. Those rights, for all persons, are protected by the rest of the Covenant. Article 27 gives additional protection to the cultural, religious, or linguistic needs of minorities, discussed by Louis Sohn (essay 11).

The Covenant includes other rights not mentioned in the Declaration, e.g., the right of detained persons to be treated with humanity, freedom from imprisonment for debt, and rights of children. The requirement (Article 20) that states prohibit propaganda for war and incitement to racial and religious hatred was also not in the Declaration. On the other hand, missing from the Covenant is any counterpart to Article 17 of the Declaration: "1. Everyone has the right to own property alone as well as in association with others. 2. No one shall be arbitrarily deprived of his property." It proved difficult to get agreement on the wording of such a right by states differing widely in political-economic philosophy; many states were particularly resistant to language that might be held to require states to provide "prompt, adequate, and effective" compensation for nationalized foreign investments. The absence of such a provision, however, can hardly be construed as rejecting the existence in principle of a human right to own property and not to be arbitrarily deprived of it.

Limitations on Rights

As in even the most enlightened and libertarian national rights systems, most of the rights in the Covenant are not absolute. The freedom of expression, in the classic reference, does not permit one falsely to cry "fire" in a crowded theater; the most libertarian societies do not permit slander; all countries impose some limits on freedom of movement in some circumstances to protect national security or public order. In the rights jurisprudence of the United States these permissible limitations are not expressed in the Constitution, although sometimes read into general phrases: search and seizure is forbidden only if "unreasonable," punishment only if "cruel and unusual," infringements on liberty only if they deny "due process of law."

The Framers of the Covenant sought to define the permissible scope of limitations as strictly as possible, although inevitably in general phrases. For example, the freedom of movement within a country or the right to leave it "shall not be subject to any restrictions except those which are provided by law, are necessary to protect national security, public order (*ordre public*), public health or morals, or the rights and freedoms of others, and are consistent with the other rights recognized" in the Covenant (Article 12(3)). Or, "the Press and the public may be excluded from all or part of a trial for reasons of morals, public order (*ordre public*) or national security in a democratic society, or when the interest of the private lives of the parties so requires, or to the extent strictly necessary in the opinion of the court in special circumstances where publicity would prejudice the interests of justice" (Article 14(1)). One can debate the merits of these and other limitations or their particular formulations, but few would question that in principle some such limitations are inevitable and probably desirable. The limitations themselves, however, are governed by law, not by the whim of the state. Whether a particular limitation on a right is permissible under the Covenant is a question of international law, and the state's action can be scrutinized and challenged as a violation of the Covenant (see Alexandre Kiss, essay 12).

Enforcing the Covenant

Like all international human rights agreements the Covenant does not eliminate the essential dependence of individual human rights on national laws and institutions. The Covenant requires states to respect the individual's rights and to "ensure" them, and the state can do that only through its own laws and institutions. Indeed, the Covenant expressly requires states to "adopt such legislative or other measures" as are necessary to give effect to rights recognized by the Covenant. The extent of that obligation and its implications for states with different legal systems are considered by Oscar Schachter in essay 13.

The Covenant's method of enforcement is described by A. H. Robertson in essay 14. There is a tendency to deprecate and depreciate it, since it is based largely on voluntary reporting, which at best tends to be self-serving and not likely to reveal violations. No doubt more intensive monitoring would be more effective. But the fact that a state has to report inevitably has some influence to induce better compliance. Further inducement will result if the Human Rights Committee develops the practice of scrutinizing these reports, asking for more information, and challenging reported claims on the basis of external evidence. A public report by a state, moreover, will be read by other governments, and by organizations and individuals both within and outside the reporting state, and their criticism of these reports will serve to improve the state's behavior. If states parties can be persuaded to assert their rights as parties to challenge violations, if more states accept the optional provisions under which the Human Rights Committee can receive complaints from other states (Article 41) or from private persons or organizations (under the Protocol) the remedial and deterrent influence of the Covenant will be further enhanced.

Permissible Reservations

Unlike some other international agreements, the Covenant does not expressly bar reservations generally or to particular clauses. In view of the character of the Covenant, one may assume that there was no intention to bar reservations; it is desirable to have states adhere to as much of the Covenant as possible, even if they insist on excluding some particular provision.* But any state may object to a reservation by another state and may even reject a treaty relation with the reserving state as regards the Covenant as a whole. Also, there can be no reservation "incompatible with the object and purpose" of the Covenant. (See Vienna Convention on the Law of Treaties, Article 19.) Major reservations that contradict the basic spirit of the Covenant would be out of order even if other parties were prepared to acquiesce in them. Surely, for a hypothetical example, South Africa could not purport to ratify the Covenant but reserve the right to maintain apartheid. Even as regards particular provisions, it would seem improper for a state to reserve a major exception permitting it to violate an important right in an important way against an important segment of its population. Even if most states acquiesced, a single objecting state might challenge the propriety of a reservation under the Vienna Convention and impugn the claim of the reserving state to be a party to the Convention.[21]

It has been suggested that those articles of the Covenant which are not subject to derogation in time of emergency ought not to be—perhaps a fortiori—subject to reservation generally. That argument is plausible, with some limitations. First, a state may wish to make a reservation to the nonderogation clause itself, and if the reservation is not "total," it might not be a reservation that defeats the object and purpose of the Covenant. Second, some clauses are not subject to derogation not because of their fundamental importance but because they are of a character to which public emergency is irrelevant and surely not "strictly required," for example imprisonment for contract debt (Article 11). That such a clause is nonderogable, then, is no sign that it

---

*Some clauses seem written as though to preclude reservation, e.g., Article 50: "The provisions of the present Covenant shall extend to all parts of federal States without any limitations or exceptions." But a reservation to that article, insisting on special treatment for a federal state, would presumably be valid nonetheless if other states acquiesced in it.

should also be not subject to reservation. Even articles that are not subject to derogation for reasons of their importance, moreover, might be treated differently for reservation purposes. The exemption from derogation is stated in terms of whole articles of the Covenant and might be deemed to exempt the entire article. But while a reservation to any of those articles as a whole may well be unacceptable as inconsistent with the object and purpose of the Covenant, a reservation to some single aspect of it might pass. Thus, for example, the right to life (Article 6) is not subject to derogation and should not be subject to reservation as a whole. But it might not be inconsistent with the object and purpose of the Covenant for a state to reserve, say, a right to impose capital punishment on persons over 17 (rather than 18) years of age. In principle, "nonderogability" should be strong but not conclusive evidence that a reservation is inconsistent with the object and purpose of the Covenant.

Interpreting the Covenant

As for any international agreement, the rights and duties created by the Covenant, and whether they are observed or violated, are determined by reference to its provisions as properly construed. The Covenant is not an exercise in rhetoric but an instrument for practical application in every society. Like any instrument, it must be read with good sense in the light of its character and purpose.

In the case of the Covenant the character and purpose are a paramount guide. The Covenant is part of the International Bill of Rights, a historic milestone in the struggle for human freedom and dignity. It is designed to help protect and ensure individual rights everywhere, and to establish a legal, political, and economic climate in which individual freedom and dignity can flourish. The Covenant, then, is not to be read like a technical commercial instrument, but "as an instrument of constitutional dimension which elevates the protection of the individual to a fundamental principle of international public policy."[22] Rights are to be read broadly, and limitations on rights should be read narrowly, to accord with that design.

Interpretation is hardly an exact science, in international or in national law, and international interpretation must take account also of differences of doctrine or style in interpretation between different legal systems, different states, courts, lawyers, or scholars. Nevertheless, international instruments are not "wide open"; words are not wholly uncertain: communication, surely agreement, would be impossible if words and sentences did not have essentially clear and indisputable meaning, whatever ambiguities or uncertainties may arise at the periphery and in unanticipated circumstances. Despite some impressions to the contrary, the provisions of the Covenant are no more ambiguous than other international or national instruments, probably no more ambiguous than instruments serving such purposes had to be. Provisions permitting derogation and limitation are in general terms and have twilight zones, but they, too, are not more ambiguous than they had to be. In any event, that lines may have to be drawn in the interpretation or application of a clause or phrase, say "public order," does not mean that they may be drawn anywhere. Every clause has a broad clear zone of unambiguous meaning with twilight only at the margin. Uncertainties and ambiguities may loom larger, however, because the application of human rights provisions, and the facts of any human rights issue, are largely in the control of the state. Other states or international bodies often do not have the interest or the ability to challenge interpretations of Covenant provisions and their applications in particular circumstances.

In principle, surely, the interpretation and application of any ambiguous or unresolved phrase is an international question, not one which the state can conclusively decide for itself. A state decides in the first instance whether a national emergency exists permitting derogation from some clauses. It does not have the sole or final say as to whether the public emergency "threatens the life of the nation", or whether the derogation was "to the extent strictly required by the exigencies of the situation." Neither does a state have the sole or final say as to whether a particular limitation which the state imposes, say on the freedom of expression, or on the right to leave the country, is a limitation "necessary" in a democratic society for security, public welfare, or public order. In these and other cases a state's interpretations and applications may be challenged by other parties, by international bodies of appropriate jurisdiction, by individuals or bodies given the right to do so by the agreement, and by world opinion.

Interpretation is the pursuit of meaning; and international law has developed rules, canons, and attitudes of interpretation, codified recently in the Vienna Convention on the Law of Treaties. "A treaty shall be interpreted in good faith in accordance with the ordinary meaning to be given to the terms of the treaty in their context and in the light of its object and purpose" (Article 31). "Recourse may be had to supplementary means of interpretation, including the preparatory work of the treaty and the circumstances of its conclusion, in order to confirm the meaning," or to determine the meaning when the text "leaves the meaning ambiguous or obscure," or "leads to a result which is manifestly absurd or unreasonable" (Article 32).

For interpreting the Covenant this means of course that we begin with the text, but we don't necessarily stop there. The *travaux préparatoires*, including all the various stages of the preparation, are relevant to resolve ambiguities and uncertainties, though obviously not against the textual grain. Since the drafting process took many years and the subjects received different degrees of attention, at different hands, the *travaux* have to be used cautiously and intelligently, but they are often indispensable to understanding the text and giving it the designed effect. Borrowed terms bring with them a freight of meaning they had in the context from which they were borrowed. Early interpretation shapes meaning and determines later interpretation. What governments applying an agreement say or act as though it means, and how other governments react; interpretation by international bodies whose job it is to monitor the implementation of the agreement, by the International Court of Justice and other international adjudicatory or arbitral bodies; by national courts or by scholars; or authoritative interpretations of similar language in other instruments—all fairly enter the process of pursuit of meaning. Interpretation, moreover, cannot be static; inevitably, it contributes to the development of various provisions, applying them to new, often unforeseen contexts and cases in the light of the purposes of a provision and the overall aims of the agreement.

A cardinal principal of interpretation is that an instrument shall be construed in consonance with its dominant purpose. In the case of the Covenant, it must never be forgotten that it is a human rights instrument, dedicated to the protection of the individual against governmental excesses. That general principle of construction is expressly developed in Article 5(1): "Nothing in the present Covenant may be interpreted as implying for any State, group or person any right to engage in any activity or perform any act aimed at the destruction of any of the rights and freedoms recognized herein or at their limitation to a greater extent than is provided for in the present Covenant." Another general principle, particularly relevant to the Covenant, is that "limitations clauses"—provisions permitting derogations from rights and limitations on rights—shall be strictly and narrowly construed. That principle is recognized in Article 5(1) and underscored elsewhere in the Covenant. Derogation where permitted is only allowed to the extent "strictly required" (Article 4(1)); limitations on rights are permitted only as "necessary," or "strictly necessary" (Articles 12(3), 14(1)).

Reference to the Declaration and Other Human Rights Instruments

Historically, spiritually, and conceptually the Covenant—like its sibling the Covenant on Economic, Social, and Cultural Rights—is a child of the Declaration and that ancestry is not irrelevant to the Covenant's meaning. Since the Declaration has been universally accepted, it is plausible to argue that it be seen as a guide to what is in the Covenant, rather than as having been rejected and replaced by it. Thus, for one example, the presence in the Declaration of Article 17 recognizing a right to own property and not to be arbitrarily deprived of it lends support to the view that such a right is intended to be protected also by the Covenant, if only by implication from Article 5(2).[23] The transformation of the Declaration into two covenants has significance for the meaning of both of them. While each Covenant rests on its own bottom, the existence of an obligation in one Covenant may suggest that it was not intended to be implied also in the other. That a provision is designated a civil-political right and included in that Covenant may also be relevant to its interpretation.

Neither the covenants nor the Universal Declaration were wholly original documents. Both drew heavily on earlier national instruments—the Declaration of Independence and the Constitution of the United States, the French Declaration of the Rights of Man and of the Citizen—and they incorporated concepts from a universe of ideas that had become a common heritage. The provision in the Universal Declaration that all human beings are born free and equal in dignity and rights, or that everyone has the right to life, liberty, and security of the person, echo the older national declarations; the accumulated meanings of their language over two hundred years cannot be irrelevant to the interpretation of that article in the Universal Declaration. Equal protection of the law, borrowed by the Universal Declaration (Article 7) and the Covenant (Article 26), brings a freight of meaning from the U.S. Constitution. The phrase "public order," translated from *ordre public,* with the original French term inserted even in the English text of the Covenant, is clearly intended to incorporate the jurisprudence of that concept in French and other civil law. Even common terms like "national security" come into international documents with national meanings, and one is entitled to, indeed one must, go to national laws and practices to determine its meaning—and its limits.

The Declaration and the covenants are comprehensive human rights agreements designed to be complete lexicons of rights. But even while these were developing, the UN was promoting other agreements on specific rights for some categories of persons. The Convention on Genocide was adopted at the same time as the Declaration. Later the Convention on the Elimination of All Forms of Racial Discrimination, the Convention on Political Rights of Women, the Convention on the Status of Refugees, and others, supplemented the covenants, expanding on particular rights and providing additional implementation machinery. While in some respects the special agreements add new obligations and are binding therefore only on parties to those agreements, in other respects they may spell out obligations already implied in the Covenant and are available therefore as sources for interpretation of the Covenant.

The Declaration and the covenants grew up while regional human rights agreements were also developing, in sight and knowledge of each other, dealing with the same problems, in the same universe, with some of the same participants. Inevitably, they drew on and reacted to each other, even when one rejected or avoided what another chose. Different agreements may have different texts as well as different contexts, but common phrases suggest common meanings, and practice under, or accepted or authoritative interpretations of the European Convention and later the American Convention, are not irrelevant to interpretation of the International Covenant.

Human Rights and Political Ideology

The Universal Declaration was written by diverse authors representing different ideologies. It expresses commitment to "democracy" but is consistent with different brands of democracy and with various degrees of economic free enterprise as with different kinds of socialism—provided the parties accept commitment to individual rights and respect the particular rights enumerated, as properly construed in accordance with their spirit and purpose.

The variety of governments that have adhered to the Covenant suggests that they at least thought their political economic systems were consistent with respect for the rights enumerated. And in fact no system claims that it must, or has the right to, violate any of those rights. Issues arise particularly as regards the right of every person "to take part in the conduct of public affairs, directly or through freely chosen representatives," and "to vote and to be elected at genuine periodic elections which shall be by universal and equal suffrage and shall be held by secret ballot, guaranteeing the free expression of the will of the electors." (In the Declaration, these rights follow the assertion that "the will of the people shall be the basis of the authority of government."[24]) Western societies tend to believe that only parliamentary multi-party democracy satisfies that requirement, not the party rule of Communist or other single party states, or military or other dictatorships ruling by decree for extended, indefinite periods. Many such systems, however, claim that the requirements of popular sovereignty and authentic vote are satisfied by occasional plebiscites and that a vote is genuine even if the individual has no choice between candidates, since he can vote "no" to the single-party slate.

In today's world, authentic parliamentary democracy is not common. The Communist states surely show no signs of modifying their system (which they claim to be more democratic than Western parliamentary systems); surely they consider their system "nonnegotiable," not anyone else's business, not a subject for discussion whether in relation to human rights or in any other context. If there is to be a universal human rights ideology, if there are to be international human rights agreements including both Communist and Western states, in the hope of protecting other civil and political rights, the West will have to acquiesce in the view that the Communist system is not intrinsically inconsistent with the Declaration and the Covenant, even while the West may hope and work for movement towards greater political freedom in Communist countries.

Other ideological differences are another matter. Accepting the Communist political system in principle does not mean that one should accept Communist interpretations or applications that are inconsistent with the very idea of individual rights or with the essential scope of a particular right. Freedom of expression, for example, can be limited for reasons of national security and public order (Article 19(*b*). That does not permit extravagant claims of the needs of national security. Nor does it permit identifying that specific, narrow exception, or the equally specific and narrow exception for "public order," with the "needs of Socialism" or the "revolution." That would essentially deny individual rights in the name of an overriding public good as a state perceived it. Similarly, limitations on other freedoms, for example, the right to leave or return to one's country, can be limited only as "necessary to protect national security, public order or public morals," not for other reasons of national or international policy or politics.

Problems in Interpretation

Some issues of interpretation suggest themselves to any reader of the Covenant, and were foreseeable when the Covenant was concluded. States identified others when they adhered, deeming it desirable to articulate reservations or understandings. Since the Covenant has been in effect and in operation, parties have been reflecting their understanding of various provisions when they report on their compliance to the Human Rights Committee, suggesting some readings which the Committee and other readers of the reports have questioned. Some issues have arisen under similar provisions in other documents. It is not possible to anticipate or hypothesize all issues; the principal ones are identified in this volume in the essays dealing with various rights. A major source and focus of issues of interpretation are the "limitation clauses," the subject of essay 12.

One set of issues that may raise particular difficulties deserves special attention: those arising out of conflicts between rights. The Covenant does not deal with possible conflicts between rights in general. In one particular case, the Covenant in effect resolves a conflict between rights: despite the provision that the state must respect the freedom of expression (Article 19(2)), the Covenant requires every party to prohibit war propaganda or any advocacy of national, racial, or religious hatred (Article 20). In other cases, the Covenant leaves the choice to the state. Some rights, for example, the right of association, may be denied if necessary "in a democratic society . . . for the protection of the rights and freedoms of others" (Article 22(2)). Similarly, Article 19(3) expressly provides that the freedom of expression may be subject to restriction necessary "for respect of the rights or reputation of others." Those provisions do not indicate which rights or freedoms of others may be protected at the expense of the freedom of association or expression, but they might well authorize states to prefer other recognized human rights, e.g., the right of privacy or the right of an accused to a fair trial (see Article 14(1)), and curtail the freedom of expression or association as "necessary" to safeguard those other rights. In other cases, the Covenant does not consider the possibility of conflict and provides no guidance as to permissible resolution. A state might argue that since it cannot literally carry out conflicting provisions, it is free to choose between them. But usually conflict will be between a principal right and some peripheral application of another, and it may be possible to derive from the Covenant some evidence as to the choice permitted to the state. In any event, if a state may be entitled to choose between individual human rights enshrined in the Covenant, it ought not be able to prefer other rights and interests which it might create by its own law for its own purposes.

It is not possible to anticipate all the issues that may arise under the Covenant. But good faith in applying the Covenant in the spirit in which it was conceived, and for the purpose for which it was created, should resolve most issues. The important and controlling considerations are: that the Covenant is a bill of rights for the individual even against his own society, even when it acts in what it sees as the public good; that derogations from and limitations upon rights are exceptional and to be sparingly and strictly invoked. Especially because the individual is at the mercy of his government and it is the government that decides in the first instance what his rights are, it is of supreme importance that all recognize that a government's interpretation or application is not final but is subject to scrutiny by other states parties, by the Human Rights Committee and other international bodies, and by organizations and individual men and women of good will who represent what the Covenant reflects, the conscience of mankind.

2

The Development of the Covenant on Civil and Political Rights

VRATISLAV PECHOTA

THE FOUNDATION of, and justification for, the International Covenant on Civil and Political Rights is stated in the first paragraph of its preamble: "In accordance with the principles proclaimed in the Charter of the United Nations, recognition of the inherent dignity and of the equal and inalienable rights of all members of the human family is the foundation of freedom, justice and peace in the world. . . ." This pronouncement was designed to provide the treaty with a philosophy inspired by past experience and present necessity, and to integrate it into the international legal order based on the purposes and principles of the Charter.

The quoted provision incorporates several significant concepts. First, the human rights enshrined in the Covenant are legal rights, not merely moral postulates devoid of any element of legal obligation. They are also universal rights, because they are based on the recognition of the equal claim of all human beings without any distinction, and because all states are equally obliged to respect them. In addition, they are international rights, since they have become a factor in international relations and, indeed, an ingredient of the peace structure of the modern world. As such, respect for them is the legitimate concern of all states, and their protection through appropriate means has become a task of international institutions. Thus, these rights have properly become subject to the international lawmaking process.

How did these concepts come to be incorporated in an international treaty? Drawing as it did on man's accumulated experience, wisdom, and aspirations, the process cannot be said to have had a single or precise beginning. The International Covenant on Civil and Political

Rights has been traced to classical ideas of divine or natural law. Eighteenth-century natural rights are definitely an authentic ancestor. Plausibly, one can find different kinds of antecedents in the traditional international law on the treatment of aliens, in nineteenth-century minorities treaties, and the work of the International Labour Organisation.* Contributing "causes" surely were Hitler and the Second World War.

The idea of an international bill of rights was conceived during the Second World War, and was prominent during the drafting of the UN Charter and the creation of the United Nations. Inevitably, the founders did no more than include the promotion of human rights among the purposes of the United Nations, requiring members to pledge themselves to that purpose singly and in cooperation with the United Nations. Elaboration of that pledge was left to organs of the organization, notably the Human Rights Commission, the only commission of the Economic and Social Council specifically projected by the Charter. The task of implementing the generalities of the Charter by creating an instrument that would spell out the rights of man was on the very first agendas of the General Assembly and its Economic and Social Council. The Commission was created and an international bill of rights was among its first assignments.

The first Human Rights Commission was a remarkable body and the cause of human rights owes much to the wisdom and dedication of the impressive galaxy of persons who composed it—notably, but not only, Eleanor Roosevelt, René Cassin, and Charles Malik.

The Legislative Process: A Preparatory Phase (1947–1948)

With dedication and energy, the Commission on Human Rights devoted itself from its first session in January–February 1947 to the task of preparing an international bill of human rights. Some of its greatest difficulties arose during its attempts to determine the kind of instrument or instruments to be drafted. Whatever the term "bill of rights" may have meant in national societies, it had no accepted meaning in the international realm; indeed, the concept of a "bill" did not exist in international law.

Some members of the Commission believed that a General Assembly declaration was feasible and were resolved to go no further than such a

* See the Introduction to this volume.

declaration, at least for the time being. In their view, assuring and protecting human rights was the concern of each state, and the Charter objective of promoting universal respect for, and observance of, these rights would best be served by a declaration. Others demanded the immediate formulation of one or more conventions; they felt that a declaration should not be prepared unless accompanied by a convention. Otherwise, they argued, the United Nations would fail to transform one of its major purposes into law. The United Nations must also ensure that this law could not be overridden by any national executive or legislative organ.

The two courses of action proposed had two different but not altogether opposed aims: a declaration proclaimed by the General Assembly would emphasize the universal character of human rights and fundamental freedoms; a convention signed and ratified by states would firmly anchor these rights and freedoms in international law.

The compromise that ensued, which resulted from the perception that there was an advantage in combining the two methods, was an agreement to start working on the drafts of the declaration and convention simultaneously. In choosing the term "covenant" to designate the international convention on human rights, the Commission indicated the solemn and inviolable nature of the obligations which states would accept by adhering to it.

In retrospect, it can legitimately be asked whether a covenant was needed after a decision had been made to prepare a universal declaration, and whether the objective sought by proponents of the covenant would not have been attained by other means, notably by the gradual transformation of the provisions of the Declaration into customary norms of international law (which eventually happened anyway). Before answering these questions, let us first examine the implications of the decision.

The concept of a covenant is an outgrowth of a legalistic view of the human rights provisions in the UN Charter. It sees international law primarily as an instrument to give effect to the pledges of states to observe those standards. If the Charter provisions are meant to constitute legal obligations, any subsequent action aimed at their progressive development should take place within the ambit of international law and should be in the form of a legally binding instrument. The original idea of a bill of rights was itself the product of legalistic thinking. So also was the interpretation given to the term. According to that interpretation, the closest international analogy to the enactment of a bill was the conclusion of a multilateral convention, which frequently serves to make up for the lack of an international legislature on the national pattern.

What, precisely, distinguishes a covenant signed and ratified by states from a declaration adopted by a resolution of the General Assembly? In the first place, at the core of an international covenant lies a meeting of minds of the contracting parties on the specific duties and obligations they intend to assume, and their agreement that the undertakings must be effectively performed. A declaration, by contrast, admits the presumption that something less than full effectiveness in terms of law is intended. A covenant leaves no doubt about the legal nature of the provisions it contains, whereas a declaration is often deemed to enunciate moral rules only. Moreover, the *vinculum juris* created by a covenant, generally absent from a declaration, places a duty on the contracting parties to bring their laws and practices into accord with the accepted international obligations and not to introduce new laws or practices which would be at variance with such obligations.

A declaration, however politically or morally weighty, is a mere expression of collective opinion and cannot normally achieve the benefits of protection that international law extends to treaties. By virtue of the principle *pacta sunt servanda,* parties to a treaty not only give up the right of nonperformance but also acquire the right to call any other party to account if they have grounds to believe that the provisions of the covenant are not being fully and effectively implemented. The exercise of this right cannot be regarded as an illegitimate intervention or an inimical act on the part of the complaining state party, nor can the concern so manifested be lightly dismissed. That some states have shown reluctance to exercise the right does not mean that states have generally looked upon the principle of mutual scrutiny as ineffectual.

The desire for implementation was, of course, the weightiest argument in favor of a covenant. Once it was agreed that special procedures for securing compliance with international standards should be inserted in the bill of rights, recourse to a treaty became all but inevitable, since no arrangements for effective international implementation could be contemplated within the framework of a declaration.

All of these considerations point to the conclusion that there was a need for a covenant on human rights. The covenant was not an accident of history, but a logical consequence of an integral design of the UN Charter to make human rights both universal and international. Time and intervening events may have reduced the differences between the Universal Declaration and the International Covenant insofar as their respective legal authority and actual impact are concerned and may have made some of the reasons for a treaty less compelling. But they have not negated the essential purpose of the Covenant, namely, to become an indispensable legal means for securing worldwide respect for, and observance of, fundamental human rights.

The Commission faced other difficulties in preparing an international bill. Conceptual problems were new and formidable. Was it feasible to commit members of the United Nations to a particular philosophy of the relationship between the government and the individual? What legal consequence should be drawn from the fact that human rights had become a subject of legitimate concern to the United Nations? What were the nature and scope of the particular rights to be internationally safeguarded? How should the idea of internationally safeguarded rights be coordinated with the established and recognized pattern of national protection of these rights?

Nothing in the records suggests that the Commission ever felt the need of a uniform theory, let alone ideology, of human rights. It did not embrace the idea that the individual had all the rights and the state all the duties. Nor did it hold the view that the spirit of "collectivity" defines the extent to which the individual is entitled to his rights. The goal of the Commission was not to achieve doctrinal consensus but to reach a set of agreements that might be justified even on highly divergent doctrinal grounds.

Most of the Commission's members believed that the obligation to respect human rights had not only a moral but also a legal character. Irrespective of the intention of the drafters of the Charter, the establishment of a universal organization devoted among other things to the pursuit of human rights on a world scale itself had significant legal consequences for its members. For one thing, it made them recognize the claim of the international community to a proper and permanent interest in the welfare of the individual. It also justified the Commission's assumption of the power to maintain these rights and, if necessary, to enforce them.

Most of the rights included within the term "human rights and fundamental freedoms" were regarded by the Commission as inherent and inalienable in the sense that they appertained to the individual as a human being and could not be taken or given away. There was, however, the claim to "new rights," which had emerged from changed social and economic conditions and seemed to challenge some of the "traditional" rights, for example, the right to own property. The Commission solved the question by relating the attainment of new rights to the broader problem of economic and social development, which had already assumed a place on the international agenda. Thus, the Commission was able to extend the concept of human rights by incorporating in it a number of economic, social, and cultural rights that were regarded by some as having a "programmatic" rather than an established legal character. It took the view that its main objective was to formulate the rights and do everything possible to assure that they were universally respected and observed. Even though the Commission recognized that the enjoyment of fundamental human rights carries with it corresponding duties of the individual, it was not the Commission's task to enumerate those duties.[1]

Finally, the Commission found that its mandate was well within the scope of United Nations responsibility as defined by the Charter, and consequently could not be considered interference in the domestic jurisdiction of member states. Domestic jurisdiction, in its view, only covered questions that had not become international in one way or another; by agreeing that questions of human rights should form the subject of an international bill, states had clearly placed them outside their domestic jurisdiction and Article 2(7) of the Charter became inapplicable.[2] This position of the Commission, however, was not to remain unchallenged after enunciation of the substantive rights was completed.

The immediate task before the Commission when it convened in January 1947 was the drafting of an international bill. The Commission decided—and its decision set an important precedent, followed by the United Nations on a number of occasions—that the term "international bill of human rights" should be applied to the entire series of documents contemplated: a declaration of human rights, a convention or covenant on human rights, and measures of implementation. This conception enabled the General Assembly first to set general principles or standards and then, building upon those general principles, to define in a convention signed and ratified by states specific rights as well as limitations or restrictions on the exercise of these rights. In accordance with this procedure, the drafting committee concurrently prepared two separate documents, one containing articles of a declaration; and the other, provisions of a convention.[3] The third component of the bill, suggestions for an effective system of implementation, remained in rudimentary form; the report merely stated that the "drafting committee acted on the assumption that the international community must ensure the observance of the rights to be included in the International Bill of Human Rights."[4]

As the Commission and its drafting committee, including three working groups, labored toward a text of a Declaration that would meet the highest standards and command the support of all member states, political cleavages became more and more apparent. The first issue on which the Commission had to compromise was the right of petition: an article to that effect, included in the draft, was subsequently deleted. The Commission was also unable to reach agreement on an article regarding the protection of minorities. Other signs of future discord could be detected in the critical attitudes of some governments toward the draft as a whole. In a statement on 18 June 1948 the Soviet delegation described the draft Declaration as "absolutely unsatisfactory" and of an "unrealistic, formal and legalistic nature."[5] Earlier, the Ukrainian delegate had withdrawn from the working group on implementation.[6]

Nevertheless, despite long discussion in the Third Committee and a barrage of amendments, the Universal Declaration of Human Rights was finally adopted by the General Assembly on 10 December 1948, basically as prepared by the Commission on Human Rights. There were forty-eight votes in favor, none against, and only eight abstentions.

Why did the Declaration outgrow its original purpose and become a document to which almost everyone, including its erstwhile critics, now attaches legal value? Its declared significance and almost unanimous approval were not the only indications of the widespread recognition and influence the Declaration was destined to exert. It had been generally assumed that the Declaration would soon be followed by a covenant with the force of a binding treaty; it was not anticipated that establishing those legal obligations would require a score of years.[7] As a consequence, the Universal Declaration was called upon to fill the gap, with profound impact on subsequent developments. For one thing, it has become a standard of reference and a practical guide for UN organs whenever human rights issues face them. Furthermore, caught by its impetus and perhaps persuaded by the overwhelming support for it that they were obliged to do so, many states have enacted legislation or amended their laws to make them correspond with the provisions of the Declaration. Finally, reliance on the Declaration and constant invocation of its provisions in various political and legal contexts—including those involving states with different social, economic, and philosophical backgrounds—set into motion its gradual transformation into a source of customary international law.[8]

The Universal Declaration set down an internationally agreed-upon minimal definition of what the international community understood by "human rights and fundamental freedoms."[9] It was on this basis that work on the draft Covenant on Civil and Political Rights, begun by the Commission even before the adoption of the Universal Declaration, proceeded after 1948.

The Drafting Phase (1949–1954)

The preparation of a treaty whose binding effect depends on its acceptance by states under their constitutional procedures is a task far different from drafting a declaratory statement. It involves studious examination of pertinent political, social, and economic conditions; coordination among the formulating body, interested international agencies, and governments; and above all, the pursuit of agreement. These inevitably consume considerable time and energy.

By the time the Commission on Human Rights was able to turn its full attention to the draft covenant, the United Nations had already developed procedures for international lawmaking. Their main features are interaction between various parts of the United Nations system, including the specialized agencies, and the participation of governments in the legislative process, not only through their representatives in the various organs, but also by written comments on the drafts prepared by United Nations bodies. In this way, governments and UN decision-making organs exercised almost complete political control over the work of the drafting body, and their attitudes, mostly politically motivated, had to be taken into account.

Spurred initially by Eleanor Roosevelt's driving enthusiasm, the Commission set to work at once and devoted much of its next six sessions to the effort.

During the fifth session (May–June 1949) it examined article by article a preliminary draft prepared by the drafting committee, which included detailed formulations of most of the civil and political rights proclaimed in the Universal Declaration.[10]

At its sixth session (March–May 1950) the Commission reexamined the draft in the light of comments and observations by governments, and formulated measures of implementation.[11]

The seventh session (April–May 1951) was devoted mostly to proposals on economic and social rights either to be included in the same covenant or to become the subject of a separate one. The Commission also dealt with measures to implement civil and political rights and revised its previous draft.[12]

By the eighth session (April–June 1952), the decision to adopt two covenants simultaneously had been made. The Commission proceeded to revise its previous drafts, formulated an article on self-determination, and adopted a preamble; but it left open the questions of implementation, reservations, and a federal-state clause.[13]

In the course of its ninth session (April–May 1953) the Commission added seven articles to the draft and revised the provisions on the establishment, composition, and competence of the Human Rights Committee, which was to become the central element of the implementation system.[14]

The drafting of the two Covenants was concluded at the tenth session (February–April 1954). The Commission adopted an article concerning reports by states on legislative and other measures to give effect to the civil and political rights, but disagreed on the inclusion of a provision regarding the right of petition. To complement the draft, the Commission added a federal-state clause and a territorial application clause previously adopted by the General Assembly.[15]

The final product clearly was not the work of the Commission alone. Almost all issues of principle had been the subject of decisions by ECOSOC and the General Assembly. The Commission had their guidance on the substantive articles, on implementation, as well as on the scope of application of the future covenant. It carried out the decisions to divide the subject matter into two separate covenants and to include the right of self-determination; it recognized that the text of the territorial clause drafted by the General Assembly was more representative of the prevailing trend in the United Nations than any of its own formulations and included it in its draft without change.

In addition to the assistance and advice of other UN bodies and nongovernmental organizations, the Commission drew upon the experience of regional efforts that paralleled the codificatiuon of human rights by the United Nations, in particular those that resulted in the adoption in 1950 of the European Convention of Human Rights.

The draft that emerged from the Commission on Human Rights was a well-balanced whole, reflecting the progress made by the idea of international protection of universal human rights since the adoption of the Charter. The quality of the draft can be measured by the clarity of the provisions on the rights to be protected, its appropriateness to the conditions of the time, and its recognition of the need for an implementation system based on national protection and international scrutiny. The draft contained six parts: a preambular statement; the right of self-determination; the general obligations of states to respect and ensure the rights contained in the Covenant, and permissible derogations from these rights; the substantive rights and their limitations; measures of implementation; and final clauses.

One or Two Covenants?

The notion that the social and economic security of man is part of the common fund of human rights, and indeed is an essential condition of his freedom, has been current for decades and was given most eloquent expression in the Universal Declaration. Yet the integration of these rights into one document with civil and political rights became a burning question, both in its own right and because it had been proposed with urgency by governments which sought to strengthen their international influence and questioned by others that feared how that influence might be used.

The Commission initially prepared a draft covering civil and political rights only, as the first of a series of covenants. But in response to a request for guidance from the General Assembly, the Commission was asked "to include in the draft covenant a clear expression of economic, social and cultural rights in a manner which relates them to the civil and political freedoms proclaimed by the draft covenant."[16]

This decision was a clear victory for those who had regarded the inclusion of economic, social, and cultural rights as a major balancing factor in the international approach toward human rights. Evidently, they suspected the motives of those Western states that had proposed separate covenants. In the General Assembly, the socialist and most of the developing countries opposed this division; they called it "erroneous, illegal and unjustified" on the ground that it defied the earlier (1948) decision of the General Assembly "to draw up a single covenant closely connected with the Universal Declaration of Human Rights, to which it had to give legal expression" (USSR). In their view, "an incomplete covenant would destroy the value of the Universal Declaration by opening the way to the argument that, inasmuch as only the provisions contained in the Covenant were binding, any part of the Declaration which was not included in the covenant was of no importance" (Mexico). It was observed that the absence of economic, social, and cultural rights was unacceptable since "those rights had become an essential part of the structure of civilized society" (Egypt), and the accusation was made that "the general public would find there a proof of the organized resistance of persons who wished to perpetuate obvious inequalities" (Poland). In an obvious allusion to public statements by the United States delegation that its government would find it difficult to accept a treaty containing economic, social, and cultural rights because they went beyond those guaranteed by the Constitution and were therefore not enforceable by the courts, one delegation bluntly suggested that "no great harm would be done if some countries used the inclusion of articles on economic, social, and cultural rights as a pretext not to ratify the covenant" (Iraq).[17]

These suspicions had been prompted in part by the proponents of the division themselves. They may have overemphasized the essential difference between the two sets of rights by suggesting that the covenant could not contain rights that "might be regarded as advantages, either material or psychological, conferred upon the individual by a social system" and that "might properly be the subject of a declaration but not, in the existing state of international law, of an international instrument with legal force" (Canada). The argument that "in the existing circumstances it would be much more useful to allow immediate promulgation of the first covenant already drafted" (United Kingdom), as "much time and effort would be needed before any agreement was reached on the definition of the rights and the means of bringing them into effect" (New Zealand), was seen as little more than a delaying tactic.[18]

The atmosphere was poisoned by the political tensions of the Korean War period. Thus, it is small wonder that little attention was paid to the fact that the controversy derived from a difference of approach rather than of purpose. It took another year and much diplomacy to diminish the suspicions. Meanwhile, at its seventh session in 1951, the Commission drafted articles on economic, social, and cultural rights, and the Economic and Social Council invited the General Assembly to reconsider its decision that economic and social rights should be included in the same covenant.

This time, the arguments concentrated more on the merits and disadvantages of the proposed division. Its proponents defined the difference between the two categories of rights in terms of their applicability: while civil and political rights were immediately applicable, economic, social, and cultural rights often called for progressive implementation. While the former protected the individual against unlawful and unjust action of the authorities, the latter would have to be promoted by the positive action of states; and they would also require different methods of international implementation. Opponents of the division advanced no less cogent views: human rights could not be so simply divided, nor could they be compared and classified according to their respective value.

As often happens with issues of principle, the resolution approving two covenants, which emerged after a long debate in the General Assembly, justified neither all the hopes nor all the fears expressed prior to its adoption. It reaffirmed the propositions of the earlier decision that "the enjoyment of civil and political freedoms and of economic, social and cultural rights are interconnected and interdependent" and that "when deprived of economic, social and cultural rights, man does not represent the human person whom the Universal Declaration regards as the ideal of the free man," and it provided that the two covenants should be prepared and opened for signature simultaneously, in order to emphasize their unity of purpose.[19]

In practical terms, the decision to prepare two instruments had both advantages and disadvantages. On the positive side, the separation made it possible to maintain the absolute character of civil and political rights and to strengthen their international implementation while encouraging a bolder approach than might otherwise have been feasible toward the formulation of economic, social, and cultural rights, notably by admitting that they could be implemented progressively. On the negative side, the division created uncertainty about the equal standing of the two categories of rights and led to duplication of a number of provisions in the covenants, raising problems of interpretation. However, the common ground and the identity of purpose, as well as the similarity of many provisions in the final drafts, make the covenants complementary and mutually reinforcing. The two covenants attained a normative unity as, together with other conventions adopted by the United Nations and its specialized agencies, they form a single body of new international law of human rights.[20]

Formulation of Substantive Rights

In defining the substantive rights, the Commission considered that the only proper course would be to distill those fundamental rights and freedoms of the individual that most members of the United Nations would regard as universal, and to ignore those modifications or departures that were judged to be local. It therefore defined and amplified, in treaty language, most of the rights set forth in the Universal Declaration: the right to life; freedom from inhumane or degrading treatment; prohibition of slavery, servitude, and forced labor; liberty and security of the person; humane treatment of persons deprived of their liberty; freedom from imprisonment for contractual obligations; freedom of movement; freedom of an alien from arbitrary expulsion; the right to a fair trial; prohibition of retroactive application of criminal law; the right to be recognized as a person before the law; the rights to privacy, home, correspondence, honor, and reputation; freedom of thought, conscience, and religion; freedom of opinion and expression; the right of peaceful assembly; the right of association; the right to marry and have a family; the right and opportunity to take part in the conduct of public affairs; equality before the law; the rights of ethnic, religious, or linguistic minorities; and prohibition of advocacy of national, racial, or religious hostility.

Conspicuously missing from the list was the right to property proclaimed in the Universal Declaration. While no one in the Commission questioned the right itself, there were considerable differences of opinion as to the restrictions to which it should be subject. At a time when property rights had lost much of their previous sanctity, it was inevitable that the Commission would find it difficult to draft a text that would command general acceptance.

Still another issue illustrates the difficulty of formulating substantive rights. At the outset it was asked whether each right should be set forth in a brief clause of general character; or whether the right, its substance, scope, and limitations, and the obligations of the state in respect of that right, should be formulated as precisely as possible. Some took the view that no list of specific obligations could be exhaustive; the Covenant should therefore contain only general provisions, and the precise scope and substance of each right should be left to national legislation. Moreover, it was argued, specific rights could be—and some in fact were—further elaborated in a series of conventions drawn up under the auspices of the United Nations and its specialized agencies. Those holding the other view considered it important to specify minimum guarantees under which each right could be fully protected, so as to make possible a case-by-case determination whether human rights were being impaired by reason of restrictive interpretation.[21]

Broadly speaking, the formulations as finally drafted reflect a balance between the two schools of thought: the provisions are sufficiently definite to have real significance both as a statement of law and as a guide to practice, but they are also sufficiently general and flexible to apply to all individuals and to allow for adjustments of national laws to suit peoples at different stages of social and political development. A good example is Article 9, on the liberty and security of persons, which sets forth in six concise paragraphs objective minimum standards for criminal proceedings that can be applied to different legal systems.

A similar problem arose in regard to limitations. Again, some believed it unnecessary, and perhaps impossible, to define in detail all the limitations permissible under each provision. According to the opposite view, however, if limitations were couched in general terms such as "public order" and "national security," there would be little guarantee that rights could not be violated.

As it happened, the course of the drafting itself presented a weighty argument for generalization: some thirty limitations were proposed on the article concerning the right to liberty and security of the person alone, and as many were suggested for the provision concerning freedom of information. As a result, the Commission chose the middle course: while specifying limitations in some instances, it settled for generalized statements and references to national law in others.

Self-determination of Peoples and Nations

The article on self-determination of peoples and nations placed at the head of the draft Covenant is a lineal descendant of Article 1(2) of the Charter.[22] Until its sixth session in 1950, the Commission acted on the assumption that only those rights pertaining to the individual were to be included in the Covenant. But in 1950 the General Assembly instructed ECOSOC to request the Commission "to study ways and means which would ensure the rights of peoples and nations to self-determination, and to prepare recommendations for consideration by the General Assembly at its sixth session."[23] As the Commission had no time to take up the matter, the Assembly decided, in response to the increasing expression of anticolonial feeling in the United Nations, that the Covenant on human rights should include an article stating, "All peoples shall have the right of self-determination." The article was to stipulate further that all states, including those responsible for the administration of non-self-governing territories, should promote the realization of that right.[24]

This initiative stimulated a heated discussion in the Commission, whose composition reflected the emerging strength of the anticolonial majority. The futility of the debate, which centered on the question of whether self-determination was a political principle or a legal right, is demonstrated by the fact of decolonization and by later developments in the political organs of the United Nations, where a series of resolutions gave practical effect to the right and declared it to be a legally binding principle of the Charter.[25] The arguments made against the right, as well as the assertion that a covenant on human rights was not the place to enunciate collective rights, were brushed aside by the majority, and the provision was formulated in a forceful and unambiguous manner.

Inspired perhaps by these and related developments, the Commission also decided to include in the new article on self-determination a clause on the right of permanent sovereignty of all peoples over their natural wealth and resources, which specified that in no case might a people be deprived of its means of subsistence.

General Provisions

The draft contained four articles setting forth the obligation to ensure the substantive rights and defining conditions under which they could be derogated from. One enjoined states to respect and ensure the rights specified in the Covenant to all persons in their territory and subject to their jurisdiction without distinction. Where the rights were not already provided for by existing legislation or other measures, states were to take the necessary steps, in accordance with their constitutional processes, to adopt such measures as might be needed to give effect to the rights. States were also obliged to ensure an effective remedy to any person whose rights were violated. This article reflects the fundamental element of human rights protection, namely, that the primary responsibility for ensuring the rights and freedoms of the individual rests with each state, and that the international character of the rights is manifested mainly by the international obligation of the state to implement them through domestic measures. The article implies that the Covenant need not be self-executing; a state may properly undertake an international obligation and subsequently adopt the necessary legislative or other measures to ensure its fulfillment. It should be noted that the Commission was loath to declare whether, by virtue of the international recognition of the rights of the individual, the latter was to be regarded as a subject of international law.

A special provision obligating states to ensure the equal rights of men and women to the enjoyment of all civil and political rights was included in the draft pursuant to a decision of the General Assembly. That provision was evidently inspired by Article 8 of the Charter.[26]

In order to enhance the peremptory character of the Covenant and provide a sound basis for the protection of human rights, another general provision embodied the principle that in case of conflict or discrepancy between a stipulation of the Covenant and rights guaranteed or enjoyed under national law or other international agreements, the provisions affording maximum protection should apply. States are therefore not free to abridge rights by reference to limitations permitted under the Covenant if their national laws or their international commitments other than the Covenant are less restrictive, and vice versa. The question of precedence was thus resolved in a manner that favors progress towards greater enjoyment of human rights, and the rule should perhaps be regarded as a general principle of interpretation when the scope of an individual right is at issue.

One of the most difficult issues concerned an "umbrella clause" designed to place a general limitation on the exercise of the rights enumerated in the draft. It was argued that the limitations permitted on substantive rights did not sufficiently provide for instances of extraordinary peril or crisis, short of war, when derogation from obligations under the Covenant might become essential for the safety of the people. Those who opposed the clause alluded to the many examples in history when emergency powers had been invoked by repressive governments to suppress human rights for reasons of political expediency. A compromise was eventually reached: it specified the nature of an emergency that would entitle a state to take measures derogating from its obligations and the kind of notifications the state was to submit on adopting such measures. The Commission was aware that a clause of that kind posed problems of interpretation. To prevent possible abuse, it enumerated the substantive rights from which no derogation was permitted under any circumstances, and it provided that measures derogating from other articles on substantive rights were subject to the obligations of the state under international law and ought not to involve any invidious discrimination. Interestingly, some members of the Commission felt that the term "international law" was open to subjective interpretation and therefore sought, albeit unsuccessfully, the inclusion of a qualifying condition referring also to the "principles of the Charter and the Universal Declaration of Human Rights."[27]

International Measures of Implementation

That the bill of rights must go beyond mere enunciation and provide for sufficient international guarantees had been acknowledged throughout the process of codification. Yet it had been recognized from the beginning that international scrutiny would function effectively only if it was assumed and generally accepted that states were prepared in good faith to fulfill their human rights obligations. Those who would be called upon to scrutinize performance should therefore not be cast in the role of grand inquisitors. Instead—to borrow the words of an eminent writer used in a different context—"they would be commentators upon departures from approved norms, advisers about how to achieve widely desired ends."[28]

The articles on implementation as drafted by the Commission by and large reflected this outlook. They provided for elaborate machinery for the adjustment of state-to-state complaints: its essential element was conciliation by a special Human Rights Committee to be composed of nine persons chosen by the International Court of Justice from a list of candidates nominated by the states parties to the Covenant. The parties were also to submit reports to the United Nations on the steps taken in pursuance of the Covenant: these reports were to be transmitted to the Commission on Human Rights (not to the Committee) for its information, study, and general recommendations. An important role was reserved to the International Court of Justice, which was to be vested with jurisdiction to adjudicate cases when the Human Rights Committee failed to achieve a solution. In addition, ECOSOC could request the Court to give an advisory opinion on any legal questions connected with any issue before the Committee.

Before making its recommendations on implementation, the Commission thoroughly studied the general issues, notably the bearing of Article 2(7) of the Charter. The Commission accepted the conclusion of the working group on implementation of its drafting committee: "the domestic jurisdiction of States, if rightly interpreted, only covered questions which had not become international in one way or another; once States agreed that such questions should form the subject of a declaration or convention, they clearly placed them outside their 'domestic jurisdiction' and Article 2, paragraph 7, became inapplicable."[29] Nevertheless, the articles on implementation were criticized both in the Commission and in the General Assembly precisely on that ground, that they contravened Article 2(7) of the Charter and the principle of national sovereignty. Thus, during the fifth session of the General Assembly in 1950 the delegation of the USSR insisted that implementation of the Covenant "falls entirely within the domestic jurisdiction of States" and demanded that the articles be deleted since "their inclusion would constitute an attempt at intervention in the domestic affairs of States."[30]

As part of the implementation procedure, the Commission considered the right of individual petition. In deciding against it, the Commission even withstood pressure from the General Assembly, which in 1950 had requested that it consider provisions for a procedure to receive and examine petitions, to be inserted in the draft Covenant or in separate protocols. As the United States representative to the Commission put it, "At the existing stage, it would be better to set up a Committee which could deal only with complaints lodged by States, and not with those lodged by individuals or groups of individuals." [31] Those in the Commission opposed to the procedure included the great powers; in fact, "opposition to petitions has been one of the very few subjects on which the five great powers have been in agreement in the postwar years." [32] Another proposal rejected by the Commission would have had the Human Rights Committee collect information on all matters relevant to the observance and enforcement of human rights and initiate an inquiry if it thought one necessary.

Other proposals for implementing the Covenant were also before the Commission. [33] One called for the establishment of an International Court of Human Rights to adjudge cases brought before it by states, individuals and nongovernmental organizations, and to render advisory opinions at the request of the Commission. Another sought the creation of a special commission to consider complaints by individuals and their organizations. A proposal for the establishment of an office of the United Nations High Commissioner for Human Rights would have vested an individual of recognized international reputation with the power to examine petitions and, if necessary, negotiate with the government concerned or refer the case to the Human Rights Committee for further action. None of these proposals, however, was seriously considered for adoption. Yet their value cannot be measured by their lack of immediate appeal but rather by the goals set by the international community for the protection of human rights and by the degree of progress toward reaching those goals. It therefore comes as no surprise that these proposals have exerted widespread influence and inspired fresh moves to add to the mechanism created by the Covenant on Civil and Political Rights.

Federal-State Application Clause

From the start, the drafters debated whether the Covenant should include a special provision to meet the constitutional problems of some federal states. The problem concerned mainly the United States, Canada, and Australia, where the jurisdiction of the federal government was not completely coextensive with the obligations of the proposed Covenant. A proposed federal clause would have enabled the governments of federal states to apply those articles they regarded as appropriate for federal action and to accept the obligation to bring those provisions they considered appropriate for action by their constituent units to the latter's attention with a favorable recommendation. Initially disposed to accommodate the concerns of the federal states, in 1947 the Commission adopted a preliminary text along the above lines.

As time went on, however, opposition to the clause grew stronger. It was argued that the clause ran contrary to the spirit of the Charter and the Universal Declaration, which recognized the universality of human rights; that it would create disparity between the rights and obligations of federal and unitary states; that it was in fact discriminatory, since it would place federal states in a privileged position and allow them fewer and less clear-cut obligations than unitary states; that it would create uncertainty as to the scope of the obligations assumed by federal states; and that there was no need for it—at least in the case of the United States—since Congress had the power to enact legislation intended to give effect to treaty obligations.

The General Assembly interjected a conciliatory tone into the controversy when it requested the Commission, through ECOSOC, to prepare recommendations "which will have as their purpose the securing of the maximum extension of the Covenant to the constituent units of federal States, and the meeting of the constitutional problems of federal States." [34]

The Commission responded by putting the clause in a different perspective: it proposed that federal states be allowed to make a reservation in respect to any provision of the Covenant to the extent that its application fell within the exclusive jurisdiction of the constituent states, provinces, or cantons. In order to meet some of the objections, the United States and Australia, joined by India, proposed that in addition to what had been tentatively agreed in 1947, the Covenant might oblige federal governments to submit information about the legislative or other measures their constituent units would subsequently take to implement the Covenant.

The question remained unresolved until 1954, when a significant development occurred. Perhaps because of the announcement by the United States that it would not sign or ratify the Covenant, the opposition gained strength and two new proposals were made: Egypt suggested that there be no clause on federal states at all; and the Soviet Union proposed that "the provisions of the Covenant shall extend to all parts of federal States without any limitations or exceptions." [35] The former proposal failed to gain majority support, but the latter was adopted by eight votes to seven, with three abstentions.

The clause thus incorporated in the draft not only precluded any special arrangements to take account of the constitutional problems of certain federal states, but also prevented such states from making reservations to meet their particular constitutional difficulties. One writer observed that "the decision of the Commission, if sustained by the General Assembly, will make it virtually impossible for at least certain federal States to adhere to the Covenant."[36] Fortunately, the prediction did not come true: Canada has ratified the Covenant, and the United States signed the Covenant containing the very same formula that had caused anxiety a score of years earlier.[37]

Territorial Clause

The Covenant was drafted when the larger part of Africa and many territories in Asia, the Pacific, and the Caribbean were still under colonial rule or had the status of trust territories. It was therefore inevitable that the extension of the future Covenant to these territories would become an issue of political principle.

At first, the drafting committee followed the pattern of some other multilateral instruments concluded under the auspices of international organizations at the time, and drafted a provision that satisfied the colonial powers. The colonial clause, as it was then called, stated that the Covenant would apply to a non-self-governing territory only when the administering state had acceded to it on behalf of such territory and that, if necessary, the state concerned should seek the consent of the government of such territories at the earliest possible moment and accede to the Covenant on its behalf as soon as its consent was obtained. At the same time, however, the drafting committee included in its report alternative proposals which extended application of the Covenant to the metropolitan territory of the signatory state and to all its trust or colonial territories.[38]

The administering states insisted on excluding dependent territories from automatic application of the Covenant on the ground that, in general, they were not responsible for legislation in the colonial territories and consequently, they had to proceed with care before securing the participation of those territories in international agreements involving domestic legislative action. But opponents of the clause argued that human rights were universal and that the effectiveness of the Covenant would be diminished if it was not made applicable to dependent territories, which needed human rights protection even more than the metropolitan states. The opponents dismissed the alleged constitutional difficulties as an "internal question"; each colonial power should reach agreement with the authorities in the dependent territories on implementation of the Covenant.

The Commission was unable to agree on a clause for the draft, and in 1950 the General Assembly dictated its own text which the Commission accepted without debate. The new clause stated that the provisions of the Covenant would be equally applicable to a signatory metropolitan state and to all the territories administered or governed by it.[39]

Admissibility of Reservations

In line with the practice for most treaties previously concluded under the auspices of the United Nations, the Commission had not initially contemplated including a provision on reservations in the Covenant. The question came to the fore under unusual circumstances. In December 1948, the General Assembly adopted the Convention on the Prevention and Punishment of the Crime of Genocide and opened it for signature by member states. In the absence of a provision either permitting or prohibiting reservations, some states attached declarations or reservations to their signature and ratification. An outcry promptly ensued over what was considered to be an inadmissible evasion of the obligations under the convention. The matter was referred by the General Assembly to the International Court of Justice for an advisory opinion and to the International Law Commission for thorough study. The Assembly recommended that the organs of the United Nations consider the problem of reservations when preparing multilateral conventions. Later, the Assembly specifically asked the Commission to include in the draft Covenant "one or more clauses relating to the admissibility or non-admissibility of reservations and to the effect to be attributed to them."[40]

A panoply of views was presented when the Commission on Human Rights took up the matter at its tenth session in 1954. At the two extremes were proposals that any state might make a reservation to any provision of the Covenant (USSR) or that no state might attach reservations to any provision (Chile and Uruguay). The argument for the former was based on the principle of sovereign equality of states, and the latter view invoked the universal character of human rights obligations. The various views between the two extremes eventually found concrete expression in two proposals: one providing that reservations might be made only to the extent that the domestic laws of a state were in conflict with or failed to give effect to a particular substantive provision of the Covenant (United Kingdom); the other providing that a state might make a reservation only if it was compatible with the object and purpose of the Covenant (the Republic of China, Egypt, Lebanon, and the Philippines).[41]

The issue was complicated both by the inflexible positions of some delegations and by the nature of the Covenant itself. On the one hand, the notion of universal human rights encompasses the totality of rights inherent in every individual and cannot admit of legitimate reservations. The Covenant granted rights to individuals and not to states. On the other hand, national traditions, laws, and legal institutions vary so greatly that some countries might find it difficult to accept all the obligations, especially since parties were obliged to give them immediate effect.

The Commission could not even agree on the applicability to the Covenant of the conclusions of the International Court of Justice in its advisory opinion on the Genocide Convention.[42] The Commission found the Court's criterion of compatibility of reservations with the object and purpose of the treaty difficult to apply to such a far-reaching and detailed convention as the Covenant, and argued that to make the admissibility of reservations contingent on that criterion would require elaborate safeguards against possible abuse.

In the end, the Commission simply transmitted the pertinent summary records of the discussion, together with the proposals submitted by the delegations, to ECOSOC and the General Assembly without any conclusions of its own. The action was not taken lightly and was not let pass without a critical gloss. The representative of India, whose views were shared by other delegates, including the Commission's chairman, commented:

> Although a higher body might more appropriately deal with those questions, the Commission should not refer its difficulties to that body passively and without any evidence of its close scrutiny of the problems involved. The Commission should not be regarded as a mere post office but should be able to give definite opinions and advice on the alternatives with which the higher body would be confronted and to provide an evaluation of the debates that had taken place. . . . Ideally, no reservations should be permitted to any part of the covenants, because they dealt with fundamental human rights and any derogation from them would weaken the effect of the covenants and their objects and purposes. Nevertheless, certain practical difficulties of implementation existed and reservations must be admitted, but only on the grounds of practical compromise. Reservations must therefore constitute the minimum practicable in the existing circum-

stances. It was difficult for the Commission to estimate the minimum accurately, but it could submit the four alternatives that had been raised.[43]

The Deliberation Phase (1954–1966)

Legislative texts of enduring significance have seldom been enacted without prolonged debate, and the United Nations effort to enunciate legal rules in the vast and intricate area of human rights is no exception.

The draft covenants were examined and eventually adopted by the General Assembly through its Third Committee (Social, Humanitarian, and Cultural). The General Assembly did not convene a special conference of plenipotentiaries but decided to allocate its own time and resources, which offered the advantage of combining diplomatic action with the overall responsibilities of the international organization. Legitimized by Articles 10 and 13 of the UN Charter, the General Assembly's involvement conveyed the expectation that the covenants, and the mechanism they were about to create, would maintain the closest possible link with the United Nations.

The deliberation stage had spanned more than a decade, and the General Assembly turned to the matter at a time when the United Nations was undergoing important changes in composition and in the order of its political priorities. Though not yet truly universal, the Assembly was fairly representative of the different legal systems and cultures of the world, and the influx of new members during that decade had more than doubled its membership. Thus, almost every state in the world (with the exception of the People's Republic of China, the two Germanys, the two Koreas, the two Vietnams, Switzerland, and several mini-states) could participate in shaping the covenants, and just as important, they would share the responsibility for the documents that ensued. Experience had already shown that, as regards the covenants, equality of states in the United Nations had real rather than just nominal value. The absence of prejudgment and prior commitment to specific political goals, and greater flexibility in thinking and attitudes, enabled the scores of small and medium-sized members of the United Nations to make an extremely useful contribution.

Employing diplomacy, statesmanship and interpersonal exchange, the General Assembly had accumulated a wealth of experience in international treaty-making. Inevitably, it inclined toward the fullest use possible of the precedents and patterns involved in those negotiations.

Among the variety of forms of negotiation in use at the United Nations, the most common is the confrontation of attitudes and the adoption of decisions by vote. Constitutionally, this represents an impeccable manifestation of community support. Pragmatically, there are other forms of equal if not greater value, such as consultative processes aimed at attaining the necessary degree of consensus. In the case of the Covenants, all these forms came into play; but when decisions were made, the Assembly almost invariably resorted to formal voting. Roll-call votes were requested more often than usual. Had the General Assembly resorted to the more laborious but reliable method of consensus, which was already gaining wide acceptance in other bodies, many differences on substantive points could probably have been reconciled rather than exacerbated by the divisive vote.

As had happened during the drafting process, public support as expressed by nongovernmental organizations remained high, despite the lack of contact between the United Nations and the general public and the inadequacy of links between the General Assembly and the nongovernmental organizations.

Substantive Changes in the Draft

The outline of the Covenant had been shaped amid conflicting ideas and working conceptions of human rights which derived from different historical formulations and social circumstances. Some were predicated on the premise that political and civil rights are definite and precise, and cannot be displaced by state interest; while others were based on the theory that rights are conferred upon an individual by government, subject to a correlative duty to conform to state policy. Given these differences, whether attempts would be made to expand or curtail individual rights depended on many imponderables.

At the same time, it was widely recognized that the effectiveness of the Covenant depended not only on the wording of its provisions but on its wide acceptance. Its structure and the character of its implementation ought to reflect the fact that within the ambit of human rights there was room for a wide divergence of state law and practice. Hence, the Covenant had to be a document of great generality, leaving the choice of specific measures to fill its broad guidelines to national institutions.

The following survey of modifications made in the Commission's draft recapitulates the interplay of the various tendencies in order to show how the Covenant was adapted to conform to felt needs.

Serious difficulties were again provoked by the provisions on self-determination. The meaning of the right and the legitimacy of its place in the Covenant were questioned. During the debate, which concentrated on the colonial aspect of the problem, its proponents claimed that self-determination was a collective right that affected each individual and was essential for the enjoyment of all other human rights; its deprivation entailed the loss of individual human rights. The controversy was compounded by the injection of the right of a people freely to dispose of its natural wealth and resources, which some delegations contended meant expropriation of foreign investments without "just compensation." A plethora of amendments resulted: some suggested deleting the article or transferring its substance to the preamble; others proposed different wording to make it more precise and definite. Some delegates believed that the whole question might be studied separately, with a view to drafting a declaration on self-determination or to preparing a special covenant on that right. The anticolonial majority, however, rejected postponement and succeeded in having the article redrafted. The fundamental right was reaffirmed, but the criticism that the earlier draft might have authorized violations of existing legal commitments was taken into account. The major changes included the omission of the word "nations" (a change that did not necessarily strengthen the concept of self-determination) and the introduction of a clause stating that the right of peoples to dispose freely of their natural wealth and resources would be exercised "without prejudice to any obligations arising out of international economic cooperation, based upon the principle of mutual benefit, and international law." The clause clearly implied that unequal treaties could be repudiated, whereas arrangements based on mutual benefit and justice, as defined by international law in force, were to be respected.

Many amendments were offered to the substantive rights defined in part 3. A large number of them would have enlarged the scope of the rights and added procedural guarantees so that the rights would be not only recognized but protected. Others would have restricted the exercise of some rights by proposing limitations based on legal and political considerations. Still others responded to new developments in human rights not addressed by the Commission's draft.

In connection with Article 6 (freedom from arbitrary deprivation of life), the issue most discussed was whether the Covenant should provide for the abolition of capital punishment. Several proposals reflected the widespread opinion that the death penalty was unjustifiable and contrary to the modern goal of punishment, which seeks to rehabilitate the offender. Although their unconditional language was not accepted, the proposals nevertheless influenced the new balance of the article. Instead of simply acquiescing in the existence of capital punishment, the new text states that "in countries which have not abolished the death penalty, sentence of death may be imposed only for the most serious crimes" and "can only be carried out pursuant to a final judgment rendered by a competent court." It was also made clear that the article could not be invoked to delay or prevent the abolition of capital punishment by any state.

Articles 7 (freedom from torture and from inhuman treatment) and 8 (dealing in general terms with slavery and forced labor) were approved without substantive changes. So was Article 9 (right to liberty and security of person), to which several amendments had been proposed. Most of the discussion was devoted to the suggested deletion of the provision: "no one shall be subjected to arbitrary arrest or detention," because the word "arbitrary" was regarded as introducing an element of uncertainty; it was proposed to replace it by the qualification that deprivation of liberty was justified only on grounds, and in accordance with procedures, established by law, that "are not in themselves incompatible with respect for the rights to liberty and security of person." Here again, the political instinct of the majority clearly preferred deliberate ambiguity to a preclusive definition suggested by the legalistic approach.

Article 10 (humane treatment of prisoners) was amplified in both general and specific ways. The Third Committee added a requirement that treatment should comprehend respect for "the inherent dignity of the human person," which implied that prisoners were entitled to respect for their physical and moral dignity, to material conditions and treatment befitting that dignity, and to sympathy and kindness. The addition of a specific provision that "accused juvenile persons shall be separated from adults and brought as speedily as possible for adjudication" reflected a growing concern about juvenile delinquency and the factors involved in its spread. Also, the Third Committee thought it desirable to include in its report a reference to the Standard Minimum Rules for the Treatment of Prisoners, adopted in 1955 by the First United Nations Congress on the Prevention of Crime and Treatment of Offenders and approved in 1957 by ECOSOC, thus indicating that states should take the rules into account in applying Article 10.

A simple statement in Article 11 that "no one shall be imprisoned merely on the ground of inability to fulfill a contractual obligation" was adopted without change.

The question of equilibrium between the rights and the limitations on them came to the fore in connection with Article 12 (freedom of movement). A rather strongly worded limitation clause placed at the head of the draft Article implied that broadly defined statutory and constitutional provisions and measures taken by the executive branch of government were given supremacy over the stated rights of the individual. To restore the balance, the Third Committee decided that the Article should begin with a statement of the rights to be enunciated rather than with a list of permissible restrictions. It deleted the words "any general laws" from the restrictions, but introduced in their place the no less controversial concept of "public order" as a ground for restraining the exercise of the rights; quite apart from its ill-defined nature, the concept is not necessarily coextensive with its equivalents in other legal systems (*ordre public, orden público, obshchestvennyi poriadok*). The Third Committee also sacrificed the provision in the Commission's draft stating that "no one should be subjected to arbitrary exile." The deletion created a noticeable void in the otherwise well-balanced article on the freedom of movement—a void made even more deplorable by the subsequent decision not to include in the Covenant a special article on the right of asylum. A related proposal on the expulsion of aliens (Article 13) was adopted without change.

The Commission's texts of the articles dealing with guarantees to be enjoyed in court proceedings (Article 14), nonretroactivity of criminal laws (Article 15), recognition of the legal personality of individuals (Article 16), and the right to privacy (Article 17), were closely scrutinized against a background of general legal principles on procedural guarantees in the sphere of personal protection. As a result, the Third Committee decided to amplify Article 14 in four important respects. In one amendment, persons charged with a criminal offense were guaranteed the right to communicate with counsel of their own choosing. Two other amendments conferred on every such person the right to be present at his trial and to trial without undue delay. The fourth stated that every person convicted of a crime has the right to have his conviction and sentence reviewed by a higher tribunal.

One issue dominated the discussion of Article 18 (freedom of thought, conscience, and religion): whether it should refer explicitly to a right to change one's religion or belief. Arab countries objected to the Commission's draft on the ground that for Moslems it is inconceivable that one could create doubt in the mind of any believer about the truth of his belief; in addition, a provision of that kind would create difficulty for the states whose basic laws were of religious origin or character. The Third Committee recognized that the paramount issue was protection of the individual's freedom of choice and accepted a formula that dodged the controversial issue. It also added a paragraph on the right of parents to ensure the religious and moral education of their children in conformity with their own convictions, a stipulation identical to Article 13, paragraph 3, of the Covenant on Economic, Social, and Cultural Rights which had already been approved.

Another important struggle illustrates how differently various participants viewed the Covenant. The occasion was the joint consideration of Articles 19 (freedom of expression) and 20 (prohibition of advocacy of national, racial, or religious hatred), during which several delegations introduced amendments that further restricted the exercise of these rights, in particular the freedom to disseminate information. These restrictions included those necessary "for the prevention of war propaganda, incitement to enmity among nations, racial discrimination, and the dissemination of slanderous rumors" and "for the promotion of peace and friendly relations among peoples and nations." Activities detrimental to the community had been condemned on several occasions in General Assembly resolutions, and the various expressions quoted had become established in United Nations vocabulary. The real issue was the old one of governmental interference, which many participants deemed lawful and even imperative in those circumstances. The opposition based its argument on the need to maintain freedom of information and to bar prior censorship.

The exchange resulted in a decision to preserve Article 19 intact, but to have it followed directly by a new provision (Article 20) imposing the duty to prohibit propaganda for war. This conflict foreshadowed the confrontation over freedom of the press that almost paralyzed UNESCO in the late seventies [44] and served as yet another reminder of the fundamental differences in the underlying assumptions about individual human rights.

The General Assembly adopted Article 21 (right of peaceful assembly) without much discussion, and Article 22 (freedom of association) with only a minor drafting change.

Article 23 (protection of the family) was discussed prior to the Third Committee's decision to include a special article on the rights of the child. It was therefore considered appropriate to strengthen the obligation of states to provide for the necessary protection of children in case of dissolution of marriage.

No changes were made in the language of Articles 25 (right and opportunity to take part in the conduct of public affairs) or 27 (protection of minority rights), but in Article 26 (equality before the law) greater emphasis was put on equal protection of the law against discrimination. Like many other provisions throughout the draft, the article repeats the Charter principle of nondiscrimination in a specific context, but in addition to the language of the Charter (race, sex, language, and religion), it prohibits other specific grounds for discrimination, namely color, political and other kinds of opinion, national and social origin, property, and birth or other status.

Two new substantive articles were proposed in the Third Committee.[45] Poland and several other states presented an article on the rights of the child, which, as adopted after some hesitation (Article 24), affirms the right of all children, without discrimination, to the full protection of their family, society, and the state, and their right to have a name and acquire a nationality.[46] Also, the USSR submitted a proposal on the right of asylum at the seventeenth session of the General Assembly. It was based on the relevant section of the Soviet Constitution and would have guaranteed the right of asylum "to all persons persecuted for their activities in support of peace and in defence of democratic interests, for their participation in the struggle for national liberation or for their scientific work." Excluded from the proposed protection were persons "who have been granted asylum for purposes of espionage, subversion, or sabotage against other States," a formula which gave rise to considerable controversy. Since its sponsor dropped the proposal at the subsequent session and no other state took it up, the idea was allowed to die.

The general provisions (Articles 2–5) did not give rise to major difficulties. The Third Committee unanimously endorsed the text prepared by the Commission and only a few drafting changes were made in Articles 2 and 4.

Prior to article-by-article consideration of the provisions concerning measures of implementation, the General Assembly had asked the Secretary-General to prepare an explanatory paper on the subject, and it had invited governments to make available their comments on it. In his study,[47] the Secretary-General provided comparative information on the working of various implementation arrangements already in existence under pertinent treaties; the comparison suggested the feasibility of some measures, such as individual petitions, which the Commission had not included in its draft. The debate in the Third Committee revealed two basic views: one insisted that any implementation other than through national legal systems was inappropriate because it would conflict with the concept of state sovereignty; the other advocated bringing the proposed implementation system up to date and upgrading it by incorporating recent developments in the field. These new developments were the entry into force of the European Convention on Human Rights, and the preparation in 1959 of an inter-American draft convention on human rights; both documents went much further in the matter of implementation than the draft Covenant, especially by providing for the right of individual petition.

There was a notable precedent in UN practice for recognizing the right of individual petition, which, perhaps more than the regional instruments, influenced the debate. The General Assembly had developed a fairly well-functioning petition system relating to implementation of the 1960 Declaration on the Granting of Independence to Colonial Countries and Peoples, which enjoyed the support of the growing anticolonial majority. Yet the idea of following that precedent here encountered a lukewarm reception. The hesitancy of the majority probably reflected the fact that, unlike the colonial petitions, the implementation system of the Covenant was designed to apply everywhere, to all situations. On the other hand, it was generally understood that no matter what the measures of implementation, they were not to be used for intervention, pressure, or for aggravating the Cold War, but for determining, studying, and removing the obstacles to the realization of the rights set forth in the Covenant.

Although the General Assembly showed no pronounced enthusiasm for mandatory provisions on complaints about human rights violations, it eventually adopted measures that in many respects go beyond what the Commission had the courage to suggest, and have the potential for further development. The Third Committee substantially amended the Commission's draft and worked out a system of implementation consisting of: a compulsory reporting procedure; an optional procedure of conciliation, which is set in motion by the complaint of one state against another state; and an Optional Protocol to the Covenant, which provides for the receipt and consideration of communications from individuals claiming to be victims of the violation of rights recognized by the Covenant. The Third Committee also changed the composition and function of the Human Rights Committee: it increased the number of members from nine to eighteen; it provided for their election at a meeting of states parties to the Covenant; and it gave the Committee the power to comment upon reports submitted to it, to tender its good offices under the optional conciliation procedure, and to consider petitions from individuals under the Optional Protocol.

Many of the Western countries would have preferred to confer complete and unconditional power on the Human Rights Committee to consider complaints, both from governments and from individuals, but they were aware that this issue was the rock on which the implementation procedure might founder. It was clearly understood that unless virtual unanimity prevailed on the provisions for implementation, adoption of the Covenant would be impossible. Moreover, no Covenant that emerged from the General Assembly with the approval of a bare majority would have had any chance whatsoever of being ratified by a substantial number of states and of providing the basis for a worldwide system of implementation encompassing 150 states.

During the debate on implementation, one issue came to a showdown: the role of the International Court of Justice. Western states felt rather strongly about the place of the Court in the system, but the aversion of the Third World countries to the Court, based on its recent performance in the South West Africa case,[48] was even stronger: the majority in the Third Committee retaliated by deleting all reference to the International Court from the Covenant.

The delegation of Jamaica made an interesting proposal, suggesting that every state designate a National Commission on Human Rights to review and report on measures taken and advise the government accordingly.[49] (Earlier, a similar amendment to the implementation articles had been submitted by Saudi Arabia.) However, the proposals were contested on the ground that they would entail constitutional changes, since the creation of a body dealing independently with human rights would not fit into the existing constitutional arrangements of most countries. The General Assembly eventually adopted a resolution commending the subject for further study. The idea seems to have borne fruit: several countries have established such a body and human rights activists in others have sought to achieve the same purpose through spontaneously created committees, watch groups, and citizens movements.

The final clauses approved by the Third Committee are identical in the two Covenants. They contain a clause denying special treatment to federal states and a clause calling for complete territorial application, exactly as they appeared in the draft prepared by the Commission on Human Rights. Although new proposals for a reservations clause had been made and discussed in the Third Committee, none was adopted. As a result, the Covenant relies on the general principles of international law governing the admissibility of reservations and their legal effects.

The Covenant was prepared by UN bodies and is linked to the United Nations by shared purpose and concern; in addition, the Covenant envisaged specific roles for the UN Secretary-General. He is designated depositary of the instrument and is made responsible for assisting in the creation of the Human Rights Committee and in the performance of its functions. Moreover, under Article 4(3) of the Covenant, the Secretary-General serves as a channel of communication among those concerned when a party derogates from its obligations. Would the Secretary-General deal with such communications merely in the context of his depositary functions, which are mostly technical in nature, or would he avail himself of his prerogatives under the Charter, which give him definite political responsibilities, especially in matters that in his opinion may threaten the maintenance of international peace and security? Presumably he would act upon communications which signal the danger of gross violations of human rights by appealing to the party concerned to desist from certain measures, by making himself available as conciliator or mediator in case a conflict should arise, or even by using his powers under Article 99 of the Charter to bring the situation to the attention of the Security Council. Conceivably, the Secretary-General also would not hesitate to reflect United Nations concern about particular human rights matters in his annual reports on the work of the Organization.

Impact of the International Milieu

The evolution of the Covenant over time clearly demonstrates how much pressure the vicissitudes of international politics exert on the legislative process. When the Commission on Human Rights started its work in 1948, the world lived in fear that the Cold War might become in fact a ruinous war among nations. There was the risk that one side would use its power in the United Nations to make the Covenant reflect its own views and to alienate the other side from the idea of codifying human rights; the fact that the Commission succeeded in navigating the murky waters of the Cold War period without detriment to its product can in large part be attributed to the personal integrity, sincerity, and lack of prejudice of most of its members.

It was not mere coincidence that pronounced progress on the most difficult issues was made during the transition from the Cold War to the period of peaceful coexistence and international cooperation. Amid new hopes for a peaceful era, the General Assembly managed to reach a consensus on the principle of international implementation and stirred the moral consciousness and political assertiveness of people everywhere, which became major factors in shaping the Covenants.

The preparation of the Covenant also coincided with the rise to prominence of the ideas of national self-determination and equality of races and peoples, and with the culmination of decolonization. It would be inexact to see as the only impact of these developments the emphasis the Covenant places on the principles of self-determination and nondiscrimination. Perhaps even more significant was the increase of the role of the Third World countries in the United Nations and the fact that they identified with the idea of the Covenant. Not only was new impetus given to the codification, but, more importantly, the power base underlying the human rights debate was altered: by sheer voting strength, the group of nonaligned and developing countries insulated the Covenant from the paroxysms of great power relationships and forced the resolution of deadlocked issues.

Another important factor that influenced the shaping of the Covenant, especially in its final stage, was the spirit of compromise generated by the policy of détente in East-West relations, based on the recognition of the strategic equilibrium after the Cuban missile crisis of 1962. But even though the moment was right for the codification of human rights on the global scale, substantive progress could not be made without compromise on many troublesome issues. Détente meant more stability in mutual relations and a substantial decrease in suspicions that the Covenant might be used to advance special interests rather than to establish universal truths or promote general well-being.

The Acceptance Phase (1966–   )

By unanimous vote in the General Assembly on December 16, 1966, the two covenants and the Optional Protocol were adopted and opened for signature.

As the underlying purposes of the covenants were to lay down rules of conduct for common observance and to be a source of legal obligation, they had to be formally accepted by states in order for their contents to become law. The legal strength of a treaty depends not only on the substance of the rules but also on the number of states that have consented to be bound by these rules. In view of the great ends the covenants were to serve, it was essential that they be universally accepted. The General Assembly recognized, however, that universality could be attained, if at all, only after long and arduous efforts in support of ratification. Consequently, it did not limit itself to calls for early signature and ratification. It applied pressure on states by asking the

Secretary-General to submit periodic reports to it on the progress of ratification, and it called upon governments, nongovernmental organizations and the Secretary-General to publicize the text of the covenants as widely as possible.[50]

Numerous international organizations, groups, and individuals in various countries joined forces in promoting the covenants. The need to win support for the covenants also inspired a literature on human rights by outstanding writers.

When the General Assembly met for its next session in 1967, the Secretary-General reported sixteen signatures but no ratifications; the Assembly thereupon issued an urgent appeal to eligible states to hasten their ratifications or accessions and reminded the members that the purposes and principles of the Charter would be greatly enhanced by the coming into force of the covenants.[51] The appeal was repeated in 1971, 1972, and 1973.[52] To stimulate ratification, the Assembly invited states to give special consideration to accelerating the internal procedures necessary for ratification and twice set specific deadlines for the deposit of ratification instruments.[53]

Yet the response was sluggish, partly because of the usual reluctance of countries to become the first to ratify a treaty that limits their freedom of action, and partly because Article 2(2) of the Covenant on Civil and Political Rights implied that each state should bring its legislation into accordance with the stipulations of the Covenant at the earliest possible moment. This interpretation was supported by the decision of the Commission on Human Rights not to include a provision allowing the necessary measures to be taken "within a reasonable time." Article 40(1) reinforced the impression that the Covenant required immediate implementation by providing that, within one year of its entry into force, each party to the Covenant should submit a report on the measures it had adopted in order to give effect to the rights. Evidently, many states thought that it would be safer first to review their laws and regulations thoroughly before proceeding with ratification. Another factor that may have accounted for the slow flow of ratifications was the difference in constitutional provisions on the execution of treaties; some constitutions provide for self-execution, while others require that the treaty be transformed into domestic law through legislation.

The General Assembly could not do much to help states resolve these problems. Therefore, instead of setting another target date which might again be disregarded, it sought to increase adherence by reexamining the vexing participation clauses. Under Article 48(1) of the Covenant on Civil and Political Rights, and under Article 26(1) of the other Covenant, only members of the United Nations and its specialized agencies, or states parties to the Statute of the International Court of Justice, could become parties to the Covenant; nonmembers were eligible only if invited by the General Assembly. The restrictive character of the clauses had been severely criticized in the Third Committee as contrary to the principle of universality. The clauses had nonetheless been maintained to enable the General Assembly to screen the international status of possible applicants. Now, eight years after its adoption, the Assembly virtually revised the articles by issuing a general invitation to all states to become parties to the covenants. The move was accompanied by the understanding that the Secretary-General, as depositary of the covenants, would, when he thought it advisable, request the Assembly's opinion before receiving a signature or an instrument of ratification or accession.

The thirty-fifth instrument of ratification, that of Czechoslovakia, was deposited with the Secretary-General on December 23, 1975, and the Covenant on Civil and Political Rights entered into force three months later. The same day, March 23, 1976, saw the entry into force of the Optional Protocol, which had received (in 1973) the ten ratifications or accessions required. As of December 31, 1980, sixty-five states representing a cross-section of the international community had become parties to the Covenant; thirteen had made declarations under Article 41 recognizing the competence of the Human Rights Committee to receive and consider state-to-state complaints; and twenty-five had become bound by the Optional Protocol.[54]

Among the parties, the Covenant has created a web of legal relationships, governed, among other principles, by the rule of *pacta sunt servanda*. The participation of more than three score states, each having the right to call to account any other participant for noncompliance, has obviously invested the Covenant with considerable potency. Moreover, as a direct descendant of the Universal Declaration of Human Rights and as an instrument anchored in the Charter of the United Nations, the Covenant carries authority that provides a proper basis for international recourse and remedy, whether or not the violating state is a party to the Covenant. This conclusion seems to follow from the fact that the Covenant, as distinguished from agreements providing for the direct exchange of reciprocal advantages, sets forth objective and universal rules of international law that no state is free to ignore.

Reservations

By December 31, 1980 twenty-nine states parties had made written statements containing reservations and declarations. No contracting party has objected in the manner prescribed by the Vienna Convention to any of these reservations or declarations.[55]

Some of the reservations clearly limit the state's obligations in some respect; others purport to interpret the scope of particular obligations. Some reservations were entered by states parties to the European Convention on Human Rights in order to bring their obligations under the two agreements into accord. Numerous statements of a declaratory nature reaffirmed attitudes previously expressed in the General Assembly. For instance, there are twelve almost identical declarations pointing out the contradiction between Article 48(1) limiting participation and the principle that all states have the right to become parties to multilateral treaties governing matters of general interest.

Two notifications under Article 4(3) of derogations for public emergency were circulated by the Secretary-General. The United Kingdom reported derogations from some of its obligations for measures it said were required by the situation in Northern Ireland. The other notification was by Chile, purporting to derogate from the provisions of the Covenant on the ground that the government proclaimed a state of siege in 1976. At its thirty-first session, the General Assembly considered the question of human rights in Chile and adopted a resolution which, apart from condemning the constant and flagrant violations, called upon the authorities to restore and safeguard fundamental human rights without delay and to respect fully the provisions of international instruments to which Chile was party. In an apparent reaction to the Chilean notification, the resolution further demanded that Chile "cease using the state of siege or emergency for the purpose of violating human rights and fundamental freedoms" and "reexamine the basis on which the state of siege or emergency is applied, with a view to its termination."[56] This indignant collective response was apparently also made in the name of the parties to the Covenant. In view of this collective rejection, the Chilean notification must be regarded as having no legal effect.

Interpretation and Application of the Covenant

Basic to the integrity and effectiveness of the Covenant is the need to secure an agreed interpretation and uniform application. By deliberate and restrictive interpretation, the Covenant might become a cover for governmental license instead of a source of meaningful legal obligation. By artful devices in domestic legislation or inconclusive phrasing of the measures giving effect to the substantive rights, the Covenant might well be rendered nugatory. It could also be put in jeopardy by effective denial of remedies.

Early Interpretation

Declarations in the General Assembly after the two covenants were unanimously adopted are a valuable source of interpretation, not merely because they indicate the member's understanding of the significance to be attached to particular terms, but also because they point out the direction in which the Covenant was expected to develop in the future.

The covenants were unanimously appraised as perhaps the most important means of assuring recognition and full respect for the freedom, equality, and inherent dignity of human beings. In freely agreeing to respect and safeguard human rights, states were not impairing their sovereignty, but rather were exercising it in order to establish an international system designed to ensure respect for human rights, which are inherent in man and older than the state itself (Uruguay). As a result, governments were accountable to each other and to the international community for the way they observed the rights of those in their charge (Cyprus). The Covenant on Civil and Political Rights defined rights and obligations that states undertook to respect and ensure immediately upon becoming parties (United States). The work had not been completed with the adoption of the covenants but had acquired new objectives and dimensions because the task was now to see that the covenants were strictly observed everywhere (USSR). The standard set by the covenants was a minimum, and great importance was consequently attached to the saving clauses in Article 5 of both covenants. No action under the covenants could restrict the enjoyment of rights afforded more extensive protection in national legal systems (United States).

Perhaps the only marked difference in the early interpretations concerned the duties of states under Article 20, which prohibits war propaganda and advocacy of national, racial, and religious hostility constituting an incitement to hatred and violence. While some regarded the provision as imposing a legal duty essential to the maintenance of peace and security in the world (USSR), others maintained that it did not obligate a state to take any action that would prohibit its citizens from freely and fully expressing their views on any subject unless dissemination of these ideas was accompanied by, or threatened imminently to promote, illegal acts (United States).

The implementation system instituted by the Covenant on Civil and Political Rights represents a compromise between those who would rely solely on the good faith of states to perform their obligations and those who held that the international community ought to know whether the provisions of the Covenant were consistently and fairly applied. Many felt that the system could be developed progressively; some even hoped that as states consolidated their progress, they would themselves continue to increase their obligations. Some expressed regret that the Assembly opted for a dual system, an obligatory reporting procedure and an optional conciliation procedure; others interpreted it as a reaffirmation of the principle of state sovereignty. Those who opposed the right of individual petition stated that the adoption of the Optional Protocol did not imply that under the Covenant the individual had become a subject of international law (USSR).

Some delegations found problems of interpretation in the wording of the substantive articles: some provisions were uneven and in places vague or too general, while others were dogmatic and unduly specific (New Zealand). These problems were aggravated by the confusion and duplication between a number of parallel articles within each Covenant and between the two covenants (Canada).[57]

All who made interpretative statements understood that the Covenant must be seen in the light of the purposes of the Charter and the stipulations of the Universal Declaration, and many expressly referred to this linkage. This has important legal consequences. If there are differences of interpretation, the choice must be validated in terms of the values expressed in the Charter and the Universal Declaration. In addition, interpretation must be judged by its effects on the purposes of the Covenant.[58]

The Development of Human Rights Obligations through the Practice of the United Nations

Not only do conventions, declarations, and recommendations of the United Nations bodies aid in interpreting the Covenant, they also reflect the strong international interest in encouraging general compliance with its standards—especially since the Covenant has not attained universality through formal acceptance by all states.

For some years the General Assembly, assisted by the Economic and

Social Council and the Commission on Human Rights, has been considering ways of making enjoyment of human rights more effective and has attempted to devise new means to improve standards of justice. Indeed, the Assembly has made its voice heard for fairness and justice on several occasions. In 1975 it adopted a declaration on the protection of all persons from torture and other cruel, inhuman, and degrading treatment; the Assembly set forth in considerable detail the standards enunciated in the Covenant and called upon all states to comply strictly with its terms.[59] Two years later, aroused by the maltreatment of political prisoners in some parts of the world, it singled out pertinent articles of the Covenant for special attention and requested states to take effective measures to safeguard the rights of political prisoners and to ensure in particular that they would not be subjected to torture and deprived of their essential rights under the Covenant and the 1975 Declaration.[60] The General Assembly has also taken follow-up action on the issue of capital punishment. Referring to Article 6 of the Covenant, the Assembly stated in 1977 that "the main objective to be pursued in the field of capital punishment is that of progressively restricting the number of offenses for which the death penalty may be imposed with a view to the desirability of abolishing this punishment,"[61] a pronouncement that shows considerable progress over the acquiescent slant of Article 6 itself. Other areas of interest to the United Nations include the international legal protection of the human rights of individuals who are not citizens of the country in which they live; the rights of persons belonging to national, ethnic, religious, and linguistic minorities; the rights of children, and the elimination of all forms of intolerance and of discrimination based on religion or belief.

Compliance with the recognized standards of human rights has been the subject of special United Nations concern, as is evidenced by the number of specific situations brought before the General Assembly and the Commission on Human Rights (e.g., alleged violations in Chile, South Africa, Equatorial Guinea, Kampuchea, and Cyprus). In dealing with these and other specific situations, the Assembly has been successful in asserting its competence against claims of domestic jurisdiction and has set important new precedents that support the view that the United Nations may assume jurisdiction where human rights are involved. Nevertheless, the need to strive for uniform standards in implementing the provisions of the Covenant has been recognized and has become a prominent task of the Human Rights Committee, set up under Article 40 of the Covenant.

The General Assembly has also conceived the idea of strengthening the international system of human rights protection through regional arrangements. Possibly inspired by the success of the European Convention and the prospect of the Inter-American Convention on Human Rights, the General Assembly appealed in 1977 to states in areas not yet having regional arrangements to consider making them.[62]

Finally, note should be taken of the endorsement the Covenant received in the Final Act of the Helsinki Conference on Security and Cooperation in Europe of 1975. By virtue of the pledge made by the participating states to comply with the human rights standards set forth in the Universal Declaration and the international covenants, respect for the obligations assumed under the Covenant now constitutes an element of the political and legal framework of détente. Moreover, the provisions of the Final Act can assist in establishing an authoritative interpretation of international instruments in force between the parties, including the Covenant on Civil and Political Rights, and may be viewed as evidence of the practice of states in respect to recognized international standards of human rights.[63]

3

To Respect and to Ensure: State Obligations and Permissible Derogations

THOMAS BUERGENTHAL

THE PARTICULAR human rights recognized and protected by the Covenant on Civil and Political Rights are specified in Part III (Articles 6–27) and are the subject of later essays in this volume. Part II of the Covenant (Articles 2–5) prescribes what it is that states parties are obligated to do about those rights, and as regards which individuals. But a state may derogate from some of these obligations to some extent in some circumstances. The state's substantive obligation as regards the recognized rights, and the limits of permissible derogations, are the subject of this essay.

The State's Basic Obligation

The crux of every state party's obligations is concentrated in Article 2(1):

> Each State Party to the present Covenant undertakes to respect and to ensure to all individuals within its territory and subject to its jurisdiction the rights recognized in the present Covenant, without distinction of any kind, such as race, colour, sex, language, religion, political or other opinion, national or social origin, property, birth or other status.

That provision indicates what it is a state undertakes, in regard to the various rights recognized in the Covenant, and to whose rights those undertakings are addressed.

Whose Rights?

By adhering to the Covenant, each state party assumes the obligation to respect and to ensure the designated rights "to all individuals" within its territory and subject to its jurisdiction. The words "all individuals" indicate that only natural persons are protected by the Covenant; corporations and other legal entities do not have "human rights." This is confirmed by the *travaux préparatoires*; "individuals" rather than "persons" was used to leave no doubt that the reference was to natural persons only.[1] The Optional Protocol to the Covenant also accords the right to file a private communication only to "individuals" who are the victims of a violation. The American Convention on Human Rights, drafted after the Covenant entered into force, refers to "persons"[2] but adds that it "means every human being."[3]

The exclusion of juridical persons from the protection of the Covenant is highlighted by contrast with the European Convention on Human Rights. The European Convention points to "everyone" as the beneficiaries of the guaranteed rights,[4] and Article 25 of the Convention accords the right of petition to "any person, nongovernmental organization or group of individuals claiming to be the victim of a violation." Churches, corporations, and other associations have consequently been able to file complaints under the European Convention;[5] such juridical persons enjoy no rights under the Covenant and therefore no remedies under the Protocol.

In some circumstances, however, measures taken by a state party against a juridical entity might constitute a violation of the Covenant if they infringe upon the rights of individuals. For example, a decision to outlaw labor unions would violate the right of individual union members to freedom of association guaranteed in Article 22.[6] A law prohibiting religious associations would presumably violate that article as well as Article 18 (freedom of religion). Measures against a juridical entity, then, can constitute violations of the Covenant insofar as they can be characterized as deprivations of an individual's right.

Individuals Subject to Territorial or Other Jurisdiction

The obligations of a state party to the Covenant apply only to those individuals who are "within its territory and subject to its jurisdiction." At first glance it would seem that the obligation applies only when an individual is both within a state's territory and subject to its jurisdiction. If so, it would not apply to nationals of the state, who are subject to its jurisdiction under international law, if they are abroad;[7] it might not apply either to those in the state's territory if they are not subject to its jurisdiction, for example, diplomats who are immune to the state's jurisdiction in many respects. In fact, however, that reading of Article 2(1) is specious and would produce results that were clearly not intended. It would compel the conclusion, for example, that a person who is temporarily outside his country no longer enjoys the right proclaimed in Article 12(4) not to be "deprived of the right to enter his own country," although that provision is plainly designed to protect only individuals who happen to be outside their country. It would be equally absurd to assume that one who avails himself of the right to leave his country, established in Article 12(2), gives up all the other rights that the Covenant ensures, including, inter alia, the right to reenter his country. Similarly Article 14(3)(d) provides for "the right to be tried in his presence" and outlaws *in absentia* criminal trials. Interpreting the Covenant as providing that a criminal defendant is entitled to protection against *in absentia* trials only when he is in the territory of the state, but not when he is outside, is patently absurd.

Article 2(1) permits and requires a different construction. Clearly, the phrase "within its territory and subject to its jurisdiction" should be read as a disjunctive conjunction, indicating that a state party must be deemed to have assumed the obligation to respect and to ensure the rights recognized in the Covenant "to all individuals within its territory" *and* "to all individuals subject to its jurisdiction." While the provision might have been drafted otherwise and the ambiguity avoided, the *travaux préparatoires* indicate that efforts to delete "within its territory" or to substitute "or" for "and" failed for other reasons.[8] It was feared that such changes might be construed to require the states parties to protect individuals who are subject to their jurisdiction but living abroad, against the wrongful acts of the foreign territorial sovereign.[9] The territorial requirement was deemed necessary because "it was not possible for a state to protect the rights of persons subject to its jurisdiction when they were outside its territory; in such cases, action would be possible only through diplomatic channels."[10] The disjunctive reading of Article 2(1) puts the Covenant in line with both the European and the American conventions which apply to those "within the jurisdiction" of the contracting state and mention no territorial requirement.

A state party which denies to an individual subject to its jurisdiction the rights guaranteed in the Covenant violates its obligations even if the individual is not within its territory at the time the violation is committed. This interpretation gains added support from the Optional Protocol, which provides that the Human Rights Committee may receive communications from individuals "subject to [the state party's] jurisdiction"; the Protocol contains no territorial limitation. Individual applicants do not have to be "within the territory" of a state party when filing their communication and they are not precluded from doing so merely because the violation took place while they were outside the state's territory. As the drafting history of Article 2(1) clearly indicates, however, the states parties assumed no obligation under the Covenant to protect individuals subject to their jurisdiction against violations committed abroad by another territorial sovereign.

Reading the jurisdictional clause disjunctively makes it clear also that the Covenant applies to any individual residing or otherwise present in the territory of a state party, whether or not he is a national of that state. Under international law, a state is deemed to have jurisdiction over all individuals within its territory. Although foreign diplomatic agents and other protected persons are generally exempt or immune from territorial jurisdiction for some purposes, if the diplomat was in fact subject to the jurisdiction of the host state in the specific instance, the guarantees of the Covenant apply.

Measures taken against an individual within the territory of a state party by governmental or intergovernmental bodies over which the state has no jurisdiction do not in general constitute a violation by the state of its obligations under the Covenant. While a state cannot ordinarily shed responsibility for what goes on in its territory, it can submit to a measure of extraterritorial jurisdiction by other states or international bodies. Thus, for example, if an individual were to allege that an international organization or court having its seat in the territory of a state party has deprived him of rights recognized by the Covenant, the complaint does not lie against the state party unless the state were otherwise implicated in the violation. The European Commission of Human Rights reached that conclusion on a number of occasions in interpreting Article 1 of the European Convention.[11] The Commission has also indicated, however, that a state may not divest itself of its obligations under the Convention by conferring judicial or legislative powers on bodies over which it lacks jurisdiction.[12] It may be possible to reconcile these ostensibly contradictory positions by suggesting that, once a state has ratified the Covenant, it has an obligation thereafter not to subject individuals within its territory to the jurisdiction of tribunals or agencies that are not bound to accord guarantees comparable to those proclaimed in the Covenant. The situation would presumably be different if a state divested itself of jurisdiction before it became a party to the Covenant by general arrangements not designed to circumvent human rights obligations.[13]

The terms "territory" and "jurisdiction" as used in Article 2(1) may take on special meaning in special situations—for example, where a state party to the Covenant is in actual control of all or a part of the territory of another state and is alleged to be violating the rights of individuals in that territory. Are the alleged victims within the "territory" or otherwise subject to the "jurisdiction" of the state party? The European Commission of Human Rights faced a similar question in *Cyprus v. Turkey*,[14] which called for an interpretation of Article 1 of the European Convention on Human Rights. That provision stipulates that the states parties "shall secure to everyone within their jurisdiction the rights and freedoms defined in Section I of this Convention." The complaint in the *Cyprus* case, which was filed by the government of Cyprus following Turkey's invasion of the island, charged Turkey with violations of the Convention in that part of Cyprus which had been invaded by Turkish troops. Although Article 1 of the Convention does not contain the territorial reference found in Article 2(1) of the Covenant on Civil and Political Rights, Turkey contended that under Article 1 of the Convention it could be held responsible only for acts committed in its "national territory." The Commission rejected this argument.

> In Article 1 of the Convention, the High Contracting Parties undertake to secure the rights and freedoms defined in Section I to everyone "within their jurisdiction" (in the French text: "relevant de leur jurisdiction"). The Commission finds that this term is not, as submitted by the respondent Government, equivalent to or limited to the national territory of the High Contracting Party concerned. It is clear from the language, in particular of the French text, and the object of this article, and from the purpose of the Convention as a whole, that the High Contracting Parties are bound to secure the said rights and freedoms to all persons under their actual authority and responsibility, whether that authority is exercised within their own territory or abroad. . . .
>
> It follows from the above interpretation of Article 1 that the Commission's competence to examine the applications, insofar as they concern alleged violations of the Convention in Cyprus, cannot be excluded on the grounds that Turkey, the respondent Party in the present case, has neither annexed any part of Cyprus nor, according to the respondent Government, established either military or civil government there.[15]

The Commission's interpretation equates the concept of jurisdiction with "actual authority and responsibility." As long as that element is present, even if a state party has not annexed a given territory or established a military or civil government in it, it is liable for acts by its agents. This analysis of the concept of jurisdiction casts light not only on the jurisdictional provisions of Article 2(1) of the Covenant generally, but also on the particular meaning of "territory" in that provision. For just as a sound test for determining "jurisdiction" is actual authority, the test for determining what is a state party's "territory" should also take into account the reality of "authority" or "control." It would follow that a state party to the Covenant which maintains actual civil or military control over a given territory is under an obligation to ensure in that territory the rights the Covenant guarantees, irrespective of whether it has formally annexed the territory or has a legal right to occupy or control it. Conversely, a state party whose territory is occupied by another state or authority would not be liable under Article 2(1) of the Covenant for violations committed by that authority or state, provided it is not in collusion with the occupier.[16]

The Character of a State's Obligations

The obligation assumed by the states parties in Article 2(1) consists of the dual undertaking "to respect" and "to ensure" the rights recognized in the Covenant. A state complies with the obligation "to respect" the rights designated in the Covenant by not violating these rights. This undertaking governs any governmental measure or state action by any official or authority at any level of government.

The obligation "to ensure" these rights encompasses the duty "to respect" them, but it is substantially broader. While the language is general and the *travaux préparatoires* are not explicit, the provision implies an affirmative obligation by the state to take whatever measures are necessary to enable individuals to enjoy or exercise the rights guaranteed in the Covenant, including the removal of governmental and possibly also some private obstacles to the enjoyment of these rights.[17] The obligation to "ensure" rights creates affirmative obligations on the state—for example, to discipline its officials and to improve administration of criminal justice and the immigration laws; the obligation to ensure may perhaps require the state to make the freedom to exercise some rights more meaningful as by providing some access to places and media for public assembly or expression; as regards some rights in some circumstances, it may perhaps require the state to adopt laws and other measures against private interference with enjoyment of the rights, for example against interference with the exercise of the right to vote and other political rights.[18]

Permissible Derogation

The states parties to the Covenant have the right in certain circumstances to take measures derogating from the obligations they assumed by adhering to this treaty. This right is spelled out in Article 4 of the Covenant:

1. In time of public emergency which threatens the life of the nation and the existence of which is officially proclaimed, the States Parties to the present Covenant may take measures derogating from their obligations under the present Covenant to the extent strictly required by the exigencies of the situation, provided that such measures are not inconsistent with their other obligations under international law and do not involve discrimination solely on the ground of race, colour, sex, language, religion or social origin.
2. No derogation from articles 6, 7, 8 (paragraphs 1 and 2), 11, 15, 16 and 18 may be made under this provision.
3. Any State Party to the present Covenant availing itself of the right of derogation shall immediately inform the other States Parties to the present Covenant, through the intermediary of the Secretary-General of the United Nations, of the provisions from which it has derogated and of the reasons by which it was actuated. A further communication shall be made, through the same intermediary, on the date on which it terminates such derogation.

Similar derogation clauses can be found in the American and European conventions on human rights.[19] An earlier draft of the Covenant article served as the model for Article 15 of the European Convention.[20] The comparable provision in the European Convention has been extensively interpreted by the European Court and Commission of Human Rights and provides a jurisprudence valuable for determining the meaning and scope of Article 4 of the Covenant.[21]

Article 4(1) of the Covenant permits states parties to avail themselves of the right of derogation to cope with "officially proclaimed" public emergencies that threaten the life of the nation. The measures taken by a state party in the exercise of its right of derogation have to meet the following tests: (a) they must be strictly required by the exigencies of the situation; (b) they must not be in conflict with other international obligations that the state party has assumed; and (*c*) they must not involve discrimination based "solely" on race, color, sex, language, religion, or social origin.

Public Emergency

Unlike the European Convention, which speaks of "war or other public emergency," or the American Convention, which refers to "war, public danger, or other emergency," the Covenant makes no reference to "war." The *travaux préparatoires* indicate that the omission was intentional and that it was motivated by an important symbolic concern. "While it was recognized that one of the most important public emergencies was the outbreak of war, it was felt that the covenant should not envisage, even by implication, the possibility of war, as the United Nations was established with the object of preventing war."[22] But the omission of specific reference to war was surely not intended to deny the right of derogation in wartime; war is the most dramatic example of a public emergency which might "threaten the life of the nation."

War, however, is not the only public emergency contemplated by Article 4(1). It can also apply to public emergencies created by natural catastrophes as well as by internal disturbances and strife. The critical element is that there must be a situation which "threatens the life of the nation."

> The main concern was to provide for a qualification of the kind of public emergency in which a State would be entitled to make derogations from the rights contained in the covenant which would not be open to abuse. The . . . wording is based on the view that the public emergency should be of such a magnitude as to threaten the life of the nation as a whole.[23]

This suggests a public emergency whose seriousness is beyond doubt and which constitutes a major threat to the nation. Interpreting the identical language in Article 15 of the European Convention, the European Court of Human Rights has defined a public emergency "threatening the life of the nation" as an "exceptional situation of crisis or emergency which affects the whole population and constitutes a threat to the organised life of the community of which the State is composed."[24] In the *Greek* case, the European Commission of Human Rights concluded that a public emergency must have the following characteristics before it can be said to "threaten the life of the nation":

1. It must be actual or imminent.
2. Its effects must involve the whole nation.
3. The continuance of the organized life of the community must be threatened.
4. The crisis or danger must be exceptional in that the normal measures or restrictions permitted by the Convention for the maintenance of public safety, health and order are plainly inadequate.[25]

These definitions and tests can be applied with equal justification to the identical language of Article 4(1) of the Covenant on Civil and Political Rights.

A public emergency, it should be emphasized, need not engulf or threaten to engulf an entire nation before it can be said to "threaten the life of the nation." Here one must distinguish between the magnitude and seriousness of a threat and the geographic boundaries in which the threat appears or from which it emanates. A "public emergency which threatens the life of the nation" could presumably exist even if the emergency appeared to be confined to one part of the country—for example, one of its provinces, states, or cantons—and did not threaten to spill over to other parts of the country.[26] A contrary interpretation is unreasonable, since it would prevent a state party from declaring a public emergency in one of its remote provinces where a large-scale armed insurrection was in progress merely because it appeared that the conflict would not spread to other provinces.

Article 4(1) also stipulates that "the existence" of the public emergency must be "officially proclaimed." (There is no comparable requirement either in the European or the American Convention.) Efforts to substitute "legally" for "officially" failed.[27] The language which was adopted suggests that the legality of the proclamation under domestic law is not the test for determining the validity and effectiveness of the derogation under the Covenant, but it would seem that the individual or body making the proclamation must have some formal or apparent authority to promulgate "official" acts. More important, "proclamation" implies publication and publicity, indicating that a public announcement must accompany the official proclamation of the public emergency.

Permissible Measures of Derogation

By Article 4(1), a state party may take measures derogating from obligations under the Covenant only "to the extent strictly required by the exigencies of the situation." Thus, although conditions may justify a state in invoking the right of derogation, the measures which it adopts derogating from obligations under the Covenant are permissible only if, and to the extent that, they are strictly required by the emergency. Article 4(2), moreover, prohibits any derogation whatever from obligations under specified articles of the Covenant. The result of Article 4(1) and 4(2) taken together is that even in a proclaimed emergency, measures derogating from certain rights are impermissible even if they might be deemed strictly required by the exigencies of the situation.

While in the first instance, of course, the state will decide whether there is an emergency threatening the life of the nation, what measures it deems necessary for coping with the emergency, whether any such measures derogate from obligations under the Covenant, and whether such measures are "strictly required," the state's decision on these questions is not final. They are issues in the interpretation and application of an international covenant, which are questions of international law, subject to scrutiny, enforcement and remedy like other issues arising under the Covenant.

In 1978, the European Court of Human Rights considered a challenge to measures taken in the exercise of a claimed right of derogation under Article 15 of the European Convention, similar to Article 4 of the Covenant. The Court said:

> It falls in the first place to each Contracting State, with its responsibility for the "life of [its] nation," to determine whether that life is threatened by a "public emergency" and, if so, how far it is necessary to go in attempting to overcome the emergency. By reason of their direct and continuous contact with the pressing needs of the moment, the national authorities are in principle in a better position than the international judge to decide both on the presence of such an emergency and on the nature and scope of derogations necessary to avert it. In this matter Article 15 § 1 leaves those authorities a wide margin of appreciation.
>
> Nevertheless, the States do not enjoy an unlimited power in this respect. The Court . . . is empowered to rule on whether the States have gone beyond the "extent strictly required by the exigencies" of the crisis (Lawless judgment . . .). The domestic margin of appreciation is thus accompanied by a European supervision.[28]

In the *Lawless* case cited by the Court, the European Court had left no doubt that it considered that it had the power to review not only whether the measures adopted by a state party were strictly required by the exigencies of the situation, but even the antecedent question whether there existed a public emergency threatening the life of the nation.[29] In the case against Greece, the European Commission of Human Rights in fact determined that the Greek military junta had failed to prove the existence of a public emergency threatening the life of the nation.[30]

The considerations invoked by the European Court to support a "margin of appreciation" presumably apply with equal force to Article 4(1) of the Covenant, and states parties to that treaty can be deemed to enjoy a comparable margin of appreciation in coping with an emergency threatening the life of the nation.[31] Although states parties, therefore, have very substantial legislative and executive discretion in dealing with genuine emergencies, the margin of appreciation would presumably be exceeded if a government could adduce no reasonable justification, given the nature of the emergency, for the severity, scope, or duration of the measures or for the manner in which such measures were applied.[32] But, as the European Court emphasized, international organs reviewing the legality of emergency measures must do so "in the light, not of a purely retrospective examination of the efficacy of those measures, but of the conditions and circumstances reigning when they were originally taken and subsequently applied."[33]

Conflicting International Obligations

Even measures strictly required by the exigencies of the situation may nevertheless be impermissible under Article 4(1) if they conflict with other obligations of the derogating state under international law.[34] The Covenant thus prevents a state party from adopting measures that violate the state's obligations under a treaty, for example, the United Nations Charter, or under customary international law.[35] Particularly relevant in this connection are humanitarian law treaties because they apply in time of war: a state which purports to derogate from obligations under the Covenant which are required also by such other treaty would be violating both agreements. Similarly, a state could not take measures under Article 4 which would violate provisions in other human rights treaties to which it is party, for example when such other treaty contains no derogation clause or[36] has a stricter derogation clause forbidding derogation from some rights for which derogation is permitted under Article 4 of the Covenant.[37]

Nondiscrimination

Article 4(1) also stipulates that the measures which a state may take in dealing with an emergency may "not involve discrimination solely

on the ground of race, colour, sex, language, religion or social origin."
The word "solely" appears to imply that the only derogations prohibited under this clause are those where the grounds listed are the sole
and exclusive reason for the discrimination. Measures having a legitimate purpose but which affect a racial or religious group in particular
would not be prohibited.[38] For example, measures taken during a public emergency in a part of the country whose inhabitants belong to a
religious minority would not be illegal merely because they affected
that group.

The Nonderogable Rights

Article 4(2) lists the provisions of the Covenant from which no derogation is permitted. These are Article 6 (right to life), Article 7 (prohibition of torture), Article 8, paragraphs 1 and 2 (prohibition of slavery and servitude), Article 11 (prohibition of imprisonment for
nonfulfillment of contractual obligations), Article 15 (prohibition
against retroactive criminal laws and penalties), Article 16 (the right to
be recognized as a person before the law), and Article 18 (freedom of
thought, conscience, and religion).[39] While the reasons for barring derogation from these Articles were not expressed, presumably some
were deemed too important to permit derogation from them even in
emergency (e.g., the right to life or to a fair trial); while, as to others,
it appeared inconceivable that derogation could be "strictly required"
even in an emergency, e.g., the prohibition on imprisonment for contract debts.

The right to life is nonderogable also under the European Convention, but that Convention provides that the prohibition against derogation does not apply to "deaths resulting from lawful acts of war."
There is no comparable provision in the Covenant. That is to be attributed, in part at least, to the fact that, unlike Article 15(1) of the European Convention, Article 4(1) of the Covenant makes no mention of
"war." The argument has been made that since the Covenant (Article
6) prohibits only "arbitrary" deprivation of life, it would be "a reasonable interpretation of this provision that death resulting from lawful
acts of war would not constitute an 'arbitrary' deprivation of life within
the meaning of Article 6."[40]

There has been some debate whether the prohibition against derogation from Article 18 (freedom of thought, conscience, and religion) applies also to Article 18(3), which provides that "freedom to manifest
one's religion or beliefs may be subject only to such limitations as are
prescribed by law and are necessary to protect public safety, order,

health, or morals or the fundamental rights and freedoms of others."
The deliberations of the Third Committee dealing with this subject
were summarized as follows:

> It was argued that, whereas the right to freedom of thought, conscience
> and religion (article 18) should, rightly, not be subject to derogation in
> time of emergency, Governments in such a situation should be free to der-
> ogate from the provisions (article 18, para. 3) which specify the permissible
> limitations on the freedom to manifest one's religion or beliefs. On the
> other hand, it was held that these permissible limitations were already
> broad enough and that it would be undesirable to give States a blanket
> authority to restrict the freedom to manifest one's religion or beliefs.[41]

The latter view prevailed and a draft amendment which would have
made Article 4(2) inapplicable to Article 18(3) was withdrawn before it
could be put to a vote.[42] The text of Article 4(2) as finally adopted
refers to Article 18 as a whole and does not exclude, even by implication, the provision of Article 18(3). It follows that no derogation under
Article 4 is permissible from any provisions of Article 18, and that the
only restrictions that may be imposed on the enjoyment of the rights it
guarantees are those expressly provided for in Article 18(3).

Notice of Derogation

A state party exercising its right of derogation must under Article
4(3) "immediately inform" the other state parties "of the provisions [of
the Covenant] from which it has derogated and of the reasons by which
it was actuated." The European Convention, which has no "immediate" notification requirement, has been interpreted to require notification within a "reasonable period," a standard which in one case was
deemed to have been satisfied by a delay of twelve days.[43] But the
express requirement of "immediate notification" in the Covenant was
intended to improve on the European Convention and a twelve-day
delay should not ordinarily be deemed satisfactory under Article 4(3).
That provision plainly calls for notice to be dispatched almost simultaneously with the proclamation of the emergency or the taking of derogating measures.
   The obligation to specify the provisions of the Covenant from which
derogation is made constitutes another improvement on the European
Convention, which requires only information about the "measures"
taken by the state party. That requirement would be met by a state
which merely declared that certain provisions of its national constitu-

tion have been temporarily suspended. Such a declaration, even if accompanied by reference to the relevant provisions of the constitution, would not necessarily indicate from which specific rights guaranteed in the Convention the state party is derogating, and some very serious infringements might consequently go unnoticed. Article 4(3) of the Covenant reduces this risk.[44]

A notification, however, that does no more than identify the provisions of the Covenant to which the derogation applies would not be sufficient. Article 4(3) also calls on the state to indicate "the reasons by which it was actuated" in exercising its rights of derogation. This phrase, read in the context of Article 4 as a whole, suggests that the state must provide some information concerning the specific measures it proposes to take, or is taking, and the reasons compelling it to do so. One of the purposes of the notice of derogation is to provide information enabling the other states parties to determine, if only in a very preliminary way, whether the derogation is consistent with the provisions of Article 4(1) and 4(2) of the Covenant. What is called for, therefore, is information that would enable others to determine the nature of the emergency, whether the measures adopted are "strictly required by the exigencies of the situation," and whether they might be discriminatory in character or inconsistent with the state's "other obligations under international law." This information must also be provided "immediately," for a notification that is incomplete in this regard does not comply with the requirements of Article 4(3).[45]

The notice of derogation under Article 4(3) is to be communicated to the states parties to the Covenant "through the intermediary of the Secretary-General of the United Nations."[46] The Human Rights Committee established under Article 28 of the Covenant (see essay 14) is not included among the addressees of the notice of derogation. This defect may be less serious than it appears, however, since the reports which the states parties must submit to the Committee (Article 40) "shall indicate the factors and difficulties, if any, affecting the implementation of the present Covenant."[47] A state party which availed itself of the right of derogation must be deemed to have encountered "difficulties" affecting the implementation of the Covenant, and its report, to be complete, should contain information relating to the derogation. The practice of the Committee supports this interpretation, despite the fact that a specific reference to derogations which had been included in the draft "General Guidelines for Submission of Reports" was deleted from the final text.[48] The deletion was explained by the Committee in the following terms:

As far as derogations under article 4 of the Covenant were concerned, several members of the Committee felt that they should not be mentioned in the General guidelines because, in particular, this might be misinterpreted as weakening the provisions of article 4(3) of the Covenant requiring that notification of any derogation and of the reasons therefor be made "immediately." The Committee decided not to refer in the General guidelines to . . . derogations under article 4 of the Covenant.[49]

Committee discussions and subsequent practice indicate that the Committee expects to be kept directly informed of derogations through the state reports and by prompt supplements thereto whenever an emergency arises after a report has been submitted.[50] Furthermore, although the guidelines do not refer expressly to derogations, they do so by implication,[51] and in reviewing state reports the Committee has already scrutinized specific derogations under Article 4.[52]

Article 4(3) requires a derogating state party to file an additional notification "on the date on which it terminates such derogation." The phrase "on the date" was used advisedly to indicate that notice should be given as soon as the termination of the derogation has been effected.[53] But failure to comply with this requirement will not validate measures taken or continued after the events which justified the public emergency and derogation have ceased to exist.[54]

Safeguards Against Abuse

Rights can be abused, sometimes for the purpose of denying rights to others. The limited authority of governments to curtail rights in some circumstances can be abused to deny rights altogether. Like other international human rights instruments, the Covenant seeks to guard against these possibilities.[55] Article 5(1) reads as follows:

Nothing in the present Covenant may be interpreted as implying for any State, group or person any right to engage in any activity or perform any act aimed at the destruction of any of the rights and freedoms recognized herein or at their limitation to a greater extent than is provided for in the present Covenant.

Article 5(1) is based on Article 30 of the Universal Declaration of Human Rights.[56] As originally drafted, Article 30 referred only to individuals, and was designed to enable the state to protect itself against individuals relying on the human rights guarantees to promote activities seeking to establish totalitarian regimes.[57] The draft was subsequently enlarged by making reference also to "groups" and "states." The addition of "states" changed the scope of the provision very substantially, for what was initially intended only as a safeguard against activities of extremist groups now applies also to regimes bent on the destruction of fundamental rights. Efforts to delete the reference to states from Article 5(1) failed.[58] The result is a provision that can play a very important role in the evolution of the human rights system established by the Covenant.

The importance of Article 5(1) results from the fact that the Covenant authorizes the state parties, under certain circumstances, to derogate from, limit, or restrict the rights it proclaims. Since governments must be granted some discretion in determining the need for such derogations, limitations, or restrictions, it is important to ensure that this authority not be used to destroy these rights altogether or to impose unwarranted limitations on their exercise. Article 5(1) stipulates, in effect, that rights and powers conferred for one purpose may not be used for another, illegitimate purpose.[59] Viewed in this light, Article 5(1) forms an integral part of all the provisions of the Covenant that authorize derogations, limitations, or restrictions.[60] Thus, a government's exercise of the right of derogation under Article 4 of the Covenant, for example, must be judged not only for its formal compliance with the requirements of that provision, but also by asking, in reliance on Article 5(1), what the government's "aim" or purpose is. If the aim in fact is the destruction of any of the rights that the Covenant guarantees, then the derogation would be impermissible even if it otherwise comports with Article 4. By focusing on the "aim" of a given activity, Article 5(1) calls for a scrutiny of motives and purposes and permits subjective elements to be taken into account in addition to the objective criteria for judging compliance with Article 4(1), Article 22(2), or others.[61]

Consequently, it is arguable that a derogation under Article 4(1) would conflict with Article 5(1) if the national emergency was created and proclaimed by a group which seized power in a state with the aim of establishing a regime committed to the denial of human rights. The European Commission of Human Rights was faced with a comparable situation in a case resulting from the rise to power of the Greek military junta, which proclaimed a public emergency and invoked the derogation article of the European Convention to suspend many fundamental rights. If in that case the Commission had not reached the conclusion that the derogation was unwarranted under Article 15(1) of the European Convention, it would have been justified in holding that the continued suspension of basic rights violated Article 17 of the Convention—the counterpart of Article 5(1) of the Convenant—because there was strong evidence indicating that the junta was using the emergency power to suppress all opposition.[62]

As applied to individuals and groups, Article 5(1) is not to be distorted and to become a tool for the suppression of rights in general. It is important to note that Article 5(1) applies only to "activities" and the "performance of acts" aimed at the "destruction" of rights or their improper "limitation." Thus, a state may outlaw a terrorist organization[63] or terrorist activities that aim at the destruction of various fundamental rights, and a member of the organization could not invoke the right of association or freedom of assembly to challenge these measures. But the individuals involved do not lose their other rights merely because they are engaged in unlawful activities. This proposition finds support in European human rights jurisprudence.[64] For example, in the *Lawless* case, the European Court emphatically rejected the contention of the Irish government that, since Lawless was engaged in terrorist activities, he was not entitled to the protection of the Convention. The Court ruled as follows:

> Whereas in the opinion of the Court the purpose of Article 17, insofar as it refers to groups or to individuals, is to make it impossible for them to derive from the Convention a right to engage or perform any act aimed at destroying . . . any of the rights and freedoms set forth in the Convention; whereas, therefore, no person may be able to take advantage of the provisions of the Convention to perform acts aimed at destroying the aforesaid rights and freedoms; whereas this provision, which is negative in scope cannot be construed *a contrario* as depriving a physical person of the fundamental individual rights guaranteed by Articles 5 and 6 of the Convention; whereas, in the present instance G.R. Lawless has not relied on the Convention in order to justify or perform acts contrary to the rights and freedoms recognised therein, but has complained of having been deprived of the guarantees granted in Articles 5 and 6 of the Convention; whereas, accordingly, the Court cannot, on this ground, accept the submission of the Irish Government.[65]

Article 5(1) of the Covenant, like Article 17 of the European Convention, prevents individuals from relying on the rights guaranteed in the Covenant for the purpose of promoting activities aimed at the destruction of the rights it proclaims. This provision does not, however, authorize the state to deprive these same individuals of their rights when they engage in other activities;[66] and even when they engage in activities aimed at the destruction of the rights guaranteed in the Covenant, they do not lose all rights, but only those that directly promote the destructive activities. Thus, although a state party may lawfully deny an individual the right actively to promote the establishment of a totalitarian regime, it would be a violation of the Covenant, not a permissible invocation of Article 5(1), to deprive him of a fair trial in criminal proceedings arising out of those activities.

Article 5(1) speaks of engaging "in any activity" or performing "any act" aimed at the destruction of the rights which the Covenant guarantees. The same language is used in Article 30 of the Universal Declaration from which the provision is derived. The legislative history relating to Article 30 indicates that these terms were used advisedly to make clear that mere expressions of opinion critical of a government or of a political system were not covered by the provision, but that what was required to come within its ambit was some "action," or steps taken in anticipation of "action," having the specific aim of "destroying" or "limiting" the protected rights.[67] This suggests that Article 5(1) should be applied by governments only when there is evidence of the "aim" to destroy or to limit fundamental rights, and when some action or measure has been taken in furtherance of this objective.

The Most-Favorable-to-Individual Clause

Article 5(2) of the civil and political Covenant has been quite appropriately labeled the "most-favorable-to-individual" clause.[68] It reads as follows:

> There shall be no restriction upon or derogation from any of the fundamental human rights recognized or existing in any State Party to the present Covenant pursuant to law, conventions, regulations or custom on the pretext that the present Covenant does not recognize such rights or that it recognizes them to a lesser extent.[69]

The purpose of this provision is to ensure that the Covenant is not used as a basis for denying or limiting other more favorable or more extensive human rights which individuals might otherwise enjoy or be entitled to, whether under international law or national law or practice.

Thus, for example, an argument has sometimes been advanced that the absence of a right-to-property clause in the Covenant would have the consequence of permitting the taking of property in the United

States without compensation, notwithstanding the contrary guarantees of the United States Constitution and laws. It is clear that Article 5(2) is designed, among other things, to prevent precisely such a result, for it specifies that rights otherwise protected may not be denied on the ground that the Covenant does not guarantee them. The fact that the Covenant affords lesser protection is not to be interpreted as reducing existing rights, and the Covenant is not to serve states as a pretext for adopting laws to reduce existing rights.

Article 5(2) also seeks to ensure that the restrictions and derogations authorized by the Covenant are not used to legalize or justify restrictions on human rights guaranteed under other instruments or laws which do not provide for such limitations. This can serve as an important canon of construction, preventing domestic courts and governmental agencies from relying on the restrictions of the Covenant to read similar limitations into less restrictive and otherwise applicable guarantees.

It should be noted, however, that Article 5(2) does not incorporate by reference or make part of the Covenant all of a state's human rights laws, or international obligations that accord individuals greater rights than does the Covenant.[70] Article 5(2) does not require states parties to continue to adhere to any domestic or international human rights standard more favorable than the Covenant.[71] But the states parties cannot rely on the Covenant as the basis for restricting other human rights obligations,[72] for justifying their failure to comply with a higher domestic or international standard,[73] or even for terminating or reducing the rights afforded by existing laws or obligations.

Conclusion

Part II defines the basic obligations of states and is the crux of the Covenant. It reflects the fundamental character of the Covenant, as not just another international agreement but as part of the International Bill of Rights, an instrument of constitutional dimension which elevates the protection of the individual against the power of the state to a fundamental principle of international public policy.

The character of the Covenant, its "object and purpose," are essential guides to the interpretation of all of its provisions, especially those provisions which deal with its basic obligations and with permissible derogations from those obligations. Few, if any, other provisions can have as pervasive effect on the enjoyment of the rights which the Covenant guarantees. If these provisions are interpreted in a manner that fails to take account of the overall objectives of the Covenant and the protective system it establishes, they will acquire a disproportionately large and unduly restrictive influence on the application of the Covenant and seriously limit the enjoyment of the rights it was designed to guarantee. Stipulations such as Article 4, which authorizes the states parties to derogate from their obligations, must therefore be viewed as applicable only in rare and exceptional circumstances and, as Article 5(1) plainly indicates, are never to be used in a manner calculated to destroy the rights which the Covenant recognizes. Other limitations and restrictions permitted by the treaty, too, must be interpreted and applied consistently with the object and purpose of the Covenant and the underlying philosophy of the International Bill of Human Rights.

4

The Self-Determination
of Peoples

ANTONIO CASSESE

A PROPOSAL to include a provision dealing with self-determination in
the covenant being drafted on human rights was made by the USSR in
1949.[1] That proposal would have imposed duties to grant self-determination only on colonial powers.[2] The USSR suggestion was not accepted,[3] but other states—Afghanistan and Saudi Arabia—later renewed
the initiative, attracting wide support among the developing states.[4]
These proposals, however, had wider scope, asserting or implying
rights not only for colonial peoples but also for peoples oppressed by
despotic governments, peoples under alien domination, and peoples of
multinational states deprived of self-determination by the central authorities.[5] Efforts by the "Socialist bloc" in the Human Rights Commission and in the General Assembly to narrow the provision so that it
would apply only to colonial peoples did not succeed, and Article 1 of
the Covenant on Civil and Political Rights as it emerged implies no
such limitation.[6]

An important addition, proposed by Chile in 1952, asserted the right
of all peoples to dispose of their natural wealth and resources.[7] That
proposal, endorsed by those that later came to be called "Third World"
states, as well as by the Socialist states, led to Article 1(2). It was an
important step in the effort of the large majority of states to change
international rules and practices governing alien properties and investments.

Opposition to the article on self-determination was strongest in the
early years by those who still had colonial possessions, notably the

United Kingdom, France, and Belgium. Other "Western" states, including the United States, were reserved, but moved toward accepting the principle.[8] In the end, however, they voted against the article because of the provision on natural resources which they saw as undermining foreign investment in developing countries.[9]

Those who opposed including the article in the Covenant made various arguments. Self-determination is a political principle, not a legal right.[10] It is too nebulous and vague a concept to be included in an international treaty.[11] It is a collective right and therefore would not fit into the Covenant, which was concerned only with rights and freedoms of the individual,[12] and its inclusion might jeopardize the Covenant.[13] The implementation system laid down in the Covenant could not be applied to self-determination.[14] Self-determination is achieved through a slow and gradual process and would not be furthered by including a provision on the subject in an international treaty.[15] As Article 1(2) of the United Nations Charter already speaks of respect for the principle of self-determination of peoples, any reaffirmation of the principle was unnecessary.[16] Since it was impossible to proclaim the right of self-determination without also providing for the right of secession, the result would be the fragmenting of states and the multiplication of frontiers and barriers among nations.[17]

While opposing inclusion of the provision, the Western states insisted that the right of self-determination, if incorporated into the Covenant, must not be limited to colonial arrangements but should apply also to the people of any state who were oppressed by their own or a foreign government.[18] This view was also held by most of the "developing states." In 1955, when debate on the provision was finally concluded, only a few states still maintained that the article should apply only to colonial situations.[19] (These states were apparently motivated by fear that the article would confer rights of secession on minorities in their territory, although the overwhelming majority of states had already indicated their view that the provision should not be so construed.)

The provision was approved by a large majority, led by Third World states, with the concurrence of the Socialist countries. The Western states maintained their opposition, perhaps not fully appreciating the significance and promise of that provision. The contribution of the Western states to the development of this article should not, however, be underestimated: they contributed to widening the scope of the article and were instrumental in effecting important changes in the text.

The Scope of Article 1

"Peoples" Entitled to Self-determination

Literal as well as more comprehensive interpretation supports the conclusion that the words *"all* peoples have the right . . . ," in Article 1 refer to any people irrespective of the international political status of the territory it inhabits. It applies, then, not only to the peoples of territories that have not yet attained political independence, but also to those of independent and sovereign states.[20]

This conclusion is borne out by the *travaux préparatoires*. While the discussions initially concentrated on self-determination for peoples in colonial states and in other dependent territories, there were increasing references to other categories of peoples as well. Representatives of several governments insisted that the rule should apply to *all* peoples, including those living in sovereign states.[21] For them, too, self-determination is "external" in part—the right to freedom from hegemony by other states. Largely, self-determination for them is "internal," the right to authentic self-government, to be free from totalitarian repressive regimes. As the delegate of India said in the General Assembly in 1950:

> Individual and political rights could not be implemented if the people to whom they had been granted lived under a despotic regime. As has been recognized in Art. 21 para. 3 of the [Universal] Declaration [of Human Rights], the will of the people should be the basis of the authority of government.[22]

And in 1951, the delegate of Syria pointed out that from the domestic point of view, the principle of self-determination "took the form of self-government, that is to say a people's right to adopt representative institutions and freely to choose the form of government which it wished to adopt."[23]

Special reference was made to peoples of federated republics and of multinational states generally. At all stages of the elaboration of the provision, Western governments referred to the federated republics of the Soviet Union, whose peoples, they said, were denied the right of self-determination by the central authorities. The USSR and other Socialist countries repudiated these allegations, insisting that the people of those republics enjoyed the right of self-determination. They did not claim, however, that self-determination was not applicable to the Soviet national republics because they were part of a sovereign state.[24] In the last stages of the drafting, moreover, the Soviet representative stressed that he had voted for the Article "because it had been clear from the debate that the word 'peoples' included nations and ethnic groups."[25] The record is clear, then, that the people of a national component of a multinational state have the right of self-determination under Article 1. Two conditions must be satisfied. First, the national group must be a member of a state made up of different national groups of comparable dimensions, not one where there is a majority and one (or more) identifiable minority groups. States contemplated include the USSR, Yugoslavia, and perhaps India. A second condition is that the national or ethnic group be recognized constitutionally, having a distinct legal status within the constitutional framework, e.g., the republics of the USSR. The rationale behind these conditions is apparently that an "ethnic group" is entitled to international self-determination only when it achieves the dimension and importance of other components of the state, both in fact and in constitutional conception.

Admittedly, there are states as to which one cannot say with confidence whether they consist of national or ethnic groups satisfying the conditions indicated, and neither the text nor the preparatory record provides guidance as to how that question shall be decided. It is to be hoped that the Human Rights Committee's practice will shed light on this delicate and explosive issue.

Self-determination also applies to the people of a sovereign state living under foreign domination, whether this domination results from annexation of territory or from direct or indirect military hegemony. This view was shared both by the proponents of the Article and by some of its opponents; it was advanced several times in the form of accusations leveled against Socialist states by Western countries, and vice-versa. These charges were clearly part of the Cold War, but irrespective of their merits, the accusations show that the states involved agreed that a state which subjects the people of another state to domination violates its right to self-determination.[26]

There was reference also to peoples of sovereign countries militarily occupied by other states: military occupation was considered a breach of the right of self-determination of the occupied peoples.[27] From 1950 to 1955, however, when the Covenant was being prepared, that issue did not have great international prominence. The drafters of the Article emphasized, rather, the general class of "peoples under foreign domination."

Minorities

The record, then, supports the view that a national or ethnic group constitutionally recognized as a component part of a multinational state is a "people" entitled to self-determination under Article 1. On the other hand, the history of the Covenant shows that minorities as such do not have a right of self-determination (and secession) generally.

The language of Article 1 provides no guidance toward a definition of "peoples" and does not support the distinction. Arguments and general statements made during the negotiation might seem to support a right of self-determination for any minority in any state that identifies itself as a "people." The Covenant as a whole, however, and especially the views commonly expressed during its preparation, compel the conclusion that the Covenant does not recognize the right of "minorities" to self-determination.

The only reference to minorities in the Covenant is in Article 27, which provides that persons belonging to ethnic, religious, or linguistic minorities shall not be denied the right to enjoy their culture, practice their religion, or use their language. That article does not speak at all to the rights of the group, only to the rights of its individual members. Article 27, moreover, seeks for such minorities rights quite different from that recognized by Article 1 for "peoples." Article 27 is designed to allow a minority to maintain its identity; the right of self-determination is more dynamic and aims at assuring the development of a community in all fields: political, economic, social, as well as cultural.

One can argue that the rights accorded to individual members of minorities by Article 27 do not necessarily imply that the group as a whole does not also have rights of self-determination. But the preparatory record is quite clear on this point. The draftsmen, and the participating states generally, intended to rule out the right of self-determination for minorities out of fear that this could disrupt and dismember sovereign states.[28] (Whether a minority can claim such a right, not under the Covenant but as a general principle of international law, is a different question.)

The Content of the Right

Internal Self-Determination

Article 1 refers not only to peoples of dependent territories but also to the peoples of sovereign states. These people enjoy the right to "internal self-determination," i.e., the right to choose their form of government and to determine the social, economic, and cultural policies of the state. This right is clearly expressed by the second sentence in paragraph 1: "By virtue of that right they freely determine their political status and freely pursue their economic, social and cultural development." [29] Although the expression is terse, the right can be understood and appreciated if the importance of the adverb "freely" is fully grasped and if, in addition, the article is read in conjunction with the other provisions of the Covenant. [30]

In stating that by virtue of this right every people freely determines its political status, Article 1 intends to convey two ideas: first, that the choice of domestic political institutions and authorities must be free from outside interference; and second, that that choice must not be conditioned, manipulated or tampered with by the domestic authorities themselves. I deal with outside interference later. Here it can be said that free determination of the national "political status" implies the right of every member of the community to choose, in full freedom, the authorities that will implement the genuine will of the people. It presupposes that every individual member of the people be allowed to exercise those rights and freedoms which permit the expression of the popular will. Article 1, therefore, of necessity incorporates other provisions of the Covenant. [31] Self-determination presupposes freedom of opinion and expression (Article 19), the right of peaceful assembly (Article 21), the freedom of association (Article 22), the right to vote (Article 25(b)), and more generally the right to take part in the conduct of public affairs, directly or through freely chosen representatives (Article 25(a)). Whenever these rights are recognized for individuals, the people as a whole enjoy the right of internal (political) self-determinination; whenever those rights are trampled upon, the right of the people to self-determination is infringed. Of course, the Covenant permits some limitations on those political and civil rights, for example on the freedom of expression and association (Articles 19(3), 22(2)). Such limitations, then, are not violations of political self-determination. Although Article 1 itself is couched in absolute terms, the fact that it operates in conjunction with other provisions results in its being subject to the same limitations provided for in those articles. In the final analysis, then, this principle suffers the same defects as the provisions of the Covenant which it incorporates: loopholes which leave wide discretion to the contracting states in imposing limitations on rights.

Despite this deficiency, Article 1 should not be underrated. It establishes a permanent link between self-determination and civil and political rights. The test for gauging whether self-determination is recognized or denied is whether or not there is a democratic decision-making process. It follows that self-determination is a continuing right that cannot be considered as implemented once and for all. This characteristic of Article 1 can be deduced from its letter and object, and was clearly stressed in the preparatory work. For example: the original text of the Article contained the words "all peoples shall have the right to self-determination"; the text which was finally agreed upon provides that "all peoples *have* the right to self-determination." In presenting the final draft, the spokesman pointed out that the tense of the verb had been changed "from the future to the present, to emphasize the fact that the right referred to was a permanent one."[32] The importance of this feature of Article 1 can be appreciated when one considers that under the principle of self-determination as articulated in later international instruments, achieving independence completes self-determination and exhausts the relevance of the principle. The Covenant adopts a different and broader view. Under the Covenant, one may continue to question whether the government of a sovereign state complies with Article 1; whether it truly recognizes its people's right to internal self-determination or has become oppressive.

What I have said regarding political self-determination applies also to economic, social, and cultural self-determination. Each of these forms of self-determination refers to a different set of provisions of the Covenant on Civil and Political Rights or of the Covenant on Economic, Social, and Cultural Rights.[33] Economic self-determination—discussed below—implies reference to the right of peaceful assembly (Article 21) and to freedom of association (Article 22), as well as to a few provisions of the Covenant on Economic, Social and Cultural Rights.[34] The same is true for social and for cultural self-determination.

External Self-Determination

Article 1(3) commits all states parties, including those administering dependent territories (i.e. non-self-governing and trust territories), to respect and promote the right of the peoples of those territories to self-determination. That means that they may freely decide on their international status, whether to form a new state or to associate themselves with an existing state. The states parties to the Covenant having responsibility for the administration of those territories are under a duty to "promote the realization of the right of self-determination . . . in conformity with the provisions of the Charter of the United Nations."

It is apparent both from the text of the provision and from the preparatory work that under the Covenant self-determination need not be offered or exercised immediately, but is to be achieved progressively.[35] But what does the reference to the UN Charter mean? When the present wording was proposed, a few Western states raised serious objections to the phrase. The representative of Australia said:

> According to the new text, the states in question were to promote the realization of the right in such territories. But the countries which had entered into trusteeship agreements were undoubtedly doing their utmost to carry out their obligations under the Trusteeship System, the objectives of which were defined in Article 76 of the Charter. If para. 3 was supposed to imply that self-determination was synonymous with the objectives of Art. 76, he strongly disagreed. Self-determination was not mentioned in Art. 76, or anywhere else in Chapter XI, XII, or XIII; and the obligations laid down in those Chapters could only be altered by amending the Charter and the Trusteeship agreements. Furthermore, the obligations assumed under the Charter in respect of Non-Self-Governing Territories and of Trust Territories were not the same; but para. 3 made no distinction between them.[36]

These objections were answered by the Representative of Lebanon:

> He realized that Chapters XI and XII of the Charter . . . contained no explicit mention of the right of self-determination, but the obligation of the Powers concerned to respect that right was clearly implicit in both the spirit and the letter of those chapters. Moreover, those Powers had always said that they were striving to promote that right. It might be contended that there was no point in repeating something that was already in the Charter. It should not be forgotten that the Charter contained a provision—Art. 2 para. 7—relating to matters essentially within the domestic jurisdiction of states, and that Chapter XI was couched in rather special terms, because it was a declaration by States concerning the interpretation they placed on their responsibilities; para. 2 of the joint proposal would give every signatory state the right to intervene if it considered that an administering Power was not promoting the realization of the right of self-determination.[37]

In my opinion, the drafters clearly intended to impose on contracting states having responsibility for dependent territories the duty, not explicitly provided for in the Charter, to grant self-determination to the peoples of those territories. The phrase "in conformity with the provisions of the Charter" means that the modalities for granting self-determination to dependent peoples are those indicated in the Charter as well as in the resolutions and in subsequent practice of the competent United Nations bodies spelling out and implementing those Charter provisions. In particular, the international bodies which watch over the process of granting self-determination are those established by virtue of the Charter, i.e., the General Assembly, the Special Committee on the Situation with Regard to the Implementation of the Declaration on the Granting of Independence to Colonial Countries and Peoples, and the Trusteeship Council. It should be added that, after the adoption of Article 1 (1955) and before the entry into force of the Covenant (1976), the United Nations system concerning dependent territories underwent significant changes in many respects: in the opinion of some authors, United Nations practice led to the abrogation of Article 73 and to the emergence of an unwritten rule whereby states having responsibilities for the administration of non-self-governing territories are duty-bound to pursue the independence of such territories, that is to say, to recognize their right of self-determination.[38] Correspondingly, the General Assembly and the Special Committee are now fully entitled to look into any question concerning the independence of those territories and to pass specific resolutions on the matter.[39] (Except for Micronesia, all trust territories have become independent). Thus, by the time the Covenant entered into force, the evolution of the United Nations practice had brought the United Nations system in line with Article 1(3) of the Covenant.

Article 1(3) applies to all states parties, including those administering dependent territories. The clear implication is that states that are not administering powers also have an obligation to promote and respect the right of self-determination by all peoples anywhere. That must be done, however, "in conformity with the provisions of the Charter of the United Nations." That precludes, for example, the use of force in violation of Article 2(4) of the Charter. It implies that every state should act in conformity with UN resolutions that suggest measures to promote self-determination generally or for particular peoples.

External self-determination also includes the right of the people of a sovereign state to be free from foreign interference which affects the international status of that state, as well as from any form of encroachment upon its independence. Thus, if a state party to the Covenant uses its military or economic power to interfere with the conduct of foreign policy of another state, it violates the right of self-determination of the people of that state. Similarly, a state violates the Covenant if it occupies the territory of another state, thereby restricting the power of the people of that state to decide freely upon the affairs of the occupied areas. In this respect, the Covenant reinforces the duty incumbent upon every state under customary international law to respect the sovereignty of other states, i.e., their political independence and territorial integrity. This restatement in the Covenant of a duty already flowing—with respect to states, not to people—from international law might seem superfluous, but Article 1, like other substantive provisions of the Covenant, benefits from the implementation procedures in section 4 of the Covenant (see essay 14). However weak these procedures may be, they supplement those existing under customary international law and under the UN Charter and can help in case of a gross breach of the right of external self-determination.

The right of self-determination, I have said, belongs also to "national" peoples in a multi-national state like the federated republics of the USSR. Unlike ethnic minorities in unitary states who are not "peoples" for purposes of Article 1, national peoples, federated in a sovereign state and enjoying distinct constitutional status, enjoy the right of external self-determination. This includes the right to independence, which the central sovereign, if a party to the Covenant, is bound to honor.

Self-Determination And The Rights Of Individuals

The Covenant takes a broad, multidimensional approach to self-determination and establishes a twofold link between the self-determination of peoples and the civil and political rights of individuals. First, external self-determination is a necessary precondition for the enjoyment of individual rights. Individuals can enjoy civil and political rights only if the community of which they are members is not oppressed by a foreign power. This was expressed time and again in the course of the preparatory work. Self-determination is the "source,"[40] the "prerequisite for the enjoyment of all other human rights";[41] "only when that right had been assured would it be possible to hope for the effective implementation of all the other rights guaranteed in the Covenant."[42] "Freedom of the individual was a snare and a delusion as long as the nation of which he was a part was not free."[43]

Self-determination and civil and political rights are closely intertwined also in the "internal" dimension of self-determination. Full realization of a people's self-determination is dependent upon true respect for the rights and freedoms of the individuals and groups making up the people. Internal political self-determination is the right to choose one's government freely and to have a government that, once chosen, is not oppressive or authoritarian. It can be achieved only if the state fully respects and guarantees those civil and political rights of individuals whose exercise enables the people to establish and express its will freely and continually. Internal self-determination, then, is the synthesis and *summa* of civil and political rights. This can be clearly deduced from the Covenant taken as a whole. It was also expressed repeatedly by participants in the drafting process: "The right of self-determination would be achieved if all the other rights which had been included were applied"; [44] self-determination is "a corollary of the democratic principle of government with the consent of the governed." [45]

Implementing the Right of Self-determination

Article 1 does not specify how the right to self-determination is to be implemented. Internal self-determination, incorporating individual civil and political rights, is implemented through the political process: through free elections (Article 25); and through freedom of expression, association and assembly (Articles 19, 21, 22). External self-determination requires an expression by the people, free from interference by governmental authorities or others. State practice provides many instances of such expression, usually by plebiscite. Whatever mode is used is, in my opinion, legitimate as long as it freely and fairly determines the desires of the people. Whether a particular mode satisfies these conditions depends on the total context. Plebiscites have sometimes been held under circumstances where they were clearly not a fair and free expression of the people's determination. Presumably, if the controlling authorities resist legitimate self-determination by a people entitled to it under Article 1, the people may secede or otherwise assert its determination, even by force.

A related question is what form self-determination may take. Nothing in Article 1 suggests any limitations on giving effect to the desires of the people. A people can decide for independence. It can choose association with any state, including the state with which it had a dependent relationship, provided that the new association is freely sought. Of course, a determination to continue such an association would in many circumstances be suspect, and unusual care would have to be taken to assure that the decision of the people was wholly free.

Disposition of Natural Wealth and Resources

Article 1(2) proclaims the general principle that one country should not exploit the natural resources of another. This paragraph, however, is not merely a reaffirmation of the right of every state over its own natural resources; it clearly provides that the right over natural wealth belongs to *peoples*. This has two distinct consequences. For dependent peoples, the right implies that the governing authority is under the duty to use the economic resources of the territory in the interest of the dependent people. In a sovereign state, the government must utilize the natural resources so as to benefit the whole people. The right of the people over natural resources, and the corresponding duty of the government, are but a consequence, in economic matters, of the people's right to (internal) self-determination in the political field. Just as the people of every sovereign state have a permanent right to choose their own form of government and to demand, through democratic means, that the conduct of national affairs be carried out in the interest of the people, so the people are entitled to insist that the natural resources of the nation be exploited in the interest of the people.[46]

Of course, in normal situations it is difficult to determine whether the central authorities of a state are using the wealth and resources for the benefit of the whole people; decisions concerning the exploitation of natural resources of necessity presuppose a wide measure of discretionary power and must take account of a number of technical and economic factors. Nevertheless, the Covenant provision can play a role where it is demonstrated that the government of a country exploits the natural resources in the exclusive interest of a small segment of the population, plainly disregarding the needs of the vast majority of the people. Similarly, a government would be in violation of Article 1 if it surrendered control over the natural resources of the country to a foreign state or private company without ensuring that the exploitation of those resources would be carried out primarily in the interest of the people.

The right of peoples over natural resources is subject to a general limitation, which in turn suffers from a major exception. The general limitation is that the free disposition of the natural wealth and resources must not impair or run counter to international treaties entered into by the central authorities with a view to promoting international economic cooperation, nor should it violate international customary rules protecting the rights of foreign investors. It is apparent from the preparatory work that this limitation on the right of free disposition over natural resources, which was pressed upon the majority of states by the developed countries, was motivated by two considerations: the fear that outside economic cooperation, so important in developing countries, might be discouraged by a rule laying down the right over natural resources in absolute terms;[47] and even more important, the intent to protect foreign investments from expropriation or nationalization without compensation.[48]

The preparatory work does not cast much light on the words "based upon the principle of mutual benefit."[49] The letter and object of the article lead to the conclusion that international treaties (and agreements with private persons) for international economic cooperation may be rescinded or disregarded by the government of a sovereign state (or by the authority of a dependent territory) if such treaties or agreements clearly benefit the foreign party only or do not provide economic and social advantages to both parties. However, the words "and international law" that follow imply that compensation must be paid to the contracting party. Together, the two clauses have the following consequence: an international treaty or agreement may be terminated by a state if it is contrary to the right of its people over its natural wealth, but this unilateral act must not prejudice obligations flowing from international law, including the obligation to provide compensation.

Developments since the draft Covenant was concluded, however, raise an important issue about the references to international law. At that time (1955), there was still a large measure of agreement that states were obligated to provide prompt, adequate and effective compensation for expropriation or nationalization,[50] although a few states claimed that compensation should be by special agreement between the states concerned ("lump-sum agreements").[51] Since then, however, international law on this subject has undergone important changes. Recent UN resolutions on the new international economic order insist that the "appropriate compensation" to be paid by the expropriating state should be governed by the "relevant laws and regulations" of that state in light of "all the circumstances that the state considers pertinent" (Article 2(2c) of the Charter of Economic Rights and Duties of States, adopted by the UN General Assembly on December 12, 1974). It is widely contended now that the traditional international rule on compensation no longer applies, although opinions differ as to what the rule now is.[52]

The question under Article 1(2) is whether the reference to international law is to the traditional customary rules existing at the time of the drafting of Article 1, or to the rules currently obtaining. I submit that the latter solution is more sound for two reasons. First, although the Vienna Convention on the Law of Treaties did not settle this delicate problem of intertemporal interpretation,[53] the International Court of Justice stated in its advisory opinion on Namibia that "an international instrument has to be interpreted and applied within the framework of the entire legal system prevailing at the time of the interpretation."[54] This, to my mind, is all the more correct when the clause at issue makes general reference to international law. Such a reference must of necessity point to the rules of international law as they change with time.

There is a second reason why the interpretation here advocated seems the correct one. Article 47 of the Covenant provides that "nothing in the present Covenant shall be interpreted as impairing the inherent right of all peoples to enjoy and utilize fully and freely their natural wealth and resources." This provision could be regarded either as superfluous, in that it merely repeats what is stated in Article 1(2), or as inconsistent with that provision, since it does not embody the clause safeguarding foreign assets and investments.[55] The fact is that Article 47 was completed and inserted in the Covenant much later than Article 1, by which time an increasingly large number of states claimed that nationalization for the purpose of realizing the right of a people "to enjoy and utilize fully and freely" its natural wealth and resources did not necessarily entail the obligation to pay compensation. Article 47, then, was adopted to "rectify," as it were, Article 1(2), or to adjust it to the evolution of international law that had taken place in the meantime. Article 47 therefore supports the suggested interpretation of the reference to international law in Article 1(2). The two provisions must be read in conjunction. It follows that if a state expropriates or nationalizes foreign assets in the exercise of its people's right "to enjoy and utilize fully and freely" its natural wealth and resources, the duty to pay compensation, if any, is governed by the rules of international law currently in force.

The interpretation suggested here is also in keeping with the general principle that if there is a discrepancy between two provisions of a treaty, the construction which gives a reasonable and consistent meaning to the conflicting clauses is preferred. According to this principle, one should try to reconcile the contradictory provisions of the treaty by finding a common denominator. Here the common denominator is found by giving the reference to international law in Article 1(2) a meaning and a scope which takes account of the purport and object of Article 47.

The last sentence of Article 1(2), "In no case may a people be deprived of its own means of subsistence," introduces an exception to what is provided earlier. It may be read to nullify even arrangements "freely made" by the people "for their own ends" if these arrangements deprive the people of its means of subsistence. It presumably nullifies the obligation to pay any compensation required under international law where such compensation would deprive the people of its means of subsistence. When many delegations, chiefly Western, objected to this provision as obscure and ambiguous,[56] some of its supporters tried to explain its meaning. Thus the representative of Saudi Arabia said that it "was intended to prevent a weak or penniless government from seriously compromising a country's future by granting concessions in the economic sphere—a frequent occurrence in the nineteenth century. The second sentence of paragraph 2 was intended to serve as a warning to all who might consider resorting to such unfair procedures."[57] The Greek delegate observed that she could not understand why objections had been raised against the provision "because the means of subsistence of the under-developed countries were so much more restricted than those of the least advanced of the economically advanced countries that the phrase could not possibly endanger the latter's public and private investments."[58] The delegate of El Salvador gave two examples of a process of deprivation of the means of subsistence of a people: "A tribe in Tanganyika had been deprived of its ancestral land and had been resettled elsewhere against its will; and in Nauru the only source of national wealth, phosphates, was being unwisely over-exploited by a British company, with the result that in about fifty years' time the population of the island would have to be resettled elsewhere because no resources would remain."[59] When the British representative objected that the examples were not pertinent, in part because the tribe did not constitute a people under Article 1,[60] the delegate of El Salvador replied that the examples he had cited "had been meant simply as examples of large human groups deprived of their means of subsistence. That, on a large scale, was what paragraph 2 sought to prevent."[61]

I sum up: Article 1 includes obligations for all contracting states. There are special obligations for those states that administer dependent territories.

—All states parties to the Covenant have the duty to respect the right of their people to internal self-determination. They must grant all the civil and political rights provided for in the Covenant which permit the full realization of that right. They must grant all the rights and freedoms provided for in both that Covenant and in the Covenant on Economic, Social, and Cultural Rights,[62] to enable their people to pursue their economic, social, and cultural development freely. States parties are also duty-bound to respect the right of self-determination of other states, refraining from interference in their internal affairs that would impair or prejudice the right of self-determination of the peoples of those states.

—Contracting states are obliged to use their natural wealth and resources so as to further the interests and needs of their peoples. They must refrain from entering into agreements (or permitting concessions and investments) which are contrary to the interests of the population; surely they must not deprive the people of its means of subsistence. Existing arrangements that prove prejudicial to the needs of the people are to be rescinded, but the other state or corporation concerned is to be paid compensation as required by present international law. No agreement or compensation, however, should result in depriving the people of its means of subsistence.

—Every state must also promote the realization of the right of self-determination of peoples in other countries or territories, but only by means consistent with the principles of the Charter and within the framework of the United Nations.[63]

—Contracting states that administer dependent territories have additional duties in regard to those territories. Such a state must "promote the realization" of self-determination by the people of the territory. They may do so progressively. They must do it in conformity with the UN Charter and the modalities provided within the UN system.

Rights and Duties under Article 1

Who are the holders of the rights corresponding to the aforementioned duties? Undisputedly, all contracting states are entitled to claim from each other the fulfillment of those duties. A major feature of the Covenant—as of all other international treaties on human rights—is that each contracting state takes on obligations concerning its domestic legal order vis-à-vis all other contracting states, and all other contracting states have a right to the observance of such obligations. Does Article 1 also confer rights on "peoples" as well? For example, does the people of each contracting state have an international right to internal self-determination vis-à-vis its own state?

The answer to this question can be found in the general system of the Covenant, but it is also contingent to some extent upon theoretical differences in approaches to international treaties. Under an essentially "dualist" approach, it would be argued that the Covenant creates duties and confers rights only upon the states parties. The "peoples" under Article 1, like individuals under other articles of the Covenant, are the beneficiaries of those rights and duties of states. They may have rights under national law if the Covenant is carried out but they do not have rights under the Covenant as a matter of international law. A different view might insist that since the states are bound under international law to grant rights and freedoms to individuals (or, as in Article 1, to peoples) the latter have rights of international character. In any event, under the Optional Protocol only individuals have an international right of "petition," but while a "people" does not have such a right, individuals might assert rights as members of a people, claiming that they are "victims" of a "violation" of Article 1 of the Covenant. (See the rights of members of minority groups under Article 27. See also essays 11 and 14.)

Subsequent Developments in the Principle of Self-Determination

Since the drafting of the Covenant was completed in 1955, the principle of self-determination has been dealt with in other important international instruments of universal scope. While these cannot affect the obligations of parties to the Covenant, they may have relevance to the interpretation and implementation of Article 1.

Article 1 was reaffirmed and to some extent developed in two major resolutions of the General Assembly. The first was the momentous Declaration on the Granting of Independence to Colonial Countries and Peoples, adopted on December 14, 1960 (G.A. Res. 1514). Paragraph 2 restates verbatim the first paragraph of Article 1 of the Covenant; paragraph 5 greatly elaborates paragraph 3 of Article 1 of the Covenant as it relates to dependent territories.[64] The second was the Resolution on Permanent Sovereignty over Natural Resources, adopted on December 14, 1962 (G.A. Res. 1803), which specifies the modalities of the exercise by "peoples and nations" of their right over natural resources and the conditions under which expropriation and nationalization of foreign assets, investments, and enterprises can take place.

These two resolutions are indicative of a fresh trend that emerged in the United Nations after the admission in 1960 of a number of newly independent countries: the tendency to place special emphasis on the right of self-determination of colonial peoples, as well as on the "economic self-determination" of both dependent peoples and other less-developed peoples, who, while enjoying political independence, are economically bound to industrialized countries and are largely dependent on their help. Clearly that trend reflected a more restricted view of self-determination than that of Article 1 of the Covenant. This narrow view was confirmed in two subsequent instruments which elaborated a full-fledged doctrine of self-determination. The first is the 1970 Declaration on Friendly Relations, a resolution of the General Assembly that although not legally binding, has great moral, political, and quasi-legislative weight in that it authoritatively sets forth the principal standards of behavior solemnly agreed to by all the members of the United Nations. The other text is the 1977 Protocol Additional I to the four 1949 Geneva Conventions on the Victims of War (see UNDOC, A/32/144 Annex I), which refers to self-determination in adopting the concept of "wars of national liberation."

While Article 1 of the Covenant took account of the views on self-determination of the less developed countries and the Socialist states, as well as of the Western countries, the subsequent instruments essentially embody the views on self-determination of the Third World and the Socialist countries only,[65] as developed in the 1950s and fully elaborated in the 1960s.[66] Under that view, the right to external self-determination devolves only upon peoples subject to a colonial regime or to foreign domination (chiefly by military occupation). Internal self-determination belongs only to the people of a sovereign country whose government pursues a policy of systematic discrimination based on race, creed, or color. The approach to self-determination in the Covenant, we have seen, is much broader as regards both external and internal self-determination. As to the latter, under the Covenant political self-determination requires the observance by all contracting states of the principal civil and political rights proclaimed in later articles of the Covenant; under the Declaration on Friendly Relations, the only requirement is that the government represent "the whole people belonging to the territory without distinction as to race, creed or colour."

While the subsequent instruments cannot detract from obligations undertaken in the Covenant, they cannot be disregarded. Even the Protocol to the Geneva conventions may be suggestive as to the definition of "peoples," although as a separate agreement defining peoples for its purposes it cannot control the meaning of "peoples" as used in Article 1 of the Covenant. The Declaration on Granting of Independence to Colonial Countries and Peoples is relevant to the interpretation of Article 1 in that it indicates the action to be taken in regard to the rights of self-determination of colonial peoples "in conformity with the provisions of the Charter of the United Nations,"[67] and the Declaration can therefore be seen as effectively incorporated in Article 1(3) of the Covenant. Thus, for example, by establishing that the transfer of all powers to the peoples of dependent territories must take place "in accordance with their freely expressed will and desire" the Declaration explicitly enunciates a concept that is implicit in the Covenant. Even more important, under the Declaration, this "will" must be expressed without any distinction as to race, creed, or color. Furthermore, the transfer must be made "without any conditions or reservations." In short, the Declaration indicates to states parties and to the competent UN bodies, as well as to the organ charged with scrutinizing the implementation of the Covenant, the Human Rights Committee, how Article 1(3) should be applied.

The 1970 Declaration on Friendly Relations might also be used to some extent in interpreting Article 1 of the Covenant. For example, paragraph 4 of the Declaration provides that "the establishment of a sovereign and independent state, the free association or integration with an independent state or the emergence into any other political status freely determined by a people constitute modes of implementing the right of self-determination by that people." Use of the 1970 Declaration also can be justified by the reference in Article 1(3) of the Covenant to the UN Charter and practice; the 1970 Declaration was intended as a blueprint for action by the UN organs and has consequently become a necessary component of United Nations practice. In other respects, however, the 1970 Declaration can be used only with caution, for it includes concepts that are at great variance with some basic conceptions of Article 1. In particular, since its view of internal political self-determination is much narrower than that of Article 1 of the Covenant, it would be unsound and improper to interpret Article 1 in the light of the narrower concept of the Declaration.

The 1962 Resolution on Natural Resources is also relevant to the interpretation of Article 1, inasmuch as it reflects, or is instrumental in shaping, those new rules of customary international law relating to expropriation and nationalization to which reference is made by Article 1(2) as read in conjunction with Article 47. In that respect one must take account also of the later Charter of Economic Rights and Duties of States which provides for "appropriate compensation," but also states that such compensation shall be paid by the expropriating state after "taking into account" its relevant laws and regulations and in the light of "all circumstances" that it considers "pertinent."[68]

Article 1 and Jus Cogens

As has been conclusively demonstrated elsewhere,[69] the general principle of self-determination has become a peremptory norm of international law (*jus cogens*) within the meaning of Article 53 of the Vienna Convention on the Law of Treaties. Numerous states have consistently maintained both in and outside the United Nations that the principle of self-determination permits no derogation. A treaty conflicting with the principle, therefore, is void. The principle of self-determination that has acquired the character of a peremptory norm, however, is probably that reflected in the Declaration on Friendly Relations.[70] That, I have noted, is narrower than the principle in Article 1 of the Covenant.

Self-determination in the Practice of the Human Rights Committee

As of 1980, the application of Article 1 has not been the subject of consideration by the Human Rights Committee established under the Covenant (see essay 14) either within the framework provided for in Articles 41 and 42 (state-to-state complaints) or that of the Optional Protocol (communications by individuals). Questions relating to the implementation of Article 1 have been raised, however, within the general reporting procedures established by Article 40. Members of the Human Rights Committee have put questions about self-determination to the representatives of five governments—the United Kingdom, the Federal Republic of Germany, the Soviet Union, the Byelorussian SSR, and Chile.

The representative of the United Kingdom was asked what was being done to speed up self-determination in his country's dependent territories.[71] In particular, what was the policy of his government if "a people expressed the desire to exercise that right but did not possess adequate resources to sustain independence?"[72] The representative of the United Kingdom replied only that the dependent territories were at various stages of constitutional development and that when territories which desired independence proved unable to meet their development needs "grants were agreed upon from the United Kingdom government to run on after independence."[73]

As the representative of the Federal Republic of Germany pointed out that his government supported self-determination in southern Africa, its representative was asked whether that meant that the government gave no aid to the apartheid regime of South Africa and prevented German individuals and companies from doing so.[74] The government's representative replied that "her country's position was one of unqualified observance of and support for the universal right to self-determination and it regarded that right as a decisive factor in evaluating the situation in South Africa."[75] That exchange may not be very meaningful, but it suggests that both that government and the committee member who asked the question interpreted Article 1(3) as requiring each contracting party to "promote the realization of the right of self-determination" not only within their own territory or in territories for whose administration they have responsibility, but also elsewhere, anywhere.

The questions put to representatives of the Soviet Union and the Byelorussian SSR concerned the "national groups" of which the USSR is composed, some of which have the status of "Union Republics," like Byelorussia. In the case of the Soviet Union, three main questions were raised: first, the "criteria for granting national groups the right to form a Union Republic, while other groups lived in autonomous republics or regions," "the meaning of 'sovereign rights' of Union Republics," and the system of legislation of the USSR as a federal state; second, about the position of "minorities and indigenous groups" living in the Soviet Union; third, about the way the right of secession conferred by Article 72 of the Soviet Constitution on each Union Republic could be advocated or implemented.[76] The representative of Byelorussia was asked about the right of secession and how it could be put into practice.[77]

The answers focused on the legal aspects of the problems only.[78] Three points, however, seem worthy of attention. First, both representatives, as well as the members of the Committee who put the questions, assumed that the right of self-determination in Article 1 applied to nations or ethnic groups of a multinational state. As regards such peoples in a multinational state, the questions concerning secession were in order. The representative of the USSR chose not to reply to questions on "the position of minorities and indigenous peoples" in the

Soviet Union. Since issues concerning minorities fall outside the scope of Article 1, strictly speaking, the Soviet representative was not required to address them in relation to Article 1. (The question is less clear as regards "indigenous peoples" which might be "peoples" under Article 1, and it would therefore have been appropriate to give the clarifications sought.) Of course, questions about minorities are wholly in order insofar as they are relevant to the special rights of members of minorities under Article 27, and the rights of individual members of those groups, like all individuals, under other articles.

When the Report by Chile was considered by the Committee in 1979, a member of the Committee drew the attention of the Chilean representative to the link between Article 1 and individual freedom. "How could there be self-determination without freedom of opinion? Article 1 of the Covenant referred to the right of self-determination of peoples, not of Governments." [79]

On balance, the Human Rights Committee members have chosen the right path as far as Article 1 is concerned. They have treated that article not merely as recognizing the right to self-determination, but as entailing detailed obligations for which states parties are accountable. They have not been content to accept general governmental assertions but have probed for details as to the implementation of those obligations.

During the early years, however, members of the Committee had not probed or addressed the obligations of the parties as regards internal self-determination. The Committee had heard reports from countries clearly having repressive, unrepresentative governments (for example, Iran, which reported in 1978), and although members of the Committee had raised questions about such repression in relation to the Covenant, with the conspicious exception of the remark addressed to the representative of Chile, cited above, Committee members did not seize the opportunity to challenge reporting countries as to restrictions on political freedoms and civil rights as denials of the right to self-determination. It is to be hoped that, in the future, members of the Committee will reaffirm and probe the implementation of that essential aspect of the right to self-determination.

5

The Right to Life,
Physical Integrity, and Liberty

YORAM DINSTEIN

HUMAN RIGHTS aim at promoting and protecting the dignity and integrity of every individual human being. If there are any rights more fundamental than others for achieving that aim, surely they are the rights to life, to physical integrity, and liberty. On these, all other rights depend; without these, other rights have little or no meaning.

The Right to Life

Article 6 of the Covenant on Civil and Political Rights proclaims that every human being has the inherent right to life. The right to life is incontestably the most important of all human rights. Civilized society cannot exist without legal protection of human life. The inviolability or sanctity of life is, perhaps, the most basic value of modern civilization. In the final analysis, if there were no right to life, there would be no point in the other human rights.

Describing the right to life as "inherent" may be questioned on the ground that legal rights never actually inhere in nature; they are always created within the framework of a legal system.[1] Still, the framers of the Covenant apparently regarded human rights as preexisting in a moral order and perhaps even in an immaculate *jus naturale*. Whether they were right or wrong is immaterial; what matters is that the right to life is validated in the Covenant as a legal right. That only this right is characterized by the Covenant as inherent may attest to its primacy and emphasize that it derives from the very fact of a human being's existence. But whether or not one accepts human rights as based on natural law or an antecedent morality, any rights and duties created by the Covenant are legal rights under international law and must be considered as binding in the international legal system.

The term "inherent" may indicate also that the framers of the Covenant felt that the human right to life is entrenched in customary international law, so that Article 6 is merely declaratory in nature and does not create new international law. Indeed, the right is also recognized in Article 3 of the Universal Declaration of Human Rights,[2] Article 2 of the European Convention for the Protection of Human Rights and Fundamental Freedoms,[3] and Article 4 of the American Convention on Human Rights.[4] If the right to life is guaranteed under general international law (and it is submitted that such is the case), obviously the right is guaranteed vis-à-vis all states (including those which are not parties to the Covenant). If the right is protected apart from the Covenant, its inclusion in the Covenant is important not only to reaffirm the right but to articulate its content and implications.

Article 6 requires that the right to life be protected by law. That is to say, each state party is obligated to have within its internal legal system a law protecting the right to life. The term "law" is broad: in general, it denotes all strata of the legal order, not only statutes (and constitutions) but also unwritten law and administrative regulations. The inviolability of life is so important, however, that a strict interpretation of "law" is here called for.[5] The international obligation requires that the right to life be protected by higher forms in the legislative hierarchy, by statute or constitutional provision.

What is the ambit of the protection that must be given to the right to life? Unfortunately, Article 6 is not specific.[6] Basically, what it tells us, by way of guidance, is that no one shall be arbitrarily deprived of his life. The emphasis must be both on "deprive" and "arbitrarily." First, deprivation of life means homicide. The right to life is not freedom to live as one wishes.[7] It is not a right to an appropriate standard of living.[8] Of course, a human being needs certain essentials—particularly food, clothing, housing, and medical care—in order to remain alive. These are aspects of the social rights to an adequate standard of living and to health which are recognized in Articles 11 and 12 of the International Covenant on Economic, Social, and Cultural Rights.[9] The human right to life per se, however, is a civil right, and it "does not guarantee any person against death from famine or cold or lack of medical attention."[10]

The right to life, in effect, is the right to be safeguarded against (arbitrary) killing.[11] To be sure, homicide may be carried out through a variety of means, including starving someone, exposing a person to extreme temperatures or contamination with disease. But, for example, the mere toleration of malnutrition by a state will not be regarded as a violation of the human right to life, whereas purposeful denial of access to food, e.g., to a prisoner, is a different matter. Failure to reduce infant mortality is not within Article 6, while practicing or tolerating infanticide would violate the Article.

Some members of the Human Rights Committee have expressed the view that Article 6 requires the state to take positive measures to ensure the right to life, including steps to reduce the infant mortality rate, prevent industrial accidents, and protect the environment.[12]

Not all deprivation of life constitutes an infringement of the right to life; only a deprivation of life that is "arbitrary." The cardinal question, therefore, is when a deprivation of life may be labeled as arbitrary. The term "arbitrary" (which appears also in Article 9 and elsewhere in the Covenant) is not easy to define. Its use in Article 6 was, indeed, criticized at the time of drafting as "ambiguous and open to several interpretations."[13] There is a conceptual question—to which we shall return—whether any action sanctioned by statute may qualify as arbitrary.[14] There are a number of practical issues regarding deprivation of life.

Is Capital Punishment Permissible?

Article 6 permits the death penalty, although it stipulates that its provisions are not to be invoked to delay or to prevent the abolition of capital punishment by any state party. The article also lays down six limitations on capital punishment: a sentence of death (a) may be imposed only for the most serious crimes; (b) must be in accordance with the law in force at the time of the commission of the crime; (c) must not be contrary to other provisions of the Covenant or to the Genocide Convention;[15] (d) can only be carried out pursuant to a final judgment rendered by a competent court; (e) shall not be imposed for crimes committed by persons below eighteen years of age and shall not be carried out on pregnant women; and (f) any person condemned to death shall be entitled to seek pardon or commutation of sentence and may be granted amnesty, pardon, or commutation of sentence even without seeking them.

The first limitation raises the question as to what constitutes a most serious crime. It was recognized that "the concept of 'serious crimes' differed from one country to another."[16] Yet no more clearly defined term was found. The second limitation merely reiterates the principle *nulla poena sine lege* which is enshrined as a general principle in Article 15 of the Covenant. The reference to other provisions of the Covenant in the third limitation signifies that there must be no discrimination in the imposition of capital punishment on the basis of race, religion, or other irrelevant grounds (as per Article 2(1) of the Covenant), that the imposition of capital punishment must be in accordance with the minimum guarantees of due process of law (spelled out in Articles 14 and 15), and must satisfy other provisions of the Covenant as well. The reference to the Genocide Convention (in Article 6(3)) is designed particularly to condemn and prevent recurrence of the Nazi experience. As pointed out by the Peruvian Delegate to the Third Committee of the General Assembly: "Nazi tribunals had committed the crime of genocide by means of mass death sentences imposed after a travesty of the judicial process."[17] Thus, capital punishment must not serve as a disguise for the implementation of a genocidal policy.

The fourth limitation hinges upon the term "competent court." A suggestion that Article 6 include a requirement that the court be independent was not favored by the framers of the Covenant on the ground that the independence of courts was provided for specially in Article 14(1).[18] The fifth requirement distinguishes between the position of minors and that of pregnant women. The sentence of death cannot be meted out at all for crimes committed by persons below eighteen years of age. The fact that the defendant reaches the age of eighteen before he is convicted or by the time he would be executed would not permit him to be executed. On the other hand, as to a pregnant woman, while the intention of the framers is subject to some doubt,[19] the text actually adopted means that the death sentence cannot be carried out in the period preceding childbirth. Pregnancy, then, only postpones the implementation of a death sentence, presumably with a view to saving the life of an innocent unborn child. The death sentence may be imposed even during pregnancy, and it can be carried out once the baby is delivered or the pregnancy is otherwise terminated.[20]

The sixth and last limitation differentiates between three terms: pardon, commutation of sentence, and amnesty. Pardon means complete release. Commutation of sentence signifies that the sentence of death will be superseded by a lighter sentence (usually of imprisonment). Amnesty is a pardon extended on a collective basis. The framers of the Covenant provided that a person sentenced to death may seek (on his own initiative) only (individual) pardon or commutation of sentence; he may, however, benefit from either, as well as from a general amnesty.[21]

Needless to say, these are all minimal limitations on capital punishment and, as long as this penalty may be resorted to, the human right to life is far from being absolute. It is noteworthy that the European and American conventions also permit capital punishment, although the latter—which is the more advanced instrument in this respect—provides that in countries which have abolished the death penalty, it shall not be reestablished, and that in no case shall capital punishment be inflicted for political offenses or on persons over seventy years of age.

The Human Rights Committee, in dealing with reports of states submitted under Article 40, has consistently supported the Covenant's commitment to the eventual elimination of the death penalty. Members warmly praised countries which reported having already done so, either formally or through disuse.[22] Other countries were pressed for details on which crimes were punishable by death and how frequently death sentences were carried out. The prevailing view was that the "most serious crimes" requirement should be read restrictively. Several times committee members expressed doubt whether crimes against property warranted the death sentence. For example, it was suggested that its application in cases of misuse of public funds constituted an excessively broad interpretation.[23] Use of the death penalty to punish "crimes against the economy" was also considered questionable.[24] Its imposition for nonviolent or political offenses (e.g., double membership in political parties) was singled out for special condemnation.[25]

Is Deprivation of Human Life Permissible in the Course of Administrative Police Action?

Article 6 ignores this important subject. In the course of its drafting, proposals were made to specify circumstances in which the taking of life would not be deemed a violation of human rights, such as (a) killing by police or other officials in self-defense or in defense of another; (b) death resulting from action lawfully taken to suppress insurrection, rebellion or riots; (c) killing in an attempt to effect lawful arrest or to prevent the escape of a person in lawful custody.[26] There was, however, opposition to any such enumeration. It was explained that "a clause providing that no one should be deprived of his life 'arbitrarily' would indicate that the right was not absolute and obviate the necessity of setting out the possible exceptions in detail."[27] By contrast, Article 2 of the European Convention explicitly states that deprivation of life shall not be regarded as contravening the article when it results from a use of force which was absolutely necessary (a) in defense of any person from unlawful violence; (b) to effect a lawful arrest or to prevent the escape of a person lawfully detained; or (c) in action lawfully taken for the purpose of quelling a riot or insurrection. In light of the *travaux préparatoires* of the Covenant, these instances of deprivation of life can probably be considered as not "arbitrary" and therefore permissible under Article 6.[28] Members of the Human Rights Committee, however, have raised questions about the use of deadly force by authorities (e.g., by the police to quell disturbances) and expressed the view that its use should be restricted. In particular, police immunity for deaths arising from the suppression of certain crimes was considered "difficult to reconcile with Article 6."[29]

Is Article 6 Violated If the State Fails to Prevent the Killing of One Individual by Another?

In principle, the obligations under the Covenant with respect to international human rights are incurred only by states and their organs acting within the scope of, or at least in connection with, their official functions.[30] Hence, the duty corresponding to the human right to life devolves only on persons exercising public authority and not on private individuals.[31] On the other hand, it may be argued that the state must at least exercise due diligence to prevent intentional deprivation of the life of one individual by another, as well as to apprehend murderers and to prosecute them in order to deter future takings of life.[32] The question came up in the course of the drafting of Article 6, and "while the view was expressed that the article should concern itself only with protection of the individual from unwarranted actions by the State, the majority thought that States should be called upon to protect human life against unwarranted actions by public authorities as well as by private."[33]

The majority view seems to be corroborated by the formulation of Article 2(1) according to which contracting parties undertake not only "to respect" but also "to ensure" to all individuals within their territories and subject to their jurisdiction, the various rights recognized in the Covenant, including, of course, the right to life. That would seem to require that the state make certain that private individuals, too, do not interfere with the enjoyment of the right to life by other individuals. This would be particularly true of mass murders. Whereas an ordinary act of murder often cannot be prevented by state officials even with due diligence on their part, the state is expected to take exceptional precaution when there is a threat of riot, mob action, or incitement against minority groups. On the other hand, it is doubtful whether due diligence, say, to cut down fatalities by preventing traffic offenses and prosecuting reckless drivers, is legally required by the undertaking to respect and ensure the right to life.[34]

Is War Forbidden as a Corollary of the Right to Life?

It has been argued that inasmuch as human lives are destroyed on a vast scale in time of war, engaging in war is an infringement of the human right to life. But as a matter of law this contention is untenable. War, assuredly, is prohibited under modern international law and constitutes an international crime.[35] But the duty of every state to refrain from war confers rights on other states and implies no rights for individual human beings. If that were not the case, it would be difficult to comprehend the two exceptions to the interdiction of war under international law—self-defense and collective security—since life is taken not only in (unlawful and criminal) wars of aggression but also in (permissible) wars of self-defense. Moreover, if the proscription of war by international law were based on, or corresponded to, the human right to life, not only interstate wars but also intrastate wars should have been disallowed. In fact, international law (as distinct from national constitutional law) does not forbid rebellions and internal conflicts, irrespective of the number of human lives lost in them.[36]

Is Euthanasia Permissible?

Article 6 does not address itself to this subject, nor, for that matter, do other human rights instruments. Evidently, the right to life is guaranteed to all human beings without exception, including the incurably sick, congenitally deformed children, senile men and women, the insane, etc. The judgment of the International Military Tribunal at Nuremberg condemned the annihilation of hundreds of thousands of "useless eaters" by Nazi Germany in the course of the Second World War.[37] The Covenant surely forbids systematic homicide by public authorities, even if carried out in order to relieve the society of the economic and social burden of maintaining hospitals, sanatoriums, asylums, etc.

The crux of the matter is voluntary euthanasia, consisting of "mercy killing" of one individual, who may demand "the release of death from helpless and hopeless pain,"[38] by another (usually, a physician or a relative of the deceased). Legally speaking, assuming that Article 6 requires the state to outlaw and prevent private homicide, the gist of the question is, "how far the consent of the victim may negate what would otherwise be a violation" of the right to life; i.e., whether waiver of the right to life is permissible.[39] Mercy killing upon the victim's request is "hardly distinguishable from assistance in suicide."[40] A legal system which penalizes attempted suicide will not condone euthanasia. But even if attempted suicide by itself is not a crime, euthanasia raises the specter of potential abuse. It is all too easy to kill "undesirables" under the guise of mercy. Several members of the Human Rights Committee felt that euthanasia was inconsistent with the Covenant. Particularly criticized was one state which had a statute mitigating the penalty for homicide when mercy was the motive.[41] If a state is permitted to excuse euthanasia, it is indispensable to assure that the consent is authentic and to set the precise form in which waiver of the right to life must be expressed to be valid. Euthanasia practiced by state officials is especially suspect and would require particularly rigorous safeguards.

Related issues have come to the fore in recent years due to the advances in modern medicine. There have been debates about the lengths to which one must go to keep a person alive through sophisticated means, and the allocation of scarce resources to save life; even the concept and definition of life and death itself have been debated. Several kinds of problems with different dimensions have arisen. First, at what point may a person be pronounced dead, so that doctors may proceed to remove a vital organ (e.g., the heart) and transplant it to another person's body?[42] Second, some medical resources, such as dialysis treatment for kidney failures, are scarce and their allocation saves certain individuals while dooming others;[43] what are the permissible standards for selection consistent with the right to life? Third, if a person is lingering in what doctors declare to be an irreversibly "vegetative" state and the vital processes of the body can only be sustained through specialized technological procedures, is it permitted to discontinue artificial life-support measures? This may be seen as euthanasia by omission.[44] The question came up before the Supreme Court of New Jersey in 1976 in the celebrated *Quinlan* case.[45] It was decided that, as a matter of domestic law, if there is no reasonable possibility of a person ever emerging from a comatose condition to a cognitive state, life-preserving systems may be withdrawn.[46] It is a plausible interpretation of the Covenant, too, that when life becomes an indignity endured without autonomy and awareness, death may be permitted to take its natural course.[47]

Does Abortion Impinge upon the Human Right to Life?

Is prenatal life protected by law, and when does the human right to life begin? Article 4 of the American Convention responds to this query expressly by stipulating that the right to life exists, "in general, from the moment of conception."[48] If the fetus has a right to life from the moment of conception, abortion is tantamount to murder and the state is obligated to protect the fetus against a prospective mother who desires to destroy it. But an attempt to introduce the words "from the moment of conception" into Article 6 of the Covenant failed.[49] That suggests that at least during most of pregnancy—until "the point at which the fetus becomes 'viable', that is, potentially able to live outside the mother's womb, albeit with artificial aid"[50]—the only human rights that have to be taken into account are those of the woman.[51] If the right of the fetus to life is not recognized, one may even speak about the human right of the woman to abortion.[52]

These and other issues concerning the right to life will have to be resolved in the application of the Covenant so that the human right to life will achieve its full development.

Physical Integrity

Freedom from Torture and Degradation

Article 7 of the Covenant forbids (a) torture; (b) cruel, inhuman, or degrading treatment or punishment; and (c) medical or scientific experimentation without free consent. The fundamental freedom from torture and degradation is also enshrined in Article 5 of the Universal Declaration of Human Rights,[53] Article 3 of the European Convention,[54] and Article 5 of the American Convention.[55] The Covenant alone includes in this freedom the right not to be subjected to medical or scientific experimentation without free consent.

The prohibition of torture may be regarded as an integral part of customary international law, and it may even have acquired the lineament of a peremptory norm of general international law, i.e., *jus cogens*.[56] There is no definition of the term "torture" in Article 7 or in other instruments. Such a definition (which, while not legally binding, is entitled to great weight) appears in Article 1 of the Declaration on the Protection of All Persons from Being Subjected to Torture and

Other Cruel, Inhuman, or Degrading Treatment or Punishment, adopted by the General Assembly in 1975.[57] The article reads:

1. For the purpose of this Declaration, torture means any act by which severe pain or suffering, whether physical or mental, is intentionally inflicted by or at the instigation of a public official on a person for such purposes as obtaining from him or a third person information or confession, punishing him for an act he has committed or is suspected of having committed, or intimidating him or other persons. It does not include pain or suffering arising only from, inherent in or incidental to, lawful sanctions to the extent consistent with the Standard Minimum Rules for the Treatment of Prisoners.
2. Torture constitutes an aggravated and deliberate form of cruel, inhuman or degrading treatment or punishment.[58]

The key elements of this definition are beyond dispute. First, torture may be either a mode of punishment (for instance, drawing and quartering) or a form of treatment having other purposes. Second, the reason motivating torture—inducing confessions, eliciting information, instilling fear (in the victim or another person) or even sheer sadism—is immaterial. Third, torture may be either physical or mental.[59] What is less clear is whether the term "torture" has a subjective element as applied to the individual, i.e., whether the victim's particular tolerance to pain may be a determining factor in establishing whether a specific act amounts to torture.[60]

Whatever the constituent elements of torture are, the term must be distinguished from cruel, inhuman or degrading treatment and punishment. As the European Court of Human Rights ruled in the *Northern Ireland* case (1978): "This distinction derives principally from a difference in the intensity of the suffering inflicted."[61] That is, the expression torture attaches a "a special stigma to deliberate inhuman treatment causing very serious and cruel suffering."[62] On that basis the Court reached the conclusion that certain techniques for interrogation in depth (sometimes called "disorientation" or "sensory deprivation") used by the British security forces in Northern Ireland in 1971[63] amounted to inhuman and degrading treatment but not to torture.[64]

The European Court of Human Rights also held in the *Tyrer* case (1978), that the level of suffering which justifies the use of the term "inhuman" is higher than that which warrants the adjective "degrading."[65] There seems to be, then, a scale of aggravation in suffering which commences with degradation, mounts to inhumanity and ultimately attains the level of torture. It is not quite clear what level of suffering inflicted merits the label "cruel," but presumably it is some-where between inhuman conduct and torture.

A further distinction is made between degrading (as well as cruel or inhuman) treatment, on the one hand, and degrading (as well as cruel or inhuman) punishment, on the other.

A degrading treatment must be both degrading and treatment. It was observed in the course of drafting Article 7 that the word "treatment" should not apply to degrading situations which might be due to general economic and social factors.[66] Thus, "treatment" must be a specific act (or omission) perpetrated deliberately with a view to humiliating the victim. What acts are to be considered degrading is less easy to answer. There is some authority for the proposition that under certain circum-stances illicit discrimination may by itself amount to degrading treat-ment.[67] The following practices also appear to deserve being subsumed under the heading of degrading treatment:

—Committing a sane person to a mental institution for psychiatric treatment because he holds certain nonconformist political views[68]
—Compelling new immigrants to go through demeaning procedures such as "virginity tests"
—Admitting a foreign laborer (*Gastarbeiter*) into a country for a pro-longed period of time on condition that he does not bring his fam-ily with him.

Punishment presumably means punishment imposed by a court fol-lowing conviction for crime. There is no consensus as to what judicial punishment can be branded cruel, inhuman, or degrading. In a sense, the mere fact of being convicted and subjected to judicial punishment is itself humiliating and degrading. But as the European Court stated in the *Tyrer* case, it "would be absurd to hold that judicial punishment generally, by reason of its usual and perhaps almost inevitable element of humiliation, is 'degrading.' "[69] Some further criteria must be used depending "on all the circumstances of the case and, in particular, on the nature and context of the punishment itself and the manner and method of its execution."[70]

Moreover, as the Court pointed out, "A punishment does not lose its degrading character just because it is . . . an effective deterrent or aid to crime control."[71] A punishment may also be cruel even though no cruelty is intended: as Bion said more than two millennia ago, though boys throw stones at frogs in sport, the frogs do not die in sport but in earnest.[72]

One school of thought maintains that capital punishment does not comport with human dignity and should be categorized as cruel and inhuman punishment.[73] Yet, as we have seen, this punishment is in fact permitted (subject to some exceptions) under Article 6. On the other hand, if the death penalty involves torture or a lingering death—if there is more to it than "the mere extinguishment of life"—it is cruel and inhuman.[74] It is submitted that public execution, which is still a frequent occurrence in some Arab and African countries, is a degrading punishment. A degrading punishment which may be regarded as irrefutably illegal under Article 7 is putting a person in the pillory and exposing him to public ridicule (as was common in days past). It must not be concluded, however, that publicity is the only relevant factor in assessing whether a punishment is degrading. As the Court in the *Tyrer* case emphasized, a punishment may be degrading even in the absence of publicity.[75] The Court, faced with a case of whipping inflicted privately as a punishment on a male juvenile under the penal law of the Isle of Man (a dependency of the British crown with its own legal system), ruled that judicial corporal punishment was degrading punishment.[76]

The position is less clear in respect of certain other judicial punishments such as solitary confinement or even life imprisonment. It is at least arguable that these two are inhuman punishments, although it is difficult to accept that life imprisonment is barred by the Covenant if capital punishment is permitted.

Medical and scientific experiments raise a number of questions, mostly in regard to circumstances which may vitiate consent. The clause banning experimentation in the absence of free consent was introduced into Article 7 in order "to prevent the recurrence of atrocities such as those committed in concentration camps during the Second World War."[77] The so-called experimentations carried out by the Nazis on inmates of concentration camps subjected the latter to, inter alia, poisons, epidemics, freezing conditions, and extremely high altitudes.[78] Such outrages can be regarded as outright torture, in which case consent is not an issue: torture, unlike medical or scientific experimentation, is unlawful even if the victim (say, for masochistic reasons) agreed to be subjected to it. With genuine medical and scientific experiments, however, free consent is the central issue. If a scientist allows himself to be infected with a microbe, or exposes himself of his own free will to radiation, with a view to advancing human knowledge, the element of consent is the touchstone of legality.[79] Still, there are problems concerning people (e.g., prisoners) who are placed in such a position that their consent to be exposed to risks through experimentation may be taken with a grain of salt.[80] Edmond Cahn speaks about the "engineering of consent" by exploiting the condition of necessitous men.[81] On the other hand, there are instances of unimpeachable experiments performed on a massive scale without seeking the consent of the persons concerned, for example, the addition of fluoride to the water supply on an experimental basis.[82] Perhaps there is room for the notion of constructive consent in such circumstances. The words "in particular" which link the two sentences of Article 7 were designed by the framers of the Covenant to make it clear that only experiments which come within the range of inhuman treatment are forbidden whereas legitimate scientific or medical practices are not hindered.[83]

Liberty

Freedom from Slavery and Forced Labor

Article 8 of the Covenant proclaims the fundamental freedom from slavery and forced labor. This human right is also enunciated in Article 4 of the Universal Declaration of Human Rights,[84] Article 4 of the European Convention,[85] and Article 6 of the American Convention.[86] There is also a series of conventions dealing with the subject: the 1926 Slavery Convention,[87] the 1930 ILO Convention (No. 29) concerning Forced or Compulsory Labor,[88] the 1956 Supplementary Convention on the Abolition of Slavery, the Slave Trade, and Institutions and Practices Similar to Slavery;[89] and the 1957 ILO Convention (No. 105) concerning the Abolition of Forced Labor.[90]

Article 8 prohibits slavery, the slave trade, servitude, and forced or compulsory labor. None of these expressions is defined in the article. The common denominator of slavery, slave trade, and servitude—as distinct from forced or compulsory labor—is that they are forbidden irrespective of the consent of the person concerned. A proposal to insert the adjective "involuntary" before the word "servitude" was opposed for this very reason: servitude (like slavery and slave trade) is prohibited in any form, whether involuntary or not, and no person may "contract himself into bondage."[91] The term "slavery" is technical and limited in scope, inasmuch as it implies ownership as chattel by another person and "the destruction of the juridical personality."[92] "Slave trade" is also an expression that should be strictly construed. A proposal to substitute for it "trade in human beings" (a phrase covering traffic in women for sexual exploitation as well as slaves) was not accepted.[93] "Servitude" is a broader term "covering indirect and concealed forms of slavery."[94] It seems to include, though it is not limited to, peonage and serfdom.[95]

The expression "forced or compulsory labour" is defined in Article 2 of the 1930 ILO Convention in the following terms (subject to five exceptions enumerated in the Article): "all work or service which is exacted from any person under the menace of any penalty and for which the said person has not offered himself voluntarily."[96] Yet this definition was not considered by the framers of the Article as "entirely satisfactory for inclusion in the covenant."[97]

Article 8 expressly states that the prohibition of forced or compulsory labor does not preclude (a) the performance of hard labor as a punishment concomitant with imprisonment pursuant to a sentence by a competent court; (b) any other work or service normally required of a person who is under detention in consequence of a lawful order of a court (or during conditional release from such detention); (c) any service of a military character (as well as national service required by law of conscientious objectors); (d) any service exacted in cases of emergency or calamity threatening the life or well-being of the community; (e) any work or service which forms part of normal civil obligations.

The difference between hard labor as a punishment (a) and service normally required of a person under detention (b) is that the former pertains to a specific punishment of "hard labor" to which a competent court expressly sentences a convicted person, whereas the latter covers ordinary prison work which all persons under detention may be required to perform.[98] Even when hard labor is imposed by a court of law, however, the hardship entailed must be within reason. As for service normally required of a person under detention, the adverb "normally" is used with a view to providing "a safeguard against arbitrary decisions by prison authorities."[99] Regarding service of a military character, as well as national service required by law of conscientious objectors (c), the question arises whether conscientious objectors are entitled to be compensated with pay equal to that received by soldiers. Proposals to deal with the subject in Article 8 failed.[100] Services exacted in times of emergency (d) do not present a problem. But what is meant by "normal civil obligations" (e)? It is noteworthy that in the case of *Iverson v. Norway* (1963), the European Commission of Human Rights refused to view the obligatory public service of a Norwegian dentist assigned (by law) for one year to a remote area in the northlands as unlawful forced labor.[101]

Another important question is whether a state may impose a general duty to work by penalizing a so-called parasitic way of life (in the style of the USSR).[102] In my opinion, such legislation must be viewed as an infringement on human rights. Every person enjoys a right to work under Article 6 of the International Covenant on economic, Social, and Cultural Rights[103] (and various other instruments). But there is no obligation to work. An "anti-parasite" law collides head-on with the prohibition of forced labor.

On the other hand, if a person does not wish to work and the state (without penalizing his conduct) withholds relief from him, this purely financial pressure does not amount to compulsion.[104] Moreover, if abstention from work is coupled with other factors, it may amount to vagrancy. Article 5(1)(e) of the European Convention expressly permits the detention of vagrants.[105] In the *Vagrancy* cases (1971), the European Court of Human Rights pointed out that the Convention does not define the term "vagrant."[106] The Court examined a definition contained in the Belgian Criminal Code, under which "vagrants are persons who have no fixed abode, no means of subsistence and no regular trade or profession."[107] There are three cumulative conditions in this definition, and the Court held that it is reconcilable with the usual meaning of the term "vagrant."[108] Thus, a person who merely has no regular trade or profession cannot be regarded as a vagrant and if detained on that ground alone, the state would be in violation of Article 8 of the Covenant.

The Right to Liberty and Security

Article 9 of the Covenant sets forth the right to liberty and security of the person. This right is confirmed in Article 3 of the Universal Declaration of Human Rights (together with the right to life), Article 5 of the European Convention,[109] and Article 7 of the American Convention.[110]

The term "right to liberty"—which may be paraphrased as the "freedom of freedom"—sounds like an abstract slogan. But it implies physical freedom and encompasses the very concrete and specific freedom from arbitrary arrest and detention, a right which is as critical as any, and too commonly dishonored in our time.

Every society uses criminal law and institutions to maintain order and justice, as well as to protect the rights of others. The procedures and sanctions of the criminal process, however, impinge on the freedom of the individual charged with and convicted of crime (and in extreme cases take his life). Such invasions of freedom are justified because they are necessary to protect society, but they are justified only if and to the extent that they are indeed necessary. The criminal process, however, is subject to failures and abuses, which are among the greatest threats to human rights, particularly to the rights to life and liberty.

Protection against inadequacies of the criminal process is a principal concern of international human rights. It is the subject of several articles in the Covenant and of a separate essay in this volume (see essay 6). In this essay, the emphasis is on one crucial aspect of that protection: the protection against arbitrary arrest and detention. Too often, in too many societies, individuals are arrested and detained without proper cause, not as part of the criminal process but in situations where the criminal law has no legitimate place.

Article 9 of the Universal Declaration [111] deals with freedom from arbitrary arrest, detention, or exile as an independent human right, separate from the right to liberty in Article 3. Article 9 of the Covenant, however, brings the freedom from arbitrary arrest or detention (though not the freedom from arbitrary exile) within the bounds of the right to liberty, as do Article 5 of the European Convention and Article 7 of the American Convention. Article 9 of the Covenant spells out this freedom as follows: "(1) No one shall be deprived of his liberty except on such grounds and in accordance with such procedure as are established by law."

Once more we encounter a reference in the Covenant (an international legal instrument) to the national legal system. The generic term "law" in its ordinary use embraces not only statutory enactments but also subordinate legislation and even unwritten ("common") law.[112] The European Court of Human Rights held in the *Golder* case (1975), that such subordinate forms of legislation may fulfill the condition "in accordance with the law," which appears in the European Convention in a different context.[113] In yet another frame of reference, the Court observed in the *Sunday Times* case (1979) that the word "law" in the expression "prescribed by law" covers "not only statute but also unwritten law." The Court added that any other interpretation would strike at the very roots of the legal system of a common-law state.[114] Still, the Court ruled that a law must be (a) adequately accessible to all citizens; and (b) formulated with sufficient precision to enable the citizen to regulate his conduct.[115] The citizen, in the Court's words, "must be able—if need be with appropriate advice—to foresee to a degree that is reasonable in the circumstances, the consequences which a given action may entail."[116] The principle governing restrictions of human rights, according to this judgment, is "the principle of legal certainty," though the Court stressed that absolute certainty is unattainable and, indeed, that excessive rigidity is undesirable.[117]

Generally speaking, the requirement that both the grounds for detention and the procedure leading to it must be "established by law" emphasizes the need to promulgate ground rules and to circumscribe the freedom of action of public officials. Not every policeman (or other state functionary) is entitled to decide at his discretion, and on his own responsibility, who can be arrested, why and how. The Permanent Court of International Justice pointed out in its Advisory Opinion in the *Danzig Decrees* case (1935) that "the principle that fundamental rights may not be restricted except by law" does not necessarily exclude the use of discretion in applying the law.[118] But the Court went on to say that there are some cases in which the discretionary powers left to a public authority are so wide that they exceed acceptable limits.[119] That statement has important implications for Article 9 of the Covenant, too.

A major question is whether the requirement that grounds and procedures of detention be established by law exhausts the injunction against arbitrary arrest and detention. This brings to the fore the meaning of the pivotal term "arbitrary." Several opinions were expressed on this issue in the process of drafting Article 9. According to one school of thought, "arbitrary" is synonymous with "illegal" or "contrary to the national legislation."[120] In other words, an arrest is arbitrary only if it is not sanctioned by law: any detention carried out under the imprimatur of law is by definition nonarbitrary and therefore permissible. On the other hand, it was argued that "arbitrary" means "unjust" and that all legislation must "conform to the principle of justice."[121] This was the position of the American Delegation in the Third Committee of the General Assembly: "Arbitrary arrest or detention implied an arrest or detention which was incompatible with the principles of justice or with the dignity of the human person irrespective of whether it had been carried out in conformity with the law."[122]

The allusion to "justice" in this context may have referred to the principle in traditional international law that a state is responsible for a "denial of justice" to a national of another state. In essence, the question is whether there exists an objective international minimum standard so that a law incompatible with it may be declared in contravention of human rights. The prevailing and better view is that Article 9 imports such an international minimum standard,[123] although proposals listing the possible grounds on which deprivation of liberty may be justified were rejected by the framers of the article.[124] As the European Court of Human Rights held in the *Winterwerp* case (1979): "In a democratic society subscribing to the rule of law . . . no detention that is arbitrary can ever be regarded as 'lawful.' "[125] It is manifestly the purpose of the Covenant to protect individuals from despotic legislation and to establish that deprivations of liberty, such as occurred under the Nazi regime, are not consistent with human rights merely because they were prescribed by national law.[126] The duties corresponding to international human rights are incurred by states. If states are free to determine the scope of their own obligations, international human rights are liable to become empty shells. Only an international minimum standard which operates independently of the vagaries of national legal systems can effectively protect human rights. The idea that no one can be subjected to arbitrary arrest or detention was imported into Article 9 of the Covenant from Article 9 of the Universal Declaration. A study of the drafting of the earlier document supports the conclusion that the intent of the framers of the original clause was to bring national legislation into line with an international minimum standard.[127]

While the content of a minimum international standard cannot be defined or enumerated, one form of arbitrariness is surely within the prohibition of Article 9—when the law permitting detention is a *lex specialis* applicable solely to John Doe und not to others. Article 9 implies that the law governing detention must be of general applicability. The arrest of a given person on legal grounds fitting only the specific occasion is arbitrary—notwithstanding the form of law supporting it—because it is capricious.

Of course, what is or is not arbitrary may depend on the context and circumstances. For example, the European Court of Human Rights pronounced in the *Engel* case (1976) that members of the armed forces are also entitled not to be dispossessed of their liberty in an arbitrary fashion.[128] Still, disciplinary penalties which would be deemed a deprivation of liberty if applied to a civilian may be permissible when imposed on a serviceman.[129]

Article 9(2) provides: "Anyone who is arrested shall be informed, at the time of arrest, of the reasons for his arrest and shall be promptly informed of any charges against him."

This right is applicable in the legitimate criminal process and expresses rights to which even those properly charged are entitled (see essay 6). But it is also designed to ensure against the abuse of the criminal process. The goal is to avoid a Kafkaesque world in which people find themselves deprived of their liberty without even knowing why.

A distinction is drawn, however, between giving reasons for arrest and informing the person of the charges against him. Reasons for arrest must be given at the time a person is arrested. The competent authorities are then given "sufficient time to prepare a detailed brief of the charges," although the period should be as short as possible.[130] Charges are, of course, more formal in character, although there is no requirement that they be imparted in writing.[131]

Article 9(3) provides in part: "Anyone arrested or detained on a criminal charge shall be brought promptly before a judge or other officer authorized by law to exercise judicial power and shall be entitled to trial within a reasonable time or to release."

There are two parts to this right. First, the freedom of action of the executive branch of government is circumscribed. A temporary administrative detention is permissible—if authorized by law—but the detainee must be brought promptly before the judiciary. The term "promptly" is not defined, but obviously it is a matter of hours or days rather than weeks or months. The European Court of Human Rights held in the *Lawless* case (1961) that administrative detention without bringing the detainee before a judicial authority is in contravention of this human right, even if its purpose is the prevention of future offenses rather than the punishment of past ones.[132]

What is the meaning of the term "other officer authorized by law to exercise judicial power"? The question arose before the European Court of Human Rights in the *Schiesser* case (1979).[133] The Court ruled that there is "a certain analogy" between such an officer and a judge, though the term "officer" has a wider meaning.[134] The exercise of judicial power "is not necessarily confined to adjudicating on legal disputes" and the officer may be an official in the public prosecutor's department.[135] Nonetheless, the Court reached the conclusion that the officer could not conceivably exercise judicial power if he does not enjoy independence from the executive and the parties.[136] In addition, the person arrested must appear before the officer who must also review "the circumstances militating for or against detention" on the basis of legal criteria.[137]

Second, once the detainee is charged, his detention may be extended (by order of a judge) on remand, although he must be brought to trial within a reasonable time. What is "reasonable time" in the context? The expression has created difficulties under the European Convention on Human Rights.[138] The European Court of Human Rights, in the *Wemhoff* case (1968), interpreted the phrase "shall be entitled to trial within a reasonable time" (which appears both in the European Convention and in Article 9 of the Covenant) as relating "to the whole of the proceedings before the court, not just their beginning."[139] It is not enough that trial begin within a reasonable time, but conviction by a court of first instance or acquittal and release must also be within a reasonable time. In the *Stögmuller* case (1969), the European Court indicated that it is not feasible to translate reasonable time "into a fixed number of days, weeks, months, or years."[140] In the *Wemhoff* case it held: "The reasonableness of an accused person's continued detention must be assessed in each case according to its special features."[141]

The Court declined to endorse the European Commission's set of seven general criteria for assessing the length of the detention imposed, preferring to rely on the specific circumstances of each case and on the reasons given by the national authorities for prolonging detention.[142] Accordingly, the Court reached different conclusions in two judgments pertaining to lengthy periods of detention delivered on the same day. In the *Wemhoff* case, the Court found that a period of three and a half years of preverdict detention was not unreasonable considering the exceptional complexity of the investigation.[143] But in the *Neumeister* case, the Court pronounced that a period of two years of detention on remand constituted a violation of human rights.[144]

Article 9(3) continues: "It shall not be the general rule that persons awaiting trial shall be detained in custody, but release may be subject to guarantees to appear for trial, at any other stage of the judicial proceedings, and, should occasion arise, for execution of the judgment."

This unusual formulation, couched in negative rather than affirmative terms, is tied in with the overall requirement in Article 9(1) that detention not be "arbitrary." It is clear that release from custody pending trial (subject to guarantees of appearance) may not be denied arbitrarily. On the other hand, there is no absolute right to such release. Applying similar provisions, the European Court has confirmed that there are three acceptable grounds for continued detention and refusal of release.[145] These are:

1. Danger of flight: if there is reason to fear that the accused will abscond because of the severity of the sentence which the accused may expect in the event of conviction;[146] or because of his character, his morals, his home, his occupation, his assets, his family ties, and all kinds of links with the country in which he is prosecuted;[147] or even because of the accused's particular distaste of detention.[148]
2. Suppression of evidence: if there is reason to fear that evidence

will be destroyed, especially as a result of the accused communicating with persons who might be involved.[149]

3. Repetition of the offense: if the accused is charged with a serious offense and there is danger that, should he be released, he would repeat it[150] or commit other offenses.[151]

The guarantees that may be required for release from custody (when granted) may vary from one country to another, and they do not necessarily have to be "of a purely financial character."[152] Yet bail is probably the most common guarantee. The forms of bail are manifold, but the common purpose is to secure the presence of the accused at his trial "by the threat that nonappearance will entail the forfeiture by the accused or some other person of a specified sum of money."[153] In practice, release from custody may be improperly denied not merely by refusal without reason to grant bail, but also by setting it at an excessively high figure. Justice Douglas of the Supreme Court of the United States stated the case lucidly: "The presumption that a man is innocent until proven guilty is in effect circumvented if a man is imprisoned, pending trial, because he cannot raise bail."[154]

Indeed, an indigent defendant who loses his freedom because he cannot provide bail may also lose the opportunity to investigate his case and to earn money he may need to press his case properly.[155] Consequently, the method of calculating bail is of crucial importance. The European Court held in the *Neumeister* case, that the purpose of the calculation of bail is to ensure the presence of the accused at his trial.[156] Assessment of bail on the basis of extraneous considerations (such as the amount of the loss resulting from the offense imputed to the accused which the accused may be called upon to make good) is therefore a violation of the individual's rights.[157] The amount of bail must be assessed principally by reference to the accused, his assets, and his relationship with any guarantors that he may have, so that the prospect of loss to the guarantors will act as a sufficient deterrent to dispel any wish to abscond.[158]

Article 9(4) provides: "Anyone who is deprived of his liberty by arrest or detention shall be entitled to take proceedings before a court, in order that that court may decide without delay on the lawfulness of his detention and order his release if the detention is not lawful."

As the the European Court of Human Rights held in the *Vagrancy* cases (1971), the purpose of this provision is to assure that detainees have the right to judicial review of the lawfulness of their arrest.[159] Hence, the right is limited to instances in which the decision depriving a person of his liberty is taken by an administrative body.[160] If the decision is made by a court in the first instance, the supervision required is already incorporated in that decision and the state need not make available to the person concerned a second judicial review.[161] For this purpose an authority is judicial in nature if it provides the fundamental guarantees of judicial procedures.[162] In the *Winterwerp* case, the Court added that it is essential that the detainee should have an "opportunity to be heard either in person, or where necessary, through some form of representation."[163]

The technique used to enable a detainee to get the necessary judicial supervision of the lawfulness of his arrest depends on the internal legal system. In common-law countries, it will usually take the form of habeas corpus proceedings, but a specific reference to habeas corpus, which had appeared in early drafts of Article 9, was deleted.[164] What ultimately counts is not the specific technique but assured access to a court.

Article 9(5) provides: "Anyone who has been the victim of unlawful arrest or detention shall have an enforceable right to compensation."

This is a very important check on the wide powers of the executive to keep a person in detention pending trial. When the executive errs or abuses its powers, it must indemnify the victim for the wrongful deprivation of his liberty. The amount of compensation may take into account not only material but also "moral" damage to the victim.[165] The right of action for compensation apparently lies only against the state as a legal person: a proposal to insert in the article "a right of action against any individual who by his malicious or grossly negligent conduct directly caused the unlawful arrest or detention" was defeated.[166]

Freedom from Imprisonment for Inability to Fulfill Contractual Obligations

Article 11 of the Covenant lays down the rule that "no one shall be imprisoned merely on the ground of inability to fulfill a contractual obligation." This right is also recognized in Article 1 of Protocol 4 to the European Convention,[167] and in Article 7(7) of the American Convention,[168] although it is not mentioned in the Universal Declaration.

The American Convention clarifies that this principle does not apply to nonfulfillment of duties of support (i.e., maintenance, alimony, and so on). This was also conceded by the framers of the Covenant, who "agreed that Article 11 did not cover crimes committed through the non-fulfillment of obligations of public interest, which were imposed by statute or court order, such as the payment of maintenance allowances."[169] Thus, the article does not preclude imprisonment for failure to pay judgment debts for damages.[170] Moreover, if a debtor has the financial means to fulfill his contractual obligation but refuses to carry out his undertaking, he is not protected by Article 11.[171] This is the implication of the clause "merely on the ground of inability": a person who is able but unwilling to fulfill contractual obligations may be punished by imprisonment.[172]

An attempt was made in the course of drafting Article 11 to restrict its scope even further to "inability to pay a contractual debt," but this was not accepted.[173] The article therefore covers any contractual obligation, namely, the payment of debts, performance of services, or the delivery of goods.[174]

Conclusion

The rights to life, physical liberty, and integrity are all (in the taxonomy of the Covenant) civil rights. As such, their roots are derived from time-honored traditions of modern civilization. Some have become generally accepted norms of customary international law, at least in their broad outlines.

It is noteworthy that whereas Article 4 permits contracting parties (under certain conditions) to take measures derogating from their obligations under the Covenant in time of public emergency which threatens the life of the nation (see essay 3), no such derogation is permitted from Articles 6, 7, 8 (paragraphs 1 and 2), and 11. That is to say, the rights to life, freedom from torture and degradation, freedom from slavery and servitude, and freedom from imprisonment due to inability to fulfill contractual obligations cannot be suspended even in time of international or internal armed conflict. In the first three instances this is so because of the quintessential nature of the rights: war or no war, emergency or no emergency, summary executions, torture, and slavery are outlawed. In fact, the temptation to perpetrate atrocities increases in time of war, when the enemy is denigrated in the public mind until it assumes a subhuman semblance; all the more reason to ensure that governments do not yield to that temptation. On the other hand, freedom from imprisonment for inability to fulfill contractual obligations is probably not subject to derogation for the paradoxical reason that it has only a marginal significance and is simply irrelevant to the crisis. Freedom from forced labor and the right to liberty and security are subject to derogation because they are, to the contrary, both significant and germane to the conduct of hostilities on the front and to the exigencies of the situation in the rear.

Notwithstanding the wide acceptance of the basic principles discussed in this paper, many questions remain regarding concrete issues of interpretation. It is to be hoped that elements of doubt and ambiguity will disappear in the years ahead and that the practice of states will redefine the exact scope of these fundamental freedoms in the largeness of spirit they demand.

6

Due Process of Law
for Persons Accused of Crime

HAJI N. A. NOOR MUHAMMAD

CRIMINAL LAW aims at regulating the conduct of individuals in their relations with each other, and in their relations with society as a whole. Its primary purpose is the preservation and maintenance of public order by protecting the fabric of society and its individual members from defined social harms. The criminal law defines socially reprehensible conduct and controls such conduct by strategies and means acceptable to the community.

As an instrument of social control, criminal law relies upon sanctions which by their very nature deprive persons of their life, liberty, or property. These invasions of basic rights are justified by the need to preserve society and to protect the fundamental rights of others. But the criminal law has often been abused with devastating consequences for individual rights. From time immemorial, tyrannical rulers have abused criminal law and process to perpetuate oppression, and to achieve their individual interests rather than the legitimate aims of a good society.

Nations which recognize the sanctity of individual life and liberty, and seek to establish an order based on human dignity and the preservation of fundamental human rights, have developed the concept of "due process of law" to guard against the abuse of criminal process and the distortion of its aims.

The genesis of the concept of "due process of law" can be traced back to Magna Carta (1215), in which the king promised that "no free man (*nullus liber homo*) shall be taken or imprisoned or deprived of his freehold or his liberties or free customs or outlawed or exiled or in any manner destroyed, nor shall we come upon him or send against him, except by legal judgment of his peers and by the law of the land (*per legem terrae*)."[1] Coke, in part 2 of his *Institutes,* equated the term "by the law of the land" with "due process of law."[2] Today the concept of "due process of law" has acquired dual significance. It includes procedural due process, a body of legal precepts and supporting institutions which require certain procedures and respect for certain values, especially (but not exclusively) in the application of the criminal law. Substantive due process embodies the "principle of legality" as well as some limitations on the power of the state under some superior law, whether "natural" or "constitutional," or international human rights laws.

Many articles of the Covenant protect substantive individual rights. This essay deals with those articles that protect the procedural aspects of "due process of law." The concept of "due process of law" as consecrating certain procedures embodies the idea of "fair play and substantial justice,"[3] and is essential to the maintenance of certain "immutable principles of justice."[4] These principles constitute the standards that society has the right to expect from those entrusted with the exercise of sovereign prerogatives. As Justice Mathews of the Supreme Court of the United States observed:

> Arbitrary power, enforcing its edicts to the injury of the persons and property of its subjects, is not law, whether manifested as the decree of a personal monarch or of an impersonal multitude. . . . . The enforcement of these limitations by judicial process is the device of self-governing communities to protect the rights of individuals and minorities as well as against . . . the violence of public agents transcending the limits of lawful authority, even when acting in the name and wielding the force of the government."[5]

The concept of "due process of law" is embodied in the common law traditions of England, the Constitution of the United States, and many modern constitutions. National systems have given expression to this concept not only in general terms, but by specific, detailed requirements, for example, the right to be represented by counsel or to have a public trial.

A significant development in human rights since the Second World War was the adoption of the fundamental concept of "due process of law" in the Universal Declaration of Human Rights and the elaboration of this concept into binding legal obligations on the states parties to the International Covenant on Civil and Political Rights.[6]

In this essay I examine the provisions of the Covenant on Civil and Political Rights which emboby the concept of "due process of law" in criminal law and procedure under the following headings: Rights of the Accused in Pre-Trial Proceedings; Rights of the Accused to a Fair Trial; Restrictions on Punishment.

Rights of the Accused in Pre-Trial Proceedings

Protection against arbitrary arrest and detention is an important element of "due process of law" and forms the central feature of any system of guarantees of the liberty of the individual. Article 9(2)–(5) of the Covenant provides appropriate guarantees for persons under arrest or detention. Although largely designated to terminate, prevent, or discourage unlawful or arbitrary detention, the guarantees apply to all persons arrested or detained, whether or not the arrest or detention is lawful and warranted.[7]

The Right to Be Informed

The first right guaranteed is that "anyone who is arrested shall be informed, at the time of arrest, of the reasons for his arrest and shall be promptly informed of any charges against him" (Article 9(2)).

Three questions arise in respect to this right: whether the information may be in general terms or must be specific; whether the information must be conveyed in any particular form; and what constitutes "time of arrest."

The European Commission, which has considered these questions in the context of the analogous provisions in the European Convention on Human Rights, held that it is sufficient that the arrested or detained person be informed in general terms of the reasons for his arrest and of any charges against him. Only later, in connection with his right to a trial, must the information concerning the charges against him be specific and detailed.[8] The European Commission has also held that the reasons for arrest, and the information regarding charges, need not be in writing,[9] and if oral need not be in any particular form.[10] In a case where an arrest warrant was read to the applicant, the Commission held that "on that occasion, the Applicant was informed promptly of the reasons for his arrest."[11]

The Human Rights Committee, reviewing the reports of states under Article 40, probed for details on pretrial procedures. In addition to emphasizing the right of a person who is arrested to be informed of the reasons for arrest, members stressed that the reasons must be set forth "at the time of arrest." It was doubted that "as soon as is reasonably practicable" satisfied this requirement.[12]

The Right to a Prompt Judicial Hearing

The second right guaranteed is that "anyone arrested or detained on a criminal charge shall be brought promptly before a judge or other officer authorized by law to exercise judicial power" (Article 9(3)).

The authority to arrest varies in different legal systems. Although, in some systems, private persons are given the right to arrest in certain specific cases, arrests are generally made by the police. Such arrests may be effected with the prior authorization (or subsequent approval) of the public prosecutor or by judicial order, which in some systems may be issued by an investigating judge or by a court of criminal jurisdiction. Detention on remand, however, is commonly authorized by judicial order only.

"Promptly" is not defined but the practice of enlightened states helps determine its meaning. The time limit within which a person held in custody on arrest must be brought before the competent judicial officer varies: in many countries it is forty-eight hours. Where periods of custody on arrest may be extended at the request of the police or public prosecutor, the period of extension is usually limited to the same length as the initial period. Ordinarily, then, delay for longer periods would violate the Covenant.

The Right to Trial within a Reasonable Time

The third right guaranteed is that a person arrested or detained "shall be entitled to trial within a reasonable time or to release" (Article 9(3)).

The European Commission has held that the requirement of prompt arraignment does not preclude imprisonment for a considerable period thereafter before the individual is brought to trial if a complicated case requires lengthy investigation.[13] The Commission has observed, however, that it had the right to evaluate whether the length of detention is consonant with the Convention.[14] Under the Covenant, too, while promptness cannot be defined precisely, a state's interpretation of the term in particular circumstances is subject to international scrutiny.

The Human Rights Committee has inquired about safeguards against unreasonably prolonged detention. The twenty-month period permitted by one penal code was considered an "extremely long period."[15] One member "expressed surprise" that a state permitted the allowable period of police detention to be doubled "during a political crisis or during the execution of international undertakings." [16]

Three questions arise: What grounds are adequate for continued detention pending trial? When can a person detained be denied bail? What constitutes "trial within a reasonable time?"

In reviewing the grounds given by the national authorities for detaining an individual pending trial, one must first consider whether the grounds relied on to prolong detention can be justified by the terms of Article 9(3), and second, whether continued detention is warranted by the facts of the case.

Initially, a person may be arrested or detained for the purpose of bringing him before a competent legal authority merely on the basis of reasonable suspicion that he has committed an offense. But what grounds are adequate for continuing detention? Applying similar provisions in the European Convention, the European Court of Human Rights observed in the *Stögmuller* case that the persistence of suspicion is not sufficient to warrant continued detention after the lapse of a reasonable time for investigation. [17]

The only basis for continuing detention, as for the original arrest, is the reasonable belief that the person has committed a crime and will be brought to trial. Article 9(3) implies that if he cannot be brought to trial within a reasonable time, he must be released; in fact, failure to bring the person to trial within a reasonable time precludes trial thereafter, and he must be released.

Even if a person is bound over for trial, detention pending trial may not be justified. A person may be remanded to detention pending trial in order to assure that he will not abscond. In the *Wemhoff* case, the European Court held that the risk that the individual may abscond must be viewed in the light of the facts and circumstances of each case and that the assessment of that risk by national authorities was subject to review. The Court upheld the validity of detention in that case. [18] In the *Neumeister* case, however, the Court held that in the particular circumstances of the case the risk of absconding did not justify detention, because other measures (e.g., bail) could effectively guarantee Neumeister's appearance at trial. Under the Covenant, too, in cases where the danger of absconding can be avoided by bail or other guarantees, it is the duty of the national authorities to see that the accused is released pending trial. [19]

Another ground for continued detention pending trial is the risk that the accused will commit a further offense. In the *Matznetter* case, the European Court held that in the special circumstances of the case the risk of further offense was sufficient to justify continued detention pending trial.[20] On the other hand, in the *Ringeisen* case, the Court held that there was no such risk and that continued detention was unwarranted.[21] Other grounds which have been found by the European Court to justify continued detention pending trial are the risks of suppression of evidence[22] and of collusion.[23] The same considerations should govern the application of the Covenant.

When Can A Person Detained Be Denied Bail?

Article 9(3) also provides that "it shall not be the general rule that persons awaiting trial shall be detained in custody, but release may be subject to guarantees to appear for trial, at any other stage of the judicial proceedings, and, should occasion arise, for execution of the judgment."

In the *Wemhoff* case, the European Court laid down the rule that "when the only remaining reason for continued detention is the fear that the accused will abscond and thereby subsequently avoid appearing for trial, his release pending trial must be ordered if it is possible to obtain from him guarantees that ensure such appearance."[24] In the *Neumeister* case, the Court noted that the bail should not be excessive, and that the amount of sureties must be fixed by reference to the purpose for which they are imposed and to the seriousness of the charge.[25] These principles would also apply under the Covenant.

What Constitutes "Trial Within A Reasonable Time"?

A person charged with crime is entitled to be tried "without undue delay" (Article 14(3c)) even if he is not detained. But an additional provision applies if the person is in detention. Article 9(3) entitles the detainee to "trial within a reasonable time or to release" from custody. The European Court, dealing with an analogous provision in the European Convention, stated that if the accused is detained, there must be "special diligence" in bringing the case to trial, and he is entitled to have his case given priority and conducted with particular expedition.[26] According to the European Court, the essential question is whether the grounds relied upon by the national authorities to justify continued detention are relevant and sufficient to show that detention has not been unreasonably prolonged.[27] As regards the criteria for assessing the reasonableness of delay, the Court observed: "The 'reasonable' or 'unreasonable' nature of the delay between arrest and sentence must be considered not *in abstracto* but in the light of specific circumstances such as the complexity of the case and the procedure followed by the applicant himself. . . ."[28]

The Right to Challenge Detention before a Court

Another right is guaranteed by Article 9(4): "Any one who is deprived of his liberty by arrest or detention shall be entitled to take proceedings before a court, in order that the court may decide without delay on the lawfulness of his detention and order his release if the detention is not lawful."

This provision lays down the principle of judicial control over every arrest or detention. The forms of such control may vary under different legal systems. In England it takes the form of a writ of habeas corpus. In other countries, an aggrieved person may have recourse to special proceedings authorized by law before a competent court or judge with a right of appeal. Article 9(4) requires every state party to the Covenant to provide some court with authority to review promptly the lawfulness of detention and to order release if detention is unlawful.

In the first *Vagrancy* cases, arising under Article 5(4) of the European Convention (which is analogous to Article 9(4) of the Covenant), the applicants complained that they had been detained in centers for vagrants by order of a magistrate (*juge de pais*) under an Act for the suppression of vagrancy, but, as the magistrate acted in an administrative capacity, they were denied the right to take proceedings before a court which could decide on the lawfulness of their detention.[29] The European Court held that this was a violation of the Convention as the applicants had no right of appeal against the administrative order relating to their detention.

The Right to Compensation

The Covenant provides that "anyone who has been the victim of unlawful arrest or detention shall have an enforceable right to compensation" (Article 9(5)).

Is this provision satisfied if there is a remedy against the official only (who may not be able to pay), or must there also be a remedy against the state? The right is generally worded and might suggest a remedy against either the individual official or against the state as a legal person.[30] The plausible interpretation is that the state must ensure that the victim's remedy is effective (see Article 2(1)), and regardless of whether there is a remedy against the state in the first instance, the state must assure compensation if the individual official cannot pay it.[31] Article 9 of the Covenant requires a remedy even if the unlawful arrest or detention was innocently motivated.[32] In the Human Rights Committee, there was approval for countries that recognized that a victim of unlawful arrest or detention was entitled to compensation for moral as well as actual damages.[33]

Rights of the Accused to a Fair Trial

The Covenant's requirements of due process in criminal proceedings relating to a fair trial raise a variety of issues. When does a trial commence and end? What are the elements of a fair trial, and what are the minimum rights of the accused? Are there special provisions governing trial of juveniles? Must there be a right of appeal? Additional questions are raised by the right to compensation for miscarriage of justice and the right to be free from double jeopardy.[34]

The right to a fair and prompt trial begins at the time a person is accused of a criminal offense, but this does not necessarily mean the time when the formal charge is made. Systems of criminal investigation and prosecution differ from country to country, and the guarantee of a fair trial should not depend upon the meaning assigned to the term "charge" by the domestic laws of a particular state. Under an analogous provision in the European Convention, the European Commission noted that in most cases it will be difficult to point to a single identifiable event in a criminal proceeding when the guarantee of a fair trial commences.[35] The Commission observed, however, that "the relevant stage is that at which the situation of the person concerned has been substantially affected as a result of a suspicion against him" even though no formal charge is made at that date.[36]

In the *Neumeister* case, the accused was first examined by the investigating judge on January 21, 1960, charged on February 23, 1961, and indicted on March 17, 1964. The European Court held that the relevant stage was the date on which the accused was charged.[37] On the other hand, in the *Wemhoff* case, the Court held that the relevant stage was the time of Wemhoff's arrest.[38] In that case, the indictment was filed more than two years after the preliminary investigation.

Taking into consideration the differences in legal systems, the right to a fair trial can be said to commence "with that act of the authorities which first substantially affects the situation of the person concerned by depriving him of that security which the law-abiding citizen is entitled to enjoy."[39]

The guarantee of a fair trial is available to an accused person throughout the criminal process, not only in the court of first instance, but also before appellate courts. In the *Delcourt* case the European Court observed:

> Criminal proceedings form an entity and must in the ordinary way terminate in an enforceable decision. Proceedings in cassation are one special stage of the criminal proceedings and their consequences prove decisive for the accused. It would therefore be hard to imagine that procedures in cassation fall outside the scope of article 6(3) of the Convention.[40]

Elements of a Fair Trial

Equality of Parties

The first element of a fair trial in criminal proceedings is the principle of equality of the parties (*égalité des armes,* "equality of arms"). This principle implies that the defendant must be given a full and equal opportunity in the proceedings before a tribunal.

The principle was considered in several cases arising under the European Convention. In the *Pataki* and *Dunshirn* cases, the applicants submitted that under the Austrian Code of Criminal Procedure they had no right of representation before the Court of Appeal, whereas the Public Prosecutor could be and was present, and that this denial of representation violated their right to a fair trial.[41] The Commission held that "the equality of arms," i.e., the procedural equality of the accused with the prosecutor, was an inherent element of a fair trial and that the proceedings concerned were not in conformity with the Convention.[42]

In the *Ofner* and *Hopfinger* cases, a draft of the appellate court's decision was sent to the Attorney General for his observations as required by the Austrian Code of Criminal Procedure, and the Attorney General expressed his agreement with the report.[43] The Commission, after a close examination of the role played by the Attorney General, observed that there was no violation of the principle of equality: the proceeding could not result in any increase in sentence and the Attorney General had not tried to influence the decision to the disadvantage of the accused without the latter being heard.[44]

In the *Delcourt* case, the applicant complained that a member of the department of the *Procureur général* attached to the Court of Cassation not only made his submission in open court but also took part in the court's deliberations as required by Belgian law.[45] The European Court observed that the department of the *procureur général* is not concerned with the prosecution of crime; its function is to advise the court. Through its opinions "it assists the court to supervise the lawfulness of the decision attacked and to ensure the uniformity of judicial precedent."[46] The Court held that in these circumstances there was no violation of the principle of equality.

The Tribunal

The second element of a fair trial is a "competent, independent and impartial tribunal established by law" (Article 14(1)).

A "competent" tribunal implies that the accused is to be tried in a court whose jurisdiction had been previously established by law, not before improvised bodies arbitrarily set up or selected.[47] The term "competent," however, can also be interpreted to require that the tribunal satisfy "legal notions of competence, *ratione materiae, ratione personae,* and *ratione loci,*" and to require also that the judges be professionally qualified.[48]

"Independent" also implies several requirements. Its primary meaning is independence from other organs of government, viewed in the context of the doctrine of separation of powers: the judiciary must not be subject to the control or influence of the executive or the legislature. This doctrine may necessitate methods of selection and procedures for dismissal of judges that assure judicial independence; it surely requires independence in fact, a judge free of influence or control by other governmental authority both in general and in relation to the particular trial. If, for instance, the court is composed of judges whose tenure is for a limited period, whose salary is subject to reduction, or who may be dismissed without good cause, and if these circumstances have a significant and continuing effect upon the actions of the court, then the court cannot be deemed independent. An "independent" tribunal is also immune to and protected from threats and pressures from mobs, individuals, or other pressure groups.[49]

Questions about the impartiality of the court may arise in a number of ways, as shown by the case law under the European Convention. The impartiality of the court may be questioned where the presiding officer made remarks adverse to the accused. In *Boeckman's Case,* the applicant objected to remarks made at his trial by the President of the Belgian Court of Appeal.[50] In a friendly settlement, the Belgian government said that while the validity of the sentence could not be questioned, it agreed that the remarks in question were such "as to disturb the serenity of the atmosphere during the proceedings in a manner contrary to the Convention and may have caused the applicant a moral injury," and paid 65,000 Belgian francs in reparation for his injury.[51]

Where cases are tried by jury, the question has been raised whether adverse press and television publicity before the trial impair the impartiality of the tribunal. In a case under the European Convention from the United Kingdom,[52] the applicant complained that the press and television had given extensive coverage to his case and that the publicity had prejudicially affected the outcome. The European Commission rejected the complaint, observing that the British Court of Appeal found no real risk of improper influence, and that the case for the Crown was so overwhelming that no jury could conceivably have returned a different verdict.[53] The Commission's opinion implies, however, that in other circumstances adverse publicity might in fact prejudice the accused and deny him a fair trial by an impartial tribunal.

A hostile attitude of a lawyer or a witness might also unduly influence a jury and prevent a fair trial. In the *Nielsen* case,[54] the question arose whether the evidence of an expert, Dr. D., improperly influenced the jury. The European Commission stated that:

> the task under the Convention is to decide whether evidence for or against the accused had been presented in such a manner, and the proceedings in general have been conducted in such a way, that he has had a fair trial. Without in any way closing their eyes to the objectionable aspects of Dr. D . . .'s statement the Commission reaches the conclusion, on an examination of the proceedings as a whole, that they do not fall short of the standard required . . . as to the right of the accused to a fair trial.[55]

The impartiality of the tribunal may also be prejudiced if the jury was not properly and fairly selected. In the *Pfunders* case,[56] six young men were convicted for the murder of an Italian customs officer in the German-speaking South Tyrol. The Austrian government alleged that the composition of the Italian jury hearing the charges violated the principle of a fair trial. According to the Austrian government, four out of six jurors were of "Italian ethnic origin and were . . . particularly liable to be swayed by the Italian press campaign, the political tension, the vehement arguments of the Public Prosecutor and of the plaintiff."[57]

In the Human Rights Committee, a major focus of inquiry has been whether adequate safeguards existed to protect the independence and impartiality of the judiciary. Doubt was expressed as to whether the requirements of Article 14(1) are satisfied by systems which exclude judges on political grounds, which provide for criminal punishment of judges (even if only for deliberately passing unjust sentences) or which grant jurisdiction to military tribunals over civilians in certain cases.[58]

A Public Trial

The third element of fair trial is that the trial be held in public (Article 14(1)). Publicity is intended to act as a safeguard against abuse by the prosecution or arbitrary action by the court.

Article 14(1) also provides, however, that "the Press and the public may be excluded from all or part of a trial for reason of morals, public order (*ordre public*) or national security in a democratic society, or when the interest of the private lives of the parties so requires, or to the extent strictly necessary in the opinion of the court in special circumstances where publicity would prejudice the interests of justice." The first grounds mentioned—morals, public order, and national security—are reasons for limiting other rights in the Covenant, for example the freedom of movement and residence and the right to leave a country (Article 12(3)). It is noteworthy, however, that Article 14, in accepting limitations for these reasons, adds the phrase "in a democratic society." While permissible limitations must always be very narrowly construed and applied (see essay 12), the reference to a democratic society underscores the especially restrictive character of the permissible limitations on public trials. That the press and the public may be excluded where the interest of the private lives of the parties so requires contemplates the possibility of private trials in exceptional cases, for example, to protect the identity of a rape victim, or in other instances where publicity might hurt the victim, his family, or other innocent persons. The special provision that the press or public may be excluded "to the extent strictly necessary in the opinion of the court in special circumstances where publicity would prejudice the interests of justice," contemplates other highly extraordinary cases where publicity might cause major public reaction and make it difficult to proceed with the trial or to assure a fair trial. But in no case is "closing" the trial to be allowed to prejudice the defendants right to a fair trial.

The Covenant provision deals only with the presence of the press at trial and does not permit restriction on reporting by the press or other coverage of any criminal proceedings. But, as we said, coverage of such proceedings by the press, radio, or television may sometimes materially prejudice a trial, especially when the trial is before a jury, and violate the right to a "fair hearing" before an "impartial tribunal."

The Covenant expressly provides that "everyone charged with a criminal offence shall have the right to be presumed innocent until proved guilty according to law" (Article 14(2)).

The presumption of innocence applies to the pretrial stage as well as during trial. During the pretrial stage, the presumption is important because it limits the use of detention on remand and, in cases where a person is detained, governs the conditions of detention. The detainee should be treated as an innocent person who is only suspected of a crime and not as a convicted person. For that reason, among others, the Covenant requires that "accused persons shall, save in exceptional circumstances, be segregated from convicted persons and shall be subject to separate treatment appropriate to their status as unconvicted persons" (Article 10(2a)).

At the trial, the proceedings must be conducted on the presumption that the accused is innocent. The basic principle underlying this guarantee is that judges in fulfilling their duties should not assume that merely because the accused has been suspected and charged he probably committed the offense. The onus of proving guilt falls upon the prosecution; any doubt should benefit the accused. Moreover, the judge must permit the latter to produce evidence in rebuttal. The judge may find the accused guilty only on the basis of evidence sufficiently strong in the eyes of the law to establish his guilt.[59] In most systems the presumption of innocence has been held to imply that guilt must be proved "beyond a reasonable doubt."[60]

The presumption of innocence applies both in accusatorial and inquisitorial systems of criminal law. At trial, under the accusatorial system, the prosecution bears the burden of proving the guilt of the accused. Under the inquisitorial system prevalent in many countries in Europe, the court must do all that is necessary to discover the truth. In either system the presumption of innocence requires that the court not be predisposed to find the accused guilty and that the accused be given at all times the benefit of the doubt.[61]

Although this principle addresses the attitude of the judge (or jury), it is incumbent on the judge to correct any impression of prejudice which may result from the behavior of the prosecutor and witnesses. If the judge fails to react to such behavior, an impression might be created that the court shares animosity toward the accused and regards him as guilty from the outset.[62]

According to a member of the Human Rights Committee, the right to be presumed innocent until proved guilty embodies a principle broader than the mere assignment of the burden of proof to the prosecution.[63] Another member questioned whether use of the term "pronounced" guilty (instead of "proved" guilty) in a state's report indicated an interpretation at variance with the spirit underlying the "presumption of innocence."[64]

The prejudicial effect of pretrial publicity on trials, especially jury trials, also relates to the presumption of innocence. Thus, in an Austrian case[65] before the European Commission, the applicant alleged that before he was convicted, the Commissioner of Police had represented to the press that the accused was a fraudulent person, and that remark was publicized by a newspaper in Vienna. The Commission observed that, under certain circumstances, information given to the press by officials before the conviction of a person accused of an offense could prejudice the presumption of innocence established by the Convention.[66] The Commission held, however, that in the instant case the applicant had failed to prove his allegation.

The presumption of innocence also came before the European Commission in regard to the admissibility of evidence of previous convictions. In a case before the European Commission, an applicant had been charged with acts of rape in 1963; evidence of a conviction for rape in 1956 and of other convictions for sexual offenses was given to a jury during the hearing. The Commission observed that "in a number of these [Council of Europe] countries information as to previous convictions is regularly given during the trial before the court has reached a decision as to the guilt of the accused."[67] The Commission held that such a procedure did not violate the presumption of innocence, "not even in cases where a jury is to decide on the guilt of an accused."[68]

Minimum Rights of the Accused

Article 14(3) provides that everyone charged with a criminal offense shall be entitled to a series of "minimum guarantees, in full equality."

These guarantees constitute essential elements of the concept of "fair trial" in criminal proceedings. The words "minimum guarantees" clearly show that the rights expressly enumerated are not exhaustive, are necessary but not always sufficient, and that a trial may not conform to the general standard of "fair trial" required by Article 14(1) of the Covenant even where the minimum rights have all been respected.[69] These minimum rights apply to all stages of the criminal proceedings, from the time when the accused is charged until his final conviction or acquittal.

The Covenant requires that everyone charged with a criminal offense must be "informed promptly and in detail in a language which he understands of the nature and cause of the charge against him" (Article 14(3a)). The European Commission observed that "an accused person has the right to be informed not only of the grounds for the accusation, that is, not only the acts with which he is charged and on which his indictment is based, but also of the nature of the accusation, namely, the legal classification of the acts in question."[70] In other words, the term "nature" refers to the offense alleged to have been committed and the term "cause" refers to the facts upon which the allegation is based. Detailed information about the nature of the charge is necessary to enable the accused to prepare his defense adequately.

The Covenant requires that the accused be given "adequate time and facilities for the preparation of his defence" (Article 14(3b)). What constitutes "adequate time" depends upon the facts of each case. For instance, in a case that came before the European Commission, it was claimed that a period of fifteen days within which a convicted person must file an appeal before the German Federal Court of Justice was inadequate.[71] The Commission held that since all that was required for the appeal was a summary statement of the grounds for appeal, the fifteen-day period could in no way be considered inadequate and does not deprive the applicant of the facilities necessary for the preparation of his defense.[72] One state reported to the Human Rights Committee that it was its practice to limit a defendant to six days to prepare his defense. In response, one committee member suggested that this limitation violated the right to "adequate time."[73]

The term "facilities" includes access to documents or other evidence which the defense requires to prepare its case. It also includes the opportunity and means for identifying and engaging counsel, and for personal communication between the accused and his counsel while the accused is in custody. "Facilities" might include also access to a library and legal materials if the accused wishes to act in his own defense.

The Covenant guarantees that a person accused of any criminal activity shall be entitled to be tried without undue delay (Article 14(3c)). The term "to be tried" means having the charges finally disposed of by the court. In this context, the period to be considered begins with the arrest or detention of the accused and lasts until he is finally acquitted or convicted. Proceedings in the appellate courts are also included and must be held without undue delay.[74] According to the European Commission, the same criteria for assessing "undue delay" apply in the context of Article 14(3c) as of Article 9(3).

The Covenant provides that every person charged with a criminal offense shall have the right "to defend himself in person or through legal assistance of his own choosing; to be informed, if he does not have legal assistance, of this right; and to have legal assistance assigned to him, in any case where the interests of justice so require, and without payment by him in any such case if he does not have sufficient means to pay for it" (Article 14(3d)).

The accused may either defend himself or obtain legal assistance of his own choosing. Presumably if he insists on defending himself the state cannot compel him to accept counsel. "Legal assistance" includes counsel as well as representation in court.[75] The accused has the right to be present at trial but, where he is represented by a lawyer, he cannot necessarily claim the right to attend every stage of the hearing.[76]

The state must provide legal assistance if the applicant does not have the means to meet the costs involved and if the interests of justice require it, whether because the accused is not sufficiently educated or competent to defend himself, because the case is complex or difficult, or because the issue is of public importance[77] and the defense should be conducted by a lawyer. The right to legal assistance is also available to the accused on appeal, whether he was convicted or, in systems that allow appeal by the government, acquitted. Since Article 14(5) gives one convicted of crime the right to have his conviction and sentence reviewed, it is plausible that the defendant is entitled to legal counsel at that stage also. The European Commission has held that "the denial to an accused person of legal assistance on appeal or the exclusion of his lawyer from the hearing of that appeal raises the issue of 'equality of arms.' "[78]

The choice of a lawyer under a free legal aid system ultimately rests with the state, and the accused cannot insist that the state pay the lawyer he selects. The European Commission has held that the state is free to regulate the use of legal aid and to exclude particular lawyers, and that generally the state is responsible for the conduct of the case by the lawyer appointed under legal aid.[79] The state's control of legal aid must not, however, impair the adequacy of the defense, the "equality of arms," or other aspects of a fair trial.

Frequent changes in representation, for example, may obstruct the defense. In the *Koplinger* case, the European Commission considered whether the frequent changes in the applicant's legal representation may have affected his right to have adequate time and facilities for the preparation of his defense.[80] The Commission observed that the legal aid system previously in force in Germany, under which a lawyer was appointed at each stage of the proceedings, was scarcely satisfactory and might be incompatible with the Convention.[81] Although courts cannot be expected to grant constant adjournments in order to enable the new lawyer to acquaint himself with the case, the individual's right to a defense must still be protected.

The Covenant guarantees the accused the right "to examine, or have examined, the witnesses against him and to obtain the attendance and examination of witnesses on his behalf under the same conditions as witnesses against him" (Article 14(3e)).

The right to examine witnesses differs under the accusatorial and inquisitorial systems. In the accusatorial system, the parties, subject to the control of the court, decide which witnesses should be examined in the case. The witnesses are examined and cross-examined by the parties concerned, although the court may put additional questions. In the inquisitorial system, the court determines who should testify and examines the witnesses. In both systems, however, the accused and the public prosecutor are on equal footing as regards summoning and hearing witnesses.

The accused is not, however, entitled to call witnesses without limit. In the *Pfunders* case, the European Commission held that the competent judicial authorities remain free to determine whether hearing a witness for the defense is likely to be of assistance in discovering the truth and to decide against calling the witness.[82]

The accused shall have the right "to have the free assistance of an interpreter if he cannot understand or speak the language used in court" (Article 14(3f)). German courts have given a liberal interpretation to the analogous provision in the European Convention. One court required the free assistance of an interpreter during the preliminary investigation.[83] Another court held that the costs incurred in providing the assistance of an interpreter could not be assessed against a foreign national.

No one shall "be compelled to testify against himself or to confess guilt" (Article 14(3g)).

This privilege protects the accused's communications and testimony. Rooted in English common law, the right against self-incrimination is considered "one of the great landmarks in man's struggle to make himself civilized."[84] There is no comparable provision in the European Convention.

Confessions coerced by physical or psychological pressures would violate the provision against torture or degrading treatment (Article 7) as well. Article 14(3g) also bars coercion by the processes of law, by subpoena, or by other demands for testifying. However, the Covenant does not address indirect pressures, such as the power of a judge or prosecutor to comment on the fact that the accused did not take the stand in his own defense. Arguably such commentary is a form of compulsion to testify.[85]

The protection in the Covenant applies only to persons accused of crime. It does not consider whether a witness in a trial or in a civil proceeding can refuse to testify because the testimony might lead to his being charged, tried, and convicted.

The Covenant contains special provisions regarding the trial of juveniles. Article 14(4) provides that in the case of juveniles, "the procedure shall be such as will take account of their age and the desirability of promoting their rehabilitation."

Most countries make special provision for young people, though the minimum age may differ between countries.[86] The Covenant does not define "juvenile." There is a provision barring capital punishment for crimes committed by those under eighteen. It does not follow, however, that Article 14(4) also requires special procedures for those under eighteen. While the Covenant speaks only to "the procedure," presumably states are required also to establish a minimum age of responsibility for crime and permissible penalties for juveniles. The Covenant places emphasis on their rehabilitation. The term "rehabilitation" is intended to incorporate the meaning of the French term "rééducation," and includes moral, physical, and educational rehabilitation.[87] Rehabilitation here is presumably intended as an alternative to certain forms of punishment after trial. (See also Article 10(3).)

In most countries, juvenile courts do not use adversary proceedings, but rather a special procedure designed to rehabilitate the offender and to shield him from the stigma of criminality. This procedure reflects sociological developments which consider the juvenile's behavior as a deviation not rooted in criminality and includes attempts to direct the offender back onto the path of socially acceptable conduct. But under the Covenant, as well as under some national laws, care must be taken that these special procedures do not disadvantage the juvenile by depriving him of rights he would have if he were an adult.[88]

The Covenant provides that "everyone convicted of a crime shall have the right to his conviction and sentence being reviewed by a higher tribunal according to law" (Article 14(5)). Review "by a higher tribunal according to law" suggests that the form of review might differ from state to state. It suggests also that the review must be "according to law" both in procedure and substance, not merely by the will or whim of an official.

Article 14(6) provides: "When a person has by a final decision been convicted of a criminal offence and when subsequently his conviction has been reversed or he has been pardoned on the ground that a new or newly discovered fact shows conclusively that there has been a miscarriage of justice, the person who has suffered punishment as a result of such conviction shall be compensated according to law, unless it is proved that the non-disclosure of the unknown fact in time is wholly or partly attributable to him."

The right to compensation of a person who suffers a miscarriage of justice complements the obligation of the state under Article 9(5) to compensate for unlawful arrest or detention.[89] It applies only when the injustice was corrected by a reversal or pardon due to some newly discovered fact. The fact might relate to the events of the alleged crime or to error or corruption in the trial. Compensation is not required if the accused was responsible for nondisclosure of the fact. There may be practical difficulties in uniform implementation of this provision and in determining appropriate compensation for different forms and degrees of miscarriage of justice.

The Covenant guarantees freedom from double jeopardy. Under the Covenant "no one shall be liable to be tried or punished again for an offence for which he has already been finally convicted or acquitted in accordance with the law and penal procedure of each country" (Article 14(7)). (Freedom from double jeopardy or the rule *non bis in idem* is not included in the European Convention.)

The double jeopardy clause precludes multiple punishment as well as multiple trials. It protects persons not only against the imposition of further punishment but also against the distress of further prosecution for the same offense. The term "finally convicted or acquitted" signifies that "all ordinary methods of judicial review and appeal have been exhausted and that all waiting periods have expired."[90] Whether an acquittal or conviction is "final" may differ "in accordance with the law and penal procedure of each country," but "final" must be applied in good faith and its application is subject to international scrutiny.

Restrictions on Punishment

The Covenant places important restrictions on the imposition of punishment (Articles 6, 7, 8, and 15).

For a proper appreciation of these restrictions, it may be useful to refer to the various theories regarding punishment. The aims of punishment have been classified as retributive, deterrent, preventive, and reformative.[91] The retributive theory rests on the idea that the wicked should be punished, and because a person is responsible for his actions, he ought to receive his just deserts. Some see punishment as society's revenge; others as society's offer to the individual of the means of expiating his crime and reconciling himself to God or to the social order. Some see punishment as preventive, as a means of protecting society by keeping the individual from repeating his crime. Others believe that punishment is for deterrence: it protects society by punishing the criminal so that he and others will be deterred from breaking the law. Finally, the rehabilitation theory states that punishment should be designed to readjust the offender to society. It is also often assumed that rehabilitation will enable him to lead a better and happier life.

No legal system adheres strictly or exclusively to any one theory. "Each of the traditional theories of punishment contains some truth; but each is defective in ascertainable ways and in different degrees."[92] Enlightened societies draw on more than one of the theories, although some admit no place for retribution. Rehabilitation of offenders has been an important goal of modern criminal jurisprudence, but few believe that it has succeeded or even that society knows how to rehabilitate. In most legal systems "legal punishment is motivated and justified in the first instance by the self-defence of society" against offenders. "In the crudest form, this means reliance on the deterrent and preventive elements in punishment."[93]

Inevitably, the International Covenant reflects the theories that motivate national systems as well as the uncertainties and confusion that surround them.

The Death Penalty

The death penalty (see also the discussion of capital punishment in the context of the right to life, essay 5) is the most extreme punishment prescribed by law.[94] Whether the state has the right to take away a man's life has often been debated. While some condemn the death penalty as a relic of a barbaric age in which "life for life" was the common form of revenge, others support it on the ground that its imposition is necessary to deter serious crime, as well as to prevent the offender from committing further crimes, and to express the moral outrage of society. During the course of the last century, there was a distinct move away from the death penalty and many have labored to demonstrate that capital punishment serves no purpose. However, the abolition of the death penalty has remained a highly controversial issue. In recent years there has been some regression: several states that had abolished capital punishment have reinstated it and others have extended it to additional categories of crime.

Those who drafted the Covenant recognized that many states were not prepared to abolish capital punishment. They strove instead to assure that adequate safeguards be provided in order that "the death penalty might not be imposed unjustly or capriciously, in disregard of human rights."[95]

Article 6(2) of the Covenant establishes safeguards against unjust and capricious imposition of the death penalty by providing: "In countries which have not abolished the death penalty, sentence of death may be imposed only for the most serious crimes in accordance with the law in force at the time of the commission of the crime and not contrary to the provisions of the present Covenant and to the Convention on the Prevention and Punishment of the Crime of Genocide. This penalty can only be carried out pursuant to a final judgment rendered by a competent court."

The death penalty, then, may be imposed only for the "most serious crimes"; the crimes which are designated "most serious" vary from country to country. For instance, in England before the abolition of the Death Penalty Act in 1969, the death penalty was available for high treason, piracy with violence, setting fire to any of Her Majesty's ships, stores, etc., and for five types of murder including murder in the course or furtherance of theft, murder by shooting and murder of a police officer acting in the execution of duty. The October 1969 Act abolished the death penalty for nearly all murders. In India, under the Indian Penal Code (Act 45 of 1860), the penalty of death may be awarded for six principal offenses: treason (for example, waging war against the government of India); perjury resulting in the conviction and death of an innocent person; murder; abetment of the suicide of a minor or insane person; attempted murder by a life-convict; and dacoity with murder (Dacoity is robbery by five or more persons).

The death penalty may be imposed only pursuant to the sentence of a competent court. Competency refers to the jurisdiction of the court and is not intended to relate to the ability of the judge or judges constituting the court (but see discussion of Article 14(1)).

The sentence of death may be imposed only in accordance with the law at the time of the commission of the crime. This restriction ensures that a law imposing the death penalty can not be made retroactive. Article 6 makes specific to the death penalty the comprehensive provision governing retroactivity of laws in Article 15(1) of the Covenant, which not only prohibits the imposition of a heavier penalty than was applicable at the time when the offense was committed but also gives the benefit of any lighter penalty provided for by a subsequent law.[96]

Finally, the sentence of death may be imposed only in accordance with law that is not contrary to the provisions of the Covenant and the Convention on the Prevention and Punishment of the Crime of Genocide.[97] The Genocide Convention is an important measure in the implementation of the human rights provisions of the United Nations Charter. The Convention makes the intentional destruction in whole or part of a national, ethnic, racial, or religious group an international crime. The *travaux préparatoires* indicate that a reference to the Genocide Convention was considered necessary since the individual's right to life could not be safeguarded adequately if the group to which he belonged was threatened with extinction.[98] Article 6(3) of the Covenant specifically provides that when deprivation of life constitutes the crime of genocide, nothing contained in Article 6 authorizes any state party to the Covenant to derogate in any way from any obligation assumed under the Genocide Convention.

The inclusion of the right to seek pardon or commutation of the sentence of death was considered essential in order to mitigate the death penalty in countries where it was still imposed.[99] A pardon is an act of mercy or clemency, ordinarily by the executive, excusing a criminal from the penalty which has been imposed on him and absolving him of guilt.[100] It makes the person who committed the crime as innocent in the eyes of the law as though he had not committed it. Pardon may be absolute or conditional; for example, conditioned on the performance of certain acts or on refraining from others, such as leaving the country or abstaining from intoxicating liquor.

Commutation of sentence is a reduction of the penalty by executive order.[101] It does not absolve the person of guilt in the eyes of the law. The power of commutation is independent of the consent of the convict and ordinarily reflects considerations of mercy or expediency, such as the health of the prisoner or the needs or unusual circumstances of his family. Not infrequently the death penalty is commuted to life imprisonment.

The Covenant specifically provides that "sentence of death shall not be imposed for crimes committed by persons below eighteen years of age" (Article 6(5)). The offender's age at the time of commission of the offense is controlling, not his age at the time of trial, conviction, or sentence. This clause and the other special provisions concerning juveniles in Article 10 recall the Roman law doctrine that "the King was with respect to youthful offenders parent rather than a punishing ruler."[102]

The Covenant also prohibits the execution of pregnant women (Article 6(5)). It delays execution of the death penalty only until the child is born. It may be urged that since the normal development of the unborn child might be affected by the mother's fear of imminent death, a pregnant woman should not receive the sentence of death in the interest of the unborn child. But it is difficult to conclude that that result is required by the Covenant as a matter of international law.

Restrictions on Imprisonment with Hard Labor

Article 8(3) provides that no one shall be required to perform forced or compulsory labor. However, it recognizes that imprisonment with hard labor is an accepted form of punishment in some countries. The Covenant does not purport to outlaw this practice, provided the labor is imposed pursuant to a sentence by a competent court.[103] "Forced or compulsory labor" is defined as "all work or service which is exacted from any person under the menace of any penalty and for which the said person has not offered himself voluntarily."[104] (See essay 5.)

Prohibition of Torture and of Cruel, Inhuman, or Degrading Punishment [105]

Article 7 provides that "no one shall be subjected to torture or to cruel, inhuman or degrading treatment or punishment."

This provision is identical to Article 5 of the Universal Declaration of Human Rights. The Covenant imposes an additional obligation that "all persons deprived of their liberty shall be treated with humanity and with respect for the inherent dignity of the human person" (Article 10(1)).

The term "punishment" implies that an offense has been committed. "Treatment" has no particular reference to crime or punishment, but the fact that a person has been convicted of a crime does not mean that he can be subjected to a "treatment" otherwise contrary to Article 7. Similarly, a state cannot administer as "treatment" what could not be imposed as punishment for crime. "The measures complained of, whatever be their description, must be assessed in each case to see whether, in the context of Article 7, they constitute any of the prohibited forms of treatment."[106]

The Covenant does not define the term "torture." The *travaux pre-´paratoires* make it clear that the word "torture" includes both mental and physical torture.[107] In the Declaration on the Protection of All Persons from Torture and other Cruel, Inhuman, or Degrading Treatment or Punishment, the term "torture" was defined by the UN General Assembly as:

> any act by which severe pain or suffering, whether physical or mental, is intentionally inflicted by or at the instigation of a public official on a person for such purposes as obtaining from him or a third person information or confession, punishing him for an act he has committed or is suspected of having committed, or intimidating him or other persons. It does not include pain or suffering arising only from, inherent in or incidental to, lawful sanctions to the extent consistent with the Standard Minimum Rules for the Treatment of Prisoners.[108]

Torture constitutes an aggravated and deliberate form of cruel, inhuman, and degrading treatment or punishment. The Declaration also provides that any act of torture or other cruel, inhuman, or degrading treatment or punishment is an offense to human dignity and shall be condemned as a denial of the purposes of the Charter of the United Nations and as a violation of the human rights and fundamental freedoms proclaimed in the Universal Declaration of Human Rights. States are enjoined from permitting or tolerating such treatment or punishment; exceptional circumstances such as a state of war or a threat of war, internal political instability, or other public emergency may not be invoked as a justification for such treatment or punishment.

The phrase "cruel, inhuman, or degrading punishment" is generally interpreted to prohibit particular modes of imposing punishment. Several cases have been brought before the European Commission and the European Court alleging that particular modes of punishment violate this principle in the European Convention.

In the *Greek* case, brought by Greece against the United Kingdom as a result of actions in Cyprus, the Commission found that the Covenant was violated by whipping and collective punishment.[109] Various forms of ill-treatment were alleged, the most common being *Falanga* (beating the soles of the feet) and *Bastinado* (repeated beatings), along with other forms including electric shocks, mock executions, and threats to shoot or kill the victim.

In the *Irish* case, the Commission declared admissible allegations made by the Irish government that persons in custody in Northern Ireland had been subjected to treatment which constituted torture and "inhuman or degrading treatment or punishment" within the meaning of Article 3 of the Convention.[110] The treatment complained of included hooding, noises, standing against a wall, deprivation of sleep, and limited diet. The Commission also held admissible an application alleging that the punishment of birching ordered by a court on the Isle of Man violated the Convention.[111]

The Commission has held, however, that *hartes lager* (sleeping hard) once every trimester as imposed by an Austrian prison,[112] solitary confinement for twenty hours a day for a period of ten months in the United Kingdom,[113] and the use of force and a straitjacket after a violent scene in prison in the Federal Republic of Germany, did not violate the Convention.[114]

The Human Rights Committee appeared to give a broad reading to the prohibition against torture or "cruel, inhuman, or degrading treatment or punishment." Contrary to the position of several countries, some members of the Committee believed that solitary confinement and corporal punishment were violations of the ban against degrading treatment. Others implied that restrictions on prisoners' rights to correspondence and regular family visits contravened Article 7.[115]

Both historically and in modern times, disproportponate or excessive punishment has been recognized as improper. The Magna Carta (1215) contained provisions specifying that punishment should be only "in proportion to the measure of the offence." The English Bill of Rights (1689) provided that "excessive bail ought not to be required; nor excessive fines imposed; nor cruel and unusual punishments inflicted." That provision is included also in the U.S. Bill of Rights.[116]

In *Weems v. United States,*[117] the U.S. Supreme Court held that disproportionate punishment violated the Eighth Amendment.[118] Although the death penalty has been held not to be cruel or unusual punishment per se, the Supreme Court held that it was an excessive and impermissible penalty for the rape of an adult woman.[119]

In the United Kingdom, in *Runyowa v. the Queen,* it was argued before the Judicial Committee of the Privy Council that the mandatory death penalty prescribed by Rhodesian law for an accessory in the crime of arson was a punishment "out of relation to that which, in particular circumstances or in reference to an offence of a particular nature, is deserved, may be an 'inhuman' punishment," and therefore unconstitutional[120] (the terms of the Rhodesian Constitution being almost identical with Article 7 of the Covenant). It has also been held in Germany that "inhuman treatment" in the European Convention includes dispro-portionate punishment.[121]

With regard to the prohibition of cruel and unusual or degrading punishment, the question may be raised whether a minimum standard can be evolved indicating at what point the punishment comes within the prohibition contemplated. Regarding similar language in the United States Constitution, Justice Brennan of the U.S. Supreme Court said:

> If a punishment is unusually severe, if there is a strong probability that it is inflicted arbitrarily, if it is substantially rejected by contemporary soci-ety, and there is no reason to believe that it serves any penal purpose more effectively than some less severe punishment, then the continued infliction of that punishment violates the command of the clause that the State may not inflict inhuman and uncivilized punishments upon those convicted of crimes.[122]

The essential tenet of the four principles enumerated above is human dignity. A punishment must not debase human dignity.

Although Article 6 of the Covenant does not outlaw capital punish-ment, the question remains whether the evolving standards of decency have now reached a point where the death penalty can be considered as coming within the prohibition of cruel, inhuman, or degrading punish-ment under Article 7 of the Covenant.

In the United States, there has been a mounting attack on the death penalty. In 1972, the California Supreme Court, in *People v. Anderson*,[123] held the death penalty per se to be cruel and unusual pun-ishment. A few months later, the United States Supreme Court in *Fur-man v. Georgia* stopped short of this position, but declared that "as ap-plied," the death penalty was unconstitutional because it was imposed in an arbitrary manner and with extraordinary frequency on blacks and the poor.[124] Later cases have further narrowed the circumstances in which, and have defined the procedures by which, capital punishment might be imposed.[125] A strong case can be made that in the very large majority of cases in all countries, the death penalty is excessive or oth-erwise impermissible under Article 7.[126]

The death penalty has been a prime concern of the Human Rights Committee. Although members have refrained from declaring whether or not execution is inherently a "cruel, inhuman or degrading punish-ment," they have stressed that the "most serious crimes" requirement for the imposition of capital punishment is best construed restrictively. In particular, it was doubted that property or nonviolent crimes merited the death sentence.[127]

Prohibition against Retroactive Application of Criminal Law

Another restriction regarding the imposition of punishment is the prohibition against retroactive application of criminal law. The Covenant provides: "No one shall be held guilty of any criminal offence on account of any act or omission which did not constitute a criminal offence under national or international law at the time when it was committed. Nor shall a heavier penalty be imposed than the one that was applicable at the time when the criminal offence was committed. If, subsequent to the Commission of the offence, provision is made by law for the imposition of the lighter penalty, the offender shall benefit thereby" (Article 15(1)).

The first clause in the above provision embodies the principle *nullum crimen sine lege*. A corollary to this principle is that a law which has been abrogated cannot form the basis of a criminal conviction if the acts were committed after the abrogation had taken effect. The *travaux préparatoires* indicate that the reference to international law in the above provision is intended to ensure that no one escape punishment for a criminal offense under international law on the plea that his act was legal under the law of his country. (See, for example, the Nuremberg Trials of the Nazi War Criminals.) The reference to international law also constitutes an additional guarantee to the individual and protects him from arbitrary action even by an international organization.[128]

This provision also contemplates that no heavier penalty be imposed than the one that was applicable at the time when the criminal offense was committed. In addition, if subsequent to the commission of the offense, provision is made by law for the imposition of the lighter penalty, the offender shall benefit thereby.

It may be questioned whether this principle contradicts the basic assumption that a penalty should be that which was authorized by the law in force at the time of its imposition. The trend in modern criminal law, however, is to allow a person to enjoy the benefit of supervening lighter penalties. Since the laws imposing new and lighter penalties are the concrete expression of some change in the community toward the offense in question, it would appear proper to allow the offenders to enjoy the benefit arising therefrom.[129] The *travaux préparatoires* indicate that the milder penal law should have retroactive effect for all offenders whether or not they have already been sentenced.[130]

Criminal procedure often appears as a collection of technical rules, but these technicalities are the expression of the civilized human conscience as it has developed over centuries. The history of liberty has largely been the history of observance of procedural safeguards. The protections of the criminal process are the ultimate safeguard for individual freedom and dignity against injustice and oppression.

7

The Freedom of Movement

STIG JAGERSKIOLD

FREEDOM OF MOVEMENT is part of the liberty of man. It has both internal and external aspects. Freedom to move within a country encompasses the right to relocate oneself and to choose one's place of residence and work, as well as the right to travel for education, occupation, or pleasure. The freedom of movement between states encompasses the right to travel abroad, to leave any country, to return to one's own country. In both aspects, the freedom is a fundamental human right. It is essential for the effective enjoyment of other human rights.

Freedom of internal movement and choice of residence allows an individual to enjoy fully the freedom of choice of occupation; he can move and relocate where jobs are available and keep his family together. Free internal movement facilitates the exercise of the right to an education, for lack of access to an education may nullify the right to it. Internal movement also fosters communication and exchange of ideas among people within a country. Free movement of individuals, especially from country to city, is vital to the economic development of states.

The movement of people has developed countries and continents. It has changed human history and shaped modern civilization. The United States, Canada, Australia, and other countries were made by the freedom of migration. It continues to be important for promoting mutual understanding and cooperation among peoples. To that extent, this right serves as an instrument of peace and reduces world tension.

A human being should be free to live where he is without being expelled or exiled. He should be free also to leave his country of residence. The freedom to leave one country for another allows an individual to choose the society in which he will live. Even if an individual never avails himself of that right, the feeling that he is free to go is important for his psychological well-being. But for the individual who finds his society intolerable, and who has made the difficult decision to expatriate himself, denial of this right may be tantamount to a total deprivation of liberty. Without the right to leave, a person may be subject to political repression, may be prevented from observing his religion, from obtaining an education or a job of his choice, or may be frustrated in his efforts to enjoy marriage and family life. Denial of this right is the source of much unnecessary suffering throughout the world.

Yet all states have denied the right to leave in times of war and some countries have prevented emigration and even temporary departure in time of peace. Some states have occasionally felt the need to limit the "brain drain," when too many trained individuals seek to leave. Some have denied the right to leave on ideological grounds, treating the desire to leave as a critical reflection on their society; temporary travel might expose their inhabitants to other ideas and wider horizons. Some states have claimed security reasons to justify denying exit to individuals; for example, on the ground that they have had access to security information.

The importance of the rights to internal and external movement is universally recognized. They are enshrined in the constitutions and laws of many states.[1] They are proclaimed in the Universal Declaration of Human Rights,[2] included as legally binding in Articles 12 und 13 of the International Covenant on Civil and Political Rights, and confirmed in the International Convention on the Elimination of All Forms of Racial Discrimination.[3] They are also protected by the European Convention on Human Rights[4] and the American Convention on Human Rights.[5]

For those who accept the theory that "natural law" limits what men and states can do, human rights are part of such natural law, and the freedom of movement is a principal "natural right." But the right to free movement has also been established us positive law in the law of many states, and as positive international law, by treaty and by customary law.

History and Antecedents of the Right

The movement of individuals has been restricted in varying degrees throughout history. Even when it was proclaimed as a natural right, it was not viewed as conferring absolute freedom. Some limits on the right were always seen as necessary and legitimate to protect important state interests. At different times in different degrees, state restrictions have tended to overwhelm the right.

In ancient times some thinkers declared that a freedom of movement existed. Socrates, for example, regarded it as an attribute of personal liberty.[6] Such a right, however, belonged only to free men, not to slaves.

In the feudalistic period, the right did not exist. Serfs were bound to live on the estates of the seigneur and there was no right to leave without the seigneur's permission. Of course, there was no right to emigrate to another country, and the seigneur could exercise his right of "porsuite" to take back one who had improperly left his territory. The agrarian system which prevailed in Europe until the end of the eighteenth century derived from these feudal legal rules and implied tight limits on individual movement.

The first major documentation of a freedom of movement is found in the original text of Magna Carta (1215). In clause 42 it set forth a right for "any person . . . to go out of our kingdom, and to return, safely and securely by land or by water, saving his allegiance to us. . . ." But that was a right only for free men. Later versions preserved this right only for merchants, reflecting the restrictive policies of the seventeenth and eighteenth century monarchies.[7] Emigration was prohibited and subject to severe penalties.

The motives of absolute monarchs for restricting freedom of movement were primarily economic. In the age of mercantilism, the power and welfare of a country were seen as depending on the number of its inhabitants. Emigration was prohibited to preserve the state's work force and economic base.

There were also military reasons for denying free emigration. A country's power and means of defense depended on the number of soldiers, and it was important to keep the entire population available for military service. Especially in unstable circumstances, a king also had strong interests in controlling the whereabouts of subjects or aliens who were considered dangerous to his security.

An individual's freedom to travel, and his freedom to choose his place of residence within his own country, were also restricted. The "passport" was introduced in its modern form in several European countries during the sixteenth and seventeenth centuries, and by the end of the eighteenth century the passport was an obligatory document for travel anywhere in Europe. It was used not only for controlling travel between countries but internal travel as well.[8]

Countering these restrictions on movement were pressures generated by interest in emigration to the New World, especially to America. Legal theorists claimed that the right to emigrate was part of natural law.[9] A general human right to leave was also in harmony with the philosophy of the Enlightenment.[10]

During the French Revolution, the passport was suppressed and the Constitution of 1791 proclaimed the right to unimpeded travel (*liberté d'aller et de venir*) as part of man's natural rights. Other constitutions, following the French example, also included this liberty, e.g., the Helvetian Constitution. But important exceptions to this freedom were soon made in France on grounds of national security, in order to stem the tide of political emigration and desertion of soldiers.[11]

In Britain, the common law did not recognize a right to freedom of movement. There was a common law writ (*ne exeat regno*) which allowed the king to prevent anyone from leaving the realm without a license, although Blackstone stressed that any restriction must be imposed by law and that the freedom could not be abridged at the discretion of the magistrate.[12] The United States followed the common law of Britain: as late as 1851 an individual had no right to leave the union without permission.[13]

In spite of this restrictive tradition, however, by the mid-nineteenth century the right to leave one's country and return to it was being increasingly recognized. The development of industry and communications brought about a relaxation in the obligatory passport system in all countries but Russia.[14] In response to, and indeed to encourage, mass immigration from other countries, in 1868 the United States Congress recognized that "the right of expatriation is a natural and inherent right of all people, indispensable to the enjoyment of the rights of life, liberty and the pursuit of happiness."[15] Many state constitutions recognized the right during this period.[16]

Writers on international law also increasingly acknowledged the right to emigrate as an absolute right based on natural law and recognized by the law of nations. The Russian lawyer of the late nineteenth century, F. De Martens, declared that "the right to emigrate is the direct consequence of the new social and political order which is based on the respect for the individual and his interests";[17] "every civilized state of our time except Russia is convinced that the right to emigrate is one of the inalienable rights belonging to every citizen."[18]

During this liberal period, even those proclaiming emigration as an absolute right acknowledged that some restrictions were legitimate in order to safeguard the interests of the state. In particular, there were rules to prohibit military personnel from leaving the country without permission. In countries where there was compulsory military training, individuals were forbidden to emigrate until this service was rendered. Restrictions also referred to obligations under civil law: e.g., one could not emigrate to avoid paying a family allowance or meeting a contractual obligation. Other regulations referred to health conditions, and some had special restrictions on women and minors. Not surprisingly, there were rules to prevent citizens from avoiding the consequences of their crimes by going abroad.

The culmination of this liberal period was an effort by the Institut de Droit International to codify the rules of emigration and to make them a part of the Law of Nations. In 1897 a conference on the right to emigrate was held and a text of a convention was prepared. It declared the right to emigrate and immigrate either individually or en masse.[19] The right was subject to limitations required by social or political necessities, but these restrictions had to be made by law and duly published. The right to emigrate was, however, dependent on there being a state to accept one as an immigrant. The convention was not adopted.[20] The First World War saw a return to strict control on entry and exit through the use of compulsory passports.

The end of the Second World War saw a revival of natural law philosophy and concern about limiting state power and guaranteeing human rights. In addition, many twentieth-century constitutions recognized the right to free movement.[21] The right was also enshrined in the Universal Declaration of Human Rights.[22]

The Declaration proclaims the right to freedom of movement and residence within a country, the right to leave any country, and the right to return to one's own country (Article 13). Like other rights in the Declaration, they are subject to restrictions imposed by law "solely for the purpose of securing due recognition and respect for the rights and freedoms of others and of meeting the just requirements of morality, public order and the general welfare in a democratic society" (Article 29).

The Covenant on Civil and Political Rights codified the rights proclaimed in the Declaration and made them binding on states parties.[23] The parameters of the right to free movement as proclaimed in the Universal Declaration are retained in the Covenant. The history of this right and its culmination in the Declaration are essential guides to the interpretation of the Covenant articles.

Some Drafting Concerns

During the drafting of the Covenant there was debate whether to incorporate a right to freedom of movement in the Covenant and, if so, to what extent and in what form. The first draft of Article 12 included only the right of an individual to leave any country, subject to certain limitations; freedom of internal movement and choice of residence were not included.[24] It was argued that these rights were subject to so many restrictions in most states that a meaningful assertion of the right could not be provided in the Covenant. That argument was rejected. The consensus was that freedom of movement, internally as well as externally, is an important human right and an essential part of personal liberty. It had been recognized in the Universal Declaration for this reason. The fact that states had denied the right in recent times made its inclusion in the Covenant even more important.[25]

The major problem during the drafting of Article 12 was that while everyone agreed that the rights to freedom of movement and choice of residence were subject to legitimate limitations, opinions differed on the scope of permissible limitations and how these should be articulated. There was concern whether it was possible to formulate limits which would adequately balance the interests of the state and of the individual without nullifying the right. The choice was between using a general limitations formula and setting forth a specific list of restrictions.

The first draft included a long list of exceptions,[26] but this was deemed too unwieldly. Efforts then focused on some general formula, like that in the Universal Declaration, which would protect the individual while safeguarding legitimate public interests.

The Commission on Human Rights first developed a draft under which the freedom of movement could be limited by any "general law" adopted "for specific reasons of national security, public safety or health."[27] Other terms were considered, such as "general welfare," "economic and social well-being," and "prevention of crime or disorder." These expressions were viewed by most as too far-reaching, so broad, in effect, as to leave no right. On the other hand, a minority saw even these general formulas as too limited and insufficient to protect legitimate public interests in curtailing individual movement.[28]

Finally, the formula now appearing as Article 12(3) was adopted: "The above-mentioned rights shall not be subject to any restrictions except those which are provided by law, are necessary to protect national security, public order (*ordre public*), public health or morals or the rights and freedoms of others, and are consistent with the other rights recognized in the present Covenant." This clause applies to freedom of internal movement, choice of residence within a country, and the right to leave any country. It does not apply to Article 13 and does not therefore limit a person's right to return to his own country.

In using the general phrases "national security, public order, public health or morals or the rights and freedoms of others," the drafters had certain legitimate state interests in mind. "National security" was included to allow a state to protect itself from political or military threats to the whole nation. Such threats must be evident and vital. The drafters were concerned primarily with control over military personnel and the security of military installations. They did not consider it legitimate for a state to curtail departure in order to maintain the nation's manpower pool, even for reasons of "security," or to curtail an individual's departure on the ground that he or she had been involved in or exposed to "classified" activities or information.

"Public order (*ordre public*)" was a particularly troublesome phrase for the drafters.[29] Public order does not simply mean the absence of disorder. The problem was finding an English language equivalent to the French expression *ordre public* and the Spanish expression *orden público,* both of which refer to the principles of the legal and political system in the country and imply notions of public security, health, and peace. The English expression "public safety" was viewed as too narrow; the notion of public safety is included in *ordre public*. "Public policy" was rejected as too broad, although some argued that it was closest to the French phrase. The compromise solution was to use "public order" followed parenthetically by the French expression to show that the English expression was not to be understood by its normal usage. (See essay 12.) Precedent for this solution was found in the Convention relating to the Status of Refugees.[30]

"Public health or morals" was included to permit restrictions for the protection of individuals. The drafters were concerned with regulations which protect legally incompetent persons and minors, and measures to prevent the spread of contagious diseases. The phrase "rights and freedoms of others" was included to allow a state to protect family support obligations and private property interests.

Any restriction on the freedom of movement is permissible only to protect one of the enumerated state interests. They must also be "provided by law." This phrase was used to insure that the source of a restriction is a general rule, usually announced by the legislative branch. It excludes bureaucratic caprice and administrative fiat, and other measures taken under executive authority, unless authorized by law and necessary for the execution of the law.

A law must be "necessary." It must bear a reasonable relation to an enumerated state interest. The law must also be "consistent with the other rights recognized in the present Covenant." This phrase was included to insure that the law was "just."[31] The law cannot be discriminatory, for discrimination is prohibited by Article 26. In addition, Article 5(1) prohibits any law which is aimed at the destruction of any right recognized in the Covenant.

Article 12 also includes a right which the drafters agreed should not be subject to the above limits: the right to enter one's own country.[32] The drafters included another right which is part of the freedom of movement: Article 13 provides protection against arbitrary expulsion. It too is not governed by the general limitation phrases discussed.

All the rights in Articles 12 and 13, however, are subject to derogation in times of national emergency under Article 4 of the Covenant. But this exception is very special and limited as indicated in essay 3 of this volume.

Freedom of Internal Movement

Article 12(1) provides: "Everyone lawfully within the territory of a State shall, within that territory, have the right to liberty of movement."

Scope

For any person lawfully within a territory, this Article establishes a right to travel within that territory subject only to possible restrictions pursuant to Article 12(3). This right belongs to "everyone lawfully within a territory." It is not restricted to nationals or citizens, or even to permanent residents; as long as the individual's presence in the country is lawful, he is entitled to move freely about the country subject only to limited restrictions justified under Article 12(3). "Everyone lawfully within a territory" includes all of a state's nationals present within its territory; the presence of a person within the state of which he is a national cannot be unlawful. Of course, nationals are subject to lawful arrest or detention pursuant to criminal process consistent with the Covenant or to lawful extradition.

Persons who are not nationals are lawfully within a territory so long as they were lawfully admitted and have complied with any restrictions that may have been imposed as a condition of entry. Since there is no general right for a foreign national to enter a country, a state can impose restrictions on entry, such as limits on the length or the purpose of stay. But the state cannot impose as a condition of entry long-term restrictions on internal movement other than those allowed under Article 12(3); otherwise, the freedom of internal movement could be effectively nullified for non-nationals.

Limits

Limits on internal movement must be imposed by law. They must be necessary to protect one of the enumerated state interests and must be consistent with the other rights in the Covenant.

National security concerns permit a state to restrict the movement of military personnel in active service. Such individuals could be restricted to a military base or prevented from travelling out of a limited area. Permanent or long-term restrictions on the movements of a substantial part of the population, however, could not normally be justified on security grounds.

A state can prohibit travel through, or limit access to, security zones or military bases within its territory. But such zones cannot be used to restrict access to substantial parts of a state's territory. Larger areas can be barred for short periods in special circumstances.

Public order restrictions on internal movement that were considered legitimate during the drafting include traffic regulations, measures directed to promote general public safety, and legitimate criminal sanctions for acts which the state is entitled to prohibit under the Covenant.[33] The state has the right to imprison individuals in accordance with law even though it restricts freedom of movement. The movement of an individual can likewise be restricted when criminal proceedings are pending against him.

In appropriate cases, a state can legitimately impose a curfew as a temporary measure; riot conditions in a city would be sufficient grounds for such a restriction, for example. But a permanent curfew is not justifiable.

During the drafting, the delegate from South Africa proposed that in the interests of good government and peace, a state should be able to proclaim reserved areas for different sections of the population and control the movement of the population between these areas.[34] That suggestion was rejected, and such restriction is not permissible under the

Covenant; restrictions on movement and access to areas of a territory based on race, sex, religion, etc. are also prohibited by the nondiscrimination provisions of Article 26.

A related question is whether a state can protect primitive indigenous populations by restricting movement to and from their territory where the restrictions are bona fide and for their benefit. The Australian delegate expressed the view that the public order concept justified this type of legislation to protect his country's aborigines.[35] In this very special case, the state may be able to do so. It may be that limiting access to a territory by outsiders while protecting the individuals' right to leave the area in question is a permissible accommodation of the rights of all concerned.

Temporary quarantines to control the spread of contagious diseases are permitted as a public health restriction.[36] States may close off access to a water supply or other contaminated area for health reasons. The rights of minors or of mentally incompetent individuals to travel can be limited but not prohibited.[37] To this end, a state could impose safeguards such as requiring adult accompaniment.

Restrictions on internal movement in favor of the rights and freedoms of others are based primarily on respect for private property rights. Although the right to own and enjoy private property and not to be arbitrarily deprived of its use are not explicitly mentioned in the Covenant, they are declared in the Universal Declaration.[38] The freedom of movement does not guarantee the right to go on or through private property.

National security, public order, or public health or morals cannot be used to justify restrictions on an individual's right to movement simply because of his political opinion, religious beliefs, sex, race, etc.[39] Thus, if a passport or other papers are required for internal travel, their denial by an administrative agency on some discriminatory basis is a violation of the Covenant. To the extent that documents are required for such travel, a state must make them available at a reasonable cost and within a reasonable time; they can be denied only on grounds, and by procedures, in accordance with Article 12(3).

Freedom of Choice of Residence

Scope

The right to freedom of choice of residence is declared in Article 12(1). This right means that residence cannot be assigned, and it implies a right to settle where one will if a place to live is available. The right applies to "everyone lawfully within the territory." It is not limited to citizens or nationals, so non-nationals lawfully within the country also have the right to choose where they will live. A state probably cannot impose a restriction as to where a non-national can live as a condition of his entry to a country. A temporary restriction might be permissible on grounds, and by procedures, within the bounds of Article 12(3).

Limits

The right to choose one's place of residence is subject to limitations that are imposed by law, necessary to protect the state interests enumerated in Article 12(3) and consistent with the other rights and freedoms recognized in the Covenant.

National security grounds would justify restrictions on residence in limited areas designated as security zones or military bases, but large areas of territory cannot permanently and normally be closed off. Military personnel in active service can be required to live in military areas or otherwise assigned a residence.

Residence restrictions cannot be used to discriminate on forbidden grounds. Individuals of different races, religions, or political belief cannot be required to live in designated areas. Neither can they be forbidden to live in particular areas.[40] The Covenant, however, addresses discrimination by governmental policy; it does not require the state to forbid or to eliminate voluntary or "de facto segregation,"[41] and it would not be permissible for the state to deny to persons who wish to live with others of the same race or religion the right to do so.

The status of protected areas such as American Indian reservations or Australia's Outback is not clear. Presumably a state may prohibit outsiders from settling in such areas, but residents of these areas cannot be prevented from living there voluntarily and they cannot be prohibited from settling elsewhere.

During the preparation of this article, one state delegate suggested that it would be legitimate to forbid movement to an urban area where an adequate supply of labor already exists and housing accommodations are inadequate.[42] This is questionable. Could a state require an individual to have a job, a certain skill, or a promise of housing as a precondition to relocation in an urban area? While the state may have a legitimate interest in planned development of its cities, such conditions would severely restrict an individual's right to move from country to city and would in effect curtail his ability to enjoy other rights guaranteed by the Covenant.

A state can legitimately set aside areas as national parks or wildlife preserves and prohibit private habitation on the grounds of public order for the benefit of its people. In establishing plans for urban development, a state may limit the amount of building or enforce other zoning restrictions even though this may affect one's choice of residence. Similarly, building codes are permissible. But a state may not establish building codes or building limits designed to deny the right of choice of residence to a class of individuals identified by race, religion or other category prohibited by Article 26.

Health concerns can also justify restrictions on residence. A state could impose density limitations to prevent health and sanitation problems caused by overcrowding. Perhaps the state may require mentally ill or diseased individuals to live in a particular place for their own welfare or for the protection of others if care is taken that the rights of these individuals are not unduly abridged.

The problem of internal exile was not specifically addressed during the drafting. If it is imposed lawfully as a criminal penalty, it is probably permitted under the Covenant; since total restriction of freedom of residence by detention in prison is permitted, internal exile is less restrictive and may be less inhumane. But internal exile cannot be used where imprisonment could not be imposed, either to punish or to interfere with what a state may not prohibit under the Covenant or as a means of keeping political dissidents out of a city.

The Right to Leave Any Country

Article 12(2) provides: "Everyone shall be free to leave any country, including his own."

Scope

This clause sets forth the right to leave a country, either one's own country of nationality or residence or any other country in which an individual finds himself; one may leave temporarily or permanently, although one who leaves "temporarily" a country not his own is apparently not guaranteed a right to return. That one has a right to leave one's own country permanently implies a right to expatriate oneself. This right is one of the most important aspects of the freedom of movement; in early drafts of the Covenant only this right was included.[43] However, this right does not guarantee that an individual will have a place to go; there is no general right of entry into another country of which one is not a national.

Limits

This right belongs to everyone but the state can limit the right to leave through restrictions imposed by law that are necessary to protect the kinds of legitimate state interests enumerated in Article 12(3) and that are consistent with the other rights and freedoms protected by the Covenant.

On national security grounds, the state can prohibit military personnel from leaving the country as long as they are on active duty. Similarly, if there is a mandatory national service requirement, individuals who have not yet served may be prohibited from leaving until service is completed.

There must be a clear threat to a vital state interest in order to justify restricting this right. States have asserted the right under this article to prohibit individuals who have had access to classified information from leaving the country. It is questionable whether the security limitation contemplates this type of prohibition. For a state to impose such a restriction permanently would severely curtail this fundamental right.

Political opinions and religious beliefs are not legitimate grounds on which to deny individuals the right to leave.[44] A state may prevent someone from leaving if there is strong reason to believe that he will engage in activities abroad that will harm his country, but this is a narrow exception; the fact that an individual may criticize the government while he is abroad does not pose the kind of threat to the security of his country which its government is entitled to prevent. The Covenant guarantees the right to freedom of thought, religion, and conscience (Article 18).

Can a state limit the emigration of scientists or other specially trained persons because it believes that a decrease in the number of people with technical knowledge would threaten its interests? The problem of "brain drain" was not addressed during the drafting. It is difficult to establish that such a problem exists, since in fact many countries have more trained technical persons than they can use and must "export" them, and state restrictions in this regard are probably not permissible. A related question arises when there is a shortage of labor in a state: can a state prohibit all emigration? Such a policy would be totally contrary to the Covenant. The right to leave is more readily subject to temporary limitations.

Difficult issues arise from the interrelation of the right to leave permanently and the right to travel temporarily. If a state has no legitimate basis for preventing an individual's permanent departure, it cannot restrict his right to travel temporarily merely from fear that he may not return. Further, it cannot achieve that end indirectly, for example by requiring his family to stay home. In the limited circumstances in which a state has a legitimate interest in preventing expatriation, it can presumably restrict a person's right to travel abroad temporarily unless it can take measures to assure his return. In those circumstances some restriction might be permissible.[45]

A state can deny the right to leave to an individual lawfully detained. It may also prevent persons subject to criminal or extradition proceedings from leaving the country. It is uncertain whether outstanding public debts are a legitimate basis for restricting the right to travel. The delegate from the Netherlands suggested that a state was entitled to prevent exit from the state if taxes were unpaid.[46] Since Article 11 prohibits imprisonment for inability to fulfil contractual obligations, breach of a contract is not a legitimate basis for forbidding exit. Are financial obligations to the state different?

A state is entitled to restrict departure for health reasons, e.g., for purposes of quarantine. But these measures should be of a temporary nature. Whether a state can permanently prohibit external travel by individuals who lack mental competence is doubtful, although some safeguards for their own protection and the welfare of others might be permitted. Certainly psychiatric evaluations are not to be abused to deny an individual the right to leave. The right of a minor to travel alone could probably be restricted, but his rights to join his family if it is already outside the country could not be denied.

If an individual is responsible for the support of a family, the state may be able to restrict his right to travel. This example was frequently mentioned as a permissible limitation on travel "to protect the rights and freedoms of others."[47] A permanent prohibition on external travel, however, would not be permissible, but a state could possibly require some guarantee that family support payments will be met. Temporary travel could not be restricted for this reason.

Generally, travel documents such as a passport may be required for individuals to leave a country. If documents are required, a state must make them available at a reasonable cost and within a reasonable time. The refusal to issue travel documents is permissible only in those special circumstances in which the individual's right to travel may be restricted. It is not permissible to restrict the right through ingenious or-ingenuous measures.[48] Discriminatory administrative policies are a violation of the Covenant.

The Right to Enter One's Own Country

Article 12(4) provides: "No one shall be arbitrarily deprived of the right to enter his own country."

Scope

While there is no general right to enter a country, this clause declares a right to enter one's own country. This right is intended to apply to individuals asserting an individual right. There was no intention here to address the claims of masses of people who have been displaced as a byproduct of war or by political transfers of territory or population, such as the relocation of ethnic Germans from Eastern Europe during and after the Second World War, the flight of Palestinians from what became Israel, or the movement of Jews from the Arab countries. Whatever the merits of various "irredentist" claims, or those of masses of refugees who wish to return to the place where they originally lived, the Covenant does not deal with those issues and cannot be invoked to support a right to "return." These claims will require international political solutions on a large scale.

Early drafts of this article dealt only with the right of nationals to enter the country of their nationality and were intended to cover also persons born abroad who had never been to the country of their nationality. However, this formula was deemed too limited by those who sought to assure the right of return to persons who were not nationals but who had established their home in a country. In a compromise based on Article 13(3) of the Universal Declaration of Human Rights, the phrase the "country of which he is a national" was replaced by "his own country."[49]

The right to enter "one's own country," then, is not governed solely by citizenship or nationality. In contrast to the European Convention on Human Rights[50] and the American Convention on Human Rights,[51] which provide only that a person may not be deprived of the right to enter the country of his nationality, the Covenant protects permanent residents. An alien, therefore, has the right to enter a country in which he has established a permanent residence. An individual may, of course, be required to submit proof of his nationality, citizenship, or residence to gain entry.[52]

Limits

The right of entry to one's country is not governed by the restrictions of Article 12(3). Some of the drafters argued that this right should not be subject to any limit,[53] but some limits are implied in the word "arbitrarily."

The term "arbitrarily" was a subject of debate in this and other contexts.[54] While some sought to limit its meaning to that which is contrary to law, a broader view prevailed, and it is clear that it includes not only what is unlawful under domestic law but also what violates other provisions of the Covenant or is otherwise unjust.

One possible limitation considered by the drafters would have permitted a state to exile its own nationals as punishment for crime. The first draft provided:

> 2. (a) No one shall be subjected to arbitrary exile;
> (b) Subject to the preceding sub-paragraph, anyone shall be free to enter his own country. [55]

A prohibition of arbitrary exile, which implies that some exile is not arbitrary, would have followed Article 9 of the Universal Declaration. This formulation was criticized on the grounds that no civilized society should practice exile and that if a provision on exile was to be included it should prohibit exile entirely. It was finally agreed that even though most countries had prohibited exile as a form of punishment, in those countries where it still existed it might be more humane to allow exile than to impose a more severe punishment such as lifetime deprivation of liberty.[56] The final draft does not mention exile because many were reluctant to appear to sanction it as a form of punishment. But exile, so long as it is imposed in accordance with law and not on grounds otherwise impermissible under the Covenant, is not clearly excluded by the Covenant.

It may be, however, that exile is now prohibited under customary international law, and it may even be *jus cogens*. Most states do not recognize it as a form of punishment. In the United States it would doubtless be unconstitutional to deny to a citizen the right of return, and as a punishment for crime, exile would be unconstitionally cruel and unusual. Exile is prohibited by the European Convention on Human Rights, which provides flatly: "No one shall be deprived of the right to enter the territory of the State of which he is a national." [57] The American Convention on Human Rights also does not recognize any restriction on the right of a national to enter the state of his nationality. [58]

The drafters clearly considered exile the only restriction on the right to enter one's own country. It was thought inconceivable, for example, that a state should prohibit the entry of one of its nationals for reasons of health or morality. [59] But the final wording of the Covenant would seem to allow other limits on the right, and while there can be no other permanent prohibitions on the right of a national to return, some temporary restrictions may be permissible. Would it be arbitrary, for example, for a state to prohibit the entry of a national temporarily because he has a contagious disease? In this and other situations the length of the restriction would be an important factor.

Protection against Expulsion

Article 13 provides: "An alien lawfully in the territory of a State Party to the present Covenant may be expelled therefrom only in pursuance of a decision reached in accordance with law and shall, except where compelling reasons of national security otherwise require, be allowed to submit the reasons against his expulsion and to have his case reviewed by, and be represented for the purpose before, the competent authority or a person or persons especially designated by the competent authority."

Scope

This article does not provide a guarantee against expulsion. It protects only an alien lawfully within a territory, and only from arbitrary expulsion. It also provides procedural safeguards for any attempt to expel him.

The article, by its language, applies to aliens. It does not address the issue whether a national can be expelled. Both the European Convention on Human Rights [60] and the American Convention on Human Rights [61] specifically prohibit the expulsion of a national from the state of his nationality. In the case of a national, it may be that expulsion and exile are the same, in which case under the Covenant a national has the "right to enter his own country," and it may be possible lawfully to expel (exile) him only as discussed in relation to Article 12(4). In any event such an act would not be covered by Article 13. An alien who is a permanent resident, too, insofar as he is protected by Article 12(4) cannot be expelled under Article 13.

A state might try to take away the nationality of an individual and then expel him. While there is no right to a nationality provided in the Covenant, other than the right of a child to acquire nationality (Article 24(3)), such a right is provided in the Universal Declaration.[62] The American Convention guarantees a right to nationality and prohibits any arbitrary deprivation of that right.[63] Under the American Convention, a withdrawal of nationality for the purpose of expulsion would be arbitrary.

Under the European Convention, which prohibits the expulsion of a national but provides no right to a nationality, a state cannot avoid this prohibition by first depriving a national of his nationality in order to expel him. The European Commission of Human Rights has gone even further, saying that even though no right to a nationality is explicitly granted in the Convention, a state cannot arbitrarily refuse to confer nationality upon an individual otherwise entitled to it if the refusal has as its sole object the expulsion of the individual.[64] This would be a reasonable interpretation of the Covenant as well. Any attempt to expel a national by first withdrawing his nationality would be contrary to the purposes and principles of the Covenant.

The procedural safeguards of this right apply to individual aliens. The Covenant does not address the issue of collective expulsion of aliens. Collective expulsion of aliens is forbidden in the American Convention on Human Rights,[65] and the European Convention prohibits collective expulsion of both nationals and aliens.[66] Under the Covenant, it would be reasonable to argue that if any attempt were made to expel aliens collectively, each one of them would be entitled to the safeguards of Article 13.

Limits

The lawful expulsion of an alien in a territory must be pursuant to "a decision reached in accordance with law." No guidelines are given as to what may constitute a lawful basis for expulsion. It was felt that states must have discretion in this matter.[67] Probably the only qualification is that it must be based on a nondiscriminatory general rule, perhaps one established by legislators.

The primary purpose of this article is to provide procedural safeguards against arbitrary expulsion. The decision, whether made by a judicial or administrative body, must be subject to review. Countries are obligated to change their internal procedures if an appeal of the decision is not presently allowed. In general, the safeguards are similar to those provided in the Covenant for a criminal trial (see Article 14). The safeguards also follow the procedure set forth in Article 32 of the Convention Relating to the Status of Refugees.[68] These protections against arbitrary expulsion are based on the premise that an alien lawfully in a country has some right to stay.

One important exception to these procedures is provided in the Article. The reasons for the expulsion and appellate review of the expulsion are not required where there are compelling national security reasons for not providing them. The phrase "compelling reasons" of national security is intended to emphasize the narrowness of the exception.

In the latter part of the twentieth century, the freedom of movement and its counterpart, the right not to be moved, promise to be of even greater concern than they were after each of the World Wars. Mass expulsions, forced relocations, and departures induced by fear or need have produced millions of refugees, notably recently in Asia and in Africa. On the other hand, many in Eastern Europe who claim the right to leave, face governments that are reluctant to permit their departure even when the applicants have a country that will admit them. In what has become the century of the refugee, the principles of the Covenant, however general and subject to exceptions, provide a humane and rational standard which all parties to the Covenant and other states must respect in good faith.

8

Legal Personality, Privacy, and the Family

FERNANDO VOLIO

WITH THE EXCEPTION of the right to life, it is impossible to determine which right or aggregate of rights protected by the International Covenant on Civil and Political Rights is of greatest importance. All are essential. All are closely interrelated. The dignity, peace, and happiness of every individual depend upon the observance of all of them. The violation of any one right not only seriously disrupts the life of the victim but also diminishes the rights of others. If, for example, a person disappears after having been detained by agents of a despotic government which even denies that such detention occurred (as happened in various Latin American countries in the late 1970s), his relatives and friends also suffer, their right to family life is violated, the liberty and safety of all are jeopardized, and civilized society is undermined. Certain rights, however, assume particular importance and deserve particular attention, notably those which protect the individual personality.

The institutions of modern society hover ominously over the individual, threatening cardinal human values. Paradoxically, the modern state, designed to humanize society and protect the individual from dominant private interests, has become the greater threat. Unofficial structures of authority, and the intricate network of social and economic relations, also reduce the individual's autonomy, leaving him isolated and disoriented, a victim of forces beyond his control. Contemporary societies endanger the very personality of the individual and invade his zone of privacy and intimate relations. The Covenant seeks to protect the individual from these forces in Articles 16, 17, 23, and 24.

Legal Personality

Article 16 provides: "Everyone shall have the right to recognition everywhere as a person before the law."

"Everyone."[1] In an age when we are still struggling to confirm what was so evident to the Romans,[2] it is necessary to emphasize that Article 16 is applicable to men and women, and to children of both sexes.[3] Each of these is a "person," with status and capacity in the legal order. Each has rights and assumes obligations. Even the just-conceived fetus is a "person" in this context, since if born alive, "its capacity to acquire rights is retroactive to the moment of its conception."[4]

Legal personality is a crucial aspect of freedom.[5] It distinguishes one man from others and permits him to assert his essential dignity *erga omnes*. It concentrates the attention of the legal order upon each human being. It gives to the essential dignity of the human being reality in law. Without it man would not be truly free, for he would be subject to injustice and injury without legal remedy.

The law gives effect to human dignity by giving the individual personal status, the power to make legal dispositions, and an area of privacy. It shields him with the principle that "that which is not prohibited is permissible."[6] Personal status permits him to exercise his liberty "endowed with rights and subject to obligations," to be someone for all practical purposes. The power to make legal dispositions permits a person to produce "legally relevant results" by putting himself into particular legal positions, such as marriage. Privacy makes possible that "inoffensive or neutral" liberty which man reserves for himself in a zone removed from disturbances by other individuals and the excesses of the state.[7] The principle "that which is not prohibited is permissible" reinforces the right to a zone of privacy within which one may act without fear of state regulation.

"Legal personality" means an individual's "personhood" in society.[8] The law gives life to an individual, for practical purposes of living in society, just as God gives him existence. Hence the graphic expression "civil death" to designate punishment, generally for political reasons, that deprives a person of his rights and leaves him on the fringe of meaningful social activity. Similarly, in earlier societies, slaves had radically diminished status as persons, becoming almost objects, denied of their inherent dignity.

"Peter is a person." He was born with that quality. But he has other attributes which distinguish him. Peter has rights. He may exercise them in pursuit of his happiness as he conceives it, but only by virtue, and with support, of the law. Legal personality is bestowed by the legal order. It is not a gracious concession by political authority, but a necessary concomitant of being a human person which enables him to live in society. The right to legal personality is indispensable to give value to man's essential dignity in daily life, giving reality to the "personhood" and protecting it against actions which would negate it.[9] Without it, there would be no effective barriers to the exercise of arbitrary power and the never-ending efforts to conceal violations of fundamental freedoms under color of legitimacy. Striking evidence of its importance is that "civil death" has been removed from the legal codes of civilized societies,[10] as has slavery, which is repugnant to the modern conscience and proscribed by democratic constitutions and laws as well as by international covenants and declarations of human rights.[11] Furthermore, when the law restricts the rights implied in "legal personality," it does so by way of exception; by narrow, explicit norms of limited character, usually relating to age, incapacity, etc. The Covenant, while permitting member states to suspend many rights proclaimed in the Covenant in a public emergency, does not permit derogation from Article 16.

When the Third Committee considered the draft article, the discussion focused on the distinction between "having a legal personality" and "having legal capacity to act." There was general agreement that "Article 16 sought to ensure that each person would be a subject rather than an object of the law, but did not attempt to address the question of a person's capacity to act, which could be restricted for such reasons as infancy or insanity."[12] Earlier discussions show that the term "legal personality" was used "for securing the recognition of the legal personality of each individual as well as his capacity to exercise rights and to assume contractual obligations."[13]

Article 16 is based upon Article 6 of the Universal Declaration of Human Rights,[14] and the opinions expressed during the debates on the Declaration are useful in interpreting the Covenant. The comments of René Cassin are particularly instructive. The principal objective of including an article relating to legal personality, he said, was to guarantee the exercise of certain fundamental civil rights "without which no human being should be forced to live," such as entering a contract, making a purchase, obtaining employment, etc. Even in countries having liberal laws, Cassin said, there is a manifest tendency to deny to aliens certain fundamental rights; e.g., the right to marry, to acquire property, to have recourse to justice, etc. Cassin characterized this tendency as "disastrous." Since the general right to enter into contracts is a fundamental civil right which was not explicitly proclaimed in the Declaration, it was necessary to include it in Article 6 with a view to protecting aliens in particular. One may not say to any human being "you are nothing" as a matter of law.[15]

It should be noted that, the term "person before the law," used in the English text, does not have the same precise meaning as the French term *personalité juridique*. The English term "covers those fundamental rights relating to the 'legal capacity' (legal status) of a person which are not explicitly mentioned in the subsequent articles of the Declaration." And "the expression 'everyone' clearly indicates that no difference may be made by a state between its own citizens and foreigners or stateless persons in the exercise of the rights included in the concept 'a person before the law.'"[16]

In sum, the Covenant requires state parties to treat every human being everywhere, male or female, young or old, alien or citizen, as a person before the law, enjoying the protections of the law and of the forces of law, with power to have rights and assume obligations: to own, acquire, and dispose of property; to make contracts; to sue, and be sued; and to invoke other legal remedies.

Another important term in Article 16 is "recognition." With the exception of its use as applied to rights generally in Article 2, we encounter it only in relation to two other rights: the right of peaceful assembly (Article 21) and the right to marry and found a family (Article 23(2)). The term was apparently intended to reinforce the right to which it applies. During the drafting discussion, it was proposed that the right to assemble, for example, "shall be guaranteed by law." Some would have drafted it along the lines of the Universal Declaration: "Everyone has the right to freedom of peaceful assembly and association" (Article 20(1)). Some, however, urged that "the right should be 'recognized' as a fundamental human right rather than *conceded* by virtue of a covenant" (emphasis added).[17] The intent of the drafters, then, was to reinforce, not to weaken, and the use of "recognition" in Article 16 (and in Articles 21 and 23) serves to reaffirm the character of those rights as fundamental liberties of every person and to render them binding norms.

Inclusion of the word "everywhere" was also the subject of debate. In 1955 the United Kingdom submitted an amendment to delete the term, since under Article 2(2) each party recognizes the rights of the Covenant only in relation "to individuals within its territory and subject to its jurisdiction." The same objection was raised later in the General Assembly's Third Committee, and it was argued that member states could accept responsibility for implementing the Covenant only within their respective jurisdictions. Nevertheless, the consensus was that the word "was not superfluous," and it was noted that it had been included in Article 6 of the Universal Declaration.[18] The inclusion of "everywhere" means that a state party cannot deny the rights of "personhood" under Article 16 even to persons not subject to its jurisdiction. A state may not deny these rights to individuals anywhere in the world, for example by cooperating in maintaining them in slavery or recognizing their slave status, or by refusing to honor their contracts or other legal dispositions on the ground that they are not legal persons.

In affirming this right "everywhere," the draftsmen desired to emphasize that this fundamental right must be fully and effectively monitored by all states parties to the Covenant. It implies an obligation upon every party to ensure rigorous compliance, not only by itself and by other parties but also by those who do not adhere to the Covenant. It may have been intended even to give the right of personality *jus cogens* status. There is an international obligation under the UN Charter to promote respect for human rights everywhere, and so-called "domestic jurisdiction" cannot hinder the establishment of an international community that is truly enlightened and peaceful and which vigorously denies refuge to forces which repress freedom. The expression "everywhere" constitutes a message of relief and hope for those persons residing in countries where the right to recognition as a person before the law is consistently and comprehensively disregarded for political reasons. It constitutes a serious warning to the governments of such countries that the international community will not remain indifferent to situations which are contrary to human dignity.

Privacy

Article 17 provides:

"1. No one shall be subjected to arbitrary or unlawful interference with his privacy, family, home or correspondence, nor to unlawful attacks on his honour and reputation.
"2. Everyone has the right to the protection of the law against such interference or attacks."

This article is, of course, one of the iron pillars of the structure erected by the slow and painful efforts of generations of men and women in many parts of the world to obtain legal protection for the ordinary activities by which they pursue happiness, as well as for the extraordinary motivations that impel them to seek glory. It asserts an aggregate of fundamental rights, linked by a common principle, addressed to the anxious and asphyxiating situation of the common man confronted by a giant and hypertrophied state apparatus. This article, then, deals with that restricted territory of exclusive action which forms a part of the individual's "freedom limits," [19] in which men take refuge when the action of the state has become unbearable or life in society exhausts them. Man realizes himself within society, since without it his gregarious nature would lose its essential nobility, but it is also man's nature to isolate himself from his peers, at least from those to whom he has lesser ties. Since time immemorial man has sought to live privately; his home has been the first redoubt for his privacy. His correspondence, his honor and his reputation have also earned the concern of the law in most societies. Article 17, however, following Article 12 of the Universal Declaration of Human Rights, expands and generalizes those elements of privacy. It creates a zone of isolation, a legal cloister for those qualities, wishes, projects, and life styles which each individual man, woman, or child wishes to enjoy or experience.

This zone of privacy is a zone of freedom. Of course, freedom must also be used to further community harmony and prosperity, since man is dependent upon society. Seeking an appropriate balance between individual freedom and collective well-being is always a complicated and wearying exercise, full of tensions and risks, but indispensable, stimulating, and rewarding. The adage of Harold J. Laski: "I do not exist only for the State, nor does the State exist only for me," eloquently expresses the narrow, balanced relationship between the individual and society. In the event of an insuperable conflict between their interests, however, it is necessary, in the last analysis, to take the side of the individual, because state power tends to reduce individual autonomy, and the state (as the legal manifestation of society) justifies its existence by promoting the well-being of the individual.

Article 17 protects rights of which "no one" shall be deprived. The Covenant uses different expressions in referring to the rights which it sets forth and protects. It adopts generic, categoric forms such as "all peoples," "everyone," "all persons," "every citizen" "any propaganda," "any advocacy," "every child," "every human being," and "no one." "No one" appears whenever the Covenant seeks to underscore a basic freedom which may not be denied to any person. It emphasizes with firmness and determination that no earthly power may deprive a human being of the protections of those norms, sacred, far-reaching, radical, inalterable, and definitive. In Article 17, that categorical effect protects values which enhance the dignity of each human being and the sanctity of his relations with those closest to him.[20]

A person's privacy, family, correspondence, honor, and reputation are protected from any interference by third parties which affects his full enjoyment of those rights. But Article 17 forbids only interference that is "arbitrary or unlawful." "Arbitrary" is used also in Articles 6 (the right to life) and 9 (freedom from arrest and detention) and was the subject of sharp and extended debate, particularly in the context of those articles. (See essays 5 and 6.) Briefly, some argued that "arbitrary" was imprecise and ambiguous, and added nothing to "unlawful."[21] In its comments on what became Article 17, the government of the United Kingdom found "arbitrary," when added to "illegality," particularly unsatisfactory as a criterion "as regards a particular person's interference with the privacy of another."[22]

The majority of the Third Committee, however, considered that the notion of arbitrariness was basic to the objectives of the Article. The principal reasons given for sustaining this thesis apply equally for the interpretation of the term in Article 17. Arbitrary means "without legal grounds" or "contrary to law," but also capricious, despotic, imperious, tyrannical, or uncontrolled. It means "illegal" as well as "incompatible with the principles of justice" and human dignity. It applies not only to laws but also to regulations and executive power and precludes abuse of discretion to jeopardize individual rights. It was urged that the Committee not reject a term which was "legally valid and commonly used in many countries and their courts."[23]

Ultimately, the view that both terms should be kept prevailed. Although a definitive, agreed reason for retaining them did not emerge, I believe such reason exists. As regards Article 17 in particular, the right of privacy there recognized is essential to individual dignity, which is in the care of the legal order, and its violation cannot and should not be sanctioned by law. Illegality, then, is itself contrary to human rights. Arbitrariness is even more odious because it departs from the idea of law, creating an abyss between force and reason, between political power and the institutions that control and limit that power. Action may be arbitrary even when it is not a violation of positive law if the legislation is itself unreasonable or capricious.[24] Action by officials, including judicial officers, is arbitrary when they abuse discretion vested in them by law, or when they manipulate legal procedures. In a particular society, such arbitrary actions may not be subject to nullification by legal procedures, and may have normative consequences and retain the character of law; those who act arbitrarily might not be held accountable. Such arbitrariness is the negation of law and of democracy.[25]

The use of both "unlawful" and "arbitrary" became relevant also to another issue during the development of Article 17. Some saw the word "arbitrary" as referring to interference by public authorities, and "unlawful" as applying to private acts. Others thought that the article should refer only to official acts; private interference could be, and generally was, adequately dealt with by national laws. The General Assembly chose the broader view, properly in my opinion, since violations are equally detrimental and odious whether committed by governments or by individuals, and state parties should be required to ensure against both kinds of violations.

During the discussion of Article 17, there were proposals to include a paragraph indicating those cases in which public authorities could appropriately interfere with a person's privacy, family, home, or correspondence. No limitation provision was added and the rights are protected without qualification. In the discussion it was emphasized that the Article "was couched in general terms, merely enunciated principles, leaving each State free to decide how those principles were to be put into effect." According to some, this meant that the article "did not limit the degree to which the State could interfere" with those rights.[26] That cannot be. Authority to limit these rights, even in the public interest, is not in fact conceded in the Article, and while some such authority is perhaps implied, it must be seen narrowly and with extreme care, taking into account the provisions of Article 5 of the Covenant. (See essay 3.)

Autonomy and Intimacy

Article 17 protects "privacy" as well as the family, home, correspondence, honor, and reputation. Although all of these may be seen as aspects of privacy in a larger sense, the right includes much besides the private matters explicitly listed.

The records of the drafting of Article 17 provide little guidance as to what was intended to be included. The provision derives from Article 12 of the Universal Declaration, but there, too, we have little indication of its scope. Some delegations indeed criticized the words "privacy," "home," and "correspondence" because "their precise legal implications were not clear."[27] But the term "privacy" has important content. Although it is an old right, and some of its manifestations have long been recognized, the right to privacy has acquired a new and special place in the law, as the means for invading the private life of individuals have multiplied and become more sophisticated and intrusive.

In its ultimate sense, privacy includes not only the security of those areas listed in Article 17—home, correspondence, family, honor, reputation—but also many rights listed in other articles: for example, the freedom of thought, conscience, and religion; the right to determine the moral and religious education of one's children; the right of association and nonassociation; and rights recognized by other articles of this Covenant and in the Covenant on Economic, Social. and Cultural Rights. Indeed, in one sense all human rights are aspects of the right of privacy. But in Article 17, privacy is related to intimacy, a kind of "spiritual zone." It is a right of seclusion. In it, alone or in the company of close ones, an individual acts according to his feelings, his will, and personality. In this situation we see man in his solitary nature; as an independent subject, he may decide how to utilize his autonomy to make his ontological liberty authentic and meaningful; he and no one else can say how his feelings, desires, and actions are to be made known to others, and thus enter the flow of interactions which constitute social life. "Intimacy is contrary to that which is public, that which is made known to all."[28] Of course, this freedom has its limits in the equal freedom with which every other man is vested and in the interests of society. Principle, and the laws of all states, suggest limits on the excesses of privacy.

Which feelings, desires, and acts—which facts and situations—are included in the concept of "privacy"? The Nordic Conference in Stockholm, in 1967, declared: "the right to intimacy is the right to live one's life in an independent manner, without outside interference." It listed the following as violations of an individual's "intimacy."

(a) interference with privacy, home, or family;
(b) interference with mental or physical integrity, or moral and intellectual freedom;
(c) attacks on honor or reputation;
(d) placement in equivocal situations;
(e) unnecessary publication of painful facts of one's private life;
(f) use of one's name, identity or likeness;
(g) scrutiny, observation or pursuit;
(h) violation of correspondence;
(i) abuse of one's means of communication, verbal or written;
(j) dissemination of information given or received in professional confidence.

The Conference specified that "the intent" of the above definition was to protect against the following:

(a) entry into enclosed areas and other properties or records;
(b) medical or physical examinations or tests of physical aptitude;
(c) painful, false or irrelevant statements about a person;
(d) interference with correspondence;
(e) interference with telephonic or telegraphic communication;
(f) surveillance by electronic or other means;
(g) tape-recording, or still or motion pictures;
(h) intrusion by the press or other mass media;
(i) dissemination of information given to or received from private assessors or public authorities subject to professional secrecy;
(j) public exposure of private matters;
(k) harassment of a person (for example, by observation or bothersome telephone calls).[29]

Scholars have made their own lists of various "activities, situations and phenomena which here and now may be declared as pertaining to privacy." One list includes:

(a) religious, philosophical, superstitious and political beliefs or ideas which the individual does not wish anyone to know about;
(b) aspects of love and sexual life;
(c) aspects of family life unknown to outsiders, especially those embarrassing to the individual or group;
(d) nonobvious physical defects or anomalies;
(e) conduct by the individual which, if known, would engender criticism or would diminish the individual's stature;
(f) health conditions the knowledge of which would affect the judgment others form for social or professional purposes;
(g) the content of oral or written communications directed solely to one or more particular persons;
(h) the past life of the subject insofar as it may serve to embarrass him;
(i) social origins which may influence social standing, including questions concerning filiation or legal status;
(j) the performance of the physical functions of excretion, or facts relating to one's own body which are held to be repugnant or socially unacceptable (body noises, insertion of fingers into natural cavities, etc.);
(k) moments of pain or extreme depression;
(l) in general, any personal data, fact or activity which is unknown to others, the knowledge of which would produce moral or physical discomfort to the subject (such as nudity, premarital pregnancy).[30]

Another list which sheds light on the interpretation of Article 17 is Prosser's, referring to the concept of privacy in American tort law. It includes:

(a) intrusion upon a person's seclusion or solitude, or into his private affairs;
(b) public disclosure of embarrassing private facts;
(c) publicity which portrays a person in a false light;
(d) use of a person's name or likeness by another.[31]

These examples of the components of the right to privacy give an idea of its scope. They include much of what is protected by the law of privacy in many countries. They include rights which go beyond the right of privacy viewed in its narrow sense, but which are part of the wider concept of intimacy which Article 17 was designed to protect. That article protects every individual on every occasion and in every context in which he requires secrecy or seclusion, even from close friends and family, and especially from the public, with regard to his physical being, disposition, moral character or habits, mental or physical health, profession, business, work or intellectual activities.

It is essential that privacy continue for as long as the individual, the holder of this singular privilege, deems it necessary. Even when the common good requires some invasion of privacy, it is justified only under order from competent judicial authorities, in accordance with the law and procedures in force, mandated by the constitutional organ empowered to do so, and in accordance with constitutional and statutory norms. It is to these legal bases that Article 17 refers when it establishes "the protection of the law" for every person who is a victim of "arbitrary or unlawful interference," excluding, therefore, actions based merely upon the caprice of the governing authorities, even though they appear under color of law.

The scope of the right of privacy has been a prominent issue in the Human Rights Committee's consideration of national reports under Article 40. (See essay 14.) Committee members indicated concern about the scope of search without a warrant or court order. The view of many members of the Committee was that under Article 17 of the Covenant, search of a home required a warrant or equivalent court order. Exceptions must be strictly limited in purpose; for example, when a felony is being committed or there is danger that an important criminal might escape or important evidence be destroyed. A state must provide a remedy for unjustified searches.[32]

The Committee discussions also indicated a broad view of the protection of Article 17, beyond matters explicitly mentioned. The inviolability of the home, it was indicated, extends to private offices. One government was asked about measures to protect individual privacy from "data banks" and other computer information.[33] Several governments were questioned about measures taken to protect individuals from the activities of the intelligence services. It was suggested that individuals should be informed when under surveillance.[34]

The Family

Elsewhere, the Covenant provides that the family "is entitled to protection" (Article 23(1)); Article 17 protects the individual against unlawful or arbitrary interference with his family. Such protection may already be included in the right to privacy: family relations are essential to one's private and intimate life and the full expression of one's personality, and the family is man's natural protection and a means of attaining many of his vital needs and noble aspirations. Article 17 protects the right of each family member to enjoy a circle of generic and unequaled loyalty; a warm, emotional atmosphere where real and edifying spontaneity reigns, and which persists even when the group is dissolved by life's contingencies. The right to family privacy is also related to other rights—the right to marry and to choose freely in marriage; the right to raise one's children at home; the right to family living and association; and the right to share, give, and bequeath property.

The Home

The home, too, is an aspect of privacy, but Article 17 accords it explicit protection also. The home has, since antiquity, constituted a manifestation of man's privacy as well as a means of protecting it, whether he lives alone, with a family, or in the company of others who join voluntarily for the purpose. In addition to providing a refuge against danger, the home makes possible a peaceful, harmonious, and warm environment for cultivating common values and transmitting them to following generations.

The home, in Article 17 of the Covenant, is above all a person's dwelling place, and it provides the principal physical ambience in which to fulfill the essentials of private life.[35] "Home" connotes habitation, the hearth, its common figurative meaning suggests the warmth of family life. For the purposes of Article 17, "home" should be read as extending to places where the individual works or carries out other activities of a private nature, similar to those that take place in the home.[36] Since home is not defined in the Covenant or in the *travaux,* the broadest definition is in accordance with the well-known adage that "it is appropriate to restrict the odious and expand the favorable."

The home is protected against "interference." That includes not only uninvited entry, but also other intrusions, such as peeping or eavesdropping, electronic surveillance, overhearing, or noise that troubles the tranquility inside. The immediate environs of the home are also protected against trespassing, intrusion, physical or mechanical or electronic surveillance, and noise.

Correspondence

The integrity and confidentiality of correspondence is another aspect of an individual's privacy that is explicitly protected by Article 17. Correspondence clearly includes written communication, and the protection extends not only during its transmission by post or messenger but also in the period before it is sent and after it is received. Correspondence also includes direct oral communication, and today must include communication by any mechanical or electronic means.

Correspondence is protected primarily against divulgence to anyone other than the intended recipient.[37] It is also protected against interruption or other interference, such as stealing a letter or purposely misdirecting or delaying it, or by "jamming" or otherwise interrupting telephone or other electronic communication.

While Article 17 speaks of "correspondence," which implies direct, personal communication between two individuals, there is no reason to limit the protection of the article in that way. It should extend to materials and documents that are not commonly called communications; for example, books, magazines, writings, prints, photographs, slides, films, records, and tapes, etc., when sent by mail, messenger, or other means of transportation or communication.[38] The ideas carried by such materials, if divulged, might jeopardize the individual responsible for them, especially if they contravene the dominant moral, religious, or political values in the society. In any event, they concern only him, and the Covenant protects his freedom to pursue his own ideas and to satisfy his curiosity or his inclinations as long as he does so within the bounds of his home or office, so as not to offend the sensitivities, feelings, beliefs, or opinions of others.

Whether as an aspect of the freedom of correspondence, of the home, or of privacy generally (or perhaps as an aspect of freedom of thought and conscience under Article 18), the Covenant protects the individual's rights even when materials are not sent by some means of communication. In *Stanley v. Georgia,*[39] a case decided by the Supreme Court of the United States, federal and state agents, in the course of a lawful search of one's home, found three rolls of film deemed to be obscene and violative of Georgia law. The U.S. Supreme Court reversed the conviction, holding that the United States Constitution protects the individual's right to receive information and ideas, and to read or observe what he pleases, within the privacy of his own home. He has the "right to be free from state inquiry into the contents of his library." Whatever the justifications for regulating obscenity, they do not "reach into the privacy of one's own home. If the First Amendment means anything, it means that a State has no business telling a man, sitting alone in his own house, what books he may read or what films he may watch. Our whole constitutional heritage rebels at the thought of giving government the power to control men's minds."[40] In my opinion, Article 17, read broadly, also protects the right to secrecy of correspondence and excludes illegal and arbitrary actions that interfere with any means of receiving and keeping ideas or information in private.

Honor and Reputation

There was little discussion of this clause during the development of the Covenant. In the Third Committee, there was some discussion as to whether "reputation" included "honor." Some felt that they are two different concepts: "a slur on an individual's honor involved a judgment of his moral conduct, whereas a slur on his reputation might concern merely an alleged failure to conform to professional or social standards."[41] Article 12 of the Universal Declaration and many legal systems use both terms. The view prevailed that "the moral integrity of man" was based on subjective (honor) as well as objective (reputation) elements.[42] Honor is a criterion which an individual applies to himself and is based upon the values by which he feels his conduct should be measured. In this sense, honor bears no relation to public opinion.[43] Reputation, on the other hand, is tied to public opinion, because it involves public recognition of an individual's qualities and merit. It is equivalent to fame or renown.

For the purposes of Article 17 of the Covenant, honor is closely related to intimacy and privacy, because when the values upon which a person bases his self-esteem have been deprecated and disrespected, he feels his honor has been impugned. For example, to say that a person is impotent, knowing that he is married and has children, affronts his dignity in an area which is not the business of any third person. An attack on reputation is less injurious since what is harmed is the opinion that people hold of a person and not his essential moral qualities. For example, if a lawyer is told that he is a failure because he loses many cases, he may be professionally discredited, but his moral dignity is not affected. Obviously, the dividing line between that which affects honor and that which affects reputation is not easy to trace. In both cases "the human moral integrity" of each person is protected; even those who are "unworthy and dishonored" have the right to repel any attack which diminishes them as persons, and to keep their "zone of honor" intact.[44] In both cases, it is a question of safeguarding a person's good name, which is indispensable to him in living and acting with a healthy sense of pride, and in participating fruitfully in common activities with the equanimity that comes from feeling respected and appreciated.[45]

The limits on the protection afforded by Article 17 are basically those established by other provisions in the Covenant. Article 19, for example, provides that freedom of expression is subject to restrictions necessary "for respect of the rights or reputations of others." But Article 17, in turn, is limited by the freedom of expression enshrined in Article 19. Presumably, the Covenant accepts modern legal doctrine regarding transgressions against honor, i.e., the law of insult, slander, and defamation. There can be no punishment or damages for historical, literary, artistic, or athletic criticism, or other judgment expressed in the fulfilment of a duty. There is also the *exceptio veritatis*, the defense of truth.

The word "attacks" (on honor and reputation) connotes intentional violence.[46] It is not a question of mere interference in matters relating to a person's honor or reputation, but of deliberate assault on them. But not all attacks are prohibited. As the *travaux* indicate, some feared that to outlaw all "attacks" might endanger freedom of thought and expression, and there were suggestions that only "abusive" or "unjustified" attacks be forbidden. It was decided to outlaw "unlawful" attacks.

"Arbitrary" was not added. It has been suggested, in reference to the same language in Article 12 of the Universal Declaration, that the omission of the word "arbitrary" was a mistake in drafting since "as it stands the word 'arbitrary' refers only to interference and does not cover attacks." Yet, "although this might not have been the intention . . . the difference exists."[47] Perhaps the drafters of Article 17 of the Covenant simply followed the text of the Declaration.[48] The omission of "arbitrary," however, is serious and unjustified: an arbitrary attack constitutes a great danger since it violates the legal order and is committed by public authority acting capriciously. The omission, surely, can not be interpreted as a license for public authorities to inflict arbitrary injury upon an individual's honor or reputation.

The growing quest for information ("data banks") on an individual's personal, professional, and public life, even in open democratic societies, brings into conflict two important values: the right of the individual to shield himself from the attention of third parties, and the right of third parties, who together comprise the public, to be informed. The complex relationship between the freedom of the press and the rights of individuals is a particular manifestation of this conflict. Article 17 of the Covenant generally resolves these conflicts in favor of the individual. Society can function without information relating to the intimate aspects of people's lives even though they may be public figures; in most cases, society, motivated by morbid curiosity or greed, infects itself with such information.[49]

The Family

Articles 23 and 24 of the Covenant properly go together with Articles 16 and 17. Here, too, it is necessary to reconcile the rights of the individual with those of society, safeguarding the individual so that necessary participation in community life does not inhibit his personality.

Article 17 took account of the family and provided for the privacy of its members. It underscored the importance of this particular human grouping and reinforced its unique solidarity. In Article 23, the Covenant elevates the role of the family to prominence in the social scheme. Article 23 begins by affirming categorically that the family is the foundation of society. This principle was never questioned during the discussions, as it was not during the preparation of Article 16 of the Universal Declaration or Article 10 of the Covenant on Economic, Social, and Cultural Rights.[50] It was self-evident, even axiomatic. The family supports and cements the social structure, organizing individuals on the basis of the most simple cell, that of parents and children. Article 23, then, refers to "the nuclear family," the group "consisting of two adults of different sexes and their descendants, all of whom live under the same roof," which "is the primary group most important to man"; in it is realized "his socialization and humanization in the sense of acculturation (the process of apprenticeship to acquire the culture of one's group)."[51] Society should protect these vital nuclei for its own benefit. But paradoxically and suicidally, society and the state have sometimes attacked the family in moments of collective, pathological aberration. The drafters of the Covenant thought it necessary to protect the family by elevating it to the rank of a fundamental human right.

Article 23 of the Covenant declares that the family is entitled to protection "by society and the State." This unusual reference to society means society in general as well as its particular components (for example, churches). This was made clear during the debate on Article 16 of the Universal Declaration from which Article 23 of the Covenant derives.[52] Article 23 protects the family as a unit, as a legal community,[53] but like other rights in the Covenant the protection afforded by Article 23 is an individual right to have and enjoy the integrity of a family.

How the family should be protected is not made explicit in the Covenant or in the *travaux*. Some indications are found in other provisions of Article 23 itself, in Articles 5 and 24, and in several articles of the Covenant on Economic, Social, and Cultural Rights. The state and society are obliged to guarantee, by law, the existence of the family and the opportunity to create one by natural or contractual union. They must not interfere with its objectives, disturb its harmony or curtail its rights.[54] They must support its integrity and facilitate resolution of the conflicts that arise from its unique relations. They must seek to preserve its bonds, or at least, to mitigate the negative impact of their dissolution. In addition, all institutions must contribute to the well-being of the family, demonstrate due respect for the emotions and the ties of human solidarity which it reflects, and refrain from actions harmful to it. For example, it was suggested that this paragraph provides "for the elimination of discrimination which . . . may be practiced against persons born out of wedlock and of the disclosure of illegitimacy in . . . official documents delivered to a third person."[55]

To Marry and Found a Family

A result of the principle that the family is fundamental, proclaimed in paragraph 1 of Article 23, is the right established in paragraph 2 for every individual "to marry and to found a family." To marry is "to live with another in a common life." It is open to question whether the state may insist that marriage be contracted only in accordance with legal formalities, prohibiting permanent nonformalized relationships. Perhaps, if the formalities are not onerous, the requirement would not violate the Covenant. An age minimum for marriage, if it is not unreasonably high, must be established as a guarantee of the harmonious development of this institution, since extreme youth and physical immaturity are serious obstacles to the achievement of the essential objectives of marriage.[56] Indeed, for a state to permit the marriage of a young child may violate Article 23(3) which bars marriage "without free and full consent," since the consent of such a minor cannot be meaningful. (The practice of allowing child brides in particular is uncivilized and a denial of the rights of children under Article 24.) A state may forbid incestuous marriages, and while the degrees of consanguinity that may be held improper are not defined, the provisions common to the major legal systems today are doubtless permissible. A state may also forbid polygamous marriages, as such marriages may be held to be inconsistent with the equality guaranteed to women by paragraph 4 of Article 23, discussed below.[57]

The sine qua non for the celebration of marriage is "the free and full consent" of the intending spouses. This provision protects both man and woman from pressures which would deny them their free will; it protects in particular the woman who, due to cultural factors prevalent in some countries, may be pressed into an unwanted union. The Covenant speaks only of the free consent of the parties and makes no reference to the consent of others, for example, parents. To require the consent of any one other than the parties would indeed infringe the right of the parties to marry. However, as was observed by the Government of the Netherlands in 1955:

> As appears from the discussions in the Commission, this provision does not exclude the possibility that the exercise of this right by minors may be subject to the consent of their parents, legal guardians, or of a public authority in accordance with the national laws of the States parties to the covenant.[58]

Since, as we have said, a state can forbid marriage by a minor, it can presumably permit it for older minors with parental consent.[59]

Equality of Rights and Responsibilities

Paragraph 4 of Article 23 provides: "States Parties to the present Covenant shall take appropriate steps to ensure equality of rights and responsibilities of spouses as to marriage, during marriage and at its dissolution. In the case of dissolution, provision shall be made for the necessary protection of any children."

This provision gave rise to substantial controversy. Opponents raised the following objections, among others: there are natural—physical and psychological—differences between men and women that are relevant to marriage; spouses in fact have, and should have, different roles and duties in marriage; governments do not always have effective control over marital matters; differences between husband and wife are imbedded in ancient traditions, religious beliefs, and practices, and eliminating such differences would require radical changes in law and custom which could not be achieved immediately. It was argued also that the rights protected by the Covenant on Civil and Political Rights were intended for immediate implementation; in this instance it would be better to adopt a provision like that in Article 10 of the Covenant on Economic, Social, and Cultural Rights which is more general and allows the rights to be realized "progressively." Others argued that Article 23(4) was unnecessary since Article 3 of the Covenant assured equality of men and women with respect to all the rights recognized by the Covenant.[60]

Those who supported paragraph 4 argued that it would be unthinkable not to include the provision, which appears in the Universal Declaration (Article 16(1)), and which embodies a fundamental right of every individual human being. The obvious inequality of women in marriage in many societies rendered the inclusion of such a provision imperative. It could not be relegated to a legal status inferior to that of other rights in the Covenant by weakening its formulation and postponing its enjoyment as under the Covenant on Economic, Social, and Cultural Rights. If parties were not prepared to make the necessary adjustments immediately "they could make reservations to the Article when ratifying the Covenant."[61]

Article 23(4) was adopted, and unless a state enters a reservation, it is obligated "to take appropriate steps" (above all to make the necessary changes in its laws) to ensure the equality of the rights and responsibilities of both spouses in all that relates to matrimony. Surely, the organs and officials of the state must not infringe upon or interfere with marital matters. This provision underscores the Covenant's dedication to the essential dignity of every human being and to the general norm of equality of the sexes (Article 3). It is particularly necessary because of engrained resistance to such equality and the organized pressures of special interest groups.[62] Article 23(4) may be addressed particularly to women, who in many cultures are in a position of inequality and disadvantage, and often in degrading submission. The weight of law and custom has often so blinded women to their degradation that they passively accept it. Provisions like Article 23(4) provide a legal basis for women to rebel and for justice to prevail.

Article 23(4) applies to marriage entered into as a natural union as well as to marriage formalized by society and law. Spouses joined in natural marriage, and their children, also require the law's protection. But formal marriage is legally more complex and obliges the state to devote special attention to that institution supported by its laws. Article 23(4) requires the state to safeguard the rights of both spouses even beyond their own will and desires. This authoritative state role, to preserve overriding societal as well as individual interests, is particularly important when the marriage is dissolved, since any child involved must be protected even against the conflicting interests of the parents. The discussion of paragraph 4 in the *travaux* indicates that protection should extend to illegitimate as well as to legitimate children, although some delegates favored protecting only the latter and leaving the protection of illegitimate children to the general provision on the rights of children (Article 24). Clearly, however, Article 23(4) covers all children, since there is no indication to the contrary, and this norm should be interpreted as broadly as possible to ensure that all children have the protection of both this paragraph and of Article 24.

The reference to dissolution includes divorce as well as death of one of the parties. The article was not meant to approve or legitimize divorce, but neither does it forbid it. The Covenant faces the realities of contemporary life by safeguarding the legitimate interests of the spouses as well as of the children.

The Human Rights Committee has focused attention on Article 23(4), examining different areas in which spouses may be treated unequally. In many countries, matrimonial property is not equally vested in husband and wife. In others, men receive a greater share of an inheritance than women. Committee members found these laws incompatible with the Covenant.

Much concern was also expressed about the consequences of marriage to a noncitizen. Many states confer citizenship automatically upon a woman who marries a citizen while requiring a man who marries a citizen to be naturalized. Members of the Committee viewed this and other inconsistent treatment as violations of the Covenant.[63]

The Committee also appeared to take the view that the Covenant required positive action to protect the family. Article 23 was understood by members of the Committee to require a wide range of legislation and social programs to guarantee equality in marriage while protecting the family institution. One frequent recommendation was to establish child-care programs for children of working mothers. Other suggestions were: economic assistance to families, especially large and needy ones; social insurance programs; and low-cost loans to young couples. Programs designed to remedy peculiar problems (for example, to facilitate the reunion of families split after the Second World War) were also suggested.[64]

The Rights of the Child

Article 24 gives every child "the right to such measures of protection as are required by his status as a minor, on the part of his family, the society and the State," without discrimination. It requires that every child shall be registered immediately after birth and shall have a name. Every child has the right to acquire a nationality.

This article did not appear in the original versions of the Covenant on Civil and Political Rights. Proposed by Poland (joined later by Yugoslavia), it was adopted with only minor amendments. Its proponents stressed that children require special protection, since their needs are in many aspects different from those of adults. It was desirable to give the principles proclaimed in the Universal Declaration of Human Rights and in the Declaration on the Rights of the Child status as legal norms obligatory for parties to the Covenant. It was also necessary to ensure equality of treatment and opportunity for every child, and to assure that children born out of wedlock suffer no diminution of their inherent rights. (The original draft specifically so provided.)

There was some feeling that this article was unnecessary, since the provisions of the Covenant apply to all human beings, and thus to children. It was argued that to dedicate a special article to children might raise doubts about the applicability of other articles to children. Special protection, moreover, was already accorded children by the Covenant on Economic, Social, and Cultural Rights. Some felt it was not necessary to protect against discrimination among children since there already was a general nondiscrimination clause in Article 2. Another objection was that the article did not specify which rights of children were to be protected. While there was agreement that children born out of wedlock should be protected against discrimination generally, some felt that giving them equal rights of inheritance might jeopardize the stability of the family. (The counterargument is that equal inheritance rights would strengthen the family, since the father would be obliged to be more responsible.)

These objections did not prevail. Although Article 2 of the Covenant protects "individuals" against all types of discrimination, and allows "every person" to seek legal remedies against the violation of his other rights, the child requires extraordinary safeguards, not only in his upbringing, but also as regards his place within the legal system, because of his vulnerability to abuse by adults.

Article 24(1) refers to "every child," and the list of forbidden bases for discrimination includes "birth." Thus, a child is not to be discriminated against because he was born out of wedlock. Such discrimination would be odious since it would punish a child for an act beyond his control.

The Human Rights Committee has shared this concern for the equality of rights of children born out of wedlock. Members have expressed the view that any statutory reference to "illegitimate children" is discriminatory, and that the Covenant requires their equality in fact, which includes legal procedures for "legitimizing" natural children, and may include requiring natural fathers to contribute to the maintenance of their children.[65]

The protections afforded a child are "such measures of protection as are required by his status as a minor," and these must be provided by the family and society (broadly conceived), as well as by the state. The language of Article 24 is sufficiently broad to protect all the rights of the child. A child is entitled to protection by his family against society and the state, and by the state and society against his family if it abuses him or neglects his interests. This protection includes attention to his physical and spiritual needs—food, shelter, health care, education, and love and affection—as well as special protections in special circumstances, for example in the criminal process.

Several specific forms of protection are mentioned. Official registration of a child at birth creates a legal base for those rights which derive from his legal personality. A child must also be distinguished with a name because a name "individualizes" a person, differentiating him from others. This requirement reinforces the rights of the so-called illegitimate child (a term modern law avoids and condemns because of its pejorative connotation). Birth registration and a name are indispensable to the protection of every child in such important matters as filiation and nationality.

In 1979, the European Court of Human Rights held that Article 14 of the European Convention, which prohibits discrimination on various grounds including "birth," requires equality in the enjoyment of rights for illegitimate children, both as regards the substance of the right and the procedure implementing it. The Court found that when a child's parentage is routinely shown by birth certificate, it is discriminatory to require the maternal affiliation of an illegitimate child to be established by the mother's voluntary recognition or by court order. The Court also held that the Convention protects the inheritance rights of illegitimate children. When a legitimate child enjoys the right to inherit from his parents' relatives who die intestate, it is violative of the Convention to deny full patrimonial rights to illegitimate children.[66]

Article 24(3) gives greater force to a principle that has already been accepted by the international public conscience, that no person may be denied a fatherland which can serve him as fertile ground in which to develop, fruitfully and with confidence, for his own and the common welfare. This paragraph reinforces and broadens the provisions of the United Nations Convention on the Status of Stateless Persons of December 28, 1954, and the Convention on the Reduction of Statelessness, of 30 August 1961. Article 24(3) favors the child over adults, since it explicitly and emphatically declares that every child shall have a nationality, whether he is born in the territory of a party or elsewhere. If he is born in the territory of a state not party to the Covenant, and the child does not have nationality at birth under the laws of some other country (say, the country of which his parents are nationals), his parents, family guardian, or some public authority must assure that he obtains the benefit of the Covenant's broad protection. Under Article 24(3) no child can be left stateless, and his status as a child grants him the right to acquire the nationality of the state party under whose wing he takes refuge, the state to whose jurisdiction he is subject within the meaning of Article 2.

In a world convulsed by wars, millions of children are left uprooted and in a state of legal chaos, in part because their birth could not be registered where they were born or where they are receiving temporary refuge. The Covenant on Civil and Political Rights, as it is ratified by more and more states, will render a particularly valuable service to mitigate that tragedy. Article 24 gives legal force to the provisions of the Universal Declaration dealing with the protection of children and the more specific provisions of the Declaration on the Rights of Children of 1959. These two important documents, in turn, serve to define the scope of Article 24 of the Covenant; the latter declaration in particular gives important content and specificity to the protections to which children are entitled.

Finally, I believe, Article 24 protects adolescents. As was indicated in discussions in the Third Committee of the General Assembly, the adolescent, also a minor, needs to be safeguarded against the abuses of adults, including his own parents, and to receive the broad protection of society and the state.

I am conscious of the magnitude of the task undertaken in this essay. The four articles of the Covenant here examined are of great importance for the defense of the rights of personality and intimacy. They occupy a central place in the essential and dynamic process of providing effective protection everywhere to the fundamental liberties of all individuals. These articles deserve continued study and exploration to develop their meaning and their promise for the unending process of enhancing human dignity.

9

Freedom of Conscience and Expression, and Political Freedoms

KARL JOSEF PARTSCH

IN THIS ESSAY, I deal with a group of rights united by a common character and designed for a common purpose: to protect the individual as homo sapiens. These rights enable man to develop his own intellectual and moral personality, to determine his attitude towards natural and supernatural powers, and to shape his relation to his fellow creatures as well as his position in the social and political order. A wide range of human activities is covered by the articles regarding the freedom of conscience and expression and the political freedoms. They reach from the prayer spoken in loneliness to active participation in the political life of the country.

I cannot here give, even in outline, the historical development of these guarantees. It is noteworthy, however, that at least one of them—religious freedom—appeared as the first fundamental human right in political instruments of both national and international character long before the idea of systematic protection of civil and political rights was developed. For example, the first operative paragraph of the "Agreement of the People" (of England) of 28 October 1647 begins with the words: "1. That matters of religion, and the ways of God's worship, are not at all entrusted by us to any human power, because therein we cannot remit or exceed a tittle of what our consciences dictate to be the mind of God, without wilful sin."

Most of the articles of the Covenant which are the subject of this essay were formulated at a very early stage of the elaboration of the Covenant. A comparison of those articles with corresponding articles of the Universal Declaration, moreover, shows their essential affinity and suggests that understanding the Covenant articles requires attention to the development of their counterparts in the Declaration.

Freedom of Religion

In the world today, there exist mainly four types of relationships between the state and religious communities: states where the civic community and the religious community are identical and law is based on and reflects religious beliefs; states where the state and the religious community are formally separated but where one creed dominates the public philosophy; states where the population belongs to more than one religion or confession (and some to none at all), and religious freedom is fully recognized with the separation of state and religion a reality; states where atheism is the official policy but religion is more or less tolerated.

Under these circumstances it is astonishing that the states participating in the formulation of an article on freedom of conscience and religion were able to find a common formula. Necessarily it was a compromise.[1]

Paragraph 1 of Article 18 of the Covenant follows very closely the corresponding article of the Universal Declaration. The later paragraphs of Article 18 have no direct counterpart, except that the limitation clause in paragraph 3 derives from the general limitation clause in the Declaration. (See essay 12.) The idea of paragraph 4—parental control of the religious and moral education of their children—was implied in the general statement in Article 26(3) of the Declaration.[2]

Paragraph 1 of the Covenant Article 18 provides: "Everyone shall have the right to freedom of thought, conscience and religion. This right shall include freedom to have or to adopt a religion or belief of his choice, and freedom, either individually or in community with others and in public or private, to manifest his religion or belief in worship, observance, practice and teaching."

It is striking that despite the variety of state attitudes towards religion there was no substantial discussion of the fundamental principle that "everyone shall have the right to freedom of thought, conscience and religion." That may be due to the "diplomatic" wording. Atheists may have been satisfied to see "thought" and "conscience" precede "religion." Liberals may have been pleased to see all three freedoms on an equal level without preference to any one of them. Strongly religious people may have regarded "thought and conscience" as corresponding not only to religion generally but even to the only true religion, the one to which they adhere.[3]

In any event, the basic formula met no opposition. Substantial debate, however, arose when the effort was made to define the content of that right in a second sentence. The Universal Declaration states that "this right includes freedom to change his religion or belief" (Article 18). That clause met opposition when the Declaration was being drafted.[4] Later, in drafting the Covenant, there was an attempt to delete it, principally by Moslem countries.[5] Some claimed that it could be interpreted to permit abuses, principally changes in personal status not based on conscience.[6] Some thought it might be viewed as encouraging missionary and proselyting activities.[7] Others claimed it was unnecessary since the freedom to change is implicit in the concept of freedom of religion, and express mention might discourage ratification by some governments.[8] But efforts to delete the clause failed, it being argued that this freedom is too important to leave to the uncertainties of interpretation by sometimes unsympathetic governments and that deletion "would be tantamount to denial of the right to change one's religion."[9] In a spirit of compromise, however, the language was changed to make explicit the right to maintain one's religion as well as to change it. The final wording recognizes the individual's right "to have or to adopt a religion or belief of his choice." That clearly implies the right to abandon a religion to which one adhered previously as well as the right to adopt a different religion.[10]

In the extended discussions, one element stands out as of utmost importance. No one who favored deleting the express mention of the right to change one's religion denied that right. All agreed that deletion of the phrase would not have the effect of denying it and that the right was implied in the first sentence of the article as part of "the right to freedom of thought, conscience and religion." In any event, the final text clearly confirms the freedom to change one's religion or beliefs by expressly guaranteeing the freedom to have and to adopt a religion or belief of one's choice.

The right is further confirmed by the express provision in paragraph 2: "No one shall be subject to coercion which would impair his freedom to have or to adopt a religion or belief of his choice." That clause reiterates "the freedom to have or to adopt a religion or belief of his choice," here in order to protect it against zealous proselytizers and missionaries. The clause also protects against coercion to support a religion other than one's own, for instance by payment of church taxes or contributions.

Paragraph 2 does not deal with the freedom to manifest one's religion; that is the subject of paragraph 3. Neither does paragraph 2 imply a general freedom to be exempt from any civil obligation incompatible with one's religion or beliefs. In one particular respect that is clearly expressed elsewhere in the Covenant. Article 8(3)(c)(ii) provides that a state may require national civilian service instead of military service "in countries where conscientious objection is recognized." That implies that states are free to recognize or not to recognize conscientious objection to military service.

Perhaps issues of conscientious objection to civic duties are an aspect of "manifesting one's religion" covered by paragraph 3 of Article 18. That paragraph provides: "Freedom to manifest one's religion or beliefs may be subject only to such limitations as are prescribed by law and are necessary to protect public safety, order, health, or morals or the fundamental rights and freedoms of others."

The limitations permitted by that paragraph apply exclusively to the freedom to manifest one's religion or beliefs. No limitations are permitted on the freedom of thought, conscience, and religion declared in Article 18(1), nor on the freedom "to have or to adopt a religion or belief of his choice" in Article 18(2). It is nonetheless astonishing that very ample and broad limitations were admitted with respect to the right to manifest one's religion.[11] (Note that this right, like the freedoms in Article 18(1) and (2), is not subject to derogation in time of public emergency. See Article 4(1).)

Limitations on rights are dealt with at length in essay 12. Here I consider briefly the special character of the limitation provision in Article 18(3). It is surely more restrictive than the general limitation clause in Article 29 of the Declaration. It is like the other limitation clauses in the Covenant in most respects, but differs from them in important ways. Like the other limitation clauses, it permits limitations only if they are prescribed by law and if they are necessary.[12] But the special character and high value of the freedom to manifest one's religion may explain the differences in Article 18(3).

Article 18(3) permits limitations to protect public safety but not "national security." Limitations may be imposed if necessary to protect the *fundamental* freedoms of others but not merely any rights and freedoms of others (see Articles 12(3), 21(1), 22(2)). It is surely significant, too, that Article 18(3) permits limitation only to protect "public safety, order, health or morals." Presumably "public" modifies "order" as well as "safety," but here it is used without the interpretative addition of the French term *ordre public*. Indeed, here even the French text does not speak of *"ordre public"* but of *la protection de l'ordre*. That clearly suggests that limitations on freedom to manifest one's religion cannot be imposed to protect *ordre public* with its general connotations of national public policy, but only where necessary to protect public order narrowly construed, i.e., to prevent public disorder.[13] A state whose public policy is atheism, for example, cannot invoke Article 18(3) to suppress manifestations of religion or beliefs.

The final paragraph of Article 18 guarantees to parents the right to determine and ensure the religious and moral education of their children. It was added at a relatively late state of the deliberations, though the problem had been discussed earlier.[14] The right belongs to the cultural and social sphere that is the concern of the Covenant on Economic, Social, and Cultural Rights, and it appears there in connection with the right to education.[15] Its incorporation in Article 18 may have been due to the fact that it was not certain that both Covenants would be ratified by all states. Article 18(4), of course, is appropriate to an article on freedom of thought, conscience, and religion; and this right may well be seen as distinct from the general educational problems dealt with in the other Covenant.

Under this article a state must permit parents to decide what kind of religious and moral education they wish to give their children. States apparently are not obliged to permit schools of general education to be run in conformity with the religious and philosophical convictions of parents.[16] The Covenant leaves open how and where religious or moral education is to take place, whether in school or outside. The state is not obliged to finance such education but only to tolerate it if the parents wish to provide it or pay for it.[17]

In comparison with the proud program established in Article 26(3) of the Universal Declaration to guarantee that "parents have a prior right to choose the kind of education that shall be given to their children," paragraph 4 seems to be very modest. It must be recognized, however, that a great number of states have a monopoly on primary and secondary education and that a legally binding covenant cannot fulfill all the wishes expressed in a programmatic declaration. Even in Western Europe the right of parents to choose the kind of education their children shall have has been highly controversial; no other guarantee in the entire European Convention with its additional protocols met with so many reservations.[18]

In sum, Article 18 guarantees very fundamental rights. The general guarantee contained in the first sentence of paragraph 1 is far-reaching. Although no definition of "thought" or "conscience" is provided, taken together with "religion" they include all possible attitudes of the individual toward the world, toward society, and toward that which determines his fate and the destiny of the world, be it a divinity, some superior being or just reason and rationalism, or chance. "Thought" includes political and social thought; "conscience" includes all morality. "Religion or belief" is not limited to a theistic belief but comprises equally nontheistic and even atheistic beliefs. The same guarantees of freedom apply to all these, and no limitation whatsoever is admitted as far as the realm of personal conscience is concerned. Such absolute freedom, moreover, applies not only to the freedom to have such convictions but also to change them and to adopt new ones. The process of maintaining such convictions as well as the freedom of individual choice are protected against all forms of direct coercion and also against indirect encroachments.

A clear distinction is made between the individual sphere and the public sphere as regards the freedom to manifest one's religion or belief. Although that freedom is guaranteed in public as well as in private— and certain forms are mentioned—such manifestations may be subjected to some limitations. Certainly manifestations of one's religion have to respect the fundamental rights and freedoms of others. Limitations to protect public safety, order, health, or morals are legitimate only if they are "necessary." The high value of the individual's interest in the freedom of manifesting his religion or belief must be given great weight against the public interests asserted; state "necessity" should not be lightly accepted in the face of personal conviction.

Freedom of Religion in the Human Rights Committee

Like other rights recognized in the Covenant, the guarantees of freedom of thought, conscience, and religion are interpreted by various bodies, both national and international: by governments considering adherence to the Covenant and possible reservations; in national parliaments comparing the national legal order with the requirements of the Covenant; by officials required to give effect to the Covenant; and by national courts in those states where the provisions of the Covenant are directly applicable. Increasingly they are, and will be, interpreted also by states parties reporting on their compliance to the Human Rights Committee established under the Covenant, by states complaining to the Committee of violations by other states (pursuant to Article 41), and by individuals transmitting communications to the Committee under the Protocol to the Covenant; the Human Rights Committee itself will interpret the Covenant in its deliberations and reports. (See essay 14.)

The interpretations reflected in the work of the Human Rights Committee, the authoritative international body charged with implementation of the Covenant, are bound to have particular significance. The records and reports of the Committee, moreover, are public and available. Because the Covenant did not come into force until 1976, however, the Committee has only a short history and the records are still meager.[19] But they already provide some guidance and hold promise as a major interpretative source for the future.[20]

It is noteworthy that no state party to the Covenant had entered any reservations to Article 18, despite the previous experiences with the European Convention[21] and the widely different views of parental rights (Article 18(4)). The early records of the Committee, however, show divergent opinions about some aspects of Article 18.

Some of the interpretations raise serious questions. For instance, the government of Cyprus considers that the freedom of religion does not apply to creeds that keep their doctrine secret,[22] for example the Druses, a view for which there seems to be no basis in Article 18.[23] And although the limitation clause, Article 18(3), clearly was intended to permit restrictions only on the right to manifest one's religion or beliefs and not on the freedom of thought, conscience, or religion—or on the right to have and adopt a religion or belief of one's choice—the USSR and Romania, as well as Barbados, purport to apply restrictions also on the "internal" sphere.[24] There have also been questionable applications of the limitation clause to various manifestations of religion and belief. It may be doubted, for example, whether limitations are permissible in order to avoid "public indignation."[25] Certainly, Article 18(3) does not permit limitations "in accordance with the Revolution."[26]

The implementation of the right of parents to ensure the religious and moral education of their children in conformity with their own conviction differs largely among the states parties according to the respective relationships between state and church. Extreme positions are taken on the one hand by Sweden,[27] with compulsory religious instruction in the schools, and on the other hand by Byelorussia and the Ukraine, where religious instruction in the schools is prohibited and the religious communities are not entitled to maintain their own educational institutions.[28] While a state may not be required to permit religious schools, the parents must be permitted, legally and practically, to assure that their children receive a religious education corresponding to their own convictions. Where religious instruction is an essential feature of the curriculum of public schools, parents should at least be allowed to insist on their children's being excused from attendance at religious worship and instruction.[29] If, on the other hand, religious instruction is prohibited in school, the obligations of state parties cannot be regarded as fulfilled if the religious and moral education is left only to the parents themselves; at least, educational activity by ministers or priests outside the schools should be tolerated. Another question raised in the Committee concerns the equality of religions under the law, especially when the state officially endorses one religion. Some members expressed concern that a state religion would receive preferential treatment and that the status of other religions might be impaired.[30]

Freedom of Opinion and Expression

It is an old commonplace that the freedom of opinion and expression is one of the cornerstones of human rights and has great importance for all other rights and freedoms. For that reason the United Nations convened a special Conference on Freedom of Information at Geneva in 1948. This conference not only prepared a draft Convention on Freedom of Information but on different occasions gave advice to the Commission on Human Rights, which was then engaged in drafting the Universal Declaration. The formulation of the article on freedom of opinion and expression for the Universal Declaration involved the fascinating process of collecting all formulations in national constitutions as well as drafts prepared by public and private political and scientific associations and organizations; the distillation of those elements not only seemed indispensable in a worldwide instrument but also was likely to be generally accepted.[31] The result was an article of only four lines (Article 19 of the Declaration):

> "Everyone has the right to freedom of opinion and expression; this right includes freedom to hold opinions without interference and to seek, receive and impart information and ideas through any media and regardless of frontiers."

This article is the basis of the first two paragraphs of Article 19 of the Covenant:

> "1. Everyone shall have the right to hold opinions without interference.
> "2. Everyone shall have the right to freedom of expression; this right shall include freedom to seek, receive and impart information and ideas of all kinds, regardless of frontiers, either orally, in

writing or in print, in the form of art, or through any other media of his choice."

Drawing on and developing the Declaration article, the Covenant provisions have several noteworthy elements:

—A distinction is implied between freedom of thought (Article 18) and freedom of opinion. In fact, there are no clear frontiers between "thought" and "opinion"; both are internal. "Thought" is a process, while "opinion" is the result of this process. "Thought" may be nearer to religion or other beliefs, "opinion" nearer to political convictions. "Thought" may be used in connection with faith and creed, "opinion" for convictions in secular and civil matters.

—A distinction is implied between freedom of opinion and freedom of expression. By implication in the Declaration and expressly in the Covenant, the freedom to hold opinions without interference is absolute; the freedom of expression may be subject to certain limited restrictions.

—The freedom of expression includes the right to seek, receive, and impart information and ideas.

—No differentiation is made among the media used to seek, receive, and impart information.

—These rights and freedoms exist regardless of frontiers. The rights of freedom of opinion and expression may be exercised not only in one's own country but internationally. They are international rights.[32]

Thus, the Covenant provision has improved on the Declaration in several respects. The distinction between the freedom of opinion and freedom of expression is sharpened. In view of their different character, they appear in separate paragraphs. This helps make it clear that the right to freedom of opinion is a private matter and is absolute with no infringement allowed, whereas freedom of expression, as a public matter of social importance, has some limits by its very nature. "The right to hold opinions" is "without interference," excluding any restrictions whatever. This is confirmed by the express statement in the limitation clause (paragraph 3) that it applies only to paragraph 2, the freedom of expression. The right to hold opinions may be seen as a special aspect of the right of privacy dealt with in Article 17, but there only arbitrary and unlawful interferences are prohibited; the privacy of thought and opinion is subject to no interference whatever.

During the discussions of this article,[33] it was suggested that paragraph 1 should bar interference only "by public authority." That suggestion was rejected. An individual has the right to freedom of opinion without interference by private parties [34] as well, and the state is obliged to ensure that freedom. Thus, the danger that the state might encourage such interference from private or so-called private sources is eliminated. It is doubtful, however, whether the complex problem of protecting a person's opinion against interferences by other individuals can be solved in this global and absolute manner.

In the Covenant, the substance and scope of the right to freedom of expression are described in detail. The three elements: "seek, receive and impart" information, as in the Declaration, were retained after some discussion. Some objected that the right "to seek" information could be misused to probe into the affairs of others and suggested a right only "to gather" information, excluding the right of active inquiry.[35] That change was not accepted. The right of active inquiry and probing, it was decided, should not be abandoned. Misuse could be prevented under the limitations clause in paragraph 3.[36] Suggestions that the object of the right—"information and ideas"—be defined and illustrated were also rejected as creating a risk of restrictive interpretation. The right applies to "information and ideas of all kinds."[37]

Similarly, there was debate whether to enumerate the media of expression. The principal media created no great difficulties: "orally, in writing or in print, in the form of art." There was discussion whether the press should be mentioned expressly, and how, if at all, visual and auditory devices should be dealt with. There was apparently reluctance to refer expressly to the licensing of radio and television. It was feared that such a provision might be utilized to hamper free expression through such media, and might even be misconstrued as authorizing the licensing of the printed word. As licensing radio and television stations for technical reasons would be permitted under the limitation clause permitting what was necessary for public order (paragraph 3), it seemed advisable not to mention it in paragraph 2. The formula "through any other media of his choice" includes all these media whether specifically enumerated or not.[38]

A different issue which will doubtless arise is whether freedom of expression implies the freedom of nonexpression, a right to remain silent, not to express one's thoughts, opinions, or beliefs. It would appear that compulsion to express one's views violates the right to hold opinions without interference under Article 18.

An interesting question that has arisen in national systems is whether the "freedom of expression" includes the right to anonymous expression. Presumably, it would be an issue under the limitation clause, whether in the name of public order (*ordre public*) a state may require that a person publishing a book or issuing a leaflet identify himself as the responsible author.[39]

Paragraph 3 of Article 19 of the covenant contains a limitation clause: "The exercise of the rights provided for in paragraph 2 of this Article carries with it special duties and responsibilities. It may therefore be subject to certain restrictions, but these shall only be such as are provided by law and are necessary:

"(a) For respect of the rights or reputations of others;
"(b) For the protection of national security or of public order (*ordre public*), or of public health or morals."

This paragraph generally resembles the other limitation clauses in the Covenant (see essay 12). But debates over the freedom of expression contributed to the development of that common approach to limitations and the general formula.

There were two main alternatives. One was to anticipate and list all restrictions on this freedom which might be necessary. This would have led inevitably to a very long list which would have to take into account the particular problems in many fields, e.g., the protection of the state against subversive activities, the law of the press and other media, the protection of the judiciary, and many others.[40] The other alternative was a formula like that in Article 29(2) of the Universal Declaration, giving in general terms the public purposes which might make restriction necessary and permissible.[41] The latter was the method chosen but, as in other limitation clauses of the Covenant, the approach of the Declaration was adapted in Article 19 to the special conditions of the freedom of expression.

The limitation clause in Article 19(3) is the only one in the Covenant introduced by a preamble. It states that the exercise of the right of expression carries with it special duties and responsibilities. This doubtless draws on Article 29(1) of the Declaration but neither the Declaration nor the Covenant defines these duties. Presumably they include the duty to present information and news truthfully, accurately, and impartially.[42] The operative part of the limitation clause has two elements. Restrictions shall be only those provided by law and only those necessary to protect certain enumerated values.[43] The formula in Article 19(3) differs somewhat from both the formula in Article 29 of the Universal Declaration and even from the other limitation clauses in the Covenant. These are dealt with at length in essay 12.

Several issues about the limitation clause have arisen in cases involving the freedoms covered by Article 19.

One question is whether the freedom of expression may be limited by a restriction imposed not by statute but by unwritten common law. In applying the analogous provision of the European Convention, the European Court of Human Rights held that a real though unwritten law would be a sufficient basis for restriction. The Court said:

> It would clearly be contrary to the intentions of the drafters of the Convention to hold that a restriction imposed by virtue of the common law is not "prescribed by law" on the sole ground that it is not enunciated in legislation: This would deprive a common-law State which is Party to the Convention of the protection of Article 10 para. 2 and strike at the very roots of that State's legal system.[44]

The European Convention requires that restrictions be "prescribed by law" (translated into French as *prévues par la loi*) while the Covenant requires that they be "provided by law," but that difference would not seem to justify a different result. Both terms are designed to assure the rule of law, the principle of legality, a knowledge of the existence of the law and accessibility to it by those affected, and sufficient definiteness as to its content and meaning. Although the Covenant was drafted later than the European Convention and the draftsmen knew the European formula but preferred a different term, there is nothing to indicate that a different meaning was intended in this respect.

Another issue that has arisen is who decides whether a limitation is justified by one of the enumerated grounds. In applying the clause permitting limitation on freedom of expression under the European Convention, the European Commission has developed the thesis that a state has a certain "margin of appreciation" in determining limitations that may be placed on the freedom.[45] But the European Commission made clear that it has not only the right but also the duty to examine whether such limitations are within the scope of permissible limitations and comply with other relevant provisions of the Convention. That thesis is valid also in the application of the Covenant. A state has a margin of appreciation in deciding what restrictions are necessary, but the state's decision is subject to international scrutiny. With all due regard to the differences between the organs of the European Convention and those established by the Covenant, the principle is the same. The latter, too, have the right and the duty to review the state's decision that a restriction is necessary, and examination by that international organ would not constitute an improper interference with the sovereignty of a state party.

As in other limitation clauses in the Covenant, restrictions under Article 19(3) must be "necessary," a stronger term than that used in the Declaration.[46] The grounds for limitation are generally the same as those in the other clauses. "National security" means here what it means elsewhere in the Covenant, and permits limitations on freedom of expression necessary to safeguard such security, for example by preventing publication of military secrets. "Public order (*ordre public*)" might permit limitations to protect other secrets in the national interest, such as in diplomatic affairs or privileged governmental matters. It might also permit barring pornographic materials, although that might come also within public "morals." False or misleading expressions about drugs might be regulated for "public health."

Article 19(3) differs from other limitation formulas in some details. While the Declaration and most other limitation provisions in the Covenant permit restrictions to protect "rights and freedoms of others," Article 19 permits restrictions necessary for "respect of the rights or reputations of others." Clearly, it was decided to emphasize that the reputations of others—listed as entitled to protection in Article 17—need to be safeguarded against slander and other harm by individuals exercising their freedom of expression. The reference to "the rights" of others without including their "freedoms" is probably without significance, especially since freedoms are commonly designated as a "right to freedom" (for example, in Article 19(2)). Whenever the limitation clause is applied, the precious value of the freedom of expression has to be carefully set against the particular purposes which have been declared legitimate. Out of the broad field of public welfare, only the smaller sectors of public health and national security appear. Although "public order" is mentioned, it is questionable whether many restrictions could be justified for *raison d'Etat*.[47] And while a state has a margin of appreciation in enacting and applying these limitations, their validity is ultimately a question of international law for international consideration.

In sum, Article 19, translating the proclamations of the Declaration into a normative text, is a remarkable achievement. The standard of protection contemplated by the Declaration has been maintained and even raised. The Covenant maintains a clear distinction between freedom of opinion and freedom of expression: the first is absolute and not subject to any restriction or interference. Expression is subject to restrictions but only in keeping with the principles of legality and necessity: restrictions must be provided by law; they must be necessary; they are permissible only for particular and specific public ends.

Freedom of Opinion and Expression in the Human Rights Committee

The general guarantee of the freedom of opinion and expression was amply discussed by the Human Rights Committee during its first sessions. It is, however, astonishing that the distinction between the right "to hold opinions" and the "freedom of expression" was hardly mentioned.[48] Nor was there discussion of the definition of "the freedom to seek, receive and impart information and ideas of all kinds," or who are the beneficiaries of these rights.

One cannot say that there was no occasion to take up these matters. The 1977 Constitution of the USSR which was reported to the Committee does not mention the right to hold opinions without interference.[49] It guarantees the freedom of speech and of the press but does not mention the freedom to seek and to receive information and ideas. The rights guaranteed, moreover, are limited to citizens, and they are subject to an important reservation: they are granted only "in accordance with the interests of the people and in order to strengthen and develop the socialist system." The reports provided by the USSR do not indicate that these gaps in the new Constitution have been filled by legislation.[50]

The discussions in the Human Rights Committee concentrated on the limitations in national legal orders on the freedom of expression, with special emphasis on the freedom of the press, radio and television, and films and art. Discussion centered on: (1) provisions of the internal legal order that were clearly impermissible under Article 19(3) of the Covenant; (2) the need for clarification of state reports; and (3), the largest group, reports raising issues as to whether a particular ideological orientation is compatible with the Covenant.

Some reports indicated clear violations of Article 19. In Iran "no discussion whatsoever was apparently permitted concerning the Constitution, the imperial monarchy and the Revolution of the Shah and the People."[51] Also questionable are restrictions deriving from the "Principles (or objectives) of the Revolution," which do not even have a legal definition.[52]

Chile reported that during the state of siege in 1973, the rights referred to in Article 19 (among others) had been restricted under the derogation clause, Article 4 of the Covenant.[53] But because notice of the derogations came after the state of siege had been lifted, it was doubtful whether this notification was still valid. A state of emergency replaced the state of siege; it was argued that under these conditions the limitation clause of Article 19(3) should have come again into force. A member of the Committee stated that under this limitation clause "freedom of opinion could not be restricted merely because the government considered it to be a threat to its own stability. . . . Any restriction on freedom of opinion required convincing proof that a clear and present danger could not otherwise be overcome." Peaceful criticism of governmental policies could never amount to such a threat.[54]

A need for clarification was felt with regard to some legal orders which used a terminology not corresponding to Article 19(3). For example, it was asked what kinds of radio and television programs would be considered "offensive to public feeling." The suspicion that aesthetic or political criteria might be implied was removed by the reply that the term covered broadcasts of an obscene nature.[55] It may be necessary, however, to assure that such broad and vague terms are not used to regulate or discourage other materials not properly covered by the limitation provision.

In Sweden, freedom of expression may be limited in the interest "of the security of the Realm" and "of the economic well-being of the people." It was explained that "security of the Realm" meant national security and that the "economic well-being of the people" had never been invoked, as no serious economic crisis had made recourse to it necessary.[56] Again, the legitimacy of such a law may be questioned, since economic crisis would not seem to warrant limitation on freedom of expression.

According to the basic law of the Federal Republic of Germany (Article 5(2)), freedom of expression is limited by the provisions of "general laws." The government expressed the view that this was permissible under the Covenant, since none of the general laws exceed the limitations permitted by Article 19(3).[57]

A number of constitutions of former British possessions which attained independence, or are still dependent territories, follow the method employed in Article 10 of the European Convention of defining permissible limitations on the freedom of expression by listing examples.[58] Since state parties are not obliged to use the same terminology but only to abide by the same standard, there can hardly be objection to this method as long as the examples listed are covered by the general clauses of Article 19(3).

A third group of issues discussed by the Committee involved states constitutionally committed to a public philosophy and which guarantee the freedoms of expression only in accordance with that philosophy, e.g., socialist ideology. There are, however, different methods of ensuring that freedom of expression is exercised in conformity with socialist standards. The most radical form is to be found in the new Constitution of the USSR (Article 50 (1)) which reads: "In accordance with the interest of the people and in order to strengthen and develop the socialist system, citizens of the USSR are guaranteed freedom of speech, of the press . . ."[59] The freedom of expression is apparently guaranteed only if used for a certain purpose, "in order to strengthen and develop the socialist system," not for other purposes, e.g., the "full development of his personality" (Article 29(1) of the Universal Declaration). In this approach, no other restrictive law is needed; major limitations are built into the statement of the right and the right exists only if it is exercised for one purpose.

A second type of provision guarantees freedom of expression on the condition that it shall not be exercised contrary to "the interests of the working people." "The interests of the working people" is not far from "the socialist system," but it is important that here only a limitation is imposed: the exercise of the freedom of opinion is legitimate so long as there is no conflict with socialist doctrine; it is not required that expression be positively motivated by a desire to strengthen and develop socialism.[60]

A third type of "socialist" system purports less severe limitations on free expression for "socialist" needs. The Yugoslav legal order, for instance, admits limitations only if based on national security and public order without providing or implying that the latter includes a political doctrine. The Yugoslav Constitution, however, admits only a one party system. One can argue that if the citizens are obliged to adhere to one political party, their choice between different political opinions and effectively their freedom to express political opinion is limited.[61]

There is a theory that all three types of "socialist" restriction are permissible as based on considerations of "public order." But "public order" is a legal concept, not a political one, and this theory is therefore self-contradictory. Moreover, even if it were accepted that in a socialist state public order is socialism, the first type of constitutional provision—as in the USSR and its closest adepts—would not be acceptable under Article 19(3). "Public order" is a criterion for limitations on a right, not for its definition. The protection of public order, moreover, must also be necessary for the limitations imposed. A comparison with the legal orders of the second type of socialist state clearly shows that a socialist state with the same attitude toward freedom of expression can function if only negative exercises of the freedom of speech are banned.[62]

Even the second type of "socialist" restriction on speech would not seem to correspond to the Covenant. A state is entitled to defend the political structure enshrined in its constitution against its enemies or even against internal subversive acts, but the Covenant does not permit a state to limit political expression directed toward peaceful political or social change. Expressions of opinion favoring changes in socialism, or even from socialism, may not be limited any more than expressions threatening the stability of the regime (as in the case of Chile), or other expressions not creating a clear and present danger of some evil coming within the purposes contemplated by Article 19(3).

The third type of restriction—that implied in the fact of a single party state—would probably not be a violation of Article 19(3) as long as the state does not interfere with expression which suggests changing such a system. I consider below whether such a system is consistent with other covenant provisions, notably Article 25.

Of the specific problems considered in this connection, the right to a free press should be mentioned. Among the members of the Committee there was a strong interest in the degree of government influence on the press. Was the press under state control? Did censorship exist?[63] Who had access to the mass media? Did the press have an obligation to report objectively and who was entitled to decide whether the press was doing so? Questions were put regarding the organization of the mass media: were they run by the state directly or by private corporations under some influence of the state?[64] Which organs were subsidized from public funds? Was there a monopoly or concentration of publishing houses which might endanger the freedom of the press? What institutions were available to guarantee the freedom of the press? Do all classes of the population have free access to mass media or is it limited to certain social or economic groups?

Very few of these questions were answered by the government representatives, and those who answered often did so reluctantly. On the basis of the information given it is impossible to draw up a true picture of the actual situation. A few illustrative examples may be given here.

Formal press censorship was not reported by any state. Only one state admitted that it had censored the press in a state of emergency.[65] In some states, however, importation of foreign newspapers and publications might be prohibited by courts. In Yugoslavia the criteria for such prohibition are offenses against the very basis of the self-management system, against national security, or the armed forces; propagation of support for aggression or other acts against humanity, international law, or the aims of the United Nations, or against peace and cooperation among states; disturbance of friendly relations between Yugoslavia and other countries; and insults to the reputations of Yugoslavia, any foreign state or international organization, or their representatives.[66] Whereas in Yugoslavia the ordinary courts have jurisdiction over such matters, in Ecuador a special court composed of prominent journalists under the chairmanship of a lawyer appointed by the Supreme Court handles cases relating to the press.[67]

The report of Yugoslavia contains an interesting remark regarding the relations between freedom of the press and the new right of citizens to be informed (Article 168 of the Constitution):[68] the introduction of this right, it was said, integrated and superseded classical "freedom of the press." A member of the Committee wished to know precisely how the supersession had taken place, whether the right to be informed and the right to freedom of expression were reconciled and how this freedom could be maintained if efforts were made to ensure adequate social influence over the mass media.[69] The answer given to these questions, that the right to be informed was not a substitute for the freedom of the press, certainly did not fully satisfy the questioner.[70]

The organization of radio and television corporations was an object of many queries. Members of the Committee were apparently aware of the problem of reconciling state ownership with free expression in these mass media. The organization of public control of films was also a major subject of discussion. Even art was not neglected.[71]

War and Racist Propaganda

The Universal Declaration contains a general provision that the specific rights and freedoms defined by it may in no case be exercised contrary to the purposes and principles of the United Nations (Article 29(3)). This clause excludes justifying propaganda for the use of force or for acts of racial discrimination as an exercise of the right to freedom of expression.[72] Proposals to insert a similar clause into Article 19 of the Covenant were not successful.[73] It was argued that such a specific limitation would not be consistent with the character of the right guaranteed and its addition might create a basis for prior censorship that would limit the free exchange of ideas.[74]

Eventually, however, the present Article 20 was adopted:[75]

"1. Any propaganda for war shall be prohibited by law.
"2. Any advocacy of national, racial or religious hatred that constitutes incitement to discrimination, hostility or violence shall be
prohibited by law."

It was also decided to put this article directly after Article 19 in order
to demonstrate the close connection between a ban on certain propagandistic acts and the freedom of expression. This placement is important for the interpretation of the article. It is practically a fourth paragraph to Article 19 and has to be read in close connection with the
preceding article.[76]

The first paragraph of Article 20 provides that "any propaganda for
war shall be prohibited by law." "War" is not defined. The Charter of
the United Nations avoids this term and speaks instead of the "use of
force" and of "aggression," and recognizes the "inherent right of individual or collective self-defense." Some have suggested other limited
purposes for which force is permissible, e.g., humanitarian intervention. The Charter also contemplates the possibility of UN military action against an aggressor. After many years the General Assembly
adopted a definition of aggression[77] which also expressly refers to the
provisions of the Charter "concerning cases in which the use of force is
lawful" (Article 6). The question has been raised therefore whether Article 20(1) of the Covenant also applies to "expressions of views in favour of the legitimate use of force in accordance with the principles of
the United Nations, namely self-defense, action under Chapter VII of
the Charter, and wars of national liberation."[78] The discussions of the
Committee confirm that the term "war" has to be interpreted in the
sense of "war of aggression."[79]

There has also been concern about the meaning of "propaganda".
The experts of the Council of Europe expressed concern that the
expression "propaganda for war" could easily be abused; it could be
invoked, for example, by a hostile critic against a scientific treatise on
military matters or against a declaration on principles of national security.[80] The term surely needs refinement, and a prohibition of materials
that do not advocate or incite to war would not be within Article 20
and would be a violation of Article 19.[81]

There may be questions also about the legislative measures states parties are obliged to enact. It is not clear whether a state must enact such
law immediately or whether it is sufficient to do so when the need

arises. At least one member of the Human Rights Committee has stated that parties are clearly obliged to enact such law whether or not circumstances require it.[82]

Also the Covenant requires that such propaganda be prohibited by law but does not prescribe what kind of law it should be. It is not required, for example, that such propaganda be made a crime.[83] State parties should be free to enact whatever legislation they deem appropriate, but a state must prohibit it; programs of education and information are not enough.[84] It appears necessary to enact a legislative provision which prohibits propaganda for war in order to give a basis for administrative measures.[85] As no penal sanction appears mandatory, a provision expressly mentioning "propaganda for war" is not required. It should be sufficient if the act of propagating war comes under a general prohibitory clause in the penal or other law.[86]

The second paragraph of Article 20 obliges states parties to prohibit "advocacy of national, racial or religious hatred that constitutes incitement to discrimination, hostility or violence." Advocacy must constitute "incitement," i.e., strong encouragement of other persons to commit acts of, or otherwise display, "discrimination, violence or hostility," perhaps within some short time. The three ends of incitement indicated are different in character. Incitement to "discrimination" and "violence" are legally defined (or definable) concepts. "Hostility" is an attitude and only a further moral qualification of the incitement. The difference between "hatred" and "hostility" is not certain; perhaps "hatred" has a strong subjective element while "hostility" suggests an attitude displayed externally. "Hostility" can exist without "hatred," but one can hardly imagine that hatred would not lead to hostility. The earlier Commission draft used the world "hostility" in order to mark the prohibited act and "incitement to hatred" in order to specify the result, but the words were later interchanged. "Advocacy of hatred . . . that constitutes hostility" is a tautology.

Three kinds of "hatred" are designated: national, racial, and religious. The word "national" is used at various places in the Covenant, not always with the same meaning. When modifying "origin," it may be identical with "ethnic."[87] Some states apparently interpret "national hatred" in Article 20(2) as meaning ethnic hatred, as appears from the fact that they report their laws prohibiting advocacy of hatred of groups of their own citizens of particular national origins.[88] On the other hand, the paragraph cannot be limited to acts committed against a state's own nationals. The French version, *tout appel à la haine nationale,* will certainly not be interpreted in this sense.

The term "racial discrimination" is defined in Article 1 of the Convention on the Elimination of All Forms of Racial Discrimination (CERD) to include distinctions on account of "race, colour, descent or national or ethnic origin."[89] The Netherlands government expressed doubts whether this definition also applies to the Covenant. In fact, it would seem that the term "race" has a less comprehensive sense here. In CERD, "national origin" is brought under "race," but in Article 12(2) of the Covenant "national hatred" appears as an alternative to "racial hatred."[90] "National origin" also appears separate from "race" in Article 26 of the Covenant, where nearly all the different criteria of Article 1 of CERD are listed.

The relationship between Article 20(2) and Article 26 is clear. Article 26 prohibits the discriminatory act as such; Article 20(2) is a special provision regarding incitement. The latter is similar to Article 2(d) and Article 4(a) of CERD, in which the obligation to punish incitement to racial discrimination is even stronger than the obligation to punish the act of discrimination itself. Article 4 of CERD even obligates states to penalize incitements to racial discrimination, not just prohibit them, although it does so "with due regard to the principles embodied in the Universal Declaration of Human Rights," namely the guarantee of the right to freedom of expression. Article 20(2) of the Covenant requires that hatred inciting to violence or hostility be prohibited but not necessarily that it be made a crime.[91] Provision in a state's constitution that such discrimination is prohibited would presumably be sufficient; an implementation in the penal code is not mandatory. Especially where no danger of racial discrimination exists because the population is mono–ethnic,[92] there would seem to be no need for provisions in the penal code. In view of the fact that the great majority of states which have ratified the Covenant are also parties to CERD, this divergence between the two instruments may not be of great practical importance.[93]

Article 20(1) and (2) are worded in objective terms: there is no special requirement of a subjective intention to stir up racial hatred;[94] if the propaganda in fact incites, it must be prohibited.

Finally, the relationship of Article 20 to Article 19 needs comment. Those in favor of the prohibition have frequently expressed the opinion that such a prohibition "could hardly be considered a threat to freedom of opinion and expression."[95] On the other hand, there are numerous opinions to the contrary. "It was feared that such a prohibition would prejudice the right to freedom of opinion and expression. . . . The article . . . contained no provision setting forth any particular right or freedom; on the contrary it could be used by any government to suppress the very rights and freedoms which the Covenant was designed to preserve."[96] Fear that the prohibition "might endanger the freedom of expression" was the main ground for four Scandinavian reservations to Article 20(1) and for the United Kingdom reservations to the whole article.[97] The President of the United States also stated: "This provision conflicts with the Constitution and thus a reservation is required."[98]

In any event, Article 20 constitutes a further limitation of Article 19. A different question is whether the limitation clause of Article 19(3) applies to Article 20 as well, even though neither article refers to the other. The relationship among all articles of the Covenant is governed by Article 5(1), under which not only is the destruction of any right or freedom recognized in the Covenant prohibited, but also no right may be limited to an extent greater than is provided for in the Covenant. Measures taken by a state to implement Article 20 which conflict with Article 19 (2)—such as the introduction of censorship or other general limitations on the freedom of expression—have to conform with the requirements of Article 19(3). Though this is not expressly stated in Article 20, its implementation has to be realized "with due regard" to freedom of opinion and expression.[99] One may say, then, that a state may do under Article 20 only what is strictly required by that article[100] and is also compatible with Article 19(3).

The Right of Peaceful Assembly

Some international instruments combine guarantees of the right of assembly and of the right of association in one article. This can be justified by several considerations. Both rights are designed to protect the right of people to come together and cooperate for some joint action or purpose. Both rights are closely connected with the formation of the common "will" of the people in a democratic society. It is sometimes difficult to distinguish between these rights. Insofar as the right of association means the right to form continuing organized collective bodies, an assembly may give rise to the foundation of an association and every association begins with an assembly; even an informal gathering may lead to the formation of an organized group. A striking example is the foundation of the first political party in the Belgian Congo by Lumumba on the ship which returned from Brazzaville to Leopoldville after President De Gaulle had promised independence to the French Congo.

On the other hand, there are differences between the two rights. The right of association includes private informal contacts, the right to decide whom one will be friendly with or spend time with for social and cultural as well as political, or commercial or other economic purposes. This may be seen as an aspect of one's privacy. Even as regards the right to form or join permanent associations, such associations may present a greater danger to public safety or security and invite different regulations for public health, order, or morals than an ad hoc gathering for only a short time. National constitutions therefore frequently differentiate between the two rights, with different reasons justifying different restrictions upon them. The control of associations may fall within the competence of different national institutions or organs than would a prohibition of assembly. One writer has said that it would be "logical" to treat them in separate articles.[101]

In the Covenant the two rights appear in separate articles for a political reason. The USSR had proposed a common article, adding that those who would use these rights against the interests of democracy should not enjoy them: dissenters should not have a right to freedom of assembly, let alone a right to freedom of permanent association.[102] The argument of the USSR was rejected on the ground that such a formulation would deprive this freedom of its very essence, and the two guarantees were separated in order to reinforce both of them and to emphasize their independent character as well as to assure these rights to those who did not agree with the party in power.

Some limitation on the freedom of assembly is implied in the formulation of the right as "freedom of peaceful assembly." While "assembly" can be a formal meeting as well as an informal gathering, while it does not require any degree of organization, the assembly must be "peaceful." Early in the drafting history it was determined that "peaceful" refers exclusively to the conditions under which the assembly is held, i.e., "without uproar, disturbance, or the use of arms."[103] This qualification should not be interpreted as referring to the object for which the assembly is called or to the opinions which may be expressed at that occasion.[104] Whether an assembly may be prohibited for such substantive reasons has to be decided on the basis of the limitation clause in the second sentence of Article 21. The wording that the right "shall be recognized" differs from the other guarantees in this Covenant and may seem weak, but the legal obligation is the same as for other rights.[105] Articles 2 and 5 of the Covenant make clear that the word "recognize" is used to express commitment. The Covenant does not purport to create particular rights (see Introduction) but states parties are to "recognize" the rights so as to respect and ensure them. (In the Covenant on Economic, Social, and Cultural Rights, most provisions express the state's obligation in terms of "recognizing" the right.) The obligation to respect and ensure the right to freedom of assembly, then, is clear. It may be noted that the insertion of a limitation clause in sentence 2 would make no sense if sentence 1 did not imply commitment.

In conformity with the traditional interpretation, "freedom of peaceful assembly" embraces not only the right to organize a meeting but also any individual's right to take part in, or to belong to, an assembly.[106]

Article 21 does not expressly state whether the right of assembly implies also the negative, the freedom to abstain from participation: may a government compel individuals to participate in a political demonstration and cause him to suffer disadvantages if he refuses? The Universal Declaration (Article 20(2)) expressly states that no one may be compelled to belong to an association. This provision was not incorporated into the Covenant in view of the "closed-shop system" of labor relations practiced in certain Anglo-Saxon states. But there was no intention to accept compulsory association or assembly in other respects. If everyone has the right freely to decide to join an assembly, he should have the right also to abstain from doing so. Freedom of choice implies a negative as well as a positive decision; freedom of assembly means the freedom to decide to assemble or not to assemble.[107]

Like the other limitation clauses in the Covenant, sentence 2 of Article 21 follows the model of Article 29(2) of the Declaration. Legitimate restrictions are defined *in abstractu,* for designated ends, not by enumeration of specific kinds or forms of restriction.[108] (This method was adopted in order to help defeat suggestions to include in this provision a ban against organizations of a fascist or antidemocratic nature.)[109] And the restrictions had to be necessary "in a democratic society."[110] While there were objections to this term because of its ambiguity, it was finally approved by a weak majority in order to safeguard the freedom of assembly against arbitrary restrictions, although whether this provision will prove effective is open to doubt in view of the diverging concepts of "democracy."

The principle of legality is expressed in Article 21 in a less strict form than in other articles. Elsewhere the restrictions must be "provided" or "prescribed" by law; here it seems sufficient that restrictions are "imposed in conformity with law," doubtless in order to allow wider discretion to administrative authorities acting under general authorizations.[111] Presumably, the police may act on the basis of a general clause authorizing them to act in the interest of public safety.

The purposes for which restrictions can be imposed are several, as in the other clauses: "in the interests of national security or public safety, public order (*ordre public*), the protection of public health or morals or the protection of the rights and freedoms of others." Attempts to reduce the number of criteria or to introduce a more restrictive definition failed.

In sum: "assemblies" can be formal meetings or informal gatherings. They have to be "peaceful," i.e., without uproar, disturbance, or the use of arms. The right is the right of the individual to participate or not to participate; it is also a right of groups or organizations to convoke an assembly or take part in it.

The limitation clause justifies governments in preventing abuse of the guarantee. But the limitations which may be imposed may only be for the purposes indicated and must be necessary in a democratic society. As with limitations on the freedom of expression, the government has a margin of appreciation, but the standards are international standards and a government's reliance on the limitation clause is subject to international scrutiny, notably by the implementing machinery created pursuant to the Covenant.

Freedom of Assembly in the Human Rights Committee

The right of assembly is subject only to one condition, that it be exercised peacefully. Limitations are permitted only in accordance with the limitation clause. Attempts to introduce other conditions or limitations on this right have no basis in the Covenant. Article 48 of the Constitution of the Ukrainian SSR, for instance, guarantees the right of assembly "in order to strengthen and develop the socialist system."[112] That may imply that the right can be exercised exclusively for the aim or purposes indicated. As with freedom of expression, even grounds which might permit restriction cannot be used as a basis for a narrow formulation of the right itself. In other constitutions "the socialist system" is a basis for limitation: freedom of assembly is not guaranteed for purposes hostile to the socialist regime.[113]

Members of the Human Rights Committee expressed doubts as to whether these formulations correspond to the criteria authorized by the limitation clause of Article 21. The representative of Czechoslovakia assured the Committee that this limitation in the Czech Constitution meant the same as "democratic order" or "public order" referred to in the Covenant. One may have serious doubts whether this interpretation is correct. As for the freedom of expression, the state cannot establish the ideology of socialism as *ordre public* to justify restricting peaceful assembly expressing disagreement or even hostility to socialism.

Other criteria for restrictions on assembly cited in state reports to the Human Rights Committee raise smaller issues. Is "public peace" covered by "public order?" [114] Can limitations in the "interest of the community" be understood as being the equivalent of restrictions in the interest of "public order?" [115] In both cases there may be doubt. On the other hand, the government experts of the Council of Europe concluded that the additional criteria mentioned in the European Convention—"for the prevention of disorder or crime"—were included in the notion of public order in the Covenant. [116] This seems sound since the delegates of the United Kingdom in UN organs repeatedly recommended the European wording as being less limiting than "public order."

In a country where different groups of political refugees exiled from their homeland are fighting with each other, it would seem legitimate to impose some restrictions on their right of assembly in the interest of public safety. (One does not even need to have recourse to the somewhat uncertain concept of "public order.") Nevertheless the Federal Republic of Germany entered an express reservation in favor of a general limitation on the right of assembly for foreigners in view of the activities of Croatian organizations in Bavaria. The Austrian government did not follow this example, although it declared that such limitations were desirable. [117] It is doubtful whether the German reservation was necessary.

Some states distinguish between assemblies on private premises and those in public places, requiring either previous notification or even a license for assemblies in public places. [118] This would seem permissible under Article 21, provided the procedure is not used to restrict the right arbitrarily.

Several segments of the population seemed to be the subject of particular concern when the freedom of assembly was discussed in the Committee: the labor force; members of the armed forces; the police; and the public administration in general. [119] Members of the armed forces and of the police are not expressly mentioned in Article 21 (as they are in Article 22). Lawful restrictions of their right to freedom of assembly could therefore be imposed only if they come within one of the criteria expressly mentioned in the limitation clause.

The Right of Association

Many of the issues arising with respect to the right of association, Article 22, are identical with those discussed in connection with the right of assembly. There are only minor differences in wording between the provisions setting forth the two rights and the permissible limitations upon them.[120]

Article 22(1) provides: "Everyone shall have the right to freedom of association with others, including the right to form and join trade unions for the protection of his interests." The right of association includes the right to come together with one or more other persons for social or cultural as well as for economic or political purposes. It includes association with only one other person as well as group assembly, casual as well as formal, single and temporary as well as organized and continuing association. As with the right of assembly, the freedom of association implies the right to decide whether to associate and the freedom not to associate.

Special attention is given to one kind of association, the right to form and join trade unions. Since that is already guaranteed in Article 8 of the Covenant on Economic, Social, and Cultural Rights and is elaborated by several conventions of the International Labour Organisation, one may even say that too much attention has been given to this aspect of the freedom of association. Other equally important forms of association—for example, forming and joining political parties—are not mentioned in the Covenant and were hardly mentioned during the drafting discussions.[121] In any event, the inclusion of the right to form and join trade unions as an example of the right of association would imply the right to form or join other organizations, including political parties; and a one-party system which excludes the formation and activity of other political parties would seem to be contrary to this provision. For this opinion, however, no confirmation can be cited from the drafting history. It has not even been clearly expressed whether this article permits the suppression of political parties. On the one hand, the majority rejected a proposal to provide for the suppression of certain political organizations. But a member of the Commission on Human Rights proposed an express provision excluding the possibility of outlawing political parties, without success.[122] National measures against political parties, under judicial control, were mentioned with apparent approval.[123]

That Article 22 creates obligations largely duplicating those of Article 8 of the Covenant on Economic, Social, and Cultural Rights may raise questions as to their relationship and mutual import. Is Article 8 a *lex specialis* which excludes the application of the general provisions of Article 22 where Article 8 applies? This cannot be, since the two articles do not create identical obligations on identical subjects.[124] The text of Article 8 may, however, give some help for the interpretation of Article 22 of the Covenant on Civil and Political Rights. Additional rights granted only in Article 8, however—for example, the right to strike— cannot be transferred into the other Covenant.

Several delegations tried to introduce into the text more elaborate provisions about trade union rights by copying almost completely the provisions of Article 8 of the Covenant on Economic, Social, and Cultural Rights.[125] They had no success. On the other hand the reference— meaningless as a matter of law—to the International Labour Convention of 1948 on Freedom of Association and Protection of the Right to Organize, which goes much further in the protection of trade union rights, has been maintained as Article 22(3).[126] This reference creates no legal obligation. Those states which are bound by that Convention have to fulfill the obligations undertaken even if their duties under the Covenant do not go as far as the Convention does.[127] Upon states not parties to the Convention new obligations are not imposed by Article 22(3). The reference does not even serve to require that obligations under the Covenant be interpreted in the same sense as obligations under the Convention.

The limitation clause of Article 22(2) is like other such clauses in the Covenant. Unlike Article 21, here restrictions must be "prescribed by law," implying legislative action and leaving less initiative to the executive branch. Restrictions must be "necessary in a democratic society" and must be "in the interests of national security or public safety, public order (*ordre public*), the protection of the public health or morals or the protection of the rights and freedoms of others." But Article 22(2) adds another sentence: "This article shall not prevent the imposition of lawful restrictions on members of the armed forces and of the police in their exercise of this right." There is no such provision, however, as regards members of the administration, as there is in Article 8(1)(c) of the Covenant on Economic, Social, and Cultural Rights. The difference probably reflects the fact that Article 8 of the other Convention includes the right to strike. One may conclude that a state party to both Covenants may restrict the right to strike for the police, for the military, and for members of the administration, but may restrict the right to join unions only for the military and the police, not for members of the administration. It cannot be denied that members of the armed forces and of the police occupy a special position and that their relationship to the state is different from that of other citizens in many regards. The argument that the clause is not necessary since restrictions could be based on "national security" or "public order" is not convincing.[128] Not all the interests in internal discipline, in political "neutralization" of the armed forces, and in protecting political parties against illegitimate influence from the armed forces and from the police, are covered by concepts like national security or public order.

The Right of Association in the Human Rights Committee

The implementation of the freedom of association has raised problems similar to those that appeared with regard to the freedom of assembly. Members of the Committee showed much interest in the formalities to be fulfilled before a new organization could take up activities. It does not seem that they regarded the requirement of such formalities to be contrary to the Covenant. Such formalities may be justified to enable the national authorities to impose legitimate restrictions.[129] Some reports from states reflected legal systems which guarantee the right of association only for certain types of activities or for certain purposes, or which constitutionally exclude independent alternative trade unions. This would seem not to be in conformity with the Covenant.[130]

A major issue discussed involved limitations on labor unions. The government of Chile was asked how it justified the ban on a number of trade unions, since such a ban seemed to be at variance with Article 22. The fact that a trade union did not share the political views of the government could not be accepted as a legitimate ground for dissolution.[131] To admit only company unions but not national trade unions certainly did not correspond to the workers' own wishes. Workers had to be organized at the national level if they were to be successful in defending their interests.[132]

The validity of the "closed-shop system" was raised with the United Kingdom. Does the provision of Article 22 exclude any coercion to join a labor union—even if committed by a private employer?[133] In addition to the fact that a provision like that in the Declaration affirming the right of nonassociation was omitted from the Covenant precisely for this reason, the United Kingdom cited an authoritative ruling of the International Labour Organisation that closed-shop agreements do not infringe the right of freedom of association.[134]

Political Freedoms

The International Covenant on Civil and Political Rights guarantees not only rights and freedoms of a personal character for all individuals; it protects also the individual's rights as a citizen, as a participant in public affairs, as a voter, and as a public servant.[135] Early drafts did not include these rights: proposals for their inclusion came later, from various sources reflecting different ideologies and doubtless having different views as to what the individual's political rights should be. The early reluctance and hesitation, and ideological differences, are particularly evident in the draft that emerged and in its subsequent interpretation.

Article 25 provides: "Every citizen shall have the right and the opportunity, without any of the distinctions mentioned in article 2 and without unreasonable restrictions:

"(a) To take part in the conduct of public affairs, directly or through freely chosen representatives;
"(b) To vote and to be elected at genuine periodic elections which shall be by universal and equal suffrage and shall be held by secret ballot, guaranteeing the free expression of the will of the electors;
"(c) To have access, on general terms of equality, to public service in his country."

The provision begins with an "umbrella clause," or "chapeau," applicable to the three rights enumerated in the three subparagraphs that follow.[136] The introductory clause provides that every citizen shall have the right and opportunity described later "without any of the distinctions mentioned in Article 2 and without unreasonable restrictions." Since Article 2(1) applies to all the rights in the Covenant, reference to it here adds no further legal obligation but was doubtless made for additional emphasis.

Since Article 2 of the Covenant prohibits discrimination of any kind, the clause regarding "restrictions" can only refer to restrictions which are not invidious distinctions like those prohibited by Article 2, but other grounds for exclusion. For instance, depriving persons of the right to vote because they are mentally incompetent, or requiring professional capacities for access to public service, are permissible if they are not "unreasonable." What restrictions are reasonable may not always be agreed upon, and again, the state has a margin of appreciation, but subject to international review and scrutiny. There may be cases in which it is not easy to distinguish between reasonable restrictions and improper discrimination. In states where a large majority of the population is able to read and write and where sufficient educational facilities are available, a literacy test before exercising the right to vote may be reasonable and legitimate.[137] If, however, a literacy test has the consequence of excluding an entire racial group from the right to participate in elections—as in certain South American states—and especially if there is evidence that such exclusion is its purpose, the test would be illegal as a measure of racial discrimination.

After the umbrella clause, three single rights follow: the right to take part in the conduct of public affairs, the right to vote, and the right of access to public service.[138] These rights differ from all other rights enshrined in the Covenant: other rights are ensured to "everyone" or to "every human being"; Article 25 guarantees these rights only to citizens. Of course, a state may do more than it is obliged to do under the Covenant and may admit aliens to one or more of these rights.

Participation in the conduct of public affairs can be realized either "directly or through freely chosen representatives." The text makes it clear that the concept of "participation" has to be understood in a broad sense. Subparagraph (a) does not guarantee direct democracy, as by referendum, but accepts the principle of representation. It is left open whether the representatives are to be chosen directly by the people or indirectly. Neither indirect election of one chamber of a parliament, nor of a President, nor the appointment of members of the government or the administration, is excluded. A proposal that "all organs of authority" should be chosen by direct elections was rejected.[139] The requirement that every citizen have the right to take part in the conduct of public affairs is satisfied if appointed officials are in some way responsible to elected representatives. The citizen has a right to participate "in the conduct of public affairs." The term is broader than "in the government of his country."[140] It includes all levels of government as well as of administration. Whether access to the judiciary is also included was not discussed.

The right to vote and the right to be elected—special instances of the right to participate in the conduct of public affairs—appear here as independent rights. When this provision was adopted during the elaboration of the Declaration, its main purpose was to guarantee freedom of elections: elections should be held and they should be free, without coercion or pressure. The name for such a requirement was found relatively late in the drafting process: elections should be "genuine and authentic."[141]

The principal question is whether one can interpret the term "genuine" as covering an election in which not more than one candidate or one list is presented to the voters and no opposition to the ruling party is allowed.[142] When the Universal Declaration was drafted, there were strong expressions that genuine elections required a genuine choice among parties and candidates and the right to vote against the government, free of any pressure. Discussions during the drafting of the Covenant were less candid. In the final discussions of the draft Covenant in the Third Committee in 1961 the delegate of Chile reported that the adjective "genuine" in subparagraph (b) had been used to guarantee "that all elections of every kind faithfully reflected the opinion of the population and to protect the electors against governmental pressure and fraud."[143]

This very diplomatic formulation avoided any allusion to a choice between at least two parties or to opposition against the government;[144] perhaps it was sought to make it possible for single-party states to adhere to the Covenant. But it is difficult to avoid the conclusion that an election in which voters have no meaningful choice between parties or candidates and cannot express that choice without compulsion or fear is not "genuine" but a violation of Article 25.[145]

Elections must be universal: everyone should be entitled to vote. There was, however, consensus that minors and lunatics might be excluded. The same consensus did not exist with regard to those "without legal capacity," a basis of exclusion which might have opened the way to arbitrary exclusions.[146] Any qualifications based on property or the level of income were considered inadmissible.[147]

The provision for a secret vote was controversial but its proponents ultimately prevailed. It was clear that there should be a distinction between the casting of the ballot (which had to be in secret) and the counting of the votes (which should be in public).[148]

Like the Universal Declaration, Article 25(2) provides that free elections shall be by "equal suffrage." Equal suffrage means that everyone has the same voting power; it does not imply that each vote has the same effect.[149]

Several governments objected that "equal suffrage" seemed to mandate proportional representation. This preoccupation seems unfounded. An electoral system "based on equality" may require proportional representation; the same is not true of election by "equal suffrage." "Suffrage" indicates the individual right of the voter and says nothing about the electoral system. Nor does it require equal effect, only that each vote be given the same weight.[150]

In comparison with the right to vote, few rules are given regarding the right to be elected. Whether age requirements are valid depends on whether they are reasonable. The same is true for a requirement that citizens may be elected to certain political offices only after they have been citizens for a certain period.[151]

The discussion of the right of access to public service confirms the thesis developed earlier. While no discrimination contrary to Article 2 should be admitted, certain requirements in the interest of the efficiency of public service could not be regarded as discriminatory. Among the reasonable requirements mentioned was a certain standard of education. Disqualifying disabilities included unsoundness of mind, conviction for high treason, or other serious offenses. Questions were raised as to whether undischarged bankrupts or people with a personal financial interest could be barred from public service under the "reasonable restrictions" clause, but no answer was given.[152]

The words "on general terms of equality" were evidently chosen to mean that specific restrictions in the interest of the efficiency of the public service would not violate the nondiscrimination rule. The term was inserted "in order to prevent certain privileged groups from monopolizing public service and to guarantee that the State had the opportunity to appoint to such services persons of the right age, competence, etc."[153]

Political Rights in the Human Rights Committee

In view of the widely differing political systems in the world, it is astonishing how few reservations or declarations to Article 25 have been made upon signature or ratification of the Covenant. The only politically substantial one was by Chile, relating to the application of Article 25(b) during the state of siege. Those by the United Kingdom to paragraphs (b) and (c) are designed to shield either remnants of the colonial regime (in the case of Hong Kong) or of traditional institutions (as in the case of the Isle of Man).[154]

This lack of reservations may have several explanations. Not all states are prepared to disclose and call attention to their own inadequacies by reserving the right to maintain them. In this case, however, another reason is probable. Article 25 does not establish clear standards for democratic and representative government. Instead of proclaiming fundamental principles, it guarantees only particular forms and formal institutions which are common to a variety of political systems but which do not play the same roles in the different systems. Universal and equal suffrage, for example, can be said to exist in almost all political systems, but it provides authentic popular government in very few. The term "genuine" election is not defined.

The wide scope permitted by the article appears also in later interpretations. The first right, namely, "to take part in the conduct of public affairs directly or through freely chosen representatives" is of a very general character. It leaves open the choice, for example, between direct and representative democracy. Two governments presenting the Covenant to their parliaments explained that this right neither conferred a right on the citizens to decide on public matters by referendum nor to elect all organs of the executive or the judiciary. The experts of the Council of Europe shared this opinion and added that it would be sufficient if those organs were elected which were usually formed by elections, mainly legislative organs.[155] The experts stressed also that such choices were open, since under Article 25 the rights are to be enjoyed "without unreasonable restrictions." This, however, misplaces the emphasis of the article and is undesirable as a mode of interpretation. That clause of the "chapeau" is designed to protect the beneficiary of the rights against illegitimate limitations; it should not be used to interpret and weaken the rights and obligations as such. The argument also is not necessary to support the conclusion because the form and the extent of civic participation is left open by Article 25(a). Not even direct elections are required.

Special problems are presented by legislative bodies which are not elected but appointed, like the Senate of Canada or the British House of Lords. In the Human Rights Committee it was asked whether the hereditary element of the House of Lords was consistent with Article 25(a).[156] The British government drew attention to the fact that hereditary peers have no vote in the election of the House of Commons, and have to choose between the peerage and membership in the House of Commons. "Because of differences in the powers and constitutional role of the two Houses, hereditary membership in the House of Lords is not seen necessarily as an advantage by those who wished to take a prominent part in public life."[157]

The right to vote and to be elected (Article 25(b)) is stronger and has a wider field of application than the corresponding guarantee of the European Convention.[158] Comparing the two texts, the European Experts concluded that Article 25(b) applied not only to national elections but also to regional and local elections, because the legislature is not expressly mentioned in the text. This *argumentum e contrario* is not absolutely convincing, though the result may be correct. In the discussions in the Human Rights Committee, regional and local elections did not receive much attention. The interest of its members focused on two questions: exclusion from the right to vote or to be elected, and presentation of candidates in elections.

Exclusion from the right to vote and to be elected was discussed at the drafting of Article 25(b). During these discussions, it was recognized that certain restrictions are reasonable and not controversial, for example, minimum age requirements,[159] the exclusion of lunatics, mentally diseased or disabled persons, and minimum residency requirements. Such restrictions appear in numerous reports of state parties. The exclusion of "disqualified persons," however, might be questionable. If disqualification has been pronounced by a judge for a certain time, in connection with punishment for some particular offense, for instance those connected with elections or for high treason, such exclusions may be reasonable. The same would be true under the principle of separation of powers for the exclusion of military personnel in active service, or public officials, from the right to be elected.[160] On the other hand, those in the military by compulsory service should not be denied the right to vote. Neither should convicts generally, irrespective of the duration of the penalty. The denial of the right to vote for bankruptcy still found in some countries is highly questionable. Though this exclusion cannot be regarded as a discrimination based on property, outlawing such persons is medieval and cannot be accepted as reasonable. The case most extensively discussed was the exclusion of illiterates in Ecuador, which Committee members found incompatible with Article 25(b).[161]

Several states were asked how candidates for elections were chosen. Bulgaria admitted that they were presented by the Communist Party and that no independent candidates were admitted.[162] The representative of the USSR gave a clearer picture of the procedure for nominating candidates. They are nominated at general meetings of public and social organizations. Electoral commissions include their names in bulletins. Every elector may strike out any candidate's name and insert one of his own choice.[163] But who is the "electoral commission," and how is it composed? Rumania and Czechoslovakia reported that all candidates are chosen by the Party. The issue whether an institutionalized one-party system was compatible with the Covenant was raised but no clear positions were taken by members of the Committee;[164] it would seem that Article 25 requires that the possibility of peaceful change by genuine partisan elections should be open.[165] There was discussion also of the permissibility of prohibiting certain political parties in order to protect a multiparty system. Members of the Committee expressed concern about the system in the Federal Republic of Germany which permits the Constitutional Court to outlaw some political parties.[166] Such measures can be justified under Article 5(1) of the Covenant if they are taken in defense of the rights and freedoms recognized in the Covenant and if the necessary procedural guarantees are given. That a suppression of all political parties by the executive—as in Chile[167]—is incompatible with the Covenant is beyond any doubt.

The right to have access to public service (Article 25(c)) certainly gives no right to an individual to occupy a particular office or charge.[168] What is guaranteed is a right of *access,* not a guarantee of enjoyment. This guarantee of access, moreover, does not exclude a policy that certain key positions in the civil service should be filled by persons who adhere to the party or policies of the government.[169] Members of the Committee, however, asked whether all civil servants—not only those in key positions—can be obliged by law to adhere to the constitutional order of the state and to actively defend that system, as in the Federal Republic of Germany. Members of the Committee made critical observations in this regard.[170] The government representative argued that special loyalty could be requested, since civil servants were appointed for life. The propriety of the methods used for inquiring into the political position of applicants for the civil service remains questionable. Since that discussion, the authorities of the Federal Republic of Germany have reexamined their practices in this respect in order to bring them into line with Articles 19, 22, and 25 of the Covenant.

It is astonishing to read in the reports of the Committee that certain states which require of their civil servants absolute conformity, and which have a well-known lack of tolerance, declared that access to public service is open exclusively on the basis of qualification and merit without any distinction on the ground of political opinion.[171]

The political freedoms discussed in this chapter are fundamental in two senses. Individual "self-government" is crucial to individual autonomy and dignity. And only where there is authentic popular sovereignty can the individual hope to enjoy the other rights enshrined in the Covenant as well as the economic, social, and cultural rights guaranteed in the other Covenant. Unlike most other rights in the Covenant, however, those I have discussed engage deep ideological differences. The prospects for the authentic enjoyment of these rights in many parts of the world are not bright. But those who care for human dignity cannot neglect these fundamental rights or accept misinterpretations and distortions of what the drafters of the Covenant intended.

10

Equality and Nondiscrimination

B. G. RAMCHARAN

EQUALITY AND NONDISCRIMINATION constitute the dominant single theme of the Covenant. Equality is of course implied in that the rights recognized by the Covenant are rights of all human beings equally, and the various provisions apply to "all persons," "everyone," "every human being," "no one." The preamble proclaims "the equal and inalienable rights of all members of the human family." By Article 2(1) a state undertakes to respect and ensure the rights recognized by the Covenant "to all individuals within its territory and subject to its jurisdiction . . . without distinction of any kind, such as race, colour, sex, language, religion, political or other opinion, national or social origin, property, birth or other status." Article 3 provides for "the equal right of men and women" to enjoy all the rights set forth in the Covenant. When a state derogates from rights in time of public emergency (Article 4(1)), the measures taken may "not involve discrimination" on forbidden grounds. Article 26 proclaims equality before the law and requires the equal protection of the law without discrimination. The law must prohibit and provide effective protection against discrimination (Article 26), and any advocacy of national, racial, or religious hatred that constitutes incitement to discrimination, hostility, or violence must be prohibited (Article 20). Several of the provisions protecting particular rights include explicit prohibitions of discrimination in regard to those rights.

Neither "equality" nor "nondiscrimination," however, is self-defining and beyond the need for interpretation, and none of these admonitions in the Covenant provides guidance as to the scope and implication of these norms. In fact, the content and reach of the principles of equal-

All views expressed in this essay are those of the author in his personal capacity.

ity and nondiscrimination are not agreed; in the national law of several countries, similar constitutional provisions have spawned an extensive and complex jurisprudence. There is also debate as to the meaning of some of the grounds for discrimination that are expressly precluded by different provisions in the Covenant.

While the Covenant does not define the relevant terms, there is some evidence of the purpose and intent of the draftsmen in the *travaux préparatoires*. For the framers of the Covenant, perhaps, the meaning of equality and nondiscrimination went without saying, deriving from its prime place as a fundamental human right and incorporating the guidance provided by the massive literature on equality and nondiscrimination in moral, legal, and political philosophy; in the constitutional and other law of different countries; in human rights jurisprudence generally; and in international law.

Equality and Nondiscrimination as Fundamental Human Rights

The inherent dignity and "the equal and inalienable rights of all members of the human family" were recognized in the opening lines of the Universal Declaration of Human Rights as "the foundation of freedom, justice and peace in the world." The claim to equality, said the late Sir Hersch Lauterpacht, "is in a substantial sense the most fundamental of the rights of man. It occupies the first place in most written constitutions. It is the starting point of all other liberties."[1]

The bedrock nature of the principles of equality and nondiscrimination in the international law of human rights were admirably brought out in an address by the Head of the Federal Political Department of Switzerland at the opening of the World Conference to Combat Racism and Racial Discrimination on August 14, 1978:

Of all human rights, the right to equality is one of the most important. It is linked to the concepts of liberty and justice, and is manifested through the observance of two fundamental and complementary principles of international law. The first of these principles, that "all human beings are born free and equal in dignity and rights," appears in the 1948 Universal Declaration of Human Rights; the second, the principle of nondiscrimination, has been solemnly reaffirmed in Article 1 of the Charter of the United Nations. It is upon those two principles that all the instruments on human rights adopted since 1945 are based. . . . The prohibition of discrimination has become a norm of positive law, as has been recognized by the International Court of Justice in respect of racist practices: To establish . . . and to enforce, distinctions, exclusions, restrictions and limitations exclusively based on grounds of race, colour, descent or national or ethnic origin which constitute a denial of fundamental human rights is a flagrant violation of the purposes and principles of the Charter.[2]

Religion

The principles of equality and nondiscrimination are reflected in the great religious and philosophical systems of the world. One of the tenets of Chinese philosophy provides: "If everyone adopts universal love and if everyone loves others as himself, will there still be those who are not dutiful?" Therefore, let "the whole world adopt universal love."[3] Hindu philosophy teaches that "one who, with equality, sees himself in all beings and all beings within himself . . . attains to the state of self-rule."[4] For Judaism and Christianity, "the common human ancestor in God's 'image' described in Genesis and the fatherhood of God to all men (Malachi 2:10) imply the essential equality of all men, supporting the idea of rights which all enjoy by virtue of their common humanity"; also "thou shalt love thy neighbour as thyself."[5] Islam commands that "he who believes in God, let him act kindly towards his neighbour."[6]

Humanitarian Movements

The principles of equality and nondiscrimination helped to inspire some of the great humanitarian movements of modern history—including the English, French, American, and Russian declarations on human rights—and the movements for the abolition of slavery and for the protection of minorities. They were amply reflected in various minorities treaties concluded after the end of the First World War.[7] They have also been included in various national constitutions or declarations of human rights.[8]

The UN Charter

In the period after the Second World War, the principles of equality and nondiscrimination were enshrined, inter alia, in the United Nations Charter (1945), the Universal Declaration of Human Rights (1948), the Charter of the OAS (1948), the American Declaration on the Rights and Duties of Man (1948), the International Law Commission's Draft

Declaration on the Rights and Duties of States (1949), the European Convention for the Protection of Human Rights and Fundamental Freedoms (1950), the ILO Convention and Recommendation Concerning Discrimination in Respect of Employment and Occupation (1958), the International Convention on the Elimination of All Forms of Racial Discrimination (1965), the International Covenants on Human Rights (1966), the American Convention on Human Rights (1969), and the UNESCO Declaration on Race and Racial Prejudice (1978).

International Customary Law

The principles of equality and nondiscrimination are now widely acknowledged as forming part of international customary law. Some have even argued that at least as regards consistent patterns of gross violation by government and societies, these principles are part of international *jus cogens,* peremptory norms binding on all as superior law. Support for the view that equality and nondiscrimination are part of international customary law comes from authoritative international instruments such as those cited in the preceding section, authoritative legal institutions such as the International Law Commission, and the International Court of Justice,[9] state practice, including pronouncements by worldwide international conferences,[10] and authoritative publicists.[11]

In their pleadings in the South West Africa cases (*Ethiopia* and *Liberia v. South Africa*), the governments of Ethiopia and Liberia invoked "a generally accepted international human rights norm of non-discrimination."[12] In the Barcelona Traction case, the International Court of Justice included among the obligations of states *erga omnes* "the principles and rules concerning the basic rights of the human person including protection from slavery and racial discrimination."[13] In its Advisory Opinion of 1971 on Namibia the International Court of Justice stated that "to establish . . . and to enforce distinctions, exclusions, restrictions and limitations exclusively based on grounds of race, colour, descent or national or ethnic origin . . . constitutes a denial of fundamental human rights" and "is a flagrant violation of the purposes and principles of the Charter."[14]

Article 9 of the UNESCO Declaration on Race and Racial Prejudice, adopted in 1978, reaffirmed that "the principle of the equality in dignity and rights of all human beings and all peoples, irrespective of race, colour and origin, is a generally accepted and recognized principle of international law."[15] The commentary to this provision states that it underlined, in forceful terms, the principle that now constitutes one of the foundations of international law: the equality of all human beings and all peoples. This principle, which was established by the United Nations Charter, has been confirmed and developed by a whole series of instruments adopted under the auspicies of the United Nations and the specialized agencies, and has been applied by the International Court of Justice on many occasions in its latest legal decisions.[16]

Articles 2(1), 3, and 26 of the International Covenant on Civil and Political Rights set forth five related principles: the principle of equal enjoyment of rights; the general principle of equality and the corollary principle of equality between men and women; the principle of equality before the law and equality before the courts; the principle of equal protection of the law; and the principle of nondiscrimination. The preparatory works of the Covenant indicate that notwithstanding differences in terminology, the principles of equality and nondiscrimination contained in the International Covenant on Civil and Political Rights were intended to be, in effect, the same principles as those contained in the Charter, the Universal Declaration, and the International Covenant on Economic, Social, and Cultural Rights. The meaning of the concepts of equality and nondiscrimination in all these instruments is to be taken from the modern international law of human rights. Thus, in the Third Committee reference was made "to discrimination in its classical juridical meaning,"[17] "to discrimination . . . in international usage."[18] It may therefore be presumed that the meaning of the concepts of equality and nondiscrimination in the modern international law of human rights were incorporated in the Covenant in all their amplitude. If these principles also have the character of *jus cogens,* that would be relevant to the permissibility of derogations from or limitations upon them. The status of these principles in international customary law also has bearing on the application and implementation of the Covenant both in the national legal systems of states parties to the Covenant and internationally. If, for example, under the law of a state party, the Covenant is incorporated and may be invoked in national law, an individual may by reference to the Covenant's provisions on equality and nondiscrimination invoke also their meaning in international customary law. States parties to the Covenant, and the Human Rights Committee, may judge a state's compliance with the Covenant by referring to the meaning of the principles of equality and nondiscrimination in international customary law.

The History of the Principal Articles

Article 2(1), the general, comprehensive equality and nondiscrimination clause, and Article 26, providing for equal protection and equality before the law, were initiated in the Commission on Human Rights. Article 3, providing for gender equality, was added in the General Assembly.[19] It was recognized that equality between men and women was already provided for under Article 2(1), but it was decided to include an express provision thereon for emphasis.[20]

In regard to Articles 2 and 26 in particular, various concepts were used in the debates without distinction. Thus, one sees references interchangeably to equality, equality before the law, equality before the courts, equal protection of the law, equality of the sexes, nondiscrimination, and nondistinction. This loose use of terminology suggests that one should seek the meaning of these articles in the light of all the relevant factors. Over the time span during which the articles were drafted (1947–1966), moreover, the membership of the UN and of the various organs was transformed and different coalitions emerged. This resulted in some inconsistencies. For instance, in the Third Committee one year, the word "nondistinction" in the International Covenant on Economic, Social, and Cultural Rights was deliberately changed to "nondiscrimination"; the following year, faced with the same issue with respect to the Covenant on Civil and Political Rights, the word "nondistinction" was left intact in Article 2(1).

Notwithstanding the holocaust during the Second World War, resulting from racial and ethnic discrimination carried to its terrible extreme, there was hesitancy on the part of some of the metropolitan or great powers to accept the implications of the principles of equality and nondiscrimination; in particular, the application of these principles to economic, social, and cultural rights was strenuously resisted. It is substantially due to a coalition of scholars, nongovernmental organizations,[21] and representatives of enlightened governments that these principles achieved the level of recognition that they did in the Covenant. The rise to independence of new states also significantly influenced the final texts.

The three articles were largely developed during the same period as the provisions on nondiscrimination in the Universal Declaration; the International Covenant on Economic, Social, and Cultural Rights; and the International Declaration and the International Convention on the Elimination of All Forms of Racial Discrimination. There is, therefore, a definite interconnection among the nondiscrimination provisions in these instruments, and the meaning of the provisions in any of these instruments draws on the related provisions of the other instruments.[22]

Positive and Negative Statement of the Same Principle

Equality and nondiscrimination may be seen as affirmative and negative statements of the same principle. Like the Charter and the Universal Declaration, the Covenant refers to "the equal and inalienable rights of all members of the human family," declaring the entitlement of all human beings to all human rights. That is reinforced by repeated references in particular articles to "all human beings," "everyone," "no one." The positive affirmation of the rights of all human beings is reinforced by Article 3, which is not couched as a prohibition on discrimination on account of gender but as an affirmation of the entitlement of women as well as men to human rights generally. Equality is decreed also in the requirement of equality before the law and equal protection of the laws, in equal access to public service and suffrage.

In adding nondiscrimination clauses to supplement the affirmative mandate of equality, the Covenant was following the UN Charter and the Universal Declaration. In all these instruments a nondiscrimination clause was added not merely for emphasis, but also from an abundance of caution. Nondiscrimination may indeed be implied in mandates of equality. But mandates of equality do not imply absolute equality without any distinction. Equality, it has sometimes been said, means equal treatment for those equally situated and, indeed, equal treatment for unequals is itself a form of inequality. The law, moreover, rarely applies to all situations and involves selections and classifications among objects based on criteria deemed to be relevant. The general requirements of equality or equal protection of the laws, then, does not mean that a state cannot select among objects for regulation or draw distinctions among them. The nondiscrimination clauses are designed to make clear that certain factors are unacceptable as grounds for distinction. Thus Article 2(1) provides that as regards Covenant rights generally, they must be ensured to all without "distinction of any kind such as race, colour, sex, language, religion, political or other opinion, national or social origin, property, birth or other status." The state must also guarantee to all persons equal and effective protection against discrimination "on any ground such as" these same listed grounds. Presumably, however, despite the principle of equality, some rights may be denied or discrimination practiced on other grounds, for example, for conviction for crime. Some possible grounds for distinction, moreover, are not mentioned, and some rights clearly imply that exclusions or distinctions are permitted on grounds of citizenship or age, for example, as regards voting; or distinctions between aliens and nationals for purposes of the right to enter a country.

Equality

An Independent Right

Although equality is implied in the fact that all human beings have the same human rights, the emphasis on equality indicates that it is a right additional to and independent of other specific enumerated rights.

Equality was defined as an independent right in a memorandum submitted by the Secretary-General of the United Nations to the Sub-Commission on Prevention of Discrimination and Protection of Minorities in 1949, one of the documents contributing to the common pool of ideas which influenced the drafting of the Covenant. The memorandum declared that the term "equality" in the Universal Declaration of Human Rights referred to moral and juridical equality, equality in dignity, formal equality in rights, and equality of opportunity, but did not imply material equality in result or in fact; it did not imply that all individuals must enjoy the benefits which those rights are designed to ensure. That is because the principle of equality as a human right does not exclude distinctions based on differences of two kinds, which are generally considered admissible and justified: (a) differentiation based on character and conduct imputable to the individual for which he may be properly held responsible (examples are industriousness, idleness, carefulness, carelessness, decency, indecency, merit, demerit, delinquency, lawfulness, etc.); and (b) differentiation based on individual qualities, which in spite of not being qualities for which the individual can be held responsible, are relevant to social values and may be taken into account (examples are physical and mental capacities, talent, etc.). On the other hand, moral and juridical equality exclude any differentiation based on grounds which have no relevance to merit or social value and should not be considered as having any social or legal meaning, whether they are innate, such as color, race, and sex; or social generic categories, such as language, political or other opinions, national or social origin, property, birth or other status.

During the drafting of the Covenants it was generally recognized that the concept of equality referred to both de jure and de facto equality.[23] This was addressed by the representative of the Ukrainian SSR in regard to the nondiscrimination provisions of the International Covenant on Economic, Social, and Cultural Rights. The Committee, he noted, was "elaborating principles of *de jure* equality; from those principles would arise the *de facto* equalization of human rights. It would be wrong to confuse those two concepts . . . equality of rights went further than mere nondiscrimination; it implied the existence of positive rights in all the spheres dealt with in the draft Covenant."[24]

Similarly, during the consideration of Article 3 of the Covenant on Civil and Political Rights, it was stressed that the "article did not merely state the principle of equality but enjoined States to make equality an effective reality, . . . and that every effort should be made to do away with all prejudice in that field. . . . The articles enshrined a principle of elementary justice, namely, equality of rights in a world where, even in the most advanced countries, women were still denied many rights."[25]

Equality before the Law and Equal Protection of the Law

As submitted by the Commission on Human Rights to the General Assembly, the draft of what is now Article 26 stated: "All persons are equal before the law. The law shall prohibit any discrimination and guarantee to all persons equal and effective protection against discrimination on any ground such as race, colour, sex, language, religion, political or other opinion, national or social origin, property, birth or other status." The first clause, affirming that "all persons are equal before the law," follows Article 7 of the Universal Declaration of Human Rights, and the Commission considered that it was important to restate that principle in the Covenant. In reply to objections that this clause might be held to mean that the law should be the same for everyone and that it might preclude the imposition of reasonable legal disabilities upon certain categories of individuals such as minors or persons of unsound mind, it was explained that the provision was intended to ensure equality, not identity of treatment, and would not preclude reasonable differentiations between individuals or groups of individuals on grounds that were relevant and material.[26]

When Article 26 was considered in the Third Committee, there was an important debate on a proposal to insert the words "in this respect" in the second sentence of the article. Both supporters and opponents of this proposal recognized that the insertion of these words could have the effect of limiting the reference to nondiscrimination in the second sentence to the content of the first sentence, i.e., discrimination on the grounds indicated would be prohibited only as applied to the enjoyment of equality before the law, i.e., in court. At the same time as the words "in this respect" were inserted in the second sentence, however, the first sentence, which had referred merely to equality before the law, was amended to state that all persons were entitled without any discrimination to the equal protection of the law (as provided in Article 7 of the Universal Declaration). With this clear affirmation of the principle of nondiscrimination, the addition of the words "in this respect" in the second sentence referred to both clauses of the first sentence and in fact restored the general nondiscrimination principle.[27] A state party must prohibit and guarantee effective protection against discrimination on the forbidden grounds, not only in court but wherever it detracts from the equal protection of the laws.[28]

The practice in the Human Rights Committee supports the broad interpretation of Article 26. During the examination of the report of the United Kingdom, it was pointed out that the authors of the report had used Dicey's concept of equality before the law as part of "the rule of law," that is, equality before the courts. The discussion of the report supported the view that while equality before the courts was indeed included in Article 26 and was expressly required by Article 14 of the Covenant, Article 26 referred not only to equality before the courts but also to the general "egalitarian" concept of "equal protection of the law" in the sense of nondiscrimination. Thus, Article 26 is not restrictive but rather has the wider egalitarian meaning in the accepted post–Second World War definition which prohibits all discrimination.[29] Similarly, during the consideration of a report of Sweden it was said that "Article 26 of the Covenant referred not merely to the, as it were, negative or passive aspect of the prevention of discrimination through guarantees of equality before the law—an aspect already covered by Article 14 of the Covenant—but also to the positive aspect of 'active protection against discrimination' on the various grounds enumerated. . . ."[30] The representative of the government of Sweden replied that he "agreed that Article 26 . . . called for positive action for the elimination of discrimination, and not merely passive measures of prevention."[31]

In 1970, the Sub-Commission on Prevention of Discrimination and Protection of Minorities adopted Principles of Equality in the Administration of Justice which may be relevant in interpreting the scope of the equality before the law and equal protection of the law provided in the Covenant. These include nondiscrimination on the grounds indicated in "equal access to the judiciary and the legal profession" and in the enjoyment of the basic elements of a fair, prompt, public trial before a competent, independent, impartial tribunal, with a right to appeal.[32]

Equal Enjoyment of Enumerated Rights

Article 2 of the Covenant requires states parties to respect and to ensure "the rights recognized in the present Covenant, without distinction of any kind, such as race, colour, sex," etc. Unlike Article 26, this article does not forbid distinction or discrimination generally, but only distinctions and discriminations in the enjoyment of the rights recognized in the Covenant. It would not, then, forbid discrimination in the enjoyment of benefits that are not rights recognized by the Covenant. But since one of the rights recognized by the Covenant is the equal protection of the laws (Article 26), distinctions forbidden by that Article are also violations of Article 2(1). Discrimination in the enjoyment of any benefit—say a tax rebate—that constituted a denial of equal protection of the laws would be a violation of Article 26, and presumably also of Article 2(1). Discrimination in the enjoyment of a particular right in the Covenant would be a violation of Article 2(1) and perhaps of Article 26 as well, even if the distinction did not involve a deprivation and violation of the particular substantive right. Thus, for example, a law setting a reasonable age for marriage does not violate Article 23(2). But setting a different (though also reasonable) age for marriage for members of a particular race or religion would violate Article 2(1) (and probably Article 26), even if did not violate Article 23.

Article 2(1) requires that the enjoyment of rights be respected "without distinction of any kind, such as race, colour, sex," etc. The clear implication is that the grounds enumerated are not exclusive and other grounds for distinction are also barred. But the grounds barred are those like race, colour, etc., "or other status." Even some "status" may be a permissible ground for denial of rights if it is relevant, for example being underage, mentally incompetent, and for some specified purposes, alienage. The Covenant does not forbid deprivation or limitation of rights for misconduct, for example upon conviction for crime.

The preparatory works do not address these or other issues that may arise, and it will be up to the Human Rights Committee to provide guidance through practice. Some guidance is provided by the application of the principle of nondiscrimination in Article 14 of the European

Convention on Human Rights. Article 14 provides that "the enjoyment of the rights and freedoms set forth in this convention shall be secured without discrimination on any ground. . . ."[33] The practice of the European Commission and Court of Human Rights indicates, first, that the principle has been held to be guaranteed only in relation to the rights and freedoms set forth in the Convention.[34] Second, it has been applied subject to a "margin of appreciation."[35] Third, in the *Sunday Times* case (1979), the European Court of Human Rights reaffirmed that "according to the Court's established case-law, Article 14 safeguards individuals, or groups of individuals, placed in comparable situations, from all discrimination in the enjoyment of the rights and freedoms set forth in the other normative provisions of the Convention and Protocols."[36] However, as held earlier in the *Belgian Linguistic* cases, Article 14 may be violated by discrimination in the enjoyment of a right under the Convention even if there is no violation of the article of the Convention recognizing that right.[37]

Nondiscrimination

In addition to the principles of equality and equal protection, the Covenant prohibits discrimination on particular grounds. Article 2 prohibits discrimination on forbidden grounds in respecting or ensuring the rights recognized by the Covenant. Article 26 forbids discrimination on the same grounds in respect of equality before the law and the equal protection of the law. Discrimination on forbidden grounds is expressly prohibited also in the enjoyment of particular rights, e.g., the rights of children (Article 18).

Article 2 forbids discrimination in the enjoyment of the rights of the Covenant. But Article 26 forbids discrimination with respect to the equal protection of the laws generally. It was argued that such a nondiscrimination clause was unnecessary in view of the general clause in Article 2, which would apply to Article 26 as well as to other rights. Some urged that even the most enlightened government might find it difficult to accept a general nondiscrimination clause applicable to rights, benefits, and laws generally (not merely to rights recognized in the Covenant). A general nondiscrimination clause might forbid also the distinctions all states make between citizens and aliens. The proposed clause might apply also to private discrimination in personal or social relationships which are not, and should not be, within the realm of law. On the other hand, others maintained that it was not enough to affirm that all were equal before the law; the article should also lay down a definite principle that there should be no discrimination on any ground such as race, colour, sex, etc. Freedom from discrimination should be established in the Covenant as an independent additional right of general applicability, not merely as a principle governing only the enjoyment of the rights recognized in the Covenant. The latter view eventually prevailed.[38]

Discrimination versus Distinction

During the drafting of the covenants, the question arose whether the word "discrimination" or "distinction" should be used. In the end both words were used interchangeably, even within the same Covenant.

During the consideration of Article 26 of the Covenant on Civil and Political Rights in the Third Committee in 1961, differences between "discrimination" and "distinction" were stressed by some representatives. The representative of Italy preferred the word "discrimination" because "there were cases in which the law was justified in making distinctions between individuals or groups, but the purpose of the article was to prohibit discrimination, in the sense of unfavorable and odious distinctions which lacked any objective or reasonable basis."[39] The following year, during the drafting of Article 2(1) of the International Covenant on Economic, Social, and Cultural Rights, the Italian, Argentinian, and Mexican delegations moved for an amendment which would replace the word "distinction" with the word "discrimination" on the grounds, inter alia, that "some distinction might be justified— for example, preferential treatment for certain underprivileged groups—and that it was discrimination which should be condemned." Moreover, they added, the term "discrimination" appeared three times in Article 24 of the draft Covenant on Civil and Political Rights which the Committee had adopted at the sixteenth session (1102nd meeting).[40] Some delegations, however, found that the proposal to replace "distinction" with "discrimination" "was questionable on legal grounds."

> First, the United Nations Charter and the Universal Declaration both employed the word distinction. Secondly, the logical meaning of 'without distinction' . . . was not that States should practice non-discrimination but they should act independently of such distinctions as might exist. . . . To make that point clear, it might even be useful to insert the words 'independently' in the place of 'without.' If the word 'discrimination' was used, in what . . . would be a misinterpretation of the intention of the authors, a State might apply unequal treatment to different groups of people and claim that that did not constitute discrimination but distinct treatment of

distinct groups. That risk was all the greater as there was no generally adopted legal definition of discrimination. Lastly, 'distinction' was the word used in legislative texts and constitutions, among them the French Constitution, which was often regarded as a model.[41]

In the end, however, it was decided to insert the word "discrimination" in the International Covenant on Economic, Social, and Cultural Rights. When the Third Committee considered a similar provision of the International Covenant on Civil and Political Rights the following year, the Italian representative again suggested that Article 2(1) should use the word "discrimination" instead of "distinction." However, the approach of the previous year did not prevail and, in the circumstances, the Italian representative did not insist on his point. As a result, the International Covenant on Economic, Social, and Cultural Rights uses the term "discrimination" and the International Covenant on Civil and Political Rights uses the word "distinction." It is clear from both debates that the drafters intended to include in both covenants the higher level of protection whichever word was used. The protagonists of each word felt that it would give the higher level of protection.[42] It appears clearly from the preparatory works of both covenants, however, that both terms exclude only arbitrary or unjust distinction or discrimination.[43]

A memorandum which the Division of Human Rights of the UN Secretariat submitted to the Sub-Commission on Prevention of Discrimination and Protection of Minorities states: "Discrimination implies, essentially, unequal and unfavorable treatment, either by the bestowal of favours or the imposition of burdens. Any of a number of grounds may underlie such unequal treatment. Four of them are mentioned in the Charter—race, sex, language, and religion. The prevention of discrimination is, therefore, the implementation of the principle of equality of treatment."[44] A later memorandum elaborated further: "The following delimitation of the meaning of the term discrimination may be suggested: discrimination includes any conduct based on a distinction made on grounds of natural or social categories, which have no relation either to individual capacities or merits, or to the concrete behaviour of the individual person."[45]

Affirmative Action

It was accepted during the drafting of both covenants that a prohibition of discrimination or distinction does not preclude positive measures taken in favor of disadvantaged groups. During the consideration of Article 26 of the Covenant on Civil and Political Rights in the Third Committee, it was recognized that "the word, 'discrimination' . . . was used . . . in a negative sense only, to mean a distinction of an unfavourable kind."[46] Similarly, it was said that the word "discrimination" conveyed the idea of a distinction made without any objective basis."[47] The representatives of Chile, Netherlands, and Uruguay pointed out that equality did not mean identity of treatment.[48]

During the consideration of the International Covenant on Economic, Social, and Cultural Rights in the Third Committee in 1962, the Indian representative pointed out that the implementation of the principles of nondiscrimination

> raised certain problems in the case of the particularly backward groups still to be found in many under-developed countries. In his country, the constitution and the laws provided for special measures for the social and cultural betterment of such groups; measures of that kind were essential for the achievement of true social equality in highly heterogeneous societies. He felt certain that the authors of the draft Covenant had not intended to prohibit such measures, which were in fact protective measures. . . . He therefore thought it essential to make it clear that such protective measures would not be construed as discriminatory within the meaning of the paragraph. The Committee might accordingly wish to add to the article an explanatory paragraph reading: "Special measures for the advancement of any socially and educationally backward sections of society shall not be construed as distinctions under this article. Alternatively, the Committee might wish to insert in its report a statement which would make that interpretation clear. . . .[49]

The point made by the Indian representative was expressly supported by the representatives of the United Kingdom, Ceylon, the Ukrainian SSR and the United States. However, it was felt that the "difficulty experienced by the Indian representative would best be met by the inclusion of an interpretative statement in the Committee's records, rather than insertion of an additional paragraph in the draft Covenant."[50] When the Third Committee discussed the nondiscrimination provisions of the International Covenant on Civil and Political Rights the following year, the Indian representative raised his point again and suggested that "article 2(1) of the draft Covenant on Civil and Political Rights should be followed by an explanatory paragraph reading: "Special measures for the advancement of any socially and educationally backward sections of society shall not be construed as distinctions under this article.' " He stated that, owing to past treatment or historical circumstances, a certain sector of the people had to be given greater privileges and protection only for a certain period of time in order to promote the rights of those people to reestablish their equality and conditions under which there would remain no need for such provisions, and equal opportunities would exist for all. If the Committee did not favor the insertion of that paragraph in the draft Covenant, a passage of similar content should be included in the Committee's report.[51] The Committee again endorsed the point made by the Indian representative.[52] The position adopted by the Third Committee followed that of the World Court, for example, in the *Minority Schools in Albania* case.[53]

In another context, the European Court of Human Rights, referring to the criteria for determining whether a given difference in treatment contravenes Article 14 of the European Convention, stated that

> the principle of equality of treatment is violated if the distinction has no objective and reasonable justification. The existence of such a justification must be assessed in relation to the aim and effects of the measure under consideration, regard being had to the principles which normally prevail in democratic societies. A difference of treatment in the exercise of a right laid down in the Convention must not only pursue a legitimate aim: Article 14 is likewide violated when it is clearly established that there is no reasonable relationship of proportionality between the means employed and the aim sought to be realized.[54]

In the Human Rights Committee one member noted that "articles 3 and 26 of the Covenant required more than restraint by the State party. They required the adoption of positive measures to prevent discrimination. . . . He did not think that affirmative action in favor of a disadvantaged group constituted reverse discrimination; in fact, it was sometimes essential."[55] Another member agreed that "Article 3 . . . clearly called for affirmative action, including social, economic and administrative measures."[56] The representative of the government of Sweden, to whom these remarks were addressed, expressed his assent.[57]

Discrimination by Private Individuals

Article 26 requires state parties to enact laws to prohibit, and to guarantee equal and effective protection against, discrimination on the grounds indicated. Clearly, the law must prohibit and prevent discrimination by state officials, and perhaps by private individuals who interfere with equality before the law, with the equal protection of the laws including equal access to public accommodations.[58] The extent to which the state must prohibit private discrimination in other respects has been debated. An early memorandum by the UN Secretariat recognized that

> there is another class of discrimination which consists in unfavourable treatment in social relations only, but not in denying legal rights to any persons. It is clear that forms of discrimination which deny legal rights may and should be fought by legal measures, while those which comprise merely social treatment must chiefly be fought by education and by other social measures.[59]

In the Human Rights Committee in 1979 a member, while agreeing that in some problem areas the private citizen should be protected not only against discrimination or interference by the State but also against private discrimination, "wondered, however, whether and to what extent such an obligation derived from Article 26."[60] In reply, it was observed that Article 26, like Article 2(1):

> prohibited discrimination on any grounds and not just on the grounds of rights recognized in the Covenant. Hence article 26 could not be interpreted as referring only to public acts. It must cover the internal system of a country and the authorities who decided who could work, occupy land and so forth. If the State owned all housing and was the sole employer, then its provisions applied to the State. In a different system, however, with private housing and numerous private employers, it was the latter who must be prevented from practising discrimination.[61]

Discrimination by private individuals was discussed during the consideration of Article 26 in the Third Committee. It was admitted that "some types of individual discrimination were a matter of legitimate personal choice,"[62] and it was suggested that "discrimination in private and social relationships . . . did not come under the law."[63] As against such legitimate "preferences of individuals in their private lives"[64] however, it was strongly denied that "discriminatory practices in matters of everyday life such as housing, restaurants, transport and access to beaches . . . were within the realm of private relationships and could not therefore be the subject of legislation. . . ."[65] The law, it was recognized, "could ensure equal treatment, equal rights and equal obligations as a citizen for every person."[66]

It may be concluded that certain types of discrimination by individuals, other than in personal and social relationships, would violate the guarantees of the Covenant and that a state party is under an obligation to take measures against such forms of discrimination.[67] In addition, private advocacy of national, racial, or religious hatred that constitutes incitement to discrimination, hostility, or violence must be prohibited by law under Article 20(2).

Distinctions between Citizens and Aliens

The rights recognized by the Covenant are human rights, not merely citizen's rights. In general they apply to "every human being" "everyone," "all persons." A suggestion to replace "persons" in Article 2(1) by "nationals" or "citizens" was not pressed.[68]

During the consideration of Article 26 in the Commission on Human Rights, fear was expressed that the prohibition of discrimination on grounds of national origin could mean the abolition of all control over foreigners. Others replied that "the application of the principle of non-discrimination had to be considered in the light of the other provisions of the Covenant. . . . A non-discrimination clause should not, therefore, be construed as prohibiting measures to control aliens and their enterprises."[69] This was also the apparently uncontested view in the Third Committee.[70] As was pointed out by the Permanent Court of International Justice, however, "the admission of foreigners to the territory of a State is a question which is not necessarily connected with the legal status of persons within its territory."[71] It was wisely cautioned in the Third Committee that "discrimination against aliens could be permissible only to the extent strictly necessary."[72]

Distinctions in the law generally between aliens and citizens, then, do not deny the former the equal protection of the laws if such discriminations are "strictly necessary." The rights recognized by the Covenant, however, explicitly apply to all persons subject to a state party's jurisdiction, aliens as well as citizens. A distinction between aliens and citizens is permitted only where explicitly provided, e.g., Article 25 (the right to vote and take part in public affairs), and Articles 12(4) and 13 (right of entry to one's country and freedom from expulsion).[73]

It has also been said that there would not be genuine equality for all citizens regardless of national origin if a distinction is made between natural born and naturalized citizens, and that such a distinction would violate the Covenant.[74]

The principles of equality and nondiscrimination in the exercise of certain specific rights have been elaborated in more detail in various United Nations studies and in standards adopted by United Nations human rights organs on the basis of those studies. Due account needs to be taken of these studies and standards in interpreting and applying the equality and nondiscrimination provisions of the Covenant.[75]

Nondiscrimination in the Matter of Political Rights

In 1962, the Sub-Commission on Prevention of Discrimination and Protection of Minorities formulated principles on freedom and nondiscrimination in the matter of political rights.[76] Article II states that "every national of a country is entitled within that country to full and equal political rights without distinction of any kind." Articles IV, V, IX, and X require equality and nondiscrimination in respect of the universality and equality of suffrage, and access to elective and nonelective public office. Article XI lists various measures which shall not be considered discriminatory, including reasonable voting qualifications and qualifications for elective or appointive office; a reasonable delay before a naturalized citizen may exercise political rights; and special measures to assure adequate representation for disadvantaged groups or balanced representation for different elements in the population.

Nondiscrimination in Religious Rights and Practices

A Special Rapporteur of the Sub-Commission on Prevention of Discrimination and Protection of Minorities submitted a set of draft principles on freedom and nondiscrimination in the matter of religious rights and practices.[77] Part 4 provided:

Public authorities shall refrain from making any adverse distinctions against, or giving undue preference to, individuals or groups of individuals with respect to the right to freedom of thought, conscience and religion; and shall endeavour to prevent any individual or group of individuals from doing so. In particular: (1) in the event of a conflict between the demands of two or more religions or beliefs, public authorities shall endeavour to find a solution reconciling these demands in a manner such as to ensure the greatest measure of freedom to society as a whole; (2) in the granting of subsidies or exemptions from taxation, no adverse distinction shall be made between, and no undue preference shall be given to, any religion or belief or its followers. However, public authorities shall not be precluded from levying general taxes or from carrying out obligations assumed as a result of arrangements made to compensate a religious organization for property taken over by the State or from contributing funds for the pres-

ervation of religious structures recognized as monuments of historic or artistic value.

In 1981, the Commission on Human Rights adopted a Draft Declaration on the Elimination of All Forms of Intolerance and of Discrimination Based on Religion or Belief. Article II provides:

> (1) No one shall be subject to discrimination by any State, institution,
> group of persons or person on grounds of religion or other beliefs. (2) For
> the purpose of this Declaration, the expression "intolerance and discrimi-
> nation based on religion or belief" means any distinction, exclusion, re-
> striction or preference based on religion or belief and having as its purpose
> or as its effect nullification and impairment of the recognition, enjoyment
> or exercise of human rights and fundamental freedoms on an equal basis.

Article III provides:

> Discrimination between human beings on grounds of religion or belief
> constitutes an affront to human dignity and a disavowal of the principles
> of the Charter of the United Nations, and shall be condemned as a viola-
> tion of the human rights and fundamental freedoms proclaimed in the Uni-
> versal Declaration of Human Rights and enunciated in detail in the Inter-
> national Covenants relating to human rights, and as an obstacle to friendly
> and peaceful relations between nations.[78]

Nondiscrimination in Education

In 1956, the Sub-Commission on Prevention of Discrimination and
Protection of Minorities adopted a resolution in which it declared that

> with a view to eliminating discrimination on grounds of race, colour, sex,
> language, religion, political or other opinion, national or social origin,
> property, birth or other status, all legislative provisions or administrative
> measures should be abolished and all practices opposed, which, for the
> purpose of discriminating against any group: (a) deprive any person or
> distinct group of persons of access to education at any level or of any type;
> (b) irrevocably limit any person or distinct group of persons to education
> of an inferior standard; and (c) establish or maintain separate educational
> systems or institutions for persons or distinct groups of persons.[79]

The Sub-Commission affirmed ten basic principles and recommended
to UNESCO to draft an appropriate international instrument for the
prevention of discrimination in education, taking these principles into

266 B. G. RAMCHARAN

account. This recommendation eventually led to the Convention against Discrimination in Education elaborated under the auspices of UNESCO.[80]

Discrimination against Persons Born Out of Wedlock

On the bases of another study, the Sub-Commission on Prevention of Discrimination and Protection of Minorities adopted a set of general principles on equality and nondiscrimination for persons born out of wedlock.[81] Article 16 states: "Every person born out of wedlock shall enjoy the same political, social, economic and cultural rights as person born in wedlock. The State shall render material and other assistance to children born out of wedlock."

The Rights of Noncitizens

The Sub-Commission on Prevention of Discrimination has also proposed a declaration on the rights of noncitizens. Article 4 of the proposed declaration states:

> Notwithstanding any distinction which a State is entitled to make between its citizens and non-citizens, every non-citizen shall enjoy at least the following rights, always respecting the obligations imposed upon a non-citizen by article 2, and subject to the limitations provided for in article 29 of the Universal Declaration of Human Rights: . . . (ii) The right to equal access to and equal treatment before the tribunals and all other organs administering justice, and to have the free assistance of an interpreter if he cannot understand or speak the language used in court;. . .[82]

Principles of Equality and Nondiscrimination in the Human Rights Committee

In its first years the Human Rights Committee did not have occasion to take firm positions interpreting the principles of equality and nondiscrimination in Articles 2(1), 3, and 26 of the Covenant. Individual members of the Committee, however, have expressed views on the content of these principles. Thus, it has been stressed that the Covenant provides not merely for formal equality in the eyes of the law or before the courts, but also establishes the equal protection of the law and nondiscrimination in fact. Members of the Committee have frequently referred to the principles of equality and nondiscrimination in this general sense. Similarly, it has been said that Articles 2 and 26 require states to take affirmative action when needed to assure equality and nondiscrimination. Members have emphasized the need to have guarantees of equal rights established in the laws of states parties. This issue has arisen particularly regarding nondiscrimination with respect to political opinion. In one instance, where the constitution of a country expressly prohibited discrimination only on the grounds of nationality, race, sex or religion, members of the Committee asked why some of the grounds on which distinction was prohibited under Article 2 of the Covenant, such as language and political or other opinion, were not reflected in the relevant articles of the constitution or the penal code. Committee members have emphatically asserted that distinctions between natural-born and naturalized citizens are in violation of the Covenant.

In considering reports of states parties, members of the Committee have posed questions and sought information relating to these articles, including:

—the adequacy of national legislation providing for equality and prohibiting discrimination;
—the extent to which human rights and fundamental freedoms are enjoyed by "every person" as distinct from "every citizen";
—information on measures taken to prevent discrimination against various groups, such as minorities and indigenous populations;
—information on guarantees against discrimination on the grounds of religion;
—information as to whether national laws provide guarantees against discrimination on grounds of political or other opinion ("Special importance" has been attached to "nondiscrimination for political reasons, since violation of that principle is liable to affect the whole institutional structure" of a country);[83]
—information on legislation and other steps by the government relating to discrimination by private persons.

Certain pronouncements by the Committee may be indicative of the interpretations which the Committee may give to Article 2. In its report for 1978, for example, "it was noted that protection of the law did not suffice to prevent discrimination in public life."[84] With reference to the report of a state party, "members expressed concern over the reference to 'illegitimate children' which seemed to constitute discrimination on the basis of birth, and asked what justification there was for the distinctions made and whether the Government had any intention of eliminating them."[85] The representative of Czechoslovakia, replying to questions by members of the Committee, stated that "regarding the application of the principle of non-discrimination . . . that principle was not provided for as such in Czechoslovak legislation but that it was applied by labour courts and in civil legal proceedings where it was the essential prerequisite for a fair trial, in the light of the general rule of the Constitution under which all citizens had equal rights and duties."[86] The Committee's report does not indicate, however, any pronouncement, either by the Committee or by individual members, as to whether failure by a state party to provide expressly for the principle of nondiscrimination constituted a violation of the Covenant.

Regarding the application of Article 3, pertaining to the equal rights of men and women, a member of the Committee expressed the view that "the words '. . . to ensure the equal rights of men and women . . .' in Article 3 of the Covenant required that the proclamation of equality should be followed by specific measures to give effect to the principle."[87] Questions asked and information requested of government representatives included:

—information on laws and measures providing for equality of men and women;
—whether national legislation provided for complete reciprocity in the obligations of spouses;
—whether foreign women married to nationals were equal before the law to local women married to foreigners;
—whether a country's religious or cultural traditions could impede equality of men and women;
—information on the respective rights of men and women regarding the devolution of property, succession, and legal representation;
—the system of property rights in marriage;
—the right of women to be elected to political office;
—information on measures to deal with the problems of working mothers with children;
—access of women to employment opportunities and to education, particularly at the higher levels;
—equality of wages;
—whether any machinery was set up to enforce legislative provisions on equality between men and women.

Replying to questions by members of the Committee, the representative of Madagascar "pointed out that it had been found necessary in Madagascar to give a preponderance of prerogatives to the husband in order to impart unity and direction to the household; and in that connexion, he explained some of the prevailing local customs which reflected the importance of the role of the wife in his country."[88] The report of the Committee does not indicate any reaction or comments by the Committee or by individual members.

Conclusion

The many provisions of the Covenant reiterating the principles of equality and nondiscrimination, and the history of their drafting, make clear the ready opportunity open to the Human Rights Committee and to others to adopt a progressive and dynamic approach to the interpretation and application of these provisions. The concepts of equality and nondiscrimination contained in the Covenant were used in the sense obtaining in the contemporary international law of human rights. They are not narrow or formalistic but "modernistic" and "egalitarian."

In probing the sense and meaning of these provisions, one must keep in mind that the principles of equality and nondiscrimination are now established parts of international customary law, and it would be difficult to deny them the character of *jus cogens,* at least as regards consistent patterns of comprehensive violations. One must keep in mind the philosophy of the United Nations, under whose aegis the Covenant came to life, particularly the importance attached to universal equality of all peoples and persons. The relationship between equality, freedom, justice, and peace remains one of the dominant concerns of the United Nations, strengthening the need for a dynamic, progressive approach to the interpretation and application of the principles of equality and nondiscrimination contained in the Covenant.

11

The Rights of Minorities

LOUIS B. SOHN

THE COVENANT ON Civil and Political Rights deals with the rights of all the inhabitants of a state equally. Article 2(1) expressly provides that the rights are to be enjoyed "without distinction of any kind, such as race, colour, sex, language, religion, political or other opinion, national or social origin, property, birth or other status," and other articles forbid discrimination on some of these grounds in the enjoyment of specific rights, e.g., the rights of children (Article 24(1)). But unlike the Universal Declaration, the Covenant (Article 27) provides special additional rights for members of minorities qua minorities. It is noteworthy that such provisions were not included in either the European or the American Convention, and a later attempt to add them to the European Convention did not succeed.

International attention to minorities has had a double aspect. States in which minorities live are sometimes concerned about the possibility of a secessionist movement by minorities, threatening the territorial integrity of the state, or about the danger of interference by other states with which the minorities are connected by ties of race, national origin, language, or religion. Over the centuries minority questions have led to interventions, aggressions, and wars, both local and general; even today they lead to friction between states, intervention by one state in another, or to appeals to the United Nations for international intervention.[1]

At the same time, there is international concern for the human rights of minorities.[2] The international community has sought to assure them equal rights and freedom from invidious discrimination. There has also been international concern to assure that minorities will flourish so as to preserve that diversity of the human race, which, since the beginning of mankind, has provided a motive power for the development of civilization and culture by weaving many strands into a single multi-colored tapestry. Even in a democratic state there is some danger that the majority which determines the laws and institutions and the behavior of national authorities may not take into account the special character and needs of minority groups.

There are several kinds of minorities. They may be composed of the indigenous inhabitants of a territory conquered by another race; members of a nation completely absorbed by another state; some inhabitants of a territory transferred from one country to another; a group that has maintained its identity though scattered among many countries by events of history; compact groups of permanently established immigrants who are trying to preserve the traditions of the country from which they came; or diverse components of a multinational, multiracial, multireligious, or culturally pluralistic state. (For further discussion, see later section in this essay, "What Is a Minority?") Because of the diversity of circumstances which have led to the emergence of minority groups in various states, it has not been easy to obtain agreement on a definition of minorities or on the rights to which they should be entitled. In particular, doubts have been expressed about the possibility of establishing worldwide standards which could be applied to all minorities, since they differ in character and circumstances from region to region, from country to country, and even in the same country.

That international human rights should provide special protections for minorities was not inevitable or universally agreed. Though provisions for the protection of religious and other minorities have been included in various treaties since the seventeenth century,[3] and in particular in several of the multilateral treaties which followed the First World War, and though one of the main activities of the League of Nations was to protect various minorities in Central and Eastern Europe and in the Middle East,[4] the Charter of the United Nations contained no provisions for the protection of minorities. It was thought that the need for such protection would be eliminated, and the political difficulties incident to the protection of the minorities would be avoided, by general recognition of the basic human rights of all.[5] This was accomplished by providing in the Charter for the promotion by the United Nations of "universal respect for, and observance of, human rights and fundamental freedoms for all without distinction as to race, sex, language, or religion" (Article 55 of the Charter).

The need for special protection for minorities, however, remained an issue. The Commission on Human Rights, established in 1946, was authorized to submit to the Economic and Social Council proposals, recommendations, and reports regarding the protection of minorities. In 1947 the Commission established a Sub-Commission on Prevention of Discrimination and Protection of Minorities and authorized it to undertake studies and to make recommendations to the Commission concerning the protection of racial, national, and linguistic minorities.[6]

The issue was active during the preparation of the Universal Declaration. The Secretariat of the United Nations, and several governments, endeavored to include in the Universal Declaration a provision for the protection of the rights of a "minority to use its own language and to maintain schools and other cultural institutions."[7] Others opposed it. They argued that in view of the nondiscrimination provisions there was no longer any need for a distinct system of protection for minorities. It was even said that the very concept of "minorities" is inconsistent with the principle of absolute equality enshrined in the Charter of the United Nations and in many national constitutions, as the term "national minority" signifies "a category of citizens whose political, economic, and social status was inferior to that of citizens belonging to the majority."[8] Where necessary, decentralization and self-management should be sufficient to secure for all national groups "an active role in realizing their position and equal social relations."[9]

Some thought an article on minorities was not only unnecessary but undesirable. The Universal Declaration should not deal with rights which did not have universal applicability, did not apply to all human beings, and did not apply in all countries in the same way. Some thought that it was undesirable to perpetuate protections for minorities because it would discourage their assimilation. Others thought it might result in cutting them off from the mainstream of national life, frustrating their emancipation and full development, and denying them equal opportunity.[10]

In the end, the Universal Declaration, like the Charter, contained a comprehensive nondiscrimination clause (Article 2), but a special article on minorities was not included. The Soviet Union reopened the matter on the floor of the Assembly and suggested a supplementary article dealing both with the right to self-determination and the linguistic and institutional rights of minorities.[11] That effort also failed.[12] At the same time, however, the General Assembly adopted a resolution stating that "the United Nations cannot remain indifferent to the fate of minorities," but that "it is difficult to adopt a uniform solution of this complex and delicate question, which has special aspects in each State in which it arises." The Assembly therefore requested the Economic and Social Council to ask the Commission on Human Rights and the Sub-

Commission on the Prevention of Discrimination and the Protection of Minorities "to make a thorough study of the problem of minorities, in order that the United Nations may be able to take effective measures for the protection of racial, national, religious or linguistic minorities."[13]

While in the early years the Sub-Commission devoted a large proportion of its work to the protection of minorities, and in particular to the question of defining the concept of a "minority," it was rather inactive on this subject between 1955 and 1971.[14] Even after Francesco Capotorti began a major study of minorities for the UN Human Rights Commission in 1971, only a very limited time was available to the Sub-Commission for that problem.

Origin of Article 27 of the Covenant

In 1950, during the discussion in the Sub-Commission of the implementation of the General Assembly's 1948 Resolution, it was again suggested, and this time agreed, that the most effective means of securing the protection of minorities would be the inclusion of an article on the subject in the proposed International Covenant on Civil and Political Rights. Issues emerged, however, as to which minorities should be protected and what rights should be granted them. In the large, the differences were between those who sought to limit protection to nationality groups, like those in the USSR, and others who favored protection for other ethnic, religious and cultural groups as well. And should the Covenant guarantee merely the freedom of a group to assert its identity, or also the right to maintain that identity by separate, independent schools, newspapers and other institutions? Should states be required only to tolerate freedom and institutions, or also to provide public financial contributions and other support for such cultural pluralism?

The first draft of the minorities article of the Covenant read as follows: "Ethnic, religious and linguistic minorities shall not be denied the right to enjoy their own culture, to profess and practice their own religion, or to use their own language." It was objected, however, that minorities as such had no juridical personality and that one should speak instead of "persons belonging to minorities"; the idea of a collectivity might be expressed by recognizing their rights "in community with other members of their group."

These amendments were approved by the Sub-Commission, which then adopted the following text: "Persons belonging to ethnic, religious or linguistic minorities shall not be denied the right, in community with the other members of their group, to enjoy their own culture, to profess and practice their own religion, or to use their own language." [15]

The Commission on Human Rights, in 1953, approved the Sub-Commission's proposal with only one amendment, designed to alleviate the fears of Latin American countries that immigrants to these countries might form separate communities asking for minority rights, and thus impair national unity and security. The Commission adopted a Chilean amendment to add at the beginning of the article the phrase "In those States in which ethnic, religious or linguistic minorities exist," [16] and the proposed article, without further change, became Article 27 of the Covenant. [17] It reads: "In those States in which ethnic, religious or linguistic minorities exist, persons belonging to such minorities shall not be denied the right, in community with the other members of their group, to enjoy their own culture, to profess and practise their own religion, or to use their own language." [18]

Basic Issues

Rights of Minority Groups or Rights of Persons Belonging to Minority Groups

While it is common to speak of rights of minorities, Article 27, we have seen, speaks of rights of "persons" belonging to certain minorities, a deliberate decision, designed to avoid giving to the group an international personality. Such international personality, it was feared, might have given a minority the capacity to vindicate its rights before a competent international institution, such as the Committee on Human Rights established by the Covenant. [19] The Optional Protocol to the Covenant gives the right to present communications to the Committee only to individuals. [20]

There were additional reasons, historical and political, favoring that conclusion. [21] Historically, the minority treaties of the 1919–1939 period also conferred rights on individuals, on persons belonging to certain minorities, although in the practice of the League of Nations the right of petition was granted not only to members of minority groups but also to the groups themselves. Politically, the danger of friction in a particular country would increase if the whole minority group rather than individuals were bringing complaints against the majority. There would also be the possibility of friction between the group and its members, especially if some of them should prefer assimilation to preservation of group characteristics. Finally, the whole conception of the Covenant required an approach different from previous attempts to protect rights of various minorities. The reason for the United Nations emphasis on human rights was to get away from the difficulties caused by the minority treaties, and the method chosen was to universalize the protection of rights of individuals; not just certain minorities, but all persons anywhere, should be entitled to certain minimum rights. It would have been inconsistent with that conception to grant special treatment to some minority groups or even to all of them.

The proponents of the new approach recognized, however, that some human rights of persons belonging to a minority group need to be exercised in community with other members of that group.[22] As the right of assembly, or the right of association, is a right which an individual exercises in concert with others, similarly the effective enjoyment of cultural, religious and linguistic rights requires acting in common with others. Thus Article 27 explicitly protects the right of a member of a minority group to act together with other members in order to enjoy these rights. A state party to the Covenant cannot require that a member of a minority practice his religion only individually and in private. Article 27, together with Article 18, guarantees the freedom to manifest one's religion or belief in worship, observance, practice, and teaching "either individually or in community with others and in public or private." And unlike Article 18, Article 27 does not permit limitations to be imposed by a state, even to the extent "necessary to protect public safety, order, health, or morals or the fundamental rights and freedoms of others."[23]

It is noteworthy that the Commission on Human Rights rejected an amendment providing that minority rights should not be interpreted as entitling any immigrant settled in the territory of a State "to form within that State separate communities which might impair its national unity or its security." But the report of the Commission stated, rather inconsistently, that the view expressed by the amendment was supported by the majority of the Commission's members.[24] The discussion on this subject in the Commission seems inconclusive. On the one hand, there was agreement about the nonapplicability of the article to immigrant groups. On the other hand, the limited rights guaranteed by the article were not considered likely to be abused (i.e., by indulging in political activity that would adversely affect national unity, or by using cultural institutions "to spread political theories").[25]

Minorities, "Peoples" and Self-Determination

One of the major obstacles to granting any special protection to minorities was the fear that they might then invoke the principle of self-determination, leading ultimately to secession. The problem was compounded by the use in the self-determination articles of the Covenants (Article 1 in both Covenants) of the expression "peoples" (instead of "nations" as in earlier versions). If all "peoples" have the right of self-determination, should not minorities also have that right? On the one hand, those Western countries which opposed the inclusion in the Covenants of a provision on self-determination insisted that such a provision would encourage a minority to claim autonomy or independence; there was no criterion to determine whether or not such a minority should be regarded as a people; and proclaiming such an undefined right might easily be construed as an appeal to secession.[26] Other states insisted that self-determination was primarily, or even exclusively, a problem of non-self-governing territories and could not be applied to sovereign countries; that self-determination applied only to national majorities living in their own territory but unable freely to determine their political status; that a minority in a community was entitled to the fullest possible safeguards, but was not entitled to obstruct the will of the majority; and that minority "rule" would be dictatorship not democracy.[27] As was pointed out, "No minority had the right to subversive action, and the article [on self-determination] would not give it that right."[28] The idea of self-determination must be reconciled with the other principles enshrined in the Charter of the United Nations; the sovereign equality, the territorial integrity, and the political independence of states. In particular, "Neither national sovereignty nor territorial integrity must be infringed under the pretext of self-determination."[29]

Article 27 is strictly limited to three specific rights and clearly avoids dealing with such broader political issues. It was understood throughout the drafting process that this restrictive formulation of the rights of persons belonging to minority groups was necessary to avoid tendencies dangerous for the unity of states and to discourage activities which might impair national unity or security.[30]

What Is a "Minority"?

The meaning of the term "minority" has fascinated international lawyers and international committees for a long time.[31] It preoccupied the

Sub-Commission on Prevention of Discrimination and Protection of Minorities in its early years, although none of its proposals for a definition proved satisfactory.[32]

An early, often cited attempt to arrive at a definition was made by the Permanent Court of International Justice in interpreting the Greco-Bulgarian Convention relating to reciprocal emigration. The Court pointed out the close connection between the Convention and the provisions of the Peace Treaty of 1919 with Bulgaria relating to the protection of minorities, and concluded that the Convention was applicable not to minorities generally, but only to persons who formed a minority in either one country or the other. While the Convention "clearly indicated that it was individuals who were entitled to take advantage of its terms," the Court noted that from time immemorial in the East "individuals of the same race, religion, language and tradition" have derived material benefits from uniting into communities. The Court then defined a community as follows:

> By tradition, which plays so important a part in Eastern countries, the "community" is a group of persons living in a given country or locality, having a race, religion, language and traditions of their own and united by this identity of race, religion, language and traditions in a sentiment of solidarity, with a view to preserving their traditions, maintaining their form of worship, ensuring the instruction and upbringing of their children in accordance with the spirit and traditions of their race and rendering mutual assistance to each other.

Whether "a particular community does or does not conform to the conception described above is a question of fact," not a question of law; and the Court found it unnecessary to consider whether, according to local law, a community is or is not recognized as a juridical person.[33]

After several of its proposals for definition were strongly criticized, the Sub-Commission on the Prevention of Discrimination and Protection of Minorities suggested in 1954 a more thorough study of the present position of minorities throughout the world, and for that limited purpose it proposed the following definition: "The term minority shall include only those non-dominant groups in a population which possess and wish to preserve ethnic, religious or linguistic traditions or characteristics markedly different from those of the rest of the population." At the same time it decided that in carrying out the study the following "considerations" should be borne in mind (which in fact added important qualifications to the definition):[34]

(i) There are among the nationals of many States distinctive population groups possessing ethnic, religious, or linguistic traditions or characteristics different from those of the rest of the population, and among these are groups that need to be protected by special measures, national and international, so that they can preserve and develop their traditions or characteristics;

(ii) Among minority groups not requiring protection are those seeking complete identity of treatment with the rest of the population, in which case their problems are covered by those articles of the Charter of the United Nations, the Universal Declaration of Human Rights and the draft international covenants on human rights that are directed towards the prevention of discrimination;

(iii) It is most undesirable to hinder by any actions [the] spontaneous development of minority groups towards integration with the rest of the population of the country in which they live, which takes place when impacts such as those of a new environment, or that of modern civilization, produce a state of rapid racial, social, cultural, or linguistic evolution;

(iv) It is highly desirable that minorities should settle down happily as citizens of the country in which they live, and therefore in any measures that may be taken for the protection of their special traditions and characteristics, including the study, nothing should be done that is likely to stimulate their consciousness of difference from the rest of the population;

(v) Minorities must include a sufficient number of persons to preserve by themselves their traditions and characteristics;

(vi) Account should be taken of the circumstances under which each minority group has come into existence, for example whether it owes its existence to a peace treaty or to voluntary immigration.

In a later study, Capotorti used the following definition:

A group numerically inferior to the rest of the population of a State, in a non-dominant position, whose members—being nationals of the State— possess ethnic, religious or linguistic characteristics differing from those of the rest of the population and show, if only implicitly, a sense of solidarity, directed towards preserving their culture, traditions, religion or language.[35]

Several objective criteria were included in this definition: in the first place, the existence, as a question of fact, of a distinct group within a State's population "possessing stable ethnic, religious or linguistic characteristics that differ sharply from those of the rest of the population."

Second, the concept of a "minority" implies a group that is numerically inferior to the majority group (this definition might have to be modified to take account of multi-minority situations where no single group forms a majority). In the third place, it is only a nondominant minority which needs to be protected. Fourth, only citizens of the state are entitled to protection as minorities; foreigners must rely on other rules of international law for their protection. In addition, there was a subjective criterion—that there must exist a common will in the group, a sense of solidarity, directed toward preserving the distinctive characteristics of the group.[36]

In drafting Article 27, there was strong emphasis on making clear that recent immigrants to South and North America should not be treated as minorities. This was the reason for including the opening phrase, "In those States in which ethnic, religious or linguistic minorities exist." It was thus agreed that the article should cover only groups "long-established on the territory of a State."[37]

Government comments on an earlier Capotorti report, apart from some dissatisfaction with his preliminary definition and some opposition to any definition, concentrated on two issues: the so-called "subjective" element—the desire of a minority group to preserve its characteristics; and the minimum size of a minority group for the purposes of this article.[38]

With respect to the subjective element, some countries emphasized the relevance of the willingness of the minority to maintain its special characteristics. On the other hand, the government of Yugoslavia made the following comment:

> The Yugoslav Government wishes to underscore its conviction that the so-called "subjective factor" is in many respects dependent on the political atmosphere, and the cultural and social circumstances prevailing in the individual social communities in which the members of minorities live and work. Historical experiences have shown that the "indifference" of the members of minorities towards their national origin, position and rights [is], as a rule, the consequence of the social and other circumstances in which they live.
>
> In societies with a prevailing negative attitude of the "majority" towards the "minority" the members of the minorities are fearful that any declaration of one's national, ethnic, cultural and other characteristics might be interpreted as a so-called 'civil disloyalty' on his part as citizen of the country concerned.
>
> Therefore, it would be inappropriate to ascribe too much importance to the need of a "declaration of desire" by the members of any minority in

order to preserve their own national, ethnic, cultural and other features and to manifest their awareness of their affiliation to a particular minority, especially in the case of a minority which has for decades been subjected to the pressures of systematic assimilation and denationalization.[39]

As to the requisite size of the minority, there was general agreement that "minority" is a group which is numerically less than 50 percent of a State's population.[40] But was there also a bottom limit, other than the implication that a group should be more than one person?[41] Some emphasized that the group should be a sizable one, as otherwise it might be too difficult to provide it with the ordinary facilities required by minorities; and it might not have enough capacity and talent to preserve its traditions and institutions.[42] The government of Sweden stated that a minority group should consist of at least one hundred persons.[43] During the discussion of the Capotorti reports in the Sub-Commission it was further pointed out that it is not only the number of persons belonging to the group that matters but also the problem of their distribution; whether, for instance, they are settled compactly in a certain area or are scattered in small numbers around the country.[44]

A definition of a "minority" is not only a question of theoretical importance, but also a practical one as the question is likely to arise whether a particular group qualifies as a "minority" in terms of the Covenant, and can, therefore, benefit from the provisions of Article 27. The guidance provided by the preparatory materials might prove insufficient in some situations.

What Kinds of Minorities Should Have Special Rights?

Article 27 is limited to "ethnic, religious, or linguistic minorities." In 1953, the Commission on Human Rights arrived at this formula after a sharp debate, in which some participants would have added "national" minorities to this enumeration while others would have preferred to limit this article to "national minorities" only. As the Soviet delegate noted, the term "ethnic or linguistic groups" was not nearly as far-reaching as "national minorities"; "an ethnic or linguistic group could form a national minority, but a group could be called an ethnic or linguistic group long before it had reached the stage of becoming a national minority."[45] He explained that a national minority, like a nation, was "an historically formed community of people characterized by a common language, a common territory, a common economic life and a common psychological structure manifesting itself in a common culture."[46]

The difference related not only to the group to be protected but extended also to the rights to be protected. As noted in the Commission's report:

> Those who were in favour of the expression "ethnic, religious or linguistic minorities" were of the opinion that persons belonging to such minorities should have the right, in community with the other members of the group, "to enjoy their own culture, to profess and practise their religion or to use their own language." Those who were in favour of the expression "national minorities" emphasized the right of such minorities "to use their native tongue and to possess their national schools, libraries, museums and other cultural and education institutions."[47]

The Commission decided to adopt the first formulation. It is not clear, however, that in adopting that formulation the Commission decided that minorities are not entitled to possess "national" schools, libraries, museums, and other cultural and educational institutions.[48]

The distinction between "national minorities" and "ethnic, religious or linguistic minorities" also caused difficulties in 1973 when a Committee of Government Experts of the Council of Europe tried to draft an additional protocol to the European Convention on Human Rights dealing with the rights of persons belonging to national minorities. Some of its members thought that certain ethnic, linguistic or religious minorities did not constitute "national minorities," while others would have interpreted the term "national minority" as broadly as possible so as to include all ethnic, religious and linguistic minorities.[49] These differences doubtless contributed to the failure to add such an article to the European Convention.

During the United Nations discussions, a distinction was made quite frequently between "genuine" national minorities and "immigrants." It was argued, for instance, that it was essential "to forestall any possibility of a provision on the rights of minorities being interpreted to mean that immigrants were entitled to claim special privileges or form separate communities which might endanger the national unity or security of the State in which they have settled."[50] This problem was taken care of, supposedly, by limiting Article 27 to "well-established historical minorities" through the insertion of the reference to "those States in which ethnic, religious or linguistic minorities *exist*."[51]

While some members of the Commission on Human Rights have considered indigenous populations as a special category of minorities, others insisted that these populations should not be treated as minorities.[52] The Sub-Commission on Prevention of Discrimination and Protection of Minorities, after its attention was called to discriminatory measures being taken in various countries against indigenous peoples,[53] appointed a special rapporteur to consider that issue.[54] The study is not yet completed.

Finally, the question has been raised whether there is a need for official recognition of a minority by a state, either explicit or implicit.[55] The Capotorti study concludes that the applicability of Article 27 to a particular minority group does not depend upon its recognition by the state concerned; if the existence of a minority group can be objectively demonstrated, the state has the duty to accord it the rights provided in Article 27.[56]

What Rights Should Be Granted to Minorities?

Article 27 did not have to deal with the most important right of members of a minority group—the right to equality, not to be discriminated against. That is provided in Article 2(1) of the Covenant, which imposes the obligation on states parties to respect and to ensure to all individuals within their territories the rights recognized in the Covenant "without distinction of any kind, such as race, colour, sex, language, religion, political or other opinion, national or social origin, property, birth or other status." Thus ethnic, religious, or linguistic differences cannot form the basis for a discrimination; and there is a positive duty to prevent discrimination against anyone on these grounds. The fact that there is no express reference here, as there is in Article 14 of the European Convention on Human Rights, to "association with a national minority," does not provide a basis for discrimination because a person belongs to a minority (see essay 10).

Article 27 is based on the assumption that in addition to protection against discrimination, members of minority groups need special rights to enable them to preserve and develop their ethnic, religious, or linguistic characteristics. Most treaties for the protection of minorities concluded after the First World War, and those concluded after the Second World War, also contained special provisions to that end.[57]

These provisions were explained as follows by the Permanent Court of International Justice in the advisory opinion relating to *Minority Schools in Albania*:

> The idea underlying the treaties for the protection of minorities is to secure for certain elements incorporated in a State, the population of which

differs from them in race, language or religion, the possibility of living peaceably alongside that population and co-operating amicably with it, while at the same time preserving the characteristics which distinguish them from the majority, and satisfying the ensuing special needs.

In order to attain this object, two things were regarded as particularly necessary, and have formed the subject of provisions in these treaties.

The first is to ensure that nationals belonging to racial, religious or linguistic minorities shall be placed in every respect on a footing of perfect equality with the other nationals of the State.

The second is to ensure for the minority elements suitable means for the preservation of their racial peculiarities, their traditions and their national characteristics.

These two requirements are indeed closely interlocked, for there would be no true equality between a majority and a minority if the latter were deprived of its own institutions, and were consequently compelled to renounce that which constitutes the very essence of its being as a minority.[58]

In the spirit of this general statement, the Court pointed out that, for a minority, having its own charitable, religious and social institutions, schools and other educational establishments is "indispensable to enable the minority to enjoy the same treatment as the majority, not only in law but also in fact." Consequently, the Court rejected the Albanian government's contention that abolition of private schools in Albania was a general measure applicable to the majority as well as the minority and that it was, therefore, not a violation of the treaty clause guaranteeing to the members of the minority "the same treatment and security in law and in fact" as was enjoyed by other Albanian nationals.[59]

The scope of the special rights to be protected has occupied the Commission on Human Rights, and its Sub-Commission on the Prevention of Discrimination and the Protection of Minorities, from the very beginning. Several issues were raised. It was agreed that members of minority groups should be entitled to enjoy their own culture, practice their religion, and use their own language. Several proposals would have expressly provided the right of minorities to use their own language in judicial proceedings, at least where the minority members did not speak or understand the language ordinarily used in courts.[60] Some proposals specified the right of minorities to establish their own schools, and a right to receive teaching in the language of their own choice in those schools.[61] There were questions also about cultural and religious educational institutions. A principal difference was between those who favored an article requiring the state only to respect the cultural rights and freedoms of the minority, and those who sought also an obligation for the state to supply or support minority institutions from public funds.[62]

Although Article 27, as it emerged, is limited to the right "to enjoy" their own culture and the right "to use" their own language, it is accepted that it includes the right to have schools and cultural institutions of their own. Plausibly the provision requires the state also to permit the use of other languages in judicial and other official proceedings by those who cannot speak or understand the official language. (This is in addition to the special right to an interpreter in criminal proceedings explicitly provided for all who need it in Article 14(3f).)

The Sub-Commission had proposed the insertion in the draft Covenant of the following article: "Persons belonging to ethnic, religious, or linguistic minorities shall not be denied the right, in community with the other members of their group, to enjoy their own culture, to profess and practice their own religion, or to use their own language." [63]

It also adopted a proposal that the General Assembly recommend that

in the interest of enabling recognized minority groups to maintain their cultural heritage when they desire to do so, Member Governments should provide adequate facilities, in districts, regions and territories where they represent a considerable proportion of the population, for:
(1) The use in judicial procedure of languages of such groups;
(2) The teaching in State-supported schools of languages of such groups, provided that such groups request it and that the request in reality expresses the spontaneous desire of such groups.[64]

A committee of the Commission on Human Rights amended this proposal by stating that governments should provide such facilities "as a minimum," and revising subparagraph 1 to read: "the use before the courts of languages of such groups, in those cases where the member of the minority group does not speak or understand the language ordinarily used in the courts." [65]

It has been widely held that by rejecting all amendments and texts which would have broadened the rights of the minorities, the Commission made clear that it favored only the more limited right of members of a minority to enjoy their own culture, to profess or practice their own religion, or to use their own language. There was, then, no obligation on the part of the government to finance their institutions, to provide special institutions for them, or to take legislative or administrative action to assist them. According to this view, Article 27 is not like the special minority treaties of the two postwar periods.

Capotorti, however, disagrees with this restrictive view. He believes that some of the rights would be meaningless were there no governmental obligation to provide assistance. In particular, adequate cultural development requires considerable human and financial resources which few minority groups possess. A purely passive attitude of governments would render the rights specified in Article 27 largely ineffective.[66]

This view is consonant with the position taken in 1978 by the World Conference to Combat Racism and Racial Discrimination, which recommended that

States adopt specific measures in the economic, social, educational and cultural fields and in the matter of civil and political rights, in order that all persons may enjoy legal and factual equality and that discrimination between majorities and minorities may be eliminated. Such specific measures should include appropriate assistance to persons belonging to minority groups, to enable them to develop their own culture and to facilitate their full development, in particular in the fields of education, culture and employment.[67]

Article 27 contains no limitations clause. Early suggestions that the rights of minorities be subject to the requirements of national security or public order did not prevail. Concerns that the promotion of minority identity might encourage secessionist sentiment, or would underscore differences leading to public disorders, were rejected. Article 27 assumes that the individual rights protected by this article are not to be sacrificed to such concerns, however sincere and bona fide. The rights protected here, however, have to be read together with other articles which Article 27 overlaps. The right to profess and practice one's own religion is protected by Article 18. Article 18(4) also expressly obligates states to respect the liberty of parents "to ensure the religious and moral education of their children in conformity with their own convictions." Article 18 is not subject to derogation even in time of public emergency (Article 4). The basic freedom of thought, conscience and religion, moreover, is not subject to any limitations whatsoever. The freedom to manifest one's religion or belief, however, may be subject to "such limitations as are prescribed by law and are necessary to protect public safety, order, health, or morals or the fundamental rights and freedoms of others" (see essay 12).

The history of the Covenant is as yet too brief to provide much guidance on specific issues. The work of the Human Rights Committee, in reviewing reports by states submitted under Article 40, has shed some light. So far the Committee has concentrated on gathering information on the legal and factual status of minorities. Queries have been made about measures taken to protect their rights, in particular their right to use their own language. In minority communities, were there schools, newspapers, radio and television stations that used the minority's language? To what extent were members of a minority group expected to learn a dominant, national language?[68] One government reported that it treated indigenous people differently from other minorities. According to one committee member, this differentiation is arguably a form of discrimination against the indigenous group.[69]

The fact that Article 27 deals with rights which, minorities apart, are also the subject of other articles of the Covenant and of other multilateral conventions, suggests issues that will surely arise. Compare, for example, cases that arose in the 1960s under the European Convention. The Convention does not deal with minorities as such, but it provides for equality, and the First Protocol to the European Convention provides in part, "No person shall be denied the right to education." In the *Belgian Linguistic* case,[70] six groups of applicants, French-speaking residents in the Dutch-speaking part of Belgium, complained that Belgian laws violated the Convention. Under Belgian law, educational instruction was in the language which is predominant in the locality. These parents, however, living in Dutch-speaking localities, wanted their children taught in French. They argued that under the Belgian law their children would be taught in Dutch and be brought up in a language different from that of their parents unless their parents went to the expense and trouble of sending the children to French-speaking schools long distances from their homes. Except for a special situation in the periphery of Brussels where the Belgian law was held to discriminate against some children, the European Court of Human Rights decided that there had been no violation. The Court said that the Convention does not guarantee children the right to be educated in the language of their parents by the public authorities or with their aid. "The negative formulation indicates . . . that the Contracting Parties do not recognise such a right to education as would require them to establish at their own expense, or to subsidise, education of any particular type or at any particular level."

Similarly, in a case involving Danish parents who objected to compulsory sex-education in the public schools, it was held that the state met its obligation to "respect the right of parents to ensure . . . education in conformity with their own religious and philosophical convictions" because the parents were free to send their children to private school.[71]

The European Convention does not contain a minorities clause, but the restrictive interpretation of the Convention language gives some support to restrictive interpretation of Article 27 of the Covenant, also couched in negative terms and granting only the right not to be "denied the right . . . to enjoy . . . to profess . . . or to use. . . ."

Implementation of Article 27

By Article 2 of the Covenant all states parties are required to adopt such legislative or other measures as may be necessary to give effect to Article 27 and the other rights recognized in that Covenant. The Capotorti report argues, moreover, that the approval of the Covenant by the General Assembly conferred upon its articles "the value of general principles no less significant than those set forth in solemn United Nations declarations"; and, in particular, that the rights conferred by Article 27 of the Covenant "can be considered as forming an integral part of the system of protection of human rights and fundamental freedoms instituted after the Second World War under the aegis of the UN."[72] Even states not party to the Covenant, then, must respect Article 27 as though it were included in the Universal Declaration.

The Capotorti study contains a detailed account of the implementation by states of the three categories of rights guaranteed to members of minority groups by Article 27.[73] Further data will become available through reports by states parties to the Covenant under Article 40 thereof.[74] It is too early to analyze these data, but in the long run they should provide an important supplement to the Capotorti study.

The rights protected by Article 27 have been the subject of proposals for special implementation by additional multilateral instruments. Several proposals for a declaration or convention to protect the rights of members of minority groups were made in the United Nations in the early years, without success[75] and the subject was revived when Capotorti suggested that a declaration be prepared which could provide guidance for governments by throwing light on the various implications of Article 27 and by specifying the measures needed for the observance of the rights recognized by the article.[76] The Sub-Commission on Prevention of Discrimination and Protection of Minorities recommended to the Commission on Human Rights that such a declaration be drafted and Yugoslavia presented to the Commission a draft declaration.[77] As revised after a preliminary discussion, the draft read as follows:

Article 1

National, ethnic, linguistic or religious minorities (hereinafter referred to as minorities) have the right to existence, to respect for and promotion of their own national, cultural, linguistic and other characteristics and to enjoyment of full equality in relation to the rest of the population, regardless of their number.

Article 2

1. Members of minorities shall enjoy all the human rights and fundamental freedoms without any discrimination as to national, ethnic or racial origin, language or religion.
2. Any propaganda or activity aimed at discriminating against minorities or threatening their right to equal expression and development of their own characteristics is incompatible with the fundamental principles of the Charter of the United Nations and the Universal Declaration of Human Rights.

Article 3

For the purpose of realizing conditions of full equality and complete development of minorities as collectivities and of their individual members, it is essential to take measures which will enable them freely to express their characteristics, to develop their culture, education, language, traditions and customs and to participate on an equitable basis in the cultural, social, economic and political life of the country in which they live.

Article 4

1. In ensuring and promoting the rights of minorities, strict respect for the sovereignty, territorial integrity and political independence and non-interference in the internal affairs of those countries in which minorities live should be observed.
2. Respect for the aforementioned principles shall not prevent the fulfilment of the international commitments of States Members of the United Nations in relation to minorities. Member States should fulfil in good faith the commitments they have assumed under the Charter of the United Nations and international instruments and under other treaties or agreements to which they are parties.

Article 5

1. The development of contacts and co-operation among States and the exchange of information and experience on the achievement of minorities in cultural, educational and other fields create favourable conditions for the promotion of the rights of minorities and for their general progress.

2. States Members of the United Nations are invited to take the needs of minorities into account in developing their co-operation with other States, especially in the fields of culture, education and related areas of particular importance for minorities.[78]

Austria suggested the addition of the following provisions:

(a) No one belonging to a national, ethnic, religious or linguistic minority shall be expelled by means either of an individual or of a collective measure from the territory of the State of which he is a national.
(b) Genocide against national, ethnic, religious or linguisitc minorities should be considered as a crime against humanity.
(c) The changing of the demographic composition of a territory in which national, ethnic, religious and linguistic minorities live is incompatible with the spirit of international human rights instruments.[79]

The Commission decided to transmit the relevant documents to the governments of Member States for their comments.[80] With one exception,[81] the governments endorsed the idea of a declaration.[82] Similarly, the 1978 World Conference to Combat Racism and Racial Discrimination recommended the preparation of an international instrument for the protection of the rights of persons belonging to minorities.[83] Most commenting governments, as well as members of the Commission on Human Rights, have proposed, however, many changes in the Yugoslav draft declaration; and the government of Austria suggested that the declaration should be prepared with the necessary care and consideration by the main United Nations organ established for the purpose of protecting the minorities, the Sub-Commission on Prevention of Discrimination and Protection of Minorities.[84] This idea was endorsed by the Commission, which requested the Sub-Commission to submit its opinion on the draft declaration, taking into account all relevant documents.[85]

While the past record on drafting documents on this subject has been quite dismal, there is perhaps a chance of success this time. It is not a task to be undertaken hastily but, if consensus can be achieved, useful guidelines for implementation of Article 27 might be obtained. As pointed out by the government of Austria, such an instrument might become "a milestone in the progressive development of the rights of the individual."[86]

12

Permissible Limitations on Rights

ALEXANDRE CHARLES KISS

FEW IF ANY of the human rights recognized in the International Covenant on Civil and Political Rights are absolute. Many of them are subject to derogation in time of public emergency. Many are subject to limitation in the public interest at any time. Some rights may be limited if they conflict with the rights of others. But limitations, like derogations, are exceptional, to be construed and applied strictly, and not so as to swallow or vitiate the right itself.

It is important to distinguish between derogation from rights in time of public emergency (dealt with in essay 3), and the permissible limitations on rights considered here. Although the circumstance permitting derogations, "public emergency which threatens the life of the nation,"[1] resembles one of the grounds for possible limitations, "national security," derogations and limitations differ in character and scope, in the circumstances in which they may be imposed, and in the methods by which they may be effected. Derogations in time of emergency are clearly intended to have only a temporary character; limitations, in contrast, can be permanent.[2] Limitations on guaranteed rights must be provided by law but there is no such requirement for temporary derogations. Certain articles of the Covenant are not subject to derogations, for example Article 18 which provides for freedom of thought, conscience and religion, yet such rights are expressly made subject to possible limitations.[3]

The limitation clauses of the Covenant developed out of Article 29(2) of the Universal Declaration of Human Rights: "In the exercise of his rights and freedoms, everyone shall be subject only to such limitations as are determined by law solely for the purpose of securing due recognition and respect for the rights and freedoms of others and of meeting the just requirements of morality, public order and the general welfare in a democratic society."

The Universal Declaration of Human Rights is the only international instrument aimed at the global protection of human rights which concentrates limitations upon rights and freedoms in a single provision. In the Covenant on Civil and Political Rights, as in all other human rights conventions, the limitations are scattered, with specific provisions—generally identical, but with some variations—applicable to particular freedoms or rights.[4] The change from a single, general clause to several particular formulas reflected a desire to tailor limitations to the extent strictly necessary so as to assure maximum protection to the individual. For example, a comparison of Article 4 of the International Covenant on Economic, Social, and Cultural Rights with Article 8(1)(a) and (c) of that Covenant illustrates the difference between a situation where limitations can be general and one where such limitations should be narrowly prescribed. Article 4, applicable to the Covenant on Economic, Social, and Cultural Rights as a whole, allows only "such limitations as are determined by law only in so far as this may be compatible with the nature of these rights and solely for the purpose of promoting the general welfare in a democratic society."

Such a general provision reflects the large and ill-determined scope of most provisions in that Covenant, which recognizes such rights as the right to work, to just and favorable working conditions, to social security, to the highest attainable standard of physical and mental health, to education, etc. On the other hand, Article 8, the only provision in that Covenant which recognizes specific rights that can be protected by courts or similar bodies against invasion by the state—the right to form or join trade unions and the right of trade unions to function freely—includes its own limitation clause in terms which are specific and narrow, and very similar to those found in the International Covenant on Civil and Political Rights or in the European and American Conventions on Human Rights. One may thus conclude that a general limitation clause was deemed sufficient for rights asserted as general principles, as in the Universal Declaration, or for rights which are difficult to define with precision. However, in providing for possible limitations on relatively well-defined rights and freedoms, such as the liberty of movement, the right to a public hearing, the freedom of thought, it was considered important to provide limitation clauses that were more stringent and pointed to the particular right.

The fact that there is no general limitation clause in the International Covenant on Civil and Political Rights has an important consequence: limitations are permitted only where a specific limitation clause is provided and only to the extent it permits. In some cases, however, the permissibility of some limitations might be implied from the character of the right although no limitation is expressed. For example, during the drafting of Article 17 of the Covenant, protecting the right to privacy, the family, the home, and private correspondence, it was proposed to add a limitation clause similar to those contained in Articles 12(3), 14(1), 18(3), but the Third Committee rejected that proposal as unnecessarily restricting the scope of the article. It was pointed out, however, that this article enunciates principles, leaving each state free to determine how those principles should be put into effect.[5] Here too, of course, a state could not impose limitations that would vitiate the right.[6]

Thus, one has to examine the limitation clauses as they relate to the particular right or freedom recognized. It is striking, however, that almost the same terms are used in all of the limitation clauses of the Covenant on Civil and Political Rights, while some other terms, used in other international instruments protecting human rights, have been omitted. Thus, terms such as "the general welfare," "economic and social well-being," or "prevention of disorder or crime" are not to be found among the grounds for limiting the rights and freedoms guaranteed by the Covenant on Civil and Political Rights. They were in fact proposed as permissible grounds for limitation on the right to movement and choice of residence in Article 12(3), but the Human Rights Commission rejected them as too far-reaching.[7] Their inclusion in other international instruments can be explained by the particular context. "General welfare" was included in Article 29 of the Universal Declaration and in Article 4 of the International Covenant on Economic, Social, and Cultural Rights. Since both articles deal with rights connected with economic and social welfare, concern for the general welfare may be a proper motivation for limiting those individual rights. The fact that Article 8(2) of the European Convention allows limitations on the right to privacy in the interest of the "economic well-being of the country" can be understood in the economic context in which the Convention was drafted; it reflected the foreign exchange regulations then common in Europe and the perceived necessity for opening correspondence to check currency violations. The term "prevention of disorder or crime" used in several provisions of the European Convention,[8] is closely connected with the terms "public safety" and "public order," and its omission from the Covenant must be considered in dealing with those terms.

The terms which appear in the limitation clauses of the Covenant on Civil and Political Rights are:

—National security	Articles 12(3), 14(1), 19(3), 21, and 22(2)
—Public safety	Articles 18(3), 21, 22(2)
—Public order (sometimes supplemented by *ordre public,* in parentheses)	Articles 12(3), 14(1), 18(3), 19(3), 21, 22(2)
—Public health	Articles 12(3), 18(3), 19(3), 21, 22(2)
—Public morals	Articles 12(3), 14(1), 18(3), 19(3), 21, 22(2).

This paper seeks to determine the significance and scope of those grounds of permissible limitation. Other expressions in the limitation clauses also deserve attention: limitations must be "provided by law," "in conformity with law," or "prescribed by law," and "necessary in a democratic society."

The Covenant provides that some rights may be limited as necessary to protect "the rights and freedoms of others." That raises the issues of conflicts between rights and the options permitted to the state in choosing between individual rights or in establishing preferences or priorities among them.*

Mode of Interpretation

All of the terms of limitation are found in several articles of the Covenant as well as in other international human rights instruments. The question arises whether they have known meaning and can be interpreted in the abstract without regard to the substance of the particular article.

Article 31 of the Vienna Convention on the Law of Treaties requires that treaties be interpreted "in good faith in accordance with the ordinary meaning to be given to the terms of the treaty in their context and in the light of its object and purpose."[9] The context comprises the text itself, including its preamble and annexes, any agreements relating to the treaty, and instruments connected with the treaty. Any relevant agreements between the parties, and rules of international law applicable between them, should also be taken into account. The stress is on the importance of context, broadly conceived. The fact that terms are used in instruments dedicated to protecting human rights is an impor-

---

* That principle of limitation is dealt with in the Introduction.

tant element in construing them. But the Vienna Convention failed to distinguish between the immediate context of a term in the provision which contains it and the more general context of the treaty as a whole and the other provisions it contains; it should require the clearest evidence to persuade one that the same terms used in different provisions of the same treaty were intended to have fundamentally different meanings. Of course, even while the same words should mean essentially the same thing in all the provisions of a text, their scope and significance may vary according to the provision in which they are included. The term "public morals," for example, may have a different significance and be applied in a different way when it concerns a possible restriction of the liberty of movement (Article 12(3)) than when it is invoked to exclude the public and the press from a trial (Article 14(1)).

One must reject also the suggestion that the preparatory work supports essentially different interpretations of the same term in different provisions. The limitation clauses of the Covenant, especially those of Articles 18, 19, 21, and 22, were drafted, revised, and adopted at different times, and as a result such terms as "national security," "public order" and "public health or morals" were variously phrased, although no difference in substance was intended. No steps were taken to conform these clauses despite suggestions that it be done in order to avoid questions of interpretation and application.[10] The *travaux* must therefore be used with caution. Moreover, according to Article 32 of the Vienna Convention, the preparatory work of a treaty and the circumstances of its conclusion are but supplementary means of interpretation which may be used only in order to confirm the ordinary meaning of the terms in their context. Recourse to the preparatory work to support different meanings of the same term may be had only if uniform interpretation would lead to a result which would be manifestly contrary to the object and purpose of the Covenant.[11] That is not the case here.

One may ask, too, how far other instruments having the same object and including the same terms are relevant for the interpretation of the Covenant. The Vienna Convention on the Law of Treaties is restrictive on this point. According to Article 31, only the Optional Protocol to the Covenant could be considered as relevant, and that protocol does not include any of the terms to be considered here. But if no other legal instrument can be cited as providing a more or less mandatory interpretation of the terms under discussion, there is nonetheless a considerable *corpus juris* regarding human rights, composed of the Universal Declaration, the two UN Covenants, the European Convention, the American Convention, and other instruments. In some cases international judicial organs have also interpreted these terms. Although evidence from such sources as to the meanings of the terms here under consideration may not be determinative as a matter of law, it cannot be neglected.

The Meaning of the Terms Used in the Limitation Clauses

All the terms under consideration—"national security," "public safety," "public order (*ordre public*)," "public health," "public morals"—have much in common and may be closely linked. All of them are difficult to define and imply a measure of relativity in that they may be understood differently in different countries, in different circumstances, at different times. All of them relate to a particular conception of the interests of a society. All directly implicate the relationship between state authority and individuals or groups of individuals. Indeed, one might ask whether all the terms do not express different aspects of a single, universal concept—*ordre public*.

"National Security"

Almost all limitation clauses include "national security" as a ground for restricting the right to which the clause applies.[12] In the Covenant on Civil and Political Rights, "national security" is a permissible basis for limiting the freedom of movement and the free choice of residence (Article 12(3)); for excluding the press and the public from all or part of a trial (Article 14(1)); for restricting the freedom of expression (Article 19(3)), the right of peaceful assembly (Article 21), and the right to freedom of association with others; and for limiting the right to form and join trade unions (Article 22).

It may be assumed that "national security" has the same meaning in all of these provisions, but none of them gives any explanation of what that meaning is.[13] Some evidence of its meaning may be found from context and from other provisions. At least there is evidence of what "national security" does not mean. "National security" is used with other terms so as to suggest that they are not equivalent but alternative. Articles 21 and 22(3), for example, permit limitations on grounds of "national security or public safety," and one may conclude that they are distinct and different grounds for limitation. That conclusion is reinforced by the fact that one clause lists "public safety" but not "national security." Article 18(3) provides: "Freedom to manifest one's religion or beliefs may be subject only to such limitations as are prescribed by law and are necessary to protect public safety, order, health, or morals or the fundamental rights and freedoms of others."

Failure to mention national security in that article justifies the conclusion that the omission was intentional and that exigencies of national security do not justify limitations on freedom to manifest one's religion or belief.[14] Similarly "national security" is regularly included together with and in addition to "public order," and must be presumed to mean something different.

Distinctions between "national security" and other terms are implied also in other human rights instruments. In the European Convention considerations of national security permit limitations on the public character of trials (Article 6(1)), freedom of expression (Article 10(2)), peaceful assembly and association (Article 11(2)), and the liberty of movement and free choice of residence (Protocol No. 4, Article 2(3)). Some of those clauses include both "national security" and "public safety" as distinct grounds. By contrast, Article 9 includes only "public safety," and one must conclude that concern for national security is not a permissible ground for limitations on freedom of thought, conscience, and religion. (The American Convention, too, sometimes uses both "national security" and "public safety," but sometimes "public safety" is included while "national security" is not.) Article 8(2) of the European Convention permits limitations on the right of privacy for national security and public safety reasons, as well as "for the economic well-being of the country." Article 10 permits limitations on freedom of expression in the "interest of national security, territorial integrity or public safety." One may conclude, then, that national security is clearly distinct from "public safety" and "public order" with which it is commonly linked, and probably also from "economic well-being of a country" or "territorial integrity."[15] That does not mean that "territorial integrity" or even "economic well-being" can never be relevant to national security, but they are not the same. A threat to territorial integrity or economic well-being is not in itself sufficient to constitute a threat to national security.

These distinctions made, it is still necessary to define the content and scope of "national security." A definition must consider the two elements of the term: "national" and "security."

The word "national" is generally used to refer to that which concerns a country as a whole. Thus, restrictions on human rights can be adopted under this concept only if the interest of the whole nation is at stake. This excludes restrictions in the sole interest of a government, regime, or power group. Limitations are not based on "national security," moreover, if their only purpose is to avoid riots or other troubles, or to frustrate revolutionary movements which do not threaten the life of the whole nation. Such grounds for restriction may sometimes fall within the scope of "public order" or "public safety," but not "national security."

The word "security," we have seen, clearly has a meaning different from public "safety" or "order," since these words are frequently used in the same clauses as alternative grounds. An explanation of "security" can be derived perhaps from the United Nations Charter. As all universal documents protecting human rights have their roots in the UN Charter,[16] it may be suggested that the term "security" used in the Covenant corresponds to the term "national security" as used in the Charter. The Charter is dedicated to maintaining "international peace and security,"[17] meaning peace between states and the security of every state. To the end of maintaining peace and security, the principal norm of the Charter, Article 2(4), forbids the use or threat of force against the political independence or territorial integrity of another state.[18] One may conclude that "national security" in the Covenant means the protection of territorial integrity and political independence against foreign force or threats of force. It would probably justify limitations on particular rights of individuals or groups where the restrictions were necessary to meet the threat or use of external force.[19] It does not require a state of war or national emergency, but permits continuing peacetime limitations, for example, those necessary to prevent espionage or to protect military secrets.[20] Presumably this ground of limitation would permit special limitations on the rights of members of the armed forces.[21]

"Public Safety"

In the International Covenant on Civil and Political Rights, the term "public safety" figures in the limitation clauses of Article 18 (freedom of thought, conscience, and religion); Article 21 (the right of peaceful assembly); and Article 22 (the right to freedom of association). Originally the term was included also in the draft of Article 12 (the freedom of movement and residence), but it was later replaced by "public order (*ordre public*)" despite objections by several members of the Third Committee of the General Assembly, who considered the latter concept too vague. They thought that the term "public safety" would make clear that the right to freedom of movement and free choice of residence could be limited only if its exercise involved danger to the safety of persons.[22] "Public safety" and "public order" are both listed in Articles 21 and 22(2), indicating that they were not considered to have the same meaning.

The term "public safety" appears frequently in the European Convention on Human Rights. In two provisions (Article 9(2), freedom of thought, conscience, and religion; and Article 2(3) of Protocol 4, freedom of movement) it is accompanied by the term "public order." In three other provisions (Article 8, right to privacy; Article 10, freedom of expression; and Article 11, freedom of peaceful assembly) it appears in connection with the "prevention of disorder or crime."[23] The drafters of the European Convention apparently considered that the expression "public safety" did not necessarily cover the prevention of disorder or crime.[24]

In the American Convention on Human Rights, the situation is similar. Out of the four limitation clauses, three, freedom of conscience and of religion (Article 12(3)); right of peaceful assembly (Article 15); and freedom of association (Article 16), link "public safety" and "public order." Article 12(3) simply states "to protect public safety, order . . . ," whereas the two other provisions state "in the interest of . . . public safety or public order." Article 22(3), freedom of movement and free choice of residence, adds to both terms a third one: "the prevention of crime", without its frequent complement in the European Convention, "or disorder."

The interpretation of the term "public safety" is particularly difficult. It cannot be assimilated to "public order," which is certainly a broader concept, but the two are apparently linked. "Public safety" apparently also includes but is broader than "the prevention of disorder or crime." The French text of the Covenant uses two different terms for the English "public safety": *sécurité* in Article 18(3) and *sûreté publique* in Articles 21 and 22. The latter term may provide some guidance when considered together with opinions manifested during the discussions in the Third Committee. Rights guaranteed by the Covenant may be restricted if their exercise involves danger to the safety of persons, to their life, bodily integrity, or health.[25] The need to protect public safety could justify restrictions resulting from police rules and security regulations tending to the protection of the safety of individuals in transportation and vehicular traffic; for consumer protection, for ameliorating labor conditions, etc.

"Public Order"

"Public order" has a central place in the limitation clauses of the Covenant. It is to be found in every one of these clauses. Most discussions of the limitation clauses have focused upon this term, which is particularly ambiguous, does not have the same meaning in different legal systems, and may not have any meaning at all in some legal systems.

In the International Covenant on Civil and Political Rights this concept appears in different forms. In most cases "public order" is followed in parentheses by the French words *ordre public* (Articles 12(3), 14(1), 19(3), 21, 22(2)).[26] However, Article 18(3), freedom of thought, conscience, and religion, envisages only "limitations as are . . . necessary to protect public safety, order, health, etc. . . ," and in the French text "restrictions . . . necessaires à la protection de la sécurité, de l'ordre et de la santé publique. . . ."[27]

The inclusion of this ground of limitation in various provisions of the Covenant followed discussions more or less parallel in every instance. As regards Article 12(3), for example, an amendment proposed that the Third Committee insert "public order (*ordre public*)" to replace the expression "public safety."[28] The discussion on this proposal was considerable. Some representatives objected that the English words "public order" were not equivalent to the French expression *ordre public* or to the Spanish words *orden público*. Others considered that such a vague expression was dangerous because it would justify far-reaching restrictions. Some members of the Committee preferred the term "public safety," which had been used in the text prepared by the Commission on Human Rights. A majority of the members, however, favored the use of the expression "public order (*ordre public*)," believing that this expression was broad enough to include the concept of "public safety."[29]

The text drafted by the Commission on Human Rights for Article 14(1) contained the term "public order" as one of the reasons for which the press and the public might be excluded from all or part of a trial. In later discussions it was argued unsuccessfully that the words "public order" in English do not have the same meaning as the French *ordre public* and should be replaced by "the prevention of disorder," which would represent what was actually intended.[30] Again at the fourteenth session of the General Assembly, the Third Committee decided that it would be useful to do as had been previously decided in drafting Article 12 and inserted in the English and Russian texts the French words *ordre public,* in parentheses.[31] A similar discussion led to the same solution for Articles 19(3) and 21; and the same result was reached without much discussion in Article 22.[32] In that case, however, a proposal to permit restrictions on association by members of the administration of the state was rejected as unnecessary because it was implied in "national security" and "public order"; it was however inserted with respect to the armed forces and the police.[33] In Article 18(3), providing for limitations on freedom to manifest one's religion or beliefs, however, essentially the same discussion resulted only in a reference to "order" without "public" and without the corresponding French term.[34]

The International Covenant on Economic, Social, and Cultural Rights also contains "public order" in the limitation clause regarding the right to form trade unions and the right of trade unions to function freely (Article 8(1a and 1c), but *ordre public* was not inserted. No specific discussion of the term "public order" is recorded.

Any attempt to interpret the term "public order" has to recognize it as a term of art borrowed from national legal systems. It must also consider the significance of the term in different legal systems, since it clearly differs from system to system. The addition in the English text of the French term *ordre public* indicates the importance of the French conception and its jurisprudence in determining the meaning and scope of this limitation.[35]

In French jurisprudence, *ordre public* has several meanings in different contexts. In French private law, a contract or a hestamentary disposition will not be given effect if it is contrary to *ordre public*[36] (serving as a kind of *jus cogens*). In a private international law (conflict of laws) case, a court will not give effect to foreign law, although its applicability is indicated, where that law is deemed contrary to *ordre public*.[37] In both these uses the term approximates closely the term "public policy" in Anglo-American law which is invoked in the same way in similar contexts.[38]

Ordre public as used in French public law is more directly relevant. There, in its principal meaning, *ordre public* refers to the "police power" of the state broadly conceived (*police administrative générale*).[39] This police power, however, must be exercised in a legal framework which includes fundamental human rights (*libertés publiques*), such as the security of persons, freedom of worship, freedom of expression, the right of association, etc.[40] The object of *ordre public* was early declared to be the maintenance of *le bon ordre, la sûreté, la salubrité publique* (good order, safety, public health).[41] The concept was held to imply authority to carry out various public functions: *bon ordre* has been understood as the maintenance of "the peace," or public tranquility; *sûreté,* as including authority to assure safety in fields such as road traffic; *salubrité publique* as the healthfulness and safety of buildings, industrial or trade installations, etc. The concept was later expanded to include esthetic elements (protection of monuments), moral elements (regulation of prostitution or pornography, special protection for the morals of children), an *ordre public economic* (consumer protection, speculation control), and an *ordre public politique* (protection of the *légalité républicaine,* or respect for the constitutional political sytem).[42] In a very broad sense, *ordre public* includes the existence and the functioning of the state organization, which not only allows it to maintain peace and order in the country but ensures the common welfare by satisfying collective needs and protecting human rights.

These functions, of course, may entail some limitations on the autonomy, rights, and freedoms of individual citizens.[43] However, the concept itself reflects the principle that there are limitations on the state's powers, especially as far as human rights are concerned; moreover, *ordre public* may itself demand respect for human rights as an element in the exercise of the public authority. A recent decision of the French Supreme Court (*Cour de Cassation*) implies that to fail to inform a person accused of crime of all the relevant elements of the charges against him is contrary to *ordre public* since the latter includes Articles 6 and 13 of the European Convention on Human Rights, the rights to due process and to an effective remedy for violation of guaranteed rights and freedoms.[44] Thus, roughly speaking, in the conflict between state authority and individual rights and freedoms, *ordre public* can be on either side. It is also a formula for resolving such conflicts in accordance with the general interest.

Both the private and public law uses of *ordre public* converge in a principle designed to assure a minimum level of public interest and social organization, consistent not only with the values of the society but with universal principles of civilization and justice. That is seen in references to *ordre public international,* which has been characterized as follows.

> Parmi les lois et les principes d'ordre public que contient tout ordre juridique, il y en a certains qui, ainsi que par exemple d'une part l'interdiction de l'esclavage et d'autre part le respect de la dignité de la personne humaine, se fondent sur des conceptions de justice et de civilisation universelle; leur denomination approprieé est pourtant celle de lois et principes d'ordre public international."[45]

For our purposes, then, *ordre public* permits limitations on particular human rights where these limitations are necessary for that accepted level of public welfare and social organization. But the human rights of individuals are part of that minimum civilized order and cannot be lightly sacrificed even for the good of the majority or the common good of all. The result is a concept that is not absolute or precise, and cannot be reduced to a rigid formula but must remain a function of time, place and circumstances.[46] In both civil and common law systems it requires someone of independence and authority to apply it by evaluating the different interests in each case.

> La notion d'ordre public s'apparente à une directive jurisprudentielle suffisamment imprécise pour permettre au juge de faire prévaloir dans chaque espèce l'intérêt général qui peut entraîner soit le respect des libertés, soit leur limitation.[47]

In this context, *ordre public* is not quite like "public policy,"[48] but the English term "public order" which the Covenant uses is perhaps even less adequate. In the debates on the Covenant it was urged that in Anglo-American jurisprudence "public order" means only "absence of disorder." The draftsmen solved the problem by using "public order" but broadened by the addition of the French concept *ordre public*.[49]

In sum: "public order" may be understood as a basis for restricting some specified rights and freedoms in the interest of the adequate functioning of the public institutions necessary to the collectivity when other conditions, discussed below, are met. Examples of what a society may deem appropriate for the *ordre public* have been indicated: prescription for peace and good order; safety; public health; esthetic and moral considerations; and economic order (consumer protection, etc.). It must be remembered, however, that in both civil law and common law systems, the use of this concept implies that courts are available and function correctly to monitor and resolve its tensions with a clear knowledge of the basic needs of the social organization and a sense of its civilized values.

"Public Health"

All but one of the limitation clauses of the International Covenant on Civil and Political Rights include "public health" as one of the possible grounds for restricting the rights or freedoms guaranteed. (The only exception is Article 14(1), which allows the exclusion of the press and the public from all or part of a trial, and its absence there is understandable, given the subject matter.)

During the drafting of the Covenant there was little discussion of this concept. Some concrete problems which were explicitly raised—such as the prevention of epidemics—fall clearly within the scope of this limitation, while others, such as the control of prostitution, might come within other grounds for restriction, such as "public morals." [50]

The European and the American Conventions on Human Rights also contain the term "public health" in all of their limitation clauses. The European Commission of Human Rights has interpreted the term broadly: for example, "public health" was held to include measures taken for the prevention of disease among cattle. [51]

Neither the inclusion of this ground of limitation nor its meaning engendered any substantial dispute or discussion in the drafting of the Covenant or of any of the other international instruments. That suggests that it corresponds to a relatively clear and accepted concept and is not likely to be a focus of controversy. Support for a comprehensive definition of public health might be adduced from Article 12 of the International Covenant on Economic, Social, and Cultural Rights:

1. The States Parties to the present Covenant recognize the right of everyone to the enjoyment of the highest attainable standard of physical and mental health.
2. The steps to be taken by the States Parties to the present Covenant to achieve the full realization of this right shall include those necessary for:
   a) The provision for the reduction of the stillbirth-rate and of infant mortality and for the healthy development of the child,
   b) The improvement of all aspects of environmental and industrial hygiene;
   c) The prevention, treatment and control of epidemic, endemic, occupational and other diseases;
   d) The creation of conditions which would assure to all medical service and medical attention in the event of sickness."

What a state is required to do by that article is surely permissible under the Covenant, even if it entails small, normal limitations on other individual rights.

"Public Morals"

"Public morals" is another term included in all the limitation clauses of the International Covenant on Civil and Political Rights. [52] In Article

14(1), the right to a fair and public hearing, the word "public" was omitted, which may mean that grounds more related to private than to public morals may be acceptable for excluding the press and the public from a trial, for example, when intimate details of private life or the reputation of a person are at stake.[53]

The jurisprudence of the European Court of Human Rights indicates that it is impossible to find a uniform European conception of morals, thus necessitating a margin of appreciation left to the states.[54]

"Public morals" here alludes to principles which are not always legally enforceable but which are accepted by a great majority of the citizens as general guidelines for their individual and collective behavior. Whether they include acts done in private, alone, or between consenting adults, has been debated. Any interpretation of the term "public morals" in the International Covenant would doubtless take into consideration the elements stressed by the European Court i.e., the primary responsibility of the state to secure the rights and liberties recognized in that Convention and the relativity and changing conception and content of morals.

A Supplementary Condition: "Provided by Law"

In the Covenant on Civil and Political Rights (and the other international instruments) the limitation clauses provide that restrictions must be "provided by law," "prescribed by law," "in conformity with law," "in accordance with law."[55] It was argued that there was a difference between some of these expressions: "prescribed by law" suggests that action must be authorized by specific legal provisions, while "in pursuance to the law" or "in conformity with the law" might be satisfied by reference to general legal principles, common law, or accepted government authority.[56] In the Covenant on Civil and Political Rights, however, "provided by law" and "prescribed by law" seem to have the same meaning; at least the corresponding expression in the French text is the same (*prévu par pa loi*).[57]

In every case the objective is to avoid arbitrary restrictions on rights by requiring that the limitation be established by general rule.[58] The corresponding terms used in the European Convention have been interpreted in this sense.[59] There is but one exception to this principle, in the provision permitting the exclusion of the press and the public from all or part of a trial.[60] This exception is understandable; the judge must decide whether the circumstances for each case are such as to require the exclusion. The authority of the judge to do so is established by the Covenant and needs no basis in specific national legislation.

The condition that a restriction must be provided by law is essentially a formal one: any restriction on recognized rights and freedoms in a state must be by general rule, normally imposed by the legislature; measures taken by the executive authority, such as the police or local administration, are excluded unless authorized by general legislation.[61] That a restriction must be provided by law does not necessarily suggest any limits on the substance of the law. In the debates in the Human Rights Commission on Article 12, however, it seemed to be agreed that in addition to serving one of the purposes indicated, all laws providing for restrictions on freedom of movement must be "just." To that end, it was suggested that the article state that the law must be in accordance with the principles of the Charter and the Universal Declaration of Human Rights. Instead the final text requires that the restriction be "consistent with the other rights recognized in the Covenant."[62] Moreover, laws limiting any of the rights must be in conformity with the fundamental principle laid down in Article 5(1): any act aimed at the destruction of any of the rights and freedoms recognized in the Covenant is prohibited.

A Key Concept: "Necessary in a Democratic Society"

Another condition included in some of the limitation clauses of the Covenant (and of other international human rights instruments) is that such limitations must be "necessary in a democratic society." Although included in Article 29 of the Universal Declaration on Human Rights, the reference to a democratic society was inserted in only three of the six limitation clauses of the Covenant: Article 14(1), right to a fair and public hearing; Article 21, right of peaceful assembly; and Article 22(2), freedom of association. When Article 14(1) was discussed in the Commission on Human Rights, the words "in a democratic society" were regarded as a salutary safeguard; opposition to the phrase on the grounds that it was ambiguous and subject to different interpretations was unsuccessful.[63] Later, in the Third Committee, some representatives stressed the usefulness of that formula to qualify the notions of "public order" and "national security" because it affords a precious guarantee against the risks of arbitrary treatment.[64] Similarly, during the discussion of Article 21 in the Commission of Human Rights, the opinion was expressed that freedom of assembly could not be effectively protected unless the limitation clause was applied according to the principles recognized in a democratic society. One answer to the objection that the word "democracy" might be interpreted differently in various countries was that a democratic society might be distinguished by its respect for the principles of the Charter of the United Nations, the Universal Declaration of Human Rights and the Covenants on Human Rights.[65]

Still, the reference to democracy was not included in Article 12, liberty of movement and freedom to choose a residence; Article 18, right to freedom of thought, conscience, and religion; or Article 19, right to hold opinions and freedom of expression. In fact, during the discussion of Article 18 in the Commission on Human Rights, a proposal to add the modifying clause "in a democratic society" did not succeed.[66] It is difficult, however, to find any basis for concluding that the omissions are significant.[67] The one specific limitation provision of the International Covenant on Economic, Social, and Cultural Rights, Article 8(1a) and (1c), concerning the right to form and join trade unions and the right of trade unions to function, includes the words "necessary in a democratic society." The same phrase appears also in some, but not all of the limitation clauses of the American Convention.[68] Like the corresponding provisions of the Covenant on Civil and Political Rights, Article 12(3) of the American Convention (freedom of conscience and religion) and Article 13(2b) (freedom of thought and expression) do not include the phrase. In contrast, the provision of the American Convention recognizing the freedom of movement and residence (Article 22(3)), mentions "necessary in a democratic society" which the corresponding clause of the Covenant, Article 12(3), does not.

In the European Convention on Human Rights, the expression "necessary in a democratic society" seems to be one of the most important concepts. It is part of each limitation clause, and it also plays a paramount role in the case law of that Convention.[69] This may be explained by the importance of an "effective political democracy" in the European countries "which are like-minded and have a common heritage of political traditions, ideals, freedom, and the rule of law."[70]

Still, the definition of that concept does not seem to be easy even where such an ideological basis exists. The European Commission of Human Rights explained that it would evaluate whether an interference in the exercise of a recognized right was necessary by paying "due regard where appropriate to legislation of other States signatory to the Convention and to international instruments on the subject."[71] In the *Vagrancy* cases, the European Court expressed the opinion that there is an *ordre public* within the Council of Europe which is a model for a democratic society.[72] In the *Handyside* case, the Court attempted to determine some elements of a "democratic society," and of one of its essential foundations, the freedom of expression. It found pluralism, tolerance, and broadmindedness to be essential elements of the concept. The margin of appreciation which states have in this field is under the control of the Court, which has the task to review, under the provisions of the Convention, the decisions of state authorities in the exercise of their power of appreciation.[73]

Here, as in regard to the concept of "public order," experience shows that the concept cannot be separated from the institutions which guarantee it: "Individual freedom, in our democratic countries, is protected by our democratic institutions. Consequently, the safeguards required, too, are inseparable from these institutions."[74]

The different concepts which may serve as grounds for restricting certain recognized rights and freedoms should be generally examined in a broader political concept, that of a model society. It may be submitted that even in the limitation clauses where no explicit mention is made of a democratic framework, the idea of democracy is always underlying, signifying that "every 'formality,' 'condition,' 'restriction,' or 'penalty' imposed in this sphere must be proportionate to the legitimate aim pursued."[75]

It remains difficult, however, to define the parameters of the notion of democratic society, even in a regional framework such as Europe, where a common heritage of political traditions and freedoms is a reality.[76] This difficulty is even greater at a universal level for the Covenant on Civil and Political Rights.

Certain elements, however, have been suggested. A "democratic society" implies political freedom and individual rights which reduce or moderate the authority of the state.[77] As expressed by Phédon Vegleris:

> . . . il est clair qu'il s'agit d'une référence à la conception d'un aménagement des sociétés humaines qu'on a voulu mettre à la base, d'une part, de l'édification d'un ordre mondial de paix et de progrès et, d'autre part, de l'intégration progressive des continents. Cette conception . . . a atteint un degré de cristallisation qui, s'il est loin d'être final, permet de discerner certains éléments ou même un certain alliage d'éléments concrets. Ces éléments sont d'une part la liberté politique dans le but de la participation du peuple 'réel' au pouvoir, et d'autre part la reconnaissance et l'opposabilité à l'Etat de certains droits essentiels et de certaines libertés élémentaires de l'individu.[78]

In line with the experience of the European human rights institutions, it should be added that a "democratic society" also implies the existence of appropriate supervisory institutions to monitor respect for human rights.

Conclusion

The limitation clauses of the International Covenant on Civil and Political Rights must be seen as interdependent. Each of the terms used is related to other terms, and a clause contained in one article cannot be separated from that used in another article, even though their actual application may lead to different results in different cases.

This interdependence implies also that the limitation clauses must be construed in the light of other articles of the Covenant having a general scope. It is important, in particular, to keep in mind Article 5(1) of the Covenant:

> Nothing in the present Covenant may be interpreted as implying for any State, group or person any right to engage in any activity or perform any act aimed at the destruction of any of the rights and freedoms recognized herein or at their limitation to a greater extent than is provided for in the present Covenant.

Clearly, that provision means that limitation clauses must be given a strict interpretation.

All the limitation clauses (with the exception of that in Article 14(1)), moreover, use the word "necessary." That indicates that restrictions on rights are permissible only when they are essential, i.e., inevitable. General rules of interpretation in international law lead to the same conclusion. Limitation clauses cannot be avoided in the system of the Covenant, which allows the adaptation of general rules guaranteeing fundamental rights and freedoms to particular situations prevailing in different states. But limitations are exceptions, and for that reason they must be interpreted restrictively.[79]

The clearest meaning of such strict interpretation is that an adequate legal justification is needed for each limitation a state would adopt. Such limitations, however, must also meet another condition: they must be acceptable in the specific political context which has been defined as a "democratic society." Even if its criteria may be difficult to determine in the abstract, this requirement eliminates forms of political organization which grant unfettered discretion to the state and its authorities. It recognizes the principle that government is limited by the concept of human rights, and that even the good of the majority or the common good of all does not permit certain invasions of individual autonomy and freedom. It does not permit pretext or paranoia. Whatever a state might do by temporary derogation in time of public emergency under Article 4 of the Covenant, it cannot insist that it is *necessary* for its national security or for *ordre public* to maintain intensive regimentation, censorship or other controls limiting freedom of movement and residence; the right to public trial; or freedom of conscience, expression, assembly, or association, which limitations are incompatible with a democratic society committed to individual freedoms and rights.

In the first instance, of course, every provision of the Covenant, including the limitation clause, are for every state party to apply and interpret for itself. The authorities of the state must decide what the Covenant requires and what it permits, including what limitations are permitted because they are necessary in a democratic society for the reasons indicated. But the conformity of any restriction to the provision of the Covenant is not a domestic matter but a question of international law. National institutions must review them in light of international law in the first instance; they are also subject to review internationally.

A principal method of limiting arbitrary power is the creation of appropriate supervisory organs. That is a major lesson of the concept of "public order" in different legal systems and of the practice under the enforcement mechanisms of the European human rights system.

This requirement of supervision and scrutiny may sometimes seem to contradict one of the conditions in the limitation clauses: that such limitations be "provided by law." As a general rule, the courts of different states must apply laws as they have been promulgated, without judging the timeliness, desirability, or appropriateness of their provisions or their conformity with the constitution or with other general principles of law. Thus, the very fact that the restrictions of guaranteed rights and liberties must be "provided by law" may remove these restrictions from judicial control, whereas the notions of "public order" and of a "democratic society" imply, as an essential corollary, some appropriate scrutiny.

In fact, this contradiction may be resolved in different ways. Some states have systems for reviewing the constitutionality of laws, whether by general or by constitutional courts. Such organs could be given authority also to review restrictions applied to the rights and liberties guaranteed by international instruments. Or, a legal system could permit international treaties to be applied by national tribunals even where such treaties may be contrary to national laws. In such a system, a national tribunal could refuse to apply a restriction which it finds to be impermissible under the limitation clause of a right or liberty guaranteed by the Covenant or another international instrument of human rights.

Finally, the review of restrictions "provided by law" for conformity with international instruments can be exercised at an international level, as is the case with the European Commission and the European Court of Human Rights. If a particular state has no national organ with authority to review the conformity of national laws to human rights treaties, the only remaining control is the international one. This underlines the importance of the task of international enforcement mechanisms to supervise state acts, legislative as well as judicial, and to decide in concrete cases whether specific restrictions are in conformity with the rights and freedoms guaranteed by international provisions. One should always keep in mind that the ultimate objective of the limitation clauses is not to increase the power of a state or government but to ensure the effective enforcement of the rights and freedoms of its inhabitants.

13

The Obligation to Implement
the Covenant in Domestic Law

OSCAR SCHACHTER

IN THIS PAPER I consider the effect to be given the International Covenant on Civil and Political Rights in the domestic law of the states parties to the Covenant. There is no general rule of international law that treaties must have domestic law effects; many treaties have no domestic legal consequences and do not require or contemplate implementation through the national legal systems of the parties. The Covenant, however, clearly requires execution through domestic legal measures. That requirement follows from the general commitment of each state party to the Covenant "to respect and ensure to all individuals within its territory and subject to its jurisdiction the rights recognized in the present Covenant" (Article 2(1)).

This basic commitment of the parties may be characterized as an "obligation of result." In itself it says nothing about the means to achieve that result. However, Article 2 goes on to specify the means by which the parties are to carry out their obligation to respect and ensure rights. In paragraph 2, the parties undertake to adopt such legislative or other measures as may be necessary to give effect to the rights recognized. That obligation as to means is conditional on their being necessary but it is an obligation nonetheless. Paragraph 3 of Article 2 adds additional obligations of means, here means of repairing violations that have occurred. It requires that an effective remedy be ensured to any person whose rights are violated. It also requires that the right to such a remedy be determined by a competent authority "provided for by the legal system of the State" and that the remedies granted be enforced by the state authorities. There is a specific obligation in subparagraph 3(b) that the state "develop the possibilities of judicial remedy." These provisions of Article 2 impose independent obligations on the states parties. It is not enough for a party to say that it respects and ensures rights (the obligation of result); it must also fulfill the obligation to use the specified means required by Article 2 through its domestic legal system, to give effect to the rights or to repair any violations.

While Article 2 is clear as to the basic requirement of implementation of the Covenant in domestic law, it leaves open questions as to the status of the Covenant in national law, the mode of application, the latitude for adaptation of national law, the self-executing effect of the Covenant in domestic law, the requirement of effective remedies, and the admissibility of reservations in these matters. We shall consider these questions in the light of the text of the Covenant, the preparatory work and the diverse national law procedures available for the execution of the Covenant.

The Status of the Covenant in Domestic Law

Does the obligation to ensure rights and remedies within the domestic legal system require the states parties to make the Covenant itself part of domestic law? A number of states have in fact done so in accordance with constitutional provisions which automatically incorporate treaties into their internal law.[1] In these cases, the Covenant has become directly mandatory for all national authorities including the courts, and (subject to local jurisdictional requirements) may be invoked by individuals in claiming redress for infringements of their rights. However, many other states parties to the Covenant do not provide constitutionally, or in practice, for the automatic incorporation of treaties into national law. These states include the United Kingdom and most other Commonwealth nations, the Scandinavian countries, and several of the Eastern European countries. In these countries, treaties enter into the body of national law only if and when legislation is specially enacted for that purpose. Without such legislation, the courts generally are not entitled to give direct effect to the treaties nor can the treaties be invoked by individuals as a basis for judicial or other remedies.[2]

The fact that this situation obtains in many countries makes it pertinent to consider whether the Covenant itself imposes an obligation that it be made part of domestic law. This question is, of course, distinct from the question of constitutional law governing the effect of treaties in domestic law. Treaties may, irrespective of constitutional law, require that they be given direct effect in a domestic legal system and, if they do, the parties are bound to follow the treaty requirement whatever their constitutional procedures for doing so. In such cases the states which do not have automatic incorporation would have to enact special legislation making the treaty part of their domestic law.

When we turn to the text of Article 2 of the Covenant, we find no requirement that the Covenant be incorporated into domestic law. What it does require (in paragraph 2) is that the parties take the necessary steps to adopt such legislation or other measures *as may be necessary* to give effect to the rights recognized (emphasis added). This phrasing leaves open the precise legal character of the measures, e.g., incorporation of the Covenant into law, other legislation, executive or administrative orders. The section leaves open, too, for determination in any specific case, whether or not legislative or other measures may in fact be necessary to ensure the rights and remedies required by the Covenant. In addition, the opening phrase of paragraph 2 refers to the condition "where not already provided for by existing legislative or other measures," thereby acknowledging that "existing measures" may make it unnecessary to adopt any new legislation or other measures.

These conclusions based on the text are in keeping with the positions taken by several governments in the course of the preparatory work relating to Article 2. It was clear to the drafting committees that many states did not provide for automatic incorporation and that in these countries the Covenant would not become part of the domestic law nor would it be directly applied by the courts. The United States representatives on various occasions laid emphasis on this situation by proposing that all states parties be placed on the same footing as those which would not make the Covenant itself effective as national law.[3] To this end, a U.S. proposal went as far as to require that "the provisions of the Covenant shall not themselves become effective as national law."[4] The U.S. was obviously concerned not so much with equality among parties as with the possibility that some of the provisions of the Covenant would be regarded as self-executing in the United States by virtue of Article VI of the Constitution (a consequence which it was thought might raise political objections in the United States). Eleanor Roosevelt, the U.S. representative in the Human Rights Commission, put it rather dramatically when she said "to begin to enforce the Covenant as such, instead of the law in conformity therewith, would throw the United States courts and other law-enforcing agencies into utter confusion."[5] However, representatives of other countries which had constitutional provisions for automatic incorporation did not share the same apprehension about confusion in their courts. They and others saw no reason why the Covenant should itself rule out direct applica-

tion by the courts if that should be the consequence of the normal constitutional practice.[6] The above-quoted U.S. proposal was decisively
rejected by the drafting committee; in fact the United States alone voted
for it.[7]

The rejection of the U.S. proposal did not mean that the drafters
favored mandatory incorporation. It simply confirmed the prevalent
view that the question of incorporation *vel non* should be left to national
law subject only to the requirement that parties fulfill their obligations
under the Covenant. This position was expressed at a later stage (1954)
by the representative of the United Kingdom in the following statement as recorded in the summary records of the Human Rights Commission:

> He pointed out that treaties under international law did not as a rule im-
> pose any requirement as to the domestic legislation of States. The ratifica-
> tion of a treaty entailed, for the states parties to it, no more than the ful-
> fillment of the obligations expressed in the treaty, whether by legislation,
> administrative action, common law, custom or otherwise. The interna-
> tional community could not ask more and had no concern with the ques-
> tion whether legislation was the method adopted. The Covenant on Civil
> and Political Rights did not, in its nature, differ in that respect from other
> multilateral instruments or international treaties.[8]

This statement was not questioned in the Commission and it may be
taken as an accurate summary of the prevailing views of the drafters as
to the intent of Article 2 on the question of incorporation. But the
observation that the "international community could not ask more and
had no concern with the question of whether legislation was the
method adopted" is an overstatement. Certainly treaties have in the
past required legislation. In the case of the Covenant, it might reasonably have been concluded that, in the absence of incorporation of the
Covenant into domestic law, remedies for its violation would tend to
be uncertain. However it cannot be said that this conclusion was drawn
in the drafting groups, nor can it be inferred that incorporation was
then considered as the preferred method of ensuring execution.

Subsequent practice has lent further support to the interpretation that
incorporation into domestic law is not required by the Covenant. A
substantial number of the states which have become parties to the Covenant have reported that the Covenant has not become part of domestic
law, whether by automatic incorporation or through special legislation.[9] Moreover these states—with a few exceptions—have maintained
that their existing national legislation and domestic legal system ensured

recognition of all the rights recognized in the Covenant and provided the necessary remedies. When these reports were considered in the Human Rights Committee established under Article 40 of the Covenant, no member of that committee raised any question as to the right of a state party to refrain from enacting the Covenant into domestic law.

Questions were raised in the Committee, however, as to whether an alleged discrepancy between the Covenant and the relevant domestic law could be considered by a court or other competent national agency when the court or national agency was entitled to act only on the basis of domestic law.[10] Could the alleged discrepancy even be raised if the Covenant was not incorporated into domestic law?[11] Representatives of the states in question responded that, although the Covenant was not part of domestic law, an aggrieved individual may invoke it in certain circumstances.[12] One such state—the USSR—reported that the Covenant, like other treaties applicable to individuals, could be referred to by individuals before tribunals and agencies even though the Covenant was not incorporated into Soviet domestic law.[13] It was not suggested, however, that the Covenant provisions would prevail over inconsistent national law. Several of the other "nonincorporating" countries informed the Human Rights Committee that, under their law, the courts will construe their domestic law, insofar as possible, to conform to the obligations of the Covenant.[14] However, they made it clear that this was a principle of interpretation and would only apply in case of ambiguity or uncertainty in the domestic law.

The Role of the Covenant in the Interpretation of National Law

That principle, it may be noted, is not peculiar to the Covenant or to human rights treaties and is not limited to "nonincorporating" states. It is widely accepted in national legal systems that domestic law should, in the event of doubt as to its meaning or application, be interpreted in a way that the result would be consistent with the country's international obligations.[15]

Since all states parties have national legislation or judge-made law relating to the rights of the Covenant and since questions of interpretation arise frequently when violations are alleged, reference to the provisions of the Covenant in such cases may prove to be a significant means of giving effect to the Covenant albeit indirectly. The experience in Great Britain in recent years is relevant in this regard, although it pertains to the European Convention on Human Rights rather than the International Covenant. The European Convention, like the Covenant, has not been made part of internal law in the United Kingdom but it has been invoked as a guide to interpretation of domestic law.[16] The rights defined in that Convention are very much akin to those of the Covenant and in that respect the problems of interpretation in the courts are similar.

These problems may be illustrated by the somewhat ambivalent positions taken by British judges. In 1975, the Court of Appeal was faced with an application for mandamus by an illegal immigrant from India awaiting deportation who requested the right to marry a woman (previously unknown to him) and who cited Article 12 of the European Convention (similar to Article 23 of the International Covenant) granting the right to marry and to found a family.[17] Although the application was dismissed, Lord Denning declared that "the immigration officers and the Secretary of State in exercising their duties ought to bear in mind the principles stated in the Convention."[18]

Later in the same year, two women from the subcontinent on being denied the opportunity to join their husbands successfully applied for mandamus in the Court of Appeal.[19] One judge on the Court (Scarman) referred to the duty of the public authorities and of the courts to have regard to the Convention in interpreting and applying the law.[20] He invoked particularly Article 8 which guarantees "respect for family life."

But in 1976, another foreign wife requested leave to remain with her husband who resided in England; she also cited Article 8 of the Convention on respect for family life.[21] In this case, Lord Denning expressly modified the statement made by him the year before. His earlier position, he said, had asked "too much of the immigration officers. They cannot be expected to know or to apply the convention. They must go simply by the immigration rules laid down by the Secretary of State and not by the convention. . . . The convention is drafted in a style very different from the way which we are used to in legislation. It contains wide general statements of principle. They are apt to lead to much difficulty in application because they give rise to much uncertainty."[22] With reference to Article 8 on respect for family life, he said: "It is so wide as to be incapable of practical application. So it is much better for us to stick to our own statutes and principles and only look to the convention in case of doubt."[23]

The comments of Lord Denning raise questions of general significance as to the role of the Covenant in interpretation of domestic law.

One question arises from his expressed reluctance to give effect to the highly general formulations of human rights of the European Convention. A similar difficulty would arise in respect of the Covenant. If national courts conclude that they cannot find adequate guidance in broadly defined human rights, the contention of governments that the treaties may be employed for interpretive purposes loses credibility. (Such judicial restraint could also limit application of the treaties even when they had the force of domestic law.) What is at stake here is whether judges reluctant to "legislate" would be prepared to undertake the difficult task of giving concrete meaning to the highly general concepts of human rights. This task would be eased if the courts abandoned traditional attitudes of strict textual construction (characteristic of British judges) and were prepared to give greater emphasis to the general purposes of the provisions, to make use of the legislative history and parimateria, and to take into account decisions of foreign courts, opinions of international tribunals (notably, the two European courts, the Court of Justice of the European Communities and the European Court of Human Rights) and, with due caution, the reports of competent international committees. Lord Denning himself eloquently stated the case for English judges abandoning their narrow traditional approach when they considered multilateral conventions which contained broad concepts and standards. He did so in an opinion on the rights of whisky distillers under a convention on carriage of goods.[24] Though this was not a human rights case (except perhaps for those who see access to whisky as a human right), its strong support of an approach that gives effect to the design and spirit of the treaty is germane to the human rights conventions. "We have for years tended to stick too closely to the letter . . . European judges fill in gaps, quite unashamedly . . . to produce the desired effect. . . . So also in interpreting an international convention . . . we should do likewise."[25] One commentator, noting the difference between these views of Lord Denning in the "carriage of goods" case and those in regard to the European Convention on Human Rights observed "with respect" that "their Lordships appear to adopt a teleological approach to matters of compensation for distillers of whisky but a literal approach to issues of respect for human rights."[26] The rebuke may not be quite fair since the interpretive problems were markedly different in the two cases. Still, the reluctance of many judges in many countries to appear to be "legislating" on human rights on the basis of general treaty provisions suggest limitations on the application of the Covenant for interpretive purposes.

In some circumstances, surely, reference to the Covenant (or European Convention) would be especially appropriate, even though it is not itself part of domestic law. There is an important opportunity for such reference when national authorities apply domestic law standards which imply wide discretion. In some situations, there is only an implied standard of "proper purposes" to govern the discretion. In many cases, authorities are subject only to broad criteria in such terms as "fair," "reasonable," "arbitrary," "abuse," and the like. In applying these terms and the implicit standards of propriety it would seem eminently reasonable to take account of the rights recognized in the Covenant and the European Convention, and more particularly the case law and relevant international decisions under these treaties. This point of view has been urged by an eminent British lawyer on the ground, inter alia, that the human rights treaties involve national commitments subject to international supervision. Even though the terms of the human rights treaties are general and uncertain, he said, "we simply have to digest them, for we cannot possibly assume that English law and practice are necessarily such as to conform to the standards of the [European] Convention." [27] This holds true also of the Covenant. One might add that in many cases, states parties to the Covenant (even if not also to the European Convention) could properly draw on the case law of the European Court and Commission in interpreting comparable provisions of the Covenant.

Another situation in which the Covenant (or the Convention) might properly be used in resolving an issue of domestic law pertaining to human rights is the not uncommon case of a statute or judge-made rule that is open to two or more interpretations. In this case, the court or agency should consider (to quote Lord Scarman in a British case) whether one interpretation "would lead to a decision inconsistent with her Majesty's international obligations under the convention while the other would lead to a result consistent with those obligations. If statutory words have to be construed or a legal principle formulated in an area of law where her Majesty has accepted international obligations, our Courts . . . will have regard to the Convention as part of the full content or background of the law. Such a Convention, especially a multilateral one, should then be considered by the Courts even though no statute expressly or impliedly incorporates it into our law." [28]

That comment highlights an additional significance for the presumption that national law is consistent with the state's international commitments both for states which have made the Covenant part of national law and for those which have not. If a state party to the

Covenant later enacted a statute (or adopted a judge-made rule), such later statute or rule would—in most states (but not all) [29]—prevail over the earlier treaty obligation, however, under the principle of *lex posterior derogat priori*. [30] It may well be in case of any inconsistency that the later statute is open to interpretation on the question relating to the obligations of the Covenant, and it would be reasonable and probably obligatory for the courts to apply the presumption that the legislature did not intend to enact rules contrary to the state's international obligations. This general "rule of presumption" of consistency with international obligations has been referred to by some parties to the Covenant (for example, Denmark and Norway) in their reports to the Human Rights Committee. [31] Although such a presumption is not conclusive under national law (and it would not apply to an unambigous law contrary to the treaty), it is likely to be significant in human rights situations where national laws permit some latitude. Of course, under international law, the application of a subsequent statute or rule inconsistent with treaty obligations constitutes an international wrong, irrespective of national law. [32] Reliance on the presumption of consistency would reduce the occasions for such breaches of international obligations, though it would not eliminate the possibility.

The Obligation to Adopt Legislative or Other Measures

In Article 2(2) the parties have undertaken to take steps to adopt such legislative or other measures as may be necessary to give effect to the rights recognized. What is meant by "to give effect" is not spelled out, but its implications merit consideration. Clearly, a right is given effect by affording remedies for its violation. The duty to provide an effective remedy is stated separately in paragraph 3; it will be discussed in the next section. A right is also given effect if its violation is avoided or prevented. Measures may therefore have to be taken for such avoidance or prevention. What measures will depend on needs and circumstances. Most obvious are educational and information activities to inform the people and officials of their rights. Administrative controls of official conduct would also help to avoid and prevent violations. Beyond that, measures may be needed for opening opportunities to disadvantaged groups (e.g., "affirmative action") and developing institutions that remove impediments to the realization of rights. Even these steps may be only a partial fulfillment of an obligation that could embrace the entire range of social structures. In short, the duty "to give effect" to recognized rights must be seen as embracing more than specific legal remedies after violation. If the obligation is taken seriously, it will require the governments and their peoples to examine, on a deeper level than has yet been done, the many diverse barriers to the enjoyment of basic rights by all.

A considerable number of the states parties have reported to the Human Rights Committee that no additional measures are required in their countries, that all rights are recognized and "ensured" and that adequate remedies are available to the individual if a violation should occur. These governmental assertions are supported by quotation of constitutional and legislative texts and explanations of judicial and administrative procedures. To a man from Mars, a large part of the world would seem safe for human rights and the Covenant virtually redundant. To an observer of contemporary events, the assertions by some governments that all necessary measures have been taken may seem incredible in the light of their actual practice.[33] Even in the case of countries with an acknowledged tradition of respect for human rights, the observer may justifiably be skeptical of the claim that existing law is adequate and that there is no need to implement Article 2(2). Thus, when the United Kingdom reported that its obligations are fulfilled by "safeguards of different kinds, operating in the various legal systems, independently of the Covenant but in full conformity to it,"[34] one may acknowledge, as a matter of general observation, that this is probably substantially the case, but still wonder about the categorical and sweeping character of the statement. The respected British legal scholar F. A. Mann has observed "we cannot possibly assume that English law and practice are necessarily such as to conform to the standards of the [European] Convention,"[35] and Lord Denning, the Master of the Rolls, referred to the terms of the Convention as "not the sort of thing we can easily digest."[36] In the light of these comments and some recent cases it does not seem excessively critical for an outsider to question the claim that no legislative or other measures are required in the United Kingdom to give full effect to the Covenant. (We shall refer later to the requirement of an effective remedy under Article 2(3) in respect of a Parliamentary Act that is alleged to violate the Covenant.)

If this doubt arises in respect of the United Kingdom, how much greater is the skepticism as regards most of the other countries making the same claim. The citation of constitutional and legislative texts—"the law on the books"—may satisfy the need for legislation, but cannot be a sufficient answer to the question of whether "other measures" are required to provide effective remedies. If it is impossible or difficult for aggrieved individuals to obtain an objective determination of their rights under the Covenant (and not simply under national law), or if state organs, including the courts, diverge in practice from the proclaimed rules, it is clear that the obligations of Article 2 are not satisfied. It is, of course, implicit that, as with other provisions of the Covenant, the determination of conformity with the requirements of Article 2 is not left solely to the state in question. Since the question involves an international obligation, the other states parties to the Covenant, and the Human Rights Committee under Article 40 of the Covenant, are fully entitled to raise questions as to the conformity of national practice with the obligations of that article. They have the right to do so, even if individuals in those states may not be able to raise the question in their national courts. The records of the Human Rights Committee for its first years of operation indicate that some members of the committee have acted accordingly. They have put searching questions to government representatives about actual practices, though the committee has just begun to go into individual cases.

A more subtle problem relating to Article 2(2) is raised by the proposal made by the President of the United States that his government ratify the Covenant with all the reservations required to ensure that existing national law will not have to be modified. This position was expressed in the message sent to the Congress in transmitting the Covenant and three other human rights treaties: "Whenever a provision is in conflict with United States law, a reservation, understanding or declaration has been recommended."[37] In explanation, it was said in an accompanying State Department communication that the treaties contain provisions which are, or appear to be, in conflict with or to go beyond the requirements of United States law and that the reservations and statements of understanding "are designed to harmonize the treaties with existing provisions of domestic law."[38] In addition, a declaration denying self-executing effect to the treaties would ensure that "the treaties would not of themselves become effective as domestic law."[39] The clarity and candor of these statements may seem commendable in comparison with the questionable claims of full conformity made by some governments. Nonetheless, the position taken by the President calls for scrutiny in the light of Article 2.

The critical legal issue raised is not whether specific reservations are admissible. It is rather whether a whole series of reservations admittedly designed to avoid any need to modify United States law can be regarded as in conformity with the object and purpose of the Covenant, especially with the "obligations of means" assumed in Article 2. The object of Article 2 was to require all parties to adopt measures wherever necessary to give effect to the Covenant. The proposed U.S. bundle of reservations is intended to deprive that requirement of any effect whatsoever for the United States. It would do so by reducing the obligations of the United States under the Covenant to the level of existing United States law so that it would be under no requirement to adopt any measures to modify existing domestic law. By attempting to avoid the need for legislation, it turns upside down the obligation of the Covenant as well as the general principle of treaty law that a party may not invoke its internal law as justification for failure to perform a treaty.[40] Under the principles of international law recognized by the International Court of Justice in its Advisory Opinion on Reservations[41] and the codification of those principles in Article 19 of the Vienna Convention on the Law of Treaties,[42] a doubt arises whether the ensemble of reservations proposed by the President would be permissible, whether they would not be "incompatible with the object and purpose of the treaty" (Vienna Convention, Article 19). It is one thing to make specific reservations on their own merits and quite another to adopt a policy of making reservations to avoid any change at all in existing domestic law. No precise precedent for this kind of situation has been found, and one may hesitate to be absolutely categorical as to the law. But irrespective of the legal issue, a serious question of good faith is bound to arise when a state purports to accept the obligations of a treaty and at the same time seeks to rule out any change in its law that would be required to comply with the treaty.

I turn now to the time allowed for a state to adopt the legislative and other measures required for it to fulfill its obligations under Article 2 of the Covenant. Whether a state must meet its obligations immediately upon adherence to the Covenant or whether it has time to do so (and how long a time) was debated at various stages of consideration of the draft covenants. A brief review of the positions advanced and the actions taken by the drafting bodies is necessary to elucidate this matter, since the text itself is silent on the point.

During the preparatory stages several representatives contended that the states which become parties to the Covenant may do so only after, or simultaneously with, taking the measures necessary to assure compliance with it. Some maintained that this requirement followed from a general rule of international law that provisions of an international instrument should be in force immediately upon ratification or accession unless the treaty itself provides otherwise.[43] Others considered that though there was no general rule of international law on the point, it was desirable because of the nature of the Covenant that states give effect to the rights in the Covenant before they adhere to it.[44] In line with these views, a proposal was made that "every deposit of instrument of accession shall be accompanied by a solemn declaration made by the Government of the State concerned, that full and complete effect is given by the law of the State to the provisions of the Covenant."[45] That proposal, however, was rejected.[46]

Most governments involved in the preparatory work considered that it was not necessary as a matter of law, nor was it desirable policy, to require that parties take measures of execution in domestic law prior to or at the time of adherence. They expressed their accord with a legal opinion of the United Nations Legal Department, which after an examination of the International Court of Justice decisions concluded that under international law the adaptation of municipal law to treaty requirements, when necessary, is not a condition precedent to a state binding itself internationally to the treaty.[47] It was also maintained by several delegates that the text of Article 2(2) should allow "a certain degree of elasticity to the obligations imposed on States by the covenant, since all States would not be in a position immediately to take the necessary legislative or other measures for the implementation of its provisions. The covenant . . . unlike ordinary conventions, concerned a vast field, so that no State could claim its legislation to be in complete harmony with all its provisions."[48] (This statement, by the way, contrasts with the subsequent claims of many of the parties, mentioned above, that their existing legislation is in complete harmony with the Covenant; the statement is nonetheless substantially accurate.)

While most representatives agreed that some elasticity was desirable in Article 2, there was considerable concern over the possibility of "excessive delays" and consequently opposition to allowing each State to fix its own time limit.[49] However, suggestions for definite time limits did not win approval. A proposal to include the phrase "within a reasonable time" was adopted at one stage and then deleted.[50] Some felt the expression was too vague to be helpful and that it would lead to unequal obligations among the states parties.[51]

One can say that the preponderant opinion within the drafting bodies was that Article 2 should not allow a prolonged period of time for a state to adopt the required measures of implementation.[52] It was especially stressed that Article 2 was not intended to incorporate the principle of "progressive implementation" expressly provided in the analogous "umbrella" Article 2 in the Covenant on Economic, Social, and

Cultural Rights. The latter provision set goals to be achieved "progressively" over time in recognition of the fact that countries could not progress faster in economic and social matters than their resources and conditions allowed. In contrast, Article 2 of the Covenant on Civil and Political Rights was seen as imposing in principle an immediate obligation but taking account of the need in some cases for time to adapt national legislation to the Covenant's requirements.[53] The distinction between the two Covenants in this respect was expressed by the representative of the United States in the General Assembly at the time of adoption of the two Covenants in 1966. She stated:

> We recognize the importance of each of the rights specified in these Covenants whether they be in the nature of goals for progressive achievement, as in the International Covenant on Economic, Social and Cultural Rights, or of obligations which States undertake to respect and *ensure immediately* upon becoming Parties, as in the International Covenant on Civil and Political Rights.[54] (emphasis added)

This statement of the United States has perhaps added significance in view of the "need" which had been stressed at earlier stages by American representatives for latitude in Article 2 to allow parties reasonable time to decide upon and enact new legislation or take other measures. A number of other delegates also underscored the view that the language of Article 2 was not intended to permit long delays or to sanction the idea of "progressive" application over time.[55] This is reflected in a 1963 report of the Third Committee of the General Assembly which said that "the notion of implementation at the earliest possible moment was implicit in Article 2 as a whole."[56] It also observed that "the reporting requirement [of Article 40] would indeed serve as an effective curb on undue delay" in implementing Article 2.[57] The fact that Article 40 required states parties to report on measures they have adopted to give effect to the rights recognized in the Covenant and to make such reports within one year of their adherence was referred to by some delegates as an indication that the measures required under Article 2 should be taken within one year after the state becomes a party.[58] While it cannot be said that this means that a definite one-year time limit should be implied in Article 2, it does not seem unreasonable to take account of that period as a good indication of the extent of the elasticity in the requirement. Whether that period may reasonably be extended in some cases would depend on the particular circumstances and would presumably take into account whether steps have been taken to achieve the necessary adaptation and the likelihood of a successful result. But certainly that elastic principle can not be stretched to justify a period of many years of delay, let alone an indefinite and uncertain undertaking to take measures in the future. To allow such "elasticity" would open the way to a significant gap between the obligation to give effect to the rights in the Covenant and the actual execution of that obligation.

Judicial and Other Remedies in National Law

Article 2(3) requires the parties to ensure that any person whose rights and freedoms are violated shall have an effective remedy. It goes on to specify that the remedy shall be granted "notwithstanding that the violation has been committed by persons acting in an official capacity." It also states that any person claiming a remedy shall have his right thereto determined by judicial or other competent authority provided by the legal system of the state party, and that any remedy granted shall be enforced by the competent authorities.

In adopting these provisions of Article 2(3), the drafting bodies rejected the views of some governments that an explicit provision on remedies was unnecessary since that was implied in the obligations to give effect to the rights defined in the Covenant.[59] It was considered desirable to make it abundantly clear that the parties must provide remedies to individuals within the domestic legal system. The paragraph does not, of course, preclude remedies on the international plane if available but it underlines the essential role of domestic remedies.

The text does not specify the nature of such domestic remedies. We may assume that undoing, repairing, and compensating for violation constitute appropriate remedies (as well as ways of giving effect to the rights in accordance with paragraph 2). If a violation is found, it must be ended and undone (if possible), and its fruits not used or repaired. Thus, "cease and desist" orders (injunctive relief) may be required. Reparation may have to include restoring the victim to his previous position if practicable. Compensation to the victim may also constitute a required remedy. That there is an express requirement of compensation to one unlawfully arrested or detained (Article 9(5)) should not mean that compensation might not be the effective remedy in other cases. Domestic law provides abundant examples of remedial action that may also be suitable for human rights violations under the Covenant. The Committee on Human Rights will probably throw light on such possibilities through its questions and comments on national reports.

The reference in Article 2(3a) to violations committed by persons acting in an official capacity was presumably intended to override a possible claim of official immunity. It may also serve to rebut a presumption that official action taken in good faith would be a valid excuse for infringement of rights or for denying a remedy. The point was made during the preparatory stage that no one should be able to avoid responsibility for a violation by claiming he acted on higher authority.[60] While much attention was given to possible violations by public officials, a proposal that "violators be swiftly brought to law, especially when they are public officials" was rejected, presumably as superfluous.[61] Perhaps that implies that remedies for violation need not include criminal punishment for those responsible for the violation.

The drafting of subparagraph (b) raised two issues: (1) whether judicial remedies should be mandatory and (2) whether the guarantee of effective remedies could be adequately met by recourse to administrative and legislative authorities.[62] Within the drafting committees strong sentiment was expressed in favor of judicial remedies as the most effective means of protection within a national system. Many delegates were dubious that effective remedies to individuals could be obtained through political bodies, especially since violations were often committed by political authorities. These attitudes, though widely held, did not in the end prevail to preclude reference to the determination of rights by administrative or legislative authorities as well as by judicial authority. For one thing, it was recognized that developed and independent judicial systems did not exist in many countries and that it would be impossible for such states to provide adequate judicial remedies quickly.[63] Moreover, it was considered desirable to underscore the duty of the legislatures and of executive officials to take effective action within their competence. Clearly in many countries—and in some situations in all countries—adequate remedies for infringements can often be granted only by such nonjudicial authorities. Even in countries with well-developed judicial systems, designated nonjudicial officials, such as the ombudsmen in the Scandinavian countries, are regarded as an especially appropriate means of protecting individuals against violations by public authorities. The reports to the Human Rights Committee by those countries stress the significance of the institution of the ombudsman.[64]

It is appropriate at this point to observe that many, though not all, of the provisions of the Covenant are capable of direct application by the courts (or by other competent national agencies) without any legislative action. Consequently, where the Covenant becomes part of national law, many of its provisions will be self-executing in the sense indicated and the courts will be able to provide some remedies without special provisions. The fact that the states parties will differ in this regard was acknowledged and accepted by the drafting bodies.[65] Clearly, the general obligation in Article 2(2) to adopt legislative or other measures as may be necessary cannot be read as a requirement for legislation that is not necessary. If the Covenant has become part of the domestic law under national constitutional or other procedures, and a court can directly apply a provision of the Covenant to give effect to the individual right in question, no legislation is required. Where such self-executing effect does not obtain, the state is obliged to adopt the legislation necessary to give effect to the recognized rights and to ensure adequate remedies.

States which have already reached the same result by virtue of their existing legislation obviously do not have to act again. Should they nonetheless choose to require new legislation as a basis for judicial action in respect of every provision of the Covenant, they are presumably free to do so as long as they do not thereby deny adequate remedies. The critical issue therefore is whether imposing a requirement of fresh legislation (which would not otherwise be necessary under existing constitutional law) would result in delaying the application of the Covenant by the courts and thereby depriving individuals of effective remedies. One can maintain that such action by a party would be inconsistent with the intent of Article 2(2) which contemplates legislation only "where not already provided for by existing legislative or other measures." Even more clearly, a legislative delay in providing for judicial action otherwise obtainable through the self-executing effect would be contrary to the categorical obligations of Article 2(3) that any person whose recognized rights are violated shall have an effective remedy and shall have his right thereto determined by competent judicial or other competent authority provided for by the legal system of the state. Ideally the problem would disappear or be *de minimis* if the necessary legislation were quickly adopted. Realistically, one must expect that legislation on complex and controversial provisions will require a good deal of time and therefore delay the application of those provisions. Such delay could in some cases mean denial of remedies.

The foregoing observations are not entirely academic in view of the proposal of the President of the United States for a "declaration" which would deny any self-executing effect to the Covenant under United States law.[66] The intended result of this declaration would be to remove all of the provisions of the Covenant from direct application and enforcement by the courts of the United States or by any competent administrative agencies until Congress enacted legislation as a basis for judicial and administrative execution. On the interpretation given above, the proposed declaration would not constitute a reservation, since it would not in itself set aside or modify the provisions of the Covenant. It would in effect place the United States in the same position as the United Kingdom and the numerous other parties that have not made the Covenant part of their internal law and directly invocable by individuals in their courts. On the other hand, it is not unlikely that the consequences of the proposed declaration, if adopted, would be a considerable delay in affording effective remedies to individuals because of the time needed for legislative action. If that delay would otherwise constitute a violation of Article 2(3), then the United States declaration may have to be seen as reserving the right to deviate from Article 2(3) in this respect.

Such delay would be even more protracted if it were decided by the President and the Senate that the requisite legislative action would have to be adopted by the state legislatures in respect of those provisions of the Covenants that concern matters over which the states exercise jurisdiction. A reservation to this effect has been proposed by the President.[67] That reservation, if adopted, may be challenged by other parties on the ground of its incompatibility with Article 50 of the Covenant which requires the Covenant to "extend to all parts of federal States without any limitations or exceptions," language which seems absolute and may suggest that a reservation to that article is not permissible. A further ground for challenging the reservation would be its probable effect in unduly delaying the provision of effective remedies under Article 2(3). Both of these possible challenges would lack legal justification if the necessary legislative action by Congress and the state legislatures were to be enacted within the elastic time limit discussed above. Since it probably could not be definitively determined at the time of ratification that this would not be the case, it may be difficult for other parties to object to the reservation on the ground that legislative delays or nonaction are possible or even likely. Perhaps if evidence of an official nature clearly supported a prediction of such protracted delays for some provisions or in some areas of the country, objections to the reservation would have an adequate foundation. But even if the reservation should be accepted, it would not provide a legal justification for a failure of the United States to meet the requirements of Article 2 within a reasonable period and in all parts of the country. As a matter of interpretation, one would not construe a reservation of the kind proposed as setting aside the basic commitments of the Covenant expressed in Article 2. If such a construction were adopted it would surely have to be held that the reservation was *ipso jure* impermissible because of its incompatibility with the object and purpose of the Covenant.

There are other implications of the obligation in Article 2(3) to ensure an effective remedy and to provide for the determination of individual rights by judicial or other competent authority. If the courts are necessarily bound by legislative enactments and may never set them aside whatever their incompatibility with the Covenant, can it be said that a truly effective remedy exists for the violation of the rights of an individual? A British judge in an opinion in 1974 stated: "In earlier times many learned lawyers seem to have believed that an Act of Parliament could be disregarded in so far as it was contrary to the law of God, or the law of nature or natural justice but since the supremacy of Parliament was finally demonstrated by the Revolution of 1688 any such idea has become obsolete."[68] Dicey has taught generations of British lawyers that "a modern judge would never listen to a barrister who argued that an Act of Parliament was invalid because . . . it went beyond the limits of Parliamentary authority."[69] While we recognize the exemplary record of British courts in human rights matters, it is undeniable that the sovereignty of Parliament imposes a theoretical and actual limitation on the judicial remedy for violations of rights by the legislature.[70] The fact that parliamentary sovereignty or its equivalent on the executive level prevails in many countries with a less admirable record than Great Britain justifies wider concern that the judicial remedy may be unavailable or insufficient. One need not go so far as to accept James Madison's praise of judicial review as an "impenetrable bulwark against every assumption of power"[71] to recognize the institution as perhaps the most effective means of limiting abuse by legislative or other political bodies. The drafters of the Covenant considered that Article 2(3) should in some way reflect the general view that judicial remedies were especially important. They did so by adding to subparagraph 2(b) a general commitment of states to "develop the possibilities of judicial remedy." Although this phrase is somewhat less than a precise legal requirement to take specific action, its inclusion is not without legal implications. At least it presents the parties to the Covenant with an opportunity, if not an injunction, to consider whether judicial review of legislation by domestic courts should not be an element in developing the possibilities of judicial remedy. Although Article 2 does not go as far as to require judicial review of legislation, it surely calls for some effective means for individuals to challenge parliamentary acts that infringe their recognized rights.

Apart from the question of judicial review of legislation, there appears to be general acceptance, at least formally, of the right of aggrieved individuals to institute official proceedings in case of alleged violations of the recognized rights of the Covenant. Virtually all the reports of the states parties under Article 40 of the Covenant have referred to constitutional and statutory provisions under which acts of public officials may be challenged. In addition, several countries have drawn attention to the role of procurators, ombudsmen and comparable officials who have the responsibility of investigating and instituting action against authorities who have abused their power or otherwise infringed on human rights.[72] Although it is not possible to assess the actual impact of these official agencies on the basis of the written reports of governments, it is not without significance that the governments provide machinery for the redress of violations on the administrative or bureaucratic level and that they relate such machinery to the obligations of the Covenant. No one would question that ideally the procurator generals, directors of public prosecutions, and parliamentary commissioners could be effective instruments for holding governmental officials accountable for their acts. The superior facilities available to such agencies and their legal and political standing can be significant factors in providing effective remedies.

The main question, of course, is whether official agencies which are part of the state apparatus are sufficiently independent to perform their protective tasks free of political restraint. Obviously, such independence is greatly qualified in many countries and perhaps almost nonexistent in some. Moreover, distinctions may have to be drawn between violations that are state policy or reflect an important state interest and individual abuses of authority or bureaucratic negligence. In the latter category the protective role of the official "watchdog" agency is likely to be much greater than in the former, though even in such nonpolitical cases objectivity and independence are not always evident. The problem of political subordination has not been overlooked by members of the Human Rights Committee as evidenced by the questions they put to representatives of states who pointed with pride to the role of procurators and other "protective" officials.[73] Although the responses of the representatives ought to be reassuring as to the independence of their officials, they were not always convincing in the light of reported cases. But such responses are some evidence of the acceptance in principle of the necessity of a measure of independence for such officials.[74] Without being unduly optimistic, this lends support to an agreed interpretation of Article 2(3) as imposing a requirement of independence and objectivity in the conduct of public officials responsible for granting remedies to individuals whose rights have been infringed.

In concluding this analysis of Article 2, it may not be superfluous to underline its central significance in the regime of the Covenant and more widely in the evolution of the international law of human rights. That significance lies precisely in the unequivocal obligation to provide an effective remedy to "any person" whose rights are recognized. That remedy is to be ensured through the machinery of the domestic legal system open to aggrieved individuals. Rights are thus brought from the lofty plane of international principles to enforceable law in concrete cases. This has sometimes been described as a "Western" legal approach that is not generally acceptable in other regions of the world. It is therefore pertinent to observe that Article 2 has now been accepted formally by states from all areas of the world—Eastern Europe, Africa, Asia, and Latin America, as well as Western Europe. All parties have declared that in pursuance of the obligations of Article 2 they ensure effective remedies to individuals. Clearly, many of them do not do so in actual practice. Their legal commitment however should not be disregarded or minimized. It affords a ground not only for international criticism but also for internal demands. Whether such demands will eventually prove effective in most countries remains to be seen; that will depend on social, political, and economic factors as well as on international legal obligations. In the meantime, Article 2 must be properly construed to serve its intended purpose of ensuring that the Covenant is given full effect in national legal systems and that individuals entitled to the rights stated therein are afforded effective means of vindicating those rights.

14

The Implementation System: International Measures

A. H. ROBERTSON

THIS ESSAY examines the measures of international implementation set out in the Covenant on Civil and Political Rights. Of course, national measures of implementation must be invoked before recourse is had to international measures. The great majority of civil rights issues can and should be settled at the national level, by courts or other national authorities. For this purpose, each state must ensure that adequate national remedies exist (Article 2(3)). (See essay 13). It is only when national remedies are nonexistent or ineffective that international remedies come into play; that is, of course, precisely when they are most required.

International law has been often deprecated because there are no formal executive institutions to enforce it. In fact, however, international obligations are generally observed, without any special "enforcement machinery." The basis of international treaty relationships is good faith; it is assumed that states accept treaty relations in good faith with the intention of respecting their obligations, and that they will respect them. And, in fact, governments generally do respect them. It has long been recognized, however, that in some areas of international agreement and convention, especially those dealing with how a state treats its own inhabitants, reliance on good faith is insufficient. That was reflected in the system established earlier in the twentieth century for implementing the International Labour Conventions. Repeated violations of human rights by states that had pledged themselves to respect such rights in the Charter of the United Nations was a principal reason for moving from the Charter and the Universal Declaration to covenants with legal obligations and machinery to enforce them.

Opponents of enforcement systems have sometimes argued that international systems intervene in the internal affairs of sovereign states.[1]

The argument is unfounded, if not disingenuous. Matters as to which states have accepted international obligations are, by hypothesis, of international concern and no longer exclusively a matter of their domestic jurisdiction. A state that has assumed obligations cannot object to measures to implement them. Surely, it is appropriate to seek such measures by agreement of the parties.

The Development of the Covenant System

Though the decision to include "measures of implementation" in the Covenants was taken in the early days of the United Nations, when the influence of the Western democracies was predominant, there were widely different opinions about the form those measures should take. Early proposals submitted to the Commission on Human Rights included an Australian proposal for the establishment of an International Court on Human Rights.[2]

René Cassin (France) proposed the creation of an International Investigation Commission empowered to consider petitions presented by individuals, coupled with the appointment of an Attorney General.[3] India suggested a conciliation committee which could investigate complaints, attempt conciliation and, if necessary, refer the matter to the General Assembly.[4] Israel proposed the creation of a new specialized agency for the implementation of the Covenants with its own Assembly and elaborate procedures for hearing complaints by states and petitions of nongovernmental organizations though not of individuals.[5] The attitude of the United Kingdom and the United States was more cautious: they proposed the establishment of a panel of independent experts from which a Human Rights Committee of five members would be selected to examine interstate complaints (but not individual petitions) and only with a view to establishing the facts.[6] The USSR was opposed to all measures of implementation, which one Soviet delegate described as "a means of interfering in the internal affairs of a State party to the Convention, and of undermining the sovereignty and independence of particular States." In 1949 the Soviet Government stated, in reply to a questionnaire, that "the implementation of the Declaration of Human Rights and the Covenant is a matter which solely concerns the domestic jurisdiction of the State" and accordingly it saw "no need for any international agreements on the subject."[7] Nevertheless, the General Assembly in 1950 requested the Commission to consider provisions for the receipt and examination of petitions from individuals and organizations (GA Res. 421-F(V)).

In 1951 Uruguay tabled a proposal for the establishment of an Office of the United Nations High Commissioner (Attorney-General) for Human Rights,[8] an idea which has been relaunched from time to time independently of the Covenant—notably by Costa Rica in 1965 and by President Carter of the United States in 1977—and has found a considerable measure of support both in the Commission and in the General Assembly, but has met with such strong opposition from certain countries that no final decision has yet been taken.

In 1950 the Commission decided that there should be some implementation measures in the Covenant, that there should be a permanent body to consider violations (thus rejecting the U.K.–U.S. proposal for ad hoc bodies), and that this organ should be empowered to consider interstate complaints. But it rejected, by narrow majorities, the possibility of access to it by nongovernmental organizations and individuals.[9]

Much further discussion took place in the Commission, the Economic and Social Council, and the Third Committee of the General Assembly during the three following years,[10] but there was little change of substance from the Commission's position in 1950, though detailed articles were drafted about periodic reports by states on the implementation of the two covenants. As a result, the draft Covenant on Civil and Political Rights submitted by the Commission to the General Assembly in 1954 called for the establishment of a Human Rights Committee of nine members, with competence to consider interstate complaints but not communications from nongovernmental organizations or individual petitions, and an obligation on states to submit periodic reports.[11]

It is useful to study the system proposed in 1954 in order to understand the changes introduced during the next twelve years.[12] The 1954 draft Covenant would have established a Human Rights Committee, its members to be elected by the International Court of Justice from a list of names proposed by the states parties. The draft envisaged that if one state party considered that another state party was violating a provision of the Covenant, it might address a communication to the latter to that effect; the receiving state would be required to provide an explanation within three months. Only if a satisfactory solution by bilateral negotiations was not reached within six months would either state have the right to refer the matter to the Human Rights Committee. The latter would normally deal with a matter only after the individual victim of the alleged violation had exhausted domestic remedies (Article 41). The Committee would have the right to call upon the states concerned for any relevant information (Article 42). The Committee would have the task of ascertaining the facts and making available its good offices with a view to a friendly solution of the matter on the basis of respect for human rights; within eighteen months of the original reference of the case to it, it would draw up a report, which would be published; if a solution was not reached the report would state the facts *and the opinion of the Committee on the question of violation* (Article 43).[13] The Committee would have the right to request (through ECOSOC) an advisory opinion of the International Court of Justice on any legal aspect of the matter (Article 44), and the states parties would also have the right to refer the case to the Court in the absence of a friendly settlement (Article 46). The Committee would submit an annual report on its activities to the General Assembly (Article 45).

Article 49 of the 1954 draft would have required states parties to submit reports on the legislative and other measures, including judicial remedies, adopted for the implementation of the Covenants;[14] these reports would be submitted to the Economic and Social Council, which might transmit them to the Commission on Human Rights "for information, study and, if necessary, general recommendations."[15] The words "general recommendations" were used in conformity with "a widely held view that the reports should not give rise to particular recommendations to individual States."[16] It will be observed that the function of studying the reports and possibly formulating "general recommendations" thereon was to be conferred on the existing Commission on Human rights and not on the new Human Rights committee. In other words, there was to be a dual system of implementation: interstate complaints would be considered by the new Human Rights Committee set up under the Covenant; periodic reports would be examined by the existing Commission on Human Rights provided for in the Charter.[17]

This implementation system proposed by the Human Rights Commission was considerably revised by the Third Committee of the General Assembly in the next stage of the drafting process.[18] The Committee accepted the idea of a permanent Human Rights Committee but increased its membership from nine to eighteen.[19] (The increase in membership was eminently reasonable since the membership of the UN had doubled since 1954). The members were to be elected by the states parties instead of by the International Court of Justice. Their term of office was reduced from five to four years. An article to the effect that the secretary of the Committee should be "a high official of the United Nations elected by the Committee" was deleted. The general view in the Third Committee was that "the best course of action was to make provisions similar to those applicable to other United Nations bodies." In so doing, the Third Committee diminished to a certain extent the degree of autonomy and standing which the Commission had wished to give to the Human Rights Committee.[20] It retained the proposal for a system of reports, but decided that they should be examined by the new Human Rights Committee and not by the UN Human Rights Commission. The reporting system thus becomes the principal measure of implementation. The possibility of interstate complaints was retained but made optional, applying only between states making a declaration recognizing the competence of the Committee to consider such "communications." This was supplemented by provisions for ad hoc conciliation commissions, if the parties to the dispute agreed.

As regards the possibility of petitions by individuals to the Human Rights Committee, it seemed at first that this would have greater chance of acceptance in the Third Committee in 1966 than in the Commission on Human Rights in 1954, since the Third Committee itself had provided for such a procedure (on an optional basis) in the Racial Discrimination Convention the previous year.[21] However, national susceptibilities were to count for more than logic; because of the influence of the African states in particular, states were reluctant to oppose such measures for strengthening implementation of the Racial Convention, but a Netherlands proposal to include an optional provision for individual petition in the Covenant was not adopted.[22] The Third committee decided that this procedure should be included in a separate Protocol to be annexed to the Covenant.[23] In retrospect, this decision seems a wise one, because the inclusion of a procedure for individual petition in the body of the Covenant, even on an optional basis, would probably have rendered its ratification more difficult in a number of countries; even without this provision it took ten years to obtain the thirty-five ratifications necessary for the Covenant to enter into force. On the other hand, the Optional Protocol providing for the right of individual petition obtained a sufficient number of ratifications to enter into force in 1976 at the same time as the Covenant on Civil and Political Rights.

The Third Committee also deleted from the draft Covenant several articles designed to permit or encourage reference of various matters to the International Court of Justice, no doubt because the diplomatic representatives in a committee representing over a hundred states in 1966 had less respect for that august body than the small number of specialists who sat on the Commission in 1954.

The changes made by the Third Committee were accepted by the General Assembly when it approved the text of the two covenants on December 16, 1966.

The Human Rights Committee

Article 28 of the Covenant provides for the establishment of the Human Rights Committee, the principal organ of implementation of the Covenant on Civil and Political Rights. This contrasts with the Covenant on Economic, Social, and Cultural Rights, where no new body was created and reports on compliance are received by the Economic and Social Council.

The Human Rights Committee consists of eighteen members. Although they serve in their personal capacities (Article 26), not as representatives of any government, they must be nationals of states which are parties to the Covenant. They must be "persons of high moral character and recognized competence in the field of human rights"; consideration shall also be given "to the usefulness of the participation of some persons having legal experience." The Commission's draft had proposed "some persons having a judicial or legal experience," but the Third Committee decided to delete the reference to judicial qualifications. The change, in fact, makes little difference, since "persons having legal experience" clearly does not exclude judges, and in any event, the clause is not mandatory.

Under Articles 29 and 30 of the Covenant, the members of the Committee are elected by secret ballot by the states parties at a special meeting convened for this purpose by the Secretary-General of the United Nations. Each state party may nominate not more than two candidates, who must be nationals of that state. The details of the election procedure are set out in Article 30. Article 31 provides that the Committee may not include more than one national of any one state and that consideration shall be given to the principles of equitable geographical distribution and representation of the different forms of civilization and principal legal systems.[24] The term of office is four years, though at the first election, nine members are to be elected for only two years, in order to avoid a complete change of membership at any one time (Article 32). Members of the Committee are eligible for reelection (Article

338 A. H. ROBERTSON

29). Articles 33 and 34 deal with the possibilities of incapacity and casual vacancies. Article 35 provides that the members of the Committee shall receive emoluments from United Nations resources, thus emphasizing that they serve in their personal capacity. This principle is further emphasized in Article 38, which requires each member of the Committee to make a solemn declaration that he will perform his functions impartially and conscientiously.[25] Article 36 provides that the Secretary-General of the United Nations shall provide the necessary staff and facilities for the functioning of the Committee.

The Covenant on Civil and Political Rights and the Optional Protocol entered into force on March 23, 1976, and the first meeting of the states parties to elect the members of the Committee took place on September 20, 1976.[26] At that election the principles of equitable geographical distribution and representation of the principal legal systems were in fact respected; five members were elected from Western Europe,[27] four from Eastern Europe,[28] two from Asia,[29] three from Africa,[30] one from North America[31] and three from Latin America.[32] The five Western Europeans were all from states which are parties to the European Convention, one of them being also a member of the European Commission of Human Rights;[33] the three Latin Americans were nationals of states parties to the American Convention on Human Rights. Only seven members of the Committee were nationals of states which had ratified the Optional Protocol providing for the right of individual petition.[34]

The early experience with the composition of the Committee underscores difficulties which have beset other UN bodies of "experts" serving "in their personal capacities." Unfortunately, some of the representatives had been, and often continue to be, government officials. That contradicts the intent of the Covenant: it not only makes it difficult for the members to devote the necessary time and attention, but also makes it less likely that they can perform their functions "impartially." The task of the Committee is difficult and delicate, and is not aided by subjecting any of its members to political pressures that are inevitable if Committee members are, or are seen as, representing governments.

Rules of Procedure

The first meetings of the Human Rights Committee, in 1977, were concerned with organizational matters, and, in accordance with Article 39 of the Covenant, settling its Rules of Procedure.[35] Rule 2 provides that the Committee shall normally hold two regular sessions each year.

The practice was established in 1977 of holding spring and summer sessions, alternating between New York and Geneva. Rule 3 deals with the possibility of special sessions, which may be convened by decision of the Committee, by decision of the Chairman in consultation with the other officers, at the request of a majority of the members, or at the request of a state party. In fact, it soon became apparent that the Committee would not be able to handle the volume of business which was likely to fall to it in the course of two regular sessions a year, particularly as the number of reports and individual communications increased and the interstate procedure entered into force. Indeed, in 1978 the Committee held three sessions and found that it was unable to complete its business for lack of time. At the fifth session (October/November 1978) the Committee decided that its work load would make three sessions a year necessary for the foreseeable future. Moreover, much preparatory work is necessary between sessions, which a number of members of the Committee who have other professional obligations find difficult to undertake. Nor can the Division of Human Rights in the UN Secretariat meet all the Committee's requirements.[36] There is a strong case for making membership on the Committee a salaried occupation to which members could devote all their time.

The two most interesting points in the Rules of Procedure concerned the publication of the proceedings and the method of voting. It was agreed that reports, formal decisions, and all other official documents of the Committee and its subsidiary bodies should be documents of general distribution, unless the Committee should decide otherwise in any particular case; the periodic reports by states parties and additional information submitted by them should also be public documents. On the other hand, documents and decisions relating to interstate complaints under Articles 41 and 42 of the Covenant, and to individual communications under the Optional Protocol, should have only restricted distribution and remain confidential.[37]

While Article 39 of the Covenant provides that the Committee shall establish its own rules of procedure, paragraph 2 stipulates that these rules shall provide inter alia (a) that twelve members constitute a quorum; and (b) that decisions be made by a majority vote of the members present. During the drafting of the Rules of Procedure, some members of the Committee referred to a tendency in recent years in various legal bodies (both inside and outside the United Nations) to adopt decisions on the basis of consensus; they urged that the Human Rights Committee should follow this method and thus "underscore the resolve of members to work harmoniously and in a spirit of cooperation." They added that "efforts had been made throughout history to incorporate moral principles into positive law. The Committee now had an opportunity to do so and should take advantage of it."[38] The argument is a good one, but it is by no means clear that the Committee would accomplish this noble aim more effectively if consensus (practically implying unanimity) is usually required. Rather, the attempt to reach consensus is liable to water down the moral principles to a lowest common denominator.

Other members argued that, while consensus was desirable if possible, to establish a rule to this effect "might considerably restrict the Committee's power of decision-making" and would be inconsistent with Article 39(2b) of the Covenant. Finally, it was agreed to incorporate in Rule 51 the method of decision by a simple majority, but to add a footnote indicating that there was general agreement that the "method of work normally should allow for attempts to reach decisions by consensus before voting. . . ."[39] In the procedures for the consideration of communications under the Optional Protocol, it was provided that a summary of an individual opinion may be appended to the collective view of the Committee (Rule 94). The point provoked a good deal of discussion; some members from the Eastern European and Latin American countries opposed the provision for individual opinions (which would frequently be dissenting opinions), on the ground that they would weaken the opinion of the majority and the moral authority of the Committee. Other members of the Committee took the opposing view, referring to "the right of dissent" implied in Article 19 of the Covenant, and drawing attention to possible situations in which the Committee might simply be unable to agree on an important point.[40] Rule 94, permitting a summary of an individual opinion, seems a reasonable compromise. This provision should prevent the Committee's work from being hamstrung by the search for unanimity and the corresponding possibilities of intransigence.[41]

In 1979, after the tenth state had made a declaration under Article 41, bringing the interstate complaint regime into force, the Committee put into effect Rules 72 to 77 of its Rules of Procedure to govern such interstate complaints. In general, these merely follow the provisions of Article 41, notably that the Committee will consider communications only if both states have declared under Article 41, and all domestic remedies have been exhausted (or have been unreasonably prolonged). Rule 75 provides that the Committee shall examine communications under Article 41 at closed meetings, but the Committee may, after consultation with the states parties concerned, issue communiques, through the

Secretary-General, for the use of the information media and the public. The Committee may, through the Secretary-General, request from either of the parties concerned additional information or observations in oral or written form and set a time limit for their submission. Under Rule 77 the parties have a right to be represented when the matter is considered by the Committee and to make submissions orally and/or in writing. The Committee shall adopt a report, in accordance with Article 41(1h), within 12 months of the notice bringing the matter to the Committee's attention, but the parties do not have a right to be present during the Committee deliberations concerning the adoption of the report. If the matter is not resolved to the satisfaction of the parties, the Committee may, with their prior consent, proceed to the conciliation procedure prescribed in Article 42.

These rules are sound, reasonable, and promising, and their promulgation did not meet with efforts to limit the Committee's powers. Doubtless they were helped by the fact that most of the members of the Committee were nationals of countries that had not submitted to this regime, and their governments were not threatened by it. The few members of the Committee from countries that had submitted to this regime were eager to see it work, and even their governments, having submitted to it voluntarily, were not disposed to try to frustrate or weaken it.

Reporting Procedures

The 1954 draft covenant had envisaged interstate complaints before the Human Rights Committee as the principal measure of implementation; a reporting procedure was added but it is clear that it was considered a less important and subordinate measure. In the final text of the Covenant, the position was reversed: the reporting procedure became the principal measure of implementation and the interstate procedure was made optional. Although that procedure went into effect in 1979, less than one-fourth of the parties to the Covenant have submitted to it. Therefore, reports by states parties and their examination by the Human Rights Committee are likely to be of cardinal importance and remain the principal means of implementation of the Covenant. Under Article 40 reports are to be presented within one year of the Covenant's entry into force for the state party concerned, and thereafter when the Committee so requests.[42]

Many tend to doubt the value of reports by states on their compliance with their international obligations. Such reports will, of course, be compiled by national officials who have a natural tendency to give the best account they can of the situation in their own country; it is unlikely that they will draw the attention of an international body to any shortcomings or failures in their national record and report violations of human rights by their government or other organs of the state. Is there then, it is asked, any value in a reporting system?

The experience of other bodies, notably the International Labour Organization which has had the longest experience,[43] shows that several elements are necessary to make a reporting system effective: the cooperation of governments in providing full information; the possibility of obtaining further (and perhaps critical) information from other responsible sources; the examination of the information thus obtained by independent persons who are not government officials; and the right of some organ or body taking part in the procedure to make suitable recommendations about any necessary improvements in the law or practice of the country concerned.

This emphasis on the need for independent scrutiny and on the power of recommending improvements is not dictated by prejudice, suspicion, or hostility toward particular governments. It results from the complex nature of modern society, the vast range of subjects with regard to which government action affects the lives of the citizens—often beneficially, but not always so—and the huge apparatus of public administration engaged in implementing that action. Officials, even with the best intentions, make mistakes; occasionally, their intentions may leave something to be desired. The greater the centralization of power in the hands of governments, the greater is the need for effective safeguards to protect the rights of the individual. In how many countries are there laws and even constitutional provisions which are beyond reproach, yet administrative action fails to correspond? It is against such general considerations that we need to look at the reporting system established by the Covenant on Civil and Political Rights.

When the Third Committee of the General Assembly was discussing the measures of implementation of the Covenant in 1966, a group of nine Afro-Asian countries[44] tabled an amendment calling for the insertion of a new article, which became, with little amendment, Article 40. It is the first article on procedures for implementation, coming immediately after the articles on the constitution and functioning of the Human Rights Committee; its adoption resulted in the deletion of the article on periodic reports proposed by the Commission on Human Rights.[45] The general view appears to have been that this proposal represented a substantial improvement over the 1954 draft. "It was also stressed that, since the procedure of conciliation envisaged was to be purely optional, care should be taken to ensure the efficacy of the only means of implementation, namely, the reporting system." [46]

Even this reporting system of limited efficacity was not accepted with general enthusiasm. In the early days, when reporting procedures were first discussed in the Commission on Human Rights, the objection was made that "any such procedure was contrary to the United Nations Charter, in particular to Article 2(7), and constituted a violation of national sovereignty." [47] This extreme and illogical view, however, was fortunately not repeated in the Third Committee; indeed, in 1963 the Eastern European representatives, reversing their earlier position, indicated that they were prepared to accept a reporting system. [48]

Of the four conditions enumerated above for an effective reporting system, the first, cooperation of governments in providing full information, is expressly required by the Covenant. It remains to be seen how well this will be achieved in practice though the early signs are reasonably encouraging. They are somewhat encouraging too as regards the other conditions—the possibility of obtaining further information, independent scrutiny, and recommendations for necessary improvement.

The Human Rights Committee has profited and learned from the experience of its earlier counterpart, the committee established under the International Convention on the Elimination of All Forms of Racial Discrimination. [49] Article 8 of the Convention provides for the establishment of a Committee on the Elimination of Racial Discrimination (CERD) of eighteen independent experts. Article 9 of the Convention contains an undertaking of the state parties to submit reports "on the legislative, judicial, administrative or other measures which they have adopted and which give effect to the provisions of the Convention." [50] The reports are to be submitted within one year of the entry into force of the Convention and thereafter every two years or on request. Article 9 also provides: "The Committee may request further information from the States Parties." It is clear that there is a rather close, but not complete, parallel between Article 9 of the Racial Discrimination Convention and Article 40 of the Covenant on Civil and Political Rights, and that the experience gained in the implementation of the former was likely to influence the practice and procedure of the new Human Rights Committee. [51]

The Committee on the Elimination of Racial Discrimination has taken its task seriously and has succeeded in imposing its authority. With the approval of the General Assembly, it has adopted the practice of inviting states parties which have submitted reports to send a representative to take part in the committee proceedings when the report is under examination. Almost all states parties have accepted such invitations and in this way a constructive dialogue has developed between the Committee and the governmental representatives, who answer questions, afford explanations, provide additional information, and so on. This procedure has the additional advantage of permitting the Committee to indicate informally that a government is not fully complying with its obligations, without the necessity for a formal decision to that effect.[52] The Committee appears to have established a basis of mutual confidence with governments (or the majority of them) which augurs well for its future work.[53]

Obviously similar problems were considered as the Human Rights Committee engaged in settling its methods of work and drawing up its Rules of Procedure.[54] The Committee quickly established its intention of following the practice of the CERD in two important respects; in requesting additional information from governments when required, and in inviting governments to send representatives to discuss their reports with the Committee and to answer questions.[55] Of course, common sense requires such action, but some governments are so extraordinarily sensitive about anything in the nature of international examination of their human rights record—invoking arguments about national sovereignty and nonintervention—that it is a distinct achievement to get them to accept even these modest measures. One member of the Human Rights Committee argued that states had agreed to accept "a reporting procedure, not an investigatory procedure" and that once they have submitted a report they have no further obligation to cooperate with the Committee.[56] The argument was even made that Article 40 of the Covenant does not contain an express provision like that in Article 9 of the Racial Discrimination Convention authorizing the Committee to "request further information from the States Parties," and that the Committee therefore should not make such requests. It is therefore a cause for satisfaction that this negative attitude has not prevailed.

As a result of these and other discussions, Rule 66 of the Rules of Procedure which contains the general provisions about the submission of reports, includes a provision that the Committee may inform states of its wishes as to the form and contents of their reports. Rule 68 provides that representatives of the states parties may be present when their reports are examined and that such a representative "should be able to answer questions which may be put to him by the Committee and make statements on reports already submitted by his State, and may also submit additional information from his State." It is clear, then, that both the Rules of Procedure and the initial practice of the Human Rights Committee are conceived in that spirit of "constructive dialogue" which is so obviously necessary.

At its session in August 1977 the Committee formulated general guidelines about the form and contents of reports, asking that they be in two parts. The first part should describe briefly the general legal framework within which civil and political rights are protected, including information as to whether they are protected in the constitution or by a separate "Bill of Rights," whether the provisions of the Covenant are directly enforceable in internal law, and what remedies are available to an individual who thinks that his rights have been violated. The second part should deal with the legislative, administrative, and other measures in force to protect each right and should include information about restrictions or limitations on their exercise. The Committee also requested that it be informed of any significant new developments at any time.[57]

At the same session, the Committee considered its first group of reports.[58] In all cases a representative of the government concerned was present to answer questions and provide further information. Questions were put by members of the Committee on such subjects as: the relationship between treaty obligations and domestic law in proceedings before national courts, and whether an individual can claim annulment of a national law or measure in case of incompatibility; limitations on grounds of *ordre public* and review of their compatibility with the Covenant; detention for political reasons; equality between the sexes; the prohibition of torture, and remedies available to victims of torture; limitations on freedom of expression, freedom of religion, freedom of assembly, and freedom of movement; the existence of minority groups and the rights accorded to them; the distinction between the treatment accorded to detained persons and to convicted prisoners; permissible length of detention; and others.

The early Annual Reports of the Committee to the General Assembly show that each report was examined carefully and in detail, usually over two or three days. Many searching questions were put to the representatives of the states parties. In some cases adequate answers were given on the spot. More often, detailed replies were promised at a later date. The effectiveness of the system will depend largely on the supplementary information provided subsequently and its careful scrutiny by the Committee.

The proper role of the Committee and the scope of its authority have been a subject of continuing debate.[59] Some members of the Committee have stressed that under Article 40(4), the Committee's function was to exchange information and promote cooperation among states parties and respect for human rights. It was not to evaluate any state's compliance with the Covenant. The Committee could study the reports submitted by states, but any comments on the reports had to be "general," not about any particular state, limited to matters of common interest and addressed to all states.[60]

Most members of the Committee, however, saw the Committee's role as one of promoting and ensuring compliance with the Covenant. Several members stressed that the Committee had the duty to scrutinize the reports received to ensure that the Covenant has been implemented, and that it should seek further information where necessary, in particular where the reports were not consistent with other information available to the Committee. The Committee should adopt a separate report on each state to be transmitted to that state relating to the fulfillment of its obligations. General comments to be included in the Annual Report would review the overall adequacy of the reports received, list difficulties in implementation and suggest solutions, and propose possible amendments to the Covenant.[61]

Despite these differing viewpoints, the Committee succeeded in adopting by consensus a draft statement on how it would proceed. The statement included principles for the Committee's guidance in formulating general comments and a list of subjects to which the general comments could be related, inter alia. The committee also confirmed its aim of engaging in a constructive dialogue with each reporting state on the basis of its periodic reports. It decided to request a second periodic report from states parties within four years of the time its first report was considered, and undertook to develop guidelines for these new reports. Before the Committee meets with the state representatives to discuss the second periodic report, a working group of the Committee would review the information received in order to identify those matters which it would be most helpful to discuss.[62]

Two major problems were revealed early in the reporting system: the delay in reporting and the Committee's need for adequate time for detailed scrutiny. The importance of the first point should not be exaggerated; as a new system begins to operate, it is not surprising if a number of states (especially those with limited resources in their national administrations) fall behind the timetable.[63] The second point is more serious. The Committee's falling behind is not surprising, since each report is supposed to cover the measures (constitutional, legislative, judicial, administrative, and other measures) designed to ensure the protection of twenty-two distinct rights and freedoms, many of them of great complexity, such as the right to liberty and security of the person (Article 9) and the right to a fair trial (Article 14). But if the Committee was behind in its work at the beginning when it had hardly begun to consider individual communications submitted under the Optional Protocol, and when the interstate procedure set out in Articles 41 and 42 was not yet in force, how will it manage in the future? [64]

The second element in an effective reporting system is the possibility of obtaining further, and perhaps contradictory, information from responsible sources other than the governments. This is provided for in the systems established by the ILO for its international labor conventions and by the Council of Europe for the European Social Charter. [65] The Covenant on Civil and Political Rights does not formally institute any similar arrangements. The nearest it comes to doing so is the provision in Article 40(3), introduced as an amendment by the United Kingdom in the Third Committee, [66] which authorizes the Secretary-General of the United Nations, after consultation with the Committee, to "transmit to the specialized agencies concerned copies of such parts of the reports as may fall within their field of competence." Both the ILO and UNESCO have expressed their willingness to cooperate with the Human Rights Committee in this respect, [67] and the appropriate provision has been included in the Rules of Procedure. [68] It would be wise not to expect too much from these arrangements for consultation with the specialized agencies, because comparatively few of the rights protected by the Covenant on Civil and Political Rights relate to matters within the competence of the ILO and UNESCO [69]; moreover, the specialized agencies do not possess a *right* to comment on states' reports and may do so only if specifically requested by the Committee (Rule 67(2)). ILO, UNESCO, FAO, and WHO have been invited to send representatives to attend the public sessions of the Committee, but their relationship to it still remains to be clarified. [70]

One special source of additional material was used early. In considering the report of Chile, which painted a wholly favorable picture of the condition of human rights in that country, the Committee referred to resolutions of the General Assembly and the report of an Ad Hoc Working Group of the UN Commission on Human Rights that indicated flagrant violations of human rights by Chile. [71] Members of the Committee used those resolutions and reports as the basis for criticizing the report in detail, challenging its assertions, and asking for further information, explanation, and justification. The representative of Chile, while responding to many of the questions, challenged the competence of the Committee to use the UN materials as a basis for questions.[72] Those UN resolutions and reports, he argued, derived from complaints by states or by private persons. Since Chile had not agreed to submit to interstate complaints (under Article 41) or to private complaints (under the Protocol), using them to impugn Chile's report would be an indirect way to subject Chile to interstate or private complaints. It was not for the Committee or any of its members, the Chilean representative argued, to express any opinion as to whether Chile was complying with the Covenant: that would constitute a form of complaint by states or individuals to which Chile had not submitted. In his view, the Committee could not look beyond the report a government submitted and could make no allegations based on any other sources.

The Committee, however, rejected these objections, and, relying on the UN materials, found that the information supplied by the report was insufficient and invited the Government of Chile "to submit a report in accordance with Article 40 of the Covenant and to furnish specific information on restrictions" imposed by Chile during the period of state of emergency.[73] The representative of Chile replied that his government considered that it had complied with its obligations under the Covenant but, although it could not accept the preambular part of the Committee's statement, it was prepared to submit a new report as requested.[74] After the Committee received a note from the Chilean Foreign Minister, challenging the Committee's action,[75] "the Committee decided to inform the Government of Chile that the Committee expected to receive the supplementary report requested in accordance with Article 40."[76]

In the Chilean case, the Committee was content to ground its challenges to a report on materials developed by UN bodies. There is no reason why the Committee must limit itself to UN sources only. From what other responsible sources could the Committee obtain information to supplement, or possibly contradict, the information furnished by governments? The answer which springs readily to mind is: the nongovernmental organizations having consultative status with the Economic and Social Council. There are several dozens of these organizations—of which perhaps the best known are Amnesty International, the International Commission of Jurists and the International League for Human Rights—which have followed assiduously the work of the Commission on Human Rights for many years, brought relevant information to its attention, and often made useful suggestions.[77] Unfortunately, certain governments have sought to restrict rather than encourage the activities of NGOs and have even talked of withdrawing completely their consultative status. In these circumstances, the organizations have not been accorded any rights to lay information before the Human Rights Committee when it is considering the reports of governments. This is a real defect in the system. That does not prevent the NGOs from supplying information to members of the Committee in their individual capacity, but this is not the same as presenting information officially to the Committee itself. Moreover, some members of the Committee are particularly sensitive on this score and have objected to the fact that the Secretariat forwarded communications from an NGO; also, that one member of the Committee, in addressing questions to the representative of Czechoslovakia, was apparently using information not included in the government's report.[78] There appears to be a tendency in the Committee to follow the practice of CERD whereby use may be made of all official publications (including opposition speeches, where they exist, and reports of intergovernmental organizations) but not of the reports of NGOs or of the press.[79]

As regards the possibility of obtaining independent information, one must conclude that the situation is far from satisfactory. One cannot but hope that the members of the Committee will succeed in overcoming this difficulty, perhaps by the intelligent use of the right of any independent expert to do his own research work and to use such sources of information as are available to him.

The third requirement which we have postulated as necessary in any effective reporting system is the independence of the persons who examine the reports. As we have seen, the text of the Covenant is satisfactory in this respect; Article 28(3) states that the members of the Committee "shall be elected and shall serve in their personal capacity." This compares with "shall sit . . . in their individual capacity" in the European convention (Article 23), and "shall be elected in a personal capacity" in the American Convention (Article 36). What is perhaps more important are the provisions of Article 38 of the Covenant requiring each member to make "a solemn declaration in open committee that he will perform his functions impartially and conscientiously"; and of Article 35 that the members of the Committee "shall . . . receive emoluments from United Nations resources." Furthermore, Rule 16 of the Rules of Procedure reiterates the requirement of a solemn declaration of impartiality, while Rule 13 requires that the resignation of a member of the Committee must be in writing to the Chairman or the Secretary-General by the member himself, thus eliminating the possibility that a government might decide to remove a member of the Committee and notify the Chairman or the Secretary-General that he has resigned.

But if the text of the Covenant is adequate in this respect, it remains to be seen whether governments will in fact apply these provisions in the spirit in which they were drafted. Regrettably, similar guarantees of the independence of international officials have not always been respected in practice. One must hope that a greater measure of independence is allowed to members of the Human Rights Committee. What one would like to see is a categorical exclusion from the Committee (and from the European and American Commissions) of persons who are salaried national officials (particularly members of permanent delegations to the UN)—not because they are not usually of the highest integrity, but because their impartiality is that much more difficult to sustain when, for the greater part of their lives, their habit and their duty is to act on the instructions of their governments, and when the prospects for their future careers depend on the goodwill and approval of their governments. It would be both logical and sensible to establish that a salaried national official position is incompatible with membership of an international organ whose members are required to serve in an independent capacity.

The fourth requirement of an effective reporting system is that the body that receives the report shall have authority to make suitable recommendations for any necessary improvements in the law or practice of the country concerned. In this respect the Covenant on Civil and Political Rights is sadly deficient. Under Article 40(4) and (5), the Committee proceeds as follows:

1. The Committee studies the reports submitted by the states parties.
2. The Committee draws up its own reports and transmits them with "such general comments as it may consider appropriate."
3. The Committee may also transmit these comments to the Economic and Social Council together with the reports of the states parties.
4. The states parties may submit to the Committee their observations on the latter's comments on their reports.

These procedures are deficient in several respects. The Committee is authorized to make "general comments" only. The term is not defined. It does not mean that these comments must be addressed to all parties and not to particular states. As drafting history makes clear, the Human Rights Committee may make recommendations to particular states parties.[80] But they must be in general terms and not relate to individual cases, and cannot therefore focus attention on specific violations and bring influence to bear to remedy them.

Moreover, the states concerned are not required to take any action on the comments made by the Committee on their reports. They "may submit . . . their observations on any comments that may be made" or may ignore them completely. And unlike other reporting systems (for example, in the procedures of the ILO and the Council of Europe), the Committee's conclusions are not submitted to an authoritative political organ empowered to make formal and specific recommendations to the government concerned. One might have thought that the Economic and Social Council would fulfill this role.[81] But there is no obligation for the Committee to submit its comments to ECOSOC. If the Committee does submit its comments to ECOSOC, there is no requirement that the governments concerned communicate to ECOSOC their observations on the Committee's comments.[82] And there is no provision that ECOSOC is to pursue the Committee's comments with recommendations for necessary remedies.

In the light of these deficiencies, much will depend on the use which the Committee makes of the possibilities offered by Article 45, which provides that the Committee shall submit to the General Assembly, through ECOSOC, "an annual report on its activities." If the Committee uses this opportunity to draw attention to situations which it considers unsatisfactory but with regard to which it cannot obtain remedial action from governments, it may help to remedy the deficiencies in the procedure under Article 40. Quite properly, the Committee was cautious in its exercise of this power during the first few years, but it may become bolder as its influence increases.[83]

It is not surprising that there are weaknesses and deficiencies in the reporting system instituted by the Covenant on Civil and Political Rights, since it is the product of the heterogeneous community of the United Nations, some of whose members oppose any system of international control at all. Seen in this perspective, the reporting system is a reasonable compromise. It will be a demanding challenge for the Human Rights Committee to make it as effective as possible.

Proceedings between State Parties

Like other multilateral international agreements, the Covenant on Civil and Political Rights is an agreement among the states parties to it, creating rights and obligations among them. Since parties to an international agreement generally can enforce it against one another by appropriate remedies, it was natural that the Human Rights Commission, in proposing the establishment of a Committee to implement the Covenant, should contemplate permitting the Committee to receive complaints by one state party alleging violation by another.

The implementing system envisaged in the 1954 draft of the Human Rights Commission involved the following stages: bilateral negotiations between complaining and respondent state; in the event of their failure, reference to the Human Rights Committee; the Committee would establish the facts and make available its good offices with a view to a friendly settlement; in the absence of such a settlement, the Committee would draw up a report on the facts and state its opinion on the question of violation; the report would be sent to the states concerned and to the Secretary-General for publication. The Committee then, was first to have a role of mediation and then, if that failed, a quasi-judicial role. The Committee would declare its opinion after proceedings of an almost judicial character; and while the opinion would not be binding on the parties, it would no doubt carry great weight.

Many of those responsible for this text would doubtless have preferred something stronger, probably a committee which, if mediation was unsuccessful, would have the power to reach a decision and not merely express an opinion; but (as happens so often in the United Nations) it was no doubt necessary to accept a weaker text as a compromise.

The Third Committee of the General Assembly, instead of strengthening the powers of the Human Rights Committee to deal with interstate disputes, did the opposite. Its most important change was to make Committee examination of interstate complaints an optional procedure. Thus, Article 41 of the Covenant provides: "A State Party . . . may at any time declare . . . that it recognizes the competence of the Committee to receive and consider communications to the effect that a State Party claims that another State Party is not fulfilling its obligations under the present Covenant." A separate declaration recognizing this competence, in addition to the act of ratification of the Covenant, is therefore required. Moreover, it is not sufficient that the state alleged to be responsible for a violation has made such a declaration. Communications can be considered by the Committee only if the complaining state has also done so. There must be (in a new sense) "equality of arms": only states which have agreed to expose themselves to this procedure have the right to use it against another state party. Furthermore, under Article 41(2), the procedure was to come into force when ten states made the necessary declarations, and that did not happen until 1979, thirteen years after the approval of the covenants by the General Assembly and nearly three years after the entry into force of the Covenant itself. By the end of 1980, only thirteen of the sixty-five states parties to the Covenant had made the declaration provided for in Article 41.[84] It is clear, then, that this procedure is not the principal measure of implementation provided for in the Covenant.

It is instructive to note the obligatory or optional nature of the systems of international control in the different human rights treaties. The European Convention on Human Rights (drafted in 1950, entered into force in 1953) makes the procedure for interstate complaints obligatory for all contracting parties (Article 24) and the procedure of individual petition optional (Article 25). The UN Covenant makes both procedures optional, while the American Convention on Human Rights (drafted in 1969, entered into force in 1978) makes the procedure of individual petition obligatory for all contracting parties (Article 44) and the procedure of interstate complaints optional (Article 45). During the conference at San José, Costa Rica, at which the American Convention was drafted,[85] it was explained quite frankly that human rights issues were inflammatory and that a system permitting interstate proceedings between American republics on such issues was politically dangerous; it was therefore considered prudent to make this an optional provision which states could accept or reject. No doubt similar considerations led the Third Committee of the General Assembly to a similar conclusion. As the Committee stated in its report, various factors of international tension and mutual suspicion still exist in the world, and it was unlikely that mandatory complaint procedures would be widely accepted.[86] It was believed that the adoption of an optional procedure would afford a satisfactory solution, and that with the passage of time "an increasing number of States Parties would no doubt accept the optional clause . . . and thereby give full effect to the system of implementation of the Covenant.[87] One may hope that this optimism was not ill-placed. In any event, it is worth recording, and bearing in mind for the future, that the Third Committee itself recognized that the system of implementation would only be fully effective when the optional provisions of Article 41 are generally accepted. It is noteworthy that the Convention on the Elimination of All Forms of Racial Discrimination, adopted by the UN at about the same time as the Covenant, provides for interstate complaints, although the procedure has not been frequently invoked. In addition, there have been state-to-state complaints under the European Convention without devastating effect on relations between the countries involved.

The second way in which the Third Committee watered down the Commission's 1954 proposals was by taking away the Human Rights Committee's right to express an opinion on the question of violation. The procedure set out in Article 41 of the Covenant envisages, in the first place, bilateral negotiations between the two states concerned; if the matter is not thus settled and domestic remedies have been exhausted, either state may refer it to the Human Rights Committee, which must examine the question in closed meetings; the Committee may call for all relevant information and the states parties may be represented and make oral and written submissions; then, the Committee is to make available its good offices with a view to a friendly settlement of the matter, based on respect for human rights; finally, if this is not achieved, the Committee is required to submit a report *which is to be confined to a brief statement of the facts,* with the written or oral submissions of the states parties attached. The functions of the Committee in relation to interstate disputes are practically limited to establishing the facts, proposing its good offices, and exercising them if the offer is accepted. As certain representatives stated in the Third Committee, the Human Rights Committee is "no longer the same as the quasi-judicial body originally proposed by the Commission on Human Rights" but "more in the nature of a functional organ."

There is, however, another procedural possibility, presented by Article 42 of the Covenant. This provides that if a matter referred to the Committee under Article 41 is not resolved to the satisfaction of the states parties concerned, the Committee may, if those states consent, appoint an ad hoc conciliation Commission, which will in turn make available its good offices "with a view to an amicable solution of the matter on the basis of respect for the present Covenant." The Commission is to consist of five members who are nationals of states which have accepted the Article 41 procedure but not nationals of the states parties involved in the dispute. Article 42 deals with the composition, method of election and procedure of the Conciliation Commission;[88] in particular, it provides that the information obtained by the Human Rights Committee shall be made available to the Commission, which may also call on the states concerned for further relevant information.

When it has completed its work, or in any event within a year of being seized of the matter, the Conciliation Commission is to draw up its report. If an amicable solution has been reached, the report will contain a brief statement of the facts and of the solution reached. If an amicable solution has not been reached, the report will contain a full statement of the facts and the Commission's view on "the possibilities of an amicable solution of the matter." Within three months of the receipt of the report, the states parties will indicate "whether or not they accept the contents of the report of the Commission" (Article 42[7c] and [7d]).

Though the relevant subparagraphs of Article 42(7) are not very clear, the text seems to give the Commission a real function of conciliation, making proposals for consideration and possible acceptance by the parties. This is rather more than merely having the Commission state "its views on the possibilities of an amicable solution of the matter." It would seem that this phrase in subparagraph (c) should rather be taken to mean that the Commission shall set forth "proposals for a possible amicable solution of the matter," because otherwise there would be little meaning in the requirement of subparagraph (d) that the state parties shall indicate "whether or not they accept the contents of the report of the Commission."[89]

One may summarize by saying that in interstate disputes the function of the Human Rights Committee is one of good offices, while that of the Conciliation Commission is of good offices and perhaps conciliation; but neither function can be exercised except in relation to states both of which have made an express declaration accepting the competence of the Committee to exercise this function and, as regards the Conciliation Commission, have consented to its appointment.

Whether state complaints to the Human Rights Committee will play an important part in protecting human rights remains to be seen. The procedure has come into force but, as of 1980, has not been used. Most of the states that have accepted it are parties to the European Convention on Human Rights and will not normally refer to the UN Committee matters which could be considered by the European Commission of Human Rights. The American States, too, are more likely to use inter-American procedures. If "state-to-state" enforcement is to develop in other parts of the world it is also likely to happen in a regional context before regional commissions. In the past, the Communist states have made it clear that they will not accept this procedure, as they are opposed to the basic principle on which it rests.

The fact that the Covenant provides for "state-to-state" complaint to the Human Rights Committee, if only on an optional basis, has raised the question whether states parties to the Covenant may refer disputes about its interpretation or application to other procedures of international settlement (for example, to the International Court of Justice). It has been argued that the Covenant is an international agreement like any other and states parties to it have the usual remedies available to states for breach of an agreement. It is relevant to observe that in Article 62 of the European Convention on Human Rights, the contracting parties agree that they will not avail themselves of other international procedures for settling disputes arising under the Convention, unless by special agreement concluded for the purpose. There is no corresponding provision in the UN Covenant. It can therefore be argued that no such limitation is implied in the Covenant. And as regards resort to the International Court of Justice, this interpretation is supported by the very broad terms of Article 36 of the Statute of the Court.

On the other hand, some have argued that the intention of the states parties was to establish special procedures for dealing with any dispute which may arise about the interpretation and application of the Covenant and that it is only by means of these procedures—and subject to the conditions and limitations pertaining to them in the Covenant—that one state is entitled to question the action of another state concerning any matter arising under the Covenant.

As regards international judicial procedures, this problem may be largely academic, since the Court is not frequently used. What may be more important is the availability of the Covenant as a basis for diplomatic protection. Under traditional international law one state is entitled to "intervene" with another state for the purpose of protecting the rights of its own citizens, principally in cases of "denial of justice." After the entry into force of the Covenant on Civil and Political Rights, a good case can be made for holding that one state party is justified in exercising the right of diplomatic protection if another state party fails to ensure any of the rights protected in the Covenant, at least where a national of the complaining state is concerned. This would give a valid justification for one state party to secure the protection of the fundamental rights of its citizens when on the territory of another state party, even if the respondent state has not accepted the provisions of Article 41 of the Covenant. And some have argued strongly that, because a breach of the Covenant is involved, such "diplomatic protection" may be provided by any state party against any other state party even on behalf of the latter's nationals, although complaint to the Human Rights Committee is not available under Article 41.[90]

Individual Communications

The real test of the effectiveness of a system of international protection for human rights is whether it provides an international remedy for the individual whose rights are violated.

In its classic conception, international law governs relations between states, and the individual has no place therein. His interests are supposed to be protected by the state of which he is a national and he has no *locus standi* before international tribunals or international organizations. In the second half of the twentieth century, however, certain inroads upon, or exceptions to, this classic doctrine have been established. Whether these inroads and exceptions are to be encouraged and further developed, or resisted and restricted, has been debated for thirty years; and the debate will no doubt continue for at least another generation. There is an immense literature on the subject,[91] and there have been and will continue to be innumerable speeches about it in United Nations organs and elsewhere.[92]

One's personal response to this issue may depend principally on one's conception of the role of the state in the modern world. If one believes that national sovereignty and the unrestricted power of the nation-state are, and should remain, the basic premises of political organization and of the law (both national and international), one will resist all attempts to permit the individual to challenge the authority of the state, in particular by the use of international remedies. If, on the other hand, one believes that the concept of the nation-state as developed in the last few centuries—and particularly in the nineteenth and twentieth centuries— is not the *summum bonum* or greatest achievement of mankind, but merely one stage in a process of constant evolution, and that the state is made for man and not man for the state, then one will welcome and encourage all attempts to protect the individual against the abuse of power by the state. To put it another way: is one on the side of Machiavelli and Hobbes or of Locke, Rousseau, and Bentham? Those who are heirs to the Bill of Rights, the American Declaration of Independence, and the French Declaration of 1789 will have no difficulty in answering this question.

To go from the general to the particular, in my view there are two practical arguments which are determinant.[93] The first is that the classic doctrine of international law simply does not work in the context of the protection of human rights. If an individual's rights are violated, this will in the great majority of cases be the result of acts by organs or agencies of the state of which he is a national. It is therefore nonsense to say that his rights will be championed by the state of which he is a national when that state is *ex hypothesi* the offender. Second, as is well known, the United Nations receives many thousands of communications each year complaining of violations of human rights throughout the world. Article 1 of the Charter states that one of the purposes of the United Nations is "to achieve international cooperation . . . in promoting and encouraging respect for human rights and fundamental freedoms for all . . . ," and there are seven other references in the Charter to the functions of the United Nations and its organs in relation to human rights. If—as was at one time the case—the organization takes no action with regard to the communications it receives, this inevitably brings it into disrepute and shows that it is failing to fulfill one of its principal functions. Both common sense and the need to preserve the reputation of the United Nations, therefore, make it necessary to adopt a constructive and positive attitude to the question of access of the individual to international remedies, notably in the system of human rights protection which the UN has launched.

These considerations led to discussions which went on for many years in different UN organs about whether the Commission on Human Rights could take any action about communications from individuals and nongovernmental organizations complaining of violations. These discussions finally led to the adoption by the Economic and Social Council in 1970 of Resolution 1503, which authorized the Commission to examine "communications, together with replies of governments, if any, which appear to reveal a consistent pattern of gross violations of human rights." [94] The procedure is complicated, involving a triple screening, and the results so far have been disappointing. It is outside the scope of this chapter to examine the Resolution 1503 procedure in detail; but its existence confirms a clear if timid recognition that the United Nations and the international human rights system cannot totally ignore individual complaints of violation of human rights.

There is also a third important argument for allowing individuals who believe that their rights have been violated to appeal to an international organ of control. If there is neither the possibility of state-to-state complaint nor a right of individual complaint, there is no meaningful vindication of individual rights beyond the general and indirect influences of the voluntary reporting system. If the international organ can be seized of interstate complaints, but there is no right of individual petition, aggrieved individuals will look for another government to champion their cause by bringing a case against the government of which they are nationals. Thus Greek citizens whose rights were violated by the military regime in their country in 1967 were led to appeal to the Scandinavian governments for help. It is obviously in the interest of peaceful relations between states that what is essentially an individual and national problem should be dealt with as such, not transformed into an international dispute between states.

When the Covenant on Civil and Political Rights was being drafted, it became necessary to face squarely the question whether the measures of implementation to be provided in the Covenant should include the right of individual petition to the Human Rights Committee. Indeed, the Commission on Human Rights had been specifically instructed to examine this problem by the General Assembly when it approved the Universal Declaration in 1948. As we have seen earlier in this essay, in 1950 the Commission considered that the Committee to be established by the Covenant should be competent to consider interstate complaints but rejected the possibility of access by nongovernmental organizations and individuals.[95] The issue was later reopened in the Third Committee of the General Assembly. In the explanatory paper on measures of implementation which he presented to the General Assembly in 1963, the Secretary-General summarized the history of the matter and the issues involved, and explained the procedures for handling individual communications which existed under the European Convention, the draft Inter-American Convention, and the Constitution of the ILO.[96]

The Third Committee discussed the matter at length.[97] After it had approved the two articles on interstate procedures (which became Articles 41 and 42) it considered the addition of a new article providing for the competence of the Human Rights Committee, on an optional basis, to receive and consider individual petitions—a text which was largely inspired by the corresponding provisions of the European Convention. Another proposal was aimed at limiting the functions of the Committee to the simple receipt and transmission of communications. A revision of the original amendment[98] set out the procedure in greater detail and would have authorized the Committee, when examining individual communications, to "forward its suggestions, if any, to the state party concerned and to the individual."

In the end, the debate turned on the question whether such a procedure should be included in the Covenant itself, on an optional basis, or in a separate protocol thereto, which would also be optional. It was decided by a very narrow majority to incorporate the right of individual petition in a separate legal text.[99]

It seems regrettable that such an important measure of implementation should be altogether absent from the Covenant itself. On the other hand, its inclusion in the Covenant would no doubt have rendered more difficult the procedure of ratification in a number of countries. There is also perhaps a certain psychological advantage in the fact that the measure is included in a separate Optional Protocol, because this fact draws more attention to the existence of the procedure of individual petition than would be the case if it were set out in an article of the Covenant. The Protocol is now included separately in the list of United Nations treaties; ratifications are published and to some extent publicized; it is thus an object of greater attention than the optional procedure in Article 41 of the Covenant. One should not exaggerate, but—on balance—nothing seems to be lost, and probably something is gained, by the fact that the Optional Protocol exists as a separate legal text.

Any state party to the Covenant which ratifies the Protocol thereby "recognizes the competence of the Committee to receive and consider communications from individuals subject to its jurisdiction who claim to be victims of a violation by that State Party of any of the rights set forth in the Covenant." Article 2 of the Protocol establishes that communications to the Committee may be submitted by "individuals who claim that any of their rights enumerated in the Covenant have been violated and who have exhausted all available domestic remedies." Article 3 provides that communications shall be considered inadmissible if they are anonymous, abusive, or incompatible with the provisions of the Covenant. Article 5(2) introduces a further precondition by providing that the Committee shall not consider a communication unless it has ascertained that the same matter is not being considered under another procedure of international investigation or settlement. This rule is eminently reasonable in itself. But this paragraph seems to place on the Committee the positive obligation of ascertaining that the matter is not being examined under another international procedure—an obligation which may be difficult to fulfill—whereas it would seem sufficient to have provided that the Committee will not examine a communication if it is shown, by the respondent government or otherwise, that the matter is being examined under another international procedure. (The Committee must also ascertain that the individual has exhausted domestic remedies, except where the application of remedies is unreasonably prolonged.)

The rule of exhaustion of domestic remedies is well known to international lawyers and is based on both justice and common sense. It is based on justice, because it would be unjust that the international responsibility of a state should be engaged on account of the action of one of its agents or tribunals when a national means of redress is available but has not been used. Equally, the rule is based on common sense, because it is in the general interest (among other reasons, as being normally quicker, cheaper, and more effective) that an aggrieved person should make use of domestic remedies, when they are available, to right a wrong, rather than address himself to an international commission, court, or other tribunal. Access to the international organ should be available, but only in the last resort, and after the domestic remedies have been exhausted. Normally, this will mean that appeals against the acts of the executive branch of the government should be addressed to the national courts before being addressed to an international organ; equally, that appeals against decisions of inferior courts should be addressed to the higher courts and, if necessary and possible, to the Supreme Court or Constitutional Court, before being addressed to an international organ. Not only are the domestic remedies likely to be speedier and perhaps less expensive; in many cases they may be more effective, because a national court of appeal or Supreme Court can usually reverse the decision of a lower court, whereas the decision of an international organ does not have that effect, even though it will engage the international responsibility of the state concerned.

All this is on the assumption that domestic remedies are available and are effective. If no domestic remedies are available, clearly there is no need to have recourse to them before the applicant can address himself to the competent international organ. Equally, if domestic remedies are theoretically available but there is unreasonable delay on the part of national courts in granting a remedy, the applicant should not be penalized as a result.

A large proportion of the applications filed with the European Commission of Human Rights are declared inadmissible on grounds of non-exhaustion of domestic remedies. It remains to be seen whether the same will be the case with the Human Rights Committee.

Article 4 and the remaining paragraphs of Article 5 of the Protocol deal with the procedure of the Committee for dealing with individual communications. They shall be communicated to the state party concerned, which within six months must "submit to the Committee written explanations or statements clarifying the matter and the remedy, if any, that may have been taken by that State." Article 5(1) states that the proceedings shall be based on "all written information made available . . . by the individual and by the State Party concerned," which would seem to exclude oral hearings and information from other sources. Communications are to be examined at closed meetings and, under Article 5(4), "the Committee shall forward its views to the State Party concerned and to the individual."

Finally, under Article 6 of the Protocol, the Committee will include a summary of its activities thereunder in its annual report to the General Assembly provided for in Article 45 of the Covenant.

From this brief summary it will appear that the procedure is not contentious, permitting argument by counsel, examination of witnesses and so on, nor is it an adjudication on the question of violation by the Human Rights Committee. Nevertheless, it marks a big advance over any measures of implementation previously established by the United Nations.[100] Much will depend on how the Human Rights Committee interprets its powers under the Protocol, particularly in forwarding "its views" to states parties under Article 5(4) and in reporting to the General Assembly under Article 6.

The Optional Protocol contains no separate provisions for rules of procedure, which means that the general provision of Article 39 of the Covenant on Civil and Political Rights applies also to action taken under the Optional Protocol, including the provision that twelve members shall constitute a quorum and that decisions "shall be made by a majority vote of the members present." The Committee Rules include a separate chapter on "Procedure for the Consideration of Communications Received under the Optional Protocol" (Rules 78 to 94).[101] The first section (Rules 78 ho 81) deals with transmission of communications to the Committee. The Secretary-General of the United Nations is the channel of communication. He is required to prepare lists of the communications received, with a brief summary of their contents, for circulation to the members of the Committee; the full text is available to them on request. A register of communications is to be kept. The Secretary-General may request from the authors of communications any necessary clarifications, particularly as regards the exhaustion of domestic remedies.

The second section (Rules 82 to 86) contains certain general provisions. Meetings at which communications are examined shall be closed (or private), but the Committee may issue communiqués for the press and general public about its activities.[102] The third section (Rules 87 to 92) deals with the admissibility of communications. The conditions of admissibility set out in the Protocol are repeated. The Committee may establish working groups of not more than five members to examine and make recommendations to the Committee about the admissibility of communications. The Committee or working group may request additional information relevant to the question of admissibility; a communication may not be declared admissible unless the state concerned has received a copy of it and has had an opportunity to comment.

Rules 93 and 94 deal with "Procedures for the Consideration of Communications," repeating essentially what is provided in Article 5 of the Protocol. Once a decision is taken that a communication is admissible, the state concerned and the individual are informed; within six months the state "shall submit . . . written explanations or statements . . . and the remedy, if any, that may have been taken by that State." These explanations and statements are to be communicated to the author of the communication for his comments. Finally, the Committee will consider the substance of the case "in the light of all the written information made available to it by the individual and by the State Party concerned and shall formulate its views thereon." These views will be communicated to the state concerned and to the individual.

There are two additions to what is specified in the Protocol. Paragraph 1 of Rule 94 reiterates the Committee's use of working groups to make recommendations about admissibility, and paragraph 3 of Rule 94, in effect, permits dissenting opinions. Lengthy dissenting opinions will not be possible, however, because a member may only request that "a summary of his individual opinion shall be appended to the views of the Committee when they are communicated to the individual and to the State party concerned." Nevertheless, this is a useful addition which should strengthen the quasi-judicial character of the Human Rights Committee when exercising its functions under the Optional Protocol and should contribute to the development of its jurisprudence.

As of January 1, 1981, twenty-five states had ratified the Optional Protocol.[103] The Committee's first Report to the General Assembly on its activities recorded the appointment of working groups to consider the admissibility of communications.[104] Since the proceedings are confidential, information was not published about the identity of the applicants, about the nature of the alleged violations or about the states against which the complaints were lodged.[105] The Committee's reports tell only the results of the procedural steps taken: decisions of inadmissibility; decisions to transmit communications to governments for their observations on admissibility; requests to applicants for further information, including steps to exhaust domestic remedies; and so on.[106] The Reports also give indications of the Committee's thinking on four topics: the standing of the author, the examination of complaints *ratione temporis,* the exhaustion of domestic remedies, and the problem of determining whether a matter is being examined under another international procedure of investigation or settlement.

In 1979 the Committee for the first time "forward[ed] its views to the State Party concerned and to the individual" (Article 5[4]) and made public what was, in effect, its first "judgment" on a private communication under the Protocol. The Committee had received a "communication" (Article 1) from a Uruguayan citizen alleging mistreatment of herself and three members of her family. Each had been charged with "subversive association" or "assistance to subversive association," and was allegedly detained without trial, held incommunicado, and tortured. The Committee brought the communication to the attention of the government of Uruguay (Article 4[1]). The government of Uruguay objected to the admissibility of the claim on the grounds that domestic remedies had not been exhausted, and that the alleged violations against the principal complainant had occurred before the Covenant entered into force for Uruguay. The Committee agreed that acts occurring before the Covenant's entry into force were beyond its jurisdiction. As regards violations alleged to have occurred after that date, however, the Committee found that no further domestic remedy remained. It decided also that the "close family connexion" permitted the author of the communication to act on behalf of the other victims.[107] When, after six months (Article 4[2]), the government of Uruguay failed to give a satisfactory explanation of its actions, the Committee formulated its views on the basis of the facts as alleged. It expressed the view that the facts disclosed several violations of the Covenant, including: torture and detainment in unhealthy conditions contrary to Articles 7 and 10(1); imprisonment after a release order contrary to Article 9(1); failure to inform the prisoners of the charges against them contrary to Article 9(2); denial of a prompt and fair trial contrary to Articles 9(3) and 14; inadequate appellate remedies contrary to Article 9(4); imprisonment incommunicado contrary to Article 10(1); and denial of political rights contrary to Article 25. The Committee expressed the view that the government of Uruguay was obligated to "take immediate steps to ensure strict observance of the provisions of the Covenant and to provide effective remedies to the victims."[108]

Relation to Regional Systems of Implementation

Any critical analysis of international systems for the protection of human rights must pose the question whether it is desirable or appropriate to have regional systems of protection in addition to the international system established by the United Nations. Are regional systems compatible with the universal system or are they likely to diminish its value and perhaps even undermine its effectiveness? In any event, how does the universal system relate and interact with regional systems?

As regards the compatibility of regional and universal systems, there is a good deal to be said on both sides of this question. On the one hand, it was possible in Europe to conclude a convention containing binding obligations and setting up new international machinery at a time when this was not possible in the worldwide framework; and though the UN covenants and the Optional Protocol are now in force, it is quite uncertain how many states will accept their optional provisions. It is likely that at least for a considerable period of time the European system will contain far more effective procedures than the universal system. Similar considerations would justify regional systems in other parts of the world.

On the other hand, it can be argued that human rights appertain to human beings by virtue of their humanity and should be guaranteed to all human beings on a basis of equality, without distinction, wherever they may live. Discrimination on grounds of race, sex, religion, or nationality is forbidden both in the United Nations texts and in the regional conventions. Equally, there should be no distinction based on geography and differences between regions. The African and the Asian should have the same human rights as the European or the American.

The two points of view can be reconciled. Human rights are and should be the same for all persons, everywhere, at all times. In other words, the normative content of different international instruments should be, in principle, the same. There may, of course, be minor differences in formulation, due to differences in drafting techniques or in legal traditions, but the basic rights and fundamental freedoms should be the same for all. The yardstick is the Universal Declaration, which sets out, in the words of its Preamble "a common standard of achievement for all peoples and all nations." No regional system should be allowed to exist which is not consistent with the norms and principles set out in the Universal Declaration.

When we come to measures of implementation, however, the answer is different. While it is desirable that the most effective system possible should be established everywhere, it is a fact that this optimum system is not at present acceptable in all parts of the world. It is therefore reasonable to set up regional arrangements which differ from each other, provided that the rights to be protected are essentially the same as those established in the Universal Declaration. This was the approach adopted by the European Convention, in which the contracting parties expressed their determination "to take the first steps for the collective enforcement of certain of the rights stated in the Universal Declaration." Other regional systems are equally legitimate if they seek to enforce, by means of regional procedures which can be accepted by a group of states in a particular area, some or all of the rights proclaimed in the Universal Declaration.

The principle of regional settlement is quite consistent with the Charter of the United Nations.[109] The Charter in Articles 33 and 52 recognizes the regional settlement of disputes and even requires members of a regional agency to "make every effort to achieve pacific settlement of local disputes . . . by such regional agencies before referring them to the Security Council." Moreover, the UN Covenant on Civil and Political Rights, in Article 44, recognizes that its provisions "shall not prevent the States Parties . . . from having recourse to other procedures for settling a dispute in accordance with general or special international agreements in force between them." Consequently, the existence of regional remedies is perfectly consistent with the Covenant. But the rights should be the same for all men and women everywhere.

Both the European Convention (and its First and Fourth Protocols) and the American Convention set out to protect the same rights and freedoms proclaimed in the Universal Declaration of 1948; both recognize this fact in their preambles, and many of the Articles in both instruments were inspired by the text of the Covenant on Civil and Political Rights or by its earlier drafts. At the same time, the system of international control in the two regional conventions is more developed and more effective than the UN system. The large majority of the parties to the European Convention have accepted the competence of the European Commission to receive individual complaints, as well as the jurisdiction of the European Court of Human Rights; the Committee of Ministers of the Council of Europe has authority to act on reports of the Commission and to supervise compliance with the judgments of the Court. The American Convention also established both a human rights commission and a human rights court and the Commission can automatically receive private complaints against any state party; if a judgment of the Court is not complied with, the Court may report the matter to the General Asssembly of the Organization of American States.

The "coexistence" of the United Nations Covenant on Civil and Political Rights and regional human rights agreements is now a fact.

In 1968, in response to an appeal from the Secretary-General of the UN, the Assembly of the Council of Europe called for ratification of the two Covenants and of the Optional Protocol "after having taken . . . the necessary decisions on the problems arising in connection with the coexistence of the European convention on Human Rights and the United Nations Covenants." It was clear that the member states of the Council of Europe wished to give favorable consideration to the ratification of the Covenants, which their representatives had taken a prominent part in drafting. At the same time, it was necessary for them to consider what problems, if any, would arise if they were to become parties to both instruments: were the same rights protected by both instruments and, if not, were the differences important; were the definitions the same and, if they were not, would this cause difficulties; would there be a conflict between the procedures of the United Nations and the Council of Europe; could the different procedures be used simultaneously or consecutively, and so on. It was decided to make a joint study of them in the framework of the Committee of Experts on Human Rights of the Council of Europe.

The experts submitted two separate reports: the first in 1968 on the coexistence of the two systems of control;[110] the second in 1970 on the differences in the enumeration and definition of the rights.[111] The conclusion of these studies was seen as an important step in permitting, or at least facilitating, ratification of the Covenants by member states of the Council of Europe.

The study made by the Committee of Experts on Human Rights led to two conclusions about the measures of implementation set out in these two treaties. As regards interstate complaints or "communications," member states of the Council of Europe should normally use the procedures provided for in the European Convention for their disputes inter se, in accordance with the principle of regional settlement of disputes before having recourse to United Nations procedures. But they should agree to accept the United Nations procedures for cases which may be brought against them by non-European states.

As regards individual applications or "communications," the governing consideration should be to secure the most effective protection of individual rights. The individual applicant should be free to choose his forum and apply either to the European Commission or to the United Nations Committee, in accordance with his own judgment about where he has the best chance of success. Once he has put in an application either in Strasbourg or in New York, however, he should not be allowed, if he is unsuccessful in one forum, to make a second attempt in the other, unless he has made an honest mistake. It should not be possible to appeal—or to appear to appeal—from the European Commission to the United Nations Committee, or vice versa. The European Convention in Article 27(1b) apparently excludes the possibility of submitting to the European Commission a case previously submitted without success to the United Nations Committee, but the Protocol, Article 5(2a), bars the Committee from considering a communication only while it is "being examined under another international procedure." The Committee of Ministers therefore recommended to member governments that when ratifying the Optional Protocol they should make a declaration or reservation to the effect that while they accept the competence of the Human Rights Committee to consider communications from individuals, they interpret Article 5(2a) to mean that a communication is inadmissible if the same matter is being examined *or has been examined* under another international procedure of investigation or settlement. Contracting parties to the European Convention which have ratified the Covenant have for the most part made a declaration or reservation to this effect.

Article 5(2a) of the Optional Protocol imposes on the Human Rights Committee the obligation of ascertaining that the same matter is not being examined under another international procedure; in practical effect that means the European Commission of Human Rights or the Inter-American Commission on Human Rights. In order to discharge this responsibility, the Committee has made arrangements for the exchange of information with the two regional Commissions, and has expressed its appreciation of their "most helpful cooperation."[112] Furthermore, the Committee has decided that the international procedures referred to in Article 5(2a) are for examination of individual petitions, and that the procedures established by the Economic and Social Council under Resolution 1503 are not included, since they refer to "situations which appear to reveal a consistent pattern of gross violations of human rights" and such a "situation" is something different from individual communications.[113] The new procedures established by UNESCO in April 1978 for handling communications from individuals relating to matters within the competence of that organization would seem to be within the compass of Article 5(2a), but the question has not been considered.[114]

As regards the comparison of the rights and freedoms protected in the UN Covenant and the European Convention, the Committee of Experts of the Council of Europe concluded that there were fifteen provisions in the Covenant which involved more extensive obligations than those contained in the European Convention, but that in many of these cases the national law of member states was already in conformity with those obligations.[115] The implication would seem to be that it was not necessary for the European states to hesitate unduly about accepting the obligations contained in the Covenant.[116] There is, generally speaking, a greater similarity between definitions of the rights in the American Convention on Human Rights and those in the Covenant. This is not surprising, because the American Convention was concluded in 1969, when the text of the UN Covenant had been available for three years. It is significant that the member governments of the Organization of American States decided to continue with the drafting of their own regional convention even after the conclusion of the UN Covenants in December 1966.[117]

It is perhaps premature to attempt to reach any firm conclusions about the relationship of the UN procedures to regional systems of implementation when the Human Rights Committee has been in existence only since 1976 and the American Convention on Human Rights in force only since 1978. Nevertheless, we can assert with some confidence that there is no incompatibility or objection in principle to the idea that universal and regional systems of implementation should coexist, provided that the conditions indicated are respected, and that measures of consultation and exchange of information between the Human Rights Committee and the Regional Commissions will occur on a continuing basis. A good start has evidently been made in establishing such arrangements. We may be reasonably confident that they will develop harmoniously in the future and thus facilitate the task—and contribute to the success of the work—of all the three organs concerned. Indeed, it is legitimate to hope that, with the passage of time, we may see the establishment of regional commissions on human rights in other parts of the world, in which case their relationship with the UN Committee could follow the pattern already established by the regional commissions in Europe and the Americas. All will have a common objective: in the words of the Universal Declaration, "to secure the universal and effective recognition and observance" of the rights proclaimed therein.

Appendixes

Universal Declaration of Human Rights

Adopted and proclaimed by General Assembly resolution 217 A(III) of
10 December 1948

PREAMBLE

Whereas recognition of the inherent dignity and of the equal and in-alienable rights of all members of the human family is the foundation of freedom, justice and peace in the world,

Whereas disregard and contempt for human rights have resulted in barbarous acts which have outraged the conscience of mankind, and the advent of a world in which human beings shall enjoy freedom of speech and belief and freedom from fear and want has been proclaimed as the highest aspiration of the common people,

Whereas it is essential, if man is not to be compelled to have recourse, as a last resort, to rebellion against tyranny and oppression, that human rights should be protected by the rule of law,

Whereas it is essential to promote the development of friendly relations between nations,

Whereas the peoples of the United Nations have in the Charter reaffirmed their faith in fundamental human rights, in the dignity and worth of the human person and in the equal rights of men and women and have determined to promote social progress and better standards of life in larger freedom,

Whereas Member States have pledged themselves to achieve, in cooperation with the United Nations, the promotion of universal respect for and observance of human rights and fundamental freedoms,

Whereas a common understanding of these rights and freedoms is of the greatest importance for the full realization of this pledge,

Now, therefore,

The General Assembly

Proclaims this Universal Declaration of Human Rights as a common standard of achievement for all peoples and all nations, to the end that every individual and every organ of society, keeping this Declaration constantly in mind, shall strive by teaching and education to promote respect for these rights and freedoms and by progressive measures, national and international, to secure their universal and effective recognition and observance, both among the peoples of Member States themselves and among the peoples of territories under their jurisdiction.

Article 1

All human beings are born free and equal in dignity and rights. They are endowed with reason and conscience and should act towards one another in a spirit of brotherhood.

Article 2

Everyone is entitled to all the rights and freedoms set forth in this Declaration, without distinction of any kind, such as race, colour, sex, language, religion, political or other opinion, national or social origin, property, birth or other status.

Furthermore, no distinction shall be made on the basis of the political, jurisdictional or international status of the country or territory to which a person belongs, whether it be independent, trust, non-self-governing or under any other limitation of sovereignty.

Article 3

Everyone has the right to life, liberty and security of person.

Article 4

No one shall be held in slavery or servitude; slavery and the slave trade shall be prohibited in all their forms.

Article 5

No one shall be subjected to torture or to cruel, inhuman or degrading treatment or punishment.

Article 6

Everyone has the right to recognition everywhere as a person before the law.

Article 7

All are equal before the law and are entitled without any discrimination to equal protection of the law. All are entitled to equal protection against any discrimination in violation of this Declaration and against any incitement to such discrimination.

Article 8

Everyone has the right to an effective remedy by the competent national tribunals for acts violating the fundamental rights granted him by the constitution or by law.

Article 9

No one shall be subjected to arbitrary arrest, detention or exile.

Article 10

Everyone is entitled in full equality to a fair and public hearing by an independent and impartial tribunal, in the determination of his rights and obligations and of any criminal charge against him.

Article 11

1. Everyone charged with a penal offence has the right to be presumed innocent until proved guilty according to law in a public trial at which he has had all the guarantees necessary for his defence.

2. No one shall be held guilty of any penal offence on account of any act or omission which did not constitute a penal offence, under national or international law, at the time when it was committed. Nor shall a heavier penalty be imposed than the one that was applicable at the time the penal offence was committed.

Article 12

No one shall be subjected to arbitrary interference with his privacy, family, home or correspondence, nor to attacks upon his honour and reputation. Everyone has the right to the protection of the law against such interference or attacks.

Article 13

1. Everyone has the right to freedom of movement and residence within the borders of each State.

2. Everyone has the right to leave any country, including his own, and to return to his country.

Article 14

1. Everyone has the right to seek and to enjoy in other countries asylum from persecution.

2. This right may not be invoked in the case of prosecutions genuinely arising from non-political crimes or from acts contrary to the purposes and principles of the United Nations.

Article 15

1. Everyone has the right to a nationality.

2. No one shall be arbitrarily deprived of his nationality nor denied the right to change his nationality.

Article 16

1. Men and women of full age, without any limitation due to race, nationality or religion, have the right to marry and to found a family. They are entitled to equal rights as to marriage, during marriage and at its dissolution.

2. Marriage shall be entered into only with the free and full consent of the intending spouses.

3. The family is the natural and fundamental group unit of society and is entitled to protection by society and the State.

Article 17

1. Everyone has the right to own property alone as well as in association with others.

2. No one shall be arbitrarily deprived of his property.

Article 18

Everyone has the right to freedom of thought, conscience and religion; this right includes freedom to change his religion or belief, and freedom, either alone or in community with others and in public or private, to manifest his religion or belief in teaching, practice, worship and observance.

Article 19

Everyone has the right to freedom of opinion and expression; this right includes freedom to hold opinions without interference and to seek, receive and impart information and ideas through any media and regardless of frontiers.

Article 20

1. Everyone has the right to freedom of peaceful assembly and association.
2. No one may be compelled to belong to an association.

Article 21

1. Everyone has the right to take part in the government of his country, directly or through freely chosen representatives.
2. Everyone has the right of equal access to public service in his country.
3. The will of the people shall be the basis of the authority of government; this will shall be expressed in periodic and genuine elections which shall be by universal and equal suffrage and shall be held by secret vote or by equivalent free voting procedures.

Article 22

Everyone, as a member of society, has the right to social security and is entitled to realization, through national effort and international co-operation and in accordance with the organization and resources of each State, of the economic, social and cultural rights indispensable for his dignity and the free development of his personality.

Article 23

1. Everyone has the right to work, to free choice of employment, to just and favourable conditions of work and to protection against unemployment.

2. Everyone, without any discrimination, has the right to equal pay for equal work.

3. Everyone who works has the right to just and favourable remuneration ensuring for himself and his family an existence worthy of human dignity, and supplemented, if necessary, by other means of social protection.

4. Everyone has the right to form and to join trade unions for the protection of his interests.

Article 24

Everyone has the right to rest and leisure, including reasonable limitation of working hours and periodic holidays and pay.

Article 25

1. Everyone has the right to a standard of living adequate for the health and well-being of himself and of his family, including food, clothing, housing and medical care and necessary social services, and the right to security in the event of unemployment, sickness, disability, widowhood, old age or other lack of livelihood in circumstances beyond his control.

2. Motherhood and childhood are entitled to special care and assistance. All children, whether born in or out of wedlock, shall enjoy the same social protection.

Article 26

1. Everyone has the right to education. Education shall be free, at least in the elementary and fundamental stages. Elementary education shall be compulsory. Technical and professional education shall be made generally available and higher education shall be equally accessible to all on the basis of merit.

2. Education shall be directed to the full development of the human personality and to the strengthening of respect for human rights and fundamental freedoms. It shall promote understanding, tolerance and friendship among all nations, racial or religious groups, and shall further the activities of the United Nations for the maintenance of peace.

3. Parents have a prior right to choose the kind of education that shall be given to their children.

Article 27

1. Everyone has the right freely to participate in the cultural life of the community, to enjoy the arts and to share in scientific advancement and its benefits.

2. Everyone has the right to the protection of the moral and material interests resulting from any scientific, literary or artistic production of which he is the author.

Article 28

Everyone is entitled to a social and international order in which the rights and freedoms set forth in this Declaration can be fully realized.

Article 29

1. Everyone has duties to the community in which alone the free and full development of his personality is possible.

2. In the exercise of his rights and freedoms, everyone shall be subject only to such limitations as are determined by law solely for the purpose of securing due recognition and respect for the rights and freedoms of others and of meeting the just requirements of morality, public order and the general welfare in a democratic society.

3. These rights and freedoms may in no case be exercised contrary to the purposes and principles of the United Nations.

Article 30

Nothing in this Declaration may be interpreted as implying for any State, group or person any right to engage in any activity or to perform any act aimed at the destruction of any of the rights and freedoms set forth herein.

International Covenant on Civil and Political Rights

Adopted and opened for signature, ratification and accession by General Assembly resolution 2200 A (XXI) of 16 December 1966

ENTRY INTO FORCE: 23 March 1976, in accordance with article 49.

PREAMBLE

The States Parties to the present Covenant,
Considering that, in accordance with the principles proclaimed in the

Charter of the United Nations, recognition of the inherent dignity and of the equal and inalienable rights of all members of the human family is the foundation of freedom, justice and peace in the world,

Recognizing that these rights derive from the inherent dignity of the human person,

Recognizing that, in accordance with the Universal Declaration of Human Rights, the ideal of free human beings enjoying civil and political freedom and freedom from fear and want can only be achieved if conditions are created whereby everyone may enjoy his civil and political rights, as well as his economic, social and cultural rights,

Considering the obligation of States under the Charter of the United Nations to promote universal respect for, and observance of, human rights and freedoms,

Realizing that the individual, having duties to other individuals and to the community to which he belongs, is under a responsibility to strive for the promotion and observance of the rights recognized in the present Covenant,

Agree upon the following articles:

PART I

Article 1

1. All peoples have the right of self-determination. By virtue of that right they freely determine their political status and freely pursue their economic, social and cultural development.

2. All peoples may, for their own ends, freely dispose of their natural wealth and resources without prejudice to any obligations arising out of international economic co-operation, based upon the principle of mutual benefit, and international law. In no case may a people be deprived of its own means of subsistence.

3. The States Parties to the present Covenant, including those having responsibility for the administration of Non-Self-Governing and Trust Territories, shall promote the realization of the right of self-determination, and shall respect that right, in conformity with the provisions of the Charter of the United Nations.

PART II

Article 2

1. Each State Party to the present Covenant undertakes to respect and to ensure to all individuals within its territory and subject to its jurisdiction the rights recognized in the present Covenant, without distinction of any kind, such as race, colour, sex, language, religion, political or other opinion, national or social origin, property, birth or other status.

2. Where not already provided for by existing legislative or other measures, each State Party to the present Covenant undertakes to take the necessary steps, in accordance with its constitutional processes and with the provisions of the present Covenant, to adopt such legislative or other measures as may be necessary to give effect to the rights recognized in the present Covenant.

3. Each State Party to the present Covenant undertakes:

(*a*) To ensure that any person whose rights or freedoms as herein recognized are violated shall have an effective remedy, notwithstanding that the violation has been committed by persons acting in an official capacity;

(*b*) To ensure that any person claiming such a remedy shall have his right thereto determined by competent judicial, administrative or legislative authorities, or by any other competent authority provided for by the legal system of the State, and to develop the possibilities of judicial remedy;

(*c*) To ensure that the competent authorities shall enforce such remedies when granted.

Article 3

The States Parties to the present Covenant undertake to ensure the equal right of men and women to the enjoyment of all civil and political rights set forth in the present Covenant.

Article 4

1. In time of public emergency which threatens the life of the nation and the existence of which is officially proclaimed, the States Parties to the present Covenant may take measures derogating from their obligations under the present Covenant to the extent strictly required by the

exigencies of the situation, provided that such measures are not inconsistent with their other obligations under international law and do not involve discrimination solely on the ground of race, colour, sex, language, religion or social origin.

2. No derogation from articles 6, 7, 8 (paragraphs 1 and 2), 11, 15, 16 and 18 may be made under this provision.

3. Any State Party to the present Covenant availing itself of the right of derogation shall immediately inform the other States Parties to the present Covenant, through the intermediary of the Secretary-General of the United Nations, of the provisions from which it has derogated and of the reasons by which it was actuated. A further communication shall be made, through the same intermediary, on the date on which it terminates such derogation.

Article 5

1. Nothing in the present Covenant may be interpreted as implying for any State, group or person any right to engage in any activity or perform any act aimed at the destruction of any of the rights and freedoms recognized herein or at their limitation to a greater extent than is provided for in the present Covenant.

2. There shall be no restriction upon or derogation from any of the fundamental human rights recognized or existing in any State Party to the present Covenant pursuant to law, conventions, regulations or custom on the pretext that the present Covenant does not recognize such rights or that it recognizes them to a lesser extent.

Part III

Article 6

1. Every human being has the inherent right to life. This right shall be protected by law. No one shall be arbitrarily deprived of his life.

2. In countries which have not abolished the death penalty, sentence of death may be imposed only for the most serious crimes in accordance with the law in force at the time of the commission of the crime and not contrary to the provisions of the present Covenant and to the Convention on the Prevention and Punishment of the Crime of Genocide. This penalty can only be carried out pursuant to a final judgement rendered by a competent court.

3. When deprivation of life constitutes the crime of genocide, it is understood that nothing in this article shall authorize any State Party to the present Covenant to derogate in any way from any obligation assumed under the provisions of the Convention on the Prevention and Punishment of the Crime of Genocide.

4. Anyone sentenced to death shall have the right to seek pardon or commutation of the sentence. Amnesty, pardon or commutation of the sentence of death may be granted in all cases.

5. Sentence of death shall not be imposed for crimes committed by persons below eighteen years of age and shall not be carried out on pregnant women.

6. Nothing in this article shall be invoked to delay or to prevent the abolition of capital punishment by any State Party to the present Covenant.

Article 7

No one shall be subjected to torture or to cruel, inhuman or degrading treatment or punishment. In particular, no one shall be subjected without his free consent to medical or scientific experimentation.

Article 8

1. No one shall be held in slavery; slavery and the slave-trade in all their forms shall be prohibited.

2. No one shall be held in servitude.

3. (a) No one shall be required to perform forced or compulsory labour;

(b) Paragraph 3 (a) shall not be held to preclude, in countries where imprisonment with hard labour may be imposed as a punishment for a crime, the performance of hard labour in pursuance of a sentence to such punishment by a competent court;

(c) For the purpose of this paragraph the term "forced or compulsory labour" shall not include:

(i) Any work or service, not referred to in sub-paragraph (b), normally required of a person who is under detention in consequence of a lawful order of a court, or of a person during conditional release from such detention;

(ii) Any service of a military character and, in countries where conscientious objection is recognized, any national service required by law of conscientious objectors;

(iii) Any service exacted in cases of emergency or calamity threatening the life or well-being of the community;

(iv) Any work or service which forms part of normal civil obligations.

Article 9

1. Everyone has the right to liberty and security of person. No one shall be subjected to arbitrary arrest or detention. No one shall be deprived of his liberty except on such grounds and in accordance with such procedure as are established by law.

2. Anyone who is arrested shall be informed, at the time of arrest, of the reasons for his arrest and shall be promptly informed of any charges against him.

3. Anyone arrested or detained on a criminal charge shall be brought promptly before a judge or other officer authorized by law to exercise judicial power and shall be entitled to trial within a reasonable time or to release. It shall not be the general rule that persons awaiting trial shall be detained in custody, but release may be subject to guarantees to appear for trial, at any other stage of the judicial proceedings, and, should occasion arise, for execution of the judgement.

4. Anyone who is deprived of his liberty by arrest or detention shall be entitled to take proceedings before a court, in order that that court may decide without delay on the lawfulness of his detention and order his release if the detention is not lawful.

5. Anyone who has been the victim of unlawful arrest or detention shall have an enforceable right to compensation.

Article 10

1. All persons deprived of their liberty shall be treated with humanity and with respect for the inherent dignity of the human person.

2. (*a*) Accused persons shall, save in exceptional circumstances, be segregated from convicted persons and shall be subject to separate treatment appropriate to their status as unconvicted persons;

(*b*) Accused juvenile persons shall be separated from adults and brought as speedily as possible for adjudication.

3. The penitentiary system shall comprise treatment of prisoners the essential aim of which shall be their reformation and social rehabilitation. Juvenile offenders shall be segregated from adults and be accorded treatment appropriate to their age and legal status.

Article 11

No one shall be imprisoned merely on the ground of inability to fulfil a contractual obligation.

Article 12

1. Everyone lawfully within the territory of a State shall, within that territory, have the right to liberty of movement and freedom to choose his residence.

2. Everyone shall be free to leave any country, including his own.

3. The above-mentioned rights shall not be subject to any restrictions except those which are provided by law, are necessary to protect national security, public order (*ordre public*), public health or morals or the rights and freedoms of others, and are consistent with the other rights recognized in the present Covenant.

4. No one shall be arbitrarily deprived of the right to enter his own country.

Article 13

An alien lawfully in the territory of a state Party to the present Covenant may be expelled therefrom only in pursuance of a decision reached in accordance with law and shall, except where compelling reasons of national security otherwise require, be allowed to submit the reasons against his expulsion and to have his case reviewed by, and be represented for the purpose before, the competent authority or a person or persons especially designated by the competent authority.

Article 14

1. All persons shall be equal before the courts and tribunals. In the determination of any criminal charge against him, or of his rights and obligations in a suit at law, everyone shall be entitled to a fair and public hearing by a competent, independent and impartial tribunal established by law. The Press and the public may be excluded from all or part of a trial for reasons of morals, public order (*ordre public*) or national security in a democratic society, or when the interest of the private lives of the parties so requires, or to the extent strictly necessary in the opinion of the court in special circumstances where publicity would prejudice the interests of justice; but any judgement rendered in a crim-

inal case or in a suit at law shall be made public except where the interest of juvenile persons otherwise requires or the proceedings concern matrimonial disputes or the guardianship of children.

2. Everyone charged with a criminal offence shall have the right to be presumed innocent until proved guilty according to law.

3. In the determination of any criminal charge against him, everyone shall be entitled to the following minimum guarantees, in full equality:

(*a*) To be informed promptly and in detail in a language which he understands of the nature and cause of the charge against him;

(*b*) To have adequate time and facilities for the preparation of his defence and to communicate with counsel of his own choosing;

(*c*) To be tried without undue delay;

(*d*) To be tried in his presence, and to defend himself in person or through legal assistance of his own choosing; to be informed, if he does not have legal assistance, of this right; and to have legal assistance assigned to him, in any case where the interests of justice so require, and without payment by him in any such case if he does not have sufficient means to pay for it;

(*e*) To examine, or have examined, the witnesses against him and to obtain the attendance and examination of witnesses on his behalf under the same conditions as witnesses against him;

(*f*) To have the free assistance of an interpreter if he cannot understand or speak the language used in court;

(*g*) Not to be compelled to testify against himself or to confess guilt.

4. In the case of juvenile persons, the procedure shall be such as will take account of their age and the desirability of promoting their rehabilitation.

5. Everyone convicted of a crime shall have the right to his conviction and sentence being reviewed by a higher tribunal according to law.

6. When a person has by a final decision been convicted of a criminal offence and when subsequently his conviction has been reversed or he has been pardoned on the ground that a new or newly discovered fact shows conclusively that there has been a miscarriage of justice, the person who has suffered punishment as a result of such conviction shall be compensated according to law, unless it is proved that the non-disclosure of the unknown fact in time is wholly or partly attributable to him.

7. No one shall be liable to be tried or punished again for an offence for which he has already been finally convicted or acquitted in accordance with the law and penal procedure of each country.

Article 15

1. No one shall be held guilty of any criminal offence on account of any act or omission which did not constitute a criminal offence, under national or international law, at the time when it was committed. Nor shall a heavier penalty be imposed than the one that was applicable at the time when the criminal offence was committed. If subsequent to the commission of the offence, provision is made by law for the imposition of the lighter penalty, the offender shall benefit thereby.

2. Nothing in this article shall prejudice the trial and punishment of any person for any act or omission which, at the time when it was committed, was criminal according to the general principles of law recognized by the community of nations.

Article 16

Everyone shall have the right to recognition everywhere as a person before the law.

Article 17

1. No one shall be subjected to arbitrary or unlawful interference with his privacy, family, home or correspondence, nor to unlawful attacks on his honour and reputation.

2. Everyone has the right to the protection of the law against such interference or attacks.

Article 18

1. Everyone shall have the right to freedom of thought, conscience and religion. This right shall include freedom to have or to adopt a religion or belief of his choice, and freedom, either individually or in community with others and in public or private, to manifest his religion or belief in worship, observance, practice and teaching.

2. No one shall be subject to coercion which would impair his freedom to have or to adopt a religion or belief of his choice.

3. Freedom to manifest one's religion or beliefs may be subject only to such limitations as are prescribed by law and are necessary to protect public safety, order, health, or morals or the fundamental rights and freedoms of others.

4. The States Parties to the present Covenant undertake to have respect for the liberty of parents and, when applicable, legal guardians to ensure the religious and moral education of their children in conformity with their own convictions.

Article 19

1. Everyone shall have the right to hold opinions without interference.

2. Everyone shall have the right to freedom of expression; this right shall include freedom to seek, receive and impart information and ideas of all kinds, regardless of frontiers, either orally, in writing or in print, in the form of art, or through any other media of his choice.

3. The exercise of the rights provided for in paragraph 2 of this article carries with it special duties and responsibilities. It may therefore be subject to certain restrictions, but these shall only be such as are provided by law and are necessary:

(*a*) For respect of the rights or reputations of others;

(*b*) For the protection of national security or of public order (*ordre public*), or of public health or morals.

Article 20

1. Any propaganda for war shall be prohibited by law.

2. Any advocacy of national, racial or religious hatred that constitutes incitement to discrimination, hostility or violence shall be prohibited by law.

Article 21

The right of peaceful assembly shall be recognized. No restrictions may be placed on the exercise of this right other than those imposed in conformity with the law and which are necessary in a democratic society in the interests of national security or public safety, public order (*ordre public*), the protection of public health or morals or the protection of the rights and freedoms of others.

Article 22

1. Everyone shall have the right to freedom of association with others, including the right to form and join trade unions for the protection of his interests.

2. No restrictions may be placed on the exercise of this right other than those which are prescribed by law and which are necessary in a democratic society in the interests of national security or public safety, public order (*ordre public*), the protection of public health or morals or the protection of the rights and freedoms of others. This article shall not prevent the imposition of lawful restrictions on members of the armed forces and of the police in their exercise of this right.

3. Nothing in this article shall authorize States Parties to the International Labour Organisation Convention of 1948 concerning Freedom of Association and Protection of the Right to Organize to take legislative measures which would prejudice, or to apply the law in such a manner as to prejudice the guarantees provided for in that Convention.

Article 23

1. The family is the natural and fundamental group unit of society and is entitled to protection by society and the State.

2. The right of men and women of marriageable age to marry and to found a family shall be recognized.

3. No marriage shall be entered into without the free and full consent of the intending spouses.

4. States Parties to the present Covenant shall take appropriate steps to ensure equality of rights and responsibilities of spouses as to marriage, during marriage and at its dissolution. In the case of dissolution, provision shall be made for the necessary protection of any children.

Article 24

1. Every child shall have, without any discrimination as to race, colour, sex, language, religion, national or social origin, property or birth, the right to such measures of protection as are required by his status as a minor, on the part of his family, society and the State.

2. Every child shall be registered immediately after birth and shall have a name.

3. Every child has the right to acquire a nationality.

Article 25

Every citizen shall have the right and the opportunity, without any of the distinctions mentioned in article 2 and without unreasonable restrictions:

(*a*) To take part in the conduct of public affairs, directly or through freely chosen representatives;

(*b*) To vote and to be elected at genuine periodic elections which shall be by universal and equal suffrage and shall be held by secret ballot, guaranteeing the free expression of the will of the electors;

(*c*) To have access, on general terms of equality, to public service in his country.

Article 26

All persons are equal before the law and are entitled without any discrimination to the equal protection of the law. In this respect, the law shall prohibit any discrimination and guarantee to all persons equal and effective protection against discrimination on any ground such as race, colour, sex, language, religion, political or other opinion, national or social origin, property, birth or other status.

Article 27

In those States in which ethnic, religious or linguistic minorities exist, persons belonging to such minorities shall not be denied the right, in community with the other members of their group, to enjoy their own culture, to profess and practise their own religion, or to use their own language.

Part IV

Article 28

1. There shall be established a Human Rights Committee (hereafter referred to in the present Covenant as the Committee). It shall consist of eighteen members and shall carry out the functions hereinafter provided.

2. The Committee shall be composed of nationals of the States Parties to the present Covenant who shall be persons of high moral character and recognized competence in the field of human rights, consideration being given to the usefulness of the participation of some persons having legal experience.

3. The members of the Committee shall be elected and shall serve in their personal capacity.

Article 29

1. The members of the Committee shall be elected by secret ballot from a list of persons possessing the qualifications prescribed in article 28 and nominated for the purpose by the States Parties to the present Covenant.

2. Each State Party to the present Covenant may nominate not more than two persons. These persons shall be nationals of the nominating State.

3. A person shall be eligible for renomination.

Article 30

1. The initial election shall be held no later than six months after the date of the entry into force of the present Covenant.

2. At least four months before the date of each election to the Committee, other than an election to fill a vacancy declared in accordance with article 34, the Secretary-General of the United Nations shall address a written invitation to the States Parties to the present Covenant to submit their nominations for membership of the Committee within three months.

3. The Secretary-General of the United Nations shall prepare a list in alphabetical order of all the persons thus nominated, with an indication of the States Parties which have nominated them, and shall submit it to the States Parties to the present Covenant no later than one month before the date of each election.

4. Elections of the members of the Committee shall be held at a meeting of the States Parties to the present Covenant convened by the Secretary-General of the United Nations at the Headquarters of the United Nations. At that meeting, for which two thirds of the States Parties to the present Covenant shall constitute a quorum, the persons elected to the Committee shall be those nominees who obtain the largest number of votes and an absolute majority of the votes of the representatives of States Parties present and voting.

Article 31

1. The Committee may not include more than one national of the same State.

2. In the election of the Committee, consideration shall be given to equitable geographical distribution of membership and to the represen-

tation of the different forms of civilization and of the principal legal systems.

Article 32

1. The members of the Committee shall be elected for a term of four years. They shall be eligible for reelection if renominated. However, the terms of nine of the members elected at the first election shall expire at the end of two years; immediately after the first election, the names of these nine members shall be chosen by lot by the Chairman of the meeting referred to in article 30, paragraph 4.

2. Elections at the expiry of office shall be held in accordance with the preceding articles of this part of the present Covenant.

Article 33

1. If, in the unanimous opinion of the other members, a member of the Committee has ceased to carry out his functions for any cause other than absence of a temporary character, the Chairman of the Committee shall notify the Secretary-General of the United Nations, who shall then declare the seat of that member to be vacant.

2. In the event of the death or the resignation of a member of the Committee, the Chairman shall immediately notify the Secretary-General of the United Nations, who shall declare the seat vacant from the date of death or the date on which the resignation takes effect.

Article 34

1. When a vacancy is declared in accordance with article 33 and if the term of office of the member to be replaced does not expire within six months of the declaration of the vacancy, the Secretary-General of the United Nations shall notify each of the States Parties to the present Covenant, which may within two months submit nominations in accordance with article 29 for the purpose of filling the vacancy.

2. The Secretary-General of the United Nations shall prepare a list in alphabetical order of the persons thus nominated and shall submit it to the States Parties to the present Covenant. The election to fill the vacancy shall then take place in accordance with the relevant provisions of this part of the present Covenant.

3. A member of the Committee elected to fill a vacancy declared in accordance with article 33 shall hold office for the remainder of the

term of the member who vacated the seat on the Committee under the provisions of that article.

Article 35

The members of the Committee shall, with the approval of the General Assembly of the United Nations, receive emoluments from United Nations resources on such terms and conditions as the General Assembly may decide, having regard to the importance of the Committee's responsibilities.

Article 36

The Secretary-General of the United Nations shall provide the necessary staff and facilities for the effective performance of the functions of the Committee under the present Covenant.

Article 37

1. The Secretary-General of the United Nations shall convene the initial meeting of the Committee at the Headquarters of the United Nations.

2. After its initial meeting, the Committee shall meet at such times as shall be provided in its rules of procedure.

3. The Committee shall normally meet at the Headquarters of the United Nations or at the United Nations Office at Geneva.

Article 38

Every member of the Committee shall, before taking up his duties, make a solemn declaration in open committee that he will perform his functions impartially and conscientiously.

Article 39

1. The Committee shall elect its officers for a term of two years. They may be re-elected.

2. The Committee shall establish its own rules of procedure, but these rules shall provide, *inter alia,* that:

(a) Twelve members shall constitute a quorum;

(*b*) Decisions of the Committee shall be made by a majority vote of the members present.

Article 40

1. The States Parties to the present Covenant undertake to submit reports on the measures they have adopted which give effect to the rights recognized herein and on the progress made in the enjoyment of those rights:

(*a*) Within one year of the entry into force of the present Covenant for the States Parties concerned;

(*b*) Thereafter whenever the Committee so requests.

2. All reports shall be submitted to the Secretary-General of the United Nations, who shall transmit them to the Committee for consideration. Reports shall indicate the factors and difficulties, if any, affecting the implementation of the present Covenant.

3. The Secretary-General of the United Nations may, after consultation with the Committee, transmit to the specialized agencies concerned copies of such parts of the reports as may fall within their field of competence.

4. The Committee shall study the reports submitted by the States Parties to the present Covenant. It shall transmit its reports, and such general comments as it may consider appropriate, to the States Parties. The Committee may also transmit to the Economic and Social Council these comments along with the copies of the reports it has received from States Parties to the present Covenant.

5. The States Parties to the present Covenant may submit to the Committee observations on any comments that may be made in accordance with paragraph 4 of this article.

Article 41

1. A State Party to the present Covenant may at any time declare under this article that it recognizes the competence of the Committee to receive and consider communications to the effect that a State Party claims that another State Party is not fulfilling its obligations under the present Covenant. Communications under this article may be received and considered only if submitted by a State Party which has made a declaration recognizing in regard to itself the competence of the Committee. No communication shall be received by the Committee if it concerns a State Party which has not made such a declaration. Com-

munications received under this article shall be dealt with in accordance with the following procedure:

(a) If a State Party to the present Covenant considers that another State Party is not giving effect to the provisions of the present Covenant, it may, by written communication, bring the matter to the attention of that State Party. Within three months after the receipt of the communication the receiving State shall afford the State which sent the communication an explanation, or any other statement in writing clarifying the matter which should include, to the extent possible and pertinent, reference to domestic procedures and remedies taken, pending, or available in the matter.

(b) If the matter is not adjusted to the satisfaction of both States Parties concerned within six months after the receipt by the receiving State of the initial communication, either State shall have the right to refer the matter to the Committee, by notice given to the Committee and to the other State.

(c) The Committee shall deal with a matter referred to it only after it has ascertained that all available domestic remedies have been invoked and exhausted in the matter, in conformity with the generally recognized principles of international law. This shall not be the rule where the application of the remedies is unreasonably prolonged.

(d) The Committee shall hold closed meetings when examining communications under this article.

(e) Subject to the provisions of sub-paragraph (c), the Committee shall make available its good offices to the States Parties concerned with a view to a friendly solution of the matter on the basis of respect for human rights and fundamental freedoms as recognized in the present Covenant.

(f) In any matter referred to it, the Committee may call upon the States Parties concerned, referred to in sub-paragraph (b), to supply any relevant information.

(g) The States Parties concerned, referred to in sub-paragraph (b), shall have the right to be represented when the matter is being considered in the Committee and to make submissions orally and/or in writing.

(h) The Committee shall, within twelve months after the date of receipt of notice under sub-paragraph (b), submit a report:

(i) If a solution within the terms of sub-paragraph (e) is reached, the Committee shall confine its report to a brief statement of the facts and of the solution reached;

(ii) If a solution within the terms of sub-paragraph (e) is not reached, the Committee shall confine its report to a brief statement of the facts; the written submissions and record of the oral submissions made by the States Parties concerned shall be attached to the report.

In every matter, the report shall be communicated to the States Parties concerned.

2. The provisions of this article shall come into force when ten States Parties to the present Covenant have made declarations under paragraph 1 of this article. Such declarations shall be deposited by the States Parties with the Secretary-General of the United Nations, who shall transmit copies thereof to the other States Parties. A declaration may be withdrawn at any time by notification to the Secretary-General. Such a withdrawal shall not prejudice the consideration of any matter which is the subject of a communication already transmitted under this article; no further communication by any State Party shall be received after the notification of withdrawal of the declaration has been received by the Secretary-General, unless the State Party concerned has made a new declaration.

Article 42

1. (*a*) If a matter referred to the Committee in accordance with article 41 is not resolved to the satisfaction of the States Parties concerned, the Committee may, with the prior consent of the States Parties concerned, appoint an *ad hoc* Conciliation Commission (hereinafter referred to as the Commission). The good offices of the Commission shall be made available to the States Parties concerned with a view to an amicable solution of the matter on the basis of respect for the present Covenant;

(*b*) The Commission shall consist of five persons acceptable to the States Parties. If the States Parties concerned fail to reach agreement within three months on all or part of the composition of the Commission, the members of the Commission concerning whom no agreement has been reached shall be elected by secret ballot by a two-thirds majority vote of the Committee from among its members.

2. The members of the Commission shall serve in their personal capacity. They shall not be nationals of the States Parties concerned, or of a State not party to the present Covenant, or of a State Party which has not made a declaration under article 41.

3. The Commission shall elect its own Chairman and adopt its own rules of procedure.

4. The meetings of the Commission shall normally be held at the Headquarters of the United Nations or at the United Nations Office at Geneva. However, they may be held at such other convenient places as the Commission may determine in consultation with the Secretary-General of the United Nations and the States Parties concerned.

5. The secretariat provided in accordance with article 36 shall also service the commissions appointed under this article.

6. The information received and collated by the Committee shall be made available to the Commission and the Commission may call upon the States Parties concerned to supply any other relevant information.

7. When the Commission has fully considered the matter, but in any event not later than twelve months after having been seized of the matter, it shall submit to the Chairman of the Committee a report for communication to the States Parties concerned:

(*a*) If the Commission is unable to complete its consideration of the matter within twelve months, it shall confine its report to a brief statement of the status of its consideration of the matter;

(*b*) If an amicable solution to the matter on the basis of respect for human rights as recognized in the present Covenant is reached, the Commission shall confine its report to a brief statement of the facts and of the solution reached;

(*c*) If a solution within the terms of sub-paragraph (*b*) is not reached, the Commission's report shall embody its findings on all questions of fact relevant to the issues between the States Parties concerned, and its views on the possibilities of an amicable solution of the matter. This report shall also contain the written submissions and a record of the oral submissions made by the States Parties concerned;

(*d*) If the Commission's report is submitted under sub-paragraph (c), the States Parties concerned shall, within three months of the receipt of the report, notify the Chairman of the Committee whether or not they accept the contents of the report of the Commission.

8. The provisions of this article are without prejudice to the responsibilities of the Committee under article 41.

9. The States Parties concerned shall share equally all the expenses of the members of the Commission in accordance with estimates to be provided by the Secretary-General of the United Nations.

10. The Secretary-General of the United Nations shall be empowered to pay the expenses of the members of the Commission, if neces-

sary, before reimbursement by the States Parties concerned, in accordance with paragraph 9 of this article.

Article 43

The members of the Committee, and of the *ad hoc* conciliation commissions which may be appointed under article 42, shall be entitled to the facilities, privileges and immunities of experts on mission for the United Nations as laid down in the relevant sections of the Convention on the Privileges and Immunities of the United Nations.

Article 44

The provisions for the implementation of the present Covenant shall apply without prejudice to the procedures prescribed in the field of human rights by or under the constituent instruments and the conventions of the United Nations and of the specialized agencies and shall not prevent the States Parties to the present Covenant from having recourse to other procedures for settling a dispute in accordance with general or special international agreements in force between them.

Article 45

The Committee shall submit to the General Assembly of the United Nations, through the Economic and Social Council, an annual report on its activities.

PART V

Article 46

Nothing in the present Covenant shall be interpreted as impairing the provisions of the Charter of the United Nations and of the constitutions of the specialized agencies which define the respective responsibilities of the various organs of the United Nations and of the specialized agencies in regard to the matters dealt with in the present Covenant.

Article 47

Nothing in the present Covenant shall be interpreted as impairing the inherent right of all peoples to enjoy and utilize fully and freely their natural wealth and resources.

PART VI

Article 48

1. The present Covenant is open for signature by any state Member of the United Nations or member of any of its specialized agencies, by any State Party to the Statute of the International Court of Justice, and by any other State which has been invited by the General Assembly of the United Nations to become a party to the present Covenant.

2. The present Covenant is subject to ratification. Instruments of ratification shall be deposited with the Secretary-General of the United Nations.

3. The present Covenant shall be open to accession by any State referred to in paragraph 1 of this article.

4. Accession shall be effected by the deposit of an instrument of accession with the Secretary-General of the United Nations.

5. The Secretary-General of the United Nations shall inform all States which have signed this Covenant or acceded to it of the deposit of each instrument of ratification or accession.

Article 49

1. The present Covenant shall enter into force three months after the date of the deposit with the Secretary-General of the United Nations of the thirty-fifth instrument of ratification or instrument of accession.

2. For each State ratifying the present Covenant or acceding to it after the deposit of the thirty-fifth instrument of ratification or instrument of accession, the present Covenant shall enter into force three months after the date of the deposit of its own instrument of ratification or instrument of accession.

Article 50

The provisions of the present Covenant shall extend to all parts of federal States without any limitations or exceptions.

Article 51

1. Any State Party to the present Covenant may propose an amendment and file it with the Secretary-General of the United Nations. The Secretary-General of the United Nations shall thereupon communicate

any proposed amendments to the States Parties to the present Covenant with a request that they notify him whether they favour a conference of States Parties for the purpose of considering and voting upon the proposals. In the event that at least one third of the States Parties favours such a conference, the Secretary-General shall convene the conference under the auspices of the United Nations. Any amendment adopted by a majority of the States Parties present and voting at the conference shall be submitted to the General Assembly of the United Nations for approval.

2. Amendments shall come into force when they have been approved by the General Assembly of the United Nations and accepted by a two-thirds majority of the States Parties to the present Covenant in accordance with their respective constitutional processes.

3. When amendments come into force, they shall be binding on those States Parties which have accepted them, other States Parties still being bound by the provisions of the present Covenant and any earlier amendment which they have accepted.

Article 52

Irrespective of the notifications made under article 48, paragraph 5, the Secretary-General of the United Nations shall inform all States referred to in paragraph 1 of the same article of the following particulars:

(*a*) Signatures, ratifications and accessions under article 48;

(*b*) The date of the entry into force of the present Covenant under article 49 and the date of the entry into force of any amendments under article 51.

Article 53

1. The present Covenant, of which the Chinese, English, French, Russian and Spanish texts are equally authentic, shall be deposited in the archives of the United Nations.

2. The Secretary-General of the United Nations shall transmit certified copies of the present Covenant to all States referred to in article 48.

Optional Protocol to the International Covenant on Civil and Political Rights

Adopted and opened for signature, ratification and accession by General Assembly resolution 2200 A (XXI) of 16 December 1966

ENTRY INTO FORCE: 23 March 1976, in accordance with article 9.

The States Parties to the present Protocol,

Considering that in order further to achieve the purposes of the Covenant on Civil and Political Rights (hereinafter referred to as the Covenant) and the implementation of its provisions it would be appropriate to enable the Human Rights Committee set up in part IV of the Covenant (hereinafter referred to as the Committee) to receive and consider, as provided in the present Protocol, communications from individuals claiming to be victims of violations of any of the rights set forth in the Covenant.

Have agreed as follows:

Article 1

A State Party to the Covenant that becomes a party to the present Protocol recognizes the competence of the Committee to receive and consider communications from individuals subject to its jurisdiction who claim to be victims of a violation by that State Party of any of the rights set forth in the Covenant. No communication shall be received by the Committee if it concerns a State Party to the Covenant which is not a party to the present Protocol.

Article 2

Subject to the provisions of article 1, individuals who claim that any of their rights enumerated in the Covenant have been violated and who have exhausted all available domestic remedies may submit a written communication to the Committee for consideration.

Article 3

The Committee shall consider inadmissible any communication under the present Protocol which is anonymous, or which it considers to be an abuse of the right of submission of such communications or to be incompatible with the provisions of the Covenant.

Article 4

1. Subject to the provisions of article 3, the Committee shall bring any communications submitted to it under the present Protocol to the attention of the State Party to the present Protocol alleged to be violating any provision of the Covenant.

2. Within six months, the receiving State shall submit to the Committee written explanations or statements clarifying the matter and the remedy, if any, that may have been taken by that State.

Article 5

1. The Committee shall consider communications received under the present Protocol in the light of all written information made available to it by the individual and by the State Party concerned.

2. The Committee shall not consider any communication from an individual unless it has ascertained that:

(*a*) The same matter is not being examined under another procedure of international investigation or settlement;

(*b*) The individual has exhausted all available domestic remedies. This shall not be the rule where the application of the remedies is unreasonably prolonged.

3. The Committee shall hold closed meetings when examining communications under the present Protocol.

4. The Committee shall forward its views to the State Party concerned and to the individual.

Article 6

The Committee shall include in its annual report under article 45 of the Covenant a summary of its activities under the present Protocol.

Article 7

Pending the achievement of the objectives of resolution 1514 (XV) adopted by the General Assembly of the United Nations on 14 December 1960 concerning the Declaration on the Granting of Independence to Colonial Countries and Peoples, the provisions of the present Protocol shall in no way limit the right of petition granted to these peoples by the Charter of the United Nations and other international conventions and instruments under the United Nations and its specialized agencies.

Article 8

1. The present Protocol is open for signature by any State which has signed the Covenant.

2. The present Protocol is subject to ratification by any State which has ratified or acceded to the Covenant. Instruments of ratification shall be deposited with the Secretary-General of the United Nations.

3. The present Protocol shall be open to accession by any State which has ratified or acceded to the Covenant.

4. Accession shall be effected by the deposit of an instrument of accession with the Secretary-General of the United Nations.

5. The Secretary-General of the United Nations shall inform all States which have signed the present Protocol or acceded to it of the deposit of each instrument of ratification or accession.

Article 9

1. Subject to the entry into force of the Covenant, the present Protocol shall enter into force three months after the date of the deposit with the Secretary-General of the United Nations of the tenth instrument of ratification or instrument of accession.

2. For each State ratifying the present Protocol or acceding to it after the deposit of the tenth instrument of ratification or instrument of accession, the present Protocol shall enter into force three months after the date of the deposit of its own instrument of ratification or instrument of accession.

Article 10

The provisions of the present Protocol shall extend to all parts of federal States without any limitations or exceptions.

Article 11

1. Any State Party to the present Protocol may propose an amendment and file it with the Secretary-General of the United Nations. The

Secretary-General shall thereupon communicate any proposed amendments to the States Parties to the present Protocol with a request that they notify him whether they favour a conference of States Parties for the purpose of considering and voting upon the proposal. In the event that at least one third of the States Parties favours such a conference, the Secretary-General shall convene the conference under the auspices of the United Nations. Any amendment adopted by a majority of the States Parties present and voting at the conference shall be submitted to the General Assembly of the United Nations for approval.

2. Amendments shall come into force when they have been approved by the General Assembly of the United Nations and accepted by a two-thirds majority of the States Parties to the present Protocol in accordance with their respective constitutional processes.

3. When amendments come into force, they shall be binding on those States Parties which have accepted them, other States Parties still being bound by the provisions of the present Protocol and any earlier amendment which they have accepted.

Article 12

1. Any State Party may denounce the present Protocol at any time by written notification addressed to the Secretary-General of the United Nations. Denunciation shall take effect three months after the date of receipt of the notification by the Secretary-General.

2. Denunciation shall be without prejudice to the continued application of the provisions of the present Protocol to any communication submitted under article 2 before the effective date of denunciation.

Article 13

Irrespective of the notifications made under article 8, paragraph 5, of the present Protocol, the Secretary-General of the United Nations shall inform all States referred to in article 48, paragraph 1, of the Covenant of the following particulars:

(a) Signatures, ratifications and accessions under article 8;

(b) The date of the entry into force of the present Protocol under article 9 and the date of the entry into force of any amendments under article 11;

(c) Denunciations under article 12.

Article 14

1. The present Protocol, of which the Chinese, English, French, Russian and Spanish texts are equally authentic, shall be deposited in the archives of the United Nations.

2. The Secretary-General of the United Nations shall transmit certified copies of the present Protocol to all States referred to in article 48 of the Covenant.

Notes

Principal UN Documents Cited

Cited As

A/2907 10 GAOR Annexes, Agenda Item 28 (Part I): Draft International Covenants on Human Rights (1955). Includes Documents: A/2907; A/2910 and Add.1 to 6; A/C.3/L.460, L. 496, L. 497; A/3077.

A/2929 10 GAOR Annexes, Agenda Item 28 (Part II): Annotations on the Text of the Draft International Covenants on Human Rights (1955).
Also appears as 18 ESCOR Supp. 6 (1955).

A/4045 13 GAOR Annexes, Agenda Item 32, Report of the Third Committee (1958).

A/3764 12 GAOR Annexes, Agenda Item 33, Report of the Third Committee (1957).

A/4299 14 GAOR Annexes, Agenda Item 34, Report of the Third Committee (1959). Also includes some other documents in A/C.3/L.795–L.833 Series.

A/4625 15 GAOR Annexes, Agenda Item 34, Report of the Third Committee (1960–61). Also includes Docs. A/4397; A/4228; and A/C.3/L.897.

A/5000 16 GAOR Annexes, Agenda Item 35, Report of the Third Committee (1961–62). Also includes Docs. A/4789 and A/C.3/L.943.

A/5655 18 GAOR Annexes, Agenda Item 48, Report of the Third Committee (1963). Also includes Docs. A/5411 and A/5462.

A/6546 21 GAOR Annexes, Agenda Item 62, Report of the Third Committee (1966). Also includes Docs. A/C.5/1102 and A/6585 from the Fifth Committee, and A/6591.

Human Rights Instruments *Human Rights: A Compilation of International Instruments,* UN Doc. ST/HR/1/Rev.1 (1978).

1. INTRODUCTION

1. Final Act, Conference on Security and Cooperation in Europe, 1(a) VII, Helsinki (1975), 14 *Int'l Leg. Mat.* 1293 (1975). The Act was adhered to by 35 states, including Byelorussian SSR, Czechoslovakia, Poland, Ukranian SSR, USSR, and Yugoslavia, who had abstained on the Declaration in 1948.

2. See H. Lauterpacht, *International Law and Human Rights,* part 1, sec. 2 (1950).

3. See generally Sohn and Buergenthal, *International Protection of Human Rights,* ch. 4 (1973). For a detailed bibliographic reference, see Sohn, essay 11, note 1.

4. These are highly impressive and still important even in the day of newer law; more than one hundred of these conventions have come into force, and many of them have been accepted by many states. See International Labour Organisation, *Chart of Ratifications: International Labour Conventions* (1 January 1980).

5. F. D. Roosevelt, State of the Union Address, 87 *Cong. Rec.* 44, 46 (1941).

6. See, e.g., G.A. Res. 285 (III), UN Doc. A/900 at 34 (1949); G.A. Res. 44 (I), UN Doc. 64 add.1 at 69 (1946).

7. In 1977 the UN Security Council called for an arms embargo against South Africa because of its race policies and accompanying violence. S.C. Res. 418, UN Doc. S/INF/33 at 5 (1977).

8. For texts, see *Human Rights: A Compilation of International Instruments,* UN Doc. ST/HR/1/Rev. 1 (1978). For a table of accessions to these instruments, see *Human Rights International Instruments: Signatures, Ratifications, etc.,* UN Doc. ST/HR/4/Rev. 2 (1980).

9. See *Human Rights International Instruments, supra* note 8. A number of states have adhered to the Convention on the Status of Refugees by way of a Protocol to that Convention and some have adhered both to the Convention and the Protocol. Seventy-nine states have adhered to the Protocol.

10. Ibid.; UN Doc. CCPR/C/X/CRP.1 para. 1 (1980).

11. Henkin, "International Human Rights as 'Rights,' " 1 *Cardozo L. Rev.* 425 (1979).

12. I draw here on Henkin, "Rights: American and Human," 79 *Colum. L. Rev.* 405, 410 (1979).

13. Covenant on Civil and Political Rights, preamble.

14. Universal Declaration of Human Rights, G.A. Res. 217 (III), UN Doc. A/810 at 71 (1948).

15. UN Charter, Art. 55.

16. Henkin, "Human Rights and 'Domestic Jurisdiction,' " in Buergenthal, ed., *Human Rights, International Law, and the Helsinki Accord* 21, 30–31 (1977).

17. *Supra* note 7.

18. See Covenant on Civil and Political Rights, Art. 2; see generally Henkin, *supra* note 11.

19. See the annual Reports of the Human Rights Committee: 32 GAOR Supp. 44, UN Doc. A/32/44 (1977); 33 GAOR Supp. 40, UN Doc. A/33/40 (1978); 34 GAOR Supp. 40, UN Doc. A/34/40 (1979); 35 GAOR Supp. 40, UN Doc. A/35/40 (1980).

20. Henkin, *supra* note 16.

21. Under the Vienna Convention, if a reservation is not prohibited by the agreement, it is permissible unless it is "incompatible with the object and pur-

pose of the agreement" (Article 19). Of course, a state may enter a forbidden reservation, in effect making a counter offer to the other parties, and if all other parties accept it there would be a new agreement (including the reservation). But if any state objected, it could keep the original agreement intact and keep the reserving state from becoming a party to the original agreement. See Advisory Opinion on Reservations to the Genocide Convention, [1951] *ICJ Reports* 15, 21.

The Vienna Convention came into effect 27 January 1980. The United States has not yet adhered to the Convention, but official spokesmen and courts have treated many of its substantive provisions as merely codifying customary international law, and they are therefore binding on the United States. See *Restatement of Foreign Relations Law of the United States (Revised)*, part 3, Introductory Note (Tent. Draft No. 1, 1980), p. 71. The text of the Vienna Convention can be found in UN Doc. A/CONF. 39/27 (1969); 8 *Int'l Leg. Mat.* 679 (1969).

22. Buergenthal, essay 3.

23. Article 5(2) provides: "There shall be no restriction upon or derogation from any of the fundamental human rights recognized or existing in any State Party to the present Covenant pursuant to law, conventions, regulations or custom on the pretext that the present Covenant does not recognize such rights or that it recognizes them to a lesser extent." See Buergenthal, essay 3.

2. THE DEVELOPMENT OF THE COVENANT ON CIVIL AND POLITICAL RIGHTS

1. See René Cassin, "De la place fait aux devoirs de l'individu dans la Déclaration universelle des droits de l'homme," in *Mélanges Offerts à Polys Modinos* 481 (1968).

See the later "Study of the Individual's Duties to the Community and the Limitations on Human Rights and Freedoms Under Article 29 of the Universal Declaration of Human Rights, Final Report by E. A. Daes, Special Rapporteur," UN Doc. E/CN.4/Sub. 2/432/Add.3 paras. 806, 815 (1980).

2. Article 2(7) of the UN Charter provides: "Nothing contained in the present Charter shall authorize the United Nations to intervene in matters which are essentially within the domestic jurisdiction of any state or shall require the Members to submit such matters to settlement under the present Charter; but this principle shall not prejudice the application of enforcement measures under Chapter VII."

3. Commission on Human Rights: Report of the Drafting Committee, UN Doc. E/CN.4/21 Annexes A, B (1947).

4. *Id.* Annex C.

5. 7 ESCOR Supp. 2, UN Doc. E/800 at 29, 31 (1948).

6. 6 ESCOR Supp. 1, UN Doc. E/600 Annex C at 34–35 (1947).

7. See E. Schwelb, *Human Rights and the International Community: The Roots and Growth of the Universal Declaration of Human Rights, 1948–63* 37 (1964).

8. This has been recognized even by Soviet jurisprudence. Thus, Tunkin in his 1975 Hague lecture acknowledged that "there are many instances when some norms of the United Nations General Assembly's resolutions have become or are becoming customary norms of international law. To this category belong certain provisions of the Universal Declaration of Human Rights. . . ." "International Law in the International System," 147 *Recueil des Cours* 143, 148 (1975).

9. Compare Buergenthal, "Codification and Implementation of International Human Rights," in A. Henkin, ed., *Human Dignity: The Internationalization of Human Rights* 16 (1979).

10. 9 ESCOR Supp. 10, UN Docs. E/1371; E/CN.4/350 Annexes I and II (1949).

11. 11 ESCOR Supp. 5, UN Docs. E/1681; E/CN.4/507 Annex I (1950).

12. 13 ESCOR Supp. 9, UN Docs. E/1992; E/CN.4/640 (1951).

13. 14 ESCOR Supp. 4, UN Docs. E/2256; E/CN.4/669 Annex II (1952).

14. 16 ESCOR Supp. 8, UN Docs. E/2447; E/CN.4/689 Annex I (1953).

15. 18 ESCOR Supp. 7, UN Docs. E/2573; E/CN.4/705 Annexes I, II, III (1954).

16. G.A. Res. 421-E, 5 GAOR Supp. 20, UN Doc. A/1775 at 43 (1950).

17. 5 GAOR C.3 (297th and 298th mtgs.), UN Docs. A/C.3/SR.297, SR. 298 (1950).

18. *Ibid.*

19. G.A. Res. 543, 6 GAOR Supp. 20, UN Doc. A/2119 at 36 (1952). Attempts were made subsequently in the Commission on Human Rights to have the decision of the General Assembly reconsidered, but without success. See the draft resolution of the USSR, UN Doc. E/CN.4/L.272 (1953) and the discussion at the 390th meeting, UN Doc. E/CN.4/SR.390 at 20–25 (1953).

20. Other conventions dealing with specific human rights problems include: Convention concerning Freedom of Association and Protection of the Right to Organize (ILO, 1948); Convention on the Prevention and Punishment of the Crime of Genocide (UN, 1948); Convention concerning Equal Remuneration for Men and Women Workers for Work of Equal Value (ILO, 1951); Convention Relating to the Status of Refugees (UN, 1951); Convention on the Political Rights of Women (UN, 1952); Convention on the International Rights of Correction (UN, 1952); Convention Relating to the Status of Stateless Persons (UN, 1954); Convention on the Nationality of Married Women (UN, 1957); Supplementary Convention on the Abolition of Slavery, the Slave Trade, and Institutions and Practices Similar to Slavery (UN, 1956); Convention concerning the Abolition of Forced Labour (ILO, 1957); Convention concerning Discrimination in respect of Employment and Occupation (ILO, 1958); Convention against Discrimination in Education (UNESCO, 1960); Convention on the Reduction of Statelessness (UN, 1961); Convention on Consent to Marriage, Minimum Age for Marriage and Registration of Marriages (UN, 1962); International Convention on the Elimination of All Forms of Racial Discrimination (UN, 1966); International Convention on the Suppression and Punishment of

the Crime of Apartheid (UN, 1973); Convention on the Elimination of Discrimination against Women (UN, 1979).

The texts of these conventions have been collected and reprinted in *Human Rights: A Compilation of International Instruments,* UN Doc. ST/HR/1/Rev. 1 (1978).

21. See generally 10 GAOR Annexes, UN Doc. A/2929 at 8–9 (1955).

22. Article 1(2) of the UN Charter includes the following purposes: "to develop friendly relations among nations based on respect for the principle of equal rights and self-determination of peoples, and to take other appropriate measures to strengthen universal peace."

23. G.A. Res. 421, *supra* note 16, at part D.

24. G.A. Res. 545, 6 GAOR Supp. 20, UN Doc. A/2119 at 36 (1952).

25. See, e.g., the Declaration on the Granting of Independence to Colonial Countries and Peoples, G.A. Res. 1514, 15 GAOR Supp. 16, UN Doc. A/4684 at 66 (1960), and the Declaration of Principles of International Law Concerning Friendly Relations and Co-operation Among States in Accordance with the Charter of the United Nations, G.A. Res. 2625, 25 GAOR Supp. 28, UN Doc. 4/8028 at 121 (1970).

26. Article 8 of the UN Charter provides that: "The United Nations shall place no restrictions on the eligibility of men and women to participate in any capacity and under conditions of equality in its principal and subsidiary organs."

27. See generally UN Doc. A/2929, *supra* note 21, at 23–24.

28. W. Gellhorn, *When Americans Complain: Governmental Grievance Procedures* 225 (1966).

29. UN Doc. E/600, *supra* note 6, at 43–44. Article 2(7) is quoted *supra* note 2.

30. 5 GAOR Plen. Mtg. 317, UN Doc. A/PV. 317 at 554 (1950).

31. UN Doc. E/CN.4/SR.105 (1949).

32. J. F. Green, *The United Nations and Human Rights* 52 (1956).

33. See generally 9 ESCOR Supp. 10, UN Docs. E/1371; E/CN.4 350 Annex III (1949).

34. G.A. Res. 421, *supra* note 16, at part C.

35. 18 ESCOR Supp. 7, UN Docs. E/2573, E/CN.4/705 at 25–27 (1954).

36. Green, *supra* note 32, at 55.

37. See *Human Rights International Instruments: Signatures, Ratifications, etc.,* UN Doc. ST/HR/4/Rev. 2 (1980). In the United States, however, the Executive Branch has proposed a reservation to the same effect. Message from the President of the United States transmitting Four Treaties Pertaining to Human Rights to the Senate, Exec. C, D, E, and F at xiv (February 23, 1978).

38. UN Doc. E/CN.4/95 Annex B at Art. 25 (1948).

39. G.A. Res. 422, 5 GAOR Supp. 20, UN Doc. A/1775 at 43 (1950).

40. G.A. Res. 546, 6 GAOR Supp. 20, UN Doc. A/2119 at 37 (1952).

41. For a full account, see 18 ESCOR Supp. 7, UN Docs. E/2573, E/CN.4/705 at 28–33 (1954).

42. Advisory Opinion on Reservations to the Genocide Convention, [1951] *ICJ Reports* 15.

43. 10 Commission on Human Rights (448th mtg.), UN Doc. E/CN.4/SR.448 at 5 (1954).

44. For the conflict over the adoption of the Declaration on Fundamental Principles Concerning the Contribution of the Mass Media to Strengthening Peace and International Understanding, begun in 1974 and resolved in 1978, *see* 18 *UNESCO Gen. Conf. Records* 63 (1974); 20 *UNESCO Gen. Conf. Records* 100, 102 (1978); cited in UN Monthly Chronicle, Dec. 1978 at 54–55.

45. See the discussion in 17 GAOR Annexes, UN Doc. A/5365 (1962).

46. 18 GAOR Annexes, UN Doc. A/5655 paras. 68–73, 77–82 (1963).

47. Explanatory Paper on Measures of Implementation prepared by the Secretary General, 18 GAOR Annexes, UN Doc. A/5411 (1963).

48. South West Africa Case [1966], *ICJ Reports* 6.

49. 21 GAOR Annex XXI, UN Doc. A/6546 paras. 557–61, 613–26 (1966).

50. *Ibid.* See also UN Doc. A/5411, *supra* note 47.

51. G.A. Res. 2337, 22 GAOR Supp. 16, UN Doc. A/6716 at 41 (1967).

52. G.A. Res. 2788, 26 GAOR Supp. 29, UN Doc. A/8429 at 83 (1971); G.A. Res. 3025, 27 GAOR Supp. 30, UN Doc. A/8730 at 71 (1972); G.A. Res. 3142, 28 GAOR Supp. 30, UN Doc. A/9030 at 84 (1973).

53. G.A. Res. 3270, 29 GAOR Supp. 31 (A/9631) at 90 (1974).

54. See *Human Rights International Instruments: Signatures, Ratifications etc.* UN Doc. ST/HR/4/Rev.2 (1980), updated.

55. *Ibid.*

56. G.A. Res. 31/124, 31 GAOR Supp. 39, UN Doc. A/31/39 at 104 (1976).

57. See 21 GAOR Plen. Mtgs. (1496th mtg.), UN Doc. A/PV/1496 paras. 63–149 (1966).

58. Compare Schachter, "The Relation of Law, Politics and Action in the United Nations," 109 *Recueil des Cours* 188 (1963). Other relevant factors in determining the standards of conduct embodied in the Covenant include preceding or subsequent treaties concluded between the parties which reveal a standard accepted by states for international law purposes, for example, the European and American Conventions on Human Rights. In addition, treaties, declarations, and recommendations adopted under the auspices of the UN, the ILO, UNESCO, and other specialized agencies, may synthesize international standards on human rights and thereby support and elaborate the Covenant provisions. The proceedings of the 1968 Teheran Conference on Human Rights should also be examined in this regard. Qualified publicists and legal scholars have contributed to our understanding of the Covenant. See also Hassan, "The International Covenants on Human Rights: An Approach to Interpretation," 19 *Buffalo L. Rev.* 36 (1969).

59. G.A. Res. 3452, 30 GAOR Supp. 34, UN Doc. A/10034 at 90 (1975).

60. G.A. Res. 32/121, 32 GAOR Supp. 45, UN Doc. A/32/45 at 144 (1977).

61. G.A. Res. 32/61, 32 GAOR Supp. 45, UN Doc. A/32/45 at 136 (1977).

62. G.A. Res. 32/127, 32 GAOR Supp. 45, UN Doc. A/32/45 at 148 (1977).

63. Compare Buergenthal, ed., *Human Rights, International Law, and the Helsinki Accord* 7–8 (1977).

3. TO RESPECT AND TO ENSURE: STATE OBLIGATIONS AND PERMISSIBLE DEROGATIONS

1. 18 GAOR Annexes, UN Doc. A/5655 para. 17 (1963).
2. American Convention on Human Rights, Art. 1(1), OAS Doc. OEA/Ser. K/XVI/1.1., Doc. 65 (1970); text reprinted in 9 *Int'l Leg. Mat.* 99 (1970).
3. *Id.* Art. 1(2).
4. European Convention on Human Rights, 213 *UNTS* 221 (1950). See, for example, Articles 2, 3. The equally authentic French text speaks of *toute personne* and *nul*.
5. F. Jacobs, *The European Convention on Human Rights* 228 (1975); Golsong, "La Convention Européenne des Droits de l'Homme et les Personnes Morales," in Centre d'études européennes, Université catholique de Louvain, *Les Droits de l'Homme et les personnes morales* 15 (1970).
6. Compare Golsong, *supra* note 5, at 27–29.
7. See A. H. Robertson, *Human Rights in Europe* 33 (2d ed. 1977). It is clear that in the absence of a territorial requirement, a national living abroad would be entitled to the protection of the Covenant against the wrongful acts of the state of his nationality. The European Commission of Human Rights has so ruled on a number of occasions. See, e.g., X v. Federal Republic of Germany, 8 *Y.B. Eur. Conv. Human Rights* 158, 166–68 (1965). See also F. Castberg, *The European Convention on Human Rights* 24 (1974).
8. 10 GAOR Annexes, UN Doc. A/2929, part II, ch. 5, para. 4 (1955); UN Doc. A/5655, *supra* note 1, para. 18.
9. The need to avoid such a formulation can be attributed to the states parties' undertaking in Article 2(1) not only "to respect" but also "to ensure" the rights guaranteed in the Covenant, which standing alone could be read to establish the obligation also to protect individuals against acts of a foreign territorial sovereign—an obligation the drafters did not wish to impose on the states parties.
10. UN Doc. A/2929, *supra* note 8, para. 4. It is difficult to read the reference to "diplomatic channels" in the last phrase of the language quoted in the text without concluding that the drafters had "state responsibility" problems in mind.
11. See, e.g., Hess v. United Kingdom, 18 *Y.B. Eur. Conv. Human Rights* 146, 174–76 (1975). See generally J. Fawcett, *The Application of the European Convention on Human Rights* 22–23 (1969).
12. See, e.g., X v. Federal Republic of Germany, 3 *Y.B. Eur. Conv. Human Rights* 280, 287 (1960).
13. Hess v. United Kingdom, *supra* note 11; X v. Sweden, 8 *Y.B. Eur. Conv. Human Rights* 272, 280–82 (1965); X v. Federal Republic of Germany, 2 *Y.B. Eur. Conv. Human Rights* 256, 300–2 (1958–1959). The courts in some Euro-

pean Common Market countries have had to face comparable issues in determining the extent to which domestic constitutional guarantees protect individuals against measures adopted by organs of the European Communities. See H. Schermers, *Judicial Protection in the European Communities* 27–29 (1976).

14. Cyprus v. Turkey, 18 *Y.B. Eur. Conv. Human Rights* 83 (1975).

15. *Id.* at 118.

16. For a discussion of the manner in which similar issues arising under the International Convention on the Elimination of All Forms of Racial Discrimination have been handled by the Committee on the Elimination of Racial Discrimination, see Buergenthal, "Implementing the U.N. Racial Convention," 12 *Tex. Int'l L.J.* 187, 211–18 (1977).

17. See Henkin, "Constitutional Rights and Human Rights," 13 *Harv. C.R.—C.L. L. Rev.* 593, 604–5 (1978). See also Williams, "The European Convention on Human Rights: A New Use," 12 *Tex. Int'l L.J.* 279 (1977).

18. The United States has in effect "ensured" civil rights by making it a crime for anyone, acting under color of law, to deprive someone of rights, or for any two or more persons to conspire to do so. See 18 U.S.C. §§242,241 (1976). It is also a crime, even for private persons not acting under color of law, to deprive someone of the right to vote and other federally protected rights by force or threat of force. 18 U.S.C. §245. Civil rights legislation (42 U.S.C. §1981) has been invoked by the courts to invalidate and enjoin private deprivations of rights, notably private discrimination on account of race. Jones v. Alfred H. Mayer Co., 392 U.S. 409 (1968); Runyon v. McCrary, 427 U.S. 160 (1967). See essay 7, at note 41; essay 10, at note 58. Compare Article 20(2) of the Covenant which requires a state to prohibit "advocacy of national, racial, or religious hatred that constitutes incitement to discrimination, hostility or violence." See essay 9.

19. See American Convention on Human Rights, Art. 27; European Convention on Human Rights, Art. 15. See generally O'Boyle, "Emergency Limitations and the Protection of Human Rights: A Model Derogation Provision for a Northern Ireland Bill of Rights," 28 *N. Ir. L. Q.* 160 (1977); Dinstein, "Derogation from International Human Rights," in *Menschenrechte in Israel und Deutschland* 63, 67–68 (1978).

20. Article 15 of the European Convention on Human Rights reads as follows:

"(1) In time of war or other public emergency threatening the life of the nation, any High Contracting Party may take measures derogating from its obligations under this Convention to the extent strictly required by the exigencies of the situation, provided that such measures are not inconsistent with its other obligations under international law.

"(2) No derogation from Article 2, except in respect of deaths resulting from lawful acts of war, or from Articles 3, 4 (paragraph 1) and 7 shall be made under this provision.

"(3) Any High Contracting Party availing itself of this right of derogation shall keep the Secretary-General of the Council of Europe fully informed of the measures which it has taken and the reasons therefor. It shall also inform the Secretary-General of the Council of Europe when such measures have ceased to operate and the provisions of the Convention are again being fully executed."

21. See Higgins, "Derogations under Human Rights Treaties," 48 *Brit. Y.B. Int'l L.* 281, 286–88 (1976–1977).

22. UN Doc. A/2929, *supra* note 8, para. 39. See also Schwelb, "Some Aspects of the International Covenants on Human Rights of December 1966," in A. Eide and A. Schou, eds., *International Protection of Human Rights* 103, 116 (Nobel Symposium 7, 1968). On the topic generally, see van Hoff, "The Protection of Human Rights and the Impact of Emergency Situations under International Law with Special Reference to the Present Situation in Chile," 10 *Human Rights J.* 213 (1977).

23. UN Doc. A/2929, *supra* note 8, para. 39.

24. Lawless case, 3 *Pub. Eur. Ct. Human Rights,* Ser. A, para. 28 (1961).

25. Greek case, 12a *Y.B. Eur. Conv. Human Rights* para. 153 (1969). The Commission's conclusion that the public emergency must be "actual or imminent" seems to be consistent with the European Court's definition adopted in the Lawless case whose authentic French text speaks of *danger exceptionnel et imminent*. The word *imminent* was omitted from the English text. See the Commission's explanation in the Greek case, para. 152. See also Higgins, *supra* note 21, at 301.

26. Support for this view can be found in Ireland v. United Kingdom, 25 *Pub. Eur. Ct. Human Rights,* Ser. A., para. 205 (1978), where the Court made the following finding: "Article 15 comes into play only 'in time of war or other public emergency threatening the life of the nation.' The existence of such an emergency is perfectly clear from the facts summarised above . . . and was not questioned by anyone before either the Commission or the Court. *The crisis experienced at the time by the six counties therefore comes within the ambit of Article 15"* (emphasis added).

27. U.N Doc. A/5655, *supra* note 1, para. 48.

28. Ireland v. United Kingdom, *supra* note 26, para. 207.

29. Lawless case, *supra* note 24, paras. 22, 28. See also Buergenthal, "Proceedings Against Greece under the European Convention on Human Rights," 62 *AJIL* 441, 445 (1968); Schwelb, *supra* note 22, at 116.

30. Greek case, *supra* note 25, para. 165.

31. Until the European Court's decision in Ireland v. United Kingdom, that tribunal had studiously avoided using the "margin of appreciation" formula that had been developed by the European Commission in the Lawless case. See Buergenthal, *supra* note 29, at 445; Higgins, *supra* note 21 at 298–99.

32. See, e.g., Inter-American Commission on Human Rights, "Report on the Status of Human Rights in Chile," OAS Doc. OEA/Ser.L/V. 2.34, Doc. 21, Corr. 1 (1974), in which the Commission ruled that "measures involving suspension of the guarantees of basic rights may in no case last longer than the actual, real, and provable situations that determine their adoption. Hence, for

example: a "state of war" which is in fact nonexistent, or which in fact has ceased to exist, cannot be invoked to justify, under international law, the suspension of such guarantees." *Id.* at 4.

33. Ireland v. United Kingdom, *supra* note 26, para. 214.

34. Comparable clauses can be found in the American and European Conventions, but no case has thus far called for an interpretation of these provisions.

35. See Partsch, "Experience Regarding the War and Emergency Clause (Article 15) of the European Convention on Human Rights," 1 Israel Y.B. Human Rights 327, 330 (1971).

36. For an analysis of this problem as it relates to the European Convention of Human Rights and the Racial Convention, see Buergenthal, "International and Regional Human Rights Law and Institutions: Some Examples of their Interaction," 12 *Tex. Int'l L.J.* 321, 324–25 (1977).

37. That may well be true of the American Convention on Human Rights, whose list of nonderogable rights is more extensive than the one found in Article 4(2) of the Covenant.

38. UN Doc. A/2929, *supra* note 8, para. 44; Partsch, *supra* note 35, at 329.

39. By contrast, Art. 15(2) of the European Convention on Human Rights prohibits derogation only with regard to four provisions: those relating to the right to life, torture, slavery, and retroactive criminal legislation. The American Convention contains a longer list (Art. 27(2)).

40. Committee of Experts on Human Rights, "Problems Arising from the Coexistence of the United Nations Covenants on Human Rights and the European Convention on Human Rights," Council of Europe Doc. CE/H(70)7 para. 74 (1970).

A similar view was expressed by at least one representative in the Third Committee of the UN General Assembly when that body considered the text of Article 4(2). UN Doc. A/5655, *supra* note 1, para. 53.

41. UN Doc. A/5655, *supra* note 1, para. 52.

42. *Id.* paras. 41–42.

43. Lawless case, *supra* note 24, para. 47.

44. This provision of the Civil and Political Rights Covenant has been taken over by the American Convention on Human Rights (Art. 27(3)).

45. The European Commission of Human Rights reached an analogous conclusion in the Greek case, *supra* note 25, paras. 80–81.

46. A similar provision can be found in the American Convention. The European Convention, on the other hand, merely provides for notification to the Secretary-General of the Council of Europe without making the states parties the ultimate addressees of the notice. But a resolution of the Committee of Ministers of the Council of Europe now requires the Secretary-General to circulate the notice to all member states. Fawcett, *supra* note 11, at 250 n.2.

47. International Covenant on Civil and Political Rights, Art. 40(2).

48. For the text of the General Guidelines, see Report of the Human Rights Committee, 32 GAOR Supp. 44, UN Doc. A/32/44 at 69 (1977).

49. *Id.* at 35–36.

50. See Human Rights Committee, Summary Records of the 43d and 44th Meetings, UN Doc. CCPR/C/SR.43–44 (1977); Summary Records of the 128th and 129th Meetings, UN Doc. CCPR/C/SR.128–29 (1979).

51. See General Guidelines, part II(b), *supra* note 48, at 70.

52. See, e.g., the review of the United Kingdom report, 33 GAOR Supp. 40, UN Doc. A/33/40 at 36 (1978); the Committee's review of Chile's report, *supra* note 50. The report by Colombia was sharply criticized by members of the Committee for failing to indicate the provisions derogated from, the difficulties causing the derogations, the extent of the derogations, and the date derogation will terminate. UN Doc. CCPR/C/SR.233 para. 13 (1980).

53. UN Doc. A/5655, *supra* note 1, para. 54.

54. See the report of the European Commission of Human Rights in the De Becker case, 2 *Pub. Eur. Ct. Human Rights,* Ser. B, para. 271 (1962). See also the Conclusions of the Inter-American Commission on Human Rights in its 1974 report on Chile, *supra* note 32.

55. See, e.g., American Convention on Human Rights, Art. 29(a); European Convention on Human Rights, Art. 17.

56. Article 30 of the Declaration does not, however, contain any language corresponding to the final phrase—"or at their limitation to a greater extent than is provided for in the present Covenant"—of Article 5(1).

57. For an analysis of this drafting history, see A. Verdoodt, *Naissance et Signification de la Déclaration Universelle des Droits de l'Homme* 272–74 (1964).

58. UN Doc. A/2929, *supra* note 8, para. 58.

59. The doctrine of *détournement de pouvoir,* as developed in French administrative law, provides the closest domestic law analogue to the concept embodied in Article 5(1) of the Covenant. Under this doctrine an otherwise lawful discretionary administrative act may be struck down if it appears that it was prompted by illegal or improper motives. See Lemasurier, "La Preuve dans le Détournement de Pouvoir," 65 *Revue du Droit Public* 36 (1959); Buergenthal, "Appeals for Annulment by Enterprises in the European Coal and Steel Community," 10 *Am. J. Comp. L.* 227, 239–42 (1961).

60. Compare Fawcett, *supra* note 11, at 253.

61. The concept of *détournement de pouvoir* (note 59) is in fact designed to take these subjective elements into account.

62. In his dissenting opinion, Felix Ermacora, one of the members of the Commission, in fact took this position. See the Greek case, *supra* note 25, paras. 214–15. See also Buergenthal, *supra* note 29, at 443 n.11.

63. See Communist Party of Germany v. Federal Republic of Germany, 1 *Y. B. Eur. Conv. H.R.* 222 (1955–1957).

64. Robertson, *supra* note 7, at 118–19; Jacobs, *supra* note 5, at 210–12.

65. Lawless case, *supra* note 24, at 45–46.

66. See the European Commission's report in the De Becker case, *supra* note 54, at 137–38.

67. See Verdoodt, *supra* note 57, at 273–74; N. Robinson, *The Universal Declaration of Human Rights* 143 (1958).

68. Sohn, "The Human Rights Law of the Charter," 12 *Tex. Int'l L.J.* 129,

137 (1977); Sohn, "A Short History of United Nations Documents on Human Rights," in *The United Nations and Human Rights* 38, 175–176 (1968). See also Vasak, "Vers un Droit International Spécifique des Droits de l'Homme," in UNESCO, *Les Dimensions Internationales des Droits de l'Homme* 707, 710 (1978), who speaks of the "clause de l'individu le plus favorisé."

69. The American Convention on Human Rights (Art. 29) and the European Convention on Human Rights (Art. 60) contain similar but by no means identical provisions.

70. Article 4(1) of the Covenant might be said to do that to the extent that it prohibits a state, when exercising its rights of derogation, to adopt measures that conflict with its other international obligations.

71. See Vasak, *supra* note 68, at 711.

72. See Committee of Experts on Human Rights, *supra* note 40, para. 85.

73. Sohn, "The Human Rights Law of the Charter," *supra* note 68, at 137–38.

4. THE SELF–DETERMINATION OF PEOPLES

1. 9 ESCOR Supp. 10, UN Docs. E/1371; 3/CN.4/350 at 47 (1949).

2. "Every people and every nation shall have the right to national self-determination. States which have responsibilities for the administration of Non-Self-Governing Territories shall promote the fulfilment of this right, guided by the aims and principles of the United Nations in relation to the peoples of such Territories. The State shall ensure to national minorities the right to use their native tongue and to possess their national schools, museums and other cultural and educational institutions." 5 GAOR Annexes, Agenda Item 63, UN Doc. A/C.3/L.96 at 17 (1950).

That the Soviet proposal was intended to restrict the right to self-determination to colonial countries appears from a careful comparison of the Soviet drafts: UN Doc. A/C.3/L.96, *supra;* 6 GAOR Annex 1, Agenda Item 29; UN Doc. A/C.3/L.206 (1952); UN Doc. E/CN.4/L.21 (1952); and of other drafts, in particular: Yugoslavia, UN Doc. E/CN.4/22 (1952); Egypt, UN Doc. E/CN.4/L.23/Rev. 1 (1952); India, UN Doc. E/CN. 4/L.25/Rev.1 (1952); and United States, UN Doc. E/CN.4/L.28 (1952). See also statements made by representatives of the Soviet Union and other socialist countries, in particular: USSR, 5 GAOR C.3 (310th mtg.), UN Doc. A/C.3/SR.310 para. 41 (1950).

3. 5 GAOR Annexes, Agenda Item 63, UN Doc. A/1559 at 28 (1950).

4. See, e.g., Mexico, UN Docs. A/C.3/SR.310 paras. 7–11 (1950), SR.311 paras. 29–32; Syria, UN Doc. A/C.3/SR.311 paras. 7–8 (1950); Saudi Arabia, UN Docs. A/C.3/SR.309 paras. 56–57 (1950), SR.310 para. 3 (1950), SR.367 para. 42 (1951), SR.398 paras. 32–34 (1952), SR.403 para. 85 (1952), SR.563 para. 12 (1953); Liberia, UN Docs. A/C.3/SR.366 para. 25 (1951), SR.400 para. 9 (1952).

5. See text at pp. 93–94, and *infra,* notes 19–22.

6. The USSR draft submitted to the Third Committee (A/C.3/L.206) was

superseded by others (A/C.3/L.216, A/C.3/L.255) which took account of the views of other delegations. UN Doc. A/C.3/SR.403 para. 40 (1952). See the explanation of the vote of the Soviet delegate on the joint draft resolution (A/C.3/L.186 and Add. 1), *id*. paras. 86–89.

In 1952, in the Commission on Human Rights, the Soviet draft (E/CN.4/L.21) mentioned only dependent territories. Egypt proposed an amendment (E/CN.4/L.23 Rev. 1) "aimed at making good" the omission of the Soviet draft by proposing a paragraph "referring to all countries without exception." UN Doc. E/CN.4/SR.255 at 10 (1952). Criticisms for that omission were voiced by the delegates of the U.S., UN Doc. E/CN.4/SR.256 at 6 (1952), and of Lebanon, SR.257 at 8. The Egyptian amendment was adopted. SR.259 at 7.

7. The first proposal of what became the present paragraph 2 was made by Chile in 1952 in the Commission on Human Rights. UN Docs. E/CN.4/SR.253 at 5–6, SR.256 at 10, SR.257 at 10–11, SR.260 at 6, 11 (1952). The Chilean delegate submitted a draft resolution (E/CN.4/L.24) which was adopted. It provided as follows: "The right of the peoples to self-determination shall also include permanent sovereignty over their natural wealth and resources. In no case may a people be deprived of its own means of subsistence on the grounds of any rights that may be claimed by other states."

8. The United States said that the promotion of the principle of self-determination was the responsibility of the Trusteeship Council and the Fourth Committee. UN Doc. A/C.3/SR.310 para. 28 (1950). This view was shared by Canada, *id*. para. 32. Brazil pointed out that the proposed article was inappropriate because the principle was already stated in Article 1(2) of the Charter. *Id*. para. 30; SR.360 para. 6 (1951).

9. A resolution in the Third Committee requesting the Commission on Human Rights to include in the Covenant an article on self-determination was supported by Third World and socialist countries while Australia, Belgium, Canada, France, Netherlands, New Zealand, Turkey, U.K., and U.S.A. voted against. Chile, China, Colombia, Cuba, Denmark, Ecuador, Israel, Norway, Peru, and Sweden abstained. UN Doc. A/C.3/SR.403 para. 58 (1952).

In 1952, the article on self-determination was adopted by the Commission on Human Rights by 13 votes to 4 (Belgium, U.K., Australia, France), with 1 abstention. UN Doc. E/CN.4/SR.260 at 4 (1952). The United States delegate voted in favor because her government "supported its inclusion in the Covenant, but she reserved the right to propose changes or additions when it came up for discussion in the General Assembly," *ibid*. The United States voted against the Chilean proposal relating to the present para. 2, SR.261 at 5.

In 1955, in the Third Committee, the article was adopted by 33 votes to 12 (France, Luxembourg, Netherlands, New Zealand, Norway, Sweden, Turkey, U.K., U.S.A., Australia, Belgium, Canada), with 13 abstentions (Cuba, Denmark, Dominican Republic, Ethiopia, Honduras, Iceland, Iran, Israel, Panama, Paraguay, Brazil, Burma, China). See UN Doc. A/C.3/SR.676 para. 27 (1955).

10. See, for instance, the note verbale of 2 July 1955 by the U.K., 10 GAOR Annexes, UN Doc. A/2910/Add.1 (1955), as well as the statement made by the

U.K. representative in the Third Committee, UN Doc. A/C.3/SR.642 para. 11 (1955); the note verbale of 20 July 1955 by Australia, 10 GAOR Annexes, UN Doc. A/2907 at 11 (1955); and the note verbale of 29 August 1955 by Netherlands, *id.* at 14.

11. Belgium, UN Docs. A/C.3/SR.361 para. 10 (1951), SR.643 para. 9 (1955); Sweden, SR.641 paras. 13, 18 (1955); Denmark, SR.644 para. 2 (1955); Australia, SR.647 para. 7 (1955).

12. France, UN Docs. A/C.3/SR.309 para. 62 (1950), SR.371 para. 20 (1951), SR.399 para. 26; Turkey, SR.310 para. 49 (1950), SR.400 para. 30 (1952); New Zealand, SR.367 para. 8 (1951), SR.400 paras. 23–25 (1952); U.K., SR.562 para. 13 (1954); Australia, SR.564 para. 13 (1954); Sweden, SR.641 para. 13–14 (1955); Netherlands, SR.642 para. 23; Belgium, SR.643 para. 8; Denmark, SR.644 para. 3; Canada, SR.645 para. 1.

13. Sweden, UN Doc. A/C.3/SR.641 para. 13 (1955).

14. Denmark, UN Doc. A/C.3/SR.644 para. 3 (1955).

15. United Kingdom, UN Doc. A/C.3/SR.309 para. 59 (1950).

16. Brazil, UN Doc. A/C.3/SR.310 para. 30 (1950).

17. Belgium, UN Doc. A/C.3/SR.361 paras. 10, 13 (1951); Australia, SR.363 para. 39; France, SR.399 para. 314 (1952): "Such an article would allow certain powerful nations to try to disintegrate other nations by instigating artificial separatist movements within peoples united by mutual consent. Even the most united nations were not proof against that danger."

Objections were also raised on a procedural plane; thus, for instance, it was contended that the Third Committee of the General Assembly and the Commission on Human Rights were not the proper bodies for dealing with the question. See United Kingdom, UN Doc. A/C.3/SR.309 para. 58 (1950); France, paras. 62–63, SR.399 paras. 27, 29 (1952); United States, SR.310 para. 28 (1950); Canada, para. 32; Turkey, para. 49; Nicaragua, SR.312 para. 5 (1950); Peru, para. 7.

18. See for instance the statements made by New Zealand, UN Doc. A/C.3/SR.649 para. 9 (1955): "If self-determination was intended to be recognized as a right, the right should be commensurate with the principle and should include the right of secession"; and by the U.K., UN Doc. A/C.3/SR.652 para. 19 (1955). See also *supra* note 17.

19. See for example: Greece, UN Doc. A/C.3/SR.572 para. 32 (1954); Saudi Arabia, SR.580 paras. 21–23, SR.582 paras. 75–76 (1954), SR.648 para. 15 (1955); Liberia, SR.644 para. 33; Syria, SR.648 paras. 7–9, SR.672 para. 25; Lebanon, SR.654 para. 39; Pakistan, SR.671 para. 23.

20. On Article 1, see: Lord, "Self-Determination Article in Human Rights Covenants," 33 *Dep't State Bull.* 808–10 (1955); Hyde, "Permanent Sovereignty over Natural Wealth and Resources," 50 *AJIL* 854–867 (1956); Graefrath, *Die Vereinten Nationen und die Menschenrechte* 54–66 (1956); Wengler, "Le droit de la libre disposition des peuples comme principe du droit international," 10 *Revue Hellénique de Droit International* 26–39 (1957); Lord, "The Right of Peoples and Nations to Self-Determination," 40 *Dep't State Bull.* 175–76 (1959); Kunz, "The

Principal of Self-Determination of Peoples, Particularly in the Practice of the United Nations," in Rabl, ed., *Inhalt, Wesen und Gegenwaertige Praktische Bedeutung des Selbstbestimmungsrecht der Voelker* 128 (1964); Arzinger, *Das Selbstbestimmungsrecht im Allegemeinen Voelkerrecht der Gegenwart* (1966); Capotorti, "Saggio Introduttivo," *Patti Internazionali sui Diritti dell'Uomo* 24–27 (1967); Schwelb, "Some Aspects of the International Covenants on Human Rights of December 1966," in Eide and Schou, eds., *International Protection of Human Rights* 110–13 (1967); Johnson, *Self-Determination Within the Community of Nations* 37–41 (1967); Mourgeon, "Les Pactes internationaux relatifs aux Droits d l'Homme," 13 *annuaire Français de Droit International* 342–44 (1967); Brügel, "Die Menschenrechtskonvention der Vereinten Nationen, *"Europa-Archiv"* (1967); Haight, "Human Rights Covenants," *Proc. Am. Soc'y Int'l L.* 99 (1968); Robertson, "The United Nations Covenant on Civil and Political Rights and the European Convention on Human Rights," 43 *Brit. Y.B. Int'l L.* 36 (1968–1969); Movchan, "The Human Rights Problems in Present-Day International Law," in Tunkin, ed., *Contemporary International Law* 248 (1969); van Dyke, *Human Rights, The United Nations, and World Community* 78–79 (1970); Mustafa, "The Principle of Self-Determination in International Law," 5 *Int'l Lawyer* 481–85 (1971); Young, *Das Selbstbestimmungsrecht als eine Vorbedingung des Voelligen Genusses der Menschenrechte* (1972); Sureda, *The Evolution of the Right of Self-determination—A Study of the United Nations Practice* 101–111 (1973); Doehring, *Das Selbstbestimmungsrecht der Völker als Grundsatz des Völkerrechts* (Referat und Diskussion der 13. Tagung der Deutschen Gesellschaft für Völkerrecht) 18 (1974); Dinstein, "Collective Human Rights of Peoples and Minorities," 25 *Int'l Comp. L. Q.* 106–11 (1976); Cassese, "The Helsinki Declaration and Self-Determination," in Buergenthal, ed., *Human Rights, International Law, and the Helsinki Accord* 86–88 (1977); Partsch, "Selbstbestimmungsrecht," *Handbuch Vereinte Nationen* 395 (1977); Partsch, "Les principes de base des droits de l'homme: l'autodétermination, l'égalité et la non–discrimination," in Vasak, ed., *Les Dimensions Internationales des Droits de l'Homme* 65–73 (1978).

21. Afghanistan, UN Doc. A/C.3/SR.309 para. 53 (1950): "Such an article would be of great benefit to all nations, especially to those which had not yet won their independence." The delegate of the same country also stated in 1951 that the draft resolution on self-determination was not directed against colonial powers: "its sole object was to protect a universal right." SR.362 para. 11. Also in 1951, the U.S. representative stated that the principle of self-determination applied, inter alia, to those peoples "which had formerly enjoyed independence but who were deprived of the possibility of governing themselves." SR.364 para. 19. The delegate of India said that "although there was good reason to make special reference to the peoples of the Non-Self-Governing Territories, it must be recognized that the field of application of the principle of self-determination was wider than that." SR.399 para. 4 (1952). The delegate of Afghanistan said in 1955 that "the problem before the Third Committee was not a colonial issue. It was unfortunate that it was sometimes regarded as such, since it was in point of fact very much broader. It should be borne in mind that the

right of peoples to self-determination . . . would have to be proclaimed even in a world from which colonial territories had vanished." SR.644 para. 10. See also the statement by the delegate of El Salvador, SR.645 para. 24; New Zealand, SR.649 para. 9; Lebanon, SR.649 paras. 29–30, 34; India, SR.651 para. 4; Egypt, SR.651 para. 32; Afghanistan, SR.652 para. 3, SR.654 para. 37; U.K., SR.652 para. 24; Denmark, SR.669 para. 6–7; Afghanistan, SR.677 para. 27.

22. UN Doc. A/C.3/SR.310 para. 14 (1950).

23. UN Doc. A/C.3/SR.397 para. 5 (1952). The representative of India reiterated this concept in the Commission on Human Rights:

"If that right meant the right of peoples to decide for themselves in political, social, economic and cultural matters, it could be averred that such a right was recognized in every truly democratic state and that it was only in totalitarian states and in countries subjected to a colonial regime that it did not exist. The totalitarian states would in any case be bound to recognize the right, in view of the provisions in the draft Covenants." UN Doc. E/CN.4/SR.256 at 4 (1952).

The representative of Lebanon, after noting that the main concern of the principle of self-determination was for non-self-governing territories, pointed out that "there were also, however, peoples deprived by their own government of an opportunity to manage their own affairs." SR.254 at 9.

See also the statements made by the representative of Greece: "It was sufficient to uphold what had been decided at the San Francisco Conference in 1945, when the principle of the right of peoples to self-determination had been closely linked to that of the free expression of the will of peoples," SR.253 at 4; and of Pakistan: "The Pakistani delegation considered it essential for the government of a country to be freely chosen by its inhabitants," *id.* at 13.

Later in 1954, the representative of Egypt stated that the right of self-determination was to be implemented "in practice by means of elections and plebiscites through which the individual expressed his wishes," UN Doc. A/C.3/SR.571 para. 4 (1954); also a view expressed in 1955 by the representative of Greece, SR.647 para. 9.

24. The United Kingdom spoke of some of the peoples of the Soviet Union, claiming that although they constituted autonomous republics of that state, the central authority did not recognize their right to self-determination. UN Doc. A/C.3/SR.311 para. 42, SR.312 paras. 14–15 (1950). The delegates of the Soviet Union, Byelorussia and Ukraine denied the allegations and asserted that the Republics of the Soviet Union enjoyed self-determination in fact. SR.311 paras. 38–39, SR. 312 paras. 14, 20. They did not claim, however, that the concept of self-determination does not apply to those republics because they are part of a sovereign state. These views were reiterated again in the Third Committee by the delegates of Czechoslovakia. SR.366 paras. 55–60 (1951); see also SR.372 paras. 14–18; Ukraine, SR.367 paras. 17–20; Yugoslavia, SR.372 paras. 2–7; Soviet Union, SR.372 paras. 26–27, SR.402 paras. 15–17 (1952); and the United Kingdom, SR.401 paras. 24–26. The view that nations of a multinational state fall within the category of peoples envisaged in the article was again stressed in

1952 in the Commission on Human Rights, UN Doc. E/CN.4/SR.254 at 3–5 (1952); and was upheld by the majority of the Commission, which adopted a text on self-determination conferring this right both on "peoples" and "all nations." This decision was confirmed in 1954 and 1955. USSR, UN Doc. A/C.3/SR. 565 para. 26 (1954); Yugoslavia, SR.568 para. 47; Ukraine, SR.641, para. 10 (1955); USSR, SR.646 paras. 12–13.

The discussions of the working party that submitted the final draft to the Third Committee in 1955 support this view. As a majority of this party had decided to delete the words "and all nations" following the words "all peoples" in the original draft, the Soviet delegate argued that the previous text "better expressed the fundamental principle of the right of self-determination" and asked whether, despite such deletions, the majority of the working party considered that they had used the word "peoples in the broad sense, that is to say, including nations and ethnic groups, as had been the intention of the old text prepared by the Commission on Human Rights." UN Doc. A/C.3/SR.668 paras, 14–15 (1955). The representative of El Salvador, in his capacity as chairman of the working party, replied in the affirmative. *Id.* para. 16.

The representative of Yugoslavia pointed out that the "elimination of the reference to 'nations' precluded any possible confusion. The word 'peoples,' which remained, was used in the widest possible sense and took in all ethnic groups, regardless of their stage of development." SR.669 para. 1.

25. UN Doc. A/C.3/SR.676 para. 49 (1955).

26. In the Third Committee, the representative of the United States pointed out that the "principle of self-determination" was applicable not only to the peoples which had not yet achieved full self-government but also to those "currently self-governing but living under the constant threat of foreign imperialism, which was striving to bring about their disintegration from within as well as from without by aggravating their duties." UN Doc. A/C.3/SR. 364 para. 19 (1951). No delegate challenged this view. The delegate of Czechoslovakia stated that "the USSR had always respected the right of peoples to self-determination, whereas some of the nations which had signed the North Atlantic Treaty were prepared to give up their right to self-determination in favor of a foreign power." SR.366 para. 58.

This view was also taken up by the delegate of Byelorussia, who noted that *"all peoples,* whatever their numbers, power or circumstances, had the right to self-determination and to evolution within the cultural environment suited to them. That principle was stated in the Charter but it was denied by the ruling circles of the United States of America, which were seeking to enslave the world" (emphasis added) SR.368 para. 15. In the Commission on Human Rights, the Belgian delegate challenged the definition of self-determination advocated by the Soviet Union, and "asked whether the Soviet Union's concept of self-determination was shared by the peoples of Estonia, Lithuania, Latvia, Poland, Romania, and Czechoslovakia." UN Doc. E/CN.4/SR.254 at 6 (1952). The Polish delegate rejected the statement as unfounded, without, however, claiming that the right of self-determination of the Polish people did not fall under the concept of self-determination to be embodied in the Covenant, as Poland was a sovereign state. He stated that "the Polish people distinguished between its real and its false friends. The Belgian representative in his statement has given a picture of the type of freedom that he advocated; that erroneous concept of freedom had formerly prevailed in Poland, but did so no longer." *Id.* at 8. The delegate of Lebanon, in listing the cases of self-determination that should be taken into account, recalled that "national governments were imposed on some peoples by foreign rule." *Id.* at 9. The same stand was taken in more general terms by the representative of the United States, who attacked a Soviet draft restricting self-determination to dependent territories by stating that "the principle of self-determination applied not only to peoples which had not yet attained independence, but also to politically independent states which needed protection from external pressure, threats, the use of force and subversive activities." SR.256 at 6. This view was echoed by Yugoslavia. The representative of Yugoslavia pointed out: "Current events clearly demonstrated that the right of both non-self-governing peoples and sovereign states to self-determination was threatened on every continent. Even in Europe small nations were the prey of other states' aggressive designs. It was common knowledge that although Yugoslavia had won its independence at the price of enormous sacrifices, today it had to defend itself against external pressure of all kinds." *Id.* at 7, 8. See also the statement made in 1951 in the Third Committee by the Yugoslav representative, UN Doc. A/C.3/SR.365 para. 11 (1951), and by the representative of Chile, SR.330 paras. 20–21 (1952). The proposals made by Yugoslavia in this regard were supported by France, UN Doc. E/CN.4/SR.257 at 4 (1952), while in 1955 the delegate of Venezuela pointed out that self-determination meant "freedom for all peoples and nations to manage their affairs in all respects without the intervention of another people or nation," UN Doc. A/C.3/SR.646 para. 42 (1955). See also Lebanon, SR.649 para. 34.

27. Yugoslavia, one of the most strenuous supporters of the article, pointed out inter alia that "no legalistic argument could refute the fact that the peoples of the European countries which had been occupied during the Second World War had been entitled not only to demand, but to fight for, their right to decide their own fate." UN Doc. A/C.3/SR.647 para. 41 (1955).

In a note verbale of June 30, 1955, Thailand pointed out that "some incidents have recently jeopardized the right of self-determination when it has been a question of the occupation of one country by another for the benefit of the latter." Thailand therefore proposed revision of Article 1 to make sure "that no country shall be tied up to another country without the full agreement of the former, obtained, say, by way of plebiscite or otherwise." UN Doc. A/2910/Add.2, *supra* note 10, at 9.

28. Afghanistan and Saudi Arabia, the authors of a draft resolution concerning the article on self-determination, deleted the word "peoples" from their draft "at the suggestion of delegations which feared that their inclusion might encourage minorities within a state to ask for the right to self-determination."

UN Doc. A/C.3/SR.310 para. 3 (1950). By request of Mexico, that word was reintroduced with the clear understanding that it should not refer to minorities.

See the following statements made in the Third Committee: Liberia, UN Doc. A/C.3/SR.366 para. 29 (1951); China, SR.369 para. 13: "the problem at issue was that of national majorities and not of minorities"; India, SR.399 paras. 5–6 (1952): "the problem of minorities, which was completely different, should not be raised in connexion with its [the right of self-determination] implementation. The sponsors of the draft resolution would never allow the article which they requested should be inserted in the Covenant to be invoked in an attempt to destroy the unity of a nation or to impede the creation of such unity. Any such attempt would be contrary to the purpose of the sponsors of the draft resolution, who recognized the basic principle of national sovereignty."

See also the statements made in the Commission on Human Rights by India, UN Doc. E/CN.4/SR.253 at 13, SR.256 at 5 (1952); Lebanon, SR.254 at 9; Uruguay, SR.259 at 5. A contrary view was expressed by Belgium, SR. 253 at 14.

See, in addition, the statements made in the General Assembly by China, UN Doc. A/C.3/SR.570 para. 16 (1954); Greece, SR.572 para. 8; China SR.642 para. 7 (1955); Canada, SR.645 para. 6; Iran, SR.645 para. 30; Venezuela, SR.646 para. 42; Greece, SR.647 para. 6; Colombia, SR.648 para. 1; Saudi Arabia, SR.648 para. 19; India, SR.651 para. 4; U.K., SR.652 para. 19; Ecuador, SR.671 para. 4; Iraq, SR.671 para. 8; Pakistan, SR.671 para. 23; Syria, SR.672 para. 26; Egypt, SR.675 para. 17.

29. The representative of Colombia stated that "an international instrument should refer to the external aspect of self-determination only." UN Doc. A/C.3/SR.648 para. 1 (1955). This view remained isolated.

30. This interpretation is borne out by the preparatory work. Thus, for instance, the representative of one of the states supporting the article, Greece, stated that the right of peoples to self-determination was "a corollary of the democratic principle of government with the consent of the governed." UN Doc. A/C.3/SR.647 para. 1 (1955). She also stated that "the right could be applied internally only by a people living in complete freedom, not by an outside authority, and plebiscites and free elections were the best guarantees of democratic application." *Id.* para. 9.

31. Resort to the other provisions of the Covenant to assess whether internal self-determination was truly implemented was advocated in the General Assembly by a state that opposed the Article, Australia. The representative of that country pointed out:

"As regards the former [internal self-determination], it was difficult indeed to determine whether or not the life of a given nation or people was governed by the principle [of self-determination]. It would seem to be contrary to the intentions of those who supported Article 1 to take the word of the Government concerned in that respect. The necessary criteria might, however, be found in the substantive articles of the draft Covenant on Civil and Political Rights. Articles 6, 7, 8, 9, 16, 17, and 20, for example, seemed to provide a more logical standard for measuring the extent of 'internal' self-determination than the simple claim that the exercise of the right of self-determination was a prerequisite of the enjoyment of other rights. The people of a society which condoned slavery or forced labor, or which denied the right of recognition to a person before the law or the right of peaceful assembly, could hardly be said to be exercising self-determination" UN Doc. A/C.3/SR.647 para. 26 (1955).

See also the statement to the same effect made by the representative of Yugoslavia, SR.669 para. 2.

32. UN Doc. A/C.3/SR.668 para. 3 (1955).

33. As almost all of the states parties to the Covenant on Civil and Political Rights have also ratified the other Covenant, the question has not arisen, in practice, whether the latter Covenant's provisions can be legitimately referred to with respect to the implementation of Article 1.

34. See, for instance, Article 8 (freedom of trade union association), as well as Articles 6 (right to work), 7 (right to just and favorable working conditions), and 9 (right to social security).

35. See, inter alia, the statement by the representative of Lebanon, UN Doc. A/C.3/SR.663 para. 34 (1955).

36. UN Doc. A/C.3/SR.669 para. 21 (1955). Similar objections were voiced by representatives of the United Kingdom, SR.670 para. 17, and of Israel, SR.673 para. 4.

37. UN Doc. A/C.3/SR.673 para. 15 (1955).

38. See, inter alia, Finger, "A New Approach to Colonial Problems at the United Nations," 26 *Int'l Org.* 143 (1972); Sinha, "Is Self-Determination Passé?," 12 *Colum. J. Transnat'l L.* 260 (1973); Engers, "From Sacred Trust to Self-Determination," 24 *Netherlands Int. L. Rev.* 85 (1977); B. Conforti, *Le Nazioni Unite* 223–26 (1979).

39. For the UN practice in implementing self-determination within established colonial boundaries, see Franck, "The Stealing of the Sahara," 70 AJIL 698–701 (1976).

40. Poland, UN Doc. A/C.3/SR.310 para. 33 (1950).

41. Ukraine, *id.* para. 47; Syria, SR.311 para. 4; Byelorussia, SR.359 para. 21 (1951).

42. India, UN Doc. A/C.3/SR.310 para. 15 (1950).

43. UN Doc. E/CN.4/SR.255 at 6 (1952). The representative of China pointed out that in his opinion the article on self-determination "should figure in both Covenants and not solely in the Covenant on civil and political rights, because the dignity and well-being of peoples depended upon the recognition, in all spheres of human activity, of the right of peoples to self-determination." UN Doc. E/CN.4/SR.253 at 3 (1952). See also the statement made in the third Committee by the representatives of Uruguay, UN Doc. A/C. 3/SR.365 para. 32 (1951); Liberia, SR.366 para. 36; Lebanon, SR.370 para. 30; Ukraine, SR.399 para. 23 (1952); Uruguay, SR. 401 para. 35; and Indonesia, SR.401 para. 45.

44. UN Doc. A/C.3/SR.310 para. 30 (1950). This point was also stressed by Denmark, SR.644 para. 5 (1955).

See also the statement made by Chile, SR.645 para. 8: "respect for human rights led inevitably to self-determination."

45. UN Doc. A/C.3/SR.647 para. 1 (1955).

46. In commenting on and warmly supporting para. 2, the representative of Costa Rica observed: "The new text mentioned 'peoples': that was quite appropriate, for . . . the people were the source of power in a state; they acted through their Government, which exercised the power vested in it, inter alia, to control the country's natural resources." UN Doc. A/C.3/SR.670 para. 23 (1955).

47. France, UN Doc. E/CN.4/SR.257 at 5 (1952); U.S.A., SR.257 at 6; Lebanon, SR.257 at 10; Australia, UN Doc. A/C.3/SR.647 para. 24 (1955); Panama, SR.650 para. 28.

48. U.S.A., UN Doc. E/CN.4/SR.257 at 6 (1952); U.K., UN Doc. A/C.3/SR.642 para. 19 (1955); U.S.A., SR.646 paras. 34–35.

49. In 1955, the representative of Syria pointed out that those words, as well as the words "and international law," had been proposed in the working party of the Third Committee by the Polish delegate, "and the Syrian delegation had considered them essential because history showed that 'international cooperation' could provide the strong with a means of oppressing the weak." UN Doc. A/C.3/SR.672 para. 25 (1955). The Greek representative noted that "as for the principle of mutual benefit, the Greek delegation had already stressed its importance in permitting countries as they attained independence, to develop their economies in absolute freedom instead of being subjected to colonial exploitation." *Id.* para. 42.

50. See the statements made in 1955 by the delegate of Chile, UN Doc. A/C.3/SR.645 para. 11 (1955); U.S.A., SR.646 paras. 34–35; Honduras, SR.647 para. 52; Peru, SR.647 para. 55; Uruguay, SR.649 para. 20; Ecuador, SR.650 para. 21; Cuba, SR.650 para. 31; Bolivia, SR.651 para. 18; El Salvador, SR.668 para. 5, SR.674 para. 8; Saudi Arabia, SR.668 para. 22; Costa Rica, SR.670 para. 24; Guatemala, SR.673 para. 28; Egypt, SR.675 paras. 18–19; U.S.A., SR.676 paras. 31–32; Haiti, SR.677 para. 3.

51. See, e.g., Giardino, "Nationalisation et indemnisation en droit international," *Etudes présentées au colloque sur de Droit Pétrolier et la Souveraineté des pays Producteurs* 39–49 (1973).

52. See, e.g., Jimenez de Aréchaga, "International Law in the Past Third of a Century," 159 *Recueil des Cours* 297–310 (1978); Brownlie, *Principles of Public International Law* 531–45 (3d ed. 1979). See also Elian, "Le principe de la souveraineté sur les resources nationales et les incidences juridiques sur le commerce international," 149 *Recueil des Cours* 7 (1976); Bedjaoui, "Non-alignment et droit international," 151 *Recueil des Cours* 337, 432–36 (1976).

53. See inter alia Yasseen, "Interpretation des traités d'après la Convention de Vienne sur le droit des traités," 151 *Recueil des Cours* 62–68 (1976).

54. "Legal Consequences for States of the Continued Presence of South Af-

rica in Namibia (South West Africa) notwithstanding Security Council Resolution 276 (1970)," [1971] *ICJ Reports* 31.

55. In 1966, a few Western delegations suggested that the contradiction between Article 1(2) and Article 47 should be eliminated by giving priority to the
former provision. They, however, did not set forth the legal reasons supporting
this view. Thus, the delegate of the United States said the following in the
Third Committee: "Article 25 of the International Covenant on Economic, Social, and Cultural Rights, which was identical with Article 47 of the International Covenant on Civil and Political Rights, was out of place in the implementation clauses. Her Government fully supported the principle expressed in
Article 25, but Article 1(2) of the Covenant provided the effective substantive
formulation on that question, and it could not be impaired by Article 25, as
other delegations had said, including some of the sponsors of Article 25." UN
Doc. A/C.3/SR.1455 para. 33 (1966). In the plenary session, the representative
of Japan said the following:

"Article 1(2) of the draft Covenant on Economic, Social and Cultural
Rights already ensures the right of peoples freely to dispose of their natural
wealth and resources. The addition of Article 25 not only duplicates Article
1(2) but also complicates its interpretation, for Article 25 does not mention
obligations arising out of international economic cooperation, based upon
the principle of mutual benefit and international law. The inclusion of Article 47 in the Draft Covenant on Civil and Political Rights is irrelevant."
21 GAOR Plen. Mtgs. (1496th mtg.), UN Doc. A/PV.1496 paras. 33–34
(1966).

56. See, for instance, the statements by the representatives of the U.K.,
UN Doc. A/C.3/SR.670 para. 15 (1955), and of the United States, paras. 30–
31.

57. UN Doc. A/C.3/SR.672 para. 36 (1955).

58. *Id*. para. 43.

59. UN Doc. A/C.3/SR.674 para. 8 (1955).

60. *Id*. para. 30.

61. *Id*. para. 33. The delegate of Australia challenged, however, the appropriateness of the remarks made by the delegate of El Salvador with respect to
Nauru. UN Doc. A/C.3/SR.675 paras. 36–37 (1955).

62. See *supra* note 33.

63. In fact, all those who spoke of the "duty to promote" the realization of
self-determination referred to non-self-governing territories only. See, for instance, the statement made by the representative of El Salvador in his capacity
as chairman of the working party charged with drafting Article 1, UN Doc.
A/C.3/SR.668, para. 6 (1955), as well as the remarks by the delegate of Lebanon, para. 34.

64. Paragraph 5 states as follows: "Immediate steps shall be taken, in Trust
and Non-Self-Governing Territories or all other territories which have not yet
attained independence, to transfer all powers to the peoples of those territories,
without any conditions or reservations, in accordance with their freely ex-

pressed will and desire, without any distinction as to race, creed, or colour, in order to enable them to enjoy complete independence and freedom."

65. As for the 1970 Declaration, see Rosenstock, "The Declaration of Principles of International Law Concerning Friendly Relations," 65 *AJIL* 730 (1971); Arangio-Ruiz, "The Normative Role of the General Assembly of the United Nations and the Declaration of Principles of Friendly Relations," 137 *Recueil des Cours* 565 (1972); Cassese, "The Helsinki Declaration and Self-Determination," in Buergenthal, ed., *Human Rights, International Law, and the Helsinki Accord, supra* note 20, at 88–92.

As for the 1977 Protocol, see Salmon, "Les guerres de libération nationales," in Cassese, ed., *The New Humanitarian Law of Armed Conflict* (1979); Bothe, Ipsen, and Partsch, "Die Genefer Konferenz uber humanitares Volkerrecht. Verlauf und Ergebnisse," 38 *Zeit. für Ausländisches Oefel. R.U. Völkerrecht* 7–10 (1978); Draper, "Wars of National Liberation and War Criminality," In Howard, ed., *Restraint on War* 135 (1979).

66. For this doctrine, see inter alia: Sahovic, "Influence des Etats nouveaux sur la conception du droit international," [1966] *Annuaire Français de Droit International* 39–42; Suković, "Self-determination as a Principle of Co-existence," 34 *V.B. Assoc. Attenders and Alumni of Hague Academy* 175–83 (1964); Bokor-Szegö, *New States and International Law* 11–51 (1970); Tunkin, *Theory of International Law* 60–69 (1974).

67. See *supra* note 63.

68. See the Charter of Economic Rights and Duties of States, Article 2(c); see also the "Declaration on the Establishment of a New International Economic Order," G.A. Res. 3201, 6th Spec. Sess., UN Doc. A/9559 para. 3e (1974).

69. Gross-Espiel, "Self-Determination and Jus Cogens," in Cassese, ed., *United Nations Law, Fundamental Rights: Two Topics in International Law* 167–73 (1979). See also Kiss, in Doehring, *Das Selbestimmungsrecht der Völker* 71, and Münch, *id.* at 90.

70. The Afro-Asian and socialist doctrine of self-determination is indeed the most widespread and is currently reflected in a number of international instruments. I therefore think that the peremptory rule on self-determination cannot but embody that doctrine—which, as I have pointed out, is much narrower than that proclaimed in Article 1 of the Covenant.

71. CCPR/C/SR.69 para. 43.

72. *Ibid.*, para. 28. See also 33 GAOR Supp. 40, UN Doc. A/33/40 para. 188 (1978).

73. CCPR/C/SR.70 paras. 20 and 21.

74. CCPR/C/SR.92 para. 50.

75 CCPR/C/SR.96 para. 18.

76. See *supra* note 63.

77. CCPR/C/SR.117 para. 27.

78. CCPR/C/SR.112 paras. 7–8, and SR.119 paras. 12,64.

79. CCPR/C/SR.128 para. 19.

5. THE RIGHT TO LIFE, PHYSICAL INTEGRITY, AND LIBERTY

1. See also H. Kelsen, *The Law of the United Nations* 791 (1950).

2. Universal Declaration of Human Rights, G.A. Res. 217 (III), UN Doc. A/810 at 71 (1948).

3. European Convention for the Protection of Human Rights and Fundamental Freedoms, 213 *UNTS* 221 (1950).

4. American convention on Human Rights, OAS Doc. OEA/SER.K/XVI/1.1., Doc. 65; text reprinted in 9 *Int'l Leg. Mat.* 673 (1970).

5. See also Garibaldi, "General Limitations on Human Rights: The Principle of legality," 17 *Harv. Int'l L.J.* 503, 550 (1976).

6. On the general problem of the concretization of human rights, see Dinstein, "Human Rights: The Quest for Concretization," 1 *Israel Y.B. Human Rights* 13, 13–14 (1971).

7. See Scheuner, "Comparison of the Jurisprudence of National Courts with that of the Organs of the Convention as regards Other Rights," in A. H. Robertson, ed., *Human Rights in National and International Law* 214, 239 (1968).

8. See Przetacznik, "The Right to Life as a Basic Human Right," 9 *Human Rights J.* 585, 586, 603 (1976).

9. International Covenant on Economic, Social, and Cultural Rights, G.A. Res. 2200, 21 GAOR Supp. 16, UN Doc. A/6316 at 49 (1966).

10. N. Robinson, *The Universal Declaration of Human Rights* 106 (1958).

11. See V. Van Dyke, *Human Rights, the United States, and World Community* 9, 10 (1970).

12. UN Doc. CCPR/C/SR.222 para. 59 (1980).

13. 10 GAOR Annexes, UN Doc. A/2929, ch. VI para. 3 (1955).

14. See the statement made by the British Delegate (Sir Samuel Hoare) in 12 GAOR C. 3 (809th mtg.), UN Doc. A/C.3/SR.809 at 239 (1957).

15. Convention on the Prevention and Punishment of the Crime of Genocide, 78 *UNTS* 277 (1948).

16. UN Doc. A/2929, *supra* note 13, ch. VI para. 6.

17. 12 GAOR C.3 (813th mtg.), UN Doc. A/C.3/SR.813 at 253 (1957).

18. See UN Doc. A/2929, *supra* note 13, ch. VI para. 7.

19. See *ibid.*

20. It is noteworthy that in the 1977 Protocols Additional to the Geneva Conventions of August 12, 1949, it is forbidden to execute the death sentence on "mothers having dependent infants" (Article 76(3) of Protocol I relating to the Protection of Victims of International Armed Conflicts) or "mothers of young children" (Article 6(4) of Protocol II relating to the Protection of Victims of Non-International Armed Conflicts). 72 *AJIL* 457, 492, 502, 505 (1978).

21. See UN Doc. A/2929, *supra* note 13, ch. VI para. 9.

22. See, e.g., 33 GAOR Supp. 40, UN Doc. A/33/40 para. 341 (1978).

23. *Id.* para. 153.

24. UN Doc. CCPR/C/S/CPR.1/Add.3 para. 7 (1980).

25. UN Doc. CCPR/C/SR.200 para. 19 (1980).

26. UN Doc. A/2929, *supra* note 13, at 29.

27. *Id*. at 30.

28. See A. H. Robertson, *Human Rights in the World* 89 (1972).

29. UN Doc. A/33/40, *supra* note 22, para. 303; UN Doc. CCPR/C/SR.221 para. 31 (1980).

30. See Dinstein, "The International Law of Civil Wars and Human Rights," 6 *Israel Y.B. Human Rights* 62, 69 (1976).

31. See J. Fawcett, *The Application of the European Convention on Human Rights* 33 (1969).

32. On the duty of due diligence vis-à-vis foreigners, see Y. Dinstein, *International Claims* 85–88 (1977).

33. UN Doc. A/2929, *supra* note 13 ch. VI para. 4.

34. See Fawcett, *supra* note 31, at 30–31.

35. See Dinstein, "International Criminal Law," 5 *Israel Y.B. Human Rights* 55, 58 (1975).

36. See Dinstein, *supra* note 30, at 62.

37. International Military Tribunal (Nuremberg, 1946), 41 *AJIL* 172, 243 (1947).

38. G. Williams, *The Sanctity of Life and the Criminal Law* 311 (1957).

39. See F. Jacobs, *The European Convention on Human Rights* 22 (1975).

40. Silving, "Euthanasia: A Study in Comparative Criminal Law," 103 *U. Pa. L. Rev.* 350, 369 (1954).

41. UN Doc. CCPR/C/SR.222 para. 6 (1980).

42. See Arnet, "The Criteria for Determining Death in Vital Organ Transplants—A Medico-Legal Dilemma," 38 *Mo. L. Rev.* 220, 234 (1973).

43. See Dinstein, "Science, Technology and Human Rights," 5 *Dalhousie L.J.* 155, 158 (1979).

44. See Williams, *supra* note 38, at 326.

45. In re Karen Quinlan, 70 N.J. 10, 355 A.2d 647 (1976).

46. *Id*. at 672 (per Chief Justice Hughes).

47. See Cantor, "Quinlan, Privacy, and the Handling of Incompetent Dying Patients," 30 *Rutgers L. Rev.* 243, 265–66 (1976–1977).

48. The meaning of the qualifying phrase "in general" is not very clear. See A. Kiss, *Population et Droit de la Vie* 14 (mimeographed text of lectures, Institut International des Droits de l'Homme; Strasbourg, 1974).

49. See 12 GAOR Annexes, UN Doc. A/3764 at 12–13 (1957).

50. The quotation is from the judgment of the Supreme Court of the United States in Roe v. Wade, 410 U.S. 113, 160 (1973) (per Justice Blackmun).

51. See B. Dickens, *Abortion and the Law* 118 (1966).

52. Politically, it is too early to regard the law on this point as settled, but the fact that the phrase "from the moment of conception" was rejected suggests that the Covenant did not recognize a right to life for the fetus at least until it is viable. The European Convention also does not recognize a right to life for a fetus. The Austrian Court, for example, held that laws permitting abortion do not violate the right to life provision of Article 2 of the European Conven-

tion. See 106 *Journal du Droit International* 144 (1979). The American Convention, Article 4, must be seen as exceptional in that it specifically protects life "in general, from the moment of conception." See also Shapiro-Libai, "The Right to Abortion," 5 *Israel Y.B. Human Rights* 120, 139 (1975).

53. Universal Declaration of Human Rights, *supra* note 2.

54. European Convention for the Protection of Human Rights and Fundamental Freedoms, *supra* note 3.

55. American Convention on Human Rights, *supra* note 4.

56. See O'Boyle, "Torture and Emergency Powers under the European Convention on Human Rights: Ireland v. The United Kingdom," 71 *AJIL* 674, 687–88 (1977).

57. Declaration on the Protection of All Persons from Being Subjected to Torture and Other Cruel, Inhuman or Degrading Treatment or Punishment, G.A. Res. 3452, 30 GAOR Supp. 34, UN Doc. A/10034 at 91 (1975).

58. *Ibid.*

59. See UN Doc. A/2929, *supra* note 13, at 31.

60. See Bassiouni and Derby, "An Appraisal of Torture in International Law and Practice: The Need for an International Convention for the Prevention and Suppression of Torture," 48 *Revue Internationale de Droit Pénal* 17, 38–39 (1977).

61. Ireland v. the United Kingdom, 25 *Pub. Eur. Ct. Human Rights,* Ser. A. para. 167 (1978).

62. *Ibid.*

63. The techniques are described *id.* para. 96.

64. *Id.* para. 167.

65. Tyrer case, 26 *Pub. Eur. Ct. Human Rights,* Ser. A. para. 30 (1978).

66. UN Doc. A/2929, *supra* note 13, ch. VI para. 13.

67. See A. H. Robertson, *Human Rights in Europe* 46 (2d ed. 1977).

68. A considerable number of such cases have been reported in the USSR. See H. Berman, *Soviet Criminal Law and Procedure* 88 (2d ed. 1972). Article 5(1) (e) of the European Convention (*supra* note 3) expressly allows the detention of persons of unsound mind. Nevertheless, the European Court held that this provision "cannot be taken as permitting the detention of a person simply because his views or behaviour deviate from the norms prevailing in a particular society." Winterwerp case, judgment of October 24, 1979, *Pub. Eur. Ct. Human Rights,* Ser. A, para. 37.

69. Tyrer case, *supra* note 65, para. 30.

70. *Ibid.*

71. *Id.* para. 31.

72. See E. Cahn, *The Sense of Injustice* 113 (1949).

73. This is the view expressed by Justice Brennan in Furman v. Georgia, 408 U.S. 238, 286, 305 (1972). His view was adopted by the majority in Coker v. Georgia, 433 U.S. 584 (1977), in which the Supreme Court held that the death penalty could not be imposed for a crime which did not involve the taking of or threat to life. Its use to punish the crime of rape was grossly disproportionate, and therefore cruel and unusual. The death penalty is permissible in the

United States for the crime of murder where the statutory criteria adequately channel the exercise of the jury's discretion. Gregg v. Georgia, 428 U.S. 153 (1976). But cf. Lockett v. Ohio, 438 U.S. 586 (1978), in which the Court invalidated a death penalty statute which limited the range of mitigating factors a trial judge was permitted to consider.

74. In re Kemmler, 136 U.S. 436, 447 (1890).

75. Tyrer case, *supra* note 65, para. 32.

76. *Id.* para 35. In Ingraham v. Wright, 430 U.S. 651 (1977), the U.S. Supreme Court held that the Eighth Amendment to the Constitution prohibits only cruel and unusual punishment upon conviction for a crime. It does not apply, therefore, to corporal punishment in public schools, and such punishment may be inflicted without prior trial or hearing.

77. UN Doc. A/2929, *supra* note 13, ch. V para. 14.

78. See J. Katz, *Experimentation with Human Beings* 292 (1972).

79. See the interesting statement made by the Polish Delegate (Ketrzynski) in 13 GAOR C.3 (1852d mtg.), un doc. A/C.3/SR.852 at 88 (1958).

80. *Ibid.*

81. E. Cahn, *Confronting Injustice* 366–67 (1966).

82. See the thoughtful statement made by the British Delegate (Sir Samuel Hoare), 13 GAOR C.3 (851st mtg.), UN Doc. A/C.3/SR.851 at 83 (1958).

83. See Note by the Secretary-General, 13 GAOR Annexes, un doc. A/4045 at 3 (1958).

84. Universal Declaration of Human Rights, *supra* note 2.

85. European Convention for the Protection of Human Rights and Fundamental Freedoms, *supra* note 3.

86. American Convention on Human Rights, *supra* note 4.

87. Slavery Convention, 212 *UNTS* 177 (1926). Text reprinted in *Human Rights Instruments* at 49.

88. Convention (ILO No. 29) concerning Forced or Compulsory Labour, 39 *UNTS* 557 (1930). Text reprinted in *Human Rights Instruments* at 54.

89. Supplementary Convention on the Abolition of Slavery, the Slave Trade, and Institutions and Practices Similar to Slavery, 266 *UNTS* 3 (1956). Text reprinted in *Human Rights Instruments* at 52.

90. Convention (No. 105) concerning the Abolition of Forced Labour, 320 *UNTS* 291 (1957). Text reprinted in *Human Rights Instruments* at 59.

91. UN Doc. A/2929, *supra* note 13, ch. VI para. 18.

92. *Ibid.*

93. *Id.* para. 17.

94. Robinson, *supra* note 10, at 107.

95. See UN Doc. A/2929, *supra* note 13, ch. VI, para. 18.

96. Convention concerning Forced or Compulsory Labour, *supra* note 88.

97. UN Doc. A/2929, *supra* note 13, ch. VI para. 19.

98. *Id.* para. 21.

99. *Id.* para. 22.

100. *Id.* para. 23.

101. Iversen v. Norway, 6 *Y.B. Eur. Conv. Human Rights* 278, 326 (1963).

102. See Berman, *supra* note 68, at 77–81. See also Burford, "Getting the Bugs out of Socialist Legality: The Case of Joseph Brodsky and a Decade of Soviet Anti-Parasitic Legislation," 22 *Am. J. Comp. L* 465, 494–502 (1974).

103. International Covenant on Economic, Social, and Cultural Rights, *supra* note 9.

104. See Scheuner, *supra* note 7, at 243.

105. European Convention for the Protection of Human Rights and Fundamental Freedoms, *supra* note 3.

106. Vagrancy cases (De Wilde, Ooms, and Versyp cases), 12 *Pub. Eur. Ct. Human Rights,* Ser. A para. 68 (1971).

107. *Ibid.*

108. *Id.* paras. 33, 68.

109. European Convention for the Protection of Human Rights and Fundamental Freedoms, *supra* note 3.

110. American Convention on Human Rights, *supra* note 4.

111. Universal Declaration of Human Rights, *supra* note 2.

112. See Garibaldi, *supra* note 5, at 520—22, 549.

113. Golder case, 18 *Pub. Eur. Ct. Human Rights,* Ser. A para. 45 (1975).

114. Sunday Times case, Judgment of 26 April 1979, 18 *Int'l Leg. Mat.* 931 (1979).

115. *Ibid.*

116. *Id.* at 951.

117. *Ibid.*

118. Consistency of Certain Danzig Legislative Decrees with the Constitution of the Free City, 3 *World Court Reports* 516, 529 (1938).

119. *Ibid.*

120. UN Doc. A/2929, *supra* note 13, at 35.

121. *Ibid.*

122. 13 GAOR C.3 (863d mtg.), A/C.3/SR. 863 at 137 (1950).

123. See Robertson, *supra* note 28, at 87. Compare Winterwerp case, *supra* note 68, para. 45.

124. UN Doc. A/2929, *supra* note 13, at 35. See for instance the proposal of the Netherlands enumerating six grounds for deprivation of liberty. 10 GAOR Annexes, UN Doc. A/2910/Add.3 (1955).

125. Winterwerp case, *supra* note 68.

126. See Hassan, "The Word 'Arbitrary' as Used in the Universal Declaration of Human Rights: 'Illegal' or 'Unjust'?" 10 *Harv. Int'l L.J.* 225, 237 (1969).

127. See *id.,* at 241–42.

128. Case of Engel and Others, 22 *Pub. Eur. Ct. Human Rights,* Ser. A at 25 (1976).

129. *Ibid.*

130. UN Doc. A/2929, *supra* note 13, at 35.

131. See C. Morrisson, *The Developing European Law of Human Rights* 117 (1967).

132. Lawless case, 3 *Pub. Eur. Ct. Human Rights,* Ser. A at 51–53 (1961).

133. Schiesser case, judgment of 4 December 1979, *Pub. Eur. Ct. Human Rights,* Ser. A.

134. *Id.* at 8–9.

135. *Id.* at 8.

136. *Id.* at 9.

137. *Ibid.*

138. See F. Castberg, *The European Convention on Human Rights* 98–101 (1974).

139. Wemhoff case, 8 *Pub. Eur. Ct. Human Rights,* Ser. A at 23 (1968).

140. Stögmuller case, 9 *Pub. Eur. Ct. Human Rights,* Ser. A at 40 (1969).

141. Wemhoff case, *supra* note 139, at 24.

142. *Ibid.*

143. *Id.* at 26. On the complexity of the case, *see id.* at 9.

144. Neumeister case, 17 *Pub. Eur. Ct. Human Rights,* Ser. A at 41 (1968).

145. See Harris, "Recent Cases on Pre-Trial Detention and Delay in Criminal Proceedings in the European Court of Human Rights," 44 *Brit. Y.B. Int'l L.* 87, 94–97 (1970).

146. Wemhoff case, *supra* note 139, at 25.

147. Neumeister case, *supra* note 144, at 39.

148. Matznetter case, 10 *Pub. Eur. Ct. Human Rights,* Ser. A at 32–34 (1969).

149. Wemhoff case, *supra* note 139, at 25.

150. Stögmuller case, *supra* note 140, at 44.

151. Ringeisen case, 13 *Pub. Eur. Ct. Human Rights,* Ser. A at 43 (1971).

152. UN Doc. A/2929, *supra* note 13, at 36.

153. Daintith and Wilkinson, "Bail and the Convention: British Reflections on the Wemhoff and Neumeister Cases," 18 *Am. J. Comp. L.* 326, 337)1970).

154. Douglas, "The Bill of Rights is Not Enough," in E. Cahn, ed., *The Great Rights* 115, 156–57 (1963).

155. *Id.* at 157.

156. Neumeister case, *supra* note 144, at 40.

157. *Ibid.*

158. *Ibid.*

159. Vagrancy cases, *supra* note 106, at 40.

160. *Ibid.*

161. *Id.* at 40–41.

162. *Id.* ut 41.

163. Winterwerp case, *supra* note 68, para 60.

164. See UN Doc. A/2929, *supra* note 13, at 35.

165. See Castberg, *supra* note 138, at 105–6.

166. UN Doc. A/2929, *supra* note 13, at 35–36.

167. Protocol No. 4 to the Convention for the Protection of Human Rights and Fundamental Freedoms, Securing Certain Rights and Freedoms other Than Those Already Included in the Convention and in the First Protocol Thereto, II *European Conventions and Agreements* 109, 110 (1963), also found at

Council of Europe, *European Convention on Human Rights: Collected Texts* 129, 130 (1979).

168. American Convention on Human Rights, *supra* note 4.
169. UN Doc. A/2929, *supra* note 13, ut 37.
170. See Robertson, *supra* note 67, at 131.
171. See Jacobs, *supra* note 39, at 183.
172. See UN Doc. A/2929, *supra* note 13, at 37.
173. *Ibid.*
174. *Ibid.*

6. DUE PROCESS OF LAW FOR PERSONS ACCUSED OF CRIME

1. J. Holt, *Magna Carta and the Idea of Liberty* (1972).
2. E. Grisworld, *The Fifth Amendment Today* 34 (1955).

The significance of both terms was procedural; the due process concept originally operated simply to place certain procedures, especially the grand jury and petit jury process, beyond the reach of the legislative process. Today the concept of "due process of law" performs a dual function. It consecrates certain procedures that must be followed and respected, particularly in the application of the criminal law, and in some legal systems, e.g., that of the United States, it also suggests substantive limitations on the powers of the state.

3. International Shoe Co. v. Washington, 326 U.S. 310, 316 (1945).
4. Twining v. New Jersey, 211 U.S. 78, 102 (1908).
5. Hurtado v. California, 110 U.S. 516, 536 (1884).
6. While my purpose is to examine the meaning of the provisions of the Covenant, reference is made also to the case law arising out of the application of the European Convention on Human Rights, since its provisions are almost identical with those of the Covenant.

For discussion of the European Convention provisions and cases, see A. H. Robertson, *Human Rights in Europe* (1977); F. G. Jacobs, *The European convention on Human Rights* (1975); J. E. S. Fawcett, *The Application of the European Convention on Human Rights* (1969); G. L. Weil, *The European Convention on Human Rights* (1962).

7. Members of the Human Rights Committee interpreted Article 9 as applying not only to detention pending criminal prosecution but also to administrative detention, for example the holding of mental patients, vagrants, juvenile delinquents, and persons held for extradition or expulsion. Un Doc. CCPR/C/SR.228 para. 4 (1980).

8. Appl. No. 343/57, 2 *Y.B. Eur. Conv. Human Rights* 412, 462 (1959).
9. Appl. No. 1211/61, 5 *Y.B. Eur. Conv. Human Rights* 224, 228 (1962).
10. See Appl. No. 2621/65, 9 *Y.B. Eur. Conv. Human Rights* 474, 480 (1966); Appl. No. 4220/69, 14 *Y.B. Eur. Conv. Human Rights* 250, 276–77 (1971).
11. Appl. No. 1216/61, Eur. Comm. Human Rights, 11 *Collection of Decisions* 1, 5 (1963).
12. 33 GAOR Supp. 40, UN Doc. A/33/40 para. 474 (1978).

13. Appl. No. 297/57, 2 *Y.B. Eur. Conv. Human Rights* 204, 210–11 (1958).

14. Appl. No. 530/59, Eur. Comm. Human Rights, 2 *Collection of Decisions* 530/59 at 4 (1959).

15. UN Doc. A/33/40, *supra* note 12, para. 269. For discussion of pretrial detention, see S. Grosz, McNutty, and Duffy, "Pre-trial Detention in Western Europe," 23 *ICJ Rev.* 35 (1979).

16. UN Doc. CCPR/C/X/CRP.1/Add. 6 para. 10 (1980).

17. Stögmuller case, 12 *Y.B. Eur. Conv. Human Rights* 364, 394 (1969).

18. Wemhoff case, 11 *Y.B. Eur. Conv. Human Rights* 796, 806 (1968).

19. Neumeister case, 11 *Y.B. Eur. Conv. Human Rights* 812, 820 (1968).

20. Matznetter case, 12 *Y.B. Eur. Conv. Human Rights* 406, 428 (1969).

21. Ringeisen case, 14 *Y.B. Eur. Conv. Human Rights* 838, 858–60 (1971).

22. See, e.g., Wemhoff case, *supra* note 18.

23. See, e.g., Ringeisen case, *supra* note 21, at 858.

24. Wemhoff case, *supra* note 18, at 806.

25. Neumeister case, *supra* note 19, at 822.

26. Wemhoff case, *supra* note 18, at 808.

27. *Id.* at 804.

28. Appl. No. 892/60, 4 *Y.B. Eur. Conv. Human Rights* 240, 252 (1961).

29. Vagrancy cases (DeWilde, Odoms, and Versyp cases), 14 *Y.B. Eur. Conv. Human Rights* 788, 824–86 (1971). Similarly, in the second Vagrancy cases the Committee of Ministers also decided there was a violation on the same grounds. 15 *Y.B. Eur. Conv. Human Rights* 694 (1972).

30. 10 GAOR Annexes, UN Doc. A/2929 para. 36 (1955).

31. In certain countries the right to compensation against the individual official is available in cases of malicious or grossly negligent conduct. The United States unsuccessfully moved to restrict the right to compensation to cases of malice. See comments by the U.S. and Egypt, UN Doc. E/CN.4/SR.148 (1950). The right to compensation has been rarely invoked under the European Convention. See Robertson, *supra* note 6, at 59.

32. See also Appl. No. 89/55, Eur. Comm. Human Rights [1955–57] *Documents and Decisions* 226.

33. 34 GAOR Supp. 40, UN Doc. A/34/40 para. 430 (1979); UN Doc. CCPR/C/X/CRP.1/Add. 3 para. 41 (1980).

34. For a general discussion of the right to a fair trial as a human right at the international level and a comparison of the guarantees provided in the Covenant, the European Convention, and the American Convention on Human Rights, see Harris, "The Right to a Fair Trial in Criminal Proceedings as a Human Right," 16 *Int'l Comp. L.Q.* 352 (1967).

35. Jacobs, *supra* note 6, at 107–8.

36. Neumeister case, 5 *Pub. Eur. Ct. Human Rights,* Ser. B, at 81 (1969).

37. Neumeister cases, *supra* note 19, at 824.

38. Wemhoff case, *supra* note 18, at 810.

39. Jacobs, *supra* note 6, at 108.

40. Delcourt case, 13 *Y.B. Eur. Conv. Human Rights* 1100 (1970).

41. Pataki and Dunshirn cases, 6 *Y.B. Eur. Conv. Human Rights* 714 (1963).

42. *Id.* at 730–32.

43. Ofner and Hopfinger cases, 6 *Y.B. Eur. Conv. Human Rights* 676 (1963).

44. *Id.* at 696–704.

45. Delcourt case, *supra* note 40.

46. *Id.* at 1128–30.

47. UN Doc. A/2929, *supra* note 30, para. 77.

48. 14 GAOR Annexes, UN Doc. A/4299 para. 52 (1959).

49. See the comments of France in 14 GAOR C.3 (964th mtg.), UN Doc. A/C.3/SR.964 para. 17 (1959).

50. Boeckman's case, 6 *Y.B. Eur. Conv. Human Rights* 370 (1963), on the admissibility of this application.

51. Boeckman's case, 8 *Y.B. Eur. Conv. Human Rights* 410, 422 (1965).

52. APPL. No. 3860/68, Eur. Comm. Human Rights, 30 *Collection of Decisions* 70 (1969).

53. *Id.* at 74–75.

54. Nielsen case, 4 *Y.B. Eur. Conv. Human Rights* 490 (1961).

55. *Id.* at 568.

56. Appl. No. 788/60, 4 *Y.B. Eur. Conv. Human Rights* 116 (1961).

57. *Id.* at 128. This part of the application, however, was declared inadmissible on the grounds of nonexhaustion of domestic remedies, as the accused had not applied for a change of venue.

58. UN Doc. A/33/40, *supra* note 12, paras. 307, 345, 530.

59. See Pfunders Case, 6 *Y.B. Eur. Conv. Human Rights* 470, 482–84 (1963).

60. A proposal to add the words "beyond a reasonable doubt" after "guilty" was rejected as unnecessary. See the debate, UN Doc. E/CN.4/SR.156 at 6–10, esp. para. 44 (1950).

61. See Jacobs, *supra* note 6, at 113.

62. See Pfunders case, *supra* note 59.

63. UN Doc. CCPR/C/SR.214 para. 87 (1980).

64. UN Doc. A/33/40, *supra* note 12, para. 126.

65. Appl. No. 2343/64, 10 *Y.B. Eur. Conv. Human Rights* 176 (1967).

66. *Id.* at 182.

67. Appl. No. 2518/65, 8 *Y.B. Eur. Conv. Human Rights* 370, 372 (1965).

68. *Ibid.*

69. See Pfunders case, *supra* note 59, at 790, interpreting the European Convention this way.

70. Appl. No. 524/59, 3 *Y.B. Eur. Conv. Human Rights* 322, 344 (1960).

71. Appl. No. 441/58, 2 *Y.B. Eur. Conv. Human Rights* 391 (1959).

72. *Ibid.*

73. UN Doc. A/34/40, *supra* note 33, para. 33.

74. See generally the Wemhoff case, *supra* note 18; the Neumeister case, *supra* note 19; the Delcourt case, *supra* note 40.

75. It was pointed out in the Commission on Human Rights that under Islamic law and in cases judged according to native tribal law and custom, the right to insist upon the assistance of a lawyer might give rise to difficulties.

UN DOC. E/CN.4/SR.107 at 6 (1949). The same point was also made at the 1958 Seminar on the Protection of Human Rights in Criminal Law and Procedure, Baguio City, UN Doc. ST/TAA/HR/2 at 16 (1958).

76. 110 *Recueil des Cours* 63 (1963). A member of the Human Rights Committee has stated that the right of the accused to attend the hearing of his case also applies to juveniles. UN Doc. CCPR/C/SR.222 para. 53 (1980).

77. 103 *Recueil des Cours* 1, 60 (1961).

78. X v. Belgium, 6 *Y.B. Eur. Conv. Human Rights* 150 (1963); X v. Austria, 6 *Y.B. Eur. Conv. Human Rights* 252 (1963).

79. X v. Federal Republic of Germany, 5 *Y.B. Eur. Conv. Human Rights* 104, 106 (1962).

80. Koplinger v. Austria, 12 *Y.B. Eur. Conv. Human Rights* 438, 488 (1969).

81. *Ibid.*

82. Pfunders case, *supra* note 59.

83. AGE Bremerhaven, 5 *Y.B. Eur. Conv. Human Rights* 362 (1962).

84. See Jacobs, *supra* note 6.

85. Compare Griffin v. California, 380 U.S. 609 (1965); Wilson v. U.S., 149 U.S. 60 (1893).

86. See Griswold, *supra* note 2.

87. UN Doc. E/CN.4/SR.167 at 16 (1950).

88. Compare In re Gault, 387 U.S.1 (1967).

89. UN Doc. E/CN.4/SR.167 at 16, 17 (1950).

90. See UN Doc. A/4299, *supra* note 48, para. 61.

91. See J. Hall, *General Principles of Criminal Law,* ch. 9 (2d ed. 1947); F. Pakenham and L. Longford, in Chapman, ed. *The Idea of Punishment* (1968); W. Moberley, *The Ethics of Punishment* (1968); H. Packer, *The Limits of the Criminal Sanction* 1968).

92. See Moberley, *supra* note 91, at 144.

93. See generally Pakenham and Longford, *supra* note 91, at 24.

94. See F. Sutherland and P. Crossey, *Criminology* 311 (10th ed. 1978); Mecafferty, "Major Trends in the Use of Capital Punishment," 25 *Federal Probation* 15–21 (1961). For bibliographies on capital punishment, see J. Mecafferty, ed., *Capital Punishment* (1973); T. Sellen, ed., *Capital Punishment* (1967).

95. UN Doc. A/2929, *supra* note 30, para. 5.

96. See Prohibition against Retroactive Application of Criminal Law, this essay.

97. G.A. Res. 260 (III), UN Doc. A/810 at 174 (1948).

98. See comments of Australia, 10 GAOR Annexes, UN Doc. A/2910/Add. 2 at 11 (1955); 12 GAOR Annexes, UN Doc. A/3764/Add. 1 para. 117 (1957).

99. UN Doc. A/2929, *supra* note 30, para. 9.

100. The Constitution of the United States confers the pardon power on the President, and state constitutions confer it on the governors.

101. Commutation may also be ordered by the sentencing court.

102. Holdsworth, *History of English Law* 473 (1924).

103. Article 8 (3b).

104. ILO, International Convention concerning Forced or Compulsory Labour (1930).

105. The European Commission has examined under Article 3 of the Convention many cases in which the applicant complained of his imminent extradition or expulsion by one of the parties to the Convention. See Jacobs, *supra* note 6, at 31–32; Fawcett, *supra* note 6, at 38–40.

106. Jacobs, *supra* note 6, at 30–31.

107. UN Doc. A/2929, *supra* note 30, para. 12.

108. G.A. Res. 3452, 30 GAOR Supp. 34, UN Doc. A/10034 at 91 (1975). See Standard Minimum Rules for the Treatment of Prisoners, adopted in 1955 by the First United Nations Congress on the Prevention of Crime and Treatment of Offenders and approved by the Economic and Social Council in 1957. 24 ESCOR Annexes, UN Doc. E/3035 (1957).

109. Appl. Nos. 5175/56 and 299/57, 2 *Y.B. Eur. Conv. Human Rights* 174, 196 (1959). In the second application, it was alleged that the British government was responsible for 49 cases of torture and maltreatment amounting to torture. As a political settlement was reached, the proceedings were dropped.

110. Ireland v. United Kingdom, 19 *Y.B. Eur. Conv. Human Rights* 512, 794 (1976).

111. X and Y v. United Kingdom, 17 *Y.B. Eur. Conv. Human Rights* 356, 370 (1974).

112. Appl. No. 462/59, 2 *Y.B. Eur. Conv. Human Rights* 382, 385 (1959).

113. De Courcy v. United Kingdom, 10 *Y.B. Eur. Conv. Human Rights* 382 (1967).

114. Kornmann v. Federal Republic of Germany, 11 *Y.B. Eur. Conv. Human Rights* 1020 (1968).

115. UN Doc A/33/40, *supra* note 12, paras. 233, 242, 374.

116. See, e.g., English Bill of Rights; U.S. Const. Amend. VIII.

117. 217 U.S. 349 (1910).

118. In Robinson v. California, 370 U.S. 660 (1962), the U.S. Supreme Court observed that the due process clause of the Fourteenth Amendment applied the cruel and unusual punishment provision of the Eighth Amendment to the states.

119. Coker v. Georgia 433 U.S. 584 (1977).

120. 1 A.E.R. 633, 641 (1966). *See* Fawcett, *supra* note 6, at 35–36.

121. N.J.W. 967 (1962). See Fawcett, *supra* note 6, at 36.

122. 408 U.S. 238 (1972).

123. 6 Cal.2d 628; 100 Cal. Rptr. 152 (1972).

124. 408 U.S. 238 (1972). For fuller discussion, see L. Derkson, *The Concept of Cruel and Unusual Punishment* 43–54 (1975).

125. In Lockett v. Ohio, 438 U.S. 586 (1978), the Supreme Court struck down Ohio's death penalty statute because it did not allow consideration of mitigating factors. As of 1980, 36 states and 2 federal jurisdictions had death penalty laws.

126. According to the Report of the Secretary-General, 21 member nations

had abolished capital punishment by law, 17 had retained it for exceptional crimes only (i.e., those subject to military law and/or committed in exceptional circumstances), 107 had retained the death penalty, and 2 nations had divided jurisdictions in which some, but not all, of the states imposed the death penalty. UN Doc. E/1980/9 (1980).

127. 34 GAOR Supp. 40, UN Doc. A/34/40 para. 153 (1979); UN Doc. CCPR/C/SR.200 para. 19 (1979).$

128. UN Doc. A/2929, *supra* note 30, para. 94.

129. *Id.* para. 95.

130. 15 GAOR Annexes, UN Doc. A/4397 para. 97 (1960).

7. THE FREEDOM OF MOVEMENT

1. See, e.g., the constitutions cited in notes 16 and 21 *infra*.

2. G.A. Res. 217 (III), UN Doc. A/811 Article 13 (1948).

3. 660 UNTS 195 (1969).

4. Fourth Protocol. 213 *UNTS* 221 (1968).

5. OAS Doc. OEA/Ser.K/XVI/1-1, D. 70; text reprinted at 9 *Int'l Leg. Mat.* 123 (1970).

6. Dialogue with Crito as reported by Plato.

7. See Aybay, "The Right to Leave and the Right to Return," 1 *Comp. L. Y.B.* 121, 130 n.4 (1977).

8. Inglès, "Study of Discrimination in Respect of the Right of Everyone to Leave Any Country, Including His Own, And To Return to His Country" UN Doc. E/CN.4/Sub.2/229/Rev. 1 (1963).

9. See, e.g., Vattel, *Law of Nations or the Principles of Natural Law,* vol. 3 (1758 ed., trans. by Fenwick 1916).

10. See, e.g., Beccaria, *Dei delitti e delle pene* (1764).

11. Reale, "Les problèmes des passports," 4 *Recueil des Cours* 97 (1934).

12. Blackstone, *Commentaries,* Book 1, ch. 1 at 125 (Lewis ed., 1900).

13. Story, *Commentaries on the Constitution of the United States,* vol. 3 at 3 (2d ed. 1851); Kent, *Commentaries on American Law,* vol. 2 at 10 (7th ed. 1851).

14. Reale, "The Passport Question," 9 *Foreign Affairs* 506 (1931).

15. Act of July 27, 1868, 15 Stat. 223; Rev. Statutes §§ 1999, 2000, 2001 (current version at 8 U.S.C. §1481, 22 U.S.C. §§ 1731, 1732). See 3 Moore, *Int'l L. Digest* § 440 (1906).

16. See, e.g., Austrian Kremsler Constitution of 1849, Article 8; Costa Rican Constitution of December 1871, Article 28; Constitution of El Salvador, August 1886, Title II, part 13.

17. *Traité de droit international,* vol. 2 at 247 (1886).

18. *Ibid.* See also Bluntschli, *Das Moderne Völkerrecht der civilisirten Staaten* 216 (1872); Praidiere-Fodere, *Traité de droit international public européen et américain,* vol. 1 at 243 (1885); Calvo, *Droit international* 23 (3d ed. 1880); Bonfils, *Manuel de Droit des Gens* 237 (5th ed. 1908).

19. See 16 *Annuaire de l'Institut de Droit International* 53 (1897); text of draft

convention is reprinted in English in Scott, ed., *Resolutions of the Institute of International Law* 137 (1916).

20. 16 *Annuaire* 242 (1897).

21. See, e.g., German Constitution of 1919, Article 112; Finnish Constitution of 1919, Article 7.

22. G.A. Res. 217, *supra* note 2.

23. G.A. Res. 2200, 21 GAOR Supp. 16, UN Doc. A/6316 (1966), entered into force March 23, 1976.

24. 10 GAOR Annexes, UN Doc. A/2929 at 38 (1955).

25. *Ibid.*

26. 7 ESCOR Supp. 2, UN Doc. E/800 Annex B, Art. 11 (1948).

27. 18 ESCOR Supp. 7, UN Docs. E/2573; E/CN.4/705 Annex I at 67 (1954).

28. 14 GAOR C.3 (954th–969th mtgs.), UN Docs. A/C.3/954–A/C.3/969 (1954).

29. *Ibid.* See also 14 GAOR Annexes, UN Doc. A/4299 paras. 14–16 (1959).

30. 14 GAOR C.3 (956th mtg.), UN Doc. A/C.3/956 para. 25 (1959).

31. UN Doc. A/2929, *supra* note 24, para. 54.

32. *Id.* para. 57.

33. See UN Doc. E/800, *supra* note 26. See also the records of discussion cited in UN Doc. A/2929, *supra* note 24, at 39.

34. See UN Doc. E/800, *supra* note 26; also UN Doc. A/2929, *supra* note 24.

35. *Id.* para. 53.

36. *Ibid.*

37. See UN Doc. E/800, *supra* note 26.

38. See G.A. Res. 217, *supra* note 2, Art. 17.

39. UN Doc. A/2929, *supra* note 24, para. 54.

40. During the Second World War, persons of Japanese ancestry in the United States, among them native-born U.S. citizens, were subjected to special residence restrictions, including curfews, detention in relocation centers and exclusion from the West Coast area. The Supreme Court upheld the restriction in Korematsu v. United States, 323 U.S. 214 (1944), accepting that "the circumstances of direct emergency and peril" made internment "a military imperative."

41. A state may, and is perhaps required to, prevent private discrimination excluding persons from housing on account of race. See essay 10, note 58 and essay 3 *supra,* note 18. Compare Shelley v. Kraemer, 334 U.S. 1 (1948); Jones v. Alfred H. Mayer Co., 392 U.S. 409 (1968).

42. UN Doc. A/2929, *supra* note 24, para. 53. See also UN Doc. E/800, *supra* note 26.

43. UN Doc. A/2929, *supra* note 24, para. 50.

44. In Kent v. Dulles, 357 U.S. 116 (1958), the U.S. Supreme Court held that "the right to travel abroad is a part of the liberty of which the citizen cannot be deprived without due process," and prohibited the Secretary of State to deny a passport on the basis of beliefs and associations. See Aptheker v. Secre-

tary of State, 378 U.S. 500 (1964). But in Zemel v. Rusk, 381 U.S. 1 (1965), the Court upheld the State Department's authority to refuse to issue a passport valid for travel to Cuba.

45. The Supreme Court of the United States has struck down various impediments to permanent residence abroad. In Schneider v. Rusk, 377 U.S. 163 (1964), the Court overturned a law rescinding the citizenship of naturalized citizens who resumed residence in their former country. Afroyim v. Rusk, 387 U.S. 253 (1967), held that U.S. citizenship could be withdrawn only with the person's consent, and denied Congress the power to withdraw citizenship from persons voting in foreign elections. As regards citizenship conferred by statute on children born abroad to a U.S. citizen, however, the Supreme Court approved a law which terminates such citizenship if certain residency requirements are not met. Rogers v. Bellei, 401 U.S. 815 (1971).

46. UN Doc. A/2929, *supra* note 24, para. 53. See also UN Doc. E/800, *supra* note 26.

47. UN Doc. A/2929, *supra* note 24, para. 53.

48. In the Human Rights Committee, a "repatriation deposit," required of all seeking to leave the country to be paid into the treasury, was criticized as overly restrictive on the freedom of movement and violative of Article 12.

49. UN Doc. A/2929, *supra* note 24, para. 60.

50. See European Convention on Human Rights, *supra* note 4, Art. 3(2).

51. See American Convention on Human Rights, *supra* note 5, Art. 22(5).

52. UN Doc. A/4299, *supra* note 29, para. 17.

53. UN Doc. A/2929, *supra* note 24, para. 57.

54. See essay 12.

55. UN Doc. A/2929, *supra* note 24, at 38.

56. *Id.* paras. 58–59.

57. See European Convention, *supra* note 4, Art. 3(2).

58. See American Convention, *supra* note 5, Art. 22(5).

59. UN Doc. A/4299, *supra* note 29, para. 17.

60. European Convention, *supra* note 4, Art. 3(1).

61. American Convention, *supra* note 5, Art. 22(5).

62. See Universal Declaration, *supra* note 2, Art. 15.

63. American Convention, *supra* note 5, Art. 20.

64. F. Jacobs, *European Convention on Human Rights* 186 (1975).

65. See American Convention, *supra* note 5, Art. 22(9).

66. See European Convention, *supra* note 4, Arts. 3(1), 4.

67. UN Doc. A/2929, *supra* note 24, paras. 63–64.

68. 189 *UNTS* 150 (1951); text reproduced in *Human Rights Instruments* at 86.

8. LEGAL PERSONALITY, PRIVACY, AND THE FAMILY

1. The Covenant deals with human rights: the rights of rational, physical persons, not of corporations, associations, or other legal persons. The Third

Committee unanimously approved changing "each person" to "each human being" to prevent Article 16 from being applied to companies. But inexplicably, the subcommittee amended the English text to read "everyone" (and the French version to *chacun*). The Spanish text retains the less ambiguous *todo ser humano*.

2. "Hominis appellatione tam feminam, cuam masculum contineri, non dubitator." (No doubt the word "man" includes the female as well as the male.)

3. In other articles, different terms are used, e.g., "each child," "all citizens," and "each individual." By using "everyone," the drafters emphasized the universal applicability of Article 16.

4. M. Planiol and G. Ripert, *Traité Pratique de Droit Civil Français* 10–11 (2d ed. 1952). The idea is contained in the adage "infans conceptus pro nato habetur quoties de commodis ejus agitur." Article 13 of the Civil Code of Costa Rica incorporates the doctrine: "The existence of a physical person commences at live birth and such person is considered already born for all purposes favorable to him for a period of 300 days preceding his birth." See also Section 9 of the American Convention on Human Rights, which protects the right to life "from conception."

5. Bidart calls it the legally relevant freedom: "a freedom capable of producing legal effects, that is to say, a juridical freedom." G. Bidart, *Derecho Constitucional; Realidad, Normatividad y Justicia en el Derecho Constitutional,* vol. 2 at 136–38 (1966).

6. *Id.* at 134.

7. Article 28 of the Constitution of Costa Rica is typical of the "zone of privacy" protection afforded by Latin American countries: "those private actions which do not disturb the moral or public order, or which are not prejudicial to third parties, are beyond the scope of the law." Compare Articles 4 and 5 of the French Declaration of the Rights of Man and of the Citizen.

8. "Person" and "legal personality" are sometimes used interchangeably. Planiel and Ripert, *supra* note 4, at 7. Marquiset, after affirming that "the human being is a subject of law and, as such, is capable of holding rights as well as obligations," adds: "personality could be defined as man's capacity to play a role in the life of the law, to be subject to legal rights and obligations." J. Marquiset, *Les Droits Naturels* 5 (1961). The terms are also linked etymologically. Capitant defines "person" as "from the latin *persona,* literally 'theater mask'; it connotes recognition of capacity to be the subject of law." H. Capitant, *Vocabulaire Juridique* 374 (1930). He then defines personality as "the ability to be a subject of law." *Id.* at 375.

9. P. Vinogradoff, *Introducción al Derecho* 47 (1967).

10. Planiol and Ripert, *supra* note 4, at 12. "Civil death has been replaced by civic degradation or legal incapacity."

11. For example, Article 8 of the Covenant prohibits slavery. The Constitution of Costa Rica commences its chapter on individual rights with a rousing condemnation of slavery and endorsement of freedom.

12. 15 GAOR Annexes, UN Doc. A/4625 para. 25 (1960). The Article was adopted without a dissenting vote.

13. 10 GAOR Annexes, UN Doc. A/2929, ch. VI para. 97 (1955). The initial draft read, "no person shall be deprived of his juridical personality." It was not adopted because " 'deprivation of juridical personality' did not have a well-defined meaning in some systems of law." *Id.* para. 98. In my view, the original version would have given greater vigor to Article 16 because the right to legal recognition implies the capacity to assert one's rights before tribunals of justice.

14. *Ibid.*

15. A. Verdoodt, *Naissance et Signification de la Déclaration Universelle des Droits de L'Homme* 108 (1964).

16. N. Robinson, *The Universal Declaration of Human Rights* 109 (1958).

17. UN Doc. A/2929, *supra* note 13, ch. VI para. 149.

18. UN Doc. A/4625, *supra* note 12, para. 25. Article 16 is based upon Article 6 of the Universal Declaration of Human Rights. UN Doc. A/2929, *supra* note 13, ch. VI para. 97.

19. M. Duverger, *Droit Constitutionnel et Institutions Politiques* 202 (4th ed. 1959).

20. There were several attempts to add "no one" by amendment to other paragraphs of the Article. For example, the United Kingdom proposed that paragraph 2 read in part: "no one shall be subject to unlawful attacks on his honor and reputation." None of these amendments was adopted.

21. UN Doc. A/4625, *supra* note 12, para. 36. The debate was not only extensive but also confusing. One delegate declared that "arbitrary" is procedural while "unlawful" is substantive; he added, "to act in an arbitrary manner [means] to act unreasonably where reasonable behavior [is] required."

22. 13 GAOR Annexes, UN Doc. A/4045 para. 46 (1958).

23. *Id.* para. 49.

24. L. Legaz, *Filosofía del Derecho* 630 (1979). According to Legaz, "arbitrariness is the negation of the law by the power which is supposed to be its custodian." He feels that law is negated when either its fundamental principles or form are disregarded, but only disregard of the latter exemplifies "arbitrariness." In that sense, the alteration of settled procedure by the state is antilegal conduct.

25. *Id.* at 639.

26. UN Doc. A/2929, *supra* note 13, ch. VI para. 100.

27. *Id.* para. 102.

28. M. Urabayen, *Vida Privada e Información* 11 (1977). Urubayen defines intimacy as "those cases which transgress the natural reserve of sexual relations or which violate personal modesty, or the revelation of sentimental manifestations towards another person." He defines privacy more broadly to include facts that for any reason "we would not like to have publicly divulged."

29. International Commission of Jurists, *The Rule of Law and Human Rights: Principles and Definitions* 63–64 (1967).

30. E. Novoa, *Derecho a la Vida Privada y la Libertad de Información, un Conflicto de Derechos* 45–46 (1977). In another part of his work, Novoa adds "tranquility or quietude" to the list. *Id.* at 46.

31. Prosser, "Privacy," 48 *Calif. L. Rev.* 383, 389 (1960). In the United States, the right to privacy includes the right of a pregnant woman to decide whether or not to terminate (abort) her pregnancy. Roe v. Wade, 410 U.S. 113 (1973). Only a compelling state interest, such as the health of the mother, may impinge on that right (by requiring a physician's approval, proper medical facilities, etc.). In Carey v. Population Services International, 431 U.S. 678 (1977), the Court struck down a number of restrictions on the distribution of contraceptives and their use by minors as violative of the right to privacy.

32. 34 GAOR Supp. 40, UN Doc. A/34/40 paras. 411, 434 (1979).

33. 33 GAOR Supp. 40, UN Doc. A/33/40 para. 348 (1978).

34. *Id.* para. 239.

35. C. Colliard, *Libertés Publiques* 293 (1972). Colliard states that "it is because the home constitutes the refuge of the family and of private life that its protection appears to be a natural consequence of the protection of the individual." A study by the International Committee of Jurists found that "until recent times, the private life of the individual was primarily what he did in the intimacy of his home, the walls of his house constituting as it were the boundary between his public and his private life." International Commission of Jurists, "The Protection of Privacy," 24 *Int'l Social Science J.* (no. 3) at 418 (1972).

36. P. Biscarretti, *Diritto Constituzionale* 727 (11th ed. 1977). Biscarretti defines the home as "any place where one has established his own habitation, where his own work is carried on, and in addition, the office, the store, one's room hallway, houseboat, etc." Capitant prefers a more narrow definition: "the place where a person has his principal establishment or the center of his interests." Capitant, *supra* note 8, at 203. Biscarretti's view is preferred by most modern authors.

37. Colliard believes that "the great principle which rules over the entire subject of letters is none other than the inviolability of correspondence . . . which appears as a transposition of a moral rule that condemns those who penetrate into the secrets of others." Colliard, *supra* note 35, at 304.

38. This is so despite the narrow meaning occasionally given to the word "correspondence" in Spanish, English, and French. Legal scholars concur with the broader reading. For example, some state that every citizen "may correspond with third parties, whether by letter or other means (telephone or telegraphic communications)." J. Auby and R. Ducos-Ader, *Droit Public* 150 (3d ed. 1967). Vasak is of the same opinion: "Correspondence should obviously include every means of communication, such as the telephone, telegraph, etc." K. Vasak, *Les Dimensions Internationales des Droits de l'Homme* 178 (1978).

39. 394 U.S. 557 (1969).

40. *Id.* at 565.

41. UN Doc. A/4625, *supra* note 12, para. 38.

42. Verdoodt, *supra* note 15, at 138–43.

43. Rather it is "the sentiment which animates man . . . and the principles which serve as norms for his actions." S. Gili, *Diccionario de Sinónimos* (1965). Casares adds that honor "is the quality which propels man to adjust his conduct

to the highest moral standards." J. Casares, *Diccionario Ideológico de la Lengua Española* (1959).

44. E. Cuello, *Derecho Penal,* vol. 2 at 579 (1943).

45. The English text permits a distinction between "honor" and "reputation." The Spanish text, however, considers the two synonymous. The American Convention on Human Rights gives "honor" and "reputation" distinct meanings, but with the implicit intent that the Spanish *honra* equal the English word "honor." To avoid confusion, Article 17 of the Covenant should also be so interpreted.

46. In Spanish, attack is synonymous with assault. In English, it may also mean a verbal assault.

47. Robinson, *supra* note 16, at 117–18. Robinson explains that an effort to reconcile the French and English texts caused the omission.

48. UN Doc. A/2929, *supra* note 13, para. 99. "The insertion of 'unlawful' before 'attacks' was intended to meet the objection that, unless qualified, the clause might be construed in such a way as to stifle free expression of public opinion." *Id.* para. 103.

49. In the United States, an official or public personality may recover damages for a defamatory statement only when made with "actual malice, i.e., with knowledge or with reckless disregard" of its falsity. New York Times v. Sullivan, 376 U.S. 254 (1964); Associated Press v. Walker, 388 U.S. 130 (1967). A private individual—who has not voluntarily become a public figure—need only prove negligence as to the statement's accuracy. Gertz v. Robert Welch, Inc., 418 U.S. 323 (1974); Time Inc. v. Firestone, 424 U.S. 448 (1976); Hutchinson v. Proxmire, 443 U.S. 111 (1979); Wolston v. Readers Digest Ass'n., Inc., 443 U.S. 157 (1979). Earlier, it was also held that a plaintiff must show knowing or reckless falsehood to recover for a false-light portrayal of his personal life. Time, Inc. v. Hill, 385 U.S. 374 (1967).

50. Verdoodt, *supra* note 5, at 162–70.

51. H. Schoeck, *Diccionario de Sociología* 309 (1973).

52. Article 16 proclaims the obligation of the state, and all groups within the state or beyond its borders, to protect the family.

53. Legaz defines the family as one of "the natural units of life and basic forms of cohabitation having roots in human nature itself" to which the law gives character and life. Legaz, *supra* note 24, at 756–57.

54. In Moore v. City of East Cleveland, 431 U.S. 494 (1977), the Supreme Court upheld the right of a grandmother and her grandchildren by different marriages to live together as an "extended family" and invalidated a zoning ordinance that prohibited it. Compare Village of Belle Terre v. Boraas, 416 U.S. 1 (1974).

55. Robinson, *supra* note 16, at 127.

56. Article 23 seems to expand the permissible age restrictions on marriage accepted in the Universal Declaration. The Declaration speaks of "full age" and has been interpreted as permitting states to require parties contracting marriage to have the ability to procreate; Article 23 speaks of "marriageable age" and

allows states to establish a legal age of majority as well as requiring physical maturity. UN Doc. 4/2929, *supra* note 13, ch. VI para 168.

57. In Zablocki v. Redhail, 434 U.S. 374 (1978), the U.S. Supreme Court invalidated, as an impermissible restraint on marriage, a statute which required court approval before a person with child support obligations could marry. The Court stated, "the right to marry is part of the fundamental right to privacy implicit in the . . . Due Process Clause."

58. 10 GAOR Annexes, UN Doc. A/2907 at 18 (1955).

59. However, the paragraph as drafted "might preclude the imposition of such requirements as parental consent to marriage in cases where persons were under age. This [is] prevalent in many countries." UN Doc. A/2929, *supra* note 13, ch. VI para. 169.

An amendment to permit consent requirements was to be added but did not appear in the approved draft.

Earlier U.S. Supreme Court decisions prohibited the state from requiring parental consent before a minor may obtain an abortion or purchase contraceptives. As long as a minor is "mature and well-informed," or the abortion is "in her best interest" the state may not interfere. Planned Parenthood of Missouri v. Danforth, 428 U.S. 52 (1976); Belloti v. Baird, 443 U.S. 622 (1979); Carey v. Population Services International, 431 U.S. 678 (1977). The Supreme Court retreated a way from that view in H. L. v. Matheson, 101 Sup. Ct. 1164 (1981).

60. UN Doc. A/2929, *supra* note 13, ch. VI paras. 155–58.

61. *Id.* para. 159.

62. Organized opposition to particular clauses has hampered ratification of the Covenant or inspired reservations. For example, Article 4 of the American Convention on Human Rights, which protects the right to life from conception, caused considerable opposition to the Convention from U.S. groups favoring legalized abortion. In Costa Rica the press vigorously opposed ratification of the Convention because of Article 14 which preserves the right to correct through the press any inaccurate or prejudicial publication.

63. UN Doc. A/33/40, *supra* note 33, para. 192.

64. *Id.* paras. 165, 181.

65. *Id.* para. 353.

66. Marckx case, Judgment of 13 June 1979, cited in 19 *Int'l Legal Materials* 109 (1980).

9. FREEDOM OF CONSCIENCE AND EXPRESSION, AND POLITICAL FREEDOMS

1. See Krishnaswami, "Study of Discrimination in the Matter of Religious Rights and Practices," UN Doc. E/CN.4/Sub.2/200 (1959).

2. Article 26(3) of the Declaration states: "Parents have a prior right to choose the kind of education that shall be given to their children."

3. See the discussion in the Commission, UN Doc. E/CN.4/SR.116, SR.117 (1949).

4. N. Robinson, *The Universal Declaration of Human Rights* 128 (1958); A. Verdoodt, *Naissance et Signification de la Declaration Universelle des Droits de l'Homme* 178 (1963).

5. Compare Egypt, UN Doc. A/C.3/SR.288 para. 26 (1950), SR. 302 para 7 (1950); Saudi Arabia, UN Doc. A/C.3/SR.289 para. 41 (1950), SR.306 para. 47 (1950), SR.367 para. 41 (1951); Yemen, UN Doc. A/C.3/SR.290 para. 62 (1950); Afghanistan, UN Doc. A/C.3/SR.306 paras. 50–52 (1950).

6. See the discussion in the Commission, UN Doc. E/CN.4/SR.116 at 8 (1949), SR.117 at 8 (1949); SR.161 at 3 (1950).

7. See, e.g., Baroody (Saudi Arabia), UN Doc. A/C.3/SR.367 para. 41 (1951).

8. See, e.g., the statement by Azmi Bey (Egypt), UN Doc. A/C.3/SR.288 para 26 (1950).

9. Beaufort (Netherlands), UN Doc. A/C.3/SR.306 para. 44 (1950); see also Cassin (France), UN Doc. A/C.3/SR.371 para. 18 (1951).

10. The government experts of the Council of Europe confirmed the opinion that the "freedom to have or adopt a religion" also includes the right to change one's religion. Council of Europe Doc. CE/H(70)7 para. 165 (1970); see also the "Memorie van Toelichting" of the Netherlands government, in *Tweede Kamer,* Zitting 1975/76, 13932 (R.1037) No. 3 at 28 (1976).

11. The constitutional orders of certain states make a clear distinction between the freedom of religion and all other rights. According to the constitutions of the United States (1st Amendment) and of the Federal Republic of Germany (Article 4), no limitations whatsoever are admitted. The constitutional jurisprudence of the United States, however, has upheld limitations on religious practice which endangers life or health or contravenes public morals.

12. In connection with Article 18, the Netherlands government took the position that the term "prescribed by law" refers to law generally, thus denying any difference between that phrase and "provided by law" in Article 19(3). See note 10 *supra;* compare note 43 *infra.* See generally essay 12.

13. Hoare (U.K.), UN Doc. E/CN.4/SR.319 at 9 (1952).

14. See UN Docs. E/CN.4/SR.116, SR.117 (1949), and SR.161 (1950).

15. Article 13(3).

16. According to Article 26(3) of the Universal Declaration and Article 2 of the (First) Additional Protocol of the European Convention.

17. See Greece, UN Doc. A/C.3/L.875, in Report of the Third Committee, UN Doc. A/4625 para. 45 (1960).

18. J. Fawcett, *The Application of the European Convention on Human Rights* 353 (1969); full texts of reservations may be found in Council of Europe, *European Convention on Human Rights: Collected Texts* 605–11 (11th ed. 1976).

19. In this chapter the results of the work of the Committee during the years 1977–1979 are systematically evaluated. See the reports of the Committee: 32 GAOR Supp. 44, UN Doc. A/32/44 (1977); 33 GAOR Supp. 40, UN Doc. A/33/40 (1978); and 34 GAOR Supp. 40, UN Doc. A/34/40 (1979). Summary Records of the first eleven sessions of the Human Rights Committee exist for

252 meetings: UN Docs. CCPR/C/SR.1–SR.252 (1977–1980). The reports of States parties are contained in UN Docs. CCPR/C/1/Adds. 1 to 53; C/4/Adds. 1 to 5; C/6/Adds. 1 to 4.

20. The Committee interprets the Covenant incidentally, often tacitly and by implication, in the course of carrying out its functions. The documents available to date reflect only examinations of reports of states parties pursuant to Article 40. In the Committee's proceedings, questions are raised by individual members, but sometimes the Committee as a whole may make evident its own interpretation of a provision of the Covenant by requesting further information on a subject. These requests have to be answered by the states parties if they deal with a matter covered by a provision of the Covenant. As the Committee is not allowed to ask questions which have no basis in the Covenant, one may conclude from such a request that the Committee is of the opinion that such a basis exists. Sometimes, however, an individual member of the Committee may ask a question which, strictly, is outside the competence of the Committee, in order to test how effective the protection of a certain right is. In connection with the right to free association, for example, a Committee member may ask whether the right to strike is guaranteed, although this right is not included in Article 22. The Committee, however, would not act within its competence if it requested further information on this subject, and the state party could legitimately refuse to answer if such a question were put to it. Unfortunately, the summary records do not always indicate precisely which questions put by individual members are covered by the request for further information. In view of this fact the records have to be used with caution; the fact that a member has put a question and that afterwards further information was requested does not always indicate that the opinion of the Committee implies a certain interpretation. (See generally essay 14.)

21. See *supra* p. 213.

22. Cyprus, UN Doc. CCPR/C1/Add. 28 at 12 (1977); its representative referred to the protection of public safety, UN Doc. A/34/40, *supra* note 19, para. 389 (1979).

23. It is noteworthy that some members brought the problem of conscientious objectors under Article 18. UN Doc. A/34/40, *supra* note 19, paras. 159 (Romania), 412 (Finland) (1979). The concept of "religion" was discussed during the first report examined by the Committee. In introducing the report, the representative of the Syrian Arab Republic mentioned that the very existence of Syria was still threatened by the expansionist policies of world Zionism. Nevertheless, he said Judaism was freely practiced in Syria and its adherents were not discriminated against. "Although the law imposed severe penalties on anyone who did not respect the religion of others, a clear-cut distinction was made between religion on the one hand and political movements and racist ideologies on the other." UN Doc. CCPR/C/SR.26 para. 61 (1977). This would imply that a member of the Jewish community could not be exposed to measures ordered against Zionists solely on the basis of his membership in this religious community.

24. UN. Doc. A/33/40, *supra* note 19, para. 444; UN Doc. CCPR/C/1/Add.33 at 21–25 (1978); CCPR/C/SR.136 para. 43 (1979); CCPR/C/1/Add.36 at 28 (1978). The Ukrainian SSR also restricts the right of parents to determine the religious education of their children. UN Doc. A/34/40, *supra* note 19, para. 280 (1979).

The Constitution of Cyprus (Article 18(8)) provides: "No person shall be compelled to pay any tax or duty the proceeds of which are specifically allocated in whole or in part for the purpose of religion in whole or in part." UN Doc. CCPR/C/1/Add.28 at 12 (1978). Compelling such duties would seem to be a form of coercion barred by Article 18(2). Less plausibly, one can argue also that such a duty is an interference with one's freedom to manifest one's own religion and not within the limitations permitted by Article 18(3).

25. Sweden, UN Doc. A/33/40, *supra* note 19, para. 79.

26. *Id.* para. 289.

27. The compulsory religious instruction in Sweden—as the representative explained—"was given in an objective and neutral manner which should not be contrary to personal beliefs." Pupils of other confessions or creeds "must in every case be given equivalent religious instruction outside school hours." *Id.* para. 91. But the reservation declared by this state to Article 2 of the Additional Protocol to the European Convention does not conform with this position. The reservation reads: "The dispensation from the obligation of taking part in the teaching of Christianity in these schools could only be presented for children of another faith than the Swedish Church, in respect of whom a satisfactory religious instruction had been arranged." Fawcett, *supra* note 1, at 353. The situation of children from atheist families is not clear. A neutral and objective instruction may be given with due regard to the doctrines of different Christian confessions. It is hardly imaginable that it conforms to the beliefs of an atheist.

28. Even among the Socialist countries there are important differences. In Hungary, denominational schools exist and are even financially supported by the state. UN Doc. A/32/44, *supra* note 19, para. 132(f). In Czechoslovakia, religious education in the public schools is optional, UN Doc. A/33/40, *supra* note 19, para. 143; in Romania it is given in places of worship and in parish halls, UN Doc. CCPR/C/1/Add.33 at 24 (1978), SR.136 paras. 32, 51 (1979); while in Byelorussia and the Ukraine the parents may instruct their children themselves and send them to religious services; UN Doc. A/33/40, *supra* note 19, para. 55, UN Doc. CCPR/C/1/Add.34 at 21 (1978), UN Doc. A/34/40, *supra* note 19, para. 280 (1979). The USSR did not answer a question regarding the parents' right. UN Doc. A/33/40, *supra* note 19, paras. 425, 444.

29. To require a special permission for this excuse could be a violation of Article 18. UN Doc. A/34/40, *supra* note 19, para. 319 (1979).

30. UN Doc. CCPR/C/X/CRP. 1/Add.4 para. 48 (1980); see also the criticism on the right to levy church taxes, UN Doc. A/34/40, *supra* note 19, para. 412 (1979).

31. See the detailed history given by Verdoodt, *supra* note 4, at 184–91.

32. The article in the Universal Declaration does not mention any limitations

on the right to freedom of expression. This is left to the general limitation clause (Article 29). For this reason, no provision regarding a possible abuse of these rights is included. The rights and freedoms embodied in the Declaration, however, may not be exercised in a manner contrary to the purposes and principles of the United Nations (Article 29(3)). This clause excludes an abuse of freedom of expression for the propagation of a war of aggression or for the incitement to any form of discrimination banned by the Charter. Verdoodt, *supra* note 4, at 191.

33. See the interventions of S. Hoare (UK), UN Doc. E/CN.4/SR.200 para. 5 (1950); R. Cassin (France), UN Doc. E/CN.4/SR.320 at 6, 11 (1952), SR.321 at 11 (1952).

34. See 10 GAOR Annexes, UN Doc. A/2929, ch. VI para. 122 (1955); 16 GAOR Annexes, UN Doc. A/5000 para. 24 (1961).

35. India, UN Doc. A/C.3/L.919; Ethiopia and six other countries, UN Doc. A/C.3/L. 929 and Add.1 and Add.1/Corr.1, in UN Doc. A/5000 paras. 9, 11, 12 (1961).

36. UN Docs. A/5000, *supra* note 34, para. 22; A/C.3/SR.1070–1078 (1961).

37. UN Doc. A/2929, *supra* note 34, ch. VI para. 125.

38. *Id.* para. 126; UN Doc. A/5000, *supra* note 34, para. 23.

39. See also Talley v. California, 362 U.S. 60 (1960).

40. Amendment papers by the U.K., UN Doc. E/CN.4/L.144 Rev. 1 (1952), which virtually reproduced Article 10 of the European Convention. See the critical remarks of K. J. Partsch, *Die Rechte und Freiheiten der Europäischen Menschenrechtskonvention* 200 (1966).

41. This model had been followed earlier by the Commission on Human Rights: see 13 ESCOR Supp. 9, UN Docs. E/1992/Annex 1; E/CN.4/640 (1951). The general formula was very ably defended by R. Cassin (France) against any attempt to insert a detailed enumeration. It was, if not the best text, at any rate the least objectionable. A detailed enumeration would neither cover any possible impairment of the rights and reputations of individuals nor protect the national community effectively against any incitement by the press to violate public order, morals, or national security. UN Doc. E/CN.4/SR.320 at 12 (1952); examples of detailed enumerations are given in UN Doc. A/2929, *supra* note 34, ch. VI paras. 128–33. The decision for a general formula following the method of Article 29(2) of the Universal Declaration helped also to avoid injecting specific political elements into Article 19 (the prohibition of war propaganda, of incitement to hatred among peoples and of racial discrimination). They were later inserted into a separate article (Article 20).

42. Former proposal by the Secretariat, in Verdoodt, *supra* note 4, at 186.

43. There are certain differences of drafting regarding both these elements in comparison with the Universal Declaration. They help interpret the final version of Article 19(3). The Universal Declaration required that restrictions be "determined by law;" Article 19(3) of the Covenant requires that they should be "provided by law"; Article 10(2) of the European Convention uses the term "prescribed by law." The theory that by these three different formulations,

different degrees of positivism are required, meets serious objections. (See also essay 12.) As far as written laws directly determine, provide, or prescribe limitations, no difference between these terms can be determined. Written norms may also indirectly be the basis of such limitations as far as a rule is logically derived from them by way of interpretation. See Garibaldi, "General Limitations on Human Rights: The Principle of Legality," 17 *Harv. Int'l L.J.* 503, 557 (1976).

44. Sunday Times case, Eur. Ct. Human Rights, Decision of 27 October 1978, 30 *Pub. Eur. Ct. Human Rights,* Ser. A, para. 47.

45. European Commision on Human Rights, 3 *Y.B. Eur. Conv. Human Rights* 310 (1960); 6 *Y.B. Eur. Conv. Human Rights* 204 (1963); 8 *Y.B. Eur. Conv. Human Rights* 174 (1965).

46. The Universal Declaration permits limitations "solely for the purpose of securing due recognition and respect for the rights and freedoms of others and of meeting the just requirements of morality, public order, and the general welfare in a democratic society."

47. See the critical remarks of Hoare (UK) UN Doc. E/CN.4/SR.200 (1950); and of Beer, UN Doc. E/CN.4/SR.321 at 9 (1952).

48. It was stated, however, that a citizen would be only punished for his "views" if those views were converted into actions. Ukranian SSR, UN Doc. A/34/40, *supra* note 19, para. 281.

49. Article 50, identical with Article 48 of the Constitution of the Byelorussian SSR and Article 48 of the Ukranian SSR Constitution.

50. See UN Doc. CCPR/C/1/Add.22 at 20 (1978) on "the right to hold and freely to express opinions," and at 13 on "the rights of aliens"; UN Doc. CCPR/C/1/Add.34 at 22 (1978); UN Doc. CCPR/I/Add.27 at 21, 13 (1978). Nor have these states made a declaration or reservation regarding eventual restrictions on the exercise of these rights by aliens as did the Federal Republic of Germany. See UN Doc. CCPR/C/2 at 5 (1977): "Art. 19 . . . in conjunction with Art. 2(1) of the Covenant shall be applied within the scope of Art. 16 of the Convention of 4 November 1950 for the Protection of Human Rights and Fundamental Freedoms."

51. UN Doc. A/32/44, *supra* note 19, para. 310.

52. UN Doc. A/33/40, *supra* note 19, paras. 62 (Libya) and 272 (Madagascar).

53. UN Doc. CCPR/C/2 at 11 (1977).

54. Tomuschat, UN Doc. CCPR/C/SR.128 para. 20 (1979); see also UN Doc. A/34/40; *supra* note 19, para. 87. Other states were asked why peaceful dissent was regarded as a threat to public security if the system was overwhelmingly accepted by the people. UN Doc. A/34/40, *supra* note 19, paras. 128 (Bulgaria) and 264 (Ukrainian SSR).

55. Tomuschat, UN Doc. CCPR/C/SR.128 para. 20 (1979).

56. UN Doc. A/33/40, *supra* note 19, paras. 205, 223.

57. *Id*. paras. 80, 92.

Note that the spokesman for the Federal Republic of Germany cited two decisions of the Federal Constitutional Court, UN Doc. CCPR/C/1/Add.18 at

26 (1977). He might have mentioned also that according to Article 19(2) of the basic law of the Federal Republic, a limitation of a fundamental right by law shall never result in an infringement on its essence, a clause which was drafted taking Article 30 of the Universal Declaration as a model and especially elaborated by the Constitutional Court in relation to the freedom of expression. A member of the Committee (Graefrath) nevertheless asked for further clarification on this very subtle and intricate question of constitutional law. UN Doc. CCPR/C/SR.92 para. 56 (1978); UN Doc. A/33/40, *supra* note 19, para. 350.

A further example mentioned by Graefrath was based on a misunderstanding. The limitation on the freedom of expression of employees forbids disclosure of the internal conditions of the enterprise. This clause is covered by Article 19(3a) of the Covenant (respect of the rights of others).

58. See Barbados, UN Doc. CCPR/C/1/Add.36 (1978); UK Dependent Territories, UN Doc. CCPR/C/1/Add.37 (1978). One of the examples is "seditious or blasphemous publications," UN Doc. A/34/40, *supra* note 19, para. 320; it was explained that neither simple criticism of the Government or of the shortcomings of the constitution was covered by this term, nor was an appeal to inhabitants to change the legislation by legal means. UN Doc. A/34/40, *supra* note 19, para. 369.

59. The constitutions of the Byelorussian SSR (Article 48) and of the Ukrainian SSR (Article 48) copy the wording verbatim. The Constitution of the German Democratic Republic (Article 27(1) in connection with Article 19(1)) is similar in substance, as is the Constitution of Hungary (Article 64).

60. Constitution of Czechoslovakia; UN Doc. CCPR/C/1/Add.12 at 15–16 (1977); the Constitution of Romania is similar: no freedom of expression "for purposes hostile to the socialist regime." See UN Doc. CCPR/C/1/Add.33 at 25–26 (1978).

61. See UN Doc. CCPR/C/SR.99 para. 25 (1978).

62. See the criticism of Sir Vincent Evans, UN Doc. CCPR/C/SR.108 para. 56 (1978); and of Prado Vallejo, UN Doc. CCPR/C/SR.109 para. 44 (1978); on the other hand, it was frankly declared that active members of a religious group could not become members of the Communist Party, whose members are required to adhere to the philosophy of dialectical materialism. UN Doc. A/34/40, *supra* note 19, para. 280 (Ukrainian SSR).

63. See UN Doc. A/34/40, *supra* note 19, paras. 160, 175 (Romania); paras. 413, 436 (Finland).

64. See *id.* paras. 87, 91, 104 (Chile); para. 200 (Spain); para. 237 (UK); paras. 413, 436 (Finland).

65. Syria, UN Doc. CCPR/C/1/Add.31 (1978).

66. UN Doc. CCPR/C/SR.102 para. 45 (1978).

67. UN Doc. A/32/44, *supra* note 19, para. 129(j); see also the BBC Complaints Commission, in UN Doc. CCPR/C/1/Add.35 at 23 (1978). In Romania, responsibility for ensuring respect for legal restrictions is vested in editorial bodies or the chief editor of each press organ. UN Doc. A/34/40, *supra* note 19, para. 175.

68. UN Doc. CCPR/C/1/ADD.23 at 28 (1978).
69. Prado Vallejo, in UN Doc. CCPR/C/SR.99 para. 29 (1978).
70. UN Doc. CCPR/C/SR.102 para. 45 (1978).
71. See the questions of Mora Rojas regarding "socialist realism," UN Docs. CCPR/C/SR.98 para. 41 (1978); SR.108 para. 39 (1978).
72. Verdoodt, *supra* note 4, at 191.
73. Proposals to adopt a specific clause prohibiting propaganda for fascism and aggression and to provoke hatred among nations were made at various times during the drafting of the Universal Declaration. See 7 ESCOR Supp. 2, UN Doc. E/800 at 33 (1948); Vishinsky, in 3 GAOR Plen. Mtgs. (180th mtg.), UN Doc. A/777 (1948); and the early work on the Covenant by the Commission on Human Rights in the 1950s (Amendments of USSR and France, in UN Doc. E/CN.4/365 at 60 (1950); discussions in UN Doc. E/CN.4/SR.174 paras. 19–69 (1950); and SR.175 paras. 2–22 (1950)).
74. Australia, UN Doc. E/CN.4/SR.377 at 6; UK, at 8 (1953).
75. In 1953 the Sub-Commission on Prevention of Discrimination and the Protection of Minorities recommended the inclusion of the following article: "Any advocacy of national, racial or religious hostility that constitutes an incitement to violence shall be prohibited by the law of the state." UN Doc. E/2250 Annex II (1953). The wording is simple and clear: advocacy of hatred (a factual act) has to be prohibited if it fulfills the requirements of a legal concept ("incitement to violence"). In any case, such disturbance of the internal peace is punishable by most penal codes. Some wished, however, to broaden the scope of the provision to include not only acts of violence but also acts of propaganda. See UN Doc. E/CN.4/L.292 (1953) on the introduction of subjective concepts as "hatred and contempt" besides "acts of violence." See also the discussion in UN Doc. E/CN.4/SR.377–SR.379 (1953). The discussion led to the compromise concerning "hatred" and "violence," so that only incitement to both was prohibited (Article 26 of the Commission draft): "Any advocacy of national, racial or religious hostility that constitutes an incitement to hatred *and* violence shall be prohibited by the law of the state" (emphasis added). The Report of the Commission, 16 ESCOR Supp. 8, UN Doc. E/2477 para. 76 (1953), speaks of a "cumulative interpretation"; see also *id.,* Annex III/A paras. 35 to 38, with the texts of the amendments. Seven years later, in October 1961 when the draft was discussed in the Third Committee, general conditions in the organs of the United Nations had changed substantially, 16 GAOR C.3 (1078–1084th mtgs.), UN Docs. A/C.3/SR.1078–SR.1084 (1961). A great number of new states from the Third World that had become members of the world organization were primarily concerned with specific problems connected with their own recent access to statehood and had few feelings for the principles of law, which they were inclined to regard as products of the colonial powers from which they had been liberated. Attempts to introduce additional restrictions into the text of Article 19 by India, Brazil, and the USSR failed. UN Docs. A/C.3/L.919–921; UN Doc. A/5000, *supra* note 34, para. 25–27. At the discussion of Article 26 of the Commission draft, the sponsors of these propos-

als referred to quite a number of conventions or draft conventions concluded under the auspices of the United Nations, and several General Assembly resolutions regarding propaganda against war, including the judgment of the Nuremberg Tribunal and the Draft Convention on Freedom of Information. UN Doc. A/5000, *supra* note 34, para. 47. Finally, in the last stage and apparently without substantial discussion, the balanced compromise reached in the Commission on Human Rights regarding the legal qualification of the factual acts was abandoned. Instead of mentioning "inciting to violence" cumulatively with propagandistic measures ("hostility"), both have been put on the same level and have to be applied alternatively. Now, discrimination, hostility *or* violence shall be prohibited by law. On the addition of the words "discrimination, hostility or" a roll call was taken. The addition was adopted with only 43 for, 21 against, with 19 abstentions.

76. A joint amendment by Brazil and seven Asian, six African, and two Eastern European states proposed separation of the article into two paragraphs, the first dedicated exclusively to war, and the second to national, racial, and religious hatred. A/C.3/L.933.

77. G.A. Res. 3314, 29 GAOR Supp. 31, UN Doc. A/9631 at 142 (1974).

78. Formulation of a possible interpretation of Article 20(1) by Finland before the Committee on Human Rights, UN Doc. A/32/44, *supra* note 19, para. 125(d); apparently also Syria does not exclude this interpretation, as it replied that implementation of Article 20(1) "had necessarily to be viewed in the context of the present political situation of resistance to external aggression"; para. 115(h) is limited to propaganda for aggressive wars. See Belgium, UN Doc. E/CN.4/SR.174 para. 52 (1950). The Memorandum of the Government of the Federal Republic of Germany regarding the Covenant addressed to the Federal Diet of June 1, 1973, Deutscher Bundestag 7, Wahlperiode Drucksache 7/660 at 37, states: "The concept of propaganda for war regards aggressions; objective deliberations or measures for psychological defense shall not be covered by this concept. 'Propaganda for War' according to Article 20(1) has to be interpreted as propaganda for an aggressive war, because Article 51 of the Charter of the United Nations expressly recognizes the right of individual or collective self-defense."

79. The penal codes of Romania, UN Doc. CCPR/C/1/Add.33 (1978); of the Ukraine, UN Doc. CCPR/C/1/Add.34 (1978); and of the German Democratic Republic, UN Doc. A/33/40, *supra* note 19, para. 179, ban wars of aggression or other aggressive acts. Article 26 of the basic law of the Federal Republic of Germany reads: "Acts tending to and undertaken with the intent to disturb the peaceful relations between nations, especially to prepare for aggressive wars, shall be unconstitutional. They shall be made a punishable offense." This provision was commended by members of the Committee. *Id.* para. 351.

When Finland, which like other members of the Nordic Council entered a reservation to Article 20(1), was asked in the Committee why it had done so, it explained that the government had hesitated to assume an obligation to prohibit war propaganda because this term could be interpreted as applying even to defensive war. In the reservation at ratification another motive is mentioned: a prohibition of propaganda for war "might endanger the freedom of expression referred to in Article 19 of the Covenant." For the text of the reservations of Finalnd, Denmark, Norway, Sweden, and the UK, see UN Doc. CCPR/C/2 (1977). The legitimacy of these reservations was questioned in the Committee. UN Doc. A/34/40, *supra* note 19, para. 414.

80. Council of Europe, Doc. CE/H (70) 7, *supra* note 10, para. 180.

81. *Ibid.* When former Article 26 (which corresponds to Article 20(2)) was discussed in the UN Human Rights Commission, a preference was given to the words "shall be prohibited by the law of the state" instead of declaring that the relevant acts "constitute crimes and shall be punished."

82. UN Doc. CCPR/C/SR.222 para. 66 (1980).

83. UN Doc. A/2929, *supra* note 34, ch. VI para. 194.

84. Multifold measures of educational or conciliatory character, as practiced in Anglo-Saxon countries, are available and may be more appropriate than penal sanctions.

85. In the case of Chile, it was objected that no legislation was enacted. UN Doc. CCPR/C/SR.129 para. 20 (1979).

86. See the report on U.K. Dependent Territories, UN Doc. CCPR/C/1/Add.37 (1978), which refers to Belize and some other territories where the acts prohibited under Article 20(1) and (2) are brought under "sedition"; see also Barbados, UN Doc. CCPR/C/1/Add.36 (1978).

87. See Article 26 of the Covenant and Article 1 of the International Convention on the Elimination of Racial Discrimination.

88. See also Cyprus, UN Doc. CCPR/C/1/Add.18 (1977).

89. Article 1(1): "In this Convention, the term 'racial discrimination' shall mean any distinction, exclusion, restriction or preference based on race, colour, descent, or national or ethnic origin which has the purpose or effect of nullifying or impairing the recognition, enjoyment or exercise, on an equal footing, of human rights and fundamental freedoms in the political, economic, social, cultural or any other field of public life."

90. *Tweede Kamer,* Zitting 1975–76, 13932 (R.1037) nos. 1–6 at 27.

91. UN Doc. A/2929, *supra* note 34, ch. VI para. 194.

92. An example of a monoethnic population is that of the Falkland Islands, according to UN Doc. CCPR/1/C/Add.37, Annex E para. 40 (1978).

93. In view of the parallelism between the two instruments, Finland has limited its reservation to paragraph 1. See UN Doc. A/32/44, *supra* note 19, para. 125(d).

94. The second report of the U.K., UN Doc. CCPR/C/1/Add.35 para. 53, reported that the Race Relations Act of 1976 has strengthened the law against incitement to racial hatred by removing the need to prove a subjective intention to stir up hatred.

95. UN Doc. A/5000, *supra* note 34, para. 46. In 1979, a member of the Human Rights Committee (Movchan) stated in UN Doc. CCPR/C/SR.136 para. 61 (1979): "He shared the view that the prohibition of Fascist and war

propaganda was not a restriction of the freedom of speech." The prohibition of such propaganda "ensured the exercise of civil and political rights."

96. UN Doc. A/5000, *supra* note 34, para. 45.

97. UN Doc. CCPRC/C/2 at 10 (1977): "The Government of the United Kingdom interprets Article 20 consistently with the rights conferred by Articles 19 and 21 of the Covenant. . . ." See also Sweden, UN Doc. CCPR/C/1/Add.9 at 26 (1977).

98. Message from the President of the United States transmitting Four Treaties Pertaining to Human Rights to the Senate (February 23, 1978) Exec Docs. C, D, E, F. The Executive Branch also recommended a text: "The Constitution of the United States and Article 19 of this Convenant contain provisions for the protection of individual rights, including the right of free speech, and nothing in this Covenant shall be deemed to require or to authorize legislation or other action by the United States which would restrict the right of free speech protected by the Constitution, laws, and practices of the United States."

99. Compare Article 4, introductory paragraph of CERD.

100. In the Human Rights Committee, the view was expressed that a law prohibiting "regionalist propaganda" and "seditious shouts or chants" was not justified by Article 20 and possibly violated Articles 19 and 22. UN Doc. CCPR/C/X/CRP.1/Add.6 para. 17 (1980).

101. Fawcett, *The Application of the European Convention on Human Rights* 223 (1969).

102. UN Doc. E/CN.4/L.126 (1952); see also the statement that dissenters should be excluded from enjoying these rights. UN Doc. A/C.3/SR.291 para. 55 (1950).

103. Eduardo Jiménez de Aréchaga (Uruguay) UN Doc. A/C.3/SR.61.

104. Robinson, *supra* note 4, at 130, with reference to the interpretation by Uruguay, UN Doc. A/C.3/SR.131 (1948).

105. The discussion of whether recognition of the right implied a commitment always, or only "in most cases," does not help very much. Cassin, UN Doc. A/C.3/SR.410 para. 39 (1952), referring to a proposal of Lebanon and Israel, UN Docs. A/C.3/L.198/Rev. 2, L.193; see also the discussions in UN Doc. E/CN.4/SR, 169 paras. 87 to 90 (1950), SR. 200 paras. 13–15 (1950).

106. Robinson, *supra* note 4, at 131.

107. Compare the discussion of the right to be silent, *supra,* text at note 38.

108. See UN Doc. A/2929, *supra* note 34, ch. VI paras. 141–143. The Third Committee only added the French term *ordre public* to the English term "public order." See A/C.3/SR.1085 para. 6 (1961); UN Doc. A/5000, *supra* note 34, paras. 51–55.

109. See the proposal of the USSR, UN Doc. A/C.3/SR.289 para. 37 (1950); similarly, UN Doc. E/CN.4/L.126 (1952) and the objections of Eleanor Roosevelt (USA), UN Doc. E/CN.4/SR.325 at 15 (1952), and those of Bracco (Uruguay), *id.* at 9.

111. France, E/CN.4/L.202 (1952)., E/CN.4/SR.325 at 9, 20 (1952), A/C.3/SR.290 para. 29 (1950); former discussions in E/CN.4/SR.169 (1950).

111. See UN Doc. A/2929, *supra* note 34, ch. VI para. 141, and Cassin (France), UN Doc. E/CN.4/SR.169 para. 74 (1950).

112. UN Doc. CCPR/C/1/Add. 34 at 22 (1978).

113. Romania, UN Doc. CCPR/C/1/Add.33 at 25 (1978); Czechoslovakia, UN Doc. A/33/40, *supra* note 19, paras. 132, 136.

114. Denmark, *id.* para. 109.

115. Belize and other U.K. Dependent Territories, UN Doc. CCPR/C/1/Add. 37 (1978).

116. Doc. CE/H (70) 7, *supra* note 10, paras. 192–3.

117. Federal Republic of Germany, BT-Drucksache 7/660 at 37, and reservation according to UN Doc. CCPR/C/2 at 5 (1977); Austrian government, Protocols of the National Council, XIV election period, Annex 230 at 45.

118. Finaldn requires prior notice, UN Doc. CCPR/C/1/Add.32 at 21 (1978); Hong Kong, CCPR/C/1/Add. 37, and Yugoslavia, UN Doc. A/33/40, *supra* note 19, para. 381, 395.

119. The labor force seems to enjoy special privileges in certain states. See G.D.R, UN Doc. A/33/40, *supra* note 19, paras. 164, 180 (no previous notification for assemblies of social organizations); and Tunisia, UN Doc. A/32/44, *supra* note 19, para. 121 (h).

120. The draft of the Commission on Human Rights was misleading: it could be interpreted as giving additional powers to the armed forces or police instead of limiting the enjoyment of the right of association by these persons. This possible misunderstanding was cleared up. See Federation of Malaya, A/C.3/SR.1088 para. 2 (1961); amendment A/C.3/L.936 Rev. 1, in Report of the Third Committee, UN Doc. A/5000, *supra* note 34, paras. 62, 72.

121. See Italy, A/C.3/SR.1088 para. 8 (1961).

122. Bracco (Uruguay), UN Doc. E/CN.4/SR.325 at 15 (1952).

123. René Cassin (France), *supra* note 106 at 11; see also (p. 240), *supra,* the practice relating to the application of Article 25.

124. A relationship as between *lex generalis* and *lex specialis* can only be assumed if similar obligations on the same legal subjects were created by the two dispositions. Such a condition, however, does not exist between the obligations undertaken under the Social Rights Covenant and those undertaken under the Civil Rights Covenant. Even if one accepts the thesis that Article 8 of the Social Rights Covenant imposes obligations which have to be fulfilled immediately, not progressively as in other obligations under the Social Rights Covenant (see U. Beyerlin, "Die Koalitionsfreiheit der Arbeitnehmer in den Menschenrechts Instrumenten der Vereinten Nationen," in Max Planck-Institut für ausländisches öffentliches Recht und Völkerrecht, *The Freedom of the Worker to Organize* 1161–63 (1980), the addressees of such obligations would always be the states parties and not the individual. But, according to the Civil Rights Covenant, he is either entitled to request from the states parties the immediate implementation of the Covenant or the immediate fulfillment of the rights embodied in the Covenant. This question is treated in essay 3. I am inclined to accept the first solution.

9. FREEDOM OF CONSCIENCE; POLITICAL FREEDOMS

125. See UN Doc. A/5000, *supra* note 34, para. 65.

126. UN Doc. A/2929, *supra* note 34, ch. VI para. 152; UN Doc. A/5000, *supra* note 34, paras. 70–71.

127. Article 5(2) of the Covenant.

128. See UN Doc. A/2929, *supra* note 34, para. 151.

129. According to the statements of Bulgaria, Romania, and the Ukrainian SSR, no such formalities had to be fulfilled by labor unions. UN Doc. A/34/40, *supra* note 19, paras. 144, 176, 282.

Frequently questions were asked as to which organ of government was competent to decide and whether this organ acted under appropriate control. See for instance UN Doc. A/33/40, *supra* note 19, paras. 63 (Libya), 311 (Iran), 381 (Yugoslavia), 406 (Jordan), and 491 (Mauritius). No clear difference was made between public institutions and private associations. In this connection, several reports mention representative councils or administrative institutions. See Hungary, UN Doc. A/32/44, *supra* note 19, para. 132(h); and Syria, CCPR/C/1/Add.31 at 3 (1978), though such institutions would not seem to be covered by Article 22 but by Article 25.

130. See the reports of Ukraine, UN Doc. CCPR/C/1/Add.34 at 23–25 (1978) Romania, Add.33 at 27; and the statements of the representatives of the USSR, UN Doc. A/33/40, *supra* note 19, para. 447; and of Byelorussia, para. 552.

131. See the strong criticism of the compulsory loyalty oath required of elected union officials. UN Doc. A/34/40, *supra* note 19, para. 88, and on the other side the statement of the government of Chile concerning labor unions, their bargaining power, and the right to strike. *Id* para. 105.

132. UN Doc. CCPR/C/SR.128 paras. 29, 35, 36 (1979). Questions to other states regarded the organization of labor unions. It was inquired whether there was only one labor union in each economic sector, UN Doc. A/32/44, *supra* note 19, para. 121(h) (Tunisia); under which conditions labor unions were recognized, UN Doc. A/33/40, *supra* note 19, paras. 311–28 (Iran), para. 381 (Yugoslavia), and para. 491 (Mauritius); and whether they were allowed to play a role in general politics, *id.* para. 406 (Jordan). Some questions referred to particular functions which are not expressly included in the provision of Article 22, for example, the right of collective bargaining and the conclusion of collective agreements. *Id.* para. 311 (Iran), para. 352 (F.R.G.), para. 490 (Mauritius); UN Doc. CCPR/C/SR.129 para. 20 (1979) (Chile). Although Article 22 does not guarantee the right to strike, there were several inquiries whether unions had the right to strike and under what conditions such right existed. UN Doc. A/33/40, *supra* note 19, para. 272 (Madagascar); UN Doc. CCPR/C/SR.136 para. 54 (Romania). It was pointed out that even a temporary suspension of the right to strike would deprive the workers of the right to bring about improvements in their economic and social conditions. UN Doc. CCPR/C/SR.129 para.20 (Chile).

133. UN Doc. A/33/40, *supra* note 19, para. 207. The proposal to insert into Article 22 a provision similar to Article 20(2) of the Universal Declaration, that no one may be compelled to belong to an association, was apparently rejected

solely to protect the "closed-shop" system practiced in Anglo-Saxon states, yet the "political closed-shop system" practiced in states with a one-party system was not mentioned.

134. UN Doc. CCPR/C/1/Add.5 at 25 (1978). This question has been referred to the European Court of Human Rights (request no. 7601/76 (Young and James) and no. 7806/77 (Webster against United Kingdom)) for a decision. On the other hand, the Netherlands Government doubted that the article applied only to restrictions by public authority and not to private interference with the right. See Memorie, *supra* note 10, at 32. Members of the Committee debated whether, under Article 22, labor unions could be excluded from political activities, submitted to state control, or denied bargaining powers and the right to strike, and whether members of the civil service or foreigners could be excluded from membership. UN Doc. A/34/40, *supra* note 19, paras. 88, 91 (Chile), 128 (Bulgaria), 201 (Spain), 247 (Ukrainian SSR), 416 (Finland).

135. Article 21 of the first draft of the Commission on Human Rights included no such provisions. Similarly, in the European Convention these rights were added only in the First Additional Protocol and in a very cautious manner. For a time it was controversial in the political organs of the United Nations whether political rights should be included in the Covenant or not. The USSR, Poland, and Yugoslavia, as well as India and Greece, regretted the absence of a provision regarding political rights in the first international covenant on Human Rights. USSR, UN Doc. A/C.3/SR.289 para. 33 (1950); Poland, SR.290 para. 3; Yugoslavia, SR.291 para. 21; India, SR.291 para. 50; Greece, SR.298 para. 26. Yugoslavia and the USSR had even taken the initiative to state that political rights should also be added to the list of rights to be defined in the Covenant. UN Docs. A/C.3/L.92, L.96. These concrete proposals were, however, rejected for procedural reasons. The General Assembly decided only to call upon ECOSOC to request the Commission to revise the draft Covenant "with a view to the addition . . . of other rights," without expressly mentioning them in detail. G.A. Res. 421-B, 5 GAOR Supp. 20, UN Doc. A/1775 at 42 (1950). Later, initiatives were taken by Belgium, Yugoslavia and Greece in ECOSOC as well as in the Commission to solicit the Commission to take up this item. UN Doc. E/CN.4/528 Add.1 paras. 28–52; see also UN Doc. E/CN.4/660 para. 17 (1952), on initiatives of NGO's. The negotiations in the Commission are in UN Docs. E/CN.4/SR.363–367 (1953); see summary of the deliberations in UN Doc. A/2929, *supra* note 34, ch. VI paras. 170–77. The basis of the negotiations were two proposals which in this matter took the text of Article 21 of the Declaration as a model. See UN Doc. E/CN.4/L.221(1953); E/CN.4/L.224 Rev. 1 (1953), a joint proposal by Yugoslavia and France. The draft prepared by the Commission was accepted by the Third Committee eight years later in 1961. UN Doc. A/C.3/SR.1096 (1961); a summary is given in UN Doc. A/5000, *supra* note 34, paras. 89–98. Accordingly, in the drafting history of Article 25 four phases have to be distinguished: the elaboration and acceptance of Article 21 of the Universal Declaration, where most of the constituent elements of the provision in the Covenant are already defined and determined;

the discussions in the General Assembly, as to whether a corresponding provision should be written into the Covenant; the elaboration of the Commission draft; and the acceptance by the Third Committee.

136. This umbrella clause resolved a controversy in the Commission as to how to eliminate discriminatory measures regarding all three of the rights while excluding unjust restrictions. Article 2(1) of the Covenant, forbidding distinctions of any kind based on race, color, sex, language, religion, political or other opinions, national or social origin, property, birth, or other status, applies to political rights as well as to other rights. Therefore, some delegations were of the opinion that it was not necessary to repeat this rule. Yugoslavia, UN Doc. E/CN.4/SR.363 at 15 (1953); France, UN Doc. E/CN.4/SR.364 at 15 (1953); U.K., UN Doc. E/CN.4/SR.365 at 4 (1953); Sweden, UN Doc. E/CN.4//SR.365 at 11 (1953). Some thought that the clause "without discrimination whatsoever" was sufficient. Belgium, UN Doc. E/CN.4/SR.365 at 9 (1953); Egypt, UN Doc. E/CN.4/SR.365 at 9 (1953). On the other hand, some delegations insisted on having discrimination clauses in each of the paragraphs, with a repetition of the forbidden criteria. See UN Doc. E/CN.4/221 (1949) (USSR); that proposal, however, omitted "political or other opinion," and was criticized by several speakers. See UN Doc. E/CN.4/SR.363 at 8, 10, 12 (1953). The "umbrella clause" was able to satisfy the representatives of both opinions. Chile, UN Doc. E/CN.4/SR.366 at 12 (1953).

137. U.S., UN Doc. E/CN.4/SR.364 at 14 (1953).

138. The insertion of the "umbrella clause" made it possible to draft the provisions regarding all three guarantees as individual rights instead of formulating objective guarantees for certain institutions, as in Article 21(3) of the Declaration and Article 3 of the (First) Additional Protocol to the European Convention.

139. UN Doc. E/CN.4/221 (1949).

140. See Verdoodt, *supra* note 4, at 205. Former drafts also used the terms of the Declaration.

141. Chile, UN Doc. A/C.3/SR.133 at 462. "Genuine" is a fancy word, nearly as bad as "classic," but it found general approval. Controversy arose only when concrete implications of "genuine elections" were suggested. The right to oppose the government, proposed by Costa Rica, UN Doc. A/C.3/SR.132 at 449, 456 (1948), and supported by the United Kingdom, at 451, was vigorously rejected by the USSR; Hitler and Mussolini, it was noted, acceded to power because they had been allowed to oppose their respective governments. UN Doc. A/C.3/SR.134 at 469–71 (1948). The reaction of the Soviet delegation was still more vigorous when Belgium proposed to insert a guarantee for the participation of more than one political party in elections. UN Doc. A/C.3/SR.133 at 464 (1948). This requirement would be contrary to the system in the USSR. There was no need for another party because the Communist party effectively cared for the interests of the workers, the only class existing in the USSR. UN Doc. A/C.3/SR.134 at 469, 471 (1948). Belgium

tried to insist, but did not obtain the support even of France and finally withdrew its amendment. UN Doc. A/C.3/SR.134 at 470, 471 (1948).

142. During negotiations in the Third Committee, the representative of Greece gave a convincing answer to this problem: the guarantee of genuine elections should involve "a choice between at least two parties, the right to organize a political opposition, [and] the right freely to exercise political control over any government." He added: "Without such basic democratic rights the building which the United Nations was attempting to erect in the field of Human Rights would lack a keystone, and there would be no certainty that people would be enabled to live under freedom, law and justice." UN Doc. A/C.3/SR. 298 para. 26 (1950). In the Commission the problem was not treated with the same frankness, although the representative of the United States had once stated that no retaliation should be admitted against any citizen who voted strictly according to his conscience. UN Doc. E/CN.4/SR.364 at 14 (1953).

143. A/C.3/SR.1096 para. 19 (1961).

144. The delegate from India suggested that more weight be given to the last passage of sub-paragraph (b), "guaranteeing the free expression of the will of the electors," by putting these words before the technical means to achieve the aim of suffrage and ballot. Though several delegations endorsed this oral proposal, an equal number opposed it and India refrained from making a formal proposal. *Id.* paras. 47, 49, 52, 57.

145. Apparently the problem was seen, but no one had the courage to decide clearly what free or genuine elections are. Apparently there was a consensus that elections need not be direct, and that indirect elections meet the required standard.

146. Australia, UN Doc. A/C.3/SR.133 at 458 (1948); similarly, Haiti, at 466 (1948); a different position was taken by Bolivia, at 456.

147. USSR, UN Doc. A/C.3SR.133 at 463 (1948); Robinson, *supra* note 4, at 132.

148. The main opposition came from two Latin American states, which contended that a rule of absolute secrecy would exclude illiterates from voting rights; these illiterates constitute 85 percent of the world population. See Haiti, UN Doc. A/C.3/SR. 132 at 450, SR.133 at 465 (1948); Guatemala, SR.132 at 454 (1948). These two states voted against the paragraph. Others believed that this objection was not pertinent. Even under the rule of secret votes, it would be possible to allow illiterates to exercise their right to vote since they could be helped by friends or neighbors. See Brazil, SR.133 at 456 (1948); Ukraine, SR.133 at 461; (1948); USSR, SR.133 at 463 (1948). The majority shared this view.

149. Such a meaning was suggested by a draft voted on by the Third Committee which read "elections . . . shall be . . . equal." This change seems to have occurred in a subcommittee. Apparently the Third Committee was not aware of the significance of this difference and no substantive change was intended.

During negotiations on the phrase "equal elections" in the Declaration, the difference between a proportional and a majority system was raised. Other problems were discussed: the size of constituencies; the elimination of racial discrimination and of property qualifications; the discrimination against women; and political discrimination. See UN Doc. A/C.3/SR.132 at 453, SR.133 at 461, 464, 465 (1948). Whether the provision would make proportional representation mandatory was not initially raised. This problem came up only at the Commission stage. Objections to the phrase "universal and equal suffrage" were raised by the United Kingdom and France. They abstained for this reason when the provision of the article was put to a vote. The delegation of the U.S voted in favor but made an explanation of its vote. UN Doc. E/CN.4/SR.367 paras. 12, 13; see also 10 GAOR Annexes, UN Doc. A/2910 and Add.1 at 7 (1955). See the following note.

150. The participants in that discussion may have been impressed by the heavy attacks of the representative of the USSR against the "the so-called majority system" which, he said, completely distorted the results of public election. Democratic principles require that "the system of election should be . . . equal." UN Doc. E/CN.4/SR.363 at 6 (1953). One should not, however, forget the difference between an electoral system entirely based on equality of effect and "an equal suffrage" which only means that each vote cast has the same weight. In 1961 the United Kingdom finally withdrew its proposal to delete the words "by universal and equal suffrage," see UN Doc. A/2910/Add.1 *supra* note 144, at 7, since the argument of the majority of the Commission set forth in the annotations by the Secretary-General appeared convincing. See UN Doc. A/2929, *supra* note 34, ch. VI para. 174. Equal "did not imply that each vote should be guaranteed identical weight by means of some kind of proportional representation in the electoral system." UN Doc. A/C.3/SR.1096 paras. 8, 9 (1961); a similar declaration was made by France, para. 50.

151. The provision does not say that all public offices should be elective, as the USSR had proposed.

152. Australia, UN Doc. E/CN.4/SR.353 at 10 (1953), SR. 365 at 15.

153. Chile, UN Doc. A/C.3/SR.1096 para. 29 (1961); similarly, United Arab Republic, at para. 64.

154. Cf. UN Doc. A/34/40, *supra* note 19, para. 324 (Hongkong); other reservations made upon signature, for example those regarding the discriminatory electoral system in Fiji, became inapplicable, since the UK ratified the Covenant after Fiji attained independence. UN Doc. CCPR/C/2 at 8, 10, 11 (1977).

155. Austria; Regierungsvorlage May 20, 1976 (NR. 230 of the Annexes to the Protocols of the "Nationalrat"—14th session) at 46; Federal Republic of Germany: Memorandum of June 1, 1973 (Drucksache 7/660 of the Bundestag, 7th session) at 38; Report of the Committee of Experts on Human Rights to the Council of Ministers of the Council of Europe, Doc. CE/H (70) 7 para. 218 (1970).

156. UN Doc. CCPR/C/SR.69 para. 3 (1978). Members also showed concern

about the composition of the legislative councils in Hong Kong and on the Falkland Islands. UN Doc. A/34/40, *supra* note 19, paras, 324, 331, 334.

157. UN Doc. CCPR/C/1/Add.35 para. 2 (1978); see also UN Doc. A/34/40, *supra* note 19, para. 231.

158. Article 3 of the First Additional Protocol to the Convention for the Protection of Human Rights and Fundamental Freedoms of March 20, 1952, states: "The High Contracting Parties undertake to hold free elections at reasonable intervals by secret ballot, under conditions which will ensure the free expression of the opinion of the people in the choice of the legislature."

159. In this regard, no common standard seems to be reached. Certain states have lowered the age limit on the right to vote and to be elected from 21 to 18 years. UN Doc. A/34/40, *supra* note 19, para. 250; others still keep to the age of 21 years, para. 324.

160. See UN Doc. A/34/40, *supra* note 19, paras. 230, 232 (UK); and para. 324 (Turkey and the Caicos Islands). The ban of any person who had engaged in political activities during the last 10 years from labor union elections in Chile was regarded as political discrimination. UN Doc. A/34/40, *supra* note 19, para. 91.

161. Compare text at 46; the language requirements in Belize are similar, according to UN Doc. A/34/40, *supra* note 19, para. 324.

162. UN Doc. CCPR/C/1/Add.30 (1978).

163. UN Doc. A/33/40, *supra* note 19, para. 448; note the similar practice in the Ukrainian SSR, UN Doc. A/34/40, *supra* note 19, para. 284, where it has also been introduced recently that deputies can be dismissed and asked to retire by the electorate.

164. See the questions put by members, UN Doc. A/34/40, *supra* note 19, paras. 252, 267; and the evasive answers given by representatives at paras. 145, 284.

165. Lallah, UN Doc. CCPR/C/SR.136 (1979).

166. Koulishev, UN Doc. CCPR/C/1/SR.94 para. 18 (1978); Evans, SR.93 para. 46.

167. UN Doc. A/34/40, *supra* note 19, paras. 90, 103.

168. Austria, *supra* note 155, at 46.

169. European Experts, *supra* note 155, para. 222; see also UN Doc. A/34/40, *supra* note 19, para. 145.

170. See Opsahl, UN Doc. CCPR/C/SR.92 para. 49 (1978); Tarnopolsky, SR. 93 para. 43; Evans, para. 51; Lallah, para. 67; Movchan, SR.94 para. 3; Koulishev, para. 18.

171. See the critical questions of Saadi and Tarnopolsky regarding the report of Romania, UN Doc. CCPR/C/SR.136 paras. 26, 56 (1979); UN Doc. A/34/40, *supra* note 19, para. 162; and the answers given at para. 178.

10. EQUALITY AND NONDISCRIMINATION

1. H. Lauterpacht, *An International Bill of the Rights of Man* 115 (1945). On equality and nondiscrimination generally, see Benn, "Egalitarianism and the

Equal Consideration of Interests," in *Nomos IX: Equality* (1965); M. Bossuyt, *L'Interdiction de la discrimination dans le droit international des droits de l'homme* (1976); I. Claude, *National Minorities* (1955); Doehring, "Non-Discrimination and Equal Treatment Under the European Human Rights Convention and the West-German Constitution, with particular reference to discrimination against aliens," 18 *Am. J. Comp. L.* 305 (1970); Dorsey, ed., *Equality and Freedom: International and Comparative Jurisprudence* (1977); Echman, "The problem of discrimination and measures which should be taken for its elimination," in *Anales de la Faculté de droit international* 237 (1971); P. Guggenheim, "Quelques remarques au sujet de l'article 14 de la Convention européenne des droits de l'homme," in *René Cassin, Amicorum Discipulorumque Liber,* vol. 1 at 95 (1969); ILO, *Discrimination in Employment and Occupation: Standards and Policy Statements Adopted under the Auspices of the ILO* (1967); Marshall, "Notes on the Rule of Equal Law," in *Nomos IX: Equality* (1965); McKean, "The Meaning of Discrimination in International and Municipal Law," 44 *Brit. Y.B. Int'l L.* 177, 177–92 (1970); Sorensen, "The Quest for Equality," [1956] *Int'l Concil.* 507; R. H. Tawney, *Equality* (5th ed. 1964); D. Thompson, *Equality* (1949); G. Van der Molen, *Discrimination and Human Rights* (1961); E. Vierdag, *The Concept of Discrimination in International Law* (1973).

2. Report of the World Conference to Combat Racism and Racial Discrimination, UN Doc. A/CONF.92/40 Annex IC (1979).

3. Mo-Tzu (5th cent. B.C. China), cited in UNESCO, *The Birthright of Man* 31 (1969).

4. Manuscriti Hindu Tradition XII, cited in *id.* at 27.

5. Henkin, "Judaism and Human Rights," *Judaism* vol. 25 at 435, 438 (1976).

6. Hadith of the Prophet, cited in UNESCO, *supra* note 3, at 33. Ancient societies in Africa, Asia, and Latin America also professed notions of equality. Aztec philosophy, for example, called for people to be taught how they should respect others. *Id.* at 32.

Even at a time when international law was not as egalitarian as it is today, some early treaties expressed concern for religious equality. See E. Vierdag, *supra* note 1, at 84.

7. See L. Sohn and T. Buergenthal, *International Protection of Human Rights* 222 (1973). See also UN Doc. E/CN.4/Sub.2/6 at 15 (1947). The treaties and declarations recognize in formal terms the principle of strict equality between individuals belonging to the minority element and others: equality of all persons before the law, equal treatment *de facto* and *de jure*.

8. See H. van Maarseven and G. van Der Tang, *Written Constitutions: A Computerized Comparative Study* 90, 108 (1978).

9. Case concerning the Barcelona Traction, Light and Power Co. Ltd., [1970] *ICJ Rpts.* 33–34; Advisory Opinion on Namibia, [1971] *ICJ Reports* 130, 131. *Cf.* Schwelb, "The International Court of Justice and the Human Rights Clauses of the Charter," 66 *AJIL* 337, 350 (1977).

10. In paragraph 13 of its Declaration, the World Conference to Combat Racism and Racial Discrimination referred to the elimination of racial discrim-

ination as "an imperative norm of international law." In paragraph 29 of its Programme of Action, the Conference recommended "that the United Nations Institute for Training and Research should organize an international colloquium on the prohibition of apartheid, racism and racial discrimination and the achievement of self-determination in international law with special attention to the principles of non-discrimination and self-determination as imperative norms of international law." The World Conference therefore felt not only that the principle of nondiscrimination (at least on grounds of race) was part of international customary law, but that it might also be among the imperative principles of international law. Although certain paragraphs of the Final Acts of the World Conference gave rise to political controversy, there was no disagreement over the above-quoted provisions. See UN Doc. A/CON.92/40, *supra* note 2. See also the statement of the representative of Italy at the Conference:

"Comme il a été énoncé par la Cour Internationale de Justice dans l'arrêt rendu en 1970 dans l'affaire de la Barcelona Traction, la règle interdisant la discrimination raciale est devenue partie intégrante du droit international général et impose à chaque Etat des obligations envers la communauté internationale dans son ensemble. Des obligations qui, par leur nature même, concernent tous les Etats. La règle internationale en question est une règle impérative, qui impose une obligation internationale d'importance essentielle pour la sauvegarde de l'être humain. De cette règle fondamentale découle l'ensemble des droits et des libertés de l'homme, que plusieurs instruments juridiques internationaux se sont chargés tour à tour de préciser, de developper, d'entourer de garanties. Parmi ces instruments une place essentielle revient à la Charte des Nations Unies qui consacre formellement parmi les buts de l'Organisation 'le respect des droits de l'homme et des libertés fondamentales pour tous, sans distinction de race, de sexe, de langue ou de religion.' "

11. I. Brownlie, *Principles of Public International Law* 596 (3d ed. 1979). See also a collection of articles by McDougal, Lasswell, and Chen, "The Protection of Aliens from Discrimination and World Public Order: Responsibility of States Conjoined with Human Rights," 70 *AJIL* 432–33 (1976); "The Protection of Respect and Human Rights: Freedom of Choice and World Public Order," 24 *Am. U.L. Rev.* 919, 1034–86 (1975); "Human Rights for Women and World Public Order: The Outlawing of Sex-Based Discrimination," 69 *AJIL* 497 (1975); "Non-Conforming Political Opinion and Human Rights: Transnational Protection against Discrimination," 2 *Yale Studies in World Public Order* 1 (1975); "The Human Rights of the Aged: An Application of the General Norm of Non-Discrimination," 28 *U. Fla. L. Rev.* 639 (1976); "The Right to Religious Freedom and World Public Order: The Emerging Norm of Non-Discrimination," 74 *Mich. L. Rev.* 865 (1976); "Freedom from Discrimination in Choice of Language and International Human Rights," 1 *So. Ill. U. L. Rev.* 1151 (1976). See also Gros-Espiell, "Non-Discrimination and Self-Determination as peremptory norms of international law, with special reference to their denial of the legitimacy of states which violate or disregard these peremptory norms,"

UNITAR Colloquium on the Prohibition of Apartheid, Racism, and Racial Discrimination and the Achievement of Self-Determination in International Law (November 1980).

12. South West Africa case, 4 *ICJ Pleadings* 493 (1966).

13. Barcelona Traction case, *supra* note 9.

14. Advisory Opinion on Namibia, *supra* note 9.

15. Declaration on Race and Racial Prejudice, Adopted by UNESCO Gen. Conf. (20th Sess.), 27 November 1978.

16. *Ibid.*

17. Pakistan, UN Doc. A/C.3/SR.1102 para. 4 (1961).

18. Argentina, UN Doc. A/C.3/SR.1184 para. 7 (1962).

19. The Secretary-General also contributed. At one stage, for example, he suggested that the General Assembly and the Commission on Human Rights "consider whether the anti-discriminatory provisions of the Covenant . . . should not be strengthened by the addition of a provision to the effect that the states parties to the Covenant undertake not to lend the assistance of their judicial, executive, and administrative organs for the purpose of enforcing or practising discrimination." UN Doc. A/C.3/534 para. 7 (1951).

20. See UN Doc. E/CN.4/528 para. 69 (1951).

21. See, for example, a memorandum of the World Jewish Congress of 27 January 1950, UN Doc. E/C.2/241 at 2 (1950).

22. As well as in the International Declaration and Convention on the Elimination of All Forms of Racial Discrimination.

23. But compare UN Doc. E/CN.4/SR.193 paras. 103, 107; UN Doc.E/CN.4/SR. 194 paras. 52–57 (1950).

24. Ukrainian SSR, UN Doc. A/C.3/SR.1183 para. 10 (1962).

25. 10 GAOR Annexes, UN Doc. A/2929 para. 34 (1955).

26. Id. para 179. *See also* Vierdag, *supra* note 1, at 126–27.

27. Tomuschat suggests that Article 26 provides merely for "equal protection in the application of the law." I do not think that the arguments he advances for this conclusion are persuasive. He admits that there was ambiguity with regard to the intention of the authors of the Covenant. This should have led him to the literal meaning of the terms. Instead, Tomuschat goes to great lengths to suggest that what appears in the Covenant as "equal protection of the law" should instead be read as "equal protection in the application of the law." Only the clearest evidence that this was the intention of the drafters could justify such a conclusion. This evidence, as Tomuschat recognizes, is distinctly lacking. C. Tomuschat, "Equality and Non-Discrimination under the International Covenant on Civil and Political Rights," in Münch, ed., *Festschrift für Hans-Jürgen Schlochauer* (1981).

28. The Permanent Court of International Justice, in its Advisory Opinion of February 4, 1932, on the Treatment of Polish Nationals and other persons of Polish origin or speech in the Danzig Territory, held that "the prohibition against discrimination, in order to be effective, must ensure the absence of discrimination in fact as well as in law." [1932] PCIJ, Ser.A/B, no. 44 at 28.

29. Report of the Human Rights Committee, 34 GAOR Supp. 40, UN Doc. para. 325 (1979); see also UN Doc. CCPR/C/SR.162 para. 95 (1979).

30. Tarnopolsky, UN Doc. CCPR/C/SR.162 para. 95 (1979).

31. *Id.* para. 16.

32. These principles were derived from a study of Equality in the Administration of Justice, prepared by its Special Rapporteur, A. Abu Ranat. UN Doc. E/CN.4/Sub.2/296 (1969).

33. The European Convention, however, does not have a provision for equal protection of the laws corresponding to Article 26 of the Covenant.

34. X v. Federal Republic of Germany, Eur. Comm. Human Rights, 39 *Collection of Decisions* 58 (1971). See also ISOP v. Austria, 5 *Y.B. Eur. Conv. Human Rights* 108 (1962).

35. Belgian Linguistic case, 11 *Y.B. Eur. Conv. Human Rights* 832 (1968); National Union of Police case, 18 *Y.B. Eur. Conv. Human Rights* 294 (1975). On "margin of appreciation," see essays 9 and 12.

36. *Sunday Times* case, Judgment of 26 April 1979, 18 *Int'l Leg. Mat.* 931, para. 70 (1979).

37. Belgian Linguistic case, *supra* note 35, at 33–34.

38. It is therefore somewhat unrealistic and unconvincing to suggest, as does Tomuschat, *supra* note 27, that the Covenant "lacks a comprehensive guarantee of nondiscrimination as meaning equality 'of' or 'in' the law." Tomuschat does not give sufficient credit to the context in which the Covenant was drafted. The Charter of the United Nations had already recognized as a main pillar of the new international order the principle of nondiscrimination. This was recognized by the International Law Commission during the preparation of the Draft Declaration on the Rights and Duties of States. The Universal Declaration of Human Rights further consolidated the principle of nondiscrimination. When this context is taken into account, it becomes very difficult to maintain that the Covenant lacks a comprehensive guarantee of nondiscrimination. As I maintained earlier, the meaning of the principles of equality and nondiscrimination was intended to be elucidated from the modern international law of human rights.

39. Italy, UN Doc. A/C.3/SR.1099 para. 10 (1961).

40. Italy, UN Doc. A/C.3/SR.1185 para. 14 (1962).

41. USSR, UN Doc. A/C.3/SR.1203 para. 16 (1962).

42. Compare the European Court of Human Rights in the Belgian Linguistic case: "In spite of the very general wording of the French version ('sans distinction aucune'), Article 14 does not forbid every difference in treatment in the exercise of the rights and freedoms recognized. This version must be read in the light of the more restrictive text of the English version ('without discrimination'). In addition, and in particular, one would reach absurd results were one to give Article 14 an interpretation as wide as that which the French version seems to imply. One would, in effect, be led to judge as contrary to the Convention every one of the many legal or administrative provisions which do not secure to everyone complete equality of treatment in the enjoyment of the

rights and freedoms recognized. The competent national authorities are frequently confronted with situations and problems which, on account of difference inherent therein, call for different legal solutions; moreover, certain legal inequalities tend only to correct factual inequalities. The extensive interpretation mentioned above cannot consequently be accepted" (Belgian Linguistic case, *supra* note 35, at 864).

43. See, e.g., the remarks of the Danish representative, UN Doc. A/C.3/SR. 1184 para. 17 (1962). See similarly the representative of Pakistan, UN Doc. A/C.3/SR.1185 para. 52 (1962). Compare I. Brownlie, *Principles of Public International Law* 598 (3d ed. 1979).

44. Definitions of the Expressions "Prevention of Discrimination" and "Protection of Minorities" (Memorandum by the Division of Human Rights), UN Doc. E/CN.4/Sub.2/8 at 2 (1947). See generally McKean, *supra* note 1.

45. UN Doc. E/CN.4/Sub.2/40 paras. 33–36 (1949). See also Vierdag, *supra* note 1, at 166.

46. Philippines, UN Doc. A/C.3/SR.1102 para. 53 (1961).

47. UN Doc. A/C.3/SR.1101 para. 24 (1961).

48. UN Doc. A/C.3/SR.1098 (1961).

49. UN Doc. A/C.3/SR.1182 para. 17 (1962). See J. Wilkinson, *From Brown to Bakke* (1979); M. Cohen et al., *Equality and Preferential Treatment* (1977).

50. UN Doc. A/C.3/SR.1183 paras. 12, 29 (1962).

51. UN Doc. A/C.3/SR.1257 para. 18 (1963). The Indian representative was supported by his colleagues from Australia and the United Arab Republic. UN Doc. A/C.3/SR. 1258 paras. 45, 48 (1963).

52. UN Doc. A/C.3/SR.1259 paras. 33–34 (1963). Compare the Third Report of the UNESCO Committee on Conventions and Recommendations, 20 UNESCO Gen. Conf., Doc. 20 C/40 para. 271 (1978): "The Committee noted . . . that a number of replies indicate that the responsible authorities have introduced preferential measures to assist disadvantaged regions . . . or to promote the education of minority groups . . . or, again, the handicapped. . . ." As already indicated in its 1968 report (15 C/11, paragraph 131), the Committee regards "differentiation which is for a protective purpose, for example to give preferential treatment to children from culturally deprived homes or backgrounds, as not amounting to discrimination within the meaning of the Convention and the Recommendation."

53. There the court recognized, "It is perhaps not easy to define the distinction between the notions of equality in fact and equality in law; nevertheless, it may be said that the former notion excludes the idea of a merely formal equality; that is indeed what the Court laid down in the Advisory Opinion of September 10th, 1923, concerning the case of the German settlers in Poland (Opinion No. 6), in which it was said that 'there must be equality in fact as well as ostensible legal equality in the sense of the absence of discrimination in the words of the law.' Equality in law precludes discrimination of any kind; whereas equality in fact may involve the necessity of different treatment in

order to attain a result which establishes an equilbrium between different situations" PCIJ [1923], ser. A/B, no. 64, at 19.

See also the Advisory Opinion on German settlers in Poland, PCIJ, [1923], Ser. B., no. 6; Advisory Opinion on Treatment and Polish Nationals and other Persons of Polish Origin or Speech in the Territory of the Free City of Danzig, PCIJ [1932], Ser. A/B, no. 44.

54. Belgian Linguistic Case, *supra* note 35, at 34. Compare the comment on the cases in F. Jacobs, *The European Convention on Human Rights* 191–92 (1975).

55. Tarnopolsky, UN Doc. CCPR/C/SR.189 para. 10 (1980).

56. Lallah, *id.* para. 14.

57. Danelius, *id.* para. 16.

58. Compare the U.S. cases upholding civil rights laws outlawing private discrimination in places of public accommodation, or private interference with access to public bodies or benefits. Heart of Atlanta Motel v. United States, 379 U.S. 241 (1964); United States v. Guest, 383 U.S. 745 (1966). Also the prohibition of private discrimination in housing and in education. Jones v. Alfred H. Mayer Co., 392 U.S. 409 (1968); Runyon v. McCrary, 427 U.S. 160 (1976). But compare Moose Lodge No. 107 v. Irvis, 407 U.S. 163 (1962) (racial discrimination by private club).

59. UN Doc. E/CN.4/Sub.2/8, *supra* note 44.

60. Tomuschat, UN Doc. CCPR/C/SR.170 para. 39 (1979). See also CCPR/C/SR.206 para. 16 (1980).

61. Tarnopolsky, UN Doc. CCPR/C/SR.170 para. 82 (1979); see also SR. 189 para. 10 (1980).

62. Saudi Arabia, UN Doc. A/C.3/SR.1099 para. 18 (1961).

63. Greece, UN Doc. A/C.3/SR.1098 para. 33 (1961).

64. Pakistan, UN Doc.A/C.3/SR.1102 para. 4 (1961).

65. USSR, UN Doc. A/C.3/SR.1098 para. 6 (1961).

66. USA, UN Doc. A/C.3/SR.1099 para. 2 (1961).

67. I therefore disagree with Tomuschat, *supra* note 27, that article 26 cannot be interpreted as an obligation incumbent upon states parties to prohibit private discrimination. This view is too broadly stated and does not take sufficiently into account the differences acknowledged by the drafters between permissible private and social distinctions and impermissible discrimination by private individuals in fields such as business, housing or transport. Tomuschat appears to argue a personal preference.

68. Indonesia, UN Docs. A/C.3/SR.1100 para. 4, A/C.3/SR1102, para. 48 (1961).

69. UN Doc. A/2929, *supra* note 26, para. 181.

70. UN Doc. A/C.3/SR.1097 para. 402 (1961).

71. Advisory Opinion on Treatment of Polish Nationals and other Persons of Polish Origin or Speech in the Danzig Territory, [1932] PCIJ, Ser. A/B no. 44 at 41.

72. UN Doc. A/C.3/SR.1102, *supra* note 64.

73. The Austrian Constitutional Court held that neither Article 14 of the European Convention, nor Article 7 of the Austrian Constitution, guaranteed aliens equality before the law, and that Austria, therefore, could limit the right of aliens to acquire real property. Erkenntnisse und Beschlüsse des Verfassungs-gerichtshofes 39 (1974, I) no. 7307 at 239; 40 (1975, I) no. 7581 at 465; noted in 106 *Journal de Droit International* 145 (1979).

74. UN Doc. 4/34/40, *supra* note 29, para. 339.

75. The study of Equality in the Administration of Justice, *supra* note 32.

76. These principles were based on a Study of Discrimination in the Matter of Political Rights, prepared by H. Santa Cruz, a Special Rapporteur of the Sub-Commission. UN Doc. E/CN.4/Sub. 2/213 (1961).

77. These principles were derived from a Study of Discrimination in the Matter of Religious Rights and Practices, undertaken by A. Krishnaswami, UN Doc. E/CN.4/Sub.2/200 (1959).

78. UN Doc. E/CN.4/L.1560 Add. 16 at 15 (1981).

79. The resolution was based on Study of Discrimination in Education by C. Ammoun, UN Doc. E/CN.4 Sub.2/181 at 172 (1956).

80. *Human Rights Instruments* at 35 (1978).

81. Study of Discrimination against Persons Born out of Wedlock by V. Saario, UN Publ. sales no. E.68, XIV 3, at 178. See generally essay 8.

82. This proposal draws on a study by Baroness Elles. UN Doc. E/CN.4/1336 (1979).

83. UN Doc. A/34/40, *supra* note 29, para. 90.

84. 33 GAOR Supp. 40, UN Doc. A/33/40 para. 209 (1978).

85. *Id.* para. 312.

86. *Id.* para. 137.

87. Tarnopolsky, UN Doc. CCPR/C/SR.142 para. 4 (1979).

88. UN Doc. A/33/40, *supra* note 84, para. 290.

11. THE RIGHTS OF MINORITIES

1. There is an abundant literature on the treatment of minorities. For a bib-liographical note, see Claude, *National Minorities; An International Problem* 215–17 (1955). For comprehensive bibliographies, see Pizzorusso, *Le Minoranze nel Diritto Pubblico Interno,* vol. 2 at 559–600 (1967); Sohn, *Cases and Materials on World Law* 538–41 (1950); Modeen, *The International Protection of National Mi-norities in Europe* 150–55 (1969); Veiter, *Das Recht der Volksgruppen und Sprach-minderheiten in Oesterreich* 813–59 (1962).

2. The most comprehensive recent view of minority questions is contained in the monumental study prepared by Francesco Capotorti for the United Na-tions Commission on Human Rights and its Sub-Commission on Prevention of Discrimination and Protection of Minorities, entitled *Study on the Rights of Persons Belonging to Ethnic, Religious and Linguistic Minorities.* It was published in installments in UN Docs. E/CN.4/Sub.2/384 and Add. 1–7 (1977); and reprinted

in UN Doc. E/CN.4/Sub.2/384 (Rev. 1 1979); UN Pub. E.78.XIV.1 (Hereinafter cited as Capotorti). It was preceded by several preliminary reports by Capotorti, which may be found in UN Docs. E/CN.4/Sub.2/L.564 (1972); E/CN.4/Sub.2/L.621 (1975).

3. Concerning the earlier treaties, see Capotorti, *supra* note 2, at 1–4.

4. An evaluation of the accomplishments and faults of the League of Nations' protection of minorities is contained *id.* at 16–26. Concerning the disputed question of the extinction of the minority treaties as a result of the changes brought by the Second World War, see *id.* at 27, relying on the UN Secretariat's "Study of the Legal Validity of the Undertakings Concerning Minorities," UN Doc. E/CN.4/367 (1950), and Add. 1 (1951). For a criticism of that document, see Feinberg, "The Legal Validity of the Undertakings Concerning Minorities and the Clausula Rebus Sic Stantibus," 5 *Scripta Hierosolymitana: Studies in Law* 95–131 (1958). See also Modeen, *supra* note 1, at 71–73.

5. See R. Russell, *A History of the United Nations Charter* 323 (1958).

6. For a short history of the Commission and the Sub-Commission, see UN Doc. ST/HR/2 (1974).

7. For a summary of these efforts by the Secretariat and by the governments of Denmark, France, the Soviet Union, the United Kingdom, and Yugoslavia, see Claude, *supra* note 1, at 157–60.

8. Comment by the government of Romania in Capotorti, *supra* note 2, at 8.

9. Statement by Dragić in *Nations and Nationalities of Yugoslavia* (1974), cited *id.* at 15.

10. For instance, China, India, and the United Kingdom proposed the deletion of the entire article. UN Doc. E/CN.4/SR.73 at 5 (1948). In supporting this proposal, Eleanor Roosevelt (United States) pointed out that

"the aim of States was to assimilate and absorb large foreign groups, and to make them part of the nation. Unless all the citizens of a given country could speak the same language, there was the danger that public order might be disrupted by persons who might not understand their duties as citizens of the country in which they were a minority. It was not a question of teaching children in a language different from that of the majority, but of adult persons who would be unable to assume their duties as citizens of the larger country" (*Id.* at 7).

While Wilson (United Kingdom) was opposed to proclaiming the principle of assimilation, he believed that "the principle of diversity in some States, far from raising cultural levels, might create minority problems." *Id.* at 12. The article on minorities was deleted by ten votes to six. UN Doc. E/CN.4/SR.74 at 5 (1948). A Soviet proposal for a more limited article was also rejected. *Id.* at 6. It suggested:

"All persons, irrespective of whether they belong to the racial, national or religious minority or majority of the population, have the right to their own ethnic or national culture, to establish their own schools and receive teaching in their native tongue, and to use that tongue in the press, at public meetings, in the courts and in other official premises" (7 ESCOR Supp. 2, UN Doc. E/800 at 44 (1948)).

11. 3 (I) GAOR Annexes 545 UN Doc. A/784 (1948).

12. The amendment was rejected by 34 votes to 8, with 14 abstentions. 3 (I) GAOR Plen. Mtgs. (183d mtg.) at 930 (1948).

13. G. A. Res. 217 C (III), UN Doc. A/810 at 77–78 (1948). It was adopted without discussion by 46 votes to 6, with 2 abstentions; 3 GAOR Plen. Mtgs. (183d mtg.) at 935 (1948). For a heated discussion in the Third Committee and the votes on many amendments to this resolution, see 3 GAOR C.3 (160th–162d mtgs.) at 716–36 (1948).

14. UN Secretary-General, "Activities of the United Nations Relating to the Protection of Minorities," UN Doc. E/CN.4/Sub.2/194 (1958); Capotorti, *supra* note 2, at 28. For a list of early studies of the Commission, see *id.* at 50.

15. UN Docs. E/CN.4/Sub.2/112 (1950); E/CN.4/Sub.2/SR.55 at 5–7 (1950); E/CN.4/Sub.2/SR.57 at 2–3 (1950); E/CN.4/358 at 19–23 (1950). See also Capotorti, *supra* note 2, at 32.

16. UN Docs. E/CN.4/674 at 5 (1953); E/CN.4/SR.369–371 (1953); Report of the Ninth Session of the Commission on Human Rights, 16 ESCOR Supp. 8, UN Doc. E/2447 at 55–56 (1953).

17. 16 GAOR C.3 (1103d–1104th mtgs.), UN Docs. A/C.3/SR.1103–SR.1104 (1961); 16 GAOR Annexes, UN. Doc. A/5000 paras. 116–18 (1961).

18. G.A. Res. 2200 A (XXI), 21 GAOR Supp. 16, UN Doc. A/6316 at 56 (1966).

19. See the statement by the United Kingdom, 10 GAOR C.3 (642d mtg.), UN Doc. A/C.3/SR.642 at 90 (1955).

20. Article 1. See essay 14.

21. Capotorti, *supra* note 2, at 35.

22. The phrase "in community with others" occurs also in Article 18 relating to the freedom of religion.

23. The 1947 draft by the Sub-Commission of a minority provision to be inserted in the Declaration of Human Rights included, however, a clause that persons belonging to minority groups shall have institutional and linguistic rights "as far as is compatible with public order and security." UN Doc. E/CN.4./52 at 9 (1947).

24. UN Doc.E/2447, *supra* note 16, at 7, 75.

25. UN Docs. E/CN.4/SR.370 at 4, 7, 9–10 (1953), E/CN.4/SR.371 at 4, 6, 7 (1953).

26. See, e.g., the statement by France in a debate on the implementation of Article 1 of the draft Covenant, 7 GAOR C.3 (445th mtg.), UN Doc. A/C.3/SR.445 at 162–63 (1952); and by Sweden and the United Kingdom in the debate on Article 1 of the Covenant, 10 GAOR C.3 (641st–642d mtgs.), UN Docs. A/C.3/SR.641–SR.642 at 86–87 (1955).

27. See, e.g., the statements by Greece in the general debate on the covenants, 9 GAOR C.3 (572d mtg.), UN Doc. A/C.3/SR.572 at 150 (1954); and in

the discussion of Article 1, 10 GAOR C.3 (647th mtg.), UN Doc. A/C.3/SR.647 at 113 (1955).

28. Statement by Saudi Arabia during the debate on Article 1, 10 GAOR C.3 (648th mtg.), UN Doc. A/C.3/SR.648 at 121 (1955). This statement was followed by the interesting remark that "minorities should be able to achieve their aims by legal means." *Id.* As the delegate from Iran recalled later:

"In the debate on article 1 of the draft Covenants, his delegation had drawn attention to the dangers of mistaken or over-simplified theories regarding the exercise of that right, which might lead to confusion and disorder; if self-determination was misused and considered as an absolute right, nothing but anarchy could result. The right could be exercised only within the limits of national sovereignty. It must not be used to undermine a sovereign Power's rights over its territory and national resources; to use the right of self determination in order to incite dissident minorities to rise against the State and imperil its stability would be as contrary to the true spirit of self-determination as aggression or subversion itself. And yet, as history went to show, groups with subversive and aggressive aims had been used by foreign Powers to overturn the governments of countries whose territory they wish to seize. Many independent countries had been the victims of irresponsible groups which had been encouraged to destroy the national unity of their own country. Furthermore, the right of self-determination must never be confused with the right of secession. Secession was the outcome not of respect for the right of self-determination but of disregard for fundamental human rights and the absence of the free consent of peoples to the exercise of the right of self-determination. . . . [No] country represented on the Committee would be in existence if every national, religious or linguistic group had an absolute and unrestricted right to self-determination."

(Statement by Iran in a discussion on recommendations concerning international respect for the right of peoples and nations to self-determination, 13 GAOR C.3 (888th mtg.), UN Doc. A/C.3/SR.888 at 257 (1958)).

29. Statement by India in the same debate, *id.* (891st mtg.) at 274.

30. 10 GAOR Annexes, UN Doc. A/2929, Agenda Item No. 28, Part II, at 63 (1955).

31. For instance, the government of Austria has noted that scholars "have not so far succeeded in formulating a generally accepted definition of the concept of minority—whether ethnic, religious or linguistic. In view of these unsuccessful efforts, it may be doubted whether a satisfactory solution of this problem is possible. Similarly, all efforts made in this field within the framework of the United Nations have failed." Capotorti, *supra* note 2, at 8.

32. *Id.* at 5–6. Capotorti also made an attempt to prepare a workable, if not generally acceptable definition. *Id.* at 11–12, 95–96.

33. Advisory Opinion of 31 July 1930, [1930] PCIJ, Ser.B, no. 17 at 19–22, 33.

34. United Nations, Report of the Tenth Session of the Commission on Human Rights, 18 ESCOR Supp. 7, UN Doc. E/2573 at 48–49 (1954).

35. Capotorti, *supra* note 2, at 96.

36. Id. at 5–7.

37. UN Doc. A/2929, *supra* note 30, at 63.

38. Capotorti, *supra* note 2, at 8–9.

39. *Id*. at 17.

40. The Yugoslav government has, however, noted that the concept of a minority is a relative one since in some localities the number of members of the minority group can be greater than that of the rest of the population. Id. at 9.

41. This was the position of the Netherlands. *Id*. at 18.

42. According to the Sub-Commission on Prevention of Discrimination and Protection of Minorites, minorities must include "a sufficient number of persons to preserve by themselves their traditions and characteristics." UN Doc. E/2573, *supra* note 34, at 49.

43. Capotorti, *supra* note 2, at 9.

44. *Id*. at 10.

45. UN Doc. E/CN.4/SR.369 at 13 (1953). The Soviet delegate also pointed out that the Genocide Convention of 1948 listed "national, ethnical, racial or religious groups."

46. *Id*. at 16.

47. UN Doc. E/2447, *supra* note 16, para. 53. See also the statements by the Soviet Union, UN Doc. E/CN.4/SR.368 at 14 (1953); India, UN Doc. E/CN.4/SR.369 at 7 (1953); the Philippines, UN Doc. E/CN.4/SR.370 at 8–9 (1953).

48. The Commission did not adopt suggestions that the article should apply only to such groups as might "wish to preserve ethnic, religious or linguistic traditions or characteristics." This, it was argued, was subjective and dangerous, "since dominant groups which did not wish to extend equal rights to certain minorities would be able to justify their action by claiming that those groups did not wish to maintain their individual character." UN Doc. E/2573, *supra* note 34, at 49.

49. See Capotorti, *supra* note 2, at 11; F. Ermacora, *Nationalitatenkonflikt und Volksgruppenrecht* 114–15, 179 (1978).

50. This view was taken especially by Latin American delegates. See, e.g., the statements by Uruguay, UN Doc. E/CN.4/SR.370 at 4 (1953); and UN Doc. E/CN.4/SR.371 at 4 (1953). In the Commission on Human Rights it was pointed out that extension of minority rights to groups of immigrants "would create a delicate problem for countries of reception which were anxious to assimilate such groups." UN Doc. E/2573, *supra* note 34, at 49–50. On the more general debate about the assimilation question, see Claude, *supra* note 1, at 80–86, 165–69. The new African states also face the issue of maintaining national unity in the face of the centrifugal effect of tribal trans-frontier links and separatist aspirations.

51. See the statement by Chile in the Commission. UN Doc. E/CN.4/SR.370 at 5 (1953).

52. It was pointed out in the debate that Mexico "was at present earnestly pursuing the incorporation within its national community of large indigenous groups which had hitherto led, so to speak, a marginal existence owing to lack of communications and the rudimentary level of economic development attained in the areas in which they lived. Those groups had remained untouched by the benefits of modern civilization, and had their own modes of thought and their own languages, but it would be sheer romanticism to make them into minorities." UN Doc. E/CN.4/SR.368 at 10 (1953).

53. Santa Cruz, *Racial Discrimination,* UN Doc. E/CN.4/Sub.2/307 Rev. 1, at 96–147, UN Pub. E.71.XIV.2 (1971).

54. José Martínez Cobo was appointed special rapporteur. For his reports, see UN Docs. E/CN.4/Sub.2/L.566 (1972), L.584 (1973), L.596 (1974), L.622 (1975), L.684 (1978); L.732 (1980).

55. Capotorti, *supra* note 2, at 12–15.

56. *Id.* at 96–97.

57. See, e.g., Claude, *supra* note 1, at 18, 137–44; Capotorti, *supra* note 2, at 18–19, 30–31. For a collection of minority provisions in recent treaties, see United Nations, *Protection of Minorities,* UN Doc. E/CN.4/Sub.2/214 Rev. 1, at 9–58, UN Pub. 67.XIV.3 (1967). According to the United Nations Secretariat, the purpose of these provisions was to protect the minorities against assimilation. UN Doc. E/CN.4/Sub.2/8 at 2–3 (1947).

58. Advisory Opinion of 6 April 1935, PCIJ, Ser. A/B, no. 64 at 17.

59. *Id.* at 19–20, 23.

60. The first draft before it, prepared by the Secretariat of the United Nations, contained the proposal that persons belonging to a minority shall have "the right to establish and maintain, out of an equitable proportion of any public funds available for the purpose, their schools and cultural and religious institutions, and to use their own languages before the courts and other authorities and organs of the State and in the press and in public assembly." U.N. Doc. E/CN.4/21 at 23 (1947). Except for the addition of the phrase "and in the press and public assembly," this text is identical with that suggested by H. Lauterpacht in his *An International Bill of the Rights of Man* 151 (1945); see also UN Docs. E/CN.4/SR.2 at 3–4 (1947), E/CN.4/AC.1/3/Add.1 at 380 (1947). A French proposal in a similar spirit suggested that such persons shall have "the right, within the limits required by public order, to open and maintain schools and religious or cultural institutions. Subject to the same limitations they may use their language in the press, at public meetings and when appearing before the courts or other authorities of the State." UN Doc. E/CN.4/21 at 66 (1947). The Sub-Commission strengthened the exception and modified the substantive clause, proposing that the persons belonging to specified minority groups (more narrowly defined than in later texts) shall have "the right as far as it is compatible with public order and security to establish and maintain their

schools and cultural or religious institutions, and to use their own language and script in the press, in public assembly and before the courts and other authorities of the State, if they so choose." UN Doc. E/CN.4/52 at 9 (1947). The words "and script" were added as a result of a proposal by the Indian expert. UN Doc. E/CN.4/Sub.2/SR.10 at 2 (1947).

61. See, e.g., the Secretariat's proposal, UN Doc. E/CN.4/21 at 23 (1947); the French proposals, *id.* at 23, 66; and the Sub-Commission's proposal, UN Doc. E/CN.4/52 at 9 (1947).

62. The Drafting Committee of the Commission on Human Rights followed to some extent the French text in proposing that minority persons shall have "the right as far as compatible with public order to establish and maintain their schools and cultural or religious institutions, and to use their own language in the press, in public assembly and before the courts and other authorities of the State." At the same time the Committee suggested that in view of "the supreme importance of this Article to many countries," this proposal should be referred to the Sub-Commission "for examination of the minority aspects." UN Doc. E/CN.4/21 at 81 (1947).

63. 11 ESCOR Supp. 5, UN Doc. E/1681 at 80 (1950).

64. UN Doc. E/CN.4/358 at 40 (1950).

65. UN Doc. E/1681, *supra* note 63, at 11 n.9. The Commission decided that it was premature to take any action on this resolution. *Id.* at 12. Finally, the Commission adopted a provision on the protection of minorities in 1953 as Article 25 of the Draft Covenant on Civil and Political Rights. In addition to the Sub-Commission's proposal, the Commission had before it the following simplified proposal by the Soviet Union:

"The State shall ensure to national minorities the right to use their native tongue and to possess their national schools, libraries, museums and other cultural and educational institutions" (UN Doc. E/2447, *supra* note 16, at 55).

There was also the following, more elaborate proposal by Yugoslavia, which was withdrawn before the final vote:

"Every person shall have the right to show freely his membership of an ethnic or linguistic group, to use without hindrance the name of his group, to learn the language of this group and to use it in public or private life, to be taught in this language, as well as the right to cultural development together with other members of this group, without being subjected on that account to any discrimination whatsoever, and particularly such discrimination as might deprive him of the rights enjoyed by other citizens of the same State" (*Ibid.*).

After adding to the Sub-Commission's text the beginning phrase "in those States in which ethnic, religious or linguistic minorities exist" (in order, as discussed before, to exclude immigrants), that text was approved by twelve votes to one, with three abstentions. *Id.* at 56. While the discussion of this final text centered mostly on objections to the Soviet and Yugoslav proposals, some comments were also made on the Sub-Commission's text. For instance, it was noted that this text would allow members of a linguistic minority "to use their language among themselves and in their schools, but would not commit governments to providing special schools for them." UN Doc. E/CN.4/SR.370 at 9 (1953).

66. Capotorti, *supra* note 2, at 98–99.

67. UN Doc. A/33/262 at 20–21 (1978). See also note 83 *infra*.

68. See, e.g., 33 GAOR Supp. 40, UN Doc. A/33/40 para. 449 (1978); 34 GAOR Supp. 40, UN Doc. A/34/40 paras. 205, 268 (1979).

69. UN Doc. CCPR/C/SR.207 para. 4 (1980).

70. Belgian Linguistic Case, 11 *Y.B. Eur. Conv. Human Rights* 832 (1968).

71. Kjeldsen v. Denmark, 15 *Y.B. Eur. Conv. Human Rights* 428 (1970); Busk-Madsen v. Denmark, 44 *Collection of Decisions* 96, 96–100 (1973); Pedersen v. Denmark, *ibid.* The three cases were joined.

72. Capotorti, *supra* note 2, at 57. It has also been suggested that the Covenants

"partake of the creative force of the Declaration and constitute in a similar fashion an authoritative interpretation of the basic rules of international law on the subject of human rights which are embodied in the Charter of the United Nations. . . . Consequently, although the Covenants apply directly [only] to the states that have ratified them, they are of some importance, at the same time, with respect to the interpretation of the Charter obligations of the non-ratifying states." Sohn, "The Human Rights Law of the Charter," 12 *Tex. Int'l L.J.* 129, 135–36 (1977).

73. Capotorti, *supra* note 2, at 57–89, 99–102.

74. See, for instance, UN Doc. A/33/40, *supra* note 68, at 15, 29, 35, 38, 45, 51, 64, 67, 72, 75, 81, 90, 93, 97.

75. See, e.g., the draft convention by Ekstrand, Masani, and Meneses-Pallares, UN Doc. E/CN.4/Sub.2/127 at 4–11 (1951). For its inconclusive discussion, see UN Docs. E/CN.4/Sub.2/SR.69 at 5–10; and SR. 70 at 2–8 (1951).

76. Capotorti, *supra* note 2, at 102. In commenting on this study, Finland pointed out that a declaration undoubtedly would promote the protection of the rights of minority persons, and consequently help such minorities to preserve their identity and their own characteristics. UN Doc. E/CN.4/1298 at 6 (1978).

77. UN Docs. E/CN.4/1261 at 45 (1977), E/CN.4/L.1367 (1978).

78. UN Doc. E/CN.4/L.1367/Rev.1 (1978).

79. UN Doc. E/CN.4/L.1381 at 2 (1978); reprinted in [1978] ESCOR Supp. 4, UN Doc. E/1978/34 at 72 (1978).

80. UN Doc. E/1978/34 at 73–74, 119 (1978).

81. Coment by Greece, UN Doc. E/CN.4/1298 at 9 (1978).

82. *Id*. at 3–8, 12–21.

83. United Nations, *Report of the World Conference to Combat Racism and Racial Discrimination,* Geneva, August 14–25, 1978, UN Doc. A/CONF.92/40; UN Doc. A/33/262, at 27. This Conference included also the following sweeping statement on minority rights (*id*. at 16–17):

"The Conference recognizes that persons belonging to national ethnic and other minorities can play a significant role in the promotion of international co-operation and understanding and affirms that national protection of the rights of persons belonging to minorities in accordance with the International Covenant on Civil and Political Rights, in particular its article 27, is essential to enable them to fulfil this role; the Conference stresses that granting persons belonging to minority groups the opportunity to participate fully in the political, economic and social life of their country can contribute to the promotion of understanding, co-operation and harmonious relations between the different groups living in a country; the Conference also recognizes that in certain cases special protection of minority rights may be called for, in particular by the adoption of effective measures in favour of particularly disadvantaged minority groups; the Conference endorses the action taken so far by the competent United Nations bodies to protect persons belonging to minorities and is confident that the future action currently envisaged will appropriately enhance the international protection of the rights of persons belonging to minorities; in the promotion and guarantee of the rights of minorities, there should be strict respect for the sovereignty, territorial integrity and political independence of the countries where they live and of non-interference in their internal affairs."

84. UN Doc. E/CN.4/1298 at 4 (1978).

85. [1979] ESCOR Supp. 6, 1 UN Doc. E/1979/36 at 83–86, 127. Among the "relevant" documents was an elaborate international draft convention on the protection of national or ethnic groups or minorities, submitted to the Commission by the Minorities Rights Group, an international non-governmental organization. UN Doc. E/CN.4/NGO/231 (1979). For the report of the Working Group of the Sub-Commission, see UN Doc. E/CN.4/Sub. 2/455/Rev. 1 (1980).

86. *Supra* note 81, at 4.

12. PERMISSIBLE LIMITATIONS ON RIGHTS

I want to express my sincere gratitude to Barbara Di Ferrante, Esq., of the Council of Europe, for her valuable assistance in the research and editing of this essay. A. C. K.

1. "In time of public emergency which threatens the life of the nation and the existence of which is officially proclaimed, the States Parties to the present Covenant may take measures derogating from their obligations under the present Covenant to the extent strictly required by the exigencies of the situation, provided that such measures are not inconsistent with their other obligations under international law and do not

involve discrimination solely on the ground of race, colour, sex, language, religion or social origin" (Article 4).
See essay 3.

2. See also Vegleris, "Valeur et signification de la clause 'dans une société démocratique' dans la Convention européenne des droits de l'homme," in Second International Conference on the European Convention on Human Rights, *Les droits de l'homme en droit interne et en droit international* 223 (1968).

3. Article 12(3) admits limitations upon freedom of movement and free choice of residence when this is necessary to protect national security. During the drafting of the article, there was discussion in the Commission on Human Rights of more exact delineation of the contents of the limitation clause. Among the restrictions which various representatives mentioned as being legitimate or necessary were those which might be imposed in a national emergency. 10 GAOR Annexes, UN Doc. A/2929 at 38 (1955). The majority, however, agreed that restrictions on freedom of movement should be provided for by law and that "such law must be just." *Id.* at 39. Article 6, the right to life, also not subject to derogation, implies at least some limitations. "No one shall be *arbitrarily* deprived of his life" (emphasis added). Capital punishment is discouraged but not outlawed. See essays 5 and 6.

4. Covenant on Civil and Political Rights, Articles 12(3), 14(1), 18(3), 19 (3), 21, 22(2). See also the International Covenant on Economic, Social, and Cultural Rights, Article 8(1) (a) and (c), G.A. Res. 2200, 21 GAOR Supp. 16, UN Doc. A/6316 (1966); European Convention for the Protection of Human Rights and Fundamental Freedoms, Articles 6(1), 8(2), 9(2), 10(2), Protocol No. 1, Art. 1 and Protocol No. 4, Art. 2(3), 213 UNTS 221 (1950); American Convention on Human Rights, Article 12(3), 13(2) (b), 15, 16(2); O.A.S. Doc. OEA/Ser. K/XVI/1.1., Doc. 65, text reprinted in 9 *Int'l Leg. Mat.* 673 (1970).

Other international conventions also contain comparable limitation clauses: the UNESCO Agreement on the Importation of Educational, Scientific and Cultural Materials of November 22, 1950, Article V; the UNESCO Agreement for Facilitating the International Circulation of Visual and Auditory Materials of an Educational, Scientific and Cultural Character of July 15, 1949; and the International Telecommunication Convention of Montreux, 1965, Article 32(2), permit restrictions on grounds relating directly to national security, public order or morals. See Buergenthal, "The Right to Receive Information Across National Boundaries," in Aspen Institute Program on Communications and Society, *Control of the Direct Broadcast Satellite: Values in Conflict* 80 (1974).

Similarly, Article 48(3) of the Treaty Establishing the European Economic Community provides that free movement of workers is subject to "limitation justified on grounds of public policy, public security or public health." A similar exception in relation to freedom of establishment results from Article 56(1), and Article 66 stipulates that Article 56(1) applies also to freedom to supply services. See A. Evans, "Ordre Public, Public Policy and United Kingdom Immigration Law," [1978] *European Law Review* 375; see also Lyon-Caen, "La réserve d'ordre public en matière de liberté d'établissement et de libre circulation," [1966] *Revue Trimestrielle de Droit Européen* 693–705.

5. 15 GAOR Annexes, UN Doc. A/4625 (1960). Article 8 of the European Convention, which protects the right to respect for private and family life, home and correspondence, includes such a limitation clause: interference by a public authority in accordance with the law is permitted if it is necessary in a democratic society "in the interest of national security, public safety or the economic well-being of the country, for the prevention of disorder or crime, for the protection of health or morals, or for the protection of the rights and freedoms of others."

6. See Article 5(1).

7. UN Doc. A/2929, *supra* note 3, at 33.

8. Articles 8(2), 10(2), and 11(2) as well as Protocol No. 4 Article 2(3). The latter, however, permits limitation of the liberty of movement for the purpose of prevention of crime, and does not mention prevention of disorder.

9. "1. A treaty shall be interpreted in good faith, in accordance with the ordinary meaning to be given to the terms of the treaty in their context and in the light of its object and purpose.

"2. The context for the purpose of the interpretation of a treaty shall comprise, in addition to the text, including its preamble and annexes:

　　a) any agreemtnt relating to the treaty which was made between all parties in connection with the conclusion of the treaty;

　　b) any instrument which was made by one or more parties in connection with the conclusion of the treaty and accepted by the other parties as an instrument related to the treaty.

"3. There shall be taken into account, together with the context:

　　a) any subsequent agreement between the parties regarding the interpretation of the treaty or the application of its provisions;

　　b) any subsequent practice in the application of the treaty which establishes the agreement of the parties regarding its interpretation;

　　c) any relevant rules of international law applicable in the relations between the parties.

"4. A special meaning shall be given to a term if it is established that the parties so intended."

10. UN Doc. A/2929, *supra* note 3, para. 112.

11. Article 32 of the Vienna Convention reads as follows:

"Recourse may be had to supplementary means of interpretation, including the preparatory work of the treaty and the circumstances of its conclusion, in order to confirm the meaning resulting from the application of Article 31, or to determine the meaning when the interpretation according to Article 31:

a) leaves the meaning ambiguous or obscure; or

b) leads to a result which is manifestly absurd or unreasonable."

12. The general limitation clause in Article 29 of the Universal Declaration does not include "national security." Neither does the general clause in Article 4 of the International Covenant on Economic, Social, and Cultural Rights. But Article 8(1) of that Covenant, providing for the right of everyone to form or join trade unions and the right of trade unions to function freely, is subject to limitations on grounds including national security.

The European and the American Conventions permit limitations based on the needs of national security similar to those of the International Covenant on Civil and Political Rights. Differences are discussed in this essay.

13. In considering limitations on freedom of thought, conscience, and religion (Article 18), it was observed that the terms "national security" and "public safety" were "not sufficiently precise to be used as a basis for the limitation of the exercise of the rights guaranteed." UN Doc. A/2929, *supra* note 3, at 49. In fact, the original draft proposals did not contain the expression "national security"; *id.* at 48. For a Netherlands proposal which does not include the term "national security," see 10 GAOR Annexes, UN Doc. A/2907 at 26 (1955).

14. In one respect, however, another provision of the Covenant seems to imply an exception. Article 8(3)(a) provides that "no one shall be required to perform forced or compulsory labour." Article 8(3)(c), however, adds that for this purpose the term "forced or compulsory labour" shall not include "any service required by law of conscientious objectors." The implication seems to be that respect for conscientious objection to military service is optional.

15. Since the European Convention was drafted before the International Covenants, it is plausible to argue that the authors of the latter deliberately discarded those grounds for limitation. Perhaps they considered that they might be included, at least in some circumstances, in the other limitation formulas, i.e., public safety, public order.

16. Charter of the United Nations, Preamble and Articles 1(3), 13(1)(b), 55(c), 62(2), 68, 76(c). See also B. Marie, *La Commission des Droits de l'Homme de l'O.N.U.* 35 (1975).

17. Charter of the United Nations, Articles 1(1), 2(3), 11(1) and (2), 15(1), 23(1), 24(1), 26, 33, 34, 37(2), 39, etc. Since the two words are always used together, "security" cannot have the same meaning as "international peace."

18. "All Members shall refrain in their international relations from the threat or use of force against the territorial integrity or political independence of any State, or in any other manner inconsistent with the Purposes of the United Nations."

19. In the context of Article 21, the right of association, the Commission on Human Rights accepted that if the activities of any group became a public danger, "the laws for the protection of 'public order', 'national security', 'or the rights and freedoms of others' could be applied." UN Doc. A/2929, *supra* note 3, at 54.

20. Compare note 3 *supra*.

21. The European Commission of Human Rights held the limitation clause of Article 10 of the European Convention (freedom of expression) applicable in a case concerning the distribution of leaflets to soldiers. It was held that the distributors must limit their conduct to accommodate the national interest. Arrowsmith v. United Kingdom, Eur. Comm. Human Rights, 8 *Decisions and Reports* 123, 131 (1977).

For the suggestion that special treatment of members of the armed forces is justified by their special status and need not invoke "national security," see essay 9.

22. 14 GAOR Annexes, UN Doc. A/4299 at 7–8 (1959).

23. A proposal by the Netherlands for Article 18 provides for limitations "in the interest of public safety, for the protection of public order" etc. UN Doc. A/2907, *supra* note 13, at 26.

24. The case law of the European Commission and the European Court of Human Rights has paid considerable attention to the restriction of guaranteed rights for the sake of prevention of disorder or crime. Many of the cases interpreting Article 8, in particular, have ruled on the applicability of this limitation. The limitation includes the necessity of interference with the correspondence right of convicted prisoners: Golder case, 18 *Pub. Eur. Ct. Human Rights,* Ser. A, at 21–22 (1975); X v. United Kingdom, Eur. Comm. Human Rights, 46 *Collection of Decisions* 136, 145 (1974); X v. Switzerland, Eur. Comm. Human Rights, 9 *Decisions and Reports* 206 (1978); X v. Federal Republic of Germany, *id.* at 207. It has also been used to permit censorship of the correspondence of imprisoned vagrants, even though such prisoners had committed no crime and had not been imprisoned upon conviction by a court. The Vagrancy Cases (De Wilde, Ooms, and Versyp Cases), 12 *Pub. Eur. Ct. Human Rights,* Ser. A at 45 (1971). A dangerous prisoner may be imprisoned far from his home if there is no maximum security prison nearer to his home. X v. the United Kingdom, Eur. Ct. Human Rights, 46 *Collection of Decisions* 112, 116 (1974). As to an alleged disruption of a family as a consequence of an order for expulsion, deportation, or extradition of one member of the family or as a result of a refusal of permission to enter the territory of the respondent state, the Commission has often found such measures justified "for the prevention of disorder or crime" where the applicant had been previously convicted on criminal charges. See, for instance, X v. United Kingdom, Eur. Ct. Human Rights, 35 *Collection of Decisions* 102, 107 (1971); European Commission of Human Rights, "Human Rights and their limitations," 4 *Case-Law Topics* 32 (1973). However, in the case of the extradition of a person whose family would probably not be able to follow, the Commission held that "such a substantial interference with the applicant's family life who does not seem to have committed any serious criminal offence in the Federal Republic of Germany, may not be justified under paragraph 2 of Article 8, on the ground of public safety or prevention of crime." Unfortunately, the Commission did not discuss the problem fully since the applicant had not exhausted domestic remedies. X v. Federal Republic of Ger-

many, Eur. Comm. Human Rights, 1 *Decisions and Reports* 77, 78 (1975). See also X v. United Kingdom, Eur. Comm. Human Rights, 39 *Collection of Decisions* 63, 65 (1972).

25. UN Doc. A/4299, *supra* note 22, at 7.

26. Article 29 of the Universal Declaration uses only the English term "public order," without the French phrase.

27. It is plausible to argue that order (and the French *ordre*) is a narrower concept than "public order" (and *ordre public*). "Order" may mean only the absence of public disorder, while as indicated below, public order and *ordre public* imply broader social policies.

28. The amendment was proposed by Argentina, Belgium, Iran, Italy, and the Philippines. 14 GAOR Annexes, UN Doc. A/C.3/L.805/Rev. 1 (1959).

29. UN Doc. A/4299, *supra* note 22, at 7–8.

30. UN Doc. A/2929, *supra* note 3, at 48.

31. UN Doc. A/4299, *supra* note 22, at 11. The Danish government later made a reservation on this point, since in Danish law the authority to exclude the press and the public from trials may go beyond what is permissible under the Covenant, and the Danish government considered that this authority should not be restricted.

32. See the discussion of this limitation in relation to Article 18, UN Doc. A/2929, *supra* note 3, at 48. See also the Netherlands proposal, *id.* at 52; in relation to Article 19(3), *id.* at 26, 54; 16 GAOR Annexes, UN Doc. A/5000 at 618; in connection with Article 21, UN Docs. A/2929 at 56, A/5000 at 9.

33. UN Doc. A/5000, *supra* note 32, at 9.

34. See *supra* note 27. The European Convention on Human Rights is less consistent in this respect than the Covenant on Civil and Political Rights. The term "public order" is used in Articles 6(1) and 9(2) next to "public safety," while Article 2(3) of Protocol No. 4 contains the expression "for the maintenance of 'ordre public'," the last words being used in French without any corresponding term in English. It was not inserted in Articles 8(2), 10(2) and 11(2), where the expressions "public safety" and "the prevention of disorder or crime" were used instead.

In the French text of the European Convention the term *ordre public* is used only in Article 6(1). Similarly, Protocol No. 4, Article 2(3) permits the limitations "nécessaires . . . au maintien de l'ordre public." In contrast, Articles 8(2), 9(2), 10(2) and 11(2) speak of *la défense* (or *la protection*) *de l'ordre,"* which is not necessarily synonymous with *ordre public.* See note 27.

As a consequence, the case law of the European Commission and the European Court under these articles do not prove helpful for the definition of the concept *ordre public,* but it may be relevant for issues about "order" in Article 18(3) of the Covenant.

The term "public order or national security" used in Article 6(1) has never been pronounced upon by the judicial bodies established by the Convention. The limitation clause of Article 2 of Protocol No. 4 (liberty of movement and freedom to choose a residence) has been invoked several times before the European Commission, which has held without further explanation that the refusal to release a lawfully detained person is clearly a permissible restriction under that provision. X v. Federal Republic of Germany, Eur. Comm. Human Rights, 9 *Decisions and Reports* 190, 192 (1978). See also Application No. 4256/69, Eur. Comm. Human Rights, 37 *Collection of Decisions* 67, 68 (1971).

In another case, again concerning a lawfully detained person, the Commission said that the notion of *ordre public* in Article 2 of Protocol No. 4 was explicitly included to cover such cases. X v. Federal Republic of Germany, 32 *Collection of Decisions* 68, 69 (1976). Article 9, which guarantees freedom of thought, conscience, and religion, subject to the possible limitations listed in paragraph 2, reads in the English version, "necessary in a democratic society . . . for the protection of public order" and, in the French version, *la protection de l'ordre*. Although there is no express mention of the French concept *ordre public* in either the English or French version, the European Court of Human Rights apparently considers Article 9(2) to be one of the *ordre public* provisions of the Convention, along with Article 6(1) and Article 2(3) of the Fourth Protocol. See Case of Engel and Others, 22 *Pub. Eur. Ct. Human Rights,* Ser. A at 41 (1977).

The term "public order" used in Article 9(2) of the Convention was also invoked before the Commission by an applicant who was serving a sentence of twenty years imprisonment for murder. He alleged that the prison authorities interfered with the exercise of his religion in that he was not allowed to grow a chin beard as prescribed by his religion, that he was prevented from doing contemplative yoga exercises, and that he was denied permission to receive a prayer chain as well as certain literature. The Commission declared the application inadmissible, finding no restriction of the applicant's right to manifest his religion. As regards the refusal of permission to grow a chin beard, the Commission accepted the Government's submission that this had been necessary in order to identify the applicant properly and concluded that such limitation was therefore "necessary in a democratic society . . . for the protection of public order." The refusal of the prayer chain was justified, according to the Commission, in the interest of the safety of the prisoner and of the maintenance of discipline in the prison. X v. Austria, Eur. Comm. Human Rights, 16 *Collection of Decisions* 20, 27 (1965).

On the subject of limitations in the European Convention generally, see Ganshof van der Meersch, "La Convention européenne des droits de l'homme a-t-elle, dans le cadre du droit interne, une valeur d'ordre public?" in *Les droits de l'homme en droit interne et en droit international* 155 (1968).

In the American Convention on Human Rights, the term "public order" has been inserted in all the limitation clauses. However, the clauses themselves vary from one provision to the other. In Article 13 (freedom of thought and expression), the limitation clause includes only "the protection of national security, public order, or public health or morals," while in Articles 12 (religious freedom), 15 (right of peaceful assembly), 16 (freedom of association), and 22 (freedom of movement and residence), the term "public safety" appears together with "public order." The French words *ordre public* were not included.

In the Treaty establishing the European Economic Community, Article 48(3) provides that free movement of workers is subject to "limitations justified by reasons of public order . . ." (*ordre public* in French). This limitation has been interpreted restrictively by the European Court.

In the Van Duyn case, it was established that the concept of public policy must be interpreted restrictively and cannot be determined unilaterally by a member state. Van Duyn v. Home Office, [1974] *Eur. Ct. J. Rep.* 1337, 1350. In the Rutili case, the Court stated that limitations on the rights of entry and residence of a community national are not permissible "unless his presence or conduct constitute a genuine and sufficiently serious threat to public policy." Rutili v. Minister for the Interior, [1975] *Eur. Ct. J. Rep.* 1219, 1231. In Regina y. Pierre Bouchereau, the Court stressed again that a restriction in the name of public policy presupposes the existence "of a genuine and sufficiently serious threat to the requirements of public policy affecting one of the fundamental interests of society." Regina v. Pierre Bouchereau, [1977] *Eur. Ct. J. Rep.* 1999, 2014. See also Bonsignore v. Oberstadt, [1975] *Eur. Ct. J. Rep.* 297; and Royer Case, [1976] *Eur. Ct. J. Rep.* 497.

35. See Ganshof van der Meersch, *supra* note 34, at 137–65.

36. "On ne peut déroger par des conventions particulières aux lois qui interessent l'ordre public et les bonnes moeurs." (One cannot derogate from laws concerning *ordre public* and good morals by private agreements).

The primary meaning of this text is that private persons when entering a contract must observe certain rules, which may be thus compared to *jus cogens* in international law. Such rules may be deduced not only from legal provisions, but also from general principles of law and, finally, from the whole philosophy of the state and its institutions. See Cour de Cassation, Decision of the Chambre civile, 4 December 1929, *Dalloz hebdomadaire* at 50 (1930). "What is at stake is the good functioning of the institutions which are necessary to the collectivity" ("le bon fonctionnement des institutions indispensables à la collectivité"), Malaurie, in Ph. Francescakis, *Encyclopédie Dalloz II* 499 (1969). "And what is considered necessary for the maintenance of the social organization" ("ce qui est considéré comme indispensable au maintien de l'organisation sociale").

37. Loussoran-Bourel, *Droit international privé* 341, 351 (1978). See also Francescakis, *supra* note 36, at 499. Some consider *ordre public* as merely a rule of conflicts of laws, i.e., conflicts between national and foreign laws resolved in favor of the first. As a matter of fact, its function has been exposed more broadly as designed "assurer globalement sur le territoire français un minimum de comformité des relations internationales avec la politique législative interne" ("to insure generally on French territory a minimum of conformity of international relations to internal legislative policy.") Francescakis, *supra* note 36, at 500.

As a rule, French courts consider foreign legislative rules violating fundamental human rights as contrary to the French *ordre public* and refuse to apply them. A. C. Kiss, *Répertoire de la pratique française en matière de droit international public,* vol. 2 at 646–48.

38. In many such jurisdictions, gambling debts, for example, will not be enforced, and agreements in restraint of trade will be invalidated.

39. Another meaning, concerned with procedure in administrative jurisdiction as distinguished from civil or penal jurisdiction, is not pertinent here. Bernard, *La notion d'ordre public en droit adminstratif* 163 (1962). See also M. Hauriou, *Aux sources du droit: le pouvoir, l'ordre, la liberté* (1933). The "procedural" meaning of *ordre public* implies that in an administrative process the government can in certain cases invoke *ordre public* arguments which have to be considered as mandatory (e.g., arguments concerning the competence of the judge, etc.).

40. Bernard, *supra* note 39, at 12.

41. Law of April 5, 1884, Article 97.

42. See Bernard, *supra* note 39, at 265.

43. *Id.* at 44.

44. Cour de Cassation, Decision of the Chambre criminelle, 5 December 1978.

45. Among the laws and principles of *ordre public* found in every legal order, there are some which are based on universal concepts of justice and civilization, for example the prohibition of slavery on the one hand and respect for the dignity of human personality on the other; their appropriate title is consequently that of laws and principles of international *ordre public.* Sperduti, "Les lois d'application nécessaire en tant que lois d'ordre public," *Revue critique de droit international privé* (1977).

For the Italian concept of *ordine publico internazionale,* see A. Ehrenzweig, *Private International Law* (1974).

Ordre public international also includes the concept of national public policy invoked in private international law (conflict of laws) cases, discussed above. See Note, "Public Policy and Ordre Public," 25 *Va. L. Rev.* 37, 39 (1938–39); UN Doc. A/2929, *supra* note 3, at 48.

46. Many have stressed the relativity of "public policy." Like *ordre public* it too cannot be a rigid formula but is a function of time and place. See, e.g., "Public Policy and Ordre Public," *supra* note 45. This relativity underscores the importance of the role played by the courts in the application and interpretation of that concept. British and American courts seem to have succeeded in constructing a flexible and intrinsically sound doctrine in this field, "to which the relativity of public policy is a matter of course." Nussbaum, "Public Policy and the Political Crisis in the Conflict of Laws," 49 *Yale L, J.* 1027, 1031 (1939). This is a characteristic shared with civil law systems.

47. Baroum Case, *supra* note 44, at 162. "The notion of 'ordre public' is like a legal indicator, imprecise enough to permit a judge in each particular case to make the general interest prevail, sometimes by respecting liberties, sometimes by limiting them."

There is some analogy between this concept and the one which was examined by the Permanent Court of International Justice in the Danzig Legislative Decrees case. There the Court used as a point of reference conformity to "sound popular feeling." The Court held that the decision whether an act falls within the fundamental idea of a penal law or whether it is condemned by sound popular feeling is left to the individual judge or to the public prosecutor to determine.

> "It is a question of applying what the judge (or the Public Prosecutor) believes to be in accordance with the fundamental idea of the law, and what the judge (or the Public Prosecutor) believes to be condemned by sound popular feeling. A judge's belief as to what was the intention which underlay a law is essentially a matter of individual appreciation of the facts, so is his opinion as to what is condemned by sound popular feeling." ([1935] PCIJ, Ser. A/B, no. 65 at 52–53)

48. "In common law systems, public policy is generally assigned a negative function. For example, in private international law, it justifies the nonapplication of the foreign law which ought to govern." E. G. Lorenzen, "Territoriality, Public Policy and Conflict of Laws," 33 *Yale L. J.* 736, 747 (1927). See also Nussbaum, *supra* note 46, at 1028.

49. For one discussion, see UN Doc. A/4299, *supra* note 22, at 7. The corresponding Spanish term *orden público,* it was explained, referred to the whole body of political, economic and moral principles considered essential to the maintenance of a given social structure. See *supra* note 45; see also Buergenthal, *supra* note 4, at 78; Ganshof van der Meersch, *supra* note 34, at 165–67.

50. See, in particular, UN Doc. A/2929, *supra* note 3, at 38–39.

51. The applicant was a farmer and a member of the Reformed Dutch Church. He had refused to sign an application for membership in the Cattle Health Service on the ground that it was against his religious conscience, and claimed that the Act of 1952 which provided for this service was a violation of his rights under Article 9 of the Convention. The Commission noted that the purpose of the 1952 Act was to prevent tuberculosis among cattle. It found that the term "protection of health" in Article 9(2) might reasonably be interpreted to cover such a health scheme which was in the interest of the community. The Commission stated that a considerable measure of discretion was left to parliaments in appreciating the vital interests of the community, although it was ultimately for the Commission to judge whether the measures taken were justifiable. The Commission concluded that compulsory membership in the Health Service was a justifiable measure for the government to take, and that there was no violation of Article 9. The application was therefore ill-founded and inadmissible. X v. Netherlands, 5 *Y. B. Eur. Conv. Human Rights* 278 (1962). See "Human Rights and their Limitations," *supra* note 24, at 35.

In another case, the applicant had been convicted for homosexual offenses and complained that his right to respect for his private life (Article 8 of the Convention) was violated. The Commission found that the exercise of this right could, in a democratic society, be subject to interference by law "for the protection of health or morals" under Article 8(2). The application was declared inadmissible but the Commission did not indicate whether the case before it came within "health" or "morals." X. v. Federal Republic of Germany, 1 *Y.B. Eur. Ct. Human Rights* 228, 229 (1955–1957). See Human Rights and their Limitations," *supra* note 24, at 29–30.

52. There are small differences in context. Most provisions speak of "public health and morals" (Articles 12(3), 19(3), 21, 22(2)), while in Article 18(3) this term appears in a longer phrase: "limitations . . . as are necessary to protect public safety, order, health, or morals."

In the Universal Declaration the term "morality" is used without the adjective. Article 29 speaks of limitations "for the purpose of . . . meeting the just requirements of morality, public order and the general welfare." It is questionable, however, whether "morality" is broader than "public morals." In the American Convention on Human Rights, the term "morals" is always accompanied by the adjective "public." In the European Convention on Human Rights, Article 9 (freedom of thought, conscience, and religion) is the only provision where there is mention of "public order, health or morals"; in all the other limitation clauses the term "morals" is not qualified. Here again, the question arises whether the authors of the European Convention intended to permit restriction to protect morality that was not "public."

53. Article 14(1) contains an express clause permitting closed trial "when the interest of the private lives of the parties so requires."

54. The decision of the European Court in the Handyside case is particularly relevant in this regard. Handyside case, 24 *Pub. Eur. Ct. Human Rights,* Ser. A (1976). The applicant had challenged his criminal conviction and the seizure, forfeiture, and destruction of the matrix and of hundreds of copies of a "school book" aimed principally at children and adolescents, parts of which were considered obscene by the British authorities in application of the Acts of 1959/1964. In its decision the Court pointed out that these Acts have an aim that is legitimate under Article 10(2) of the European Convention, namely the protection of morals in a democratic society. The decision stressed that the protection machinery established by the Convention is subsidiary to the national systems in safeguarding human rights. The Convention leaves to each contracting state the primary task of securing the rights and liberties it includes. As far as "morals" are concerned, the Court found that it was not possible to find a uniform European concept of morals in the domestic law of the various European states. National laws better reflect current views of the requirements of morals which, especially in our era, vary from time to time and from place to place. By reason of their direct and continuous contact with the vital forces of their countries, state authorities are in a better position than the international judge to give an opinion on the exact content of these requirements as well as on the necessity of a restriction intended to fulfill them. Consequently, Article 10(2) leaves to the states a margin of appreciation which is not unlimited; the European Commission and Court are responsible for ensuring the observance of the state's obligations. Thus, the Court's task under Article 10 is to supervise national legislation as well as the decision applying it, even when such decisions

have been given by an independent court. The European Court concluded that the fundamental aim of the judgment of the British Court applying the 1959/1964 Acts, the protection of the morals of the young, was a legitimate purpose under Article 10 of the Convention. See also Cohen Jonathan, "Cour européenne des droits de l'homme (Chronique de jurisprudence 1976–1977)" 14 *Cahiers de droit Européen* 341, 350 (1978).

In several other cases, no distinction was made by the European Commission between morals and other grounds for restricting recognized rights and freedoms. See X v. United Kingdom, Eur. Comm. Human Rights, 39 *Collection of Decisions* 63 (1972); X v. Austria, Eur. Comm. Human Rights, 24 *Collection of Decisions* 20 (1967). In another case, where a man convicted of homosexual offenses under Article 175 of the German Penal Code complained that the police had searched his home and seized his documents, the application was declared inadmissible on the ground that there was no interference with the exercise of the right to privacy (Article 8) "insofar as such interference is provided by law and constitutes a measure which, in a democratic society, is necessary for the prevention of disorder or crime and for the protection of public morals, which was the position in this case." X. v. Federal Republic of Germany, 3 *Y. B. Eur. Conv. Human Rights* 184, 190 (1960).

55. But see *supra* notes 51 and 54.

56. Article 29 of the Universal Declaration uses yet another form: "In the exercise of his rights and freedoms, everyone shall be subject only to such limitations as are determined by law."

57. Such restrictions "as are provided by law" in Article 19(3), freedom of opinion and expression, is in the French text "restrictions . . . expressement fixées par la loi." It has been suggested that these terms should be interpreted as including not only statutes formally enacted by the legislature but also customary and judge-made law, even when not in writing. In support, it may be noted that during the drafting of Article 29(2) of the Universal Declaration the term "prescribed" was replaced in the English text by "determined," but that may not be relevant for interpretation of the Convention where the term "prescribed" is used.

58. O. Garibaldi, "General Limitations on Human Rights: The Principle of Legality," 17 *Harv. Int'l L. J.* 503, 556–57 (1976).

59. Case of Klass and Others, 28 *Pub. Eur. Ct. Human Rights,* Ser. A (1979); and also X v. Belgium, Eur. Comm. Human Rights, 9 *Decisions and Reports* 13, 19 (1978).

In the Handyside case, *supra* note 54, at 16, one of the questions considered by the Court was whether there was a law authorizing the limitation.

60. Article 14(1) of the International Covenant on Civil and Political Rights. See also Article 6 of the European Convention. Article 8(5) of the American Convention provides only that "criminal proceedings shall be public, except insofar as may be necessary to protect the interests of justice."

61. "Ce que ces dispositions exigent, c'est que les limitations soient 'prévues par la loi.' Et ceci couvre aussi bien un régime restrictif établi par une loi—ou

un acte réglementaire pris conformément à la loi—que les applications indi-
viduelles qui peuvent être faites des réglementations en vigueur." Vegleris, *supra* note 2, at 222. (What these provisions require is that the limitations be
provided by law. This includes a restrictive rule established by law—or a reg-
ulatory act taken in conformity with the law—as well as possible individual
applications of regulations in force.)

62. UN Doc. A/2929, *supra* note 3, at 39.

Other limitation provisions in the Covenant (Articles 18(3), 19(3), 21 and
22), do not refer to "other rights recognized by the Covenant" but, in different
formulas, permit limitations necessary to protect the rights and freedoms of
others. On their face those clauses may be broader, since they seem to permit
limiting the particular covenant rights not only to protect other rights under
the Covenant but even other rights and freedoms not recognized by the Covenant. There is no evidence, however, that any difference was intended by the
different formulas used.

63. UN Doc. A/2929, *supra* note 3, at 42–43.

64. UN Doc. A/4299, *supra* note 22.

65. UN Doc. A/2929, *supra* note 3, at 54.

66. *Id.* at 49.

67. The difference in the texts may reflect only that the clauses were drafted
at different times, and that in other respects, too, the drafting process was not
a single, coherent process. Or, perhaps, the omission of the phrase from Article
12 may reflect only the feeling that freedom of movement does not implicate
the ideology of democracy, as does, for example, freedom of the press. On the
other hand, omission of the phrase from Article 18 (freedom of thought, conscience and religion) and Article 19 (right to hold opinions and freedom of
expression) may reflect the feeling that those rights are so sacrosanct that it was
undesirable to stress that even democratic societies are entitled sometimes to
limit them.

68. Articles 15 (right of assembly), 16(2) (freedom of association), and 22(3)
(freedom of movement and residence).

69. See X v. Austria, Eur. Comm. Human Rights, 16 *Collection of Decisions*
20 (1965), where the Commission's decision upheld the right of prison authorities to refuse a prisoner a religious magazine which also dealt with martial arts,
as an act necessary in a democratic society for the protection of public order. In
another case, the Commission upheld the refusal of prison authorities to allow
a prisoner certain objects necessary for the practice of his religion as being a
decision necessary in a democratic society for the protection of the rights and
freedoms of others. X v. United Kingdom, Eur. Comm. Human Rights, 5
Decisions and Reports 100, 101 (1976). The same formula was used in X v. Austria, Eur. Comm. Human Rights, 13 *Collection of Decisions* 42, 53 (1964), and
X v. Netherlands, Eur. Comm. Human Rights, 23 *Collection of Decisions* 137,
138 (1967).

70. Preamble of the European Convention.

71. Marckx v. Belgium, Eur. Comm. Human Rights, 3 *Decisions and Reports*
112, 134 (1976).

72. "Finally and above all, the right to liberty is too important in a 'democratic society' within the meaning of the Convention for a person to lose the benefit of the protection of the Convention for the single reason that he gives himself up to be taken into detention. . . . When *the matter is one which concerns ordre public within the Council of Europe,* a scrupulous supervision by the organs of the Convention of all measures capable of violating the rights and freedoms which it guarantees is necessary in every case." Vagrancy cases (H. R. De Wilde, Ooms, and Versyp Cases), 14 *Pub. Eur. Ct. Human Rights,* Ser. A, at 36 (1971).

Compare a recent decision in which the Commission declared its task was "to consider whether the penalties imposed on the applicants were prescribed by law and whether they were necessary in a democratic society for any of the criteria enumerated in Article 10(2)." X v. Belgium, Eur. Comm. Human Rights, 9 *Decisions and Reports* 13, 19 (1978).

73. "The Court's supervisory functions oblige it to pay the utmost attention to the principles characterising a 'democratic society.' Freedom of expression constitutes one of the essential foundations of such a society, one of the basic conditions for its progress and for the development of every man. Subject to Article 10(2), it is applicable not only to 'information' or 'ideas' that are favourably received or regarded as inoffensive or as a matter of indifference, but also to those that offend, shock or disturb the State or any sector of the population. Such are the demands of that pluralism, tolerance and broadmindedness without which there is no 'democratic society' " Handyside case, *supra* note 54, at 23.

74. Intervention by P. H. Teitgen during the debates of the preparatory works of the European Convention on Human Rights on August 16, 1950. Council of Europe, *Collected Edition of the "Travaux Préparatories" of the Convention for the Protection of Human Rights and Fundamental Freedoms,* vol. V at 292 (1950).

75. Handyside case, *supra* note 54.

76. The matter was raised at the Parliamentary Assembly of the Council of Europe by the Dutch Minister of Foreign Affairs. He referred to the limitation clauses in the European Convention on Human Rights and observed that the notion of a democratic society had never been defined in the context of that Convention. He expressed his appreciation of the difficulties implied by the task of defining or, if not defining, indicating the parameters of the notion of a democratic society. The main problem is that "democracy is a continuously evolving process. Democracy at a standstill is dead. Democracy has to live in the hearts and minds of our citizens; and their thoughts, their ideas are constantly developing." Council of Europe, Parliamentary Assembly, Doc. AS (30) CR 19 at 31–33. On the *caractère evolutif* of the concept, see Vegleris, *supra* note 2, at 239.

77. Vegleris, *supra* note 2.

78. *Id*. at 237: "It clearly refers to the concept of the organization of human societies based, on the one hand, on the construction of a world order of peace and progress and, on the other hand, on the progressive integration of the con-

tinents. This concept . . . has attained a degree of crystallization which, although it may be far from final, makes it possible to discern certain elements or even a certain mix of concrete elements. These elements are, on the one hand, political liberty with the goal of real participation in power by the people and, on the other hand, the recognition of and the ability to enforce against the state certain essential rights and certain elementary liberties of the individual."

Compare P. H. Teitgen, *supra* note 74, at 290–292: "In all the countries of the world freedoms have to be defined and limited. Suppose we take the case of a democracy. The limitation imposed will be valid only if it has as its aim the public interest and the common good. The State, in a democracy, may limit an individual freedom in the interests of the freedom of all, in order to allow the collective exercise of all the freedoms, in the general interest of a superior freedom or right, in the public interest of the nation. The restriction which it imposes is a legitimate one precisely by reason of the fact that this is the goal which is aimed at: it sets a limit upon freedom in the general interest, in the interest of the freedom of all. . . .

"The internal legality of the restrictions which any State may impose upon an individual freedom will beyond a doubt depend upon whether its nature is democratic or totalitarian."

79. The Permanent Court of International Justice stated that "an exception to the principles affirmed in the preceding paragraphs . . . does not . . . lend itself to an extensive interpretation." Nationality Decrees issued in Tunis and Morocco, [1923] PCIJ, Ser. B, no. 4. In another case the Court said that when a provision which constitutes a derogation from the rules is generally applied, and is strictly in the nature of an exception, no further derogation is allowed. Polish Upper Silesia, [1926] PCIJ, Ser. A, No. 7 at 22.

Against such considerations one might refer to another general principle of interpretation in international law: "in case of doubt a limitation of sovereignty must be construed restrictively." Free Zones of Upper Savoy and the District of Gex, [1931] PCIJ, Ser. A/B, No. 46 at 167; also *id.,* Ser. A, No. 24 at 12 (1930); S. S. Wimbledon case, [1923] PCIJ, Ser. A, No. 1 at 24–25. As regards the international instruments protecting human rights, however, one should recognize that these rights derive from the inherent dignity of the human person (Preamble of the Universal Declaration and both Covenants). Fundamental rights and freedoms are not grants by states to their citizens, which could be considered a limitation of the sovereignty, but are preexisting rights. That is clearly the meaning of the Covenant. In a report to the Sub-Commission on Prevention of Discrimination and Protection of Minorities, Mrs. E. A. Daes, Special Rapporteur, stated:

"The Special Rapporteur considers that the following principles should govern every limitation, restriction or interference in the exercise of the rights or freedoms of the individual: . . .

"4. *The principle that human rights and freedoms are absolute and that limitations or restrictions are the exceptions*

This principle is fundamental for the protection of the rights and freedoms of the individual. Consequently, a restrictive interpretation should apply to the provisions or restrictions on the exercise of certain rights of the individual." UN Doc. E/CN.4/Sub. 2/432/Add. 3 para. 806, 815 (1980).

13. THE OBLIGATION TO IMPLEMENT THE COVENANT IN DOMESTIC LAW

1. The following states parties to the Covenant have constitutional provisions pursuant to which the Covenant has become part of their national law upon ratification or accession: Austria, Colombia, Cyprus, Ecuador, Federal Republic of Germany, Iran, Mali, Senegal, Syria, Tunisia, Yugoslavia, and Zaire.

2. O'Connell, *International Law* 58, 61 (2nd ed. 1970); MacDonald, "International Treaty Law and the Domestic Law of Canada," 2 *Dalhousie Law J.* 307 (1975).

3. UN Doc. E/CN.4/SR.125 at 11 (1949).

4. *Ibid.* See also 10 GAOR Annexes, UN Doc. A/2929 at 18 (1955).

5. UN Doc. E/CN.4/SR.138 at 12 (1950).

6. UN Doc. E/CN.4/SR.125 at 7–9 (1949), especially statements of representatives of Philippines, Egypt, and Lebanon.

7. *Id.* at 18–19. The vote was 1 in favor, 9 against and 4 abstentions.

8. UN Doc. E/CN.4/SR.427 at 10 (1954).

9. Among these countries are United Kingdom, Denmark, Norway, Sweden, Finland, Guyana, and Mauritius. The Eastern European socialist countries which do not automatically incorporate treaties per se into domestic law include the USSR, German Democratic Republic, Bulgaria, and Czechoslovakia. See notes 10 and 11 *infra,* relating to Czechoslovakia, and note 13 on the USSR.

10. In the 1978 session of the Committee, several members of the Committee raised this issue with the representative of Czechoslovakia, inquiring particularly whether an individual claiming a violation had the right to invoke the Covenant though it was not part of domestic law. See, for example, C. Tomuschat, UN Doc. CCPR/C/SR.64 para. 64 (1978); Sir Vincent Evans, SR.65 para. 37 (1978); A. Movchan, SR. 65 para. 42.

11. The response of a government representative in one instance, that it was not "possible" for a discrepancy to occur (because national law ensured all rights) was less than persuasive. Statement of the representative of Czechoslovakia, UN Doc. CCPR/C/SR.67 paras. 3, 4 (1978). The position stated here, that the Covenant could not be incorporated in domestic law in Czechoslovakia, is inconsistent with the doctrine previously established in Czechoslovakia that treaties are *ipso jure* transformed into internal law.

12. See, for example, the reports of Denmark, UN Doc. CCPR/C/1.Add.4 at 3 (1977), and of Norway, *id.* Add.5 at 1 (1977). See also the statement of Sir Vincent Evans on United Kingdom practice, *supra* note 10.

13. See Report of Human Rights Committee, 33 GAOR Supp. 40, UN Doc. A/33/40 para. 432 (1978). For general analysis of Soviet treaty law bearing on the question of the right to invoke treaties, see Blishchenko, "International

Treaties and their Application on the Territory of the U.S.S.R.," 69 *AJIL* 819 (1975).

14. See reports of Denmark and Norway, *supra* note 12.

15. Sørensen, "Report Concerning Obligations of a State Party to a Treaty as regards its Municipal Law," in A. H. Robertson, ed., *Human Rights in National and International Law* 13 (1968).

16. R. v. Miah, [1974] 1 W.L.R. 683; R. v. Secretary of State for the Home Department, ex parte Bhajan Singh, [1975] 3 W.L.R. 225.

17. *Ibid.*

18. *Id.* at 230. See also 47 *Brit. Y.B. Int'l L.* 359 (1974–75).

19. R. v. Secretary of State for the Home Department, ex parte Phansopkar and ex parte Begum, [1975] 3 W.L.R. 322.

20. *Id.* at 339, 341. See also 47 *Brit. Y.B. Int'l L.* 360–61 (1974–1975).

21. R. v. Chief Immigration Officer, Heathrow Airport, ex parte Salamat Bibi, [1975] 1 W.L.R. 979, [1976] 3 All E.R. 843, 847–8.

22. [1976] 3 All E.R. 843, 847–48.

23. *Ibid.*

24. James Buchanan & Co. v. Babco Forwarding and Shipping, [1977] 2 W.L.R. 107.

25. *Id.* at 112.

26. Crawford, "Decisions of British Courts during 1976–1977," 48 *Brit. Y.B. Int'l L.* 351 (1976–77).

27. Mann, "Britain's Bill of Rights," 94 *Law Q. Rev.* 512, 521 (1978).

28. Pan-American World Airways v. Department of Trade, [1976] 1 *Ll. L.R.* 257, 261–62. (C.A.) Also quoted in Crawford, *supra* note 26, at 348.

29. In a number of countries treaties have a normative rank superior to statutes and therefore prevail over subsequent as well as prior statutory rules. The following states parties to the Covenant fall in this category: Colombia, Cyprus, Ecuador, Mali, Senegal, Tunisia, and Zaire.

30. Subsequent statutes prevail over treaties in Austria, Federal Republic of Germany, Netherlands, Syria, the United States, and Yugoslavia, as well as in those countries (*supra* note 9) where treaties do not become part of domestic law.

31. See *supra* note 12. Under Danish law, discretionary powers of administrative officials must be exercised in such a way that their acts—whether decisions or regulations—must conform to international treaty obligations. This is a legal obligation enforceable by judicial review. UN Doc. CCPR/C/1/Add.4 at 4 (1978).

32. See Article 27 of the Vienna Convention on the Law of Treaties.

33. Reports that domestic law provisions are fully adequate to fulfill the obligations of the Covenant have been made, inter alia, by Chile, Czechoslovakia, German Democratic Republic, Libya, and the USSR.

34. UN Doc. CCPR/C/1 Add. 17 at 1 (1977).

35. Mann, *supra* note 27.

36. Lord Denning, *supra* note 21.

37. Message from the President of the United States, transmitting four treaties pertaining to human rights, Sen. Exec. C, D, E, and F, 95th Cong. 2d Sess. iii–iv (1978).

38. *Id.* at vi.

39. *Ibid.*

40. Article 27 of the Vienna Convention on the Law of Treaties. For divergent views, see Correspondence, 74 *AJIL* 155–157 (1980).

41. Advisory Opinion on Reservations to the Convention on Genocide, [1951] *ICJ Repts.* 15.

42. Article 19(c) provides in effect that a state may not formulate a reservation which is "incompatible with the object and purpose of the treaty."

43. U.N. Doc. A/2929, *supra* note 4, para. 7.

44. See, for example, comment of United Kingdom in UN Doc. E/CN.4/365 at 14 (1950).

45. UN Doc. E/CN.4/374 (1950).

46. UN Doc. A/2929, *supra* note 4, para. 17.

47. UN Docs. E/CN.4/116 (1950); E/CN.4/SR.4/SR.138 at 13 (1950).

48. UN Doc. A/2929, *supra* note 4, para. 8.

49. *Id.* para. 9.

50. *Ibid.* The proposal was adopted provisionally in 1949 and deleted in 1952 at the 8th session of the Commission on Human Rights. The vote for deletion was close: 9 in favor, 8 opposed, one abstention. UN Doc. E/CN.4/SR.329 (1952).

51. For discussions in the Commission, see UN Docs. E/CN.4/SR.327–329 (1952).

52. See Schwelb, "The Nature of the Obligations of the States Parties to the International Covenant on Civil and Political Rights," in *René Cassin, Amicorum Discipulorumque Liber* (1969).

53. UN Doc. A/2929, *supra* note 4, para. 10.

54. 21 GAOR Plen. Mtg. (1496th Mtg.), UN Doc. A/PV/1496 para. 124 (1966).

55. See, for example, 18 GAOR C.3 (1257th–1258th mtgs.), UN Docs. A/C.3/1257, 1258 (1963), especially statements of representatives of United Kingdom, USSR, Netherlands, Jamaica, Peru, Sudan, and Italy.

56. 18 GAOR Annexes, UN Doc. A/5655 para. 23 (1963).

57. *Ibid.*

58. UN Doc. A/C.3/1258 paras. 6, 16, 19 (1963).

59. UN Doc. A/2929, *supra* note 4, para. 14.

60. *Id.* para. 15.

61. *Ibid.*

62. *Id.* para. 16.

63. *Ibid.*

64. Sweden, UN Docs. CCPR/C/1/Add.9, CCPR/C/SR.52,53 (1978); Denmark, UN Doc. CCPR/C/1/Add. 4 (1977).

65. See *supra* notes 4, 5, and 6 and accompanying text. As noted above, a

proposal by the United States intended to render the Covenant non-self-executing was rejected.

66. See document referred to *supra* note 37, at vi.

67. *Id.* at xiv.

68. Lord Reid, in Pickin v. British Railways Board, [1974] A.C. 765 at 782.

69. Dicey, *Lectures on the Law of the Constitution* 59 (2d ed. 1886).

70. The United Kingdom has accepted judicial review of its legislation through its adherence to the European Court of Human Rights.

71. James Madison, speech of June 8, 1789. 1 *Annals of Congress* 457 (Gales and Seaton's History [1834–56]).

72. See, for example, reports of Democratic Republic of Germany, UN Docs. CCPR/C/1/Add. 13, CCPR/C/SR.65 (1978); the USSR, UN Docs. CCPR/C/1/Add.22 (1978), CCPR/C/SR.108, 109, 112 (1978); Ecuador, UN Doc. CCPR/C/1/Add.29 (1978); Sweden, UN Doc. CCPR/C/1/Add.9 (1978); United Kingdom, UN Docs. CCPR/C/1/Add. 17, CCPR/C/SR.7 para. 3 (1978).

73. See UN Doc. CCPR/C/SR.67 on report of German Democratic Republic, especially comments of W. Tarnopolsky at 4, 5; J. Prado Vallejo at 8, 9; Espersen at 8; see also UN Docs. CCPR/C/SR.64, 65 on report of Czechoslovakia.

74. See, for example responses of representative of German Democratic Republic, UN Doc. CCPR/C/SR.68 at 3 (1978); and of representative of Czechoslovakia, UN Doc. CCPR/C/SR.64 at 3 (1978).

14. THE IMPLEMENTATION SYSTEM: INTERNATIONAL MEASURES

1. A collection of extracts from official UN documents discussing this problem may be found in L. Sohn and T. Buergenthal, *International Protection of Human Rights* 556–739 (1973). A summary thereof is given in a book review by the present author in 8 *Human Rights J.* 292, no. 1 (1975). The issues are well summarized in 10 GAOR Annexes, UN Doc. A/2929 paras. 24–39 (1955); and in 18 GAOR Annexes, UN Doc. A/5411 (1963). See also E. Schwelb, *Human Rights and the World Community* (1964).

2. 9 ESCOR Supp. 10, UN Doc. E/1371 at 36–49 (1949). The different stages in the drafting of the Covenants are described in some detail in Sohn, "A short history of United Nations documents on human rights," in The United Nations and Human Rights 101, 120–162 (1968). See also two articles by Schwelb: "Measures of Implementation in the U.N. Covenant on Human Rights," 12 *Tex. Int'l L. J.* 141 (1977); and "Notes on the Early Legislative History of the Measures of Implementation of the Covenants," in *Mélanges Offerts a Polys Modinos* 270–89 (1968). For a general background, see Humphrey, "The U.N. Charter and the Universal Declaration . . ." and Hoare, "The U.N. Commission on Human Rights," both in E. Luard, ed. *The International Protection of Human Rights* (1967). For the machinery actually established by the Covenant on Civil and Political Rights, see Das, "Institutions et Procédures issues des conventions relatives aux droits de l'homme . . . ," in

K. Vasak, ed., *Les Dimensions Internationales des Droits de l'Homme* 409–31 (1978) (cited below as "UNESCO Manual"). An English edition of this important work is in preparation (1979). See also two articles by Mower, "The Implementation of the U.N. Covenant on Civil and Political Rights," 10 *Human Rights J.* 271 (1977); and "Organizing to Implement the Covenant: First Steps by the Committee," 3 *Human Rights Rev.* 122–31 (1978). In addition, see the articles in Volumes 19, 20, 21 of *Review of the International Commission of Jurists* (1977–78) (cited as *ICJ Rev.*).

3. UN Doc. E/CN.4/AC.4/1(1947).

4. UN Docs. E/CN.4/452 at 1–4 (1950), E/CN.4/SR.168 at 3–5 (1950).

5. UN Doc. E/CN.4/353/Add.4 (1950).

6. UN Doc. E/CN.4/274/Rev.1 (1949).

7. UN Doc. E/CN.4/353, cited in Sohn, *supra* note 2, at 136.

8. 13 ESCOR Supp. 9, UN Docs. E/1992 at 15, 40–43; E/CN.4/640 (1951).

9. UN Doc. E/CN.4/SR.178 at 4–5, 11–13 (1950).

10. Sohn, *supra* note 2, at 144–62.

11. 18 ESCOR Supp. 7, UN Docs. E/2573, E/CN.4/705 (1954).

12. A most useful document for this purpose is UN Doc. A/2929, *supra* note 1.

13. This provision was the result of an amendment by the United Kingdom based on Article 31 of the European Convention on Human Rights.

14. Article 47 contained a general safeguard of the jurisdiction of the International Court of Justice. Article 48 set out special procedures for implementing Article 1 of the Covenant on the right of self-determination.

15. This provision corresponded to Article 20 of the draft Covenant on Economic, Social, and Cultural Rights.

16. UN Doc. A/2929, *supra* note 1, ch. VII para. 176, ch. IX para. 19.

17. The Secretary-General's commentary explains: "It was considered that the Human Rights Committee would be a quasi-judicial organ set up for the very specific purpose of receiving complaints alleging non-observance of the covenant . . . and that to transmit reports to the committee might be . . . to invite it to pass judgment without being seized of a complaint by a State Party, and would prejudice its autonomy and independence." *Id.* ch. VII para. 174.

18. The issues presented to the Third Committee are summarized in UN Doc. A/5411, *supra* note 1. The discussions and decisions of the Third Committee are summarized in its Report to the General Assembly, 21 GAOR Annexes, UN Doc. A/6546 (1966). Sohn, *supra* note 2, also summarizes the discussion at 164–68.

19. It is interesting to compare the different systems adopted by the regional organizations. The European Commission of Human Rights, established under the European Convention on Human Rights of 4 November 1950, consists of a number of members equal to the number of High Contracting Parties (twenty in January 1981). By contrast the Inter-American Commission of Human Rights, established by resolution of the Ministers for Foreign Affairs of the Organization of American States in 1959 (and subsequently made a statutory

organ of the Organization by the Protocol of Buenos Aires of 1967), consists of only seven members. This system is repeated in Article 34 of the American Convention on Human Rights of 1969.

20. The Third Committee considered that the Human Rights Committee as established by the Covenant "was no longer the same as the quasi-judicial body originally proposed by the Commission on Human Rights, which would have remained in virtually permanent session . . . [it] would be more in the nature of a functional organ holding periodic sessions." UN Doc. A/6546, *supra* note 18, para. 308.

Moreover, by limiting its autonomy, they committed an error. The Committee is not, strictly speaking, a "United Nations body," i.e., subject to the control of the General Assembly (even though it sends the Assembly an annual report). It is an emanation of the states parties created by virtue of a separate treaty, and it is important to insure its independence from the political organs of the UN. In its first report to the General Assembly, the Committee pointed out that it "was not a United Nations body but a conventional organ established by the States parties to the Covenant." 32 GAOR Supp. 44, UN Doc. A/32/44 para. 19 (1977). The General Assembly, in its Resolution 32/66 of 8 December 1977, noted "with appreciation" this report and expressed its satisfaction "at the serious way the Committee is undertaking its functions." It did not disagree with the Committee's statement about its autonomy.

21. See International Convention on the Elimination of All Forms of Racial Discrimination, Article 14, 660 *UNTS* 195.

22. The Netherlands proposal was endorsed by Canada, Colombia, Costa Rica, Ghana, Jamaica, Nigeria, Pakistan, the Philippines, and Uruguay.

23. The vote to accept the proposal by Lebanon was 41 votes to 39, with 16 abstentions. See UN Doc. A/6546, *supra* note 18, paras. 478–85.

24. Compare Article 9 of the Statute of the International Court of Justice, which requires that "the representation of the main forms of civilization and of the principal legal systems of the world should be assured."

25. The same principle is established in Article 23 of the European Convention and in Article 36 of the American Convention.

26. At that time there were 44 parties to the Covenant and 16 to the Protocol.

27. Cyprus, Denmark, Federal Republic of Germany, Norway, United Kingdom.

28. Bulgaria, German Democratic Republic, Romania, USSR.

29. Iran, Syrian Arab Republic.

30. Mauritius, Rwanda, Tunisia.

31. Canada.

32. Colombia, Costa Rica, Ecuador. The election of officers at the first session of the Committee in March 1977 equally respected the principle of geographic distribution: the Cypriot member was elected chairman; the three vice-chairmen were from Bulgaria, Mauritius and Norway; the *rapporteur* from Colombia.

33. Torkel Opsahl of Norway. The British and Danish members of the Committee were also members of the Council of Europe's (intergovernmental) Steering Committee on Human Rights.

34. The members from Canada, Colombia, Costa Rica, Denmark, Ecuador, Mauritius, Norway.

35. The Rules of Procedure are found in the first Annual Report of the Human Rights Committee to the General Assembly, UN Doc. A/32/44, *supra* note 20, Annex II.

36. See the discussion of these problems in "The Human Rights Committee," 20 *ICJ Rev.* 27, 27–28 (June 1978). General Assembly Resolution 32/66 (1977) specifically drew attention to the obligation of the Secretary-General to provide the necessary staff facilities required by the Committee, but in 1978 the Director of the Division of Human Rights informed the Third Committee that he did not have the necessary staff.

37. UN Doc. A/32/44, *supra* note 29, paras. 46–47.

38. *Id.* para. 28.

39. *Id.* paras. 29–32.

40. *Id.* paras. 86–89.

41. "The New Human Rights Committee," 19 *ICJ Rev.* 19–22 (December 1977). As of 1980 there has been no occasion to invoke majority rule.

42. The 35 states which first ratified the Covenant were to deposit their first reports by March 23, 1977 (one year after the Covenant entered into force).

43. The International Labour Organisation (ILO) reporting system is highly developed. The ILO constitution provides that states which have ratified the international labor conventions produced by the ILO will submit periodic reports on the way they are implemented. These reports are examined by a special Committee of Experts on the Application of Conventions, consisting of independent persons appointed by the Governing Body of the ILO. The reports and the findings of the experts are submitted by the Governing Body to governments and to the International Labour Conference with its tri-partite structure. They are examined by the Conference Committee on the Application of Conventions, consisting of representatives of governments, employers, and workers; the latter will, of course, always be ready to challenge overcomplacent statements by government representatives. Rather similar arrangements have been established by the European Social Charter of 18 October 1961, which institutes a system of periodic reports, to be examined by a Committee of Independent Experts (assisted by a representative of the ILO).

For the ILO procedures, see C. W. Jenks, *Human Rights and International Labour Standards* (1960); "The ILO and Human Rights, Report presented to the International Conference on Human Rights," Teheran (1968); Valticos, "L'Organization Internationale du Travail," in *UNESCO Manual, supra* note 2, at 442–79. For the UNESCO procedures, see "L'UNESCO et les droits de l'homme," *id.* at 479, 506. For the European Social Charter, see *infra* note 65.

44. India, Iran, Libya, Nigeria, Pakistan, Senegal, Sudan, United Arab Republic, Upper Volta.

45. UN Doc. A/6546, *supra* note 18, paras. 372–97, 546–50.

46. *Id*. para. 380. On the effectiveness of the reporting system, see also Mower, *supra* note 2, at 287.

47. UN Doc. A/2929, *supra* note 1, ch. VII para. 161.

48. Both the Commission and the Third Committee drafts required that states should report "on the measures they have adopted which give effect to the rights recognized herein *and on the progress made in the enjoyment of those rights*" (emphasis added). See, e.g., UN Doc. A/2929, *supra* note 1, ch. VII paras. 162–66; UN Doc. A/6546, *supra* note 18, para. 382. That requirement, some argued, implied that the rights and freedoms set out in the Covenant are to be implemented by the contracting parties "progressively." This strained interpretation is not compelling. It would reduce the obligations under the Covenant on Civil and Political Rights to the status of those under the Covenant on Economic, Social, and Cultural Rights, which expressly provides that they are to be realized "progressively"; that provision was in recognition of the difficulty of implementing a number of them (e.g., the right to work) in many, if not all, countries. Civil and political rights, on the other hand, are generally capable of immediate implementation and were intended to be so applied. A state should put its laws and administrative practice in compliance with the Covenant before ratifying it, or within a reasonable time thereafter.

The reference in Article 40(1) to the "progress made in the enjoyment of those rights," was not intended to weaken the obligation of immediate implementation. But there may be certain legislative or administrative measures which require amendment, and Article 2(2) expressly recognizes this possibility. Moreover, it would be foolish to pretend that no further progress can be made in the enjoyment of the human rights in any country, even after it has ratified the Covenant.

The states are obligated to report "the measures they have adopted" to give effect to the rights set out in the Covenant, "the progress made in the enjoyment of those rights," and under Article 40(2), "the factors and difficulties, if any, affecting the implementation of the present Covenant." The United States proposed an amendment to the effect that reports should relate to "the legislative, judicial or other action taken"; but certain speakers opposed it on the ground that it was more restrictive than "measures," and the amendment was not adopted. See UN Doc. A/6546, *supra* note 18, para. 384.

49. The Convention was approved by the UN General Assembly on December 21, 1965, G.A. Res. 2106-A, 20 GAOR Supp. 14, UN Doc. A/6014 (1965), and opened for signature on March 7, 1966. The Convention entered into force on January 4, 1969 and by December 31, 1980 had been ratified by 108 states, making it the most widely ratified of all UN Conventions. The text is reprinted in *Human Rights Instruments* at 24.

50. The Convention also provides for the competence of the CERD to examine interstate disputes (Articles 11 to 13) and, as an optional procedure, individual communications.

51. Further information may be found in Buergenthal, "Operating the U.N.

Racial Convention," 12 *Tex. Int'l L.J.* 187 (1977); Schreiber, "La Pratique Récente des Nations Unies dans la Domaine de la Protection des Droits de l'Homme," 145 *Recueil des Cours* 333–38 (1975); UNESCO Manual, *supra* note 2, at 375–409.

52. Buergenthal, *supra* note 51, at 201.

53. Schreiber, *supra* note 51, at 338.

54. See, e.g., the first two Annual Reports of the Human Rights Committee to the General Assembly; UN Doc. A/32/44, *supra* note 20, and 33 GAOR Supp. 40, UN Doc. A/33/40 (1978). See also the notes on the Committee meetings in 19 *ICJ Rev.* 19 (1977); 20 *ICJ Rev.* 24 (1978); and 21 *ICJ Rev.* 16 (1978).

55. See *infra* note 85.

56. 20 *ICJ Rev.* 25 (1978).

57. UN Doc. A/32/44, *supra* note 20, at 69–70.

58. The Committee considered the reports of the Syrian Arab Republic, Cyprus, Tunisia, Finland, Ecuador, and Hungary. In 1978 the reports of Sweden, Denmark, Czechoslovakia, Madagascar, Iran, Federal Republic of Germany, Yugoslavia, Jordan, USSR, Mauritius, and Byelorussian SSR were received; the follow-up reports of Ecuador and Libya were also considered. In 1979, Chile, Bulgaria, Romania, Spain, Ukrainian SSR, and the United Kingdom dependent territories submitted reports; and follow-up reports from Finland, Cyprus, Syria, and the United Kingdom were submitted.

59. A full discussion took place, for example, in 1980. See UN Docs. CCPR/C/SR.231–SR.232 (1980).

60. UN Docs. CCPR/C/SR.231 paras. 9–17, SR.232 paras. 3–18.

61. UN Doc. CCPR/C/SR/231 paras. 2–8, 18–30 (1980). The Committee on the Elimination of Racial Discrimination does not merely promote cooperation and respect for the Convention, but monitors compliance with it. Reports of states parties are carefully scrutinized by the Committee for insufficiency and for evidence of violation or other noncompliance, and states are asked to answer questions or supply additional materials. In examining the reports and other statements by the reporting state, members of the Committee regularly refer to legislation and to other official documents and statements of the reporting state and to documents of intergovernmental organizations. The reports of the Committee are not limited to general statements about states generally but address issues of compliance of individual states. See, e.g., Decision 1 (XVIII), Information supplied by Cyprus relating to conditions in Cyprus, 33 GAOR Supp. 18, UN Doc. A/33/18 at 94 (1978).

62. UN Doc. CCPR/C/SR.260 (1980). The statement reads in part:

"(b) In formulating general comments the Committee will be guided by the following principles:

"They should be addressed to the States parties in conformity with article 40, paragraph 4 of the Covenant;

"They should promote co-operation between States parties in the implementation of the Covenant;

"They should summarize experience the Committee has gained in considering States reports;

"They should draw the attention of States parties to matters relating to the improvement of the reporting procedure and the implementation of the Covenant, and

"They should stimulate activities of States parties and international organizations in the promotion and protection of human rights.

"(c) The general comments could be related, *inter alia,* to the following subjects:

"The implementation of the obligation to submit reports under article 40 of the Covenant;

"The implementation of the obligation to guarantee the rights set forth in the Covenant;

"Questions related to the application and the content of individual articles of the Covenant;

"Suggestions concerning co-operation between States parties in applying and developing the provisions of the Covenant."

63. A state is required to submit a report within one year after the Covenant comes into force for that state (Art. 40(1a)). Of the 35 initial reports which should have been received by March 22, 1977, only 16 arrived on time. Reminders were sent governments and the facts reported to the General Assembly. As of January 1, 1981, 65 states were parties to the Covenant, and 60 reports were due (a year having elapsed since entry into force), of which 44 had been received. Reports had not been received from four states whose reports were due in 1977, three states whose reports were due in 1978, four whose reports were due in 1979, and five whose reports were due in 1980. In addition, supplementary information requested by the Committee from some governments had not been supplied. At its tenth session (1980) the Committee agreed to send reminders to the states with reports outstanding and resolved to mention Jamaica, Rwanda, and Uruguay (whose reports were due in 1977) in its Annual Report to the General Assembly as having failed to fulfill their reporting obligations under Article 40. (Lebanon, also delinquent since 1977, was not to be mentioned due to "special difficulties" experienced in preparing its report.)

64. In 1978, the Committee held three sessions and found that only a small number of reports could be examined at each session. It reviewed the reports of 6 states (Czechoslovakia, Denmark, German Democratic Republic, Libyan Arab Republic, Sweden, and the United Kingdom) at its third session (January–February 1978); 6 states (Federal Republic of Germany, Iran, Jordan, Madagascar, Norway, and Yugoslavia) at its fourth session (July–August 1978); and 4 states (Byelorussian SSR, Mauritius, the USSR, and a supplementary report by Ecuador) at its fifth session (October–November 1978).

65. For details of the ILO system, see references in *supra* note 43. On the European Social Charter, see A. H. Robertson, *Human Rights in Europe* 140–150 (1963); Tennfjord, "The European Social Charter," 9 *European Yearbook* 71 (1961); Sur, "La Charte Sociale Européenne," 22 *European Yearbook* 88 (1974). The European Social Charter institutes a system of periodic reports which are

examined by a Committee of Independent Experts (assisted by an ILO representative); employers and workers organizations at the national level then comment on the report, followed by their international counterparts; the governmental Social Committee adds its appraisal; and both the Parliamentary Assembly (of the Council of Europe) and the Committee of Ministers may add their recommendations.

66. UN Doc. A/6546, *supra* note 18, paras. 378, 385.

67. 17 *Human Rights Bull.* 63 (1977).

68. Rule 67 para. 1 provides for the transmission to the Specialized Agencies of copies of such parts of the reports as fall within their competence.

69. At its fourth session (July/August 1978), the Committee agreed that extracts of reports concerning Articles 22 and 24 of the Covenant be sent to UNESCO, but no agreement was reached as to how specialized agencies should comment on state reports. Cooperation with specialized agencies is discussed in some detail in the Committee's Annual Report, UN Doc. A/33/40, *supra* note 54, at 103–5.

70. In December 1978 the General Assembly requested the Commission on Human Rights to review the whole question of cooperation between United Nations bodies and Specialized Agencies concerned with human rights (Resolution 33/54).

71. Report of the Ad Hoc Working Group to inquire into the situation of human rights in Chile, UN Doc. A/33/331 (1978), and the report of the Ad Hoc Working Group submitted to the Commission on Human Rights, UN Doc. E/CN.4/1310 (1978).

72. See 34 GAOR Supp. 40, UN Doc A/34/40 para. 107 (1979); the general discussion of the report of Chile is at paras. 70–109.

73. *Id.* para. 108.

74. *Id.* para. 109.

75. *Id.* Annex V at 119, Letter dated 9 July 1979 from the Minister of Foreign Affairs of Chile.

76. *Id.* para. 66, and Annex.

77. On the work of NGOs in the human rights field, see Archer, "Action by Unofficial Organizations on Human Rights," in E. Luard, ed., *The International Protection of Human Rights* 160 (1967). The NGOs played a significant role in strengthening the human rights provisions of the Charter at the San Francisco Conference in 1945. See also Humphrey, "The U.N. Charter and the Universal Declaration . . . ," *id.* at 39. Further light on the role of NGOs is shed by M. Moskowitz, *International Concern with Human Rights* (1974).

78. 20 *ICJ Rev.* 27 (1978).

79. See *infra* note 91.

80. UN Doc. A/5411, *supra* note 1, para. 22.

81. As it does under the previously existing system of periodic reports operated by the UN Commission on Human Rights.

82. Though Rule 71(2) provides that the Committee may transmit to ECOSOC the governments' observations, if any.

83. The system's lack of power results from the reluctance of some govern-

ments to permit United Nations "interference" in what they consider to be domestic matters. In the 1954 drafts the Commission's function was limited to making "general recommendations," in keeping with the "widely held view that the reports should not give rise to particular recommendations to individual states. . . ." UN Doc. A/2929, *supra* note 1, para. 19. However, this narrow construction of the Commission's reporting function was adopted when the draft still provided for obligatory interstate complaints and the reporting system was of secondary importance. It does not necessarily apply today when the reporting system is the primary implementation mechanism.

84. Austria, Canada, Denmark, Finland, Federal Republic of Germany, Iceland, Italy, Netherlands, New Zealand, Norway, Sweden, and the United Kingdom.

85. See also A. H. Robertson, *Human Rights in the World* 122–39 (1972).

86. UN Doc. A/6546, *supra* note 18, para. 184.

87. *Id*. para. 413.

88. *Id*. para. 308.

89. Article 42 in its present form is based on an amendment proposed by nine states (India, Iran, Libya, Nigeria, Pakistan, Senegal, Sudan, the United Arabic Republic, and Upper Volta). Paragraph 7 provided that the Conciliation Commission should present a report "containing such recommendations as it may consider proper for the amicable solution of the matter." *Id*. para. 441. The French representative proposed changing the phrase to "containing its views on the possibilities of an amicable solution of the matter." *Id*. para. 446. This amendment was intended to weaken the powers of the Conciliation Commission, and was adopted by a large majority. *Id*. para. 468. Nevertheless, the phrase makes little sense unless it is understood to empower the Commission to make suggestions for a possible amicable solution.

90. See Henkin, "Human Rights and 'Domestic Jurisdiction,' " in T. Buergenthal, ed., *Human Rights, International Law, and the Helsinki Accord* 21 (1977); but compare Frowein, "The Interrelationship Between the Helsinki Final Act, the International Covenants on Human Rights, and the European Convention on Human Rights," *id*. at 71.

91. See the many works cited in Sohn and Buergenthal, *supra* note 1, at 19–21; Council of Europe, *Bibliography on the European Convention on Human Rights* 42–46 (3d ed. 1978).

92. See references given in note 1 *supra,* and note 94 *infra*.

93. My views are set out more fully in a treatment of the right of individual petition under the European Convention on Human Rights, *Human Rights in Europe* 149–53 (2d ed. 1977).

94. The discussions which finally led to the adoption of ECOSOC Resolution 1503 are reproduced at length in Sohn and Buergenthal, *supra* note 1, at 739–856, and summarized in 8 *Human Rights J.* 293 (1975). The procedures are described by Schreiber in "La Pratique Récente des Nations Unies dans le Domaine de la Protection des Droits de l'Homme," 145 *Recueil des Cours* 351–58 (1975); and in the UNESCO Manual, *supra* note 2, at 322–27.

95. UN Doc. E/CN.4/SR.178, *supra* note 9, at 3–4.

96. UN Doc. A/5411, *supra* note 1, paras. 37–42.

97. The text summarizes the Report of the Third Committee, UN Doc. A/6546, *supra* note 18, paras. 474–85.

98. Submitted jointly by Canada, Colombia, Costa Rica, Ghana, Jamaica, the Netherlands, Nigeria, Pakistan, the Philippines, and Uruguay.

99. UN Doc. A/6546, *supra* note 18, para. 485. Most of the Soviet, Asian, and African states voted in favor. Most of the Western group and Latin American states voted against. Among the abstentions were: Brazil, China, Cyprus, Greece, Israel, and Turkey. When it came to the vote in the General Assembly on December 16, 1966, the Optional Protocol was approved by 66 votes to 2 with 38 abstentions.

100. The Committee on the Elimination of Racial Discrimination will have slightly greater powers, when considering individual communications under Article 14 of the Racial Discrimination Convention, because it "shall forward its *suggestions and recommendations,* if any, to the State Party concerned and to the petitioner." But this is also an optional procedure which will enter into force when ten States have accepted it, which had not occurred as of 31 December 1980.

101. The rules are set out in UN Doc. A/32/44, *supra* note 20, at 61–66.

102. This may not be easy. At the third session of the Committee (January/February 1978) it was not possible to reach agreement on the text of the communiqué. 20 *ICJ Rev.* 24 (1978).

103. Barbados, Canada, Colombia, Costa Rica, Denmark, Dominican Republic, Ecuador, Finland, Iceland, Italy, Jamaica, Madagascar, Mauritius, Netherlands, Nicaragua, Norway, Panama, Peru, Senegal, Suriname, Sweden, Trinidad and Tobago, Uruguay, Venezuela, and Zaire. UN Doc. E/CN.4/1444 (1981).

104. UN Doc. A/32/44, *supra* note 20, at 5. Three members of the first group and two of the second group were nationals of states parties to the Optional Protocol.

105. 19 *ICJ Rev.* 22 (1977) reports that one was a joint communication signed by 18 persons and referring to alleged violations by the government of Uruguay of the rights of 1,200 named individuals.

106. UN Doc. A/32/44, *supra* note 20, at 37.

107. UN Doc. A/34/40, *supra* note 72, at 126.

108. *Id.* at 129.

109. There is a good deal of literature on the problem of "coexistence" of the European Convention and the UN Covenant. In English: by the present author in [1968–69] *Brit. Y.B. Int'l L.* 21–48 (1968–9); and in *Human Rights in the World* 80–110 (1972); Buergenthal, "International and Regional Human Rights Law and Institutions: Some Examples of Their Interaction," 12 *Tex. Int'l L. J.* 321–430 (1977); Cançado Trindade, "The Domestic Jurisdiction of States in the Practice of the United Nations and Regional Organizations," 25 *Int'l and Comp. L.Q.* 715–65 (1976). In French: P. Modinos, "Co-existence de

la Convention Européenne et du Pacte . . . des Nations Unies," *Revue des Droits de l'Homme* 41–69 (1968); M-A. Eissen, "Co-existence de la Convention européenne et du Pacte . . . des Nations Unies," *Zeitschrift für auslandisches offentliches Recht und Völkerrecht* 237–62, 646–49 (1970); J. De Meyer, *Co-existence de la Convention européenne et du Pacte . . . des Nations Unies* (1969); Vegleris, "Le principe d'égalité dans la Déclaration Universelle et la Convention européenne . . .," *Miscellanea Ganshof van der Meersch* 565–88 (1972); Velu, "Le droit à la liberté et a la sécurité—étude comparative . . . ," *Revue de droit pénal et de criminologie* 67–213 (1968).

110. Council of Europe, "Report of the Committee of Experts to the Committee of Ministers on the Problem of the co-existence of the two systems of control," Doc. CM (68) 39 (February 1968).

111. Council of Europe, "Report of the Committee of Experts on Human Rights to the Committee of Ministers," *Human Rights: Problems Arising from the Co-existence of the UN Covenants on Human Rights and the European Convention on Human Rights,* Doc. CE/H (70)7, (1970).

112. UN Doc. A/33/40, *supra* note 54, at 99–100.

113. *Ibid.*

114. *Id.* at 104–5.

115. Council of Europe, Doc. CE/H (70)7, *supra* note 111.

116. Subsequently, the Committee of Ministers of the Council of Europe decided to include in the organization's medium-term plan of work for 1976–1980 a study of the possibility of extending the European Convention to include some of the rights included in the Covenants but not in the Convention. In a "Declaration on Human Rights," adopted on April 27, 1978, the Committee of Ministers decided to give priority to this work, notably as regards rights in the social, economic, and cultural fields.

117. A. H. Robertson, *Human Rights in the World* 122 (1972).

Index

Abortion, 122; right to (U.S.), 444*n*31, 446*nn*59, 62

Abuse of state's right of derogation, safeguards against, 86-91

Accused, *see* Criminally accused

Adolescents, 207-8. *See also* Juveniles

Affirmative action, 259-61, 267, 319

Afghanistan, 92

Africa, 184, 336, 474*n*50

Afroyim v. Rusk, 441*n*45

"Agreement of the People" (of England), 209

Aliens, 4, 33, 58, 187-88, 239, 257, 266; right to enter country of permanent residence, 180-81; protection from expulsion, 182-84; distinctions re, 263-64, 266

American Convention on Human Rights, 15, 28, 71, 73, 74, 80, 115, 249, 294, 338, 349, 350, 414*n*46, 416*n*69, 498*n*19; derogation clause, 78, 79; capital punishment, 118; freedom from torture, 122; right to life, 122, 442*n*4, 446*n*62; freedom from slavery, 126; right to liberty and security, 128, 129; freedom from imprisonment for debt, 135-36; freedom of movement, 180-81; right to enter own country, 182; protection against expulsion, 182; right to nationality, 183; minorities, 270; limitations, 291, 481*n*12; terminology, 296, 298, 306, 445*n*45, 488*n*52; system of international control in, 353, 366; individual complaints in, 359; relation to international implementation system, 366-69; non-derogable rights, 414*n*37; "public order," 484*n*34

American Declaration on the Rights and Duties of Man, 248

Amnesty, 116, 117

Amnesty International, 348

Anglo-American law: "public policy" in, 300

Apartheid, 14; *see also* International Convention on the Suppression and Punishment of the Crime of Apartheid

Appeal, *see* Review

Arab countries, 58

Arbitrary (term), 57, 140-45; arrest and detention, 19, 129-31, 133; deprivation of life, 56-57; relation to "unlawful," 57, 130-31, 191-92; right to life, 115-16; capital punishment, 118-19; punishment, 163; expulsion, 173; freedom of movement, 181, 182; right to privacy, 191-92

Arbitrary action, 164

Argentina, 258

Armed forces, *see* Military personnel

Arrest, arbitrary, 128, 129, 130-32, 135-36, 140-45

Arrest and detention, 191, 325

Asia, 184

Assembly, right of, 59, 97, 98, 188, 230-34, 295, 297, 305, 309

Association, right of, 30, 59, 73, 97, 98, 102, 235-37, 295, 297, 305, 309; and privacy, 193

Asylum, right of, 19, 60

Australia, 166, 175, 333

Austria, 5, 148, 151, 289, 473*n*31; Code of Criminal Procedure, 146; Constitutional Court, 429*n*42, 470*n*73

Autonomy, 12, 13, 185, 190, 192-96, 244, 309

Bail, 134, 142, 143, 162

Barbados, 215

Barcelona Traction case, 249

Belgian Congo, 230

Belgian Linguistic cases, 257, 286, 467*n*42

Belgium, 92, 147; Criminal Code, 128; Court of Appeal, 147-48

Belize, 463*n*161

Bidart, G., 442*n*5

Bion, 124

Birth, registration of, 207; *see also* Children

Blackstone, Sir William, 169

Boeckman's Case, 147

"Brain drain," 167, 178

Brennan, William Joseph, 163

Buenos Aires, Protocol of, 498*n*19